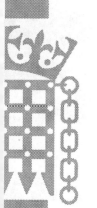

H(

European l   ... Committee

7th Report of Session 2007–08

The Future of the Common Agricultural Policy

Volume II: Evidence

Ordered to be printed 26 February 2008 and published 6 March 2008

Published by the Authority of the House of Lords

London : The Stationery Office Limited
£29.00

HL Paper 54–II

CONTENTS

Page

Oral Evidence

Written Evidence

Written Evidence was also received from:

The British Independent Fruit Growers' Association
Mr.Philip Colfox
Food Security
Sub Rosa

This has not been not been printed, but is available for inspection at the
House of Lords Record Office (020 7219 5314).

We would like to take the opportunity to thank all our witnesses for their
submissions to our inquiry.

The Report of the Committee is published in Volume I (HL Paper 54-I) and
the Evidence is published in Volume II (HL Paper 54-II)

Minutes of Evidence

TAKEN BEFORE THE EUROPEAN UNION COMMITTEE D

WEDNESDAY 4 JULY 2007

Present	Bach, L	Moynihan, L
	Brookeborough, V	Palmer, L
	Cameron of Dillington, L	Plumb, L
	Greaves, L	Sewel, L (Chairman)
	Miller of Chilthorne Domer, B	Ullswater, V

Memorandum by the Department for Environment, Food and Rural Affairs

Overview

Q1. *What should be the long term objectives of the CAP?*

1. In December 2005, Defra and HM Treasury published a vision for the Common Agricultural Policy (at: www.defra.gov.uk/farm/capreform/vision.htm) which set out long term goals for how a reformed CAP could support a profitable and sustainable farming sector. That vision proposed that within 10 to 15 years, European agriculture should be:

— internationally competitive without reliance on subsidy or protection;

— rewarded by the market for its outputs, not least safe and good quality food, and by the taxpayer only for producing societal benefits that the market cannot deliver;

— environmentally-sensitive, maintaining and enhancing landscape and wildlife and tackling pollution;

— socially responsive to the needs of rural communities;

— producing to high levels of animal health and welfare; and

— non-distorting of international trade and the world economy.

2. In order to achieve that, the CAP needed to be reformed further so that it constituted:

— a free, fair and level playing field throughout the EU for farmers to produce and market their goods in a single market, as in other sectors of the economy;

— central to this, the integration of agriculture within EU competition policy on the same basis as for other sectors with rules set at the EU level;

— a clear framework, set at EU level, to define the goals of EU agricultural policy, focussing in particular on maintaining the environment and promoting sustainable rural development, particularly in the more environmentally sensitive regions of the Union;

— within this framework and in the long-term, targeted, non production distorting measures defined and applied at Member State, regional and local levels to achieve these goals in accordance with local priorities and consistent with EU competition policy;

— import tariffs for all farm sectors progressively aligned with the much lower level prevailing in other sectors of the economy;

— no price support, export refunds or other production or consumption subsidies;

— social and welfare benefit support as determined by the Member States would be available to farmers on the same basis as other members of society but there would be no income or production support payments which treat agriculture differently from other sectors; and

— EU spending on agriculture would be based on the current Pillar II and would support these objectives as appropriate, allowing a considerable reduction in total spending by the EU on agriculture and bringing this into line with other sectors.

Q1. *Does the title "Common Agricultural Policy" aptly fit your perceived objectives of the policy?*

3. There would continue to be a common European policy, precluding unfair competition between Member States, but one very different from that now in place. Price support would be phased out as would other direct support to farmers; agricultural markets would progressively open up; and there would be a central rather than a peripheral role for rural development measures, including those targeted on protection and enhancement of the rural environment.

Q1. *What do you consider to be the main pressures on the CAP as it currently is?*

4. We strongly welcomed the direction of recent reforms, which we expect will have a positive effect. But the evidence is clear that the CAP still gives rise to substantial economic and fiscal costs for the EU's consumers and taxpayers, and represents very poor value for money. The CAP is also inequitable, both within the EU and internationally, whilst market price support has contributed to the intensification of EU agriculture, with associated environmental costs.

5. What is more, much of the CAP is holding back the competitiveness of European farming in the context of a globalising economy. Farmers need to be freed from the constraints, bureaucracy and distortion of a managed market, so that they can become fully connected with consumer demand and responsive to market opportunities.

6. In summary, in the context of globalisation, increasing environmental pressures, and the EU's Lisbon Agenda for economic growth, the current CAP is not serving the long term interests of European farming or society.

THE REFORMED CAP

Q2 *What has been your experience so far with the reformed CAP? What has worked well and less well? And where can lessons be learned?*

7. The policy landscape under the CAP has changed considerably through implementation of recent reforms.

8. The 2003 reforms should encourage a more market-oriented focus to farm businesses. In particular, the decoupling of direct payments from production allows farmers to re-assess what they do in order to maximise their farm's returns from their own skills and resources. It is regrettable that this message has been obscured by the significant problems associated with the introduction of the Single Payment to farmers in England. We are determined that the right lessons are learned from that experience, so that we move to a stable platform for making payments. RPA and Defra are working closely with industry stakeholders to that end.

9. While it is too early to reach a conclusive view, emerging anecdotal information suggests that the introduction of cross compliance (linking CAP payments to compliance with a range of environmental, public, plant and animal health and welfare standards) is reinforcing the base level of responsible farming practice. Beyond that the continued flexibility provided by voluntary modulation, has enabled the funding and delivery of Environmental Stewardship, a key policy tool in improving the environmental performance of farming.

10. Recent reforms are, therefore, moving the policy framework towards a point where farmers would be able to compete freely in the market, unhindered by the historic constraints of the CAP, and rewarded for the responsible management of our landscape and natural resources.

11. The nature of farming and the fact that the sector is made up of many thousand individual businesses, mean time is needed for policy change to take effect on the ground. The Agricultural Change and Environment Observatory Programme has been set up to monitor changes arising from CAP reform and other key drivers, and to assess the consequent implications for the environment. Their first review is at: www.defra.gov.uk/farm/policy/observatory/pdf/execsummary-ar06.pdf

12. The Observatory is an important means for identifying environmental risks from a changing agriculture sector and an important part of the evidence base for charting progress towards our vision for English farming, set out by David Miliband in his Speech at the Oxford Farming Conference in January 2007. That vision is of a farming sector which is profitable in the marketplace, continuing to produce the majority of the food we consume, even when the subsidies have gone; making a positive net environmental contribution, notably in respect of climate change, but also more widely; and managing the landscape and the natural assets that underlie it.

THE SINGLE PAYMENT SCHEME

Q3. Do you consider the Single Payment Scheme to be a good basis for the future of EU agricultural policy? What changes might be made at the EU level to the Single Payment Scheme, including to the rules governing entitlements, in the short and/or the longer-term?

13. The introduction of the Single Payment Scheme (SPS) reduced economic distortions and environmental pressures associated with the schemes it replaced, and so represented a significant landmark in the evolution of the CAP. However an agricultural income support measure of this sort has no place in a sustainable CAP and the benefits arising from cross-compliance can not begin to justify the €33 billion per annum cost across the EU.

14. A managed phase out of the SPS requires, in the short term, a move to full decoupling and significant simplifications in the scheme rules (eg abolishing set-aside, reducing the number of other types of SPS entitlements and introducing both less rigid land eligibility rules and more proportionate control requirements, particularly for smaller claims). Those should be actively considered in the forthcoming CAP Healthcheck.

MARKET MECHANISMS

Q4. What short and longer-term changes are required to the CAP's market mechanisms? Suggestions made by the Commission have included re-examination of certain quotas, intervention, set-aside, export refunds and private storage payments

15. In line with our vision we want to see early fundamental reform, leading to abolition of the intervention price system and all the associated policy instruments, such as production quotas, set-aside, planting bans, aids for storage, processing and distillation, other withdrawal mechanisms and export refunds.

16. Farmers need clarity about such changes so that they have sufficient time to plan and a transitional process which enables them to adjust effectively, focusing in particular, on early simplification measures and better consumer and market alignment.

RURAL DEVELOPMENT

Q5. What is your view on the introduction of the European Agricultural Fund for Rural Development (EAFRD)? Do you consider that it is meeting its objectives thus far? Is it suitably "strategic" in nature, meeting the needs of rural society as a whole rather than being restricted to aiding the agricultural industry? How well is it being co-ordinated with other EU and national policies on regional and rural development?

17. The EAFRD implements Pillar II of the Common Agricultural Policy. Introduced by the new Rural Development Regulation (1698/2005) in 2005, the EAFRD only entered into being on 16 October 2006. The move to the current arrangements is a welcome improvement compared to the arrangements that applied from 2000–06. However, it is too early to be definite about the practical benefits which will arise, and there is certainly scope to go further. The rural development programming period which is supported by the EAFRD began on 1 January 2007. As at 7 June 2007, only 2 (of the expected 94) new rural development programmes had been approved.

18. In principle, however, the new Rural Development Regulation and EAFRD is a welcome step since it requires member states to adopt a more strategic approach to their rural development policies from the outset. Under the UK Presidency of the European Union, Community Strategic Guidelines for Rural Development were adopted which set out priorities for rural development at European level. Additionally, under the EAFRD Member States must also provide a National Strategic Plan for Rural Development to complement their more detailed Programmes. However, until all, or at least the majority of, new programmes have begun formally it is impossible to say whether or not the EAFRD will prove to be more strategic in practice.

19. That said, it is already clear from the volume of European regulations, accompanying guidelines and Commission requirements alone, that Member States must provide a considerable amount of detailed information in order to get programmes approved. The implementation and controls requirements also combine to provide a complex operating environment for Rural Development Programmes. Arguably, the effectiveness (or otherwise) of the Fund will in one sense be gauged by how easy it is for Member States to deliver rural development policy "strategically" and effectively, without falling foul of the detailed rules governing implementation.

20. In England, EAFRD funding will be targeted strongly on schemes that deliver environmental benefits through improved land management, notably in respect of maintaining and enhancing biodiversity and helping to protect natural resources. This approach is both consistent with the Community Strategic Guidelines and the Vision for the CAP published jointly by Defra and Treasury in 2005.

21. In terms of integration with other EU and national policies on regional/rural development, the Commission implementing rules do require programmes to contain a considerable amount of information about demarcation with other funds/policies in order to promote complementarity and avoid dual-funding.

Q6. *Is there a case for a higher level of EU financing of rural development? Do you have a view on the extension of compulsory modulation from Pillar I (Direct payments) to Pillar II (rural development)?*

22. Since 2001, the United Kingdom has used the voluntary modulation mechanism to increase the level of EU financing for rural development by transferring funds from Pillar I to Pillar II of the CAP. The UK is in favour of greater compulsory modulation as we believe that Pillar II represents better value for money than Pillar I.

23. In all policy areas, and looking ahead to the EU Budget Review, the Government believes that spending through the EU Budget should represent value for money, should add value compared to spending through national budgets, should be proportionate, and should be properly managed.

WORLD TRADE

Q7. *What benefits can the EU's World Trade Organisation obligations create for EU agriculture, and consequently, for the EU economy as a whole?*

24. The Doha Development Agenda (DDA) has the potential to improve market access significantly (by reducing import tariffs) for EU exporters in to third country markets; to significantly reduce trade distorting domestic support globally; and to eliminate all export subsidies by 2013. This is in line with the UK's CAP Vision paper (see page 13)—helping to foster an internationally competitive industry without reliance on subsidy or protection; and one which is non-distorting of international trade and the world economy.

25. In addition to the benefits to the developing world that the DDA has the potential to bring, an ambitious outcome will benefit EU consumers by improving their access to imports and reducing prices in the EU; will allow EU producers and processors improved market access to third countries for their exports; and allow processors an increased range of imports. It is difficult to be prescriptive about the levels or amounts involved in the absence of a DDA deal and given the complexities of individual commodities. However, assessments of the impact of the Uruguay Round suggest that the benefits could be considerable.

26. Whilst recognising we need to manage any kind of transition carefully, we believe that opening up the EU market will be positive for consumers and competitive businesses and so for the EU economy as a whole. WTO obligations also provide for international sanitary and phyto-sanitary standards and a disputes procedure for managing world trade.

ENVIRONMENTAL PROTECTION AND CLIMATE CHANGE

Q8. *To what extent has the system of cross-compliance contributed to an improved level of environmental protection?*

27. Cross compliance measures have been phased in since 2005. Cross compliance applies to all farmers claiming direct payments including the Single Payment and, as of 2007, claimants for new land based Pillar II Rural Development schemes. Cross Compliance consists of two parts: Statutory Management Requirements, derived from 19 existing EU directives and regulations, which all farmers have to comply with irrespective of whether they receive direct payments; and an obligation on farmers to keep their land in Good Agricultural and Environmental Condition (GAEC).

28. It is too early to reach a conclusive view on the impact of cross compliance, but some anecdotal information is emerging. For example, the 2006 annual survey of farmers for Momenta (the cross compliance advice provider) indicated that:

— 40% of farmers have changed their practices to meet cross compliance; and

— 35% have noted environmental or other benefits, such as increased wildlife and reduced runoff from fields.

29. Other changes noted in some parts of the country have been a decrease in blocked public rights of way.

30. These are encouraging signs, which Defra's monitoring and evaluation programme will be looking to investigate further in 2008/09. However, we also recognise that the EU legislation makes the administration of cross compliance restrictive and burdensome in places, and we are engaging with the EU review/report process with the objective of enabling more flexibility and simplification. Furthermore, Defra's Regulatory Impact Assessment estimates that the costs to farmers of cross-compliance are modest relative to the size of the budget for direct payments and that the benefits of cross-compliance could be achieved much more cost effectively.

Q8. *How is it linking with other EU policy requirements such as the Water Framework Directive?*

31. The Water Framework Directive is not incorporated into the current cross compliance arrangements but a number of cross compliance measures contribute, in some respects, to reducing diffuse water pollution. In order to keep their land in Good Agricultural and Environment Condition farmers are obliged to draw up a simple risk-based soil management plan—Soil Protection Review—to identify and resolve soil-related problems on their land. They must not cultivate or apply fertilisers, manures or pesticides to land within 2 metres of the centre of any watercourse, and they must prevent overgrazing and unsuitable supplementary feeding to reduce damage to natural or semi-natural vegetation and potential erosion. Statutory Management Requirements cover, among other things, the protection of groundwater from various pollutants, the use of sewage sludge on agricultural land, Nitrate Vulnerable Zones, and restrictions on the use of plant protection products.

32. The European Commission has established a Strategic Steering Group to assess the extent to which agriculture needs to contribute to the delivery of WFD objectives and to help Member States to optimise the contribution from Rural Development programmes, and is also considering the role of cross-compliance. The current mandate runs from 2007–09.

Q9. *How can the CAP contribute to mitigation of, and adaptation to, climate change?*

33. The 2003 CAP reforms were not designed for the purpose of climate change mitigation and adaptation, but they may foster changes in agricultural practices and market responses, which bring about some reductions in greenhouse gas emissions, improvements in the efficient use of inputs, or a reduction in the volume or intensity of agricultural activity. For instance, as noted in the Climate Change Programme 2006, decoupling of direct payments from production is likely to lead to a reduction in livestock numbers and an associated decrease in methane emissions estimated at some 0.68 MtCe per annum in 2010. Similarly, it is expected that trends towards lower input agriculture and better soil nutrient management will be reinforced with a consequent reduction in nitrous oxide emissions.

34. The extension of cross-compliance from 1 January 2007 claimants to new land based Pillar II Rural Development schemes will result in an increasing focus on some aspects of environmental management that, together with changes driven by decoupling, may have positive effects on greenhouse gas mitigation. For example, the requirement to implement Soil Protection Reviews should help to reduce soil organic matter loss (and therefore carbon loss). Defra's cross compliance monitoring and evaluation programme in England will be looking to assess the impacts of cross compliance in 2008–09.

35. Environmental Stewardship (ES) and previous agri-environment schemes, under which farmers receive payments for environmental "goods", though not designed to address climate change at present, have encouraged low-input agriculture and are likely to have contributed to decreased emissions (eg through decreased fertiliser use, buffered waterways against fertiliser run off, and reduced grazing intensity). Defra-funded research into the impact of ES on greenhouse gas emissions is due to be published shortly. This will contribute to the Defra and NE review of progress on ES which has just begun. Under the review of progress ways of increasing the scheme's contribution to climate change mitigation will be examined.

36. Under the Rural Development measures we have supported the establishment of perennial energy crops to encourage additional sources of biomass.

Q9. *What do you consider the role of biofuels to be in this regard?*

37. The CAP currently offers a production based energy aid payment of €45 per hectare to support the growing of crops for energy use. However, as a production linked subsidy, such a payment involves undesirable economic and trade distortion. The Government's preferred approach is to stimulate *demand* for bio-energy for heat, electricity and transport fuels. To stimulate renewable electricity we have introduced the Renewables Obligation and the Government is undertaking work on potential measures to support renewable

heat. We will, be introducing a Renewable Transport Fuel Obligation (RTFO) from April 2008 to require the UK's fuel suppliers to ensure that a minimum level of their total fuel sales are from a renewable source. Since similar mechanisms are being introduced in other Member States, the need for production based subsidies should be eliminated in due course.

38. The European Union set a reference value of 5.75% biofuel penetration for 2010 under the Biofuels Directive, and more recently the European Union Spring Council has endorsed a binding target for 2020 of 10% to be achieved by all EU Member States for the share of biofuels in overall EU transport petrol and diesel consumption, to be introduced in a cost-efficient way. The binding character of this target is subject to a number of important conditions, including second generation fuels becoming commercially available and production being sustainable. For example, the contribution of biofuels to climate change mitigation depends upon the extent to which it displaces fossil fuel emissions once account has been taken of the whole production, processing and distribution cycle. This can vary considerably by feedstock and by production conditions.

39. Further consideration needs to be given to how best to promote "second generation" biofuels from perennial energy crops, which, together with forestry material and wastes provide better carbon savings returns per hectare than annual crops thus reducing pressure on land.

FINANCING

Q10. *Do you consider the current budget to be sufficient?*

40. Rural development expenditure has been maintained at roughly its current level and once the EU modulation agreed in 2003 is included, that means that the focus of the CAP on rural development in the current financial perspective is greater than under the last one.

41. As set out in the Government's CAP Vision paper, we believe there is a strong case for expenditure under the CAP to be substantially reduced. In all policy areas, and looking ahead to the Budget Review, the Government believes that spending through the EU Budget should represent value for money, should add value compared to spending through national budgets, should be proportionate, and should be properly managed.

Q10. *Do you consider co-financing to be a possible way forward in financing the Common Agricultural Policy?*

42. In line with the views set out in the Government's CAP Vision paper, we think that Pillar I should be phased out by 2015–20. Co-financing of Pillar I is one of a range of ways of managing the phase out of Pillar I that could be considered. But Pillar I co-financing is not an end in itself.

ENLARGEMENT

Q11. *What has been the impact on the CAP of the 2004 and 2007 enlargements and what is the likely impact of future enlargements of the EU on the post-2013 CAP?*

43. The 2004 and 2007 enlargements have resulted in some additional costs to the CAP which have so far been absorbed within the budgetary ceilings agreed in 2002. While these ceilings will come under increasing pressure as higher payments continue to be phased in in the newer Member States, the Financial Discipline Mechanism (FDM), agreed as part of the 2002 Brussels Agreement, ensures that the ceilings cannot be breached. Current estimates suggest that the FDM will not be activated before 2009.

44. Enlargement has highlighted problems with existing CAP market management instruments, particularly in the cereals sector, where there has been a large increase in intervention. As a consequence, the Commission has proposed the abolition of maize intervention.

45. The CAP needs to adapt in order to absorb new Member States into the EU in future—for which the UK is a strong advocate. Our vision is clear about the benefits we see to both old and new Member States from the changes we are proposing.

SIMPLIFICATION OF THE CAP AND OTHER ISSUES

Q12. *How could the CAP be further simplified and in what other ways would you like to see the Common Agricultural Policy changed in the short and/or the long term?*

46. The Commission Communication on CAP Simplification was published in October 2005. As Presidency, we prioritised progress on the dossier, and reached agreement on Conclusions at the December 2005 Agriculture Council. In these we achieved a high level of ambition, including a request to the Commission for an Action Plan with concrete proposals. Ambition is increasing in the Action Plan, and new measures relate to simplification of cross compliance requirements, a clear concern for farmers.

47. We believe that the best way to ensure that simplification proposals tackle the right issues is to put in place the necessary evidence base first. This is why we have led a project at EU level to accumulate all available data on administrative burdens in the agriculture sector. This was presented to the Commission and Member States in April, where the Commission encouraged Member States to develop simplification proposals on the back of the evidence. We will be working with colleagues in Europe to make progress, looking forward to the 2008 Health Check of the CAP, as an opportunity to deliver real simplification benefits to farmers, through steps such as the abolition of compulsory set-aside.

11 June 2007

Examination of Witnesses

Witnesses: MS SONIA PHIPPARD, Director, Food and Farming, MR ANDREW LAWRENCE, Deputy Director CAP Reform & EU Strategy, and MR SIMON HARDING, Deputy Director, Economics and Statistics, Department for Environment, Food and Rural Affairs, examined.

Q1 Chairman: Good morning. Thank you very much for coming today and helping us with the very start of this inquiry into the future of the Common Agricultural Policy. It seems as though it is almost every year we have a session on the future of the Common Agricultural Policy, but progress is being made. This is an evidence-taking session. There will be a transcript distributed to you afterwards for you to have a look and see whether it is accurate. Would you like to start by making any initial comments?
Ms Phippard: I was not particularly planning to make any initial comments, except perhaps simply to update you. We provided you with a written note of Defra's current position and view in response to your questions. Since we finalised that there has been a little more progress in the sense that the June Agriculture Council concluded decisions on the reform of the Fruit and Vegetables regime. The Portuguese Presidency has made a start by confirming that they want to get ahead and, if they can, to complete reform of the Wine regime within their presidency, which is ambitious but an excellent ambition. The Commissioner has confirmed that her timetable for the immediate next steps, the so-called Health Check, will indeed be to publish a public consultation paper in the course of the autumn. There will obviously be some discussion at the Agriculture Council, but what she is very keen to do is to engage citizens, certainly public opinion in general, in terms of the immediate future of the CAP. It is likely that the consultation document on the EU Budget Review will be published early in the autumn and that will probably begin to ask some questions and to give some flavour of the longer term, although obviously I can only speculate as to the precise

content. The process continues to move, hence our active engagement with it.

Q2 Chairman: Looking forward to 2020, what do you see as the defining characteristics of the CAP? What would it look like? What would its main features be?
Ms Phippard: My hope, and the UK's hope, is that the CAP would be in some ways broader but also better focussed than it is at present. At the moment it tends to be defined largely by the money it spends, which is not tremendously effective or healthy, although it has very understandable effects on behaviour. I would hope that by 2020 it would be defined much more clearly in the minds both of the European Commission and also of farmers and the public by the outcomes that it is seeking to achieve. It clearly continues to be a series of regulations which enable the Single Market within the EU for agricultural products and delivers to the citizen the things that really matter around food safety and food security—the supply of food—but it is also focused on the other outcomes that are important from farming, the so-called public goods, environmental public goods, and also the enhancement and protection of our rural areas. That means that the financial flows will be very much focused on those public goods. The UK's ambition by 2020 is of it being entirely focused on those public goods, many of them environmental but not necessarily exclusively so, and with a suitable balance and framework between any national funding that may exist at that stage.

Q3 *Chairman:* If the exclusive focus would be on public goods in terms of financial flows, what elements of the CAP would fall away?

Ms Phippard: Essentially the present Pillar I and all its works. In other words, payments which are exclusively income support and the market measures which also form part of Pillar I,—intervention, export subsidies and price support of various kinds.

Q4 *Chairman:* That is a very ambitious objective. To get there, who are your friends?

Ms Phippard: We have quite a number of friends, surprising though this may seem.

Q5 *Chairman:* Apart from the Treasury!

Ms Phippard: We have friends within the United Kingdom, of course. Overseas there are now a number of other Member States who are looking at a pretty radical reform of Pillar I, some who have been long-standing friends and friends of reform—ie the Swedes and the Danes. The Germans are pretty clear that further reform is needed. They are currently engaged in a very active internal debate between the Federal Government and the Lander, but it is reform-oriented. The former Dutch Minister had published a paper setting out his views, but there is no doubt that the Dutch government is looking for further reform. The list also includes some of the Baltic states, the Estonians and Latvians—the Latvians have published a document—and some of the other new Member States, the Maltese and the Czechs. There are a number of other Member States who, I think, without necessarily going quite as far as us, would definitely support the enhancement of Pillar II at the expense of Pillar I. In other words, they see the value of moving the funding much more clearly to targeted public goods rather than across-the-board payments.

Q6 *Lord Bach:* Can I remain general and really follow on from what the Chairman was asking you. You talk about progress towards the abolition of direct payments and the end of the Single Payment Scheme. Can you just enlarge a little bit on that? I presume and hope that it is Defra's policy that those direct payments will end in due course? When do you think direct payments as such, whatever they are called, will end?

Ms Phippard: As you know, the Defra-Treasury paper aims for a target end-date of between 2015 and 2020. If I look at statements from the Commission, on the face of it, in an agriculture context, it is likely to be at the latter end of that window, because there are quite a lot of Member States who would see the next Financial Perspective, 2013 to 2020, as a transition period. That is in the Agriculture context. However, the major debate on financial issues will happen in the context of the Budget discussions,

which will be at the Heads of Government and Finance Minister level. Where I hope we and most other Member States would be entirely at one is that, as they look at the financial pressures on the CAP, the public goods element of the spend (ie Pillar II as it currently is), they will see it is far better value than Pillar I. I would hope that the pressure from that angle will be to bring Pillar I down while protecting, and indeed potentially enhancing, Pillar II. As to how fast that will move, I am not sure it is for me to speculate.

Q7 *Lord Bach:* Is it not important that it moves pretty quickly? Is it Defra's present policy that we should lead the way towards that happening pretty quickly or that we should be in a pack of well-wishers and just go along with them? That is an important decision to make. Up until now I think we have had a reputation with our European colleagues, sometimes good, sometimes not so good, of being prepared to be way out on this, hopefully to lead the others to the Promised Land. What is your view?

Ms Phippard: I think we will continue to lead the debate. I think it is only us and Sweden who have said unequivocally, with a timescale, that Pillar I payments should come to a complete end and we will continue to do that because it is abundantly clear to us—and our economic evidence every time reinforces this message—that Pillar I is simply not good value for money for anybody. Equally, there are still demands which potentially we are not meeting either at EU or national level on the environmental and public goods side. There are great benefits from moving ahead with change. We have said, and we remain clear, that that has got to be done over a manageable timescale, but we will be pressing for ambitious decisions in the context of the Health Check, the Budget Review and all other discussions that happen. We would hope for some very firm and clear decisions in that series of discussions over 2008/09 and probably the first couple of years of the new Commission.

Q8 *Lord Bach:* You say in your document that the good things about cross-compliance do not outweigh the huge cost there is under Pillar I and direct payments. Just expand on that a bit. There are other ways of doing the environmental good works other than Pillar I, are there not?

Ms Phippard: Yes. Cross-compliance has two elements, the first of which is simply obeying the law. It is quite clear that cross-compliance in its first year, from the work of our own Environmental Observatory and others, has helped to sharpen focus on obeying the law because it adds an extra sanction. Nevertheless, that is the law and it is inspected, regulated and enforced. The second half is more obvious value added, the good agricultural and environmental condition, but it is at a fairly basic general level. Certainly within England what we have seen as the major way of going beyond that is our entry-level Environmental Stewardship Scheme and we have currently structured that scheme so that we have a spectrum, with cross-compliance as the very basic level and then entry level stewardship. We are looking to encourage the vast majority of farmers or at least the vast bulk of land within that scheme. That is one obvious way. The other is looking at law enforcement and other more specific incentives.

Q9 *Chairman:* That is a bold way forward that you have outlined to us. Do I take it that the Territorial Administrations have signed up with equal enthusiasm to that objective?

Ms Phippard: I think the Territorial Administrations would join us in the direction of travel. The 'Vision' paper was published by Defra and the Treasury; it was not a joint document. We have some very new Territorial Administrations and so I think it would be rash of me to speak for them in detail, but we work very closely with them. We do not have differences in the basic direction of travel. We might have some differences in nuance and probably in speed.

Q10 *Lord Cameron of Dillington:* You told us who your friends were. But, probably because we ought to actually hear evidence from them, who are the enemies on the Continent?

Ms Phippard: Probably the most vocal is France, as a very significant beneficiary of the CAP, but they, too, have their range of allies. Of the new Member States, Poland is probably the leader, with Hungary as well. Among the other older Member States, the Irish are conservative on a number of things, although not everything. But on spend they are. Luxembourg, Austria, Greece and Finland for geographical reasons are also conservative.

Q11 *Lord Cameron of Dillington:* The Commission refers to the 'European Model of Agriculture'. I think I know what it means and I suspect the words 'family farm' occur several times during any definition of it. Perhaps you might like to comment on that. In what way do you think the economic and maybe social conditions have changed in the last ten years and may be continuing to change, hopefully, regarding the structure of the countryside and the rural economy which is going to make the job of implementing your policies easier?

Ms Phippard: Just on the European model of agriculture—interestingly, it does not mention the 'family farm'. Any joint EU Ministerial discussion tends to bring those words out. One of the points that we tend to make is that the family farm itself is an immensely variable feast. There are some extremely large, efficient family business farms in lots of parts of

Europe as well as, it has to be said, the rather small ones. The European model talks about versatility, sustainability, competitiveness, and it also talks about the continuing process of reform. I think the one aspect of the European model where we tend slightly to pause is an emphasis on agriculture happening everywhere in the EU. I think we would say where that makes environmental and market sense rather than inevitably. Coming on to your second question, we have seen a number of changes in the last ten years. One is that EU agriculture has been influenced, albeit probably with a rather slower, dampened effect, by global trends much more than by its own protectionist framework. We have seen the impact of global price changes, global markets, et cetera shaping European farming to a much greater degree and that has been obvious in farms tending to increase in size, whilst the number of those employed in agriculture has generally been falling. There is a real enthusiasm on the part of farmers in much of the EU to be market orientated. "Stop telling us to be market orientated, that is what we want," is something we hear quite a lot, and that is not just a UK phenomenon. There is a real appetite to respond to the market. In a number of cases that has fed through into strong farmer support for things like decoupling payments. We await with interest to see whether that will happen in those parts of the EU where governments have insisted on retaining coupled payments. The other thing that has happened within the last ten years, which is more EU-orientated, is Enlargement, which has further extended the versatility and the variety of models. It has taken us back in some ways to some of the challenges that the EU 15 faced earlier, because we have some very, very large numbers of non-sustainable farm "businesses" in a number of the new Member States. We have that extra challenge. On the other hand, we have a larger market and a lot more players who are looking for the competitive model that is going to enable them to survive.

Q12 *Lord Greaves:* Can I just pick up on that question of the new Member States and the restructuring that is needed? If you take a longer view, people used to talk about going into the Common Market and inefficient French farmers. Farmers in the Paris basin are no more inefficient than farmers in East Anglia, perhaps less so. A huge transformation took place in France with the rural reorganisation, which really predated the CAP in many ways and the whole place was transformed. That kind of reorganisation needs to take place in Poland and Bulgaria and some other places. It is going to be very expensive and somebody is going to have to pay for it. How does that fit in with CAP reform?

Ms Phippard: I would say it fits very well. The evidence is pretty clear that across the board Pillar I-type payments are not the way to achieve that. Pillar I-type payments tend to stultify and slow down structural change because they give everyone a comfort zone in which they sit. Also, decoupled payments tend to result in people continuing to do what they have always done, whereas a greater focus on Pillar II, particularly in those cases, the Axes 1 and 3, payments for farming innovation and for more major rural development and restructuring, seem to us to be two useful levers, but frankly, so, too, are some elements of European policy outside the CAP. The UK has made it clear that we would see those Member States as major recipients of structural funds because of their rural problems. They have far too many farmers, but the problem goes way beyond farming. There is a major skills issue. There is a major question of where the populations sit and so on. So the quite substantial sums that are and will flow to them under structural funds are important to them.

Q13 *Lord Plumb:* There are two parts to my question, one of which is to do with food security. There is a lot of confusion over food security. I am sure the commercial farmers have told you how important it is. Secondly, there is confusion over how European agriculture is going to fit into the competitive pattern which we are already facing and what part they should play in that, recognising what is happening in Brazil and China and various places where they are exporting large quantities of food at a price way below our cost of production. On the food security point, in your paper of December 2006 you say "Food security should not be confused with national security, which is a pure public good. Food itself does not have 'public good' characteristics." I fully accept that self-sufficiency makes little sense. In today's international world we have to face competition as it is. As we see the reform of the CAP and support many of the measures that are being proposed at the moment, how is that going to fit in? The structure of farming will change. The structure of agriculture right through Europe will change. There may be closer ties between agri-business and the farming community as we see the development of the marketing of products and so on. Those really are my two concerns which I think need clearing up, because of the confusion that obviously exists. We are not just talking about food, of course, we are now talking about fuel. You will know that at the Royal Show the buzz word in the whole of the show was fuel rather than food, as we see that development taking place.

Ms Phippard: Let me reiterate what we said certainly in both that December paper but also in the 'Vision'. It is quite important that food security is not confused with either self-sufficiency or national security. The UK, and indeed the EU, have relied very heavily on effective trading relationships as part of our food security for many years. The Second World War obviously, in those particular national security circumstances, challenged that. Current assessments of national security issues—and food is an essential of life—indicate that maintaining secure and stable trading relationships and enhancing those are absolutely key to our food security and our fuel security as a nation. That said, we do indeed recognise that the liberalisation of trade has impacts on who produces what and where. We have done quite a lot of analysis already of what those impacts are likely to be and we are continuing to try to enhance and take forward that analysis and to share that with our counterparts around Europe. It is worth emphasising again that Europe, in food trade terms at the moment, is pretty much in balance. If you do it in euros or pounds, we export a lot of high-value-added products. We import quite a lot of commodities, some of which we cannot produce here, some of which we could but do not. By and large, as we look ahead, that continues to be the pattern against a world where we will face more competition from cheaply produced commodities but where the global population is growing and the global demand for the high-quality, high-value-added type of products that the EU produces is also growing. However, that is an enormously across-the-board picture and not much comfort to the individual sector or farmer. So below that we are trying to make sure we do understand and can discuss with both farming interests here but also the rest of our European counterparts what the more detailed impacts will be, whether there are consequences which—probably not, frankly, from a food point of view but maybe from a rural policy point of view—would lead to a drastic change in the rural economy in a particular area or environmental impacts.

Mr Harding: I think one of the most important points that our paper made was that, if you are interested in food security, then you need to realise that there are a huge variety of threats to our food security and food supplies and that only some of those threats are of a nature that would make it helpful to actually grow lots of food on your own sovereign territories. There is not really a very direct connection between how much food you grow domestically and the level of security that you attach to your supplies of food. There are a great many other influences, such as energy supplies, logistical systems, the possibility of terrorist attacks, et cetera. There is a long list which is enumerated in that paper. The second point to make is about the data itself. We have published figures of about 60 per cent for what we call food self-sufficiency and about 70 per cent for self-sufficiency in what we call indigenous products, such as things that we typically grow in Northern Europe. Those figures are calculated on the basis of shares of value.

It takes account of the prices of the products that we are buying. Obviously there is a huge mix of food products, including a lot of processed products, things to which a lot of value has been added beyond the farm gate. That is not really the same thing as our nutritional requirements. If you were to look at our nutritional requirements and ask the question! Are we going to starve or feel hungry? The answer to that would be a great deal different and the relevant figure would be a great deal higher. If you take into account the problem of obesity and over-eating, you would probably say that we were 110 per cent self-sufficient at the moment. That is for the UK and the situation is even more favourable for the EU as a whole, from where we get most of our food imports at the moment. Unless we are cut off from Europe, then the UK is at least as food secure as Europe is. As far as European food security is concerned, in the sense of purely growing the stuff, the estimates that have been made of the probable impact of radical trade reform suggest a wide range of possibilities, but most of the studies seem to indicate that changes in the output of European agriculture could be less than 10% and could be between 10% and 20% and is less likely to be any more than that. If you apply those levels of changes to what we already produce, you do not get an alarming picture of moving into a marginal food supply.

Q14 *Chairman:* Do you not think you are likely to run into an argument from supporters of Pillar-I type payments? The argument would be along the lines that we live in a dangerous world, we have climate change, we do not know what the impact of climate change is going to be, we have the strongly emerging economies in the Far East and China, with food consumption likely to go up. So, it might be argued, in those circumstances should we not play it safe and put food security at the top of the list and, in order to do that, protect Pillar I payments? Do you see that as an argument that you might have to confront?

Ms Phippard: It is an argument that we have to confront. There are a number of arguments advanced for protecting Pillar I but they nearly all centre around either the view that in certain parts of Europe farming might stop if you took it away or you have to safeguard in some way the present pattern of European agriculture. The response to that is that the pattern of European agriculture has changed, is changing and will continue to change. Pillar I has had some impacts on it, most of it not tremendously helpful because in a number of cases it has encouraged over-production of the wrong things (hence the sugar reforms that we are rather painfully trying to go through at the moment) rather than helped to support food security as defined by those who take that line of argument. Yes, the argument will be presented. I think the other response to it is

that, if you are seriously looking at food security in a European security sense, let us look at the value of Pillar I payments against all the other things that we are doing to spend on European security. I would push the argument gently towards the Budget Review, where we need to look at all European spend and the outcomes that Europe is trying to achieve and ask whether seriously maintaining Pillar I simply on that basis would make any sense either absolutely or relatively.

Q15 *Lord Plumb:* Are you concerned about the balance of production? I am in danger of talking about British agriculture and the Chairman will be very angry with me if I do. Let us look at it in European terms. We are seeing quite a measure of change at the moment. Three herds are going out of production every week for instance. The milk supply situation is desperate. The cost of feed going into those animals is increasing. That is not just a British problem, that is a European problem. My own worry is that we see that getting totally out of balance and that is not going to be of interest to the consumers in European countries.

Ms Phippard: I think the answer would be 'yes', at a quite high level. That is why we set up the Agricultural Change and Environmental Observatory, which is looking at what is happening here, particularly focused on England, to try and make sure that within our own shores we are aware of changes and, if there are trends which are worrying for any reason, we can spot those. The big balance question at the moment, it seems to me, is the one that is prompted by the fuel debate, where there are a variety of issues. There are the people who estimate that, if we were going to produce all our fuel as biofuel, or a large proportion of it, then the whole of Europe would become a mass production of non-food crops. That has all kinds of downsides. Hence the UK's very firm view, which I think is shared across Europe, is that, as we look at the fuel alternatives, we need to be very, very clear both about looking for the most efficient sources of them, which may not be European, and at the environmental impacts of those sources. There are also concerns about the impacts in developing countries if the biofuel market does well and, therefore, rather as we heard some years back, about niche crops displacing essential production for feeding of the local population. The same concerns apply to biofuels. As responsible world citizens we have to keep a pretty clear eye on all of that. So responsible purchasing and doing everything we can through our broader energy and biofuels policies to make sure that we purchase in a responsible manner which does not have adverse social and environmental impacts is vitally important.

Q16 *Lord Greaves:* I am old enough to remember the Second World War and the 1940s. In those days every scrap of food was consumed and yet nowadays there is huge wastage. When we talk about the level of production and over-production or whatever, production for what? There is a vast amount wasted that the supermarkets will not accept because it is not the right shape of carrot or whatever it is. It is said that people waste 50% of the food that they buy, as it is then thrown away. People do not seem to eat half of the food that goes on the plates nowadays. We were all taught to eat up every last scrap, which is why some of us find it difficult keeping our weight down. Is not the presumption, which I suppose has been there in public policy ever since the Corn Laws were abolished 175 years ago, that food should be as cheap as possible and that the whole of competition policy and all the rest of it should be geared at getting it to be as cheap as possible? Is there not a basic flaw in that at a time when so much is wasted? How do we marry up these different things?

Ms Phippard: I do not think that, from a public policy point of view, I would argue that food should be as cheap as possible. I hope I will not get shot by any fellow members from elsewhere in government for saying that. I think what we should argue is that food should be affordable for all and that public policy which simply adds costs to food without benefit cannot be sensible. Equally, there is a good argument for enabling the market to recognise things like the full environmental cost of the production of food and making consumers more aware of that. At the moment there are environmental costs which are not reflected in consumer prices. There is a lively debate beginning around whether that is right and whether there are markets which should be developing that to take account of that kind of value. I think the answer is that we should not be asking consumers to pay for the costs of a policy which does not deliver those goods. Artificially inflating prices has done nothing to help handle that over-purchase and waste. This is a very real challenge both in terms of helping consumers to understand the rather complex thinking around sustainable consumption but also looking at how markets function in terms of environmental costs.

Q17 *Lord Greaves:* By historical standards food prices are incredibly cheap now. We are not paying for all sorts of extra things, are we?

Ms Phippard: Within Europe we are still paying twice over for the Pillar I aspects of the CAP. I do not think removing that will make a vast difference one way or the other to consumer behaviour. I think the way you tackle consumer behaviour is a different thing. I do not think inflating food prices through the CAP, even if we were to do it to a ludicrous extent, would be a very good way of influencing consumer behaviour.

For most European citizens food is still a relatively low proportion of their total budget. Perversely, however, it is in the very poorest parts of Europe, mostly the new Member States, where food still is a very significant proportion of the budget. Those are probably the areas where healthy, accessible, safe food is still a much bigger need. It seems to us that having a policy which has perverse effects on price cannot be right.

Q18 *Viscount Ullswater:* I am going to take you back to structures, if I may. You argue very strongly, both in your paper and today, for the phasing out of Pillar I payments. As we have seen in some other regimes, do you think there will be a pressure from Member States to have part of that payment funded by what I think in the wine regime they call "national envelopes"? I am just wondering whether there is a pressure for national envelopes to be developed and whether that will have a direct impact on EU competition policy. Before I leave that, I wanted to go a little bit into Pillar II, where your evidence indicates that there are going to be 94 new Rural Development Programmes. Is that right?

Ms Phippard: Yes.

Q19 *Viscount Ullswater:* Is that not going to be costly? Will that really benefit the rural community? It certainly will not benefit the consumer of food. If that is the case, this huge number of policies and perhaps the development of national envelopes, are we not really repatriating agriculture back to the Member States? Your comments please.

Ms Phippard: In terms of the phasing out of Pillar I, there are a number of different ways in which people may call for national spend. The Dutch certainly have floated the idea of co-financing. Some are doing rather more what you were suggesting, going for more traditional State Aids, ie purely national financing. Our view on co-financing would be that it is something of a red herring when it comes to Pillar I. It does not seem to us that it is a particularly helpful step on the way to reducing Pillar I. If you are going to keep an across-the-board Pillar I with the same rules for everybody, then the theory that brings co-financing into Pillar II does not apply. While I do not think we would automatically say "no, never", we would very much want to understand where on earth it fitted in. At the moment it is not very obvious to us that it is a logical step to take. On the question of State Aids—ie purely national spend—to replace, Pillar I-type support, again we would very much query it as a replacement to Pillar I because why give income support to some or all farmers in a certain Member State? We would need to be absolutely clear it was not anti-competitive. At the moment the State Aid rules certainly would not allow it. In a simpler CAP world, where the payments were focused entirely on public goods, then I imagine we would need to revisit the current State Aid rules which reflect the large sums of European money that go in. Either way, I am not attracted to the prospect of State Aids replacing Pillar I. As you come to Pillar II-type measures, it seems to me that the arguments are slightly different. I think there is a question of making sure that we look at Pillar II against your entirely well-founded concerns about bureaucracy, and that we should not be funding at a European level from a taxpayer point of view or forcing through a European level of bureaucracy and inspection and enforcement things which should be entirely down to Member State discretion. As long as activities are proper public good which do meet competition and State Aids rules, if we go that way for certain types of activity, which may currently be either within Pillar II or on people's wish-lists for Pillar II, allowing state aids is something we should think through. It is an entirely reasonable area to explore and really to work out what should be done at EU level and what should be done at national level. As for the 94 Rural Development programmes, the UK is guilty of four of them, because we have one each for England, Scotland, Wales and Northern Ireland. Germany has Lander and Spain has 17 Provinces. That is how we get to 94. Each one is actually reasonably large and obviously has a measure of regional integrity which would be defended vigorously either by the Scots, the Catalans, the English or whoever. I think that allowing that measure of regional segregation is not a bad thing. One of the things we have argued about Pillar II is that it does need to be flexible and locally responsive. Clearly in the UK we have very much welcomed and taken full advantage of the ability to use regional flexibility. However, one of the things we will certainly be wanting to address with other Member States and the Commission as we look forward is how we can simplify Pillar II, not only what is in there (we have got to have only the right things in there) but some of the rules around it which are complex. We are pretty confident there is scope for some simplification as we go forward. We have made one step within England, in the Entry Level scheme, something which is much simpler than a traditional Pillar II measure—at least we hope so—at the application and paying agency levels. But looking at the scope for rather simpler approaches within Pillar II and some of the bureaucracy around it is one of the things we very much want to do. Our experts have been a bit distracted by jumping through the hoops of getting in the present Rural Development programme, so we are rather at the beginning of that. But we certainly intend to do it.

Q20 *Viscount Ullswater:* I am concerned about the finance. Will some of the finance for Pillar I be transferred to Pillar II? Is that phased? Or is it discreetly financed by different parts of the budget?

Ms Phippard: The limits on CAP expenditure apply to Pillar I and Pillar II. We are transferring money from Pillar I to Pillar II by modulation, both the compulsory modulation which applies to all the old Member States and, in the UK and Portugal, voluntary modulation. The Commissioner has made it clear that one of her ambitions both for the Health Check and looking further ahead is taking that process further. In the Health Check they are looking to increase the rate of compulsory modulation over the next few years and the UK has made it clear that it supports that ambition. I think the question as we look further ahead, beyond 2013, is whether you look rather more radically at both Pillars and, instead of quite a complicated system of effectively top-slicing each Member State and indeed each farmer, you actually look at the financing of the two Pillars afresh and start again with new sums dedicated to the specific funding pots within the overall CAP that fund Pillar I and Pillar II. But this is a Budget Review-level discussion rather than a Health Check discussion.

Q21 *Chairman:* Can I push you a little bit on the co-financing of Pillar I? It could be argued that one of the benefits of co-financing is that National Treasuries have to pick up the direct cost and that creates the opportunity for a little bit of financial discipline.

Ms Phippard: That obviously depends very much on the rules for co-financing. It would certainly enhance Finance Ministries' interest in the cost, particularly Finance Ministries in Member States who are net recipients rather than net contributors—which is why I said that we would not automatically rule it out if it was on a route to somewhere. My suspicion is that there will be quite a lot of pressure from Finance Ministries anyway, given lots of aspirations for the EU budget, to look pretty hard at Pillar I and possibly quite hard to get a measure of agreement on co-financing for it. It does risk being something of a distraction, although it is not something we should ignore and certainly not completely rule out.

Q22 *Lord Cameron of Dillington:* The Rural Development policy has got four Axes and we seem to focus mainly on the Environment Axis. I have always seen rural economic development as a way of taking the dependence of farmers away from their food production into other businesses, or even the whole rural economy and employment, and that would seem to me to be a very good Axis to focus on. Are we not interested in the other three Axes?

Ms Phippard: I think the answer is that we are certainly interested in rural development in its broadest sense and driving forward innovation, diversification, et cetera. There is no lack of interest and we have both consulted and taken very seriously the opportunity in Axes 1 and 3. In England we are doing 3 and 4 together. I think the question as we go forward is, certainly in our economic situation and the economic situation of most of the older EU Member States, whether this is the only and the best focused way of achieving those outcomes. The sums—and I am very conscious of it from previous responsibilities for the sustainable farming and food strategy in England—available through Axes 1 and 3, although welcome, are trivial compared to the sums available on the whole skills agenda through funding for Learning and Skills Councils or the funds that still flow to old Member States through structural funds, so we need to make effective use of those and indeed national funding to the RDAs in England and equivalents elsewhere in the UK. It seems to us that the question about those Axes is not their desirability as outcomes but whether it is the best use of scarce CAP funding. Our assessment in England was that for the environmental needs to be met through agri-environment schemes, et cetera, under Axis 2, we needed to put as much as possible in there. That said, it looks rather different as you go east. We said in the 'Vision' document and would still firmly stand by the fact that in those countries that have a major rural restructuring/reskilling task ahead of them every possible channel needs to be open to them for at least a transitional period, probably quite a long transitional period looking at experience elsewhere in Europe. CAP rural development funding is an effective lever. Again, however, we need to make sure it is well targeted and works sensibly with those other levers.

Q23 Baroness Miller of Chilthorne Domer: In answer to the question before last you mentioned starting afresh with rural development funding, which would obviously be quite good for the UK as we have had a rather bad deal recently because of the fact that successively we have had a very low historical base to go forward on. If we were to start afresh, what do you think the objective criteria would be as a basis for any funding? Again, how much commonality is there between different States on those criteria? Is that even a horizon document at the moment?

Ms Phippard: The Commission did develop, and there was agreement on, objective criteria for allocating the proceeds of compulsory modulation. That allocation key depended on agricultural land area, agricultural employment and GDP, so measures of current competitiveness and agricultural land need, which seemed to us the sort of place to start and there obviously already has been a measure of agreement around that. If we stick with our present 3—Axes Rural Development Programme, you need to capture something which is about land area, rural disadvantage and environmental value. So you have agricultural employment and need on

the one hand and then the wider rural need. Is there general agreement around it? Well, it is quite hard when some people are sitting on disproportionate gains from the current system. At the moment I do not think we could expect the Austrians or the Finns to vote with alacrity in that direction. I think we have to have that debate. The Commission, and the Council, has already agreed that at least some measure of debate needs to happen in the context of the Health Check and it clearly needs to happen in the run-up to the next Financial Perspective, because for us and for some others to have a rural development share based on patterns of spend in the early Nineties will by 2010-2011 be completely ludicrous. We would argue that it is fairly ludicrous now.

Mr Lawrence: It is worth adding that the new Member States of course were entitled to so-called SAPARD funding—the Special Accession Programme for Agriculture and Rural Development—and they did not have a historic reference period which the EU could use by which to judge what they should get. So there is another model potentially there. Sonia has mentioned the compulsory modulation work but there is another model in the way in which the criteria are put together for new Member States to access that money.

Ms Phippard: The other point to make about the new Member States is that they will be very strong allies of ours in having another thorough look at all of this because they are very conscious that a lot of money was put into old Member States.

Q24 Baroness Miller of Chilthorne Domer: Can I just push towards this ultimate end point. If you did get to that point where the SAPARD view of the world did come to be accepted within the EU, what sort of a tool would we then use or develop to see whether value for money was being delivered? We have already mentioned that there are 94 different rural development plans, and obviously it will be important then to say "Well, actually, you have developed your rural area, so in future you should not have as much of the funding." That is going to be immensely contentious, so it is going to need immensely strong tools to actually measure so that people can come to an objective agreement. Do you see that work being done by the Commission at all?

Ms Phippard: It is beginning, but you are right to hint that it is complex. It is difficult stuff. The European Court of Auditors have begun to make a start and provide some reporting and thinking around the evaluation of agro-environment measures and investment support, the two main aspects of Pillar II. The other thing we can do is, for all Member States, all their regions, all 94 rural development programmes come in, to look at the scope of what is in there and the tools there are now to evaluate the type of measures that people are using. The evaluation is getting better, in my view; but we have a long way to go. Rural development in its current form is still relatively young by EU standards and it is complicated stuff. We have quite a lot of work in hand within the UK to try to understand better environmental benefits and their value and the contribution of any specific scheme to that benefit. It is not easy, but I think there is a very real will at both European level and certainly domestically to enhance that, and a slight tension with our European Commission colleagues to ensure that they do not make excessive demands for extra statistical information, which acts as a burden on all Member States, but do have the evidence base that they need really to get a stronger handle on value for money and the contribution of rural development. So yes, it is very much on their agenda.

Q25 *Lord Palmer:* I have two questions, the first of which you have almost answered when answering Lord Greaves and Lord Cameron's supplementary. Perhaps I can ask Mr Lawrence this one. If we think last time the CAP was reformed back in 2003, it was of course before the recent enlargement. What changes, if any, does the Government consider ought to be necessary to accommodate the needs of the diverse agriculture situations in the new Member States? And, my particular concern, what about any future enlargement?

Mr Lawrence: As you say, the 2003 reform was before enlargement, although it was pretty clear that enlargement was going to happen, so it was certainly in light of and in anticipation of that. I think our vision pretty much answers the question about what you could and should do and I think there have been inquiries in this Committee, and others as well, looking at the impact of enlargement and how the CAP should adjust and that is very much, as Sonia has explained, the focus upon restructuring and modernisation of their agricultural systems. I know I was in Romania not long ago and the challenge put to us was that they have 4 million farms, of which 2 million need to find something else to do.

Q26 *Lord Greaves:* Only 2 million!

Mr Lawrence: That might be Step One. That is the sort of level of challenge and, as Sonia said, that is what our vision is really trying to look towards as we look towards future enlargement with Croatia and Turkey, to make sure that the CAP is structured such that we can help this change happen rather than, as Sonia has described, having a system around Pillar I which potentially keeps people on the land, puts land prices up, and makes it more difficult for people to start and to move and to change.

Q27 *Lord Palmer:* I ought perhaps to declare an interest in that I am a farmer in Scotland and am therefore in receipt of a Single Farm Payment, but a recurrent theme of critics of the CAP over the years is that it is not 'common'. They point to the different situation for farmers where the Single Farm Payment is historic and, of course, others where it has been replaced by the regional flat rate payments to continue partial coupling in some Member States, to rural development programmes that seem to provide differing, competitive benefits and differences in administrative rigour. How much importance in reality does the Government attach to the notion of—dreadful expression—the level playing field?

Ms Phippard: The answer is that a level playing field is certainly important to avoid distortion of competition and there are various aspects of the distribution of funding under the current CAP which are inequitable and will need to change over time. But that does not necessarily mean uniformity. The different approaches that have been taken to the distribution of Pillar I funding do not seem to us seriously to alter the level playing field, at least in the medium term, because they are by and large decoupled, even where there is a measure of coupling aiming to maintain production in a certain way. Those farmers are arguably disadvantaged by the fact that they also have to stick with a lot of the old bureaucracy that went with the old coupled payments. So there are some things that need simplifying and levelling out and there is little doubt that the Commission have that very much in mind as they look ahead. They are not particularly happy with the diversity of approaches to Pillar I that there are. They have a problem they know they have to tackle between the new Member States, who are on the SAPS scheme (the area payments scheme) and the old Member States, and a couple of the new ones who are on the single payment scheme; and they rather prefer the philosophy behind the new Member States' scheme, which is the area-based sort of approach that England is moving gently towards, and one or two of the other old Member States have approached. I suspect the Commission will come up with some thinking around some fairly drastic simplification but that will be as they look to post—2013, and I think our view on that would be slightly similar to my comments on co-financing. In principle, yes, fine, let us explore it but let us make sure it is not a huge distraction when the general direction of travel is to reduce the sums available. As we know, redistribution is extremely painful, so looking at the relative impacts of likely reducing funding in Pillar I and redistribution, we will have to look at the detail.

Mr Lawrence: That is what I would have said.

Q28 *Lord Plumb:* Since you obviously recognize the importance of a level playing field, one area, of course, where there is no level playing field is in the field of money and the gap of 20 per cent between the value of the euro and the value of sterling—and there are other countries, of course, who have not necessarily adopted the euro but they do not have the gap that we have in this country. What would you recommend a farmer to do? Should he take his money in euros or not?

Chairman: You have to get this into CAP reform somehow!

Q29 *Lord Plumb:* Chairman, it is right in the middle of CAP reform. If you give me the right answer, I will leave now.

Ms Phippard: I think he should support the reduction of the Pillar I payments very speedily, so that he no longer faces this difficult dilemma.

Q30 *Lord Plumb:* But surely there are payments through Pillar II also.

Ms Phippard: There are Pillar II payments.

Mr Harding: From an economic perspective, they can already have their payments in euros if they want to, and the sensible thing to do, if 16% of your income comes in foreign currency, is to make sure that 16% of your outgoings are in a foreign currency as well. There are ways in the market that that can be achieved. It requires a level of sophistication that a lot of farmers do not yet seem to possess, but it is possible.

Lord Plumb: Chairman, I am aware of the procedures. I wanted an answer.

Chairman: You are not getting one!

Q31 *Viscount Brookeborough:* My Single Farm Payment may not be big but it certainly looks better in euros! You have already mentioned briefly sugar, fruit and vegetables, and wine, which are at different stages of conclusion, although they are by no means actually reformed in practice yet. Would you like to comment on the progress and on what you feel about them, and to indicate to what extent the Health Check should actually look at them, accepting that some of them are so new at the moment that there is not going to be much to say?

Ms Phippard: As you say, they are all three at rather different stages. For sugar: the reform was done, although I think everyone recognized in 2005, when the reforms were agreed, that it was a staging post and would need to be returned to in due course, but 'in due course' is well beyond the likely Health Check timing. The issues around sugar at the moment are about the fact that the EU was spectacularly over-producing and had serious trade challenges. The Commission and the Council concluded that we needed to take out around 6 million tonnes of EU production. The first two years of the restructuring scheme have only seen the achievement of about a third of that, whereas it had been hoped that we

would be well over halfway in Years One and Two. So the discussions that are going on now and will be concluded before the Health Check are about how to get that reduction in EU production back on track.

Q32 *Viscount Brookeborough:* Knowing where you are at the moment, do you think this next stage is going to succeed?

Ms Phippard: I think the Commission's will is pretty clearly that it will, and the nature of the original reform package is such that, if the Council do not reach agreement now on amendments to the restructuring package, there will be uncompensated quota cuts across the board at the end of the four-year process. So I hope very much—and I am sure here we are completely at one with the Commission—that against that background all Member States will agree to something which allows that quota reduction to happen with compensation in the next two years.

Q33 *Chairman:* Would you agree that at the moment the burden of the sugar reform has fallen almost entirely on the ACP countries?

Ms Phippard: I am not sure that I would agree with that. What I would say is that what has happened so far in sugar reform has been some of the change in European production that we all wanted to see and mostly in the areas that everyone anticipated it happening. So it is true that that has been not desperately burdensome because it has been well compensated, but there has been some real will to change—the Italian approach, for instance, has taken it seriously. There are, however, a number of Member States where sugar beet does not look like the natural local product where movement has been rather slower and finding ways of ensuring that the reduction happens is important. In terms of EU sugar refining, there was an important element of the package which is about enabling our refiners also to remain competitive and a measure of protection for them during the transition period. That has worked to an extent but there obviously has been an impact. We have our continued import obligations and we will continue to honour those; we have no choice. But that is now widely recognized around Europe and calls, for instance, which there were from some of the beet producer organisations simply to cut the refining allowed as though you could just do that have actually been modified in the light of commercial trade law reality.

Q34 *Viscount Brookeborough:* What about fruit and vegetables, very briefly?

Ms Phippard: Fruit and vegetables, we think, basically is concluded, at least at political agreement level and is a good outcome. Obviously, it has to be carried through. Good news because it leads to full decoupling of those aids over a transitional period but the various calls that there were along the way for certain sectors within fruit and vegetables to be completely ring-fenced and maintain coupled payments were defeated in the final decision with sensible transition to the new single payment. The risk and crisis management elements, which we look at with a certain wariness, because certain Member States promote risk and crisis management in a way that looks to us remarkably like market support by the back door, are actually all firmly in industry hands; they are all owned by the producer organisations, effectively co-operatives of fruit and vegetable producers. They are 50-50 funded, so there is serious industry funding for them. And, although in some cases some of the measures do not seem to us ideal, nonetheless the firm industry ownership and responsibility seems to us to be a good outcome. Wine—we wait to see the Commission's proposals.

Q35 *Chairman:* I thought you had them.

Ms Phippard: They have been quite widely leaked and I think there our view is broadly to welcome the direction of travel but there are certainly some aspects we will want to explore fairly carefully, especially at some of what they can do in the national envelopes—and national envelopes are, alas, not national spend but EU spend allocated to individual Member States. We will want to be very sure that— the risk and crisis-type point I was making a moment ago—we are not introducing market support measures by the back door through that. We also have a small UK—England and Wales—interest in all of this and one significant concern, which is that we remain below the radar of the EU regime. We are at present, but we are incredibly close to the bottom and, because they have extended the planting ban till 2013 in the latest proposal, there is a high risk— depending on the weather, a near certainty—we would go over it, so we need to try and ensure that that does not happen, because the last thing we want is our small but promising wine sector disadvantaged

Q36 *Viscount Brookeborough:* But it is true that the planting that has taken place and is taking place this year will put us over in three years' time?

Ms Phippard: Yes—unless it all gets washed away . . . ..

Q37 *Lord Greaves:* Proposals to get rid of the milk quotas and Set Aside. The whole of the history of the CAP is littered with bureaucratic interventions in the market to try and patch things up which by and large do not work. Set Aside did not stop production subsidies continuing to rise on cereals, for example, and milk quotas have not maintained adequate milk prices to producers and so on. The whole thing is perverse, but dismantling them once they are in

existence causes all sorts of other problems on the way. What problems do you see from getting rid of them? What on earth is the justification for Set Aside in the context of a Single Farm Payment? There is absolutely no logic at all. It is just crackers. What problems do you see, what effects do you see on agriculture throughout Europe of doing away with this?

Ms Phippard: That is precisely what we have argued in terms of the relationship between Set Aside and the single payment, and I am glad that that now seems to be generally recognised. There is a lot of anxiety round the removal of Set Aside, much of which seems to us to be misplaced, and the anxieties are basically that instantly all those Set Aside areas will be in full production and that some environmental benefits, which have definitely accrued from having a Set Aside system, will all be lost. Actually, our evidence suggests that in fact farmers removed from coupled subsidies generally are taking some sensible decisions about productive and fallow land and leaving unproductive land fallow above and beyond compulsory Set Aside. By and large they choose as Set Aside areas their least productive land. Moreover, the whole theory that Set Aside provides a magic protection for certain land for environmental purposes has been completely undermined by the decision to allow non-food crops on that land, so it is not a total protection now; it is a *de facto* protection for some of the compulsory Set Aside land. What we are doing is obviously talking to our environmental stakeholders, advisers and so on, to try and make sure we really have understood the problem, rather than the slight scare stories around it. As I said, I think our assessment is that there is not a major catastrophe about to happen but we are making sure that we have looked at the specific impacts and have the measures, possibly through cross-compliance, possibly through environmental stewardship, if there are risks of very specific losses. A lot will, of course, depend on the market and the price for cereals generally, both for food and non-food uses. I am afraid it is back to monitoring and making sure we have got the measures that may be needed, but I do not think I am in crisis mode. The UK Government assessment is that it is not a major crisis but we are talking to the Commission, we are talking to other Member States; indeed, we are going to do that informally next week to a number of them to see what their assessment is. Milk quotas—again, as you say, this is something which was generally opposed by most of the industry when it arrived and is now regarded, at least in some Member States, as an essential part of life as they know it. Our own industry has, by and large, now come firmly and publicly to the view that the time has come to end the system as planned in 2015. We have a good deal of analysis, both done and in hand, and in discussion with industry, about price impacts and so on. But actually the important thing seems to us to be to have a debate about how we get there rather than trundling along to 2015 as if it is not going to happen or it might be postponed and then everyone falls off a cliff. Again, there are quite a number of Member States—a larger list than my list of our allies on all other subjects—who fully agree that, and our Dutch colleagues are holding a seminar in Brussels next week precisely to talk about the so-called soft landing, the various options for managing an end to quotas, probably looking at options like increasing the quantity of quota; cross-border trading is one option which people canvassed, not one we are so keen on; how the super levy applies; should some of those controls come off gradually over the period.

Q38 Chairman: This is the first time we have specifically mentioned the Health Check. Most of our discussions had been at a more general level of pushing the horizon out a bit. It might be useful to get your view on what you think will specifically come out of the Health Check.
Ms Phippard: Handily, the Commissioner has been very clear in a number of speeches about her wish list. It seems to us that there will be a range of issues under the simplification banner: simplification of the single payment scheme and cross-compliance, and that includes abolition of Set Aside, removal of things like the ten-month rule, which was discussed and pressed for this year but the Commissioner very firmly said, "No, that is one I'm going to return to in the Health Check," and probably a further round of discussion and, we would hope, some simplification around cross-compliance conditions which again has been in discussion under the German presidency with more to come. Further moves towards full decoupling: we would hope to see a trajectory to 100% decoupling. I think we will see most of that probably proposed by the Commission. Further compulsory modulation, as we have touched upon, from Pillar I to Pillar II. She has also suggested that even if the WTO round, the DDA, has run into the sand, she would expect to see the EU commit to the full end of export subsidies by 2013 and further cuts in intervention and price support, so the end of not just dairy quotas but potato starch quotas and so on. She will look at things linked to the coupling point—like the energy scheme, a little coupled payment which does not have a vast impact on energy crops but has a lot of bureaucracy attached.

Q39 Lord Cameron of Dillington: One of the areas of policy that has risen dramatically up the agenda since 2003 is the whole question of climate change. In this country farmers and foresters represent less than 1% of the population but we produce more than 7% of the greenhouse gases. Whilst obviously the former

figure is greater on the Continent, I suspect the latter figure is probably very similar. Is this likely to feature as part of the Health Check, do you think? I would hope that all the various Departments of Agriculture are doing some thinking about how they can mitigate the agricultural emissions of greenhouse gases. Maybe this is a separate item?
Ms Phippard: No. I think it is very much in everyone's thinking. Obviously, we touched earlier on the fuel issue, and that is an aspect of the mitigation debate. But the role of agriculture and agricultural land in mitigation more generally, carbon sequestration and so on, I think people are aware of. For ourselves domestically, we are reviewing our environmental stewardship scheme and are looking at the role of environmental stewardship in both mitigation and adaptation. One of the reasons for cracking on with that is that we anticipate that that sort of issue will arise as we look at rural development, etc, in the context of the Health Check. An interesting question is whether, as the Commission looks, for instance, at further compulsory modulation, the argument for that will be the growing climate change needs in rural development. It is a pretty obvious driver. It is certainly one that the Commissioner has picked up. This is an issue which I almost invariably find I am discussing when I visit other Member States, talking about bilateral and multilateral future of CAP issues. When you think about public concerns and the public understanding and support for CAP, and the longer term future, the role of agriculture and climate change is clearly something where by and large the public do have understanding, sympathy, active support. But again, it is quite complicated stuff. You have to be clear about where Pillar II can play an important part.

Q40 Lord Moynihan: I listened with great interest to your assertion that food prices should not be as cheap as possible but should be affordable, and you cited the example of environmental costs as a reasonable upward distortion on prices. Can you help the Committee by defining "affordability" in greater detail?
Ms Phippard: I think what I was suggesting there was, as we have discussed, that the price of food relative to income in Europe has fallen steadily over time. Affordability is an extremely difficult issue in terms of people's choices and so on, and the Government has been very clear that actually enabling people to make informed choices is the most important thing. I think I would define affordability in this context as ensuring that the population, whether here or elsewhere in Europe, has access to safe, healthy food in a way which they can purchase it without having to take decisions which critically affect the rest of their lives. That is not an economist's definition. Simon may be able to provide something much

neater and more technical than that, but it seems to me that that it is in that territory of making sure that people are not financially so constrained that, in making sensible decisions about how to deploy their income, they are under-provided with food.

Q41 *Lord Palmer:* The interesting thing is that, if one goes back 40 years, 40% of the total income for every family in the UK was in fact spent on food, and today, to answer Lord Moynihan's question, that figure has actually dropped to single figures. It is a very big difference over 40 years.

Ms Phippard: But it is still up to about 30% in one or two of the new Member States. I think that was the point I was making. It does vary hugely. Affordability does not actually seem to me to be a very live issue for the vast bulk of the UK population. Nevertheless, it does vary a bit depending on family circumstances. There are people in the UK for whom it is an issue.

Q42 *Lord Moynihan:* Perhaps your colleague can give us the economist's definition.

Mr Harding: Economists do not use the concept of affordability at all. But, since you have given me the opportunity and clearly have a thirst to know about it, the Government defines poverty as, I think, 60% of the median household income. If we look at people who have 60% of the median household income and see how much of that they need to spend on food, that might give you an assessment of affordability. But, as Sonia says, if food only accounts for 8% of the average household bill, that is not very much, and we must remember that 93% of that 8% is actually value added after the farm gate, so it is all the packaging, transport, retailing, etc.

Q43 *Lord Moynihan:* If that is your motive, you would want it as cheap as possible?

Mr Harding: If you are interested in poverty, then you will certainly want food not be an issue for the householder defined as being in poverty. But, of course, the whole social security system is engineered in a way that enables social security payments to reflect the cost of food and other essential items anyhow, so hopefully this is not an issue in that sense.

Q44 *Baroness Miller of Chilthorne Domer:* Does the assessment, then, of the family tax credit level actually take into account the price of food?

Mr Harding: I believe it would, yes. I am not from that Department, but I believe it does. **Viscount Brookeborough:** Food has to be affordable for the lowest income group that does not get other grants such as tax credits and then the tax credits must make up for it.

Chairman: I think we are on a wild goose chase!

Q45 *Baroness Miller of Chilthorne Domer:* Just on that one, I would be grateful if you would confirm that in writing because I understood it did not.

Mr Harding: I will check it out for you.

Chairman: We thank Lord Moynihan for that helpful question. We particularly thank all of you. Thank you very much indeed for a very good session.

WEDNESDAY 11 JULY 2007

Present	Bach, L	Palmer, L
	Brookeborough, V	Plumb, L
	Cameron of Dillington, L	Sewel, L (Chairman)
	Jones of Whitchurch, B	Ullswater, V
	Moynihan, L	

Memorandum by The Royal Society for the Protection of Birds

INTRODUCTION

The Common Agricultural Policy (CAP) underwent its third and most significant reform in 2003, but the need for further reform has never been so urgent. There is a need for a review of the objectives for the CAP (with or without a revision to the Treaty itself) and an assessment of how well it currently achieves these. For example, the bulk of the CAP is now expended on the Single Payment which is described by the European Commission as an income support for farmers, but there seems to be no evidence about how efficiently it does this, or whether support is directed at social groups most needing it.

To the extent that the CAP is an environmental policy, evidence strongly suggests it is failing. Biodiversity decline is continuing across Europe and agricultural intensification is one of the main drivers of this loss, whilst agricultural expansion, often to meet demand in affluent countries, is the principal cause of loss worldwide. The need to reduce greenhouse gas emissions from all sectors, including agriculture, which is responsible for approximately 10% of EU greenhouse gas emissions, is increasingly urgent, whilst the impacts of climate change are already being felt and will place further stress on wildlife. Furthermore, the pressure on our land base to increase production is increasing exponentially as agriculture is relied upon to feed a global population that is growing both in size and affluence, and is now being turned to produce fuel, heat and power.

Farmland makes up almost three-quarters of Europe's land, and provides a crucial habitat for many species, but farmland biodiversity is in crisis across the continent. Farmland bird populations in Europe, which, as indicator species, reflect the welfare of farmland wildlife as a whole, fell by 44% between 1980 and 2005. In the EU-15, where this decline was most serious, populations fell by over 40%, and for some species as much as 60%, whereas the decline in the new Central and Eastern European Member States has been more moderate as agricultural intensification slowed following the collapse of the Soviet Union, but already populations are beginning to decrease again.

The intensification of agriculture is the main driver of this collapse in farmland bird populations, but the abandonment of traditional farming systems also represents a critical threat. Wildlife in Europe has co-evolved with traditional farming systems and many species depend on their continuation for the provision of appropriate habitats.

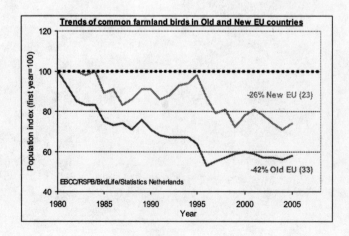

OVERVIEW

1. The CAP, and its aims, as enshrined in the Treaty of Rome 50 years ago, is no longer appropriate for dealing with the social and environmental problems faced by rural areas in the EU. Increasing agricultural productivity, stabilising the agricultural market, assuring the availability of food at a fair price to consumers and ensuring a fair standard of living to farmers were appropriate aims half a century ago. Today, they fail to deal with the urgent challenges of our time, such as reversing biodiversity decline, mitigating and adapting to climate change, and ensuring the continuation of ecosystem services that provide adequate clean water and healthy soils. Like all areas of policy, the CAP must evolve as our needs evolve and knowledge develops.

2. The aims of the CAP should reflect what we as a society genuinely need and expect from our land, including sustainable agriculture, healthy biodiversity, landscapes and clean water.

3. The RSPB therefore proposes that the EU transforms the CAP into a *common* policy for rural land use with an appropriate level of subsidiarity allowing national and regional programming to account for differing priorities—not dissimilar to the current European Agricultural Fund for Rural Development. There is a clear rationale for such a common policy: because land management is associated with externalities that affect the whole of the EU and directly impact on EU level commitments, the costs of addressing these externalities imposes costs that individual states may perceive as a competitive disadvantage and yet generates benefits for the whole EU.

THE REFORMED CAP

4. The fundamental driver for reform was bringing agricultural production more into line with world markets through the decoupling of agricultural support. The RSPB supported the broad thrust of this reform because of the incidental benefits this would afford to the environment, and indeed decoupling appears to have brought some benefits of de-intensification (sheep in the uplands, optimal input use for arable farming), but cautioned that decoupling could lead to accelerated abandonment of High Nature Value farming across Europe. Thus, the environmental impacts of the reform needed to be understood and managed; and resources made available for environmental mitigation (eg through agri-environment). This has been imperfectly achieved and highlights the need for a sophisticated understanding of the likely variable impacts of further reform, and good environmental impact assessment as part of future reforms. Domestically there have been some welcome benefits from the 2000 and 2005 reforms, particularly the expansion of agri-environment schemes and the creation of a clearer environmental baseline through cross-compliance. The UK could better capitalise on the positive experiences of reform so far when it makes the case for further reform across the EU.

THE SINGLE PAYMENT SCHEME

5. As much as 78% of the total CAP budget goes to the Single Farm Payment, but we await clarification on the question of what the payment is for. It is a highly inefficient income support; it secures little positive environmental gain; and it seems powerless to prevent abandonment of farming in High Nature Value areas. We therefore believe it should be phased out and replaced with payments that can efficiently secure public goods. Meanwhile, we think that all CAP payments should be linked to rigorous baseline standards of environmental performance through and improved and harmonised cross-compliance scheme.

6. Decoupling payments from production has lessened the incentive to intensify and will therefore deliver environmental benefits relative to the pre-2003 system of support. However, environmental criteria were not well considered in the calculation of direct payments, and farmers that reduced production during the reference period as part of an environmental scheme may even be penalised by the system. Indeed, the historical allocation of payments, which has been the preferred method of distribution in most Member States, will favour those with the most intensive production practices during the reference period.

MARKET MECHANISMS

7. The RSPB is broadly content with bringing the agriculture sector more closely in line with market conditions, provided that tools are in place to mitigate environmental impacts of market reform (eg the loss of set-aside, abolition of market mechanisms), and that adequate funds are available for positive purchase of public goods.

RURAL DEVELOPMENT

8. The "second pillar" of the CAP has funded valuable measures to deliver environmental public goods in a number of countries—for example the conservation of valuable hay meadows, protection of habitat for stone curlews and bustards and "broad and shallow" measures to ensure better environmental management of environmental features in the wider countryside. The UK countries have developed some imaginative agri-environment schemes based on clear science; these have great potential to deliver results and give farmers a long-term incentive to build the environment into their farm businesses. Environmental payments through the rural development measures represent the most promising part of the CAP, but they lack funding, receiving only 20% of the total budget, are often misused, and can even be used for environmentally destructive practices. There is an urgent need for the UK to commit more funding to agri-environment: we are very supportive of many of the UK schemes but concerned that lack of resources will compromise them. This would help the UK develop a counter-case to the inappropriate use of Rural Development funds in some Member States which includes:

    i.   Funding unsustainable drainage and irrigation expansion;

    ii. Funding inappropriate afforestation;

    iii. Using agri-environment to pay for practices that do not have a demonstrable environmental benefit, or for practices that would be followed anyway;.

    iv. Less Favoured Area payments that go to farmers that are not practicing environmentally friendly farming.

9. The high level of subsidiarity permitted in schemes funded through the European Agricultural Fund for Rural Development (EAFRD) means that their success in meeting their objectives depends on Member States and regional Governments for successful implementation, and while there are many examples of schemes successfully delivering on their objective, there are equally many failing schemes as a result of poor implementation. Research[1] and our own experience[2] with agri-environment schemes suggest that if the following rules are followed they will deliver:

    i.   The scheme rewards farmers for delivering public goods and should be well targeted at the achievement of measurable specific environmental outcomes (such as the conservation of certain species or habitats)

    ii.   Schemes must be backed by a budget sufficient to deliver their aims

    iii. The scheme design should be based on good science

    iv.   Management required should be agronomically feasible and practical

    v.   The scheme design should be an iterative process

    vi.   Schemes should be targeted initially at existing biodiversity interest where is can be demonstrated that there is real potential for habitat species recolonisation

    vii. Monitoring of the environmental impact of agri-environment schemes necessary, and the results should feed into further design stages

    viii. Stakeholders, including farmers and environmental experts, should and involved throughout scheme design and implementation

10. These rules should be a requirement for future rural development schemes, and greater power needs to be granted to the Commission so that they ensure these requirements are met as part of the scheme approval process. All EAFRD measures need to be screened to ensure that they are indeed contributing to, and not acting contrary to, the overall goals of the EAFRD.

FINANCING OF RURAL DEVELOPMENT

11. In the long term we see a complete diversion of CAP funding to create a single sustainable land management and rural development fund, but accept this should be phased. We urge the UK to be cautious in this regard since the 2005 budget deal brokered by the UK is widely perceived as a device whereby EU funding for rural development and the environment actually falls as modulation creates funding through one stream whilst core funding is cut back. This approach undermines the concept of creating a sustainable and reformed CAP, and leaves the UK politically isolated with its laudable reform agenda.

[1] Evans AD and Armstrong-Brown S (2002) The role of research and development in the evolution of a "smart" agrienvironment scheme. Aspects of Applied Biology 67: 253-262.
[2] BirdLife (2005) Agri-environment schemes and biodiversity: lessons learnt and examples from across Europe.

12. Maintaining co-funding of rural development measures would ensure Member States feel ownership of the policy and increase the domestic pressure for accountability, but higher rates of EU funding should be made available for lower income countries.

13. Increased modulation into a co-funded instrument would increase the cost of the Common Policy to Member States, but this could be prevented by progressively introducing co-funding to Pillar I, and, in the long-term, applying degressivity to total spend or reducing the co-funding requirement for rural development expenditure.

ENVIRONMENTAL PROTECTION THROUGH CROSS-COMPLIANCE

14. Cross-compliance is likely to deliver some benefits depending on how it is implemented at the Member State level. It has, as a minimum, given a significant boost to the importance of farmers complying with European law, but overall there is no evidence yet that it has contributed to a significantly improved level of environmental protection, due to inconsistent and inadequate implementation. Furthermore, there will be problems demonstrating its effectiveness in delivering environmental benefits as there are no measurable targets or output monitoring. Nor should it be assumed that the Single Payment is commensurate with public goods delivered since the payments are massively disproportionate to any additional requirements over the regulatory minimum.

15. Cross-compliance has been implemented with a very high level of subsidiarity and flexibility, much greater than that allowed for Rural Development measures, for example. Only the UK, Germany, Sweden and Austria have comprehensively implemented the good agricultural and environmental (GAEC) requirement to protect landscape features. In the UK this has seen welcome protection for hedges and water courses. Other countries have either ignored this requirement or have translated it into such vague language that removing or damaging landscape features will still be acceptable. There is an opportunity to address this issue during the CAP Health Check.

16. Another critical farmed habitat in the EU that is supposedly offered protection by cross-compliance is permanent grassland. This is one of the most valuable farmland habitats in Europe, but many Member States still allow it to be ploughed up, irreversibly destroying its biodiversity value, on condition that, at the national level, the overall amount of permanent grassland remains within 10% of the amount present in a reference year.

17. Since the demand cross-compliance places on farmers, and consequentially the benefits it delivers, are disproportionately small relative to payments, it appears the bulk of the direct payment scheme is not about maintaining these standards but about improving farmer incomes. On the RSPB's conventionally managed 181ha arable farm in Cambridgeshire, for example, it was calculated that the costs of implementing cross-compliance were approximately €75 compared to €27,000 received in direct payments.

18. Cross-compliance does not currently include requirements that specifically address the Water Framework Directive although the requirement in England to leave 1m buffer strips alongside watercourses may contribute. Again the CAP Health Check provides an opportunity to more closely link the Water Framework with cross-compliance and the CAP.

CLIMATE CHANGE

19. Agriculture is responsible for 9% of greenhouse gas emissions in the EU. Much of this is a result of unsustainable, intensive practices such as the excessive application of artificial fertilisers and pesticides. For example, in the life-cycle of wheat production, 51% of emissions are associated with the manufacture and use of nitrogen fertiliser. Every sector has to reduce its greenhouse gas emissions if we are to avoid dangerous levels of climate change and reduce our emissions by 60% by 2050.

20. Bioenergy could play an important but limited role in reducing EU greenhouse gas (GHG) emissions, but it also poses a number of environmental risks. Bioenergy requires large amounts of land if it is to become a significant renewable energy source. Indeed, our energy and fuel needs are so great that bioenergy represents a potentially limitless new pressure on our land resource that threatens to leave little room for wildlife conservation and natural habitats. Our aim must therefore be to optimise the food and fuel we can generate whilst preserving natural and semi-natural habitats and moving towards a low carbon, sustainable agricultural system.

21. The second problem presented by bioenergy, and particularly biofuels, is the variability in GHG savings according to different production pathways. Producing biofuel from wheat, for example, offer up a range of GHG savings compared to conventional petrol, as high as 77% and as low as 17% (ie an increase in emissions). Support for bioenergy should therefore be contingent on delivering significant and quantified GHG savings and meeting minimum sustainability standards that ensure unacceptable damage to biodiversity and the environment is not caused.

22. Within the scope of our vision for the role of an EU sustainable land management and rural development policy, it is important to stress the need to ensure public money is spent to deliver public goods. The production of biofuels, or any other agricultural product, cannot be seen *per se* as a public good that should be publicly supported. GHG emission reduction and carbon storage on the other hand, however, can be seen as a public good. Farming can deliver for climate change mitigation through decreased emissions, increased soil carbon storage and substitution of fossil fuels with less carbon intensive fuels. It is the climate benefit that can justify targeted public support.

23. Climate change will also pose very significant adaptation challenges to agriculture, and it is likely that we will see changing cropping and agricultural practices as climatic conditions change. This may present unforeseen challenges for biodiversity conservation that will need to be monitored.

24. Climate change thus places a further importance on improving the sustainability of agriculture practices and the value of farmed land for wildlife. The quality of agricultural habitats will determine the ability of many species to move effectively between protected areas in order to follow their shifting climate envelopes, ie the areas with the climatic conditions appropriate for the species in question. EU support for farming and land management must secure the provision of corridors and transition habitats such as managed coastal retreat to facilitate adaptation. Similarly, extreme weather events and decreased water availability will require a much more ecologically sensitive land management of watersheds and agriculture will have a key role to play. The €50 billion expended each year on the CAP should be assisting in this process, but there is little sign it currently that it is doing so.

FINANCING THE CAP

25. The 2005 budget deal was unsatisfactory from the point of view of adequately financing EU obligations relating to the Natura 2000 network, EU BAP commitments and the potential demands of the Water Framework Directive. Added to this will be the potential land management costs of climate change adaptation and mitigation. Much of this problem stemmed from the agreement by Heads of Government in 2002 that largely protected Pillar I of the CAP to 2013, alongside an unwillingness of reformist Member States in 2005 being prepared to underpin rhetoric about CAP reform with hard cash reality.

26. The lack of a level playing field in financing of Pillar I and Pillar II—with Pillar I payments effectively being "free" to Member States at the point of delivery whilst Rural Development measures must be match-funded. This can be redressed by introducing national co-funding for Pillar spend, and/or reducing national co-funding for Pillar II measures, perhaps on a sliding scale depending on their European priority.

ENLARGEMENT

27. The 2004 and 2007 enlargements have brought very large areas of highly environmentally important farmed land into the EU and thus present huge environmental challenges and opportunities these enlargements present. The modernisation of agriculture in these new Member States needs to be achieved in a way that respects, and capitalises on, this environmental resource. Experience gained through the accession of Spain and Portugal, which have seen significant environmental losses and a move towards agriculture that is often unsustainable in the long term (for example relying on unsustainable supplies of fresh irrigation water) suggests pathways for more ecologically based modernisation in countries such as Bulgaria and Romania. RSPB is actively working with Birdlife partners in these countries to help develop Rural Development Programmes that will enable farmers to preserve the natural environment whilst developing their farming in a way that is sustainable for the long term. However, the task presented is huge and urgent if massive environmental losses are to be avoided, and this requires wholesale political and financial commitment at the EU level, something the UK government would be well placed to spearhead if it chose.

SIMPLIFICATION OF THE CAP

28. The RSPB has no problem in principle with the principle of CAP simplification; indeed, as a significant agricultural landholder we share the frustrations of farmers with administrative burdens imposed under the CAP such as the Single Payment application process. As such, we have not opposed simplifying the administrative process of cross-compliance, whilst seeking to ensure that the underlying environmental objectives are not diluted. Thus there is a need for simplicity to be balanced with efficiency—a greater focus in a reformed CAP will inevitably involve greater complexity to deliver real environmental benefits, compared to approaches such as Less Favoured Area payments which are fairly simple to administer yet often deliver little public benefit. The experience with the Single Payment System in England highlights the need to take a long view and reserve complication for where it will deliver real benefits: thus we are sceptical about Pillar I payment capping or redistribution, except where this will have clear environmental benefits. This philosophy underlies the following comments on future prospects for reform:

In the short term:

29. Cross-compliance as a tool could be playing a more effective role in protecting the European countryside from the most environmentally damaging practices, such as habitat destruction; and in implementing basic measures to reduce water pollution and ensure the health of soils. It is clear from recent reviews, however, that this potential is far from being fulfilled in most Member States, resulting in widely varying standards in environmental protection across the EU. This must be addressed urgently and cross-compliance schemes should be revised in all Member States. The programming approach used in EAFRD measures could provide a model for harmonising cross-compliance whilst maintaining the flexibility required given the differences in circumstance between Member States.

30. The LFA scheme should be reformed so that it specifically targets High Natural Value Farming, as defined by the European Environment Agency, and made conditional on basic management requirements that ensure beneficial farming practices continue. This should be part of a package for HNV farming that also includes targeted use of Axis 1 and 3 type Rural Development measures to improve the rural economy in a sustainable way, through, for example, building local and added value food chains.

31. There is scope for an initiative to improve the quality of Rural Development expenditure across the EU through starting immediately on a process of review and networking of experience in the new Programmes.

In the longer term:

32. As explained above, we want to see establishment of a sustainable rural development policy for the whole of the EU, building on the current Rural Development Regulation but targeted at sustainability, with support for land management structured according to the pyramid model and based on the principle of public money for public goods at its core.

33. The central element of this fund should be a sustainable land management axis, equivalent to the current Axis 2 with tiered layers of intervention and payment. Alongside this axis, Axis 1 and 3 measures should be used to tackle the social and economic challenges faced in the more marginal rural areas of the EU, but they should be explicitly targeted at improving sustainability of farming and land management in these areas (thus addressing EU objectives for climate change, water and biodiversity) and properly assessed to ensure they do not cause environmental harm.

June 2007

Examination of Witnesses

Witnesses: DR MARK AVERY, Director of Conservation, DR SUE ARMSTRONG-BROWN, Head of Countryside Conservation, and MR HARRY HUYTON, Agriculture Policy Officer, Royal Society for the Protection of Birds, gave evidence.

Q46 Chairman: Good morning. Thank you very much for coming along and helping us with our inquiry on the CAP, the Health Check and the slightly longer term future as well. Let me explain, although you know the ropes as well as I do. We are taking evidence in a formal session. There will be a minute taken and you will get an opportunity of looking at the record and doing any factual corrections which are necessary. We are also being sound broadcast, so it is possible that somewhere in some distant place someone may be listening to us. Would you like to start by making any opening comments and then we will go straight on to questions and answers?

Dr Avery: Let us go into the questions. We are here to answer your questions.

Q47 *Chairman:* Thank you very much. I was wondering if you could kick off by explaining your vision of the CAP as we look forward and what you see achievable in the relatively short term through the 2008 Health Check, and what you see as taking longer, coming into the context of the post-2013 period?

Dr Avery: Absolutely. The Common Agricultural Policy has been around for a long time and it is changing a lot. Clearly, it started as a mechanism to provide funding for production and it is moving away from that. Where we are at the moment is that there are the remnants of production subsidies enshrined in a Single Farm Payment, which is now a payment without a policy aim, we would say, but there has been movement from Pillar I to Pillar II and we would like to see that movement of public funding continuing to move towards Pillar II to deliver these things called public goods. We think that has to happen in a way which keeps farming in the countryside. The RSPB is very much in favour of the farmed countryside, and the thing which makes this industry different from other industries is the public benefit which derives from farming. Public benefit we might get on to later, but it includes things like landscape and wildlife, which are important side-effects of farming. They are things which come out of farming but there is no market for the song of the skylark, even though the song of the skylark is a wonderful thing which comes out of the way that we manage the countryside. So we would like to see the emphasis of public funding moving towards rewarding land managers for those public goods and away from incentivised production, because that is what the market should deal with. So in the short-term the big prize in the 2008 Health Check is to have modulation up to 20% to continue that movement and retain voluntary modulation as well, so that individual Member States can do more of this, and we would like to see the UK continuing to lead in this area. In the longer-term, I think quite a lot of reform of CAP comes down to Treasuries looking at the budget and just wanting to reduce it. There is a danger in that because we do want to see farming continue and we do want to see public support, but we want that public support to be tied into those public goods. So how one moves further in that direction is clearly difficult and what everybody has to struggle with.

Q48 *Chairman:* That seems to be a defence of present levels under the CAP?

Dr Avery: For Pillar II to do as much good in delivering environmental and other public goods as it could do we believe that that money has to continue to go in there, and in the UK there is not enough money, we would say, at the moment going into agri-environment schemes. So many farmers will be disappointed that they cannot sign up for higher-level stewardship schemes at the moment because there is not enough money there, and that does seem to derive from the 2005 budget agreements which the UK engineered under our Presidency. So they seem to cut the good bits of CAP and leave the bad bits of CAP.

Q49 *Chairman:* I have got to ask you, I suppose, what you think the level of support amongst the other Member States is for the type of policy direction you are advocating?

Mr Huyton: I think there are an increasing number of Member States who are looking to Pillar II of the CAP as the future of public support, but it is clear that a lot of the big players are not yet on-side. Here the UK has got a clear role to play in leading this agenda at the EU level. The RSPB is a partner of Bird Life International and we work closely with them, so I work with the RSPB equivalent in the 26 other Member States. We have recently agreed a joint revision for the future of the CAP which we will be launching in Brussels, with the Commissioner's help in fact, this year. I think that shows that there are people throughout the EU who subscribe to this model and it is about giving them a louder voice and helping them to get this message across.

Q50 *Chairman:* Are the Poles enthusiastic supporters?

Mr Huyton: Some of them are more enthusiastic than others, that is true! Pillar II is playing a role in Poland. They do have an agri-environment scheme in its early stage which will be delivering public benefit and we hope that will highlight how effective this mechanism can be.

Dr Avery: I think it is clearly a challenge for a Europe-wide policy to deliver the different things which are needed in terms of public goods in different Member States. From the wildlife point of view, which is the one we understand the best, the UK has experienced some of the biggest declines in farmland biodiversity. We know particularly about farmland bird declines, which have been greater in the UK than elsewhere in Europe. So sitting here in the UK we would like to see Pillar II mending some of that damage which has been done to the UK countryside. If you go to Poland, that has not started yet—well, it has started, but it is at a very different position. It is a wildlife-rich country and yet it has the CAP as well, so it is quite a challenge for policy that a whole EU policy measure can do good in very different situations at different ends of Europe.

Chairman: Thank you very much. Let us move on.

Q51 *Lord Plumb:* You said that you were concerned that we maintain a viable farming industry and you want to see, therefore, environmentally friendly farming and environmental issues fitting well into this particular pattern. You refer in your evidence several times to one of the causes of the difficulties and that one of the results of the CAP in the past has been a move towards more intensification. I would submit that there has been de-intensification since the 1990s and there is a faster move in that direction now than there was. Do you not accept that, whilst there have been income difficulties in farming over recent years—which you well understand, I am sure—for many farmers, the object of farming is not exclusively profit? There is plenty of land and farms around which include sporting activities and residential comfort, and therefore surely it would be very helpful to explore further the possibilities of how environmental development can be maintained in those areas and how it can be developed further? I believe there are many, many farmers who are now becoming much more interested in the carrot which is being held out for them for moving much more into the environmental interests of the whole field. To what extent do you see this developing as time changes?

Dr Avery: We would agree with you that many farmers are interested in participating fully in environmental schemes and that farming is not solely a business for making money. If it were, then lots of people ought to have left this industry in past years, although of course at the moment wheat prices at least are picking up quite dramatically. We would say that there are many opportunities for farmers in taking a more environmentally friendly approach to their farming. Part of that is through signing up to the schemes, but there are other ways that farmers can make money from a good environment as well—through tourism, through diversification, bed and breakfast, and all those types of ways of making money out of a good environment.

Dr Armstrong-Brown: It is a very interesting area that you have raised there, and I think a better understanding of the interplay between a land management business, for whatever purpose, and the environmental good it can deliver is essential as we go forward, particularly so in the new Member States, where we are actually actively trying to raise the question of how to have a different model for agricultural development in those areas which does capitalise much more so than in the past on these other benefits. At the moment these countries have a choice between staying as they are, which is in a very undeveloped state with a poor quality of life in some areas in the countryside, and following the historic western agricultural development model. But that does have downsides, as we have learned, as well as benefits. So it is an excellent time to be exploring

these issues and trying to seek a better way of these countries developing and getting the quality of life benefits, the production benefits, and so on, that are required but also retaining some of the environmental delivery they are currently doing. I do think it is crucial to ask this, and ask it in Europe, and get that debate going now ahead of the Health Check and the Budget Review so that some decisions can be made with those questions in mind.

Q52 *Lord Plumb:* If farming is to remain viable, then obviously farmers have got to look more so (and welcome the opportunity of doing so) at market forces because that is where their income, hopefully, is going to come from. Are you concerned about the balance of farming, though, because market forces are already showing that in the arable sector farmers are going to do much better this year. That is going to be, of course, at the expense of the livestock sector, because there is a 30% increase in the cost of the feed going into animals at the moment and that, of course, is going to be a further burden in the livestock area? Is this not a problem from your point of view of the lack of balance, or further lack of balance that there might be in the development of agriculture in the future?

Dr Avery: That must be good news for farmers, that some of them –

Q53 *Lord Plumb:* Is it good news for birds?

Dr Avery: I will come on to that. It must be good news for farmers that their commodity prices are going up, although, as you say, in some sectors of agriculture that will be bad news because they are customers of another sector of farming. I was quite surprised at the Royal Show last week, whenever it was, that I was being told by people in milk that things were looking up for dairy farmers.

Q54 *Lord Plumb:* Really?

Dr Avery: Well, I was told that by people in the milk industry and I expressed the same slight surprise that you do, but I am not an expert on this. I suppose our worries are that profitable farming does mean that many farmers, because they are environmental enthusiasts, will put more of their own money back into environmental improvements in their farms, but we cannot be sure of that. The other aspect of rising commodity prices is that agri-environment schemes look less competitive compared with growing winter wheat if you are getting £120 a tonne for it. So there is a very difficult and unpredictable balance there, and that is why we believe the public funding for agriculture should be much more directed at delivering those public goods so that it is clear that there is a mechanism to allow many farmers who want to do great things for the environment to do it. Now, if the price of commodities rockets, then it will be more difficult for those environmentally-friendly schemes to compete and that might get us to a position eventually where regulation might have to come in to assist. But at the moment we are wedded towards a voluntary agri-environment scheme and we know that lots of farmers want to join those schemes. At the moment, the problem is that there is not enough money for the schemes to allow all those farmers who wish to participate to do so.

Mr Huyton: We know at the moment that, where farmers have got into schemes, those payments have been worthwhile. We did a recent evaluation of them and one of the options under the entry-level stewardship schemes, skylark plots, found that even at the current wheat prices they are competitive. The important thing is that we continue to have that balance and that these options continue to be competitive, and I think to do that we need to regularly review the payment levels, which are all based, of course, on an income for GOM calculation, which will change when you are at different commodity prices. So as long as we keep that under regular review and keep agri-environment competitive, there should not be a problem.

Q55 *Chairman:* Let us just check. Your view on the Single Farm Payment is that the environmental requirements behind the Single Farm Payment just do not actually deliver, is that right?

Mr Huyton: I think when you take an EU—level look at cross-compliance, it has not quite delivered its promise as being a consistent baseline across the Member States for environmental protection, which is what I think we all hoped it would be. So in some countries where cross-compliance has been implemented, let us say thoroughly, it has provided that baseline and we would put England and the UK in that category, but in other countries that has not happened. What we have seen is that the legislative part of cross-compliance, the complying of existing European law, has been translated by many countries in such a way that makes it pretty much impossible to apply at the farm level because it is so vague, and then the good agricultural and environmental condition part of cross-compliance has been implemented very differently in different countries. One of the key things in that part of cross-compliance was the protection of landscape features like hedgerows, stone walls, and such like. Here, Germany, Sweden, Ireland have all implemented that literally. We have said, "OK, those features are now protected and we cannot remove them." Other countries have not. Some have simply ignored it and others have again adopted such vague language that anyone could find their way around it. So cross-compliance allowed Member States a significant level of subsidiarity and it is clear that that level was to much and we have not got that consistent baseline.

Dr Avery: Cross-compliance in this country has been very easy for farmers to meet. There was a whole lot of fuss about cross-compliance from the CLA and the NFU about how terrible it was going to be, and it is easy for practically all farmers to meet cross-compliance. So I think the lesson there is that industry over-reacted to it. It is dead easy and it is not much more than meeting legal requirements, so that is fine. But we cannot say that it is doing very much at the moment.

Q56 *Viscount Ullswater:* Some people have suggested that farming is going to split in two directions, one towards the commercial area of farming where it can survive on world prices; and, if the prices of growing particularly increase, whether it is for food or biofuels, you can see the eastern side of the country becoming a sort of cereal-growing area, and because production subsidies have been reduced you can see the livestock area having to be supported by the rural policies, which you have talked about before. What do you see, therefore, as being the balance on biodiversity, which obviously you are concerned about, whether the East of England is going to be devoid of that and the West of England is going to have all the bird life? Is it something which you recognise as being a concern?

Dr Avery: We recognise that further polarisation of agriculture may happen. We would not agree with your painting of the picture where the wildlife would be under those scenarios, because in terms of agri-environment schemes they will still play quite a big part even in the cereal parts of the country, and the agri-environment schemes we have at the moment are quite good at dealing with many of the needs of wildlife in cereal-dominated areas. So we would not say that all the birds will disappear from the east of the country. If anything, I think we would be more worried about the west of the country, which looks attractive—I grew up in the West Country—the fields are still green and there are still hedges. But actually the intensity of grassland management is so great there at the moment that that is one of the places where wildlife is disappearing. It is more difficult to hear the song of the skylark or to find nesting lapwings on the western side of the country than it was when I grew up there, or on the eastern side of the country. The polarisation in wildlife will not be quite the same, and we need to avoid that happening, but I think there are other ways that livestock farmers can tap into markets. Locally grown meat is one real opportunity which livestock farmers have which a cereal farmer does not have. A cereal farmer is growing a commodity and you do not care where the wheat which goes into your bread comes from really, whereas I do go and buy my lamb from the local farmer in Northamptonshire, and I hope he remains a livestock farmer because I like him, I like his farm and I like being able to buy my food locally. Now, he has moved his business to tap into people like me and there is more scope for more farmers to do that, I think.

Mr Huyton: Yes, and that is exactly the kind of thing that Axis 1 of the Rural Development Regulation can help support, setting up the local supply chains, helping farmers add value to their products because of the added public benefit they are delivering on their farms. So there is something very positive that Axis 1 can be doing there.

Dr Avery: There may be other ways of making money from land as well. There is a lot of talk about the eco-system services that land management delivers, which is the kind of new jargon, but things which are included in there are things like flood alleviation. So, if you are a farmer on the Somerset levels, then it may be more difficult to make your money out of producing milk—maybe—but in future perhaps you will get paid to allow your land to flood so that Bridgewater or Taunton does not. We have had floods recently. Perhaps public money directing land use in different directions will create new opportunities for farmers to tap into that. In the uplands there is an awful lot of carbon in the peat soil and there maybe different forms of land management. Maybe we will be paying farmers to farm carbon instead of farming sheep on the tops of our hills in future. So it is not certain. The future of farming has never been certain. It is probably more uncertain now, but there are things out there which might lead to new income streams for farmers if the agricultural industry is prepared to adapt and change.

Q57 *Viscount Ullswater:* I gather from what you are saying that you cannot see a time when agriculture or land management can rely entirely on the marketplace from its outputs and that there will need to be a form of public money going into it in order to preserve not only the physical aspects of the countryside but also the biodiversity that you require?

Dr Avery: I think there are two things there, and I think it would be rash for farmers in this country to think that they could compete brilliantly on world markets when the price of land and the price of labour in this country are going to be much higher than in other parts of the world. So it is going to be difficult. The playing field is not level, for a start, but from the point of view of biodiversity we definitely do not think that the market alone will deliver wildlife in the countryside because all the experience of the last few decades shows that it did not and there is no reason to assume that it will in the future. That is why we think that agriculture is different from other industries. Agriculture produces wildlife, landscape and other public goods, providing you get the right

type of agriculture, and it is fair for the public to support farmers to produce that because there is no market for farmers to tap into through the song of the skylark. So, yes, we would like to see public support providing it is the right type of public support.

Q58 *Lord Bach:* The right type of support is the crucial question, is it not? Reading your paper, the single payment scheme is not the right type of support because it is effectively, you would argue, a continuation of paying for production? Is that how you see it? It is a double question. The way you would see it is that the only way in which farmers should be paid is not for producing in any sense at all but that it should be so that real environmental benefits can be gained from the land and it should not have anything at all to do with production, or do I read you wrongly?

Dr Armstrong-Brown: Yes, there are two elements there, as you said. We do see the Single Farm Payment as a stepping stone. It was a step away from production-related payments and compensation payments, but it does need to move on from being that. It was put in place for a reason, which we understand, but in some respects it was a political fix which was needed to move away from that system, as well as being something which served its own goal as well. We recognise that it was necessary, but we do not think that it has any longer a very strong tie to any policy objective in the EU. It is not even an income support payment in any real sense because of the way it is distributed. That said, we do not want to see it whisked away, leaving us with just Pillar II alone as it currently stands, and we do see a need for further movement in a phased way so that in relation to the support which is given to farmers through Pillar II there is not a sharp change from Pillar I. Currently the whole system is geared towards having some sort of "income support payment" through Pillar I. We do see the need for that to change. You mentioned, though, whether we support any kind of production payment. There are very clear World Trade Organisation drivers against that kind of payment which need to be adhered to. The one place where we see a specific payment for an environmental benefit or another public benefit—it could be a social benefit—not being as clear cut is in most cases, in the agri-environment system, in high nature value farming areas, where these areas are in a fairly traditional state and not really particularly able to take up agri-environment payments just at the moment. Also, the way in which agri-environment payments are calculated, as you know, relies upon income from growing and, if you are talking about incredibly low income areas, you are left with a zero sum gain. There is not very much you can pay them for in the agri-environment system. There we do see a role for payments for high nature value systems to sustain them until they are in such a state that there can be more explicit payments for individual public benefits.

Q59 *Viscount Ullswater:* Are you saying that you need to keep sheep on the uplands and cattle on the marshes in order to get the orchids and whatever are the requirements?

Dr Armstrong-Brown: Yes. There are particular land management techniques—cattle grazing is a very good example—which are required to deliver the environmental benefits you might want, but there it is very delicate. You would not be allowed any more to say, "We are paying you to produce beef on this land," but you can pay for the environmental benefits that come from producing beef on that land.

Q60 *Viscount Ullswater:* From grazing the land?

Dr Armstrong-Brown: Yes.

Mr Huyton: Throughout Europe there are high natural value habitats which depend upon a certain level of grazing throughout the Continent.

Q61 *Viscount Brookeborough:* You highlight in your paper that the enlargement of the EU has brought in Members with important environmental assets, and it is not surprising because they are very much behind, less developed and less intensive than we are. Your evidence suggests that these may be at risk if the CAP is applied in these regions and you have given the examples in your evidence of Spain and Portugal. I think it would be quite interesting to hear how they have suffered, in your opinion, since their accession. But could you describe these assets in the areas of the new Member States and how they are integrated at present with their domestic economies and what new risks you see to them?

Mr Huyton: I think the new Member States, particularly Central and Eastern European Member States, bringing with them the kind of burden of general biodiversity you would associate with traditional farming practices, have a real wealth of biodiversity. I have a couple of figures here. Corncrakes—91% of the EU's population in the new Member States, so 152,000 pairs compared with the 800 pairs we have in the UK and the five pairs we have in England. So it is an absolutely massive disproportionate concentration of Europe's biodiversity—100% of Aquatic Warblers; 75% of White Stork. A project the RSPB was involved in recently was mapping the biodiversity hot spots of Europe and it looked at the species richness of farmland birds across the Continent. I do not know whether you can see this. It is quite small. We have copies that we can leave, but you can see the big red blotch over there on Eastern Europe, which represents the species richness relative to the rest of the Continent. That is a hugely important asset, but

what we are seeing at the moment is that the new Member States are essentially playing catch-up on agricultural development, quite understandably, and they are capitalising on the available Pillar I subsidies and the Pillar II subsidies to develop in the way we have developed our agriculture. Of course, with that will be the negative impacts on wildlife which we have already seen here and in the EU15. We and other organisations compile a farmland bird indicator for across Europe and, if you look at the indicator for the EU new Member States, you will see it is significantly higher than here. Now it is beginning to tail off already as this investment happens through the money coming in from the CAP.

Dr Avery: One of the things that maybe it is worth saying is that we framed quite a lot of our answers in terms of farmland birds because that is what we know most about. But, if you go to Eastern Europe—and I do not know Eastern Europe well—it is amazing, the landscapes and the richness of the countryside for wildlife which, when you come back to the UK, you can only find remnants of, and you tend to find it on nature reserves. So the RSPB's nature reserves in Cambridgeshire, on the Nene washes, is the closest you can get to the wildlife richness of Eastern Europe. You can stand there and hear Corncrakes singing and Black-tailed Godwits singing, and that is about 20 miles from where I live. I go there often because it is so fantastic. Now, if that place disappeared, my next port of call to have that experience would be Eastern Germany. We are talking about birds here, but there is also the landscape, the quality of life and the richness of the countryside—it is only when you travel abroad from the UK that you realise how much we have lost in this country, and if we had kept more of it we would value it very highly. So, if the Accession States go down the same route over a much longer period of time than we have done in this country, the effect of the CAP could be to wreck Europe's wildlife in the Accession States, and that does not seem to be a very sensible way to go.

Q62 *Viscount Brookeborough:* If, as you suggest, the CAP were to evolve into a Rural Development Policy, to what extent do you think such a policy might address these risks? In your paper you use fairly extreme terms, "However, the task presented is huge and urgent and this requires a whole set of political and financial commitments." Will this not ultimately mean that, although the CAP may have changed into a rural policy, we will actually be putting more money into maintenance of the land than we are currently into the CAP?

Dr Armstrong-Brown: I think one crucial thing to recognise is that starving these areas of funds will not necessarily guarantee the continuation of that biodiversity. It might, but it would not necessarily be the most obvious way to do it. So allowing European money to flow into these areas does not seem to be a bad thing, but allowing it to flow in the wrong way and incentivising the wrong behaviour does. We believe, and there is evidence to show, that if you put the emphasis as an area develops on some of these non-commercial aspects to simply bring them up alongside the economic and quality-of-life social benefits that people are seeking, the role of the CAP needs to be through these rural developments which already exist to keep up with the change and ensure that the environmental benefits maintain pace with the changes—which are going to happen, and we accept them. We do not want to see these areas fossilised, but we do need to see a new development model so that they can develop in a more sustainable way. We would also see social benefits, we believe. At the moment these areas are gearing up quite a big rural depopulation issue. People will move out of farming. They will not be able to find jobs there any more if they follow the Western model. If rural development policies are used to boost eco-tourism to find the kinds of niche food and added value of other agricultural products which have been described already, there is a far higher chance of thriving rural communities being sustained in some of these areas, even though they will not look exactly like the ones that are there now.

Q63 *Viscount Brookeborough:* You believe it can become sustainable, because it is such a massive task and the population is already moving out of those areas? To a certain extent you are denying them the social advancement that the EU has promised.
Dr Armstrong-Brown: That is an incredibly important point and the last thing we would want to do is to say, "Choose birds not jobs." For a start, it is not that argument anyway. Agri-environment schemes are linked to higher levels of rural employment than Single Farm Payment areas anyway. We have various examples of that. We do recognise there will be a change, but you are right to highlight the urgency and the importance of this. It is going to be quite difficult. We do have decades of history of the wrong sort of development to draw on and not all that much experience of the right sort. We have one decade of learning about good agri-environment schemes and the types of schemes that are now in Axes 1 and 3, but we need to bring all that and apply it as fast as we can. Otherwise, as you say, it will be too late.

Q64 *Viscount Brookeborough:* Would you say something about Spain and Portugal as to what has changed since their accession and how it has been detrimental to the environment? Secondly, because you are particularly involved with birds, what about the extensive shooting of songbirds in other countries

of Europe? I notice that we were blue on your chart, which seemed to be for the lowest preservation levels. I come from Ireland and you had us especially low.
Mr Huyton: I am afraid Ireland is particularly blue!

Q65 *Viscount Brookeborough:* But after all the damage which is done day by day in farming—and I am not protecting it at all—there is extensive shooting of songbirds throughout a lot of the rest of Europe?
Dr Avery: I can deal with the shooting of songbirds, to give my colleagues some time to think about the rest of the answer to the question. The shooting of songbirds is not a good idea and quite a lot of it which has come about in Southern Europe and the Mediterranean is illegal, and it is illegal under the Birds Directive.

Q66 *Viscount Brookeborough:* But they do not do much about it?
Dr Avery: Well, there has been progress, but not enough progress. We would certainly say that the spring shooting, in particular, of birds like Turtledoves, which are migrants—Turtledoves are farm birds in this country but spend the winter on the other side of the Sahara—by the French in South-West France and in other parts of Southern Europe is bound to decrease the population. Having said that, all the research which has been done actually shows that it is changes in farming which have driven the big decline in Turtledoves right across Europe. They are dependent upon seeds during the summer, particularly Fumitory, which used to be a fairly common weed and is now a rarer plant. So, even if the bird is shot illegally—and we are against that—the thing which has actually driven its decline is these big land use changes right across Europe.
Mr Huyton: I can comment a little on Spain, but before I do, if you do not mind, I would like to add quickly to what Sue was saying earlier because of the difference between Pillar I and Pillar II. I think the way to look at it is that Pillar I is essentially financing capital-intensive agriculture, whereas Pillar II is financing employment-intensive agriculture, and we have got an increasing body of evidence of that. We are involved in a study of the agri-environment in Wales, Tir Gofal, for example, which looked at the social and economic benefits of this scheme, and it found that this scheme, which costs the Welsh Government £11 million a year, is generating an additional expenditure in the Welsh economy of £21 million a year and is helping to create an equivalent of 385 full-time jobs because these need more manpower to deliver than the Single Farm Payment, and such like. That was just in addition to what we said before. On your question of what is happening in Spain and Portugal, in Spain we have continued to see a decline in the agricultural area as the more

marginal areas, which are also some of the best areas for biodiversity when they are managed appropriately, are being abandoned. So low-intensity, un-irrigated arable land, for example, has been abandoned. I think the figure is that between 1996 and 2006 the utilised agricultural area has declined by 10%. That overall figure masks the big expansion in the area under permanent crops, which is predominantly irrigated and usually in the areas that are most water-scarce. A similar pattern, I understand, is happening in Portugal, which of course is using, like Spain, its rural development money to finance an ever-growing programme of irrigation. I think that is all I can say on those countries.

Dr Avery: Irrigation is certainly one of the big problems in both Spain and Portugal.

Q67 *Viscount Brookeborough:* They have had several drought years in Portugal and Spain, have they not?

Dr Avery: They have, but the last decade or so has allowed irrigation schemes to be put into areas of low intensity agriculture which were phenomenally important for wildlife, such as the Steppes areas of Extremadura which hold globally threatened species of birds like the Lesser Kestrel and the Great Bustard. You go back to areas which were rich in those species and you find that there is wheat growing there, or tobacco, or other crops, because irrigation has been put in place. That is understandable, but it is going to eat away at the tourist industry and you wonder whether the bottom will fall out of that means of farming, but it will have done the damage in the meantime.

Mr Huyton: These countries actually really show quite clearly the different results you get through investment in agri-environment and through funding intensive practices like irrigation and such like. In Portugal there is a fantastic example of an agri-environment scheme in an area called Castro Verde, which has helped to protect the Great Bustard, which is declining everywhere in Portugal apart from where this agri-environment scheme covers it. There are all sorts of associated benefits relating to eco-tourism, if you want to go out and watch them. Meanwhile, you have the ongoing investment in irrigation infrastructure in areas which are suffering from water scarcity and that water scarcity will only continue to get worse in the future with climate change.

Dr Avery: Just briefly, it may be worth saying that we are clearly keen on agri-environment schemes, I am sure that shines through! We are partly keen on agri-environment schemes because our experience of them in the UK is that the UK has brought in good agri-environment schemes—not perfect agri-environment schemes, we would like to see them done better and we would like to see more money in them, but they

have worked. They have delivered much of what was intended and we can envisage how, with tweaks to the system, they could deliver even more for public money. There are other examples across Europe where agri-environment schemes have worked well, but there are some spectacular examples of where they have worked really badly, and that is where Member States have introduced agri-environment schemes which could never work. They were not well-designed. So we are in favour of them partly because we think they are a good idea and partly because we have had good experience in the UK. But that does not mean that they have been perfect everywhere they have been put in place.

Q68 *Baroness Jones of Whitchurch:* But is it not inevitable that they have to be subsidised? Are there any agri-environment schemes which can just be profitable in their own right? Or are the schemes you are promoting inevitably going to be subsidised?

Dr Armstrong-Brown: Could you clarify that? We were actually talking about the fact that the scheme is a subsidy and it is a payment for a specific purpose rather than a general subsidy, but they can lead to farmers being more profitable. So there is quite a lot of examples with some of the rural development grants of people setting up farm shops, people setting up business parks on their farms in disused farm buildings where people can tele-work, and so on, which then do lead to a more often viable bottom line for that farm, and that would be an ideal situation.

Q69 *Baroness Jones of Whitchurch:* The question is, in relation to the schemes which are being funded by this money, is it inevitable that they have to be subsidised or could you envisage a situation where they would be economical in their own right? Or is the whole of our funding project for ever more going to be based on some subsidies to make the environmental balance worthwhile?

Dr Avery: One example, I guess, is organic farming, where the environmental benefits from organic farming are reasonably well-documented and clear. The RSPB would say that generally speaking on biodiversity grounds organic farming is a good thing. It is clearly more complicated than that, and I am not going to say anything about whether organic food tastes better or is safer for you. But in terms of biodiversity benefits organic farming does deliver benefits. There is public money going into that, but the market is providing a lot of the support and the incentive for more farmers to go organic. So that is an example of where there is a shift in the way a rather small but growing proportion of farmers are farming their land and they are absolutely making money out of the environment, if you like, by farming in an environmentally-friendly way. That is probably the best example.

11 July 2007   Dr Mark Avery, Dr Sue Armstrong-Brown and Mr Harry Huyton

Q70 Baroness Jones of Whitchurch: Yes. Could you envisage using that money as a sort of seed corn, and then people will stand on their own two feet in five or ten years' time?

Dr Avery: I suppose another example, which you might be surprised to hear the RSPB say, would be management for game shooting. The best types of pheasant and partridge shooting, which are done to deliver an income from the shooting, do have environmental benefits for wildlife. That is absolutely true. A lot of farmland birds benefit from that type of management. So that is another. We are clearly struggling to think of a long list of ways where you make money from doing environmentally the right thing without public support, but those are two. Organic farming is not without any public support, but it is not completely dependent upon public support.

Dr Armstrong-Brown: I do think it is quite important to recognise that a lot of the time we are dealing with a market failure, so we do strongly believe that there will need to be some sort of public support—not for everything, and examples in addition to those are rare things which will make money in their own right. But basically it is not usually going to be in any producer's interest not to produce if his business is production. But if the environmental benefit you are after depends upon not producing on a little bit of the land, there is always going to be a market failure there and the only two ways you can address it are through regulation or through some sort of incentivisation really, unless the market changes in such a way that it recognises the efforts being made. I know some supermarkets are very interested. We were speaking to some of them about how some of those benefits to the consumer can be paid for through the consumers rather than through policy, but I cannot really see a way in which these sorts of incentives will never be required. So I do not think we will get to that golden market system which delivers us all the farmers' requirements, clean water, all the climate changes, et cetera, that we want from the countryside just on its own.

Q71 Lord Cameron of Dillington: I would just like to follow up a little bit on the Chairman's question on cross-compliance with a couple of other questions. From what you say about the application of cross-compliance in other countries it has been fairly lax in some areas. Does that mean you see that the future of cross-compliance should involve a greater degree of prescription from Brussels? And, if so, how does that equate with the statement you made earlier about the dangers of having EU-wide policies when you have got different topographies, different habitats, different climates, and so on?

Mr Huyton: As we said, I think it is clear it is not working at the moment, so the approach we have at the moment is too far on the subsidiarity scale towards the Member States, but at the same time we need the flexibility because obviously the environmental situation between Member States and between regions varies widely. So we need to maintain some broad flexibilities. We need to bring it back a bit more towards the control of Brussels or the EU, but the way we think this could be done is through a programme of approach similar to what we get under the rural development programmes at the moment. So, the EU sets a strategic framework, Member States submit their proposals and the EU does a final sign-off to make sure that the different proposals coming from all different Member States adequately meet the requirements and reflect a similar level of environmental protection. I think that would be a good model because that retains the flexibility. Member States still write their own programmes, they still look at how this applies to the Member States, but there is this check to make sure that they are ticking all the boxes and they are not missing anything out.

Q72 Lord Cameron of Dillington: My second question relates to that. Reading your evidence, reading between the lines, I get the feeling that you are slightly torn between the benefits of cross-compliance, which is in a way like regulation because everyone is going to take Pillar I money and therefore will apply to all farmers, compared with if you put all the money into Pillar II and you only have environmental schemes, which were kind of acting in competition with food production in the marketplace and it would only be taken up by some farmers. Is that a true analysis of the dilemma you find yourselves in?

Dr Armstrong-Brown: We do not really see it as a dilemma, actually. We feel quite calm about this one. We do feel the need for a common baseline for everybody, you know, there is a speed limit in towns! There is a clear argument for that. Whether or not it needs to be delivered through cost-compliance or some other route is open to question. Actually, if the Single Farm Payment were to be phased out you would not have anything to hang your cost-compliance on, so you would need to have another way. That baseline can be envisaged and is necessary, and every hectare of land should be at a certain standard for the environment.

Q73 Lord Cameron of Dillington: So, even if Pillar I disappeared, you would want to see an introduction of regulation to apply?

Dr Armstrong-Brown: We would like to see some way of establishing good farming practice, how to manage land on behalf of yourself and others to a minimum standard. But we do recognise that to go beyond that—you cannot require everybody to be self-funding, to make a huge effort, if it is not in their business interests, unless there are some further enhancements on top. But we do see the need for both of those approaches, the baseline and the extra thing which not all farmers may choose to go into. But we do see a baseline that everybody should adhere to as being necessary.

Q74 *Lord Plumb:* You abolish the Single Farm Payment and you introduce regulation, because you would have to introduce regulation to make sure you have got suitable environmental practices by farmers. You have got a market out there working away which is sending pretty strong signals to farmers. With that sort of combination, what do you think the impact would be on European agriculture in terms of its shape and numbers?
Dr Armstrong-Brown: The economists would argue that we already are there. It is not necessarily a view that any of us completely believe, but with decoupled payments in theory they do not impact on farming choices because they are not attached to them. Now, we all know that is not actually the case and there is recoupling going on at the level of the individual.

Q75 *Chairman:* You are almost having your cake and eating it, are you not, with your argument? One minute you say you want to get rid of the Single Farm Payment and the next minute you are saying, "Well, it's decoupled and it's not –
Dr Armstrong-Brown: We will have our cake and eat it when we can keep all the money and its all in Pillar II, and that is what we are aiming for. But your question, I think, was about the changes to European farming and I think we can see some of them already. What we are seeing now is a continuation of some of the trends that already existed. So abandonment was going on and intensification was going on. Decoupling has released some of the restraints on both of those processes and now there is an adjustment to a freer market. What we would like to see is the bit of the equation which has not yet been put fully into place, which is alongside the decoupling rural development schemes which provide that market for the public good that does exist in some ways but not entirely yet. If that were to be the case, then what European farming would look like would depend on your development policy if you were incentivising through the new CAP. What we would like to see it do is allow profitable farming to integrate a lot of measures that look after the environment alongside those activities, so we would probably see some abandonment continuing. That might not always be a terrible thing, but we would like to see, in high nature value farming areas, abandonment stemmed through those rural development policies

and those traditional farming customs which deliver such high quality environmental goods retained. Where it is sensible to have more intensive agriculture, where the market will dictate that that is the case—East Anglia is a good example, and the West Country for livestock farming—we would like to see those rural development policies ensuring the delivery, alongside production, of the environmental goods that we seek to get from those areas. That is how we would see it changing from the system we have now, if what we would like to see were to come to pass. Without strong rural development policies and well-funded agri-environment schemes, we would probably see this polarisation that Viscount Ullswater was talking about earlier continuing. We would see more abandonment. We would very likely see much more cyclical behaviour in the markets, which is already starting and will happen anyway, and the perturbations which Lord Plumb was raising earlier. We would anticipate those would happen anyway, but it could be moderated a little bit through the rural development programme if that were seen to be desirable, which we think it would be.

Q76 *Lord Cameron of Dillington:* It would seem appropriate if I ask some questions on the budget at this stage. You obviously want, as you were saying—and all the money is going to Pillar II in the long run—that money to be spent achieving good results from what you were talking about as market failures. How do you see this evolving? At what level? Do you get Parish Councils asking for what they particularly want in terms of their local habitat and environment? I am talking about Axis 2, I know, but you are very keen on Axis 2 and you are probably not the right people to discuss the other Axes with. But is it at District Council level, Local Authority level, Regional level? And what criteria would be applied from Brussels, because it has to be a European-wide policy?
Dr Armstrong-Brown: Are you talking about the specific delivery priorities? Or are you talking about the overall policy objectives, because I think you could come at it from either end, and you probably need to do both?

Q77 *Lord Cameron of Dillington:* I am taking the overall policy objectives as given, because you want to improve the countryside in terms of habitats and the environment. There are lots of different things and you are particularly concerned about habitats and the way wildlife is managed and looked after. Other people might go for landscapes, but let us take the policy objectives. It is actually the delivery and how you would ensure that there was an even spread of funds across Europe, because you have got to have a single market. At what level would you apply these policies in terms of delivery?

Dr Armstrong-Brown: That is a very good question. The more local you get, the more fine-tuned your delivery can be, but there needs to be a good overview. We do have a fairly good understanding of some aspects, especially for the farmland birds, where the real hot spots are and where you can do some good, and where some basically are not there, so there is no point in targeting agri-environment measures, if we are talking about Axis 2. One of the reasons why schemes have failed in the past is that they have simply been targeted at things that are not there and therefore have not delivered them. You do need to have that knowledge. It does not necessarily have to be done at a Council or District level, because those data are held at different scales by different organisations and in different countries as well. There certainly has to be local involvement. There is actually a consultation process going on now for England, delivering the environmental stewardship scheme, which is broken down by government office region, which is one of the places you could start. But it would rather depend—if you are talking about a very rare moth, you might need to go incredibly local. If you are talking about lapwing, nationally we have a fairly good understanding of pretty much where you would be likely to deliver a benefit if you targeted a measure for them.

Q78 Lord Cameron of Dillington: So in your vision of the long-term future you would probably divide the funds up, give some locally and have some sort of national policies? Is that how you see it? Perhaps you have not worked out the details?

Dr Armstrong-Brown: We have not got the detail, but to answer your question at a sort of headline level, there has got to be a common acceptance of the headline objectives of the Pillars, otherwise it is not a common policy. How to actually deliver those in specific places will rely on the knowledge of individuals who know where these things are. I do not really think national and local finances would be the only way to do that.

Mr Huyton: Part of the way we see this thing delivered is the system of having a basic entry level scheme available to everyone. That would ensure that some funds are going everywhere, so that every farmer who wants to do something more for the environment and join this scheme can, and that money should be available across the EU. But then there are these kind of more advanced schemes which target specific environmental priorities, be it a specific species or a specific environment problem. So it may be a catchment area which is particularly prone to water pollution, and such like. I guess the targeting of those more advanced measures would be based on your environmental priorities.

Q79 Lord Cameron of Dillington: Can I just step back then to the middle term. In your written submission you talk about having Pillar I co-founded by Member States. Why are you suggesting this? And how would you retain a single market if you did have co-funding?

Dr Armstrong-Brown: That is almost a necessity because, if you were to start putting all the money from Pillar I into Pillar II, which is co-founded, the budget would double. So, if you switched the co-funding requirements away from exclusively falling on Pillar II and make the remnants of Pillar I co-funded, you could contain the overall budget. It would also be a very interesting test for how committed Member States really were to Pillar I payments. At the moment there is resistance to change.

Q80 Lord Cameron of Dillington: So you are assuming that some Member States would support their agriculture differently from ours?

Dr Armstrong-Brown: I think it is very likely, although that is my opinion rather than a fact. But people who argue very strongly against reform may do so partly because at the moment there is no cost to the State from Pillar I payments, apart from what they are contributing to the overall budget. If that state had to contribute part of the cost of Pillar I payments but Pillar II payments were less restricted in that way—that would help remove the brake on Pillar II payments, caused by having to co-finance them at the moment, with the policy weight now falling on the objectives serviced by Pillar II—would it not make more sense to make that easy to be delivered through European funding streams and, if the Member States strongly wished to have a large Pillar I, ask for a contribution from the Member States to support it? It is cutting the same size cake in a different type of pattern.

Lord Cameron of Dillington: I think I had better leave it there.

Q81 Lord Moynihan: Could I ask you and your colleagues to travel somewhat further afield than Spain and Portugal and the natural habitats of Eastern Germany into the rather complex area of world trade? It was noticeable in your very helpful evidence that you did not comment on the implications of changes taking place in the world market as a result of trade liberalisation, the potential impact of rising real incomes and a high demand for renewable energy crops, et cetera. What sort of impact do you feel this might have on the environment in Europe, and indeed globally?

Mr Huyton: Globally, the biggest drive of biodiversity decline is agriculture expansion—agriculture expansion in places like Brazil and Indonesia, which is feeding the global commodities market, and we know that an increasingly liberalised agricultural market will accelerate that pattern. The European Commission did a sustainability impact assessment of the Doha round for trade negotiations and one of their key environmental findings was that we would accelerate rainforest destruction. So that is a fact. Of course, at the same time the areas which are less competitive at the global level would experience more of a depression, which could be particularly worrying if it is those areas which are practising the traditional form of agriculture which is delivering environmental benefits. That is one of the reasons behind our thinking that these areas need specific targeting in Europe, because I suspect that will be the biggest risk from the biodiversity perspective of increased liberalisation in the EU. There is this bigger question about commodity prices going up as a result of changes in diets and increasingly a growing population. There is not a lot we can do about that. But on the other side an increased demand for biofuels is driving commodity prices up, and there is more we can do about that. The biofuels market is a publicly created market. It is created through public intervention and subsidy in the form of tax incentives, obligations, and such like. So we have more of a say there and I think that, if we start seeing serious problems in terms of habitat destruction at the global level, then we will need to rein in the biofuels market. We have been urging the Government here and the European Commission to ensure proper monitoring of land-use change globally, agriculture expansion and intensification is in place so that we can see the response to these two patterns and so that we can inform our domestic policies on biofuels as a result of that.

Dr Avery: It is difficult to see that the outlook is particularly rosy, is it not? We live on a small and beautiful planet. There are already more than six billion people living here. If everybody had the same standard of living that we have in this country, we would need three planets. The population is growing and going to grow. What has happened because of that in history is that we have eaten into rainforests, savannahs and natural habitats to a growing extent; and it is quite difficult to see that that is going to stop, which depresses me enormously. But I am afraid the RSPB does not have the answer to that up our sleeves, and I am not sure who does. It would be wrong for us to come here and say, "Oh, it's all very simple and it's all going to work out OK," because my suspicion would be that it is not.

Q82 *Lord Moynihan:* Is the global land-use change going to be covered in the document you referred to earlier, namely the launch in Brussels with your colleagues on the 27th?

Mr Huyton: It is one of the key challenges to agriculture policy in Europe's rural areas which we outline in that document.

Dr Avery: You did mention biofuels, and maybe we should say just a little more on biofuels now. Biofuels vary enormously in their greenhouse gas emissions savings. They have been treated as all being the same, and they are not. Clearly, one of the worrying things is that growing biofuels creates an incentive to cut down more of tropical rainforest than we are doing already: and rainforest destruction counts for about 20% of greenhouse gas emissions at the moment. So it would be bizarre if we cut down rainforest and create greenhouse gas emissions from doing that to create biofuels, some of which have a rather poor record themselves in saving greenhouse gas emissions, but that seems to be one direction we might be heading in. I think some of the enthusiasm for biofuels is a con. It is an environmental con and clearly it will create great pressure on food production globally as well. You cannot grow food and biofuels on the same bit of land very easily, and that does come down to how many people there are on this planet and how much we are trying to get out of it. So I am depressed, I am afraid. I am usually an optimist, but this seems too big a problem for us to crack very easily.

Q83 *Lord Moynihan:* I appreciate your frankness on the subject. There is a very specific point, which goes back to your comments earlier on the high natural value of farming and the decoupling of support that would lead to a loss of high natural value farming. You suggest that the Less-Favoured-Area payments should be designed to protect this sector. I wonder if you have made an analysis on whether or not this can be made consistent with the 'green box' requirements of the WTO or not?

Dr Armstrong-Brown: There is an issue there, because of the way in which the 'green box' is constructed. We do believe in the short-term that is not the biggest problem for these areas. The problem is to find some way of retaining them until any possible legal wrangle can be untangled. It is possible there might be an issue, but we do not think it is a particularly serious one and there is certainly much more urgency to get some payments in place which would actually retain these first. In the longer run, the ideology behind the setting for the 'green box' and the world trade rules which relate to agriculture, it is worth asking questions about whether it is going to guarantee the delivery of the things which are emerging as priorities now, the social and environmental things which are emerging as priorities now. One certainly would not want to throw the baby out with the bathwater, but if it becomes impossible to support areas of land management which are delivering huge environmental good but are not economic, surely that is wrong? We would then start to challenge the rules around the green box and suggest that income for GOM payments were not necessarily the best way to sustain these systems.

Lord Moynihan: Thank you very much indeed.

Q84 Chairman: If we are talking about a concern with global warming, maintaining livestock on the uplands is not a very good idea, is it? The fewer cows, the better?

Dr Armstrong-Brown: The greenhouse gas emissions from the livestock? I think the few which are in the uplands do not really emit quite as many as the vast numbers in intensive feed herds in the lowlands.

Lord Plumb: Are you including sheep in that, Chairman?

Chairman: Yes, I include sheep.

Lord Moynihan: It depends on the quality of the food production!

Q85 Viscount Brookeborough: In your paper, in the Rural Development paragraph, you say that funding inappropriate afforestation is not a good thing. Could you go a bit further into that, because quite clearly the clearing of the rainforest is a very, very bad thing. What in the UK is 'inappropriate afforestation' if you accept that we desperately need timber from somewhere, no matter how much paper you recycle, and so on?

Dr Avery: I think in the past, in the same way that we have encouraged unsustainable farming practices, we have encouraged unsustainable forestry. So afforestation in the uplands, for example—which is a terribly bad place to grow trees, actually—they do not grow very good trees—where you need to drain soils in order to be able to grow the trees has led to increased run-off.

Q86 Viscount Brookeborough: But there is a tremendous amount of work going on to, if you like, in layperson's language, create sponges and the run-off from forests which are currently being planted, or re-planted, is very, very much less.

Dr Avery: This is just like agriculture, it depends on the forestry, does it not? So, rows and rows of sitka spruce trees on the side of a hill which has had moor grips put into it to allow them to grow there probably is not very sustainable forestry and increasing tree growth across the uplands with native species might actually lead to carbon sequestration flood risk management and a richer environment and a better landscape.

Q87 Viscount Brookeborough: I am inclined to agree with you about trees on the uplands, and so on. But unfortunately we have got to have them somewhere. Are you then suggesting that we should grow it on lowlands, or where, because you have already said that biofuels being grown on lowlands will take away

food production and we could run into problems on that? Somewhere these trees are going to have to grow.

Dr Avery: I think we will have to take that away and think about it some more and come back to you.

Q88 Chairman: What you have said, then, about forestry is fair for, say, 20 years ago, but forestry policy has changed significantly over the last 10 or 15 years?

Dr Avery: It has, I think that is fair. But we are left with the mistakes of previous forestry policy and the Forestry Commission and landowners are now left at the felling of the first crop of trees with the decision of whether they continue with forestry or go back into some other land use in many of those places.

Q89 Viscount Brookeborough: But we still have the lowest percentage of our land of any European state under forestry, and therefore it is a Government aim to increase that, because otherwise we are relying on other forests which are unsustainable, such as rainforests?

Dr Avery: Yes, I think that is true. I am not sure that, if we were starting from scratch, we would have a State forestry service now. We do not have a State agricultural department or a State fishing fleet. The Forestry Commission was brought into being after the First World War because we were worried that we needed a strategic supply of pit props. We do not need those any more. Many of the places where we are trying to grow trees at the moment are not the best places to grow them; and, if we are looking at the pure economics of forestry, we probably would not do it in many of the places where we are doing it.

Q90 Chairman: British forestry is not economic forestry any more, is it? It is recreational and environmental forestry—in England. There is virtually zero commercial forestry in England being planted now.

Dr Avery: I think there is almost zero economically profitable forestry, but the State still owns large amounts of land and manages large amounts of land, and the Forestry Commission's aim is to grow trees on that land. We would actually say that there might be better uses for quite a lot of that land than growing trees.

Q91 Lord Palmer: We are nearly at the end and I was intrigued to hear what you were saying about biofuels. I must remember to send you the latest press release from the NFU about how, if the land taken out of set-aside was to grow enough oilseed rape to meet our RTFO, a lot of your fears in fact, I think, would be put aside. But a yes or no answer, please: are you concerned that support for the production of biofuels would actually have a damaging impact on bird life? You used to say it did, but you have slightly changed your stance over the years, particularly when Lord Bach was Minister! I put that on the record.

Dr Avery: If it is a yes or no answer, then the answer is yes, we are still concerned.

Lord Palmer: What do you consider to be the main challenges for agriculture as a result of climate change? And what role might a new Rural Development policy based on the current EAFRD play in assisting farmers to adapt to these challenges?

Q92 *Chairman:* That could be a "Don't know" if you like!

Dr Avery: We could have a go at that, but it would be fair to say that nobody, I think, who could appear before you would know the answers with any great certainty here. Clearly, some of the challenges that climate change will set for agriculture will be in moving to new crops and new ways of farming. So maybe one can just look a bit further south in Europe to see what British agriculture might look like, but it may not be quite that simple. Another challenge will be that agriculture, like all other industries, will have to be looking at its carbon emissions and looking at ways to do its job with lower emissions. I think, as we touched on earlier, there are some quite big opportunities for land management in terms of looking at whether places like the uplands have a different future, which is in being carbon sinks, and managing upland peat and soils in different ways to stop them being degraded, to stop them drying out, to stop them emitting greenhouse gases, maybe a softer management approach to restore those uplands so that they are not adding much carbon— they may be adding carbon to what is there at the moment, but they stop losing carbon. There is quite a lot of work which is now beginning to be done to look at those issues and it may be that upland farmers will be paid for farming carbon rather than farming sheep in 20 years' time. That might be one of the things that land management delivers as a public good. Flood risk management may be another thing which is produced in that way.

Lord Palmer: Thank you very much.

Q93 *Lord Cameron of Dillington:* I cannot let you get away with just a "Yes" answer to the previous question. Could you expand on why growing crops for biofuels is damaging for bird life?

Dr Avery: We would love to. We were not asked to give a wider answer.

Q94 *Lord Cameron of Dillington:* No, I realise that. I thought you were getting away too easily!

Mr Huyton: One thing I would say is that, while the NFU is saying that they can produce enough to meet the Renewable Transport Fuel Obligation, there is a reason why all our processing plants are being sited next to major ports and that is because a lot of it will come from outside the UK and outside the EU, because biofuels is a global commodity market which the UK cannot necessarily compete on. So that is just something to be aware of. It is not where the market will deliver the biofuels from, unless the market is regulated in some way. We are concerned in that short-term biofuels do need land, so they will need to be grown on set-aside. Set-aside has inadvertently had a range of benefits for farmers in particular throughout Europe, so that is a worry. Also, it is the first sign of this land use pressure. Biofuels need land and I think the NFU's own calculations suggest that you would need 1.2 million hectares of land producing oilseed rape and wheat to meet this obligation, and that is a lot of land when you consider how much arable we have in the UK. So this idea of losing habitats that are important—in the UK that might be set-aside and in Eastern Europe that might be permanent grassland, which would be a very big worry from the biodiversity perspective. It is one of our most important farmed habitats in Europe. Then perhaps in the longer term there is an idea that biofuels, and bioenergy as well, will mean new crops, which will represent quite a big ecological shift in terms of the nature of our farmland. So Miscanthus and short rotation coppice bring with them a range of challenges for wildlife that we need to make sure that we manage. We know very little about what kind of habitat Miscanthus will offer for wildlife. We suspect it will be pretty poor because it is extremely fast-growing dense grass which has got very little space for any kind of wildlife to access, but the research needs to be done so that we know what the impacts of these new crops will be and how we should manage them. There is also a concern particularly of these new perennial crops being planted very close to processing stations and creating monocultures in permanent crops.

Dr Avery: We are not against biofuels and we would say that there may well be a place, and probably there is a place, for the right type of biofuels in this country and abroad. But it would be wrong to say that all biofuels are good and they are all going to be great for the environment, they are all going to save lots of greenhouse gas emissions and therefore they are the green crop which will have no downsides at all. Not all people are the same, not all environmental organisations are the same, and not all biofuels are the same. We would be nervous that, with the bandwagon that is biofuels at the moment, too many people jump onto it without thinking about it, particularly since, if biofuels are going to have a bigger place in UK farming, it will only be if public money goes into supporting them. And, if public money goes into supporting them, we ought to be very clear about their greenhouse gas emission benefits (and not all biofuels are the same) and we ought to look at their other environmental benefits and disbenefits (and not all biofuels will be the same on that basis either). So let us look carefully and properly, and saying, "Let's use all of next year's set-aside to grow biofuels" does not feel like the most informed and careful look at the subject to us.

Q95 *Viscount Ullswater:* Is that the same attitude you take towards the growing of GM crops?

Dr Avery: I am happy to touch on that. The RSPB opposed the herbicide-tolerant GM crops, the three crops which were proposed and went through the farm-scale evaluations, and I think actually the results of the farm-scale evaluations showed that our worries about those particular crops were indeed justified, which is why they did not receive Government approval to go ahead. But GM crops generally we are neutral on. In fact, we have quite close contacts with the biotechnology firms and I always suggest to them that the challenge for them is to come forward with a GM crop which we could support because it has big environmental benefits, and that is possible. But none of the companies has yet come close to coming to us to say, "Here's one that you're going to like."

Q96 *Lord Cameron of Dillington:* There is a gap in the market!

Dr Avery: Absolutely, it is a gap in the market. It takes quite a long time to develop the crop.

Q97 *Lord Plumb:* One of your major concerns was the use of fertilizers and pesticides, and so on and so forth. Do you not accept that, if we move towards genetic modification, that in turn will reduce the quantity of fertilizers quite considerably and in many areas almost eliminate the use of pesticides in the way that they do? But on that particular point, reading your evidence, you are concentrating on those areas. Do you not accept that season by season, as we see the changes, particularly taking the present season, the big problem at the moment is blight, blight in potatoes? We shall have no potato crop in this country or in other parts of Europe, Holland in particular, where there is not spraying dealing with blight. Farmers are having to spray every third day to try to control the blight. To say, therefore, that we should either eliminate or considerably reduce this is totally ignoring the fact that you have got to live with nature and not try to do things which are slightly different?

Dr Avery: There are several statements and questions all together in what you said.

Q98 *Lord Plumb:* Well, answer me yes or no!

Dr Avery: I certainly cannot answer yes or no to that. In terms of inputs to GM crops, we would still say that you need to look at these on a GM-crop-by-GM-crop basis. The rhetoric from the biotech companies about herbicide-tolerant crops was that they would need less pesticide, which was indeed true, but less pesticide that would have a more harmful impact on the environment because those crops would have been modified to allow broad spectrum herbicides to be used which would kill all the weeds. That was what they were supposed to do. So this is like saying that drinking a shot of neat alcohol will do you less harm than drinking a couple of pints of shandy. It is not true. It is a smaller amount of alcohol or pesticide, but the impact it has is a lot bigger. So our position on GM crops is that we are philosophically neutral, but we await with interest the industry coming along with the GM crop which the environmental movement can get behind, and probably the RSPB would be one of the first environmental organisations to back a GM crop that really was good. But I have not seen one yet. I have not even had a sniff of one yet.

Q99 *Lord Plumb:* Go to India and look at the cotton crop and then you decide.

Dr Avery: That may be true, but not for the UK.

Q100 *Chairman:* One specific: something which could come out of the Health Check would be the abolition of set-aside. Views?

Dr Avery: As we said, set-aside has done environmental good accidentally. It was not an environmental scheme. The RSPB supported set-aside when it came in, but it has done good. It is going to disappear and it makes sense in policy terms that it does disappear. Why would you have a system for limiting production when your funding is not based on production? But we would like to see the accidental but real benefits of set-aside somehow incorporated into the future, so we would not want to lose the environmental benefits of set-aside. That is one reason why we are keen on more money going into agri-environment schemes which could take up the slack if set-aside disappears, as it surely will at some stage.

Q101 *Chairman:* I think we are just about done. If you could rack your brain, is there anything you would like to say but you have not had the opportunity of saying?

Dr Avery: I think not, but if there is something –

Dr Armstrong-Brown: It has been touched on, sort of, through some of the conversations we have had. For a more positive outcome from the Health Check and the Budget Review that is coming up to happen, for a new CAP to evolve, there is going to have to be a catalysis mechanism to get that debate going in

Europe. It is very live in this country. It is extremely good. There is high-quality thinking going on. I do not think you get such high-quality debates everywhere else in Europe, and I do think they are necessary to think through these things properly. Through our partner organisations in Bird Life International we are trying to do some of it, but I do think there is a major role for the UK Government here to lead that debate in a positive way which actually requires mental engagement from people rather than posturing. I do think that is absolutely crucial and it will be one of the things that makes the new CAP good or bad, depending on how it is done.

Chairman: Thank you very much indeed. Thank you for your time and your help.

WEDNESDAY 18 JULY 2007

Present	Bach, L	Palmer, L
	Brookeborough, V	Plumb, L
	Cameron of Dillington, L	Sewel, L (Chairman)
	Jones of Whitchurch, B	Ullswater, V
	Miller of Chilthorne Domer, B	

Memorandum by the National Farmers' Union of England & Wales

The NFU is very pleased to respond to submit evidence to the European Union Committee (sub Committee D) of the House of Lords on the future of the CAP. The NFU has more than 50,000 farming members in England and Wales and represents the great majority of full-time commercial farmers.

INTRODUCTION

1. The NFU had advocated the principle of decoupling some ten years before it came into effect. The NFU was virtually the only farm organisation in Europe to support the Commission's proposals for a radical reform of the CAP.

2. Reality has proved disappointing. In order to gain a majority in the Council in 2003 the Commission accepted a number of compromises and special national arrangements, which have resulted in very different implementation of the reform in different Member States. What is worse, the British government decided to adopt a radical and complicated system in England which has so far proved beyond the ability of Defra and its Agencies to implement correctly or effectively.

3. Wales, Scotland and Northern Ireland chose different models, so that even within the United Kingdom the same producer will be treated very differently, depending on the post code. The NFU represents farmers in England and Wales. This reform has meant that interests of farmers in England and Wales, and their views on further change, are now in some respects different.

4. What was intended to be a simpler common policy has now become more complicated and less common. The priority for the NFU, both short and long term, is to revert to the original intention of a simple common policy.

OVERVIEW

5. The NFU profoundly believes that European agriculture has passed a critical turning point. A combination of rising world population, and economic growth particularly in Asia, and global warming which is simultaneously creating demand for renewable energy and reducing production capability in some parts of the world, has significantly altered the balance of supply and demand. The issue is not now simply food security, as it was when the CAP was devised, but an amalgam of food, energy and environmental security.

6. All these mean that land, and land-based production, are key strategic issues for Europe. The long term objective of the CAP must be to preserve Europe's production potential. The title Common Agricultural Policy aptly describes that objective.

7. The NFU is not persuaded by the argument that the Common Agricultural Policy should be scrapped and replaced by a Common Rural Policy. The justification for a CAP is that agriculture is an industry with extensive government involvement and financial support, where farmers compete in an open single European market. A common policy is required to avoid competitive distortions. It is possible that financial support will decline in future, but in view of the strategic importance of farming it is unlikely that government involvement will reduce. No such justification attaches to a common rural policy, any more than for a common urban policy. There is, certainly, a need for a European policy framework to support under-developed regions, some of which may be rural, but that is a different issue.

8. The main pressures on the CAP have been relatively constant over the years. The main ones are:

— Budgetary demands, particularly as the EU is expanding to include relatively poor countries with relatively larger farming sectors;

— The tension between subsidiarity in an ever-larger and more diverse Europe and the need to maintain fair competition in a single market;

— International pressure for greater liberalization and lower state support (it is disappointing that the efforts of the EU to make its policy non trade distorting have not been more widely recognized at home and abroad.)

— The need to maintain public support for the policy; and

— The need to maintain Europe's productive capacity while respecting the obligation to produce in a sustainable way.

THE REFORMED CAP

9. The significant change made in 2003 was to decouple support from production. This requires a total change in behaviour by the producer, who should not use the decoupled payment to subsidise current production; and by the rest of the food chain, which needs to recognise that supply will in future only be secured if the price offered is remunerative.

10. It was always recognized that these behavioural changes would not occur overnight; but progress has been frustratingly slow, particularly in the beef, sheep and dairy sectors. There have been some encouraging developments in contractual relations in the liquid milk sector this year, and the NFU believes that an appreciation of the dynamics of decoupling was one of the factors behind these moves. If so, this could be a turning point.

11. Implementation of the Single Payment Scheme in England has been a disaster. The story is well documented and has been the subject of a number of investigations. Many factors have contributed to the failure, but the most critical was the government's insistence on implementing a complicated and radical scheme in the belief that this would, in some way, advantage English farmers. In reality because it proved impossible to administrate it has caused financial hardship to thousands of farmers and exposed the UK to a huge risk of budgetary disallowance. And, because it has meant different treatment of farmers both in the UK and in the EU, it has created the perception, and in some cases the reality, of competitive distortions.

12. The NFU does not disagree that moving to a flat rate payment in England is ultimately the right approach. But this should have been attempted in phased steps, at a common pace throughout the EU. The lesson is that CAP Reform is a long distance race. Setting off at a sprint is not a winning formula.

THE SINGLE PAYMENT SCHEME

13. Despite the woeful inadequacy of the English implementation, the NFU believes that the Single Payment Scheme is a sound basis for the future of Europe's policy, for the foreseeable future. The scheme has, in principle, much to offer in terms being non-trade and non-market distorting. The urgent need is for incremental changes to make the SPS both more common and simpler. The CAP Health Check is a golden opportunity to make those changes. A priority is to reduce the number of different entitlements; this can be done by:

— Abolishing the separate "authorisations" for fruit and vegetable production in countries (like England) that are operating an area-based system.

— Abolishing set aside, which has no place in a decoupled system.

14. Other changes that the NFU is advocating in the Health Check are:

— Abolition of the partial decoupling option.

— An increase in the minimum area, (at the option of Member States) from 0.3ha to 5 ha.

— An increase in compulsory EU modulation, to allow a corresponding decrease in voluntary national modulation.

15. Even with these changes, the EU would still go into the next financial period, beginning in 2013, with three very different single payment schemes operating in parallel, namely:

— "historic" payments, in most of the old EU members states (including Wales and Scotland).

— Flat rate area payments, most notably in England and Germany.

— A "simplified area scheme" in most of the 12 new member states.

16. The NFU's insistence on a common policy means that it must support a move to a single system at some point, and our attachment to simplicity points to the new member state model; the key issue is one of timing. The NFU would certainly not support a headlong rush to a uniform system; it must be done in phases and together. The first step in the process would be for all "old" EU member states to move to an area based system, but, as signalled in the introduction, this does put English and Welsh farmers into opposition. English farmers would like the transition to be relatively short and start as soon as possible—in the health check if that is feasible—while Welsh farmers would like the process to be gradual and delayed as long as possible.

17. We mentioned simplicity in the previous paragraph. A move to a flat-rate system would mean that the entire system of payment rights/entitlements could be removed, with claimants making an annual subsidy application on the basis of hectares farmed, as already happens in most new member states. The payment entitlements introduced under the SPS will then simply have been a mechanism for converting previously coupled support based on livestock numbers/cropped area/sugar beet tonnage etc into a per-hectare payment over a transitional period.

MARKET MECHANISMS

18. The NFU recognises that the importance of market management is greatly reduced and further trade liberalisation will at some point render it inoperable. The key here is export subsidies, for once they are abolished there will be no guarantee that any produce taken off the market will ever find an outlet. Public intervention or private storage aids are more likely to weaken than to strengthen the market.

19. The NFU agrees with the Commission that milk quotas should end in 2015.

20. Set aside has no place in a decoupled system. In a freer global market place, insofar as set aside does impact on the market price it is much more to the benefit of our trading partners in the rest of the world, who do not idle land. In a decoupled system, farmers will increase or decrease their area of arable crops according to the forward price signals. The environmental benefits claimed for set-aside can be better achieved by other mechanisms.

21. The EU has signalled that the EU is ready to eliminate export subsidies. The NFU accepts this, provided that other forms of export aid, such as bogus food aid, over-generous credit and state trading enterprises are eliminated in parallel.

22. In the longer term there is a strong case for introducing some form of risk management, and some EU countries already have arrangements in place. There are a large number of practical problems that would need to be resolved; the NFU is following this issue closely.

RURAL DEVELOPMENT

23. It is too soon to form a judgement on the EAFRD, given that the programmes for the UK 2007–13 have yet to be submitted to the Commission, let alone approved.

24. The NFU supports most of the measures under Axis 2 (land management), but is more sceptical of the potential measures under Axis 1 (improving competitiveness) and Axis 3 (the wider rural community). In England these measures are determined and administered by the Regional Development Agencies.

25. Our experience so far does not give us confidence that these measures will be well targeted or effective. For example, £98 million has been ring-fenced by Defra under Axis 1 to help deal with the environmental challenges of the livestock sector, but this risks being so widely diffused as to render it ineffective. Similarly, the NFU fears that an opportunity to use funds under Axis 3 for kick-starting local power generation projects will be missed.

26. The NFU hopes that these concerns will be proved groundless, and that the RDAs will take on their new role in rural development effectively and efficiently. But until that has been demonstrated there is no case for higher levels of funding.

27. The NFU strongly supports an increase in compulsory EU modulation in the CAP Health Check. These extra funds must be used in the UK to make a corresponding reduction in voluntary modulation rates.

28. The NFU would also like to draw attention to potential distortions of competition that could arise from rural development progammes that are being run in some other member states that have a very generous allocation of core European funds. For example, Ireland is proposing to operate programmes that are close to being coupled support for beef and sheep production.

WORLD TRADE

29. As an exporting region with internal prices generally above world levels, the process of trade liberalisation in agriculture was always going to be difficult for the European Union, and our interests tend to be more defensive than offensive.

30. If there is to be a conclusion of the Doha Round, the European Union will have to go beyond its initial offer, particularly on the level of tariff reductions. This will cause serious difficulties for some sectors of European agriculture.

31. By the same token, some of our competitors, most notably the USA, will have to make serious changes to their internal support arrangements. While the EU has reduced its support, and made much of it non trade distorting, the USA has increased support and much of it—notably the counter-cyclical payments—is very trade distorting. The reduction of such programmes is the major gain that the EU can expect from the WTO Round.

32. The gain to the European economy is more likely to come from a further liberalisation of trade in manufactured goods and services. It is important that a WTO settlement includes these issues and is not restricted to agriculture.

ENVIRONMENTAL PROTECTION AND CLIMATE CHANGE

33. Cross compliance and agri-environmental schemes (which now cover more than 4 million hectares of farmland) have made a positive contribution to environmental protection. The full extent of the improvement is yet to be quantified, but the fact that these measures are in place should allow a moratorium on new prescriptive legislation through, for example, the Water Framework Directive and the proposed Soil Framework Directive.

34. Agriculture has a major role to play in climate change mitigation and adaptation.

35. Agriculture is only a minor contributor to CO_2 emissions, but is a major producer of other greenhouse gases like Nitrous Oxide and Methane. The NFU believes it is urgent to find integrated and cost-effective ways of reducing these emissions, and is a partner in a project to find ways by which British agriculture can continue to produce, while reducing its environmental footprint. Integrated solutions are vital; when addressing greenhouse gas issues we must not create new environmental problems.

36. The NFU applauds the binding EU commitments of 20% of energy production and 10% of transport fuel from renewable sources by 2020.

37. In the short term, production of bio-ethanol and bio-diesel are the most easily accessible opportunities, and production in the USA, Brazil and Germany have already had an impact on world cereal, sugar and oilseed prices.

38. In the medium and longer term other types of renewable energy production are likely to be much greater land users; this would include micro-generation from bio-digesters and local CHP plants. The enhanced Renewable Obligation Certificates proposed in the May Energy White Paper should provide an important stimulus to investment in such technology. The NFU believes that Rural Development Programmes in England and Wales should be used strategically to support these types of development.

39. The NFU has the ambition that every farm in England and Wales should have the opportunity to become a net energy exporter.

FINANCING

40. The budget for 2007–13 seems, on the face of it, to be inadequate to finance the accession of Bulgaria and Romania and any other new member states that may arrive in this period. So far, however, the CAP budget has kept well within its limits.

41. A serious issue for the NFU is the historical legacy of inadequate core funding of Rural Development in the UK, which has lead to a level of national modulation that will rise to 14% in England, while being unknown in virtually the whole of the rest of Europe. This is an issue that must be addressed in the next funding period.

42. The NFU is strongly opposed to co-financing and agrees with the Commission that this would be a step to the disintegration of the CAP.

43. In our view, it would require a Treaty change to make co-funding obligatory on Member States, and this would inevitably be resisted by the poorer Member States. The most likely way that it would come about would be to introduce the same mechanism that applies to pillar 2 funding, namely that European funding would be contingent on a certain level of national funding. This is precisely what led to a chronic level of under-funding of rural development in the UK.

ENLARGEMENT

44. Apart from the budgetary aspects, noted above, the experience of enlargement has been of net benefit to agriculture in the old member states, including the UK. Far from providing low priced competition, the general experience has been that accession countries have proved to be valuable new markets for high quality products. There is no reason to suppose that future enlargements will not follow the same pattern.

45. British agriculture, and horticulture in particular, increasingly depend on migrant labour. The NFU regrets the restrictions that were placed on immigration from the 2007 accession countries; and is very concerned at the impact that the phasing out of the well-established Seasonal Agricultural Workers Scheme (SAWS) will have.

SIMPLIFICATION

46. Our views on simplification have been covered in answers to other questions.

June 2007

Examination of Witnesses

Witnesses: MR PETER KENDALL, NFU President, MR MARTIN HAWORTH, Head of Policy and MS CARMEN SUAREZ, Chief Economist, National Farmers Union of England and Wales, examined.

Q102 Chairman: May I welcome you and thank you for coming along to help us with our review of CAP, with the two elements—the health check immediately and then looking further forward to further reform of the CAP. I will start by saying that this is obviously a formal evidence session. There will be a transcript available, which we will send to you afterwards, and you can see if there are any corrections that need to be made. Also, we are being webcast; so there is a possibility that somebody somewhere might be listening to what we are saying. Do you want to start by making any opening statements of a general nature? Or would you prefer to get on with questions and answers?
Mr Kendall: I think you have had our submission. I am more than happy to pick up questions about what we have already said.

Q103 Chairman: In your evidence, you made the obvious point that the factors behind the CAP have changed very much from when it was originally put together. Now, you state, those main drivers are "an amalgam of food, energy and environmental security". Can you talk briefly on how you see those factors coming together and influencing the development of the CAP, particularly towards the future?
Mr Kendall: Thank you very much indeed for the invitation to be here today, particularly for having the chance to expand on some of the questions regarding our evidence. I think that it has happened in a remarkably short period of time that we have

seen a very major shift in how we view agricultural production and land as a resource. I have not been involved in the NFU that long, but I was Deputy President three years ago. In that period of time we have seen an enormous change of emphasis, looking at land, whether it is producing food, energy, the environmental agenda, with climate change coming to the fore; whereas, when we embarked on CAP reform in 2003, we were still looking at how we managed some of yesterday's problems rather than the challenges of tomorrow. When we reflect back on the origins of the CAP and coming out of seeking food security within Europe, there are now those additional dimensions. We are looking at the fact that we have a more volatile climate; we have new demands on land use from energy; and we could have a very long debate on the rationale behind the use of renewable energy, energy crops and biofuels in itself. The major dynamic evident in the dairy sector at the moment is the global drivers of population growth and dietary change. There are countries like India and China, where we have seen a bigger increase in milk prices—and global skimmed milk powder would be the best indication of that—and we have seen it in cereal prices in the last years. We are now seeing a whole load of global drivers which mean that we have to look differently at how we view the CAP going forward. Rather than just reducing agricultural support, I think that we now need to have a policy which makes sure that our agricultural land is in the best condition and is a valuable resource that is available; because I believe that we will need it more than we have done, probably since that post-war period.

Q104 *Chairman:* That gets us on to the future role of government, does it not? You make the point in your evidence that you think that, because of the strategic importance of farming, governments are unlikely to reduce their level of intervention. Intervention has two elements to it, does it not? One is policy intervention and regulation; the other is financial intervention. Again, what do you see as the nature of government intervention? How will governments intervene in farming in the future, in the context of interventions that do not distort competition?

Mr Kendall: I think that is enormously challenging, as we sit here now with a United States' Farm Bill at a fairly developed stage at this moment in time. Some of the soundings we are picking up are that it might actually have more of an interventionist role than a less interventionist role, coupled with their driver for renewable fuels. It tells me that the world will be a very difficult place to evaluate, going forward. How we call upon the Government or the EU to be involving itself in those markets is therefore incredibly challenging. When we look at why we have support payments from within Europe, why we have a Common Agricultural Policy, we have to examine some of the differences we have within Europe, our environmental challenges and responsibilities—and, probably more importantly, the irresponsibilities we have—and the protection, the cross-compliance we put on our farmers. I am a cereal grower from East Anglia, and there is also the fact that my markets are distorted by agricultural policies around the globe. Although there may be some really positive signals coming through for alternative uses, I am convinced that we will see volatile markets. When new land comes into production, you will see some years when it all clicks, you will get very high yields and you will see prices fall. You will still see the impact globally where countries will be placing those surpluses on to world markets; we will be paying export restitutions to distort the global marketplace. We do have to look at an agricultural policy which helps with some of our additional challenges in our environmental management—in how we make sure that we preserve and look after the countryside in the way we have done as an industry, I think pretty impressively, in recent times; but also to make sure that we are not disadvantaged through other countries' policies. That also brings me to the CAP, where I think that we have made some very good commitments on removing export restitutions, on making commitments on reducing tariffs on imports, on opening our markets up to imports from developing countries. However, we have ended up with a CAP which, to me, is less "common". Certainly in my farming memory—for the 24 years I have been

farming—we do have, even within the island of the United Kingdom, four different systems. We also have a very varied system in Europe, where we see France, with 40 per cent of all suckler cows, maintaining full coupling on beef production. When we look for the market to send the right signals to my members within the UK, therefore, we will not see those true market signals. We therefore need to see an agricultural policy that helps us to meet those environmental challenges and that actually puts right some of the distortions which are occurring in the global marketplace.

Q105 *Chairman:* You have said "put right some of the distortions in the global marketplace". How do you put right those distortions?

Mr Kendall: I am looking at the fact that we do have a role for a payment system and support for farmers. It would be crazy if we damaged our production base because, over a number of years, a country that had a surplus was placing it on the world markets. You would see a small percentage of global production traded in the marketplace driving and dictating those global prices—which would cause me either to under-invest or take land out of production, because of other countries' distortions. I therefore think that there is a role for supporting agriculture while those distortions exist on a global basis.

Q106 *Lord Bach:* Let me press you on that a bit because, as My Lord Chairman has said, it is a crucial point. The question in principle is: why should government provide financial support to farming? Of course, we will all agree that they should provide support for real disadvantage and poverty in rural or urban areas, and perhaps also to assist in making our environment a better place. But what other private industries enjoy this level of taxpayers' financial support—or, indeed, any financial support these days? You talk about extensive government involvement, and of course there is; but that applies to many other industries as well. How, in 2007, can there in principle be any case at all for having taxpayers' money paid to support farming in this country?

Mr Kendall: I would personally love the idea that I was in an industry that was entirely on its own, no one coming to me and saying, "You are receiving handouts or support from the Exchequer". I can tell you that there are many, many of my members who would feel that would be a great place to be. I have recently been out in Herefordshire with suckler cow farmers, looking at the situation they face. As I do, I repeat the example of what the French suckler cow industry is having. I also see some of the statements coming out from the new President of France about wanting to build more and stronger red lines around certain sectors of their industry and agriculture. If we are going to lose some of our critical mass in the United Kingdom while other people distort and have a role in those marketplaces—it is the same with the United States, which up to now, through their food aid programmes, have had a significant impact on global marketplaces—I think that our land as a resource, our farming industry—and I am not going to say "farmers" because that could be interpreted as being self-indulgent—and the way we manage it will be a really critical resource. We should be looking at ways in which we do not see the industry either under-invest or scale back or actually export that production in the short term. I therefore think that there is a role for government to play. Whether it is on the same scale, whether it is in exactly the same form, is where we should be having an adventurous debate, going forward. However, I think that it is crazy if we run an experiment in England—not even in the UK but just in England—that could see some of our very good infrastructure, some of our very skilled practitioners, go and do other things, because we underestimate the value of what they do.

Q107 *Lord Bach:* "In principle" is my question. In principle, there cannot be any justification, can there, for taxpayers paying for private farming? If somehow distortion, which seems to me to be the only argument put forward now for continued financial support, was lessened or even removed altogether, would you agree that there would be absolutely no case at all for financial support from the taxpayer for farming in this country?
Mr Kendall: I think the distortion is a big part of it. There is the aspect of—Carmen, as our chief economist, has reminded me—the role of public goods, in the fact that we are managing our environment in a very different way. I have a number of fields on my farm in Bedfordshire that are nine or ten acres, surrounded by large hedgerows, with footpaths across them. I can promise you that the management and looking after them in that state is very different to if I were prairie farming in Iowa, for example, in very different environmental conditions. So I do think that we offer a number of benefits through looking after the countryside. We look after 70% of the land area in the United Kingdom. A debate that we should be having, going forward, is that a public good should also be in preserving that land in a good productive capacity; that we do not just leave it to the market entirely. I have had some really quite concerning emails and pictures from the North East at the moment, where whole potato crops have been absolutely wiped out because of extreme weather. I am not going to say whether this is climate change or a symptom of climate change, but we do seem to be seeing more frequent extreme weather conditions. How we look after and maintain that land in a good productive capacity, because of those

increasing challenges coming round the corner— whether it is climate change, energy security, population growth, demand challenges—is important, and I put that as a public good, as well as the environmental management that I think the farming industry provides so competently.

Q108 *Lord Bach:* Do you think other industries could argue a like case from their own points of view—how fundamental they are, how they are faced with all kinds of difficult problems, and how the community would be affected badly if things went wrong? Why should they not argue the same case?
Mr Kendall: I think that some have in the past.

Q109 *Lord Bach:* But they have failed. They do not get the money now.
Mr Kendall: But we do have government intervention in certain areas of our lives, whether it is health, transport, education, and we do have a role for government. I think that the land is an important resource. It is something that we should be looking at now. I acknowledged earlier as to whether it should be in a reduced role; but, as we look at the role of government in agriculture, I do press very strongly that it should be across the trading area in which we operate, which is Europe, and not just in England or the UK, as some sort of experimental type of policy.

Q110 *Lord Plumb:* Looking across the role in Europe—and obviously we have to make comparison between the situation here and in other European countries—I think that you have already referred to many of the important effects that the reform has had. You make the point very clearly, quite rightly of course, that it is incomplete: it is an ongoing situation. Most of the evidence that we are receiving—and you will not be surprised at this—is suggesting that there should be a transfer of money from Pillar I to Pillar II. In other words, there should be concentration on the areas where farmers can be seen to be more environmentally friendly. I think that consumers might respond better if that can be explained to them. Yet the trend is already confirmed that there is a widening food trade deficit, as part of the overall trade deficit. How concerned are you when consumers regard cheap food as a priority? Does the reform of the CAP fit well as far as you are concerned? Does it benefit consumers in this country? How does it compare in other European Union countries as against in the United Kingdom? If so, why and how?
Mr Kendall: It is quite a complicated question, which I would expect from one of my predecessors!
Lord Plumb: I might say in passing that the question you had three times over from a former minister was one which I received many times, many years ago!

Q111 *Lord Bach:* And look what has happened now!

Mr Kendall: Perhaps I could pick up on the first, rural development—the Pillar I to Pillar II transfer—and then maybe Martin will want to pick up on some of the benefits of the cheap food policy. It is an interesting experiment that is already going on—the transfer from Pillar I to Pillar II—and again I can pick England out as an example of what is going on. My business will have 17% sliced off my support payment this year. This is a difficult area for me because I represent farmers in England and Wales. In Wales it will be 0% on top of the EU modulation. Instead of 5% with 0% national, I will have 12% English and then 5% EU. I think that this current year it is going up to 19% in England, within two years. We have done some figures comparing the impact this might well have on a standard-type farm, if you compared an 80—hectare dairy farm with a million litres in Scotland with, say, Northumberland, or even going into Holland. Over the period of the next rural development that will affect a farm in England over one in Scotland by £25,000, compared to one in Holland by £30,000—over that five-year rural development period. When they have the challenges of a nitrate-vulnerable zone regulation coming, they will have to make a lot of investment in how they handle dirty water, slurry storage, *et cetera*. To me, that is a distortion that I have real concern about. Farmers who may be just as skilled, just as creative, as between one country and another, because we have made that decision and have moved money from Pillar I to Pillar II here, but not in those other countries, we will create almost unintended consequences. If I meet a young guy in his early thirties saying, "Actually, I do not have that £25,000 to make that investment", I will be disappointed, because I want my farmers to be competing with the very best in Europe, planning for the future and doing so wherever possible on that—and I know it is a widely overused phrase—level playing field. I think that there is a case for the moving of money from Pillar I to Pillar II. We have grave concerns over how effectively that money is spent. I would be very concerned about how it might happen at different speeds in different countries, because of the very poor historic allocation of rural development money. If we started with a blank sheet of paper and looked at rural development spend, we can see the UK having 7% rather than the just over 3% we currently have. That will put us in a much better place and we will have a much lower need for the modulation we currently have. I know there are arguments for moving that money very quickly and I think we should do it, if it happens evenly throughout Europe. However, we should also make sure that it is well spent and used to preserve that productive capacity, because I think the challenges facing us are very important and I would be concerned. You may have

seen the comments, written in a lighthearted way in the farming press, where I have suggested provocatively that thatching bus shelters where buses no longer run is not of great use. We need to worry about our productive capacity, our investment in our structure and also in our agricultural capability, and I would not want to see that lost too much.

Mr Haworth: Lord Plumb mentioned that the CAP has been associated with a cheap food policy, and that has obviously benefited consumers. Our view is that that period may now be coming to a close and that we are in a period where food prices are likely to be higher, and possibly sustainably higher. If that does prove to be true, it also links back to the question posed by Lord Bach. Obviously, the case for ongoing support, at least at its current level, would be less if that does prove to be true. We in the NFU did support the CAP reform in 2003, and indeed advocated it, because we thought that it would help to make farmers more focused on the market rather than on trying to get the maximum support that they could, even though that is not what the market or consumers were requiring or asking them to do. To some extent, the reform has succeeded in that; but it has not succeeded to the extent that we hoped it would, for a couple of reasons. One is that we had wanted to see this policy applied uniformly across Europe, and that has not proved to be the case. It has been implemented in different ways in different countries and, unfortunately, a degree of coupling has remained in some countries; and that has led into the distortions that Peter mentioned. The second unfortunate thing that has happened is that, because of the way that the policy was implemented in England and the problems that we had, a lot of farmers have been concerned, or their mind has been on the difficulties of implementation and the lateness of payments, rather than on the market and how they should respond to that new system—and that is obviously extremely unfortunate. We do therefore see that the policy has not been uniform; it has impacted in different countries in different way. We can argue about who has benefited and who has lost out of the process, but for us a priority now is to get back to a more common policy—and a simpler policy.

Mr Kendall: Could I make one comment about cheap food? I have a real concern that some of the policies, some of the ways that agriculture has behaved globally, have delivered food that is too cheap. I think of the very public riots in Mexico, as they were painted, as an indication of a policy where the Americans had been supporting more and more production of maize within the United States, making counter-cyclical payments that made sure that the farm incomes were high but the global price was low. Therefore, those other developing countries, like Mexico for example, had not been able to afford to produce their own maize. We have been talking about some of the renewable energy dynamics that are driving prices at the moment. Many of the African states we talk to are actually wanting higher global prices in some of these staple products, so that they can bring their agricultural land back into use, so that they can make that investment. I think that cheap food and a cheap food policy globally have significantly damaged not only the development of countries but also the investment in core agricultural production.

Q112 Lord Plumb: Still on food policy, you speak a little confidently in your paper on possible improvements in the milk sector. Is that really so at the moment? Is one not concerned about the growing imbalance in agriculture? The cost of feed at the moment is increasing by 30%, and that of course is making it more difficult for the producer. In that context, I understand that the gap at the moment between the cost of production and the price paid to the farmer is something like 4p a litre. When I go into the supermarket, as I did last night to pick up a litre of milk, they charge me 85p for it. I know that is a supermarket and I know that it is after normal hours, and so on. Nevertheless, there seems still to be a huge gap, and a total misunderstanding therefore by the consumer of what the producer actually receives and what effect it is having on the imbalance, as I see it, of the industry.

Mr Kendall: I think that, when you held my job, Lord Plumb, you were a mixed farmer. My job becomes more challenging because I am now purely an arable farmer. I have enjoyed the benefits of the recent price hikes but, as my brother reminded me this morning, it is no good having these high prices until you get it in the shed—and it is looking incredibly flat and weatherbeaten at this moment in time. Prices may go higher therefore, if we fail to get this harvest completed and gathered in. On the issue of milk, however, I do have some real optimism for the dairy sector, when I see people looking to divert milk from perhaps cheese production to skimmed milk powder, and they can be paid over 26p a litre for that. While farmers are still receiving 17p or 18p, and I know there have been some good movements recently, it is how you move from those long contracted arrangements, some of which last a year into the future at those lower prices. What is happening in the marketplace, which is strongly driving milk prices up, will take some time to come through. Most of the dairy farmers I meet at the present time see those very strong global dynamics and those strong market signals. Cheese prices are already moving; skimmed milk powder has moved enormously. My challenge to both retailers and processors is to make sure farmers get that return sooner rather than later. Otherwise, faced with the increased food prices and

other challenges they face, they will not be here for the long term and they will make short-term decisions. I believe that the long-term signals are much stronger and much more encouraging. Where we do have a problem with the high grain prices at the moment is particularly in the lamb and beef sector, where the markets are not responding and where we have real challenges on a global basis. Again, we are trying to represent to retailers the need for pigs and poultry—where the chains are quite short, where they do see those impacts quite quickly—that they are remedied; that those price changes respond in that case, and are passed back to the farmers and the producers. I am, like you, Lord Plumb, worried that we see an increase in one sector or one part of agriculture and—because of the imbalance in the balance of power between retailers and producers—that is not passed back quickly enough, to ensure that we raise all of the sectors into a profitable position fast enough.

Q113 Lord Plumb: Should the EU intervene in the relationship between the different sectors? How does COPA see this? Obviously this is a matter that you discuss with all your colleagues in Brussels.
Mr Kendall: For those who are not aware of how COPA works, we now have 27 countries. That makes forming a collective view within Europe challenging, to say the least. I have a French president of COPA— and I am now a vice-president—who usually starts a sentence with "*Non*". That is how he usually approaches a response on most subjects.

Q114 Lord Plumb: Nothing new in that!
Mr Kendall: We try to say, "How can we develop the argument or work with people to find a solution?"— which is hopefully how, within the NFU, we try to work policy. We want the marketplace to work as effectively as possible. I think that there is a role for the Competition Commission in the balance of power between retailers and producers, and that is a role which we encourage. For example, how we look at the dairy market in the European perspective rather than just the UK perspective. However, I do not think that the European Commission should be involved in trying to balance up different sectors. It should encourage the market to work fairly and effectively.

Q115 Chairman: Can we ask a very quick specific question, in relation to what you said about milk and your optimism there, and take that in the context of the health check? I assume therefore that you are quite content to see the abolition of quotas?
Mr Haworth: Yes, we accept that the abolition of quotas will take place in 2015. There does not seem to be an agreement at European level to stop them before that or after that. We think that there does

need to be a period to allow us to exit from what has been in place as a policy for more than 20 years, but we fully accept that they will go. Of course, if these high prices remain, it will be much easier than if we were in a period of low prices. I think it is worth noting here, with the CAP, that we have been accused for a long time of maintaining prices way above world prices. It is worth pointing out that, if the world price was operating in the dairy sector at the moment, producers would be getting over 27p a litre and the actual average price is 17p—which is a remarkable turnaround. For the first time ever, there are no stocks at European level and there are no export subsidies operating at the European level; so we are in a quite remarkable turnaround period.

Q116 *Lord Plumb:* Does that mean a world shortage?

Mr Haworth: Yes, it does. It means that, because we have the rising demand, particularly from China and India, there is effectively a world shortage, particularly of skimmed milk powder, where the price has increased in a dramatic way in the last six months. More than 50%, I think.

Ms Suarez: Yes.

Q117 *Viscount Brookeborough:* Mr Kendall, you are an arable and possibly a grain baron! I was wondering whether you could tell us very briefly, along the lines of what you have just said about milk, about the grain price—forgetting for one moment the bad weather, which will obviously have an additional effect. Could you tell us about grain prices, where they are going, and are you doing better?

Mr Kendall: A number of our organisations start by telling you about how the costs have escalated, and you could put it in that perspective. To start with, I have not suffered so much from the bad weather as many people have. In many respects, I am in a much better place than I was two years ago. I think that there is a lot of distortion in what is causing the current changes in grain prices. I am picking out wheat and barley—grains as opposed to maize—on a global basis. The maize price has changed enormously because of the drive for ethanol within the United States. Within the wheat market particularly, probably less than three million tonnes of wheat globally would go into ethanol production. The main driver of the wheat price, therefore, would be the fact that, if you go east of Berlin, they have had very severe droughts, very poor crops, and there was the Australian drought of last year where production fell from 24 million tonnes to less than 9 million tonnes. Those have been the key drivers. Even this year they are expecting that we will have the third biggest wheat harvest ever, but it will still be significantly below consumption. I think that the drivers of the wheat price, therefore, are global

demand coupled with areas where drought has impacted on meeting that increasing challenge. Where is it going to go? I probably would not be the President of the NFU and would be working in the money markets or trading grain if I knew where they were going to go! I have risk management tools in place in my business. I carry options for next year already, to make sure that I protect myself against downturns in prices. We are aware that there is significant land that can come into production in other parts of Eastern Europe and around the world. You are seeing from the response of things like phosphate prices and nitrogen prices that people will be using more inputs globally to step up production. If that all clicks, I can see the prices returning to lower levels; but, as you say, climate change seems to deliver us more volatile growing conditions. It is very difficult to predict. I can already get in excess of £100 a tonne for my wheat for November 2009. I have made some coverage for 2008 harvest, which I have not even planted yet, but I will be looking to 2009 at some point.

Q118 *Lord Bach:* A question on partial decoupling. You make a strong case—I believe, anyway—for the ending of partial decoupling. Can you give us some examples of the ways in which continued coupling in specific Member States has disadvantaged our farmers? If payments were fully decoupled, would the problem then arise of the coexistence across the EU of payments based, on the one hand, on area production and, on the other, on historic production? Would that be the next problem? Would that come to the fore, as it were, if we got rid of coupling?

Mr Kendall: We are already in discussions with the Commission about the Health Check for next year and how they will respond, but we have made strong representation on the need to remove partial coupling from the system, because we think it distorts decisions. There is the example I gave about the French suckler cow premium being kept in place. I would even include in that the Irish, where they are using their rural development budget to give a top-up for the keeping of suckler cows to be termed as a coupled support payment, which goes with that keeping of animals in Ireland. They have very generous rural development budgets, as you are well aware. I am already picking up worrying comments from the Commission that, maybe in areas such as beef, they would permit full coupling to remain in place following the Health Check, and going even further forward. That bothers me because, if it means that people are not making the right rational choice on what they are doing with their resources—and they do have 40% of the suckler cows in France—that will impact on some of the decisions that my farmers and members are making within the UK. That is a concern, and the beef one is a good example. On the grain one, for example in Spain and again in France, you receive less money if you do not produce. That was therefore impacting on some of the decisions made within those countries, but I think that the global prices have moved those sectors that were only partially coupled in grains—in, say, France and Spain—to be less of a problem, less of a hindrance on the marketplace. When we look at how that might impact on the existence of area versus historic payments, we have to look at the fact that the Commission has encouraged the new Accession countries to keep their simplified systems, rather than moving to our system. That indicates to me that the Commission are moving, or want the original 15 to move, towards an area-based system that is based on a regional-type payment rather than the historic. I see it from a very difficult perspective, as I have said, because I represent Welsh as well as English farmers. I can understand, having seen how some of the transfers have occurred in England—and we have had many discussions on some of the challenges in getting that money sorted and the implementation of the complicated system we had in England—my members in Wales are very keen to keep a simple, historic system until they can see how easy it is or whether it is possible easily to implement a regional hybrid or a regional system, as we have in England. The appetite for that in Wales, therefore, is not strong—I can promise you that. However, there is a feeling within Europe that that is the logical way to go, looking then at certain levels of agricultural production in those countries where you would have different regions, as we do in England now—the two lines of three regions—to represent the sort of agriculture that is going on in those areas.

Q119 Lord Cameron of Dillington: This is really a continuation of that question, concerning the Single Farm Payment. Obviously, that has not gone very well in this country. One of the suggestions you make is that the minimum area should go from 0.3 ha to 5 ha, which I suspect is an opening bid to the Commissioner. I think that he said 3 ha. You may like to comment on that. My main question, however, is this. If, as you are suggesting, in the long run we get to an overall area payment across the EU—which I think that certainly most of us would favour—how would you allocate that? Would it be the same area payment in every region, allowing for the differential—as we have in England with the less favoured areas? Would it be the same in Eastern Europe and new Member States as the old Member States? How do you think this is going to work? Also, what do you think the reaction of the WTO would be to the whole question of farm support in a decoupled way like this?

Mr Kendall: I will pick up the first comment you made about the 3 ha and the Commission, because I was being accused of being a cereal baron from East Anglia and it may be perceived to be difficult for me to make that comment from the NFU's perspective. However, one of the big challenges we have had as an industry is the 40,000 new claimants that came into the SPS system. A friend of mine in the grain trade who owned half a hectare where I live gleefully told me how he had spent £1,000 to get a cheque for, I think, £50 in his first year. I think that we are seeing lots of those sorts of complications, where people have had really complicated systems to map and sort everything out for very small "pony paddocks", which has not been the most efficient use of resources; particularly when some of our members—and I am very keen that we see younger people coming into farming, building, looking forward, looking at the industry for the long term—sometimes have not had the money six months after their counterpart might have had it in Scotland, Ireland or in Europe. Where we can simplify it, where we can make the system work well, so that people can plan and build businesses—I think that is incredibly important. Comments on how we might look at the European perspective and the WTO I will leave to Martin.

Mr Haworth: We have always said that we see CAP reform as an ongoing process. We would see it as a series of transitions, if you like. We, the NFU, were not actually favourable to going to an area payment in England in the first instance. Although we do accept that that was a sensible place to get to, we would prefer to see that happen in some sort of equal transition across Europe, rather than our going alone, as it were, even in the UK. We would therefore see this as a series of transitions. We do therefore see the next step as moving to the whole of Europe going to some sort of area payment. The logic that is applying here is that you cannot justify a historic allocation for very long. If that is true, you cannot also justify the historic allocation of the budget for very long, because it is based on historic production levels. Therefore, we would see a movement towards a common European level of payment. Whether that will be by every country having the same or every country dividing up its region into different qualifies of agricultural land, as we have done in England, or regions, as they have done in Germany, I do not know. However, we do see this as a series of transitions. Of course, there is the other transition that might happen, which goes back to the question by Lord Bach, that we may see all this being phased out; so there may come a period when we are not talking about very much anyhow—but that might be over a longer period of time.

Ms Suarez: As to the last question concerning WTO, under the current definition there is in principle nothing that would prevent having different levels of payments in different countries or having, as we have in the case of England, different levels of payments within the same country. The current definition of what are Green Box payments allows for that. When we talk about how the Green Box might be defined in the future, we are talking about the next round of negotiations, not the current round. Taking into account the current impasse in the Doha Round, we are probably talking about quite a bit further ahead and, as Martin has indicated, maybe at that stage we will be discussing other issues.

Q120 *Lord Cameron of Dillington:* Just to go back to what Martin was saying, you do foresee, some time after 2013, even area payments and the support generally being phased out, do you?
Mr Haworth: There are two possibilities. Either that they will start to be phased out or their nature will change and they will be for something specific, and they may be permanent in that case. That is a debate that has to take place at some point.

Q121 *Chairman:* Could you just continue a little on the "something specific"?
Mr Haworth: There are people who are advocating that the payments change in their nature to be a payment for environmental goods or for rural development or for the coming European rural policy. There are areas there, where there are payments for services which are cases of market failure, where there is a justification for a permanent payment—so long as the market failure exists. It becomes quite a kaleidoscopic picture, made up of different elements here. Part of the justification of the payments is a transition, if you like, away from price support, and part of the payment might be justification for a permanent market failure; so providing services which the market will not provide, like environmental enhancement.
Mr Kendall: We try, as an organisation, to be very engaged in this sort of discussion. I can promise you that, in Europe, there is always this challenge. When I was first appointed deputy president, I remember sitting in the COPA Council, where they asked for any comment on decoupling first. Of course I gave the NFU's line, that we were very engaged with government about finding ways of fully decoupling—to find that I was followed by 26 people who told me that I was unhinged, in all senses and purposes! So, when we talk about phasing out, when we talk about how they are used, we want to be part of a debate that does not disadvantage English or UK farmers but shows a pragmatic concern about how the industry moves forward. Comments have been made about my background in farming, but there are parts of the United Kingdom in less favoured areas, where they manage really critical parts of the environment, where we will have to be engaged in a quite proactive

way to avoid abandonment and cessation of important parts of landscape management and farming.

Q122 *Viscount Ullswater:* That comes on quite neatly to the question which I am going to put to you. In your paper you point out quite strongly that set-aside has no place in a decoupled system and you want to see it abolished immediately. Also, in your paper you say that farmers will increase or decrease their area of arable crops according to forward pricing. I think that you have given us an indication of your own views about how that stimulus could work. However, some witnesses have said that set-aside has had some environmental benefit and they would not want to see that benefit lost in a transitional period. I think that you also claim that it can be achieved by other means. I would like you to identify what means you think those are. As to your last comments about other landscape features—the fells in Cumbria, for instance—you either want to keep the sheep on or you want to reduce the number, or whatever it is, in order to keep them in good repair. Is that not in a way a market distortion as well? How can we get these environmental benefits that we want and perhaps avoid being accused of market distortion?
Mr Kendall: Perhaps I could start with the set-aside question. I think that there is an enormous hidden impact in set-aside. To me, it almost epitomises an indifference to productive land. It almost says, "We don't need this as a resource". I think it is a really dark cloud that hangs over agriculture and I hope that we can move away from it as soon as possible. On my farm I am allowed to grow industrial crops on my set-aside, so that is how I would utilise my set-aside land—which is allowed through EU rules already at this moment in time. On Monday this week, the Commission recommended that it be set at 0% for next year; so we are seeing the impact of set-aside already being reduced and underway. Where I am nervous about the reactions to the environmental benefits is in how you use set-aside. Some people used set-aside in grass margins, by woods, next to hedges, next to watercourses, et cetera, and took a percentage out on a semi-permanent basis, and that made a big environmental impact. I have spent some time recently at the Game Conservancy Trust at Loddington. Many of you will be familiar with some of their work. They have 60 scientists analysing the impact of environmental management on the countryside. I am not sure if it is an official term but, when they see us spraying off set-aside, they refer to it as the "slash and burn" management of set-aside. That would not have positive environmental benefits. Therefore, we do see environmental benefits from where we are semi-permanently managing margins of grass areas, maybe through other cover-crop

management. Where, in the majority, it is being used on a rotational basis, the environmental benefits have been much less significant. I would refer you to the Game Conservancy Trust to give you detailed analysis of what that has been; they are pretty scientific in their analysis, and they say that it would be quite small. That is what leads us to our recommendation that there are other ways of delivering the environmental gains. We have to look at the agri-environment schemes that are currently in place. I am actually an enormous optimist about what is occurring in the countryside at this time. We have a whole host of factors that are coming together. There is decoupling. I still hear people talking about over-grazing, but the drivers for over-grazing, for stocking levels that are not economic, are not there now. The payment to put more livestock units on a hectare are no longer there, because of decoupling. The impact of cross-compliance is very significant in terms of farmers' behaviour. It is not just about the periods when you cannot plant your hedgerows or your margins; it is any discretion to those areas, and you lose a significant amount of your payment. I think that it has people focused much more on that resource protection, therefore, than just the simple cross-compliance might indicate. Add on to the decoupling the cross-compliance, the Entry-Level scheme and the agri-environment schemes that are now right across the board—over four million hectares in Entry-Level schemes and agri-environment schemes—and I think that we are seeing an explosion of good environmental outcomes in the countryside. Do we need to monitor that explosion of good outcomes before we rectify any negative impact from set-aside? Or do we look to—and I think that the Game Conservancy Trust are very well placed to do this—understand what the impact of removing set-aside will be, and then look at any small adjustments that might need to be made in agri-environment schemes to deliver those outcomes? It is very easy to say that we have to replace all that land that is currently set-aside with other agri-environment schemes. Let us look at what we need. Let us measure what is being delivered. If we project five years forward—and I see that the margins that have gone in around watercourses, the hedgerow management is different, the new planting of woodland and hedgerows—I think that we are seeing some fantastic outcomes in the rural environment. We have not touched on landscapes. The other point was about distortion if we try to keep livestock or types of production in other areas. I think that one of the major conundrums for us is that the payments need to be for the environmental outcomes. It will, I am sure, cause somebody to say that there is livestock in an area that otherwise would not be there; therefore their production has the potential to overhang the market. That is a concern and a

conundrum which we face, and it is one where the priorities have to be weighed up.

Viscount Ullswater: It will be a conundrum which remains.

Chairman: Let us move on to climate change.

Viscount Brookeborough: You support very strongly the EU commitment to 20% of energy production and 10% of transport fuel from renewable sources. What changes do you foresee in land use with these targets coming in? Do you think that government is supporting them strongly enough?

Q123 Chairman: The other one is: do you think that they are achievable?

Mr Kendall: What changes to land use? Again, I think that the market will make some of those decisions: to choose to say whether it incentivises, or whether we find, for example, that willow and miscanthus have a stronger demand for land use rather than the conventional crops, such as those which I grow. I am aware that there have been a couple of large bioethanol announcements. BP and ABF made a big announcement a couple of weeks ago, to use over a million tonnes of wheat as their primary feedstock. British Sugar have their ethanol plant involving sugar beet, which they are looking to use. There is also a private equity-backed business, Ensus, which is also building another one in the North East, which will take in excess of a million tonnes of cereals. We think that will meet the UK's target of 5% by 2010 for petrol, because the ethanol goes into the petrol market. On the point of whether the Government is doing enough, I think that the Renewable Transport Obligation will drive the 5% from the UK sources and I think that will be done largely from traditional patterns of cropping.

Q124 Viscount Brookeborough: But this will be a distortion of the market, will it not, because it is false?

Mr Kendall: We have to look at the calorific values of grain. If I go back to my grandfather's days on the farm, a third of the farm would have been growing oats for feeding the horses to provide the horsepower for the cultivation of the land. A third of the farm was traditionally used for powering the farm. Looking at today's values of oil, I think it has come off its peak of $78 to about $76 now. That delivers a calorific value of wheat, just for burning, of in excess of £110 a tonne. It is a new dynamic between food, fuel and energy which, when oil was $20 a barrel, was not in people's consciousness. There is now a new dynamic that we will live with, and it will put a new tension into the marketplace. Where the big potential comes for the 20% by 2020 is both in new technologies and in by-products and waste. There are some really great examples. Bedfordia, who now call themselves Biogen, have their anaerobic digestion plant not very far from where I farm in Bedfordshire. They are taking green waste. It was on the news on Monday night, and they were shown collecting waste, for example from the food industry in Bedford and Milton Keynes, which was going into the pig slurry, and in turn producing methane which is burned off for renewable electricity generation. They are helping with the waste product collection and green waste in Bedford and Milton Keynes; they are helping make the slurry, which otherwise would be more of an environmental challenge for them. They have much more stable digesters as a result, and they produce green energy. The fourth win, I like to think, is that it is also a great positive for farming—about the smart solutions we can deliver. I think that anaerobic digestion could help us meet some of these targets quite ambitiously. When I look at the straw on my farm—and at the moment I chop every single acre of straw—I see the quarter of a million new homes that they wish to build every year for the next 15 years, and the directives now to put more and more district combined heat and power in place, into those new developments, we can see smart ways of using by-products, co-products from agriculture to help do that. We also have to look at our forestry as a resource. I think that we can go a big way towards the 20% by 2020, but also we have the other opportunities of second-generation renewable fuels, biofuel, and the cellulosic technology. It is very difficult to call when that will be commercial. I know that it is up and running now but the cost, because of the way of blasting the cellulosic starch from cellulose to make that ethanol, is incredibly prohibitive at this time. To deliver the targets within Europe, I think that we need some of that second-generation. Equally, I do not think that we should have a closed mind. We have had some figures in recently from Africa, where they think there are 380 million hectares of partially denigrated land that in some way could be producing feedstock for renewable fuels. This is an opportunity, as I said earlier, for developing countries to help us produce renewable energy, drawing CO_2 from the atmosphere and producing renewable energy. It is converting the sun on a yearly basis, rather than drawing on those resources from millions of years ago.

Q125 *Baroness Miller of Chilthorne Domer:* I am very glad to hear you being so enthusiastic about the potential there. What I want to ask you about is biodigesters. One of the frustrations to me is that we are still hearing a lot of talk about investment in slurry storage and almost no discussion—partly following the disastrous Holdsworthy experiment in my neck of the woods—about moving to this next generation of biodigesters. Do you think that is because the message about the potential benefits have not got through enough so that the capital investment is still being looked at in just slurry

storage terms? Or do you think it is because that initial step needs to be subsidised from the rural development payments?

Mr Kendall: We had some interesting announcements in the White Paper before David Miliband moved on to the Foreign Office, advocating double ROCs, so that there would be twice the incentive for anaerobic digestion and other combined heat and power schemes. I thought that was a big incentive. Talking to people within the industry, they think that is a big incentive; that it puts us almost on a par with the German renewable energy law. ROCs are not as certain or as predictable as the German scheme. The German scheme would have given you a renewable energy price through to 2027. People were therefore bringing packages together that helped them with the finance, construction and management, and they knew that after a certain period of time they were in profit. The whole package came together in a contained way, and they were able to look at the finance over that period of time. We think the ROCs are a big incentive. The figure I have been given is that it takes from about 10 eurocents to 15 eurocents per kilowatt hour that the biodigestor would be producing. The German system starts at about 17 for the small plants and comes down to about 14 or 13.5 eurocents for the bigger plants. So we think that we are on a pretty good par. One of the reasons we need political unity behind this is to know with certainty for the long term that people can make those plans, and we can try and get people to bring these packages together. At the moment, as you so rightly said, I still hear people talking about slurry storage rather than looking at the anaerobic option. We have made some recommendations on rural development, which Martin may want to touch on.

Mr Haworth: We do see a role for the rural development programme here and we are slightly frustrated that it has not been taken up at central government level in the form of a recommendation, if you like, for the RDAs. We do see the possibility of using part of the rural development programme to encourage things like local initiatives to produce combined heat and power, whether it be for schools or for new housing estates. We do think that there is an opportunity there, which we hope will not be missed but we are slightly concerned that it might be.

Q126 *Baroness Miller of Chilthorne Domer:* Whom do you see as your major partners within this? Surely the EEA is there, trying to deal with some of the run-off issues? The RDAs could be taking action without a recommendation from central government if they had a bit more innovation, could they not? Who do you think your partners are in bringing this all together?

Ms Suarez: It will probably have to be a combination of different actors. We must not forget that to some extent the RDAs do have access to some of the rural development funds, but 80% of the rural development funds have been allocated to help environmental schemes and for outside the domain of the Regional Development Agencies. Out of the money that the Regional Development Agencies have, they have received a strong indication from Defra as to where to allocate some of the money. Within those indications, combined heat and power, for instance, does not appear; so to a very large extent they find that their hands are tied. However, we must not forget that the Regional Development Agencies also have roles which go beyond the management of the rural development programme and they have access to other types of funds. They also have funds for the private agencies in the community and to some extent they can act as "marriage brokers", encouraging contact between providers of sustainable energy and, for instance, the people who are building housing estates and the like. I think that it is therefore establishing a partnership. It is a new area and, as such, it is very difficult to say exactly who will be the main drivers there. It is a question of communication of the benefits of working together.

Q127 *Baroness Miller of Chilthorne Domer:* May I finally push you on that link with the EEA and run-off from slurry applied wet, as opposed to post-digester when it is applied dry? Is that something that has been explored as a big benefit?

Mr Kendall: We have certainly spent a lot of time talking to the Environment Agency about that, but their budgets are very limited and so they have severe problems in that area as well. I am very keen on the principle of demand pull, rather than supply push. I use the example of the Renewable Transport Fuel Obligation. It gave certainty that the market would require 5% by a certain time period, and we have now seen the businesses coming out and making those investment decisions. I do want to see combined heat and power, for example, where, in new housing developments, they have a much stronger drive to make those a part of the planning condition, part of the driver going forward. Again, I think that we should be looking at waste disposal; ways of making anaerobic digestion part of the solution, rather than just an option going forward. If we make the demand a certainty, I think that people will find ways of business coming together to deliver those outcomes.

Q128 *Chairman:* Going back to biofuels, is there not at least a theoretical danger that, in supporting the development of biofuels, we will just be introducing an old-fashioned production subsidy?

Mr Kendall: The balance on this is whether we look at the support for biofuels as a subsidy or a tax credit. If, for example, we are producing a renewable fuel that is a 60% or 70% saving on CO_2 emissions, should we tax it and treat it in the same way as we do a fossil fuel, or even the tar sands that are being pulled out of Canada, for example? If we say that we will treat them in a more balanced way and we will tax them according to their green credentials, the problem is that the Treasury does not like that or welcome that; because, if you look at what has happened in Germany, they have lost a lot of revenue. The way of providing some certainty, therefore, is not to treat it on the basis of its "greenness"—which you could ask companies to demonstrate and to show how much CO_2 they were saving—but to introduce market certainty by saying, "We want to be driving this market forward", and the development and evolution. Why I think that a 5% target is so important, as we have in the UK, is because this will put in train the supply chains, the development, that will lead us to put second-generation in place. We are not talking about enormous quantities; we are talking about quite a measured response with 5%, which we think we can deliver, with some imports, through some of our set-aside land and some of our exportable surplus. It will give—with, for example, BP and Ensus building their plants up in the North East—the expertise and the technology drive that will make our adoption of second-generation, the use of the by-products, the use of straw, even the manures and slurries, a much more exciting opportunity—and realistically being able to deliver that. There was some criticism yesterday about some of the environmental impacts. Peak oil will soon be with us, whether it is with us already or whether it soon will be with us. Yes, of course, we must be more efficient in our use of fossil fuels; but we need to find other energy sources. I think that the 5% target is a small toe-in-the-water, which allows us to start driving the technological evolution that will deliver much more sustainable and better second-generation outcomes.

Q129 *Viscount Brookeborough:* You mention in Paragraph 35 of your paper the greenhouse gas emissions from farming. They have recently appeared in the press, and I am not sure that the general public has focused on them previously. Could you tell us something about how you think there might be found, as you say, "integrated and cost-effective ways" of dealing with this?

Mr Kendall: Yes, and one of them would be what we have been talking about with anaerobic digestion. If you look at the carbon emissions from agriculture, they are pretty small; they are less than 1%. Unfortunately, if you take all our other contributions to greenhouse gases, agriculture goes to 7%, because of its methane and its nitrous oxide. One of the enormous challenges—and my very first comments were about how rapidly things have changed in global terms and our focus on climate change—is that the research and development in the last 25 years has not been focused on how we work with the livestock industry to reduce methane emissions. It is quite a new preoccupation to focus on methane emissions from cattle. I think that we shall have to look at how we can vary diets; how we can change grazing patterns; whether we use different grasses. There is work going on now to understand that; but, as I have said, most of the focus of the research and development was not in that area. Now that the understanding of the impacts of climate change is so real and so vivid for us, we realise that we need to put in those resources. One of the reasons why I am so worried about government spend on R&D at this moment in time is because this is long-term R&D work and we need to be helping and stimulating that research and development from farming. I think that we could look at the methane emissions and the way we treat and house cattle, how we look at diets, and we must have some more R&D spend. However, if we did have anaerobic digestion, for example, and we were able to capture and store the dirty waters, the manures and get more stable digestion; if we could incentivise people to inject rather than to sprinkle and spread the dirty water, that again would reduce it. At the moment, we are trying to understand the science of nitrous oxide emissions. Perhaps I may, while I have such a fantastic audience, make another plea, namely about agricultural building allowance. The last Budget made the point that agricultural building allowance should be abolished, going forward and retrospectively. We need a significant amount of investment both in the poultry and dairy sectors, which are good examples, and the pig industry—because of IPPC requirements, because of better emission control for greenhouse gases. And yet, in the UK alone, we have removed agricultural building allowances. In Ireland, for example, you write off a new agricultural building, which hopefully will be significantly more environmentally friendly, at 15% a year for six years and 10% in year seven. I have people who have made significant investments in recent years in new poultry housing in free-range. Because we are going to scale down the use of battery cages over the next four or five years, we need something like 10,000 ha of free-range egg production. Those buildings will not have agricultural building relief, and so they will not be having the smart environmental performance which I think that other countries in Europe will have. We are lobbying really hard in terms of better environmental investment in buildings, where we need that incentive. Otherwise, that production will go elsewhere.

Q130 *Viscount Brookeborough:* Perhaps this becomes more important because, with climate change, if we get less cold winters people will be more inclined to keep their cattle out longer. I live in Northern Ireland, and we can obviously put our animals out earlier in the spring and keep them out later. This will therefore be working the other way, whilst we are trying to capture it all and use it in biodigesters.

Mr Kendall: Equally, there are the extreme weather patterns and how much dirty water we need to store. I need these investments to be encouraged, rather than to find that this can happen in other parts of Europe and not here.

Q131 *Baroness Miller of Chilthorne Domer:* Could I ask if you happen to have a top-of-your-head figure for what the Treasury saved by removing that allowance? Do you think you could tell us, just to get an idea of what sort of a saving it is?

Mr Kendall: It is partly a simplification scheme. Again, when they look at the general processes, they sometimes do not see quite the impact that this will have on better practice. Agriculture and climate change are so important, this is a case for being treated slightly differently.

Chairman: Let us move on to rural development.

Q132 *Lord Cameron of Dillington:* To some extent, we have had conversations about rural development already and you are obviously anti voluntary modulation, for level playing field reasons. We gather that. I get the impression, however, and both you and Martin have mentioned it, that, with the agricultural economy going as it is, you are not against compulsory modulation, providing we keep a level playing field. You have mentioned various areas where Pillar II funds could be used that may be compatible with WTO, et cetera. In a general way, what sort of criteria do you see being applied to Pillar II so that we kept this level playing field and so that it did not become a long-term drug to various parts of this industry, and maybe other rural industries? At the moment, it is divided into four axes. Do you see those remaining? How do you see this being played out?

Mr Kendall: I will ask Carmen to come in on that, but perhaps I could first speak to compulsory modulation. We have to acknowledge that there are some sectors at the moment, particularly with the recovery of dairy (it is not going as fast as I would like) and also beef and sheep, where to talk about high levels of compulsory modulation—and I know that we are in a decoupled world where it should not be affected—until those market prices respond, we have to be cautious about how far that compulsory modulation goes. However, uniform compulsory modulation is definitely preferable to national modulation.

Ms Suarez: Concerning the fairness of what we would like rural development to do, I think that the first issue to be addressed is to ensure that there is a fair allocation of the resources of the rural development funds. So far, the criterion that has been used to allocate funds to the different Member States has been on the basis of historical allocations; so problems have become perpetuated over time. That means basically that the UK gets very little, because the UK used to get very little. I think that is probably the biggest issue. On the basis of what rural development is supposed to do—that is, addressing some of the issues that are related to land management and some of the issues that relate also to people living in rural areas—criteria such as the percentage of land that is agricultural land, or the percentage of people living in rural areas, will definitely give the UK a much fairer and definitely much higher allocation of rural development funds. Concerning the axes, it is always very difficult to talk about classification, because any classification, especially of policy measures, ends up being artificial almost by definition. Even now we look at the way in which different programmes are classified as within one axis. Taking the example, for instance, of biodigesters, will they be a competitive-placed measure and therefore something that would fall within Axis 1 of rural development? Or do we consider that the biodigester is being used to provide energy in a village, in a rural area? Is that something that is addressing a problem of infrastructure in a rural area, and therefore could be classified within Axis 3? I do not think that we should get too hung up on the different definitions of the axes. What is certain, however, is that issues of competitiveness in the agricultural sector, land management, and quality of life in rural areas are important, but we should try to look at solutions that can address all those issues simultaneously, without looking too much at the percentage which goes into one axis or the percentage which goes into another. As Peter has already mentioned, it is clear that the importance of land as an input of production is increasing over time, and the importance of the competitiveness of the agricultural sector is definitely very important. It is quite interesting that the UK seems to be out of kilter with other Member States when it comes to the allocation of rural development funds, and has decided to put much less money into competitiveness measures than other Member States. That is probably something that we should call into question. Last but not least, we must not forget that some of the rural development programmes that we have in place are programmes which were designed at a time when the problems that people were trying to target were substantially different to those which we have now. If we think about the Entry-Level scheme or the Higher Level scheme, at the time when they

were designed climate change was not the concern that we have right now. Within any process of ongoing review of those programmes, we probably need to look at whether they are really addressing the issues about which we are concerned right now.

Q133 *Lord Cameron of Dillington:* In terms of where the programmes are coming from, maybe they should be all three. But should they be pan-European programmes, Member State programmes, regional programmes, even County Council programmes or Parish Council programmes? How do you see that? *Ms Suarez:* "Subsidiarity" is probably the magic word! I think that it is necessary to have a very clear European framework—to avoid, amongst other things, that rural development funds end up doing what they are not supposed to do. The example of the Irish Government using rural development funds implicitly to support production is something that has been very much commented upon. There has to be a very clear framework as to what rural development funds can and cannot do. It is only natural that there will be some degree of flexibility, not only because of different preferences within different Member States but, even going to the regional or local level, it is quite clear that issues such as flood prevention will be more relevant in some parts of the country than in others. A very clear framework, therefore, but some scope for flexibility at the national and regional level.
Chairman: We turn now to world trade.

Q134 *Baroness Jones of Whitchurch:* You have already described to us very graphically the effect that the USA subsidies have been having in terms of the grain market, on a global basis, and we do not know what will happen in terms of the Doha Round. From your perspective, however, what would be a good solution from Doha? I know that we can fantasise—but what is a practical, good solution that would strengthen our hand in terms of the market longer-term?
Mr Haworth: We would certainly like to see a lot of progress made on the issue of internal support. We think that Europe has done a tremendous amount to make its own support system non-trade distorting. That has not always been sufficiently recognised by our partners, but we have made big progress; whereas the Americans—to use that example, because it is such a flagrant example—have actually moved in the other direction. They have increased the volume of their support and in some cases have made it more trade-distorting. A serious attempt to tackle that in the Doha Round is therefore essential in our view, and one of the few positive things that we could expect from the Doha Round. Farmers in this country have accepted that export subsidies do need to be phased out, and we would like to see that

discipline also extended to all countries. They do not always subsidise exports in the same way and they do it in less overt ways, but those too should be phased out. Those are the two biggest issues we would like to see out of the Doha Round.

Q135 Baroness Jones of Whitchurch: In your evidence somewhere you used the phrase that our position is defensive rather than offensive. Do you think that we have almost become paralysed by what was happening at Doha? That we could almost be doing more outside of the negotiations to boost exports, with or without the export subsidies? Do you think that there is a stronger global market out there that the EU is not really addressing in the interim?
Mr Haworth: The problem that Europe has, or has had, is that it is a region that has had a high level of internal prices and yet is a major exporter. It is very difficult to see how we can continue that position during the trade liberalisation round. Europe is a large exporter and some of its exports would come from high value-added products, like Scotch whisky, special cheeses, et cetera. By and large, they will find markets whether or not there is trade liberalisation. There is obviously some scope for improving those markets; for example, some countries have differential and unfair taxes on imported alcohol, and those can be addressed. By and large, however, the high value-added products are going to find their markets in any case. Rather, it is the bulk commodities that are the issue. Europe will benefit if global trade is opened up, from the fact that Europe will not be such an attractive market. If the South East Asia markets are opened up, we will see America, Australia and New Zealand targeting those markets more than Europe, and of course we will benefit indirectly from that. Whether there is much that can be done outside Doha is difficult to say. Europe is engaged in a lot of bilateral negotiations which, if the Doha Round does not make progress, will clearly be substituted for Doha; but that is a process which we see as quite a dangerous one, because we will end up with a lot of different bilateral relationships rather than an overall, multilateral framework—which we would prefer. We would prefer it because, first, we do want to see discipline in world trade, and the multilateral process is the only way to get multilateral rules that are respected; that cannot be done at a bilateral level. Second, the multilateral Doha process is the only way to put discipline on subsidies. That cannot be done bilaterally either. By and large, therefore, our strong preference would be to see progress at the multilateral level in Doha.

Q136 Baroness Jones of Whitchurch: Do you feel that the EU, if you like, bats for you? If you take a specialist cheese manufacturer, they could almost make their own markets. They could literally go round the world to trade markets and try to market their materials. What is the benefit in the EU acting for British farming interests? Do you ever see any advantage? You talked about it being indirect. I wondered quite how indirect it was.
Mr Haworth: Yes, we would see advantage. Take the specialist cheese as an example. There are very restrictive import terms into the United States, which effectively limits the volume of special cheeses going into America. That is a huge potential market—and one which certainly needs a lot of good cheese, from my own experience!

Q137 Baroness Jones of Whitchurch: There was a food programme on at the weekend, where there were a whole lot of cheese manufacturers who had gone to a trade place in New York. So they obviously can penetrate?
Mr Haworth: They can penetrate, but the volume that has been there up to now is limited. That is one thing, therefore. It is clearly better to do that at a European level than it is at a national level. The other big benefit that we can get is in protecting geographic designations, which is a very important issue to some of our partners—the Italians, for example—but which should also be important to us. If we can protect some of the important designations that we have against fraud and mislabelling, that is important.

Q138 Lord Plumb: In the interests of time, My Lord Chairman—because I know that you will be angry if I ask a question which requires a long answer!— could we ask the President to ask his Chief Economist if she would write to us and tell us what effect currency values have on world trade? I am thinking, of course, of both the dollar and the euro.
Ms Suarez: With great pleasure!
Chairman: I think that we could have a very depressing discussion on US trade policy, actually. I think that it will get worse rather than better.

Q139 Lord Cameron of Dillington: Both you, Peter, and Martin have hinted—with provisos, I agree— that perhaps there is less need for agricultural support into the long-term future. Yet, in your written submission, you say that the CAP needs more funds to deal with enlargement, including Romania, Bulgaria, and so on. It would seem to me that the obvious solution to these two divergent concepts is the principle of co-financing of Pillar I, and yet you are against co-financing. Discuss!
Mr Kendall: There are a number of issues on co-financing. I suspect that our historical perspective of how the UK has fared with rural development budgets, the arrangements that grew out of the Fontainebleau Accord and what-have-you, have

meant that often the UK has been poorly funded. We therefore have a historical perspective that has not always left us with the greatest confidence that we would be co-financed in the same way. I think that there are issues, and we recognise that in the European Commission there are quite strong views on the fact that compulsory co-financing requires changes in the Treaty of Rome, because they become taxation measures—and that would cause real problems for some of the Accession countries, and how they would react. There are therefore some real concerns about how co-financing would come in. Bearing in mind that Commissioner Fischer-Boel has been so strongly in favour of more uniform EU modulation and less national modulation, this would be required to be uniform if it was not to be distorting. We do have some concerns, therefore, that co-financing would need a major shake-up within the EU, and would be unpopular with the Accession countries if it imposed taxation requirements on them; and that, again batting for UK farmers, we would not come out of it as well as some of our counterparts.

Q140 *Chairman:* You have indicated that you signed up to the 2003 reforms generally, and you see the Health Check as an opportunity of achieving some of the strategy behind the reforms. I suppose the crunch question is: to what extent is that view shared by your colleagues in Europe?

Mr Kendall: That is a very interesting one. As I have said, in my new role as a Vice-President of COPA, it is a difficult one to try and get consensus on. But there are a significant number of countries which are engaged in and wanting to have an open and sensible debate about the way forward. Denmark and Sweden, for example; Italy are quite good partners of ours; and I think that the Germans want to have a proactive debate in a number of these areas. Also, some of the Accession countries want to see a simplified model having some resonance round the rest of Europe. As I said, the chairman of COPA-COGECA is currently a Frenchman; so how proactive COPA can be on that will be interesting to

see. We certainly intend to be actively involved in not saying, "We can't do anything" but, rather, "How can we move forward?", and we want to be positive and engaged.

Chairman: So "*Non*" becomes "*Peut-être*"!

Q141 *Lord Palmer:* Going back to the question asked by Lord Brookeborough, would you agree that, under our obligations for the RTFO, it is relatively complicated having to deal with four different ministries, ie Defra, Department for Trade and Industry, Department for Transport and, finally, the Treasury? Have you had any experience that these ministries are perhaps not talking to each other on the same wavelength?

Mr Kendall: I think that it has made for very, very complicated discussions on the RTFO because of the way that it has been spread. We have been advocating for some time that there should be one ministry taking the lead on many of these issues. I know that you have had a very active role in helping on some of these areas. Even if it is something that we do want to see simplified, we do need to see some sensible drivers. I do think that the way the RTFO is now in place is giving some certainty. What I am concerned about is some of the drivers that are being put on the accreditation schemes that will be put in place. We do want sustainable standards in place. We do want to make sure that we are not adding to environmental degradation in other parts of the world. We have to make sure, however, that we deliver an industry in the UK that is realistic. If, for example, our counterparts in France accept that cross-compliance provides environmental protection, we have to be careful that we do not raise the bar too much so that, again, this start of the journey of evolving to second-generation is not curtailed because of getting that wrong. I think that some of the conflict between the different departments is slowing that process of putting that accreditation in place.

Chairman: I think that is it, unless there is something we have missed that you think we desperately ought to know. If not, thank you very much indeed for your time.

Supplementary memorandum by the NFU

In the course of our session of oral evidence to the Committee's enquiry on the future of the CAP, we were requested to supply some further information on the impact of exchange rate fluctuations on the agricultural sector, and on the effects of the proposed phasing out of the Agricultural Buildings Allowance.

EXCHANGE RATE FLUCTUATIONS

1. The impact of exchange rate fluctuations on the agricultural sector is multifaceted. As a trading sector, exchange rate fluctuations of the domestic currency with respect to the currencies of our competitors and/or the currencies most commonly used in international transactions impact the international competitiveness of the sector and add to the risk of the transaction, while the very existence of different currencies compounds

the transaction costs associated with trade. As a recipient of payments originated in the EU budget (and, therefore, denominated in Euros), exchange rate fluctuations of sterling with respect to the Euro will lead to changing levels of agricultural support. The paragraphs below will develop these issues in further detail.

2. Given the importance of our economic and policy relation with the Euro zone, fluctuations between the Euro and sterling and resulting from the status of the UK as a non-Euro zone country merit special and separate consideration, especially as some of our main competitors will not be facing them.

3. UK agricultural trade is dominated by trade with the EU, as over ⅔ of both agricultural imports and agricultural exports are conducted with EU-25 countries. [See Table 1 below]. In total, trade with the EU in agricultural goods represented over £22 million in 2005 (of which £15.5 million were imports and £6.5 million were exports). The majority of trade conducted with the EU-25 is conducted in Euros or Euro-pegged currencies (as the new member states prepare their markets for convergence in order to fulfil their ambition to be part of the Euro zone).[1]

Table 1

TRADE IN FOOD, FEED AND NON-ALCOHOLIC DRINKS

	2000	*2001*	*2002*	*2003*	*2004*	*2005*
Imports from the EU-25 (£ million)	10,841	11,742	12,413	13,979	14,728	15,845
Imports from EU-25 as proportion of total Imports (%)	64	64	65	67	67	68
Exports to the EU-25 (£ million)	5,431	5,283	5,726	6,435	6,375	6,459
Exports to EU-25 as proportion of total exports (%)	62	62	64	65	66	65

Source: DEFRA

4. The importance of EU trade is even more evident when focusing on (specific) indigenous products. Table 2, below, exemplifies the importance of EU imports and exports: for all the major indigenous products, except for sheep, EU imports and exports account for between 70% and 100% of all trade.

Table 2

RELEVANCE OF EU TRADE BY COMMODITY TYPE, 2005

	EU Imports as% of total imports	*EU Exports as % of total exports*
Cereals	73	81
Sheep	10	99
Pork	98	89
Bacon and Ham	100	96
Poultry	89	86
Butter	100[2]	70
Cheese	94	83
Eggs	85	72

Source: DEFRA

5. It should be noted that the impact of exchange rate fluctuations on trade flows will not be equal across all sectors, as those with more integrated and domestic supply chains will feel the impact less than those which are European or global markets. As an example, the cereals (wheat) market is considered a global commodity, with international performance varying depending on exchange rate fluctuations (especially as UK wheat is usually priced with reference to French wheat). This is demonstrated below by the relationship between the

---

[1] The only exception being Slovenia, who has already joined the Euro zone.
[2] Butter import figures are distorted by New Zealand product which is imported via Denmark.

€/£ exchange rate and net trade in wheat, where an exportable surplus of more than £350 million in 1995 was reduced to a trade deficit of almost £50 million in 2002.

Figure 1

EXCHANGE RATE (EURO/£) AND WHEAT TRADE

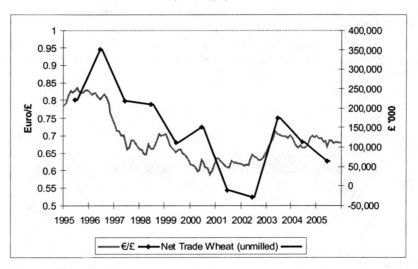

Source: NFU calculations

6. In addition to the impact of exchange rate fluctuations on international competitiveness, it should be noted that all transactions conducted in a foreign currency will be subject to transactions costs, with the EU Commission estimating that these transaction costs equal a "deadweight" of 1.2% of trade value. Over the period 2000–05 the deadweight loss on agri-food trade from the rest of the EU can be estimated to be in excess of £1.2 billion. This transaction cost is growing as trade increases, and represents a significant cost to the UK agri-food chain which could be reduced by entry to the Euro.[3]

7. Moreover, at the individual level and for small firms, transaction costs can be as much as 1–3% of any particular transaction. It should be noted, however, that only a portion of the transaction costs will accrue to farmers—more specifically, farmers stand to lose a share of the transaction costs related to exports. Over the six year period 2000 to 2005, this can be estimated to be in excess of £0.4 billion, roughly equal to the value of the annual barley crop. A portion of these transaction costs (dependent on the market power of the farmers respect to other economic agents in the supply chain) will accrue to farmers.

8. Transactions in a different currency involve a higher risk than that associated with transactions taking place in the same currency. Although in some cases it is possible to insure against the risk in a particular transaction, this involves an obvious cost that makes the product more expensive and, therefore, less attractive in international markets. Moreover, it is not always possible to insure against the risk in an ongoing trade relation, due to the several uncertainties involved (uncertain quantity, uncertain price, uncertain exchange rate). This might result in a discouragement to trade and a loss of potential markets for UK farmers when compared with their competitors in the Euro zone.

9. With market related payments, and more recently the single farm payment, priced in Euros and then converting to sterling at a predetermined exchange rate,[4] UK farmers and growers are also exposed to exchange rate risk on the support payments. This is demonstrated by the year-on-year variability in support payments and the losses over the period 1999–2007 can be estimated as being in excess of £1.5 billion, as the exchange rate used to convert farm support payments remains above that which it would have entered the Euro at its inception in 1999 (1€ = 0.705978 £).[5]

---

[3] Of course, transactions costs apply to all international trade exchanges. The overall value of transaction costs for the agri-food sector the 2000-2005 period can then be estimated at £1.5 billion.

[4] Currently payments are calculated on the exchange rate for last trading day of September, with a high associated level of risk. The NFU would like to see the exchange rate calculated on the average over a one-month period as under previous schemes.

[5] The losses are calculated by comparing the actual rate applied to support payments as compared with the exchange rate of 1Euro = 0.705978 £. If the UK had become a member of the Euro zone at its inception, the entry rate would have been very close to the market rate at that time.

Table 3

LOSSES IN SUPPORT PAYMENTS DUE TO STRONG STERLING

£m	1999	2000	2001	2002	2003	2004	2005	2006	2007
Market Related Payments/SPS	212	255	567	208	10	83	91	104	33

Source: NFU Calculations

10. As a result of the factors highlighted above, the incomes of UK farmers are intrinsically linked to developments in the Euro-sterling exchange rate. The chart below shows the strength of this relationship over time.

Figure 2

FARMING INCOMES AND EXCHANGE RATES (EURO/£)

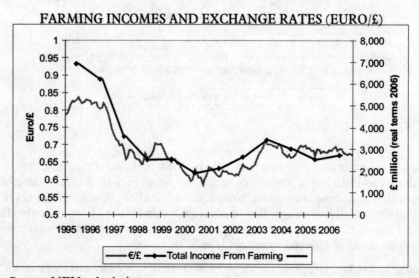

Source: NFU calculations

11. Concerning our exchanges with non-EU countries, it should be noted that with the exception of the relation between exchange rate fluctuations and support payments (specific to the Euro), all the factors highlighted above apply also to the impact of changes in the value of sterling with respect to other currencies. Of these, special mention needs to be made of the $, given its status as currency of choice in a large percentage of the transactions with non-EU countries. For instance, transaction costs associated with agricultural exports during the 2000–06 period can be estimated (assuming 1–3% of transactions costs on exports, see above) to be in excess of £0.1 billion and as high as £0.3 billion.

12. As it would be expected, there is a certain degree of correlation between the competitiveness of specific agricultural commodities and the $/£ exchange rate, though the relation is weaker than in the case of the €/£ exchange rate (see Figure 3 below for wheat).

Figure 3

EXCHANGE RATE ($/£) AND WHEAT TRADE

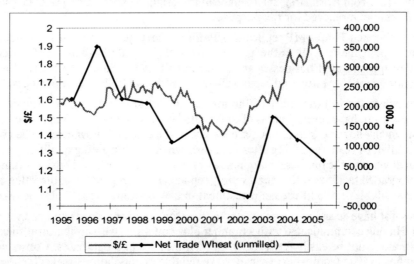

Source: NFU calculations

13. Given the lack of relation between the dollar exchange rate and support payments and the lower percentage of trade conducted in dollars, the relation between farming incomes and the $/£ exchange rate, though existent, is weaker than the one between farming incomes and the €/£ exchange rate.

Figure 4

FARMING INCOMES AND EXCHANGE RATES ($/£)

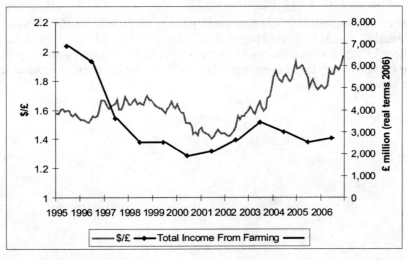

Source: NFU calculations

THE EFFECT OF PHASING OUT AGRICULTURAL BUILDINGS ALLOWANCES

1. The 2007 Budget announced the phasing out of both industrial buildings allowances and agricultural buildings allowances. Agricultural buildings allowances give relief in tax computations for capital expenditure incurred on the construction of agricultural buildings, fences and certain "other works". The allowance is given at the rate of 4% per annum with the result that qualifying expenditure is written off against taxable profits over 25 years.

2. Agricultural buildings allowances will be phased out from 2008–09. The allowance will reduce to 3% in that year, 2% in 2009–10, 1% in 2010–11 and be abolished from April 2011.

3. Phasing out will apply to allowances on expenditure already incurred but not yet fully relieved as well as new, future investment. For example, a qualifying investment of £100,000 in 2005–06 will receive writing down allowances of £4,000 in 2005–06, £4,000 in 2006–07, £4,000 in 2007–08, £3,000 in 2008–09, £2,000 in 2009–10 and £1,000 in 2010–11. From April 2011, the balance of the original expenditure (£82,000) will become a "tax nothing" and will remain unrelieved for tax purposes.

4. On 5 June 2007, Stephen Timms MP replied to a Parliamentary question from Jim Paice MP that, for the 2010–2011 financial year, the receipts to the Treasury from the staged phasing-out of agricultural buildings allowances given to incorporated businesses are expected to be £5 million. The figures for unincorporated businesses could not be reliably estimated separately from industrial buildings allowances.

5. In order to calculate the full tax effect of the loss of agricultural buildings allowances for a particular business, it is necessary to have several pieces of information: the value of qualifying expenditure incurred to date in respect of which allowances have not yet been given; the value of allowances to be given in the course of 2007–11; the number of years remaining after 2011 over which the remaining qualifying expenditure would have been written down; and the business' marginal tax rate. Furthermore, if the business is intending to invest in additional or upgraded facilities rather than simply replacing existing facilities, the value of the allowances which will not be available on the future net investment in new buildings should also be taken into account.

6. The NFU does not have access to our members' accounting and tax records and cannot therefore extract this information. Having communicated with a number of accountants with agricultural clients, it is also clear that the information cannot be easily retrieved from their systems and databases. Consequently, we do not currently have sufficient data from which we can make reliable extrapolations regarding the overall value of the agricultural buildings allowance.

7. In the course of discussing the issue with members, we have however been given a number of specific examples of its effect and we have summarised some of these on the attached spreadsheet (not printed).

8. These examples illustrate that:

9. the impact of phasing-out on individual businesses is considerable. (A further large poultry business has estimated that it will lose agricultural buildings allowances worth £126K per annum in tax terms once these have been fully phased out);

10. significant balances of unrelieved expenditure can exist among unincorporated farming businesses as well as incorporated businesses; and

11. incorporated farming businesses do not necessarily pay tax at the full rate of corporation tax and cannot therefore be presumed to benefit from the proposed 2% rate cut. Those who pay tax at the small companies' rate will suffer a double "hit" because the small companies' tax rate is to be progressively increased, while the overall impact for those who pay tax at the marginal rate will depend on where their taxable profits lie within the marginal rate band.

November 2007

WEDNESDAY 17 OCTOBER 2007

Present   Bach, L   Moynihan, L
           Brookeborough, V   Palmer, L
           Cameron of Dillington, L   Plumb, L
           Greaves, L   Sewel, L (Chairman)
           Jones of Whitchurch, B   Ullswater, V

Memorandum by Natural England

INTRODUCTION

1. This evidence is submitted on behalf of Natural England, the statutory body working to conserve and enhance England's natural environment, for its intrinsic value, the well-being and enjoyment of people and the economic prosperity that it brings. Its role is to ensure that England's unique natural environment, including its land, flora and fauna, freshwater and marine environments, geology and soils, are protected and improved. Natural England also has the responsibility to help people enjoy, understand and access the natural environment.

2. In this evidence, we have attempted to answer the questions listed in the "Call for Evidence" issued by the Committee on 30 April 2007. The total length of this evidence exceeds the recommended 6 pages, but the key points are summarised in the "overview and summary" section below:

OVERVIEW AND SUMMARY

Q1a. *What should be the long term objectives of the CAP? Does the title "Common Agricultural Policy" aptly fit your perceived objectives of the policy?*

3. The current title of the Common Agricultural Policy does not fit either the current objectives of the policy or the direction in which Natural England would like it to evolve. Whilst we welcome the 2003 reforms, particularly the introduction of decoupling, these have stimulated debate about what the first pillar of CAP is for. It seems to have lost its original purpose, without finding a new one. Natural England believes that the long term objective of the policy should be to help secure the future of the rural environment by paying farmers and other land managers for forms of land management that are vital for maintaining and restoring environmental features but which cannot be secured, in sufficient quantity or quality, through the market or through advice and regulation alone. .

4. This view is based on three facts:

    i.   Although the agricultural industry is relatively small in terms of its contribution to the economy (at least in Western Europe), it is critical in terms of its influence over the health of our environment. Farmers manage a very high percentage of Europe's land area and are one of the principal forces shaping our environment.

    ii.   There is ample evidence that modern commercial farming can no longer be relied on to deliver a high quality rural environment as an automatic, free, by-product.

    iii. The rural environment is likely to face many new pressures in the years ahead, including the need to deal with the global and local consequences of climate change.

5. Looking forward, Natural England sees a need to use the land wisely, flexibly and sustainably so that it can supply the wide range of services that we will all require—reconciling the need for food, energy and water with allowing natural systems such as floodplains to function and maintaining landscapes rich in wildlife for people to enjoy.

6. There are unresolved questions about what the best European framework would be to achieve this, though it is clear that this framework will need to ensure the integration of the CAP with European environmental regulation and funding, and with European Structural Funds. However whatever this structure, we see a clear need for large-scale, long-term public funding to help safeguard the rural environment in England and across Europe in the face of the many and growing pressures that it faces.

7. CAP should however have wider ambitions than simply paying to secure the environmental management of land year by year. A reformed CAP should be aimed at helping to build a new social contract between farmers and the rest of society, where farmers see one of their primary roles being to manage the environment, including its landscape, biodiversity and natural resources, and where the public sees farmers as guardians of the environment and agrees that they are happy to pay farmers for these "public goods" through taxation. This contract would also involve farmers moving towards more environmentally and economically sustainable production of food that consumers want to buy and are prepared to pay a fair price for.

Q1b. *What do you consider to be the main pressures on the CAP as it currently is?*

8. Listed below are what Natural England considers to be the main pressures on the CAP. In each case the description includes a short commentary on how CAP could respond to these pressures:

  i.   Pressure to reduce spending on CAP: A growing number of Member States are becoming concerned at the scale of CAP spending, particularly given its perceived lack of purpose since the 2003 Reforms. We believe there is a need for continued large scale spending on land management but this can only be justified by a further major reform of CAP along the lines described above. .

  ii.   Continued strong support in some member States for income support payments for farmers: This seems to be largely driven by concerns for rural communities and the rural environment in geographic areas where traditional farming methods are still widely employed. We believe that a proposal to re-focus CAP on the maintenance of the rural environment has the potential to recognize and address these concerns and could be used to widen the base of support for further reform.

  iii. Changing global context: There are some calls for CAP to help farmers to adapt to a rapidly changing environment where they face significant challenges in an increasingly competitive global market for agricultural products, demanding expectations from consumers for high quality and low price, changing regulatory and tariff regimes and, on top of all this, the uncertainties and opportunities of climate change. By contrast, some aspects of CAP are also under pressure as some farming sectors experience a revival in prosperity, driven in part by the growing demand for bio-energy. We recognise that there may be a need to help the farming industry adapt to change but we must manage the environmental side-effects and beware of re-introducing measures that distort markets and recreate the sort of long term dependency on public subsidy that existed before the recent rounds of CAP Reform.

THE REFORMED CAP

Q2. *What has been your experience so far with the reformed CAP? What has worked well and less well? And where can lessons be learned?*

9. Natural England is fully aware of the problems of implementing the Single Payment Scheme in England, but there are many other organisations better qualified than us to provide evidence on this subject. Our evidence therefore concentrates on the environmental effects of the 2003 CAP Reforms.

10. Disentangling the impacts of the 2003 Reforms is complicated by the fact that they were the latest in a series of reforms. The need for an environmental dimension and moves towards some decoupling were addressed in earlier rounds, particularly the 1992 MacSharry reforms and Agenda 2000. However, the 2003 Reforms added two key new dimensions. These were a further shift towards decoupling income support payments from production and the introduction of cross-compliance as a condition applying to nearly all payments linked to land and its management.

DECOUPLING

11. England was one of the first Member States to take full advantage of the opportunity to decouple income support payments from production and so provides something of a test bed for understanding the environmental impacts of these latest reforms.

12. Factual data on the actual changes that have occurred as a result of decoupling is still limited. The initial results from Defra's Agricultural Change and Environment Observatory (ACEO) suggest that change in the immediate aftermath of decoupling has been slow. Land managers appear to be taking time to consider their options, given that in many cases they are still receiving very similar levels of payment. A survey commissioned

by the ACEO[1] has shown that only 26% of farmers indicated that they intended to change their farming system in the next five years, whilst 44% were uncertain. The same survey included a Comparison of five investment strategies and identified that the use of the single payment to "substitute" for the previous production linked payment was the strategy that farmers were most likely to adopt, followed by use of the Single Payment as a "pension".

13. Despite this "inertia", there are indications that decoupling will have significant impacts over time. Forecasting work done so far for the ACEO[2] and research in Wales[3] indicates that these will include both positive and negative impacts, although it is difficult to be completely accurate in relation to "cause and effect", given the wide range of drivers (additional to the CAP) which impact on land management decisions.

14. In summary, the potential environmental implications of the anticipated changes in farming practices include:

— *Biodiversity*—potential risks in the arable sector relate to increases in block cropping and shifts to simplified crop rotations which could reduce habitat diversity. When prices are low, there could be an increase in fallow land, which could potentially be beneficial to biodiversity, although this will depend on how it is managed. In lowland areas of high nature conservation, there are concerns that it will become harder to find the grazing animals needed to maintain these areas, particularly where cattle are needed. In upland areas a reduction in the stocking rate of over-grazed land will provide benefits, particularly for heather moorland, although issues with under-grazing may begin to emerge. Upland ecosystems may also be affected by a move away from cattle, which are important in the control of bracken and other coarse vegetation.

— *Landscape*—over the longer term there could be major changes in landscapes as the balance and nature of livestock and cropping enterprises alter. In some areas there may be increasing homogeneity and loss of distinctiveness due to either larger scale intensive management in productive areas or, conversely, increased extensification and near-abandonment in marginal areas. The landscape will also be affected as land leaves productive agriculture for leisure and other uses. The maintenance of landscape features may also decline in these circumstances;

— *Water quality*—Changes in types of crop and livestock, cropping practices and the degree of intensity of livestock production are likely to be particularly important in affecting the potential for reducing water pollution. Risks of localised negative impacts remain through increased stocking rates on dairy farms. There is some evidence to suggest that farmers are making increased use of buffer strips of uncultivated land alongside water courses and other sensitive habitats following CAP reforms, which will help to reduce the risks of water pollution.

— *Soils*—Significant changes in levels of compaction and erosion, and possibly organic matter, are considered particularly likely through changes in the balance of crops grown and in methods of livestock production. Potential risks for localised negative impacts are linked to move to larger, more intensive dairy farms and increases in maize production. There are also potential issues arising from bio-crop production, depending on the location and type of management.

— *Air quality*—declines in the beef herd, extensification and potential reductions in fertiliser use are important factors leading to reductions in emissions. Some localised risks for ammonia emissions exist through more intensive production on dairy farms.

— *Climate change*—declines in the beef herd and reductions in fertiliser use should lead to reductions in greenhouse gas emissions, particularly methane and nitrous oxide.

— *Pesticides*—extensification may lead to less herbicide usage.

15. Across Europe, there is concern that decoupling may have some adverse consequences in some areas where traditional farming systems have survived. In Spain, for example, production linked Pillar I payments have provided an incentive for some extensive producers in marginal areas to manage their traditional olive groves. Also, in La Vera, Extramadura, CAP pillar I support for the goat, sheep and cattle sectors has helped to maintain extensive grazing in areas where it contributes to maintaining diverse and attractive landscapes.

---

[1] Research project EPES 0405/17: Research to Understand and Model the Behaviour and Motivations of Farmers in Responding to Policy Changes (England). Final Report November 2006.
[2] See "CAP Reform—Implications of farm level change for environmental implications", CSL/CCRU, October 2006.
[3] ADAS, 2007, Review of Indicators for assessing the impacts of agri-environment schemes and recent CAP Reforms on biodiversity in Wales.

CROSS-COMPLIANCE

16. Working to a common framework, Member States have implemented cross compliance in a variety of ways, particularly in respect of the development of Good Agricultural and Environmental Condition (GAEC). It is therefore difficult to estimate the environmental benefits and dis-benefits of cross compliance across Europe. Even in England, there are difficulties. These are partly due to the fact that cross-compliance has only been operational since 2005 and partly because the monitoring and evaluation system is still under development. However, we think Cross-compliance has a valuable role to play in establishing baseline standards for land and environmental management and in improving farmer awareness of environmental issues.

17. Natural England believes that cross-compliance is a powerful tool to ensure that minimum standards are met. We do however recognise the widespread concern about the level of bureaucracy surrounding the administration and enforcement procedures relating to cross-compliance. We support moves to simplify these processes, but strongly believe that simplification should not be achieved at the expense of lowering environmental standards.

THE SINGLE PAYMENT SCHEME

Q3. *Do you consider the Single Payment Scheme to be a good basis for the future of EU agricultural policy? What changes might be made at the EU level to the Single Payment Scheme, including to the rules governing entitlements, in the short and/or the longer-term?*

18. Although environmentally speaking, the Single Payment Scheme is undoubtedly an improvement on the production based subsidies that preceded it, Natural England does not consider that the Single Payment Scheme is a good basis for the future of EU Agricultural Policy. We think a key principle for future reforms of CAP should be that public funds should be used to produce public benefits. Although there are potential environmental benefits from the cross-compliance standards attached to the Single Payment, these mostly relate to better compliance with statutory requirements. The Single Payment remains essentially an income support payment, not a payment for positive environmental management.

19. Natural England consequently believes that over time resources should be progressively shifted from the Single Payment to the Rural Development Programme, and especially to the Axis 2 Measures including agri-environment, where payments can be used to directly secure positive environmental management. We believe that such a shift could address the negative consequences of decoupling listed in our answer to question 2 as well as retaining the positive benefits.

MARKET MECHANISMS

Q4. *What short and longer-term changes are required to the CAP's market mechanisms? Suggestions made by the Commission have included re-examination of certain quotas, intervention, set-aside, export refunds and private storage payments.*

20. Natural England's general view is that the remaining market mechanisms are an anachronism in a decoupled world and should be phased out. However, in doing so it is important to manage any environmental side-effects. In the case of set-aside, for example, Natural England would not oppose the abolition of set-aside, provided there were to be a commensurate increase in Pillar II funds to deliver the environmental benefits that set-aside has been providing. Natural England is currently helping to support research aimed at establishing the extent to which set-aside has had beneficial environmental side-effects and would be pleased to make the results available to the Committee when the research is complete. A recent survey[4] has shown that set-aside can be directly linked to a recovery in woodlark numbers in England.

---

4   Unpublished results of 2006 national survey: BTO, RSPB, Natural England & the Forestry Commission, England,

RURAL DEVELOPMENT

Q5. What is your view on the introduction of the European Agricultural Fund for Rural Development (EAFRD)? Do you consider that it is meeting its objectives thus far? Is it suitably "strategic" in nature, meeting the needs of rural society as a whole rather than being restricted to aiding the agricultural industry? How well is it being co-ordinated with other EU and national policies on regional and rural development?

21. Natural England believes that EAFRD should not be primarily either about the agricultural industry or rural society. Instead, it should be about payment for the management needed to maintain the quality of the rural environment.

22. Natural England therefore supports Defra's decision to weight the England Rural Development Programme as heavily as possible towards Axis 2 and the delivery of environmental benefits. We feel this should be the main purpose of EAFRD, at least for England. There is a clear need to secure the rural environment, there is a clear case for public funding, based on the absence of suitable market mechanisms, and there are no adequate alternative sources of funding.

23. Safeguarding the rural environment does moreover produce wider benefits. There is good evidence from the economic valuation literature that people value a high quality natural environment. In the specific context of agri-environment schemes a number of studies have attempted to value the benefits of Environmentally Sensitive Area (ESA) schemes (one of the predecessors to Environmental Stewardship). All yielded positive benefits and estimated people's willingness-to-pay to be in the region of £25 per person.

24. On the economic side, it is extremely difficult to estimate all the economic benefits of an attractive environment, but there have been attempts to measure some of the more direct economic effects. It has for example been estimated that across the UK green agricultural systems, including organic systems and land in agri-environment schemes, support 41,000 FTE jobs and contribute £840 million in value added.[5] In another study, of the Lake District ESA, it was calculated that this scheme had generated enough building work on historic farm buildings to create 25-30 FTE jobs in the local economy.[6]

Q6. Is there a case for a higher level of EU financing of rural development? Do you have a view on the extension of compulsory modulation from Pillar I (Direct Payments) to Pillar II (Rural Development)?

25. There is a clear case for a higher level of Rural Development funding in England. Although Defra did well in negotiating the budget for the 2007–13 Rural Development Programme for England (RDPE), it is obvious to Natural England, as the body responsible for delivering the largest part of this programme, that the demand and need for environmental management will continue to exceed the available budget. This situation is likely to be reinforced by the additional pressures of adapting to climate change.

26. The maintenance of the Agri-environment Scheme budget within the overall RDPE funding is our first priority and, given that the UK receives a disproportionately small allocation from the core EAFRD budget, this can only be achieved through a high rate of modulation.

27. We also support modulation in principle, as it is the main tool available at the moment for transferring resources from Pillar I to Pillar II. Natural England does however recognize the concern that some farmers in England have expressed at the relatively high level of voluntary (national) modulation that Defra has agreed to levy in England. We would therefore support an increase in the rate of Europe-wide compulsory modulation, both as a way of reducing the disparities between farmers in different countries and as a way of moving more of CAP funding into Pillar II.

28. However, given the underlying imbalance in the allocation of Pillar II money to Member States, and the fact that we only retain 80% of the proceeds from compulsory modulation, it is very unlikely that agreement will be reached on a rate of compulsory modulation that is sufficient to maintain, let alone increase, the scale of our current commitment to agri-environment funding. There is also a wide variation in spending on Rural Development, across Europe and even between the countries of the UK. It is therefore vital to maintain the flexibility to continue to apply an appropriate level of voluntary, national modulation in each of the countries of the UK.

---

[5] Soil Association, 2006, Organic Works: Providing more jobs through organic farming and local food supply.
[6] English Heritage 2005, Building Value. Public benefits of historic farm building repair in the Lake District.

WORLD TRADE

Q7. *What benefits can the EU's World Trade Organisation obligations create for EU agriculture and, consequently, for the EU economy as a whole?*

29. In brief, Natural England agrees that trade liberalization is likely to produce net economic benefits for the EU. Trade liberalization is however likely to have complex environmental side-effects, some of which will need intervention to manage and mitigate. Pillar II funding can help to do this in relation to the adverse impacts arising within Europe, but more thought is needed on how adverse impacts can be avoided in other countries.

30. Because Pillar II is important in mitigating the effects of trade liberalization, it is important that future World Trade Organisation (WTO) rules do not constrain its legitimate use.

31. There is a voluminous literature on agricultural trade liberalisation covering a host of liberalisation scenarios. Much of it focuses on how regional (continental) output and trade flows might change under a new set of rules (eg the global GTAP model). The OECD, World Bank, UN and some development NGOs tend to lead research in this area. As a result, the analysis of impacts is often very aggregated, and since the EU is a trading bloc, the impacts of liberalisation scenarios tend to be assessed at this level.

32. Whatever the scenario modelled, most analysis concludes with a similar direction of travel for the EU. In general, market liberalisation will lead to increased competition for EU producers and output levels and prices are likely to fall as a result. Clearly the extent of liberalisation will determine the degree of change. The main losers would most likely be developed country producers (excluding notable cases like New Zealand and Australia). EU consumers would gain (in the form of lower prices) along with key non-OECD country producers (eg India, Brazil, Argentina, etc).

33. As with decoupling, the *environmental effects* of trade liberalisation are more difficult to assess. The consensus in the literature is that trade liberalisation, although good for growth, can have negative impacts on the environment and these need to be guarded against where possible. Defra has recently completed some work in this area looking at liberalisation in different commodity regimes.[7] The overall conclusion is that the speed of liberalisation is important and whilst there are likely to be positive environmental gains in the EU (of a similar nature to those from decoupling), the international environmental impacts are likely to be negative as a result of increased output overseas. Most research concludes that the EU has adequate systems in place (such as agri-environment schemes and regulations) to guard against what negative impacts might result but the same can not be said for other countries.[8] The EU could, therefore, be legitimately criticised to some extent for "exporting environmental degradation" if the net environmental impact of trade liberalisation is negative overall.[9]

ENVIRONMENTAL PROTECTION AND CLIMATE CHANGE

Q8. *To what extent has the system of cross-compliance contributed to an improved level of environmental protection? How is it linking with other EU policy requirements such as the Water Framework Directive?*

34. For the reasons set out above in our answer to Question 2, it is very difficult to assess the contribution made by cross-compliance. This is currently the subject of a review commissioned by Defra, which should be reporting shortly. A preliminary assessment by the Land Use Policy Group[10] concluded that in broad terms it seems likely that cross compliance will:

— have a positive impact on specific environmental issues including water quality, soils, biodiversity and landscape and historic environment.

— help improve compliance with the Statutory Management Requirements (SMRs) where there have been compliance issues (eg Groundwater & Nitrates Directives).

— improve compliance with other environmental regulations.

— Add value to agri-environment schemes by helping to reduce the gap between normal farming systems and practices and agri-environment schemes and by enabling agri-environment schemes to focus on environmental maintenance and enhancement, as opposed to protection.

35. Natural England believes that cross-compliance needs to evolve into a mechanism for codifying acceptable baseline standards of environmental land management.

[7]   Defra (2006) "The environmental impacts of trade liberalisation and potential flanking measures".
[8]   See also European Commission work on Sustainability Impact assessment of WTO reforms (University of Manchester).
[9]   Potter (1999) Agricultural liberalisation and its effects', Report for the UK Countryside Agencies.
[10] Land Use Policy Group Briefing—Cross Compliance, April 2007.

Q9. *How can the CAP contribute to mitigation of, and adaptation to, climate change? What do you consider the role of biofuels to be in this regard?*

36. Natural England is of the view that land managers can make an important contribution to both adaptation and mitigation of climate change.

37. There has been an overall reduction in greenhouse gas pollution from agriculture both across Europe and in the UK since 1990.[11] This has been in part due to the implications of various CAP reforms, mainly from a reduction in livestock numbers, but also other policy drivers such as the Nitrates Directive.

38. Despite these reductions, projections are that by 2020 UK agricultural emissions will be nearly back to 2004 levels (ie around 15% below 1990 by 2020).[12] It would appear, therefore, that the sector is not on course to deliver the scale of contribution that will be required across the economy if the UK is to meet the 26–32% reduction that the Climate Change Bill proposes by 2020. This suggests that there is a need for agricultural policies such as CAP and the funding streams that flow from it to be playing a more defined and direct role in ensuring that the sector delivers more on climate change.

39. For example, research by Defra into the contribution that Environmental Stewardship makes to mitigation has found that most options under ELS and HLS, especially habitat creation and buffer strips, will result in reduced emissions (due to less inputs and energy use) and enhanced carbon storage in soils and vegetation. However, the research has calculated that the annual contribution ES as a whole makes to reducing greenhouse gas pollution is only equivalent to 0.5% of total UK emissions.[13] Although this is still a useful contribution, it could be significantly higher if climate change were a specific target in the design and delivery of the scheme.

40. Furthermore, there has not been (to our knowledge) any assessment at the UK or EU level of the contribution that Pillar I mechanisms, especially cross-compliance, are making to reducing emissions and enhancing carbon storage.

41. It is even harder to assess or quantify the contribution that CAP is making to delivering adaptation for the natural environment. Natural England believes however that Environmental Stewardship has the potential to make a major contribution in this area. Environmental Stewardship is currently encouraging practices that will conserve and enhance the existing natural environment, and the integrity of the existing features of the natural environment will be a key factor in determining resilience to climate change. Natural England has contributed to a recent report[14] that identifies a range of practical actions that can help habitats and species adapt. Many of these can already be facilitated using Environmental Stewardship.

42. If there is a more significant shift of support from Pillar I to Pillar II and a greater focus on providing public goods, then in our view CAP would have the potential to improve the contribution of the sector to mitigation and adaptation. To do this, all aspects of CAP, both Pillar I and II, will need to be "climate-proofed', so that they are making a clear and direct contribution to mitigation and adaptation.

43. However, it is important that we do not concentrate too much on financial incentives from public subsidy as a long-term solution. There will always be limited funding available and CAP alone will not deliver the scale of contribution required from the sector. We also should, as a matter of principle, be exploring what can be achieved through market mechanisms.

The Role of Bio-energy

44. There is considerable debate about the extent to which bio-energy crops (both perennial crops for biomass heat and power and annual crops for transport biofuels) will or will not contribute to greenhouse gas pollution abatement.

45. There is also much speculation about the extent to which the increased global demand for biofuels will lead to significant changes in land use in England. Simple extrapolations of the amount of land that may be required to meet for example the EU Directive on biofuels or the Renewable Transport Fuels Obligation (RFTO) do not take into account the fact that the biofuels market will be global and that production will come from countries and regions which have the most suitable conditions and can produce the fuel at the lowest cost. However, production in these areas may also have the greatest overall impact on the natural environment.

46. For the emerging bio-energy industry to be sustainable, it will need to both minimise the impact on the natural environment and optimise the contribution to reducing greenhouse gas pollution.

---

[11] UK GHG emissions from agriculture have fallen by 15% (1990—2005) and by 14% across the EU-15 (1990–2003).
[12] UK Climate Change Programme (2006), Defra.
[13] 1.03 million tonnes of carbon equivalent a year.
[14] Defra 2007: Conserving Biodiversity in a changing climate: Guidance on building capacity to adapt.

47. Natural England believes that urgent action is required to establish agreed standards and methods of accreditation for sustainable bio-energy production both domestically and overseas. There is also a need for more evidence to be gathered on the economic viability of biofuel production in England relative to the rest of the global economy and the consequence for current land use.

FINANCING

Q10. *The Commissioner has expressed her dissatisfaction at the financing agreement reached by the Member States at the December 2005 Council. Do you consider the current budget to be sufficient? Do you consider co-financing to be a possible way forward in financing the Common Agricultural Policy?*

48. The December Financial Settlement made it harder to fully exploit the potential of the Rural Development Programme. It did nothing to address the imbalance in the share of the core EAFRD budget allocated to the UK and by squeezing the overall budget for Pillar II, it sent an unfortunate message to Europe. Although the voluntary modulation arrangements negotiated by the UK government has allowed the UK to mitigate this impact the overall budget for Pillar II is still not sufficient to fully meet the scale of need.

49. £3.9 billion will be available for the next Rural Development Programme in England over the next seven years, of which £2.9 billion will be available for Environmental Stewardship. This is a very good settlement in the circumstances, but does not provide sufficient funds to meet the current and likely future scale of need. Estimates of the size of programme needed to fully deliver on the existing objectives of Environmental Stewardship vary, but we would need in the order of £500-£700M per year by 2013 to do this. However, this estimate is incomplete as it does not take into account the substantial extra resources needed to meet the challenge of climate change, nor the cost of purchasing the environmental benefits currently provided by set-aside.

50. Because of this scale of need, Natural England is convinced that a further, large scale transfer of resources is needed from Pillar I to Pillar II. We do not yet however have a view on whether the overall level of CAP funding is sufficient. This is largely because, if Pillar I were to be drastically reduced, we think that it would be necessary to revise both the scope of Pillar II and the basis on which Pillar II payments are calculated, as many farmers do currently choose to use their Pillar I payments to help underwrite their fixed costs. Our current estimate is that this would require a substantial further increase in the Pillar II budget, though this would not be so large as to replace Pillar I.

51. This is a complex area that urgently needs further research and testing. Natural England is currently commissioning research to assess the implications of phasing out Pillar I. Initial findings will be available in the autumn and the final report is due in January 2008.

52. Natural England's primary interest is in ensuring there are sufficient funds to meet the environmental needs identified. The extent to which this should be done by co-financing is primarily a political decision which it would not be appropriate for us to comment on.

ENLARGEMENT

Q11. *What has been the impact on the CAP of the 2004 and 2007 enlargements and what is the likely impact of future enlargements of the EU on the post-2013 CAP?*

53. Following EU accession in 2004, Polish agricultural businesses saw a tenfold increase in subsidies (CAP and other subsidies) and higher prices. This led to a 142% increase in agricultural business income, higher energy use, more intense and simplified land use, use of manufactured bought-in feed in place of on-farm production, replacement/improvement of machinery, and increased use of more productive plant and animal breeds15. A key environmental issue is the need to conserve Polish rural landscape structure, biodiversity and soils eg by preventing excessive land consolidation, decline of landscape features, reduction in crop diversity and further decline in extensive farming and other practices where these maintain natural and landscape values (eg prevent intensification or abandonment).[15]

54. The current CAP is therefore both part of the problem and part of the solution. Pillar I payments and even elements of Pillar II have fuelled rapid change in the countryside, but other parts such as agri-environment have at least the potential to be part of the solution. It could be argued that enlargement strengthens both the case for having a European level programme and the case for further reform. The case for having a European level Programme is that enlargement has brought into the EU several countries with large areas of internationally important wildlife habitat but with limited ability to fund its conservation, and they need an

---

[15] WWF Poland, Polish national report for the WWF /LUPG project Europe's Living Countryside, Warsaw 2005.

element of cross-subsidy. The argument for further reform is that, given the current balance of funding in CAP, the present policy probably does more harm than good.

55. Enlargement seems likely to increase the pressure on the Rural Development Programme budgets in the older Member States. Given the scale of the issues faced by some of these new member states we should accept the need for an element of cross-subsidy, subject to two important caveats:

— further reform, so that we are not subsidising habitat destruction.

— increased overall funding for Pillar II, so that important environmental management here in England is not squeezed too hard.

56. Enlargement also increases the range of variation between member states. We now have a Europe that consists of countries at very different stages of development and with very widely differing land management and rural development needs. This reinforces the point made earlier that it is extremely unlikely that a single, Europe-wide rate of compulsory modulation will provide every member state with the right level of Rural Development Programme funding. It strengthens the case for continuing to allow member states to apply additional voluntary modulation at national level.

SIMPLIFICATION OF THE CAP AND OTHER ISSUES

Q12. *How could the CAP be further simplified and in what other ways would you like to see the Common Agricultural Policy changed in the short and/or the long term?*

Simplification

57. In the timescale of the CAP Health Check, there are a number of ways of simplifying the CAP:

— Abolishing Set Aside, with appropriate environmental follow up measures incorporated into Pillar II. See answer to Question 4.

— Simplification of Cross-compliance, without diluting the standards it sets. See answer to Questions 2 & 8.

— Completion of decoupling. See answer to question 2.

— Further simplification through the introduction of a flat rate SPS.

Other short and longer term changes

58. As already mentioned, Natural England would support an increase in the rate of compulsory modulation as part of the CAP Health Check, though not at the expense of the ability to raise voluntary modulation.

59. In the medium term, we would favour a much larger scale transfer of funding from decoupled income support payments to payments that help farmers and land managers to maintain the quality of the rural environment. This can be summarized as paying for public environmental goods in areas of market failure.

60. In terms of the current structure of the CAP this would mean arguing for the phasing out of Pillar I and the expansion of Pillar II, and more specifically the measures available under Axis 2. However, looking to the longer term, we need to keep the mechanisms available to us under review.

61. Agri-environment schemes, together with basic regulatory framework, are currently the only major policy instruments available in England to conserve and enhance the natural environment on a sufficient scale. Whilst we strongly believe that the role of agri-environment schemes needs to be expanded, we also recognise a number of limitations and therefore the dangers of over-reliance on this approach. Potential problems include:

i. The schemes effectively "rent" environmental goods and services from land managers rather than "buying" them. The implication is that the continued provision of a high quality natural environment is completely dependent on government funding in perpetuity.

ii. The determination and specification of target outputs has to be undertaken by government rather than the beneficiaries, which perpetuates a "subsidy" mentality.

iii. Scheme payments tend to be based on "input activities" rather than actual outputs. This can reduce the incentives for the development of new and novel approaches to delivering environmental goods and services by suppressing the role of entrepreneurship.

iv. Many of the environmental improvements we seek need to occur at a scale that greatly exceeds individual holdings—implying some degree of co-ordination.

62. In response, Natural England will lead the new thinking around the development of agri-environment policy going forwards and explore new ways and mechanisms to deliver a high quality natural environment that complements the current Environmental Stewardship programme.

11 June 2007

Examination of Witnesses

Witnesses: DR HELEN PHILLIPS, Chief Executive Officer, and MR DAVID YOUNG, Executive Director—Strategy and Performance, Natural England, examined.

Q142 *Chairman:* Dr Phillips, thank you very much indeed for finding time with your colleague to come and talk to us about the CAP Health Check and the way forward on CAP reform. Perhaps you would like to say a few opening words, setting the scene of how you see the future developing, and then we will go through a question and answer session if that is okay. *Dr Phillips:* That would be great. Thank you for that opportunity. We are going to be slightly disgraceful in our few opening words, hopefully giving you the hooks for some of the key recommendations we would like to see flow from your report, and also to indicate some of the key areas where we think we might have a fruitful discussion later in the session. As you will be aware, Natural England is just over a year old. We had our first birthday at the beginning of October. One of our roles is the delivery of Environmental Stewardship. It means that we will be administering £2.869 billion pounds' worth of CAP funds, which is the bulk of the rural development programme for England between now and 2013. However, in our role also as champion of the natural environment it means that we have a much wider interest in the Common Agricultural Policy. We want to ensure that it supports environmental protection and improvement but, at the very least, does not act or work against it. We see three main opportunities now for securing reform of the CAP. The first is the current review of Environmental Stewardship. Flowing from that, we would like to see the securing of better environmental outcomes through this investment of public money and also a better understanding of what has been achieved with the public money invested to date. That primarily will be around improved targeting of Higher Level schemes, getting better geographic literacy on the Entry Level schemes, and also making sure that we get an environmentally useful successor to the Hill Farm Allowance. That is the first one and, I realise, very current and slightly outwith your interest in today's session. The second is the CAP Health Check, which clearly offers the opportunity to make adjustments to the current framework between now and 2013. A good example of the things we would like to see flow from this is in Set-Aside, where we have seen a policy measure that is a sensible policy measure of itself but with rather clumsy implementation, and where we have real concerns about the environmental degradation that will flow from that decision. On 26 September 2007, European Union agriculture ministers approved the Commission's proposal to set the compulsory set-aside rate at 0% for autumn 2007 and spring 2008 savings. We would therefore like to see the opportunity taken to adjust that within the context of the CAP Health Check. Also, for a very clear direction of travel to be set out, in terms of going away from income support and subsidy to farmers for meeting that would be basic operating requirements in any other industry, and all the investment which goes into that, to payments of public money in return for public goods and environmental goods and services. Also, an increase in compulsory modulation, but one which does not undermine voluntary modulation; as you will be only too well aware, 50% of the English requirement for agri-environment funds comes from voluntary modulation. More compulsory modulation would be a good thing because it would get us away from Pillar I towards Pillar II; but, by the same token, we recognise that we do not have similar starting points across Europe in each of the different countries. If we want to keep the notion of a Common Agricultural Policy, therefore, we do need to reflect the fact that people may need to progress at different speeds towards that common policy. Last but by no means least, the EU Budget Review provides the opportunity for a much more fundamental review of spending priorities. If we think about some of the other challenges that are coming now that we have not had in previous programmes, there is, for instance, adequate funding for climate change and the impacts of climate change; a substantial reduction in income support, reinforcing that direction of travel away from Pillar I towards Pillar II, and that coming much more to the fore; also, a fair distribution of rural development funds, recognising what is fair and sensible rather than having to live with historical accident. Beyond that, and perhaps more controversially given the fact that we have a number of you around the table who are already in our agri-environment schemes, how, in the longer term, we secure these environmental goods and services in perpetuity, rather than find ourselves in the position of renting them for a certain period of time, and often that benefit can be lost once the scheme stops. That is a canter round some of our aspirations for the short, medium and longer term, in terms of CAP reform.

Q143 *Chairman:* I think that my opening question follows on quite nicely from what you have said. You argue in your evidence that you have the impression that Pillar I has lost its original purpose and has not really found a new one. You go on to say that in the longer term the CAP should be to "help secure the future of the rural environment by paying farmers and other land managers for forms of land management that are vital for maintaining and restoring environmental features . . . which cannot be secured . . . through the market". It is therefore a market failure role that is available. Would you like to talk more about that?

Dr Phillips: Yes. We did use rather mouthful terms there! As we see it, the original purpose of the CAP was to secure a stable supply of safe and affordable food, reasonable standards of living for UK farmers and, at the same time, allow the industry to adapt, modernise and develop. Since then, agriculture has changed beyond recognition and I do not think that we can any longer depend on a high-quality environment as a by-product of commercial farming. That is before you factor in new changes such as climate change and the fact that we need a more resilient countryside as part of our adaptation response; also, I suppose, where it is you view the arguments around food security and whether or not food security equates with food self-sufficiency; and, of course, the improved commodity prices bringing great fortune to some sectors of the agricultural industry but by no means all. Given those changes, we think that the EU policy should be directed towards securing environmental goods and services that are not rewarded by the prices paid for in our food. We therefore talk, perhaps a bit romantically, about a new social contract between farmers and the rest of society: one where farmers see one of their primary roles as the protection and stewardship of the countryside, in return for which taxpayers are willing to make that investment in the longer term— I suppose also coupled with more economically and environmentally sustainable food production practices, where those externalities are captured in the price of that commodity and that people are willing to pay a fair price.

Q144 *Chairman:* Could I be a bit brutal and say, Yes, that is a very attractive argument which you develop for the maintenance of support through the CAP. But, as you said when you started off, originally the CAP was there to secure a plentiful supply of relatively cheap, safe food. It has done that. We do not need it. Why not abolish the CAP and, if we want environmental programmes, go through a totally different support mechanism?

Dr Phillips: We need to think about the restructuring of CAP in the wider sense. Our focus is very much on rural development and sustainable agricultural practices. You have to think about land use in the wider context. There is a lot of pressure on land. There is pressure on land for food, for fuel, for development, for a whole range of things. It is about the extent to which we need to see some intervention in that use, so that we can secure goods and services we need now but also the goods and services we might need in the longer term.

Mr Young: There are new challenges that have emerged, climate change being just one of them; there is also global trade liberalisation. One of the great benefits in Europe is that CAP has enabled liberalisation of markets in Europe whilst protecting environmental standards. That is something the EU can be proud of. Further trade liberalisation will require consistent standards across the world; so it is important that the EU maintains its mechanism for ensuring that food production is subject to appropriate standards, including those for climate change protection, and ultimately advocates them globally as a universal standard to which all countries can aspire.

Q145 *Chairman:* That is justification for keeping the CAP, is it?

Mr Young: There will be a continued wave of trade liberalisation. A consequence of not having a CAP is that we place at risk all of those public goods that will not be delivered by the market mechanisms. That is the practical reality.

Chairman: We may come back to that at some stage.

Q146 *Lord Plumb:* Following on My Lord Chairman's question, and related to trade liberalisation, you said earlier that there is ample evidence that modern commercial farming can no longer be relied on to deliver a high-quality rural environment as an automatic free by-product. At a conference yesterday, your Vice-Chairman was trying to tell us that it is possible and he sets that example. In fact, at this very moment, he is showing round his farm colleagues from various countries of the world, and showing them that you can have 600 cows on your commercial farm; that you can produce food, fibre and fuel, all from crops on that farm, and it can still be environmentally friendly. That is a point he was emphasising yesterday to people from South America, North America, and indeed from all over the world—not from Africa. When we talk about liberalisation of trade, therefore, you say that it has an environmentally positive impact within the European Union but you think that it then becomes more complex when it is global. I would like you to expand on that a bit. Are we talking about China? Brazil? Are we talking about the areas that are sending in these vast quantities of products? Again, we had the WTO as well as the World Bank represented yesterday and so all of these things were coming out, loud and clear. It is perfectly obvious that, when you start talking about environmentally friendly farming, we are talking one language and it seems that the rest of the world is talking another. I am all for setting examples, but if we are going to go on importing those products—and more products come from developing countries than from all the other countries put together—it is a different world that we are in. We have to accept what is, not just what we hope could be. I would like to hear a little more on that.

Dr Phillips: There are almost two elements to that. You start with the very positive example of Mr Christensen and the way in which he farms. We would like to see all farmers farming in an environmentally—

Q147 *Lord Plumb:* He is not alone, you know. There are a lot of them.

Dr Phillips: Absolutely. At the end of the day, we do not by any manner of means want to be paying for every environmental good and service we want. If we get ourselves into that position—let us be frank—there will not be enough money to go round. Farmers look after 75% of the land area of Europe; they look after over 70% of the land area of England. It is about that partnership; it is about what it is that farmers are willing to do in terms of how they look after the land which, absolutely and utterly, underpins the partnership we have with them in terms of agri-environment schemes and what flows from that. There is a very interesting dynamic happening at the moment in Set-Aside and the discussions we had with some of the farming unions in that context. Perhaps I could paraphrase them. They ran along the lines of, "Higher commodity prices are great. They have been a long time coming. Not sure that you are actually going to be able to entice us into agri-environment schemes any more, because it is more profitable with wheat at £110 per tonne. Don't be asking us for cross-compliance measures, because we don't want more regulation; we want less regulation, please". Somewhere in that cycle, we need to think about how we procure at a fair price those environmental goods and services that only farmers can provide for us and that we do need to have. How that has been achieved in Europe, is effectively, to say that, with the kind of liberalisation across Europe, there has been a public investment in buying some of those goods and services. You could say that they are variable but, by and large, there has been something of a fairly level playing field in terms of environmental standards set out. I think that the challenge is the one of scaling that up. We do not have a lot of evidence, frankly, about what is the offset issue when you are buying more food from other parts of the world, but it does not take a genius to work out that we are eating more or less the same, or more; that we are producing less

and it is coming from somewhere else, possibly somewhere else with lower environmental standards; and that we are going to see environmental degradation. It is often not going as far afield as China. We want to make sure with the new Accession Countries that some of the implications of CAP will not mean more intensification and/or land abandonment in what are pretty high-value nature farming areas with low resilience. I think that it is about how the Common Agricultural Policy, either in its current manifestation or in the direction in which we would like to see it go in the future, becomes a blueprint for sustainable agriculture. That, in turn, flows into standards, and those standards can be set at a global level. Our view is that the World Trade Organization will have limited objection to that, because it can be shown to be non-trade—distorting, and environmental standards are an important matter at a global level.

Q148 *Lord Palmer:* Your written evidence suggests that cross-compliance has been applied in a variety of different ways among European Member States. Could you give us some examples of what you see as good and less good applications? You go on to suggest that cross-compliance should become a means of establishing baseline standards for good farming within the United Kingdom; but, if Pillar I were to be phased out, would not the incentive which the Single Farm Payment provides for compliance also disappear? How then do you envisage the baseline standards being met, and indeed enforced?

Dr Phillips: It is important to consider cross-compliance in its two facets: the Statutory Management Requirements—which, when I am being unkind, I call "money for nothing"—and Good Agricultural and Environmental Condition. A very good example is Requirement 14—I am sorry to be slightly nerdy—of Good Agricultural and Environmental Condition, which prevents the roots of hedgerows being churned up and which also protects diffuse pollution going into watercourses. There are some other less good examples; for example in Denmark, where, through some of the Single Farm Payment measures, the cross-compliance does not actually require good landscape protection measures. The issue is that we must not continue to pay farmers for meeting basic environmental requirements. There are legal requirements that are effectively being paid for through the Single Farm Payment. If we say that is a flawed philosophy in this day and age, how do you protect the additional requirements such as the Good Agricultural and Environmental Condition ones? My view is that it will become a qualifying criterion for those who wish to enter into agri-environment schemes and that, for those who do not, the basic and huge suite of things that has been secured through cross-compliance will be secured through regulation. I do not mean heavy-handed regulation; in fact, I may mean considerably lighter regulation than we currently experience, much of which is quite input-focused, but more risk-based, proportionate regulation.

Q149 *Viscount Ullswater:* When you look at Europe and all the different conditions for farming in Europe, are you suggesting that each country should have its own view about how cross-compliance works? I think that what you have described is very current for the UK, but when you go to Poland and see some of what we would describe as very rural areas, where a lot of the work is done by hand and machinery has not got in in quite the same way that it has here, is it not right that they should be able to create their own standards and not have a common standard throughout the CAP?
Dr Phillips: I would be arguing for a slightly more radical step than that, which is that we should not be having Pillar I. We do not want to be either subsidising or consequently inflicting undue regulation on people for meeting basic operating requirements; and I would say that those basic operating requirements should be common, as enshrined, as they currently are, in EU directives and other legislative mechanisms.

Q150 *Lord Bach:* First of all, I played a small part in setting Natural England up and I am delighted that it is doing so well and has so many staff who can come here today.
Dr Phillips: They are not all ours!

Q151 *Lord Bach:* Are they not? How do I tell! However, I want to come back to what My Lord Chairman was asking you at the start, and it is a fundamental question. If I agree that Pillar I has served whatever purpose it once had, is there not a question about where that money goes to? In other words, if we agree that farmers should not be paid for producing what they produce, why should farmers be paid by the taxpayer for doing what they ought to do anyway in terms of environmental protection? Are there other groups in society who are so protected if they offend against environmental good practice?
Dr Phillips: Hear, hear! I entirely agree with that assertion. The issue, then, is what is it we want to pay farmers for, that have a price and are not going to be delivered through other mechanisms? Currently—and this is a very up-and-down picture in terms of how the flow of agri-environment funding goes—if you were to average it out, there is £414 million a year going out of the door to farmers, through Environmental Stewardship. We reckon the need—and this is very much a finger-in-the-air estimate—is somewhere between £500 and £700 million a year.

That factors in, for example, Biodiversity Action Plan requirements, but it only partially factors in water Framework Directive requirements and does not estimate or cost out climate change and climate change adaptation requirements. There is therefore a substantial number of environmental benefits that need to be bought. If you think that the Single Farm Payment is seven times the amount of money that goes to farmers through agri-environment schemes, you can see that there could be a substantial shift of monies from Pillar I to Pillar II, whilst at the same time probably making it quite possible for Treasury to have a reform dividend in that process; albeit, I should say for the purpose of completeness, that that £500 to £700 million is quite a loose estimate. There is quite a lot that has not been added in to it. It is also based on the premise that we must recognise that a lot of the environmental goods and services farmers currently deliver are in effect propped up. God bless it! It is the one good thing about the Single Farm Payment, namely the infrastructure support that goes through the Single Farm Payment. We would therefore need to recognise the fact that that would no longer be for free, and there would need to be some adjustment to reflect that cost to the farmer.

Q152 *Lord Bach:* How do you work out what should be paid to the farmer for environmental purposes and what should not? I know it is a very rough figure, the half a billion that you mentioned; but what is it about that that farmers should be paid for and paid for by the taxpayer, and about the rest of the environmental considerations that the farmer should look after himself? How do you draw those distinctions?
Dr Phillips: The funding formula at the moment is interesting territory. It is based on income foregone. It is something that we are beginning to give some consideration to. In many ways, it will be quite difficult to get away from income foregone. Imagine that you are a farmer standing in a field: it is the mental calculation you do in your head about, "What is it that can come from this land that is in front of me?". There is a good example, for instance, with our SSSIs. We have a PSA target to get SSSIs back into favourable condition; we are struggling massively to do that. We should be at 83% by the end of this year. With a fair wind, we will be at 81%, and that is because it is getting harder to do. The further you get in the programme, the more expensive the measures and the more difficult to achieve. It is about what the cost of that is. Do we actually want to be doing a deal with farmers that says, "What is the cost to you of securing this environmental good and service, together with the profit you require?" Or is it on the basis of income foregone, with all the implications of that when commodity prices go up? The implications of that, if prices go up, is that you have either to change the areas in which you are buying the

benefit—so classic horn-and-corn territory—and, having said that, the environmental goods we need, for example the habitats we want to protect, are not necessarily transferable from one area to another. You may therefore have to face the almost inevitable reality that you can buy less in periods of high commodity prices.

Q153 Lord Greaves: Or pay more for it?

Dr Phillips: That would be nice, but that is a predication on the total available funding for the Common Agricultural Policy. We would love that as a recommendation.

Mr Young: I think that behind your question is a deeper point. You could assume that the environment is in a good, healthy condition now and that we need some basic, light-touch regulations, and it will be all right. However, the reality is that the environment is highly degraded; it is highly fragmented. With the advent of climate change, there will be significant new, additional risks to the natural environment. The question is what is the share of the cost to secure the natural environment for the future? Can we realistically expect farmers to pay for it all?

Q154 Lord Bach: Or the taxpayer to pay for it?

Mr Young: Or indeed the taxpayer. Nonetheless, it is our position that we believe absolutely that the natural environment should be secured for the future and we need to find a partnership as to how that should be delivered.

Q155 Chairman: In the rest of the planning system, people who find that they do not get planning permission for activities that they wish to engage in could well argue that that is income foregone; that they are being penalised. But we do not give them any compensation for that; we just say that it is counter to planning policies. Why should farmers get compensation for income foregone, if it is in fact delivering a planning objective?

Dr Phillips: If you think about a simple example, if somebody wants planning permission to build a hotel, the profit that comes from that hotel goes to them. It is not that we are trying to secure the hotel as a public good and service for society or the community more widely. We are actually talking about buying things that society needs, such as clean water, improved habitats, reducing flood risk, connecting habitats in the face of climate change. You could therefore argue that there is more benefit to society than there is to the individual who is producing those benefits on behalf of society.

Q156 Baroness Jones of Whitchurch: We could turn that argument round. You picked a hotel, but you could say that house-builders are meeting a social

need. They make a profit out of it. We do not pay them necessarily in that way.

Mr Young: I think that there is a difference as well. The planning system aims to allow and permit various forms of development. We do not have a planning system at this stage which articulates a vision for the natural environment. The natural environment is not embedded properly within spatial planning in this country. We do not have systems where we identify where we need those environmental goods and services in different parts of the country suited to different regional needs. If we did, I think we would be supportive of your argument; indeed, it is something we might argue for. However, at this point in time we do not and therefore there is no effective planning of environmental protection for the future.

Q157 Lord Greaves: Farming is more or less excepted from the planning system—not entirely but very substantially. The argument being put, I think, is that farming ought to be part of the planning system; but I think that argument was lost, if it was an argument, 45 or 47 years ago and it would be very difficult to bring it back now. I want to go back to the basic level, the Pillar I stuff, the cross-compliance. If that is to be abolished, then what you are suggesting is that there should be some form of regulation which farmers are subjected to but not paid for. The farmers I talk to about cross-compliance at the moment tend to shrug their shoulders and say, "Yes, in principle it's OK. We've got to do it and we do it because we need the Single Farm Payment". Whether or not they think it is a good thing, they accept it because they can see the sense, in that they are delivering something for the money that they get. That seems to be a widespread point of view. If you continue to require cross compliance-type measures from farmers but no longer pay them anything for that, first of all you have a problem of convincing farmers that it is a good idea and, linked to that, you have a real problem of enforcing it. You said "a much lighter regulation regime"; I think that you will need to have a much stronger regulation regime, to make sure that whatever it is that you are asking for—whether it is the present cross compliance-type measures or whether it is other things altogether—will be carried out.

Dr Phillips: There are two facets to that. In many ways, Lord Bach put the argument more succinctly than I would probably manage. The issue is this. If you think about process industry regulation, it is subject to the IPPC directive, to air quality requirements, and a whole host of waste management requirements. We do not say that the process industry should have a payment from somebody in order to help them meet those environmental standards and requirements; yet that is the situation we have got ourselves into, culturally and historically, with agriculture. I think that we need to make sure that we do not let incentives subsidise regulation. There are a range of levers you can use to get environmental outcomes. There is regulation, advice, advocacy, incentives, and practical action. At the moment, however, we know that the Common Agricultural Policy, as you said yourself, is probably not sufficient to meet the totality of the requirements, particularly if we need to pay more against increased commodity prices. So why is it that we allow some of that incentive money, which really needs to be earmarked very carefully for buying those things that nothing else can buy, to support and subsidise regulation?

Q158 Lord Greaves: I accept the case that is being made. I understand that completely, and the case Lord Bach put forward. What I am asking about is the regulatory regime which would be necessary to enforce that. Would that be part of Natural England's remit? Or who would do it?
Mr Young: We mentioned earlier that, if Pillar I was phased out and there was no Single Farm Payment, the basic conditions, the baseline standards, would be the eligibility criteria for agri-environment schemes. We have targets in place to achieve 60% of agricultural land in what we call our Entry Level Scheme. That would then pick up at least 60% of the agricultural area. In addition, as Dr Phillips mentioned earlier, we are trying to make our Entry Level Schemes more geographically literate, which means identifying in different parts of the country where the most important environmental goods and services need to be delivered. That would include the areas where it was most important that those regulations came into effect. We would therefore be targeting agri-environment schemes to the key areas of need, and the eligibility criteria would be those minimum environmental conditions. I cannot say to you that I can answer the question, "What would happen with the remaining 40%?". It is a wider question of broad-based regulations: the Water Framework Directive, the Soil Directive, the Birds and the Habitats Directives, and all of those sorts of things, some of which we administer, others of which the Environment Agency administers. Essentially, however, we would secure those basic standards by linking the conditions as eligibility criteria for agri-environment.
Chairman: We are getting into an interesting dialogue, but we have to move on, I am afraid.

Q159 Viscount Brookeborough: Your evidence indicates that decoupling has been important. You do not say a great deal about whether you think it has had a really good effect or not, except that you use the word "inertia". Presumably, therefore, you are suggesting that, if it is having an effect, it is not quick enough. How far do you think the effect of decoupling has been masked, or you might say almost overrun, by the strengthening of some agricultural markets? Would you foresee greater environmental impacts if agriculture prices should fall to levels nearer the average of the past decade, accepting that at the moment the grain and milk price in particular is going in entirely the opposite way?
Dr Phillips: The first thing we have to say is that it is pretty early days in terms of decoupling. We need more time to see outcomes through. It undoubtedly has been complicated by the realities of commodity prices and these will probably delay, or possibly defer, the effects of decoupling. This effect is difficult to estimate. Income support through the Single Farm Payment of itself dilutes the economic signals, particularly at times of low prices. Our partnership with the agricultural industry through agri-environment has largely been at times of low commodity prices, albeit we have been through one previous cycle of boom-and-bust. It is about how we persuade good environmental practices as a matter of course, as Lord Plumb referred to earlier, but also how we adjust the rates to reflect the market realities. It is whether that is a case of our having a greater quantum of money, of our being able to offer more money to out-compete commodity prices, or whether the implications of that are fewer environmental goods and services, or perhaps our having to be quite counter-intuitive and being able to almost buy the environmental goods and services that are available to us through the market at the point at which they are available, and sometimes having to put off for a longer period of time some specific habitats or species or other requirements that we might need in a specific geographic locality at a particular point in time.

Q160 Viscount Brookeborough: You suggest that there is a lack of statistics. What do you personally believe is happening out there, in some of the farms? I live in Northern Ireland—I accept that you are England—and we are seeing quite a big change in what people are doing. You suggest that maybe the inertia is partly as a result of Single Farm Payments. I would put it the other way: the very fact that Single Farm Payments are there is allowing quite a lot of change to take place. We are definitely seeing people go out of milk—although I think their decision to go out of milk was about two weeks before the price rise! However, people did cut down on the number of stock immediately. I accept that they may not be your statistics, but is this not happening in England and only happening with us? Or are we simply not collecting the information that we should be? Things will change, or we are seeing them changing very quickly, from the point of view that the markets have dictated that there will be 0% Set-Aside. That will produce 1.6 million hectares of extra land. This will distort all these lovely plans that people have in place for decoupling Single Farm Payments and whatever, will it not?

Mr Young: You have rightly identified that there are significant variations in the way in which people are responding across the country. If we compare the uplands with the arable areas, for example, the capacity of the upland areas to respond to the price signals is limited by the fact that the prices have not changed a great deal for farmers in the uplands; whereas there have been very substantial changes in arable areas. On the face of it, therefore, there will be significant differences, overlaid, from our point of view, with where the environmental benefits are that we want to secure. They are often separated. We might want to secure the environmental benefits in an area where there is no incentive to change, whereas we are less interested in areas where there are major changes being driven through by the decoupling. There are these two different, competing issues. You have this floor price, if you like, created by the Single Farm Payment, which clearly buffers price signals from the market and then, in some parts of the agricultural sector, you now have these very substantial price increases which are pulling people towards changing their cropping, and things of that nature. They are complex things to model, and we are doing some work with Defra on that at the moment. As Dr Phillips said, it is very early days to be able to see where it is heading. We think that it is likely to go in two ways. One is a high degree of extensification—high volume, low inputs; and, at the other end, moving towards niche markets. We are only just picking up signals, as you are, and I do not think that the evidence base is clear in the UK, let alone across Europe.

Dr Phillips: The other thing related to that, which is very important, is that we must not lose the support of the UK taxpayer or the European taxpayer. If they see that they are subsidising the achievement of basic operating requirements at the same time as paying a higher price for their food, it makes it rather a bitter pill to swallow. 80% of the taxpayers who live in cities and towns are getting enormous benefit from what farmers are producing. Unless we can make that very direct connection between what the money is going for and what the benefits are, we will find it very hard to support a programme for which we find it very difficult to see that, for the foreseeable future, we will not have a need.

Q161 *Viscount Brookeborough:* So we have to be more flexible in the areas that we can support?

Dr Phillips: Much more flexible, and a much more direct link about what a public pound has been spent in return for.

Q162 *Lord Plumb:* Modulation is very much related to Pillar I. You want to get rid of Pillar I. You will not get rid of Pillar I until 2014, at best. I think we need to face that, because it has hardly started. A lot of farmers are just beginning to understand what Pillar I is about. A lot of people have not yet been paid. I think that it is rather early days to be saying that we get rid of something, before it has been seen to be properly operating. You want to see an increase in modulation on Pillar I. Is this fair to the United Kingdom? Is it not very much related to structure? If you take the average-sized holding in Romania, for instance—three hectares—how will that relate, if you have a modulation that is increased, to the structure of farming and to the individual farmer?

Dr Phillips: I think that we need to take modulation as compulsory modulation and voluntary modulation. We know that Commissioner Fischer-Boel is obsessed with compulsory modulation and the increase in it, and is very anti voluntary modulation. In our view, compulsory modulation is a good thing on a number of fronts. One is that it gets more money out of the Single Farm Payment and into looking after rural development, in particular buying environmental goods and services. However, we would be anxious about compulsory modulation being sold to the CAP Health Check in such a way that it said that voluntary modulation was not required. As I have already mentioned, 50% of the Environmental Stewardship programme in England is supported by voluntary modulation. As to the funding formula—which I will not endeavour to describe to you, but no doubt David will be able to—every pound of compulsory modulation will not equate with a pound reduction in voluntary modulation—

Q163 *Lord Plumb:* I accept that.

Dr Phillips: . . . because of the complexities of the way in which it works. I think that we need to be very careful. The other thing we need to do is get away from this mantra that high levels of voluntary modulation are some kind of English peculiarity. We talked earlier about the need for a Common Agricultural Policy and, if we still believe in driving towards commons standards for sustainable agriculture across the EU, it is not a level playing field; everyone has not started from the same place; there are a lot of historic accidents as to how funding is distributed; and I think that we need to accept the reality that different economies are in a position to move at different speeds. The fact that you could have a substantial sum of voluntary modulation, with the ability to do that kind of flexing in terms of the speed at which different Member States move towards this common view, is an important tool that can be used in just that way.

Q164 *Lord Cameron of Dillington:* One of the new aspects of land management generally since the last CAP reform is the whole question of climate change. It is a new card that has to be played. I wonder how you feel that any CAP reform could influence the quite considerable impact that agriculture has on climate change in terms of greenhouse gases, and whether perhaps it ought also to look at mitigation concerning the impact of climate change on the natural environment—or maybe that has nothing to do with CAP.

Dr Phillips: Very much so. As you say, there is a very considerable impact of agriculture on climate change. It is accountable for 9% of greenhouse gas emissions across the EU and the second-highest producer of methane in the UK after the energy industry. It is a big impact. It is therefore very important that we think about what the contribution of agriculture is on two fronts. One is mitigating the rural impact in terms of contributing towards climate change. For me, that is all about sustainable practices; for instance, less use of fertilizers, more sensible use of agricultural wastes; but also thinking about what contribution agriculture can make, both in terms of mitigating and adapting to climate change. I think that there is an absolutely and utterly unique role here for agriculture; it is a very important one and one that no other sector can play. If we think about mitigation straight off, there is the better management of peat soils. We have just had a piece of work done, in collaboration with Durham University, which shows that, if you let peat soils continue to degrade at the current rate, we will have a net contribution of carbon emissions of 400,000 kilotonnes a year. Yet, if we were to embark on a programme of peat restoration, we would have a net sink of carbon of 40,000 kilotonnes a year. Peat restoration costs millions of pounds, but it does not cost tens of millions of pounds. When you come from the environmental sector, you can begin to talk yourself into what a lot of money this is. When you think about the investments in some other carbon management and mitigation measures, it is actually a very cost-effective way of going about carbon mitigation. There is also the role of adaptation. If you think about species and habitats' requirements to move in the face of new climate change scenarios, a landscape-scale response will be required. It is not just about what can be achieved on a particular farm or a particular holding; it is about how, for example, we can get wildlife corridors established in such a way that we can see migration either northwards, or eastwards, or uphill. That will involve co-ordination, joint working, and investment in it in a way that we have never invested in it in the past. If you think about the Climate Change Bill and the requirement to report on climate change adaptation every five years—a pretty mild measure but nevertheless we are

glad to see it—we will have to be able to point to what some of the land use responses to that have been, and agri-environment schemes would lend themselves terrifically to making that a reality. It is something we could point to on a map that we have managed to do in terms of joining up these landscapes and these habitats. As I said in an earlier answer when I gave you what the additional requirement is, that is without factoring in that requirement. We must think about that not only in terms of the economics of CAP, but also in the economics of the investment we are making in carbon management more widely.

Q165 *Lord Cameron of Dillington:* One of the problems is that food is an international commodity, and you were talking about the difference between food security and food self-sufficiency. In the future, there will be a real problem with world food security. The IPCC has just produced a report saying that northern Europe is probably one of the best places to produce food for the world because every other area will be very badly affected by droughts, flooding, storms, and so on. If we stop producing food because we have a greater priority for the environment, are we not exporting the climate change problems elsewhere? In China, the Yellow River now fails to reach the sea for a large part of the year because there is so much irrigation and production going on in that area. I think that one has to look at it in a world situation.

Mr Young: It brings us back to our earlier point about the need for fully international standards that are accepted globally for sustainable agriculture. Simply because we do not have that level playing field at the moment, we have to be very careful that we do not walk away from appropriate standards for the natural environment in Europe. As I mentioned before, we think that there has been a very considerable effort to allow agriculture to adjust structurally to be more responsive to markets, to expand its production, while retaining those environmental standards. It is really important, therefore, that that continues to be a core part of the purposes of CAP or its successor and, as Dr Phillips said, becomes something of a blueprint for sustainable agriculture globally.

Dr Phillips: There are the very practical things that we need to see. We could do lots about our 2010 target or our 2050 target by contracting agriculture in the UK. That is clearly not the answer if it is going to go somewhere else. However, there are at least three ways to reduce emissions: production methods with a lower greenhouse gas contribution; practices which encourage the retaining of carbon in soils; but, equally importantly, food prices that reflect the externalities.

Q166 Lord Cameron of Dillington: Touching on another area, the question of biofuels, you talk about international accreditation, which we certainly supported in our report on that subject. How would you see that international accreditation working?

Dr Phillips: Biofuels can make an important contribution to energy security and to environmental protection, if it is done in the right way. If we take the example of biofuels from wheat, you can see a net greenhouse gas saving of somewhere between plus-77% to minus 7%, depending on what the production pathway has been. That is just one of a number of examples. It totally underlies the fact that any accreditation system needs, for us, to be based on two central planks. One is what the total greenhouse gas coefficient is; the second is what the other elements of the sustainability of its production are, not least of all biodiversity. However, in that regard we need to make sure that we avoid production subsidies for biofuels, because, with that, we will see all the things that we do not want, such as very big monocultures of biofuels. I think that the mechanism that the EU immediately has at its disposal is to make sure that no bio-energy, other than those produced in accordance with this standard, is accepted as part of the contribution to the UK target on bio-energies.

Q167 Viscount Ullswater: Perhaps I could go back to these agri-environment schemes. I think that originally the agri-environment policies evolved from policies concerned primarily with agricultural production. Dr Phillips, in your evidence as well as in what you have told us today, you were concerned about renting them rather than buying them. We have not moved to the stage of buying them yet. I would like to hear what you think about the future, because I notice also from your written evidence that you said that Natural England would lead on developing new agri-environmental schemes. Is your concept to develop the SSSIs, to develop the SPAs, to give your wildlife corridors or landscape features? How will you buy these? How will they be secured, in the sense of having purchased them for future enjoyment of the landscape?

Dr Phillips: I wish I knew the answer to how to get them in perpetuity rather than rent them. I suppose that it is just being faced with the awful reality of the expiry of the classic schemes. We have had some fabulous environmental benefits from, for example, the Countryside Stewardship Scheme. Needless to say, we have to model when those schemes fall out of payment. When you look at the schemes that will be coming out and you try to see what the options are for those schemes in the future, there is only a portion of them that will be suitable for Higher Level Stewardship and some of them that will be suitable for Entry Level Stewardship. You think that there is something very wrong in a situation where, almost

overnight, you can reverse the effect you will be having on that landscape. Of course that will not always be the case because, as Lord Plumb said earlier, a lot of agri-environment payments are actually about winning hearts and minds, and once these practices are established they continue. However, it is not always the case. We therefore need to give some serious consideration, in the context not only of the Health Check but of the wider suite of CAP reforms, to how we get some mechanisms to do that—but in a way that does not frighten farmers from participating in these schemes in the first place. Nobody wants to think that their land is being nationalised by the back door, but it is a ripe area for further consideration. If I understood the second part of your question about SSSIs, SPAs, and the linking of that to the climate change adaptation point, it is a very helpful prompt. We certainly do not think that the only way in which we can get climate change adaptation is by applying incentives to farmers and land managers. We were very actively considering what our role in landscape designation could be in that regard—so that we designate areas of outstanding natural beauty, national parks, and so on. They have done spectacularly well in terms of their original purpose. However, if we were to say in a similar way that we maybe should not be thinking about what some of the modern pressures and requirements of those are, are the criteria for designation actually achieving the full suite of objectives in the same way? It is not that we are suggesting that farmers should be single-handedly charging to the rescue on that, but looking at what the other options are and how we could augment and support it.

Mr Young: Also, a key part of what we are doing is focusing on where the most important areas are that will need to be secured for the future. At the moment, the agri-environment schemes are very broad-based, but we are working with the Environment Agency and other organisations to home in on where the areas that are delivering the multiple benefits for the environment are which will be compromised by climate change or other things, for which we may need new levers and mechanisms. So we are taking some of the early first steps to try to answer the questions, I suppose, albeit we do not have the perfect answers to them.

Dr Phillips: We share with you a frightening fact. If you look at where the rural development funding has been invested over the last programme and compare it with where it is planned to invest that money for the period 2007-13, there is quite a big mismatch. What we have done for the period 2007-13 is to take regional targeting statements, which some of you may be familiar with—it is a kind of list of everything that rural development funding could possibly do for the rural environment—and to overlay those geographically. At the end of the day, it was decided that this was a multi-objective scheme for multifunctional agriculture. You think, "This shouldn't be a slavish criterion, but it should certainly inform judgments about where the funding goes". If a key requirement of that judgment is to get the most benefits in any particular location, there is only about a 50% match between where that funding is currently going and where it will go in future. That is not to say that you could do a wholesale shift, because there will be examples, for instance, where there is a particular species or scheduled ancient monument that is out there, where there is no other benefit that will come for it and where it needs to be looked after; but if you take the principle that by and large it is about getting the most multiple benefits, there is a considerable mismatch. That has been a lot of our focus in terms of the current review of Environmental Stewardship that I mentioned, about getting better targeting of HLS and targeting geographically on ELS.

Q168 *Viscount Ullswater:* Do you see a balance between the East of England and the West of England—corn and horn? Do you see an equal balance between the two?
Dr Phillips: I am not sure I know what you mean by an equal balance.

Q169 *Viscount Ullswater:* Where are you looking to improve the environment? Is it in the uplands? Is it in the West Country? Or is it in East Anglia and Lincolnshire? They are two very different environments and I am wondering where the balance might be in the funding.
Mr Young: The targeting that we are doing is being done at both a national level and at a regional level. The sorts of outcomes that we might want to secure in one part of the country will vary from others. In the uplands, there are important areas for biodiversity protection, carbon mitigation, and so on. In the arable areas, we will obviously need to pay particular attention to things, certainly in the Environment Agency, such as water quality. We need to make sure that the targeting reflects what it is we need that land to be delivering in terms of public goods. It is also giving us an opportunity to look at what we want, as well as where the priorities should be. We are doing that both nationally and regionally.

Q170 *Chairman:* Can I ask you this? You may think that it is an impertinent question, and I really want a very short answer. I think that you have demonstrated quite clearly how rural development spend can contribute and does contribute to the rural environment. Can I ask you the question the other way round? How does agri-environment spend enhance rural development?
Dr Phillips: There is some pretty compelling evidence about prosperous rural environments being dependent on high-quality environments. At the risk of being equally impertinent, I would move beyond the rural to the urban, because I think that we get very fixated about this being money for rural communities. We need to link it to the fact that it is a benefit more for urban communities often than it is for rural communities.
Chairman: Thank you very much indeed. It has been a great pleasure.

WEDNESDAY 17 OCTOBER 2007

Present   Bach, L   Moynihan, L
                   Brookeborough, V   Palmer, L
                   Cameron of Dillington, L   Plumb, L
                   Greaves, L   Sewel, L (Chairman)
                   Jones of Whitchurch, B   Ullswater, V

Memorandum by the Environment Agency

SUMMARY

The Environment Agency welcomes this opportunity to submit evidence on *The Future of the Common Agricultural Policy*. In particular we are keen to emphasise:

— In the longer term, sustainable rural land management requires that the Common Agricultural Policy (CAP) should be replaced with an adequately funded European common rural policy, addressing issues across the whole rural environment and economy. Public money should be used to secure public goods and services, including clean water, healthy soils and robust wildlife.

— In the shorter term, the CAP Health Check should deliver a policy in which there is a greater transfer of funding from Pillar I (direct payments) to Pillar II (rural development) through a significantly higher rate of compulsory modulation, whilst retaining the ability for the UK to use voluntary modulation if needed. This would be allied with simplified and robust cross compliance protecting the environment.

— It is essential that CAP reform allows us to provide greater resources to Rural Development Programmes in England and Wales, in order to deliver all that is required.

— The CAP should ensure that the production of energy crops does not cause environmental degradation or loss of biodiversity and takes place within the context of overall energy use being significantly reduced.

1. INTRODUCTION

Almost three-quarters of the land in England and Wales is used for agriculture. Whilst there are positive environmental outcomes from farming, there are also many negative ones and costs. For example, almost half of groundwaters used for public drinking water supply now require some form of treatment, due in large part to nitrate pollution, whilst monitoring and/or removing pesticides from water costs consumers around £120m p.a. It has been estimated that agriculture contributes to 14% of total flood events costing £128m p.a.

Taken individually, very few farms create substantial environmental problems, but the combination of small problems from over 100,000 farms adds up to a significant environmental impact. We consider that tackling these issues requires a spectrum of solutions, from regulation to advice and including the justified use of incentives to purchase public goods and services. Our work seeks to influence all of these issues to improve environmental outcomes.

RESPONSES TO QUESTIONS

Our responses to specific questions/points in the consultation are as follows.

Q1. *What should be the long-term objectives of the CAP? Does the title "Common Agricultural Policy" aptly fit your perceived objectives of the policy? What do you consider to be the main pressures on the CAP as it currently is?*

Our objective when seeking to influence rural land management is to reduce overall environmental impact, minimising negative effects and increasing positive ones. Through regulation and advice we promote sustainable rural land management and encourage land managers to safeguard natural and cultural heritage. We wish to see publicly funded incentives used appropriately to support this work. It is our view that the long-term objective of the CAP should be to promote sustainable development across the rural environment and economy as a whole, with agriculture as an important component.

Over the next 10–15 years we see land management expanding beyond traditional farming and forestry to cover the provision of a growing range of environmental goods and services, including adaptation to climate change. We want to see "traditional" environmental interests such as soil and water conservation, biodiversity conservation, access and cultural issues recognised as being critical in adaptation to climate change and building robust rural economies.

The Environment Agency has a long-term vision for rural landscapes in England and Wales where:

— Agriculture is profitable and provides net environmental benefit as part of a thriving rural economy.

— Land managers have adapted to climate change, reducing flooding impacts and planning for drought.

— Through the Water Framework Directive (WFD), land managers understand and accept their polluting impacts on the environment and are working to reduce them.

— Agricultural production uses low carbon techniques, for example with minimal inputs of energy and artificial fertilisers, using waste streams to generate energy.

— Biomass and biofuel crops help mitigate climate change without environmental damage.

This vision is based on a number of principles, including the recognition that a high quality environment is a social and economic asset, giving businesses a competitive edge and improving the quality of life for both rural and urban populations.[1] We also believe that recipients of public subsidy should provide a range of services to society including sustainable management of soil, water and air, maintenance of locally distinctive landscapes and enhanced biodiversity. This should be underpinned by compliance with minimum statutory standards related to the environment, animal welfare, public health and countryside access.

Delivering this vision will require both tactical and strategic changes to the CAP. In our view the current aims of the CAP are confused and unclear, it has moved away from its aims as expressed in the Treaty of Rome but has not clearly articulated its new end objectives. In the longer term EU strategy should be to:

— Replace the CAP with an adequately funded European common rural policy that aims to secure sustainable land management in light of European Union (EU) commitments on climate change, water and biodiversity.

— This new European common rural policy should pay for the public benefits delivered by rural land management where those benefits are not rewarded through the market.

— Such support should help regenerate the rural economy, by directly sustaining and creating jobs in land management and by supporting related activities. There should also be investment support for a wider range of rural business development, training and capacity building and for changes in land management and land acquisition which bring added environmental benefits.

The move towards de-coupled support in the 2003 CAP reforms and the accompanying emphasis on a sustainable EU rural development policy is a welcome step in the right direction and has reduced negative impacts of the CAP. However, much more needs to be done to ensure that in the short-term financial support to the agricultural sector is directly linked to sustainable land management and clearly defined environmental outcomes. A favourable outcome from the CAP Health Check would be the first step towards achieving this longer-term vision. The key changes we would like to see are:

— A further transfer of funding from Pillar I to Pillar II through a significantly higher rate of compulsory modulation, emphasising a direction of travel that progressively strengthens Pillar 2 and removes Pillar 1.

[1] Land Use Consultants (2005) The environment, economic growth and competitiveness—the environment as an economic driver. Prepared for European Regional Policy Group, October 2005.

— Continued ability to raise additional funds through voluntary modulation.

— Cross-compliance conditions maintained and streamlined through tighter targeting underpinned by appropriate environmental standards.

— Administrative improvements to the implementation of cross compliance such as tolerance for minor non-compliance and harmonisation of control rates.

— Measures taken to ensure that if set-aside is abolished, the scale of environmental benefits are retained.

— Biofuel production to be associated with strict environmental standards and a requirement to provide a net reduction in greenhouse gases.

Q2. *What has been your experience so far with the reformed CAP? What has gone well and less well? And where can lessons be learnt?*

Factual data on the changes that have occurred since decoupling began to be implemented in UK are limited, hampered by the fact that many changes in land management take place relatively slowly, at least at first, so environmental changes take time to emerge. It is also often difficult to relate cause and effect, given the wide range of decisions unrelated to the CAP which affect land management.

Work to predict impacts indicates that there will be both positive and negative effects. For example, there is evidence to suggest that farmers are already making increased use of buffer strips of uncultivated land alongside water courses and other sensitive habitats which will help reduce the risks of diffuse water pollution. On the other hand, there are potential risks to biodiversity in the arable sector from an increase in block cropping and simplified crop rotations that could reduce habitat diversity.

We expect that the introduction of cross compliance and Good Agricultural and Environment Condition (GAEC) rules will bring about a gradual improvement in basic environmental management standards on farms, regardless of how they are changing due to other policy drivers. The Environment Agency has Competent Control Authority status for cross compliance relating to Groundwater Regulations, the Nitrate Action Programme and Sewage Sludge Regulations. To date, minor breaches of the Nitrate Action Programme (ie poor record keeping) are one of the most common non-compliance issues. We consider that over time (and for as long as it remains), cross compliance should be extended by adding more simple controls over a wider range of topics.

Our recent report with the National Farmers Union (NFU) and Farmers Union of Wales (FUW) into the state of the farmed environment[2] strongly indicated the need to reduce diffuse water pollution from farming. Our early experience with the England Catchment Sensitive Farming Delivery Initiative indicates that farmers are capable of significantly reducing their environmental impacts once they accept that there is a need to do so, and realise how they can achieve it. The means of reducing impact differs from farm to farm. Sometimes it is a matter of better compliance with regulation, other times it requires changes in land use or land management outside the requirements of regulation. In the latter case some additional incentive is required and rural development funding will be essential for this.

Q3. *Do you consider the Single Payment Scheme (SPS) to be a good basis for the future of EU agricultural policy? What changes might be made at the EU level to the SPS, including to the rules governing entitlements, in the short and/or longer term?*

Our long term vision for rural land management (see Q1) is that the CAP, and therefore the SPS, is replaced with an adequately funded European common rural policy that aims to secure sustainable land management in light of EU commitments on climate change, water and biodiversity. Public money should be used in return for the delivery of public goods, including clean water, healthy soils and robust wildlife.

The SPS, which is intended as "income support", is a flawed basis from which to deliver the environmental outcomes we are seeking. However, there is evidence that it is not an effective way to deliver income support either as it is diverted into capital value. In the short-term the continuing presence of the SPS offers opportunities to restrict further environmental damage via cross compliance. However, as the SPS reduces in value so the influence of cross compliance will decrease, particularly in the face of improved commodity prices. This emphasises the need to develop a robust, well-funded and properly targeted rural policy.

---

[2] Environment Agency, NFU & FUW (2006) Good Farming, Better Environment, December 2006.

Q4. *What short and long-term changes are required to the CAP's market mechanisms? Suggestions made by the Commission have included re-examination of certain quotas, intervention, set-aside, export refunds and private storage payments.*

Set-aside currently provides a reservoir of largely uncropped land over about 3% of agricultural land in England and Wales. This includes highly intensive arable areas where there is low cover of semi-natural habitat and participation in agri-environment schemes is low. Evidence suggests, although introduced for purely market management reasons, set-aside has delivered environmental benefits for biodiversity, soil and water protection. However these benefits largely depend on how set-aside is managed and do not accrue when set-aside land is used to grow industrial crops.

The Environment Agency, working with the other UK countryside and environment agencies as the Land Use Policy Group, recently commissioned research into alternative policy options for retaining the largely accidental environmental benefits of set-aside.[3] This indicates that the most realistic and beneficial way to retain the environmental benefits of set-aside would be to develop a package in which:.

— General widespread environmental protection benefits arising from set-aside are delivered through adapted cross compliance conditions;

— Specific, high value, environmental benefits arising from set-aside are delivered through agri-environment targeted measures;

Q5. *What is your view on the introduction of the European Agricultural Fund for Rural Development (EAFRD)? Do you consider that it is meeting its objectives thus far? Is it suitably strategic in nature, meeting the needs of rural society as a whole rather than being restricted to aiding the agricultural industry? How well is it being co-ordinated with other EU and national policies on regional and rural development?*

It is still very early to comment on whether EAFRD is meeting its objectives. The Rural Development Programmes (RDP) for 2007–13 are the first to operate in the reformed CAP environment post-2003, and these programmes are yet to be approved. EAFRD has a legacy of focus on the agricultural industry, and a relatively small amount of funding is dedicated to the wider rural community.

Agri-environment schemes have traditionally been the main focus of rural development in UK. These schemes have now been in operation for over a decade, and there is clear evidence they have generated positive environmental outcomes. In our view, agri-environment schemes are essential to raise the general level of performance on resource protection and reduce soil erosion and water pollution. They are a positive mechanism for engaging with the farming community.

Of all the human activities contributing to pollution, farming is one of the most significant: Over 75% of the land area of England and Wales is farmed, contributing on average to 60% of nitrate and around a third of phosphate pollution. Failure to tackle diffuse water pollution is very likely to result in the UK failing to achieve the objectives of the Water Framework Directive (WFD) in 2015. It has been identified as the main threat to achieving "good ecological status". WFD objectives aim to ensure that the water environment is in a fit state to serve the needs of the whole community. Early work on the WFD indicates that to achieve the objectives will require use of a full suite of measures from regulation to incentive. Defra has built full use of its agri-environment programme, Environmental Stewardship, into its baseline assumptions on how to achieve WFD objectives in England and we welcome this.

In England and Wales most EAFRD funding will be spent in the agri-environment objective of Axis 2, and its application is restricted because it must be related to income foregone by the land manager. This is an area of concern in the uplands, where income achievable per hectare is relatively low, meaning that agri-environment schemes are much less attractive. If significant management effort or change of practice is required, or particularly capital expenditure, then the schemes are unlikely to attract entrants. EAFRD should provide a mechanism more easily tailored to achieving environmental objectives in the uplands, which are areas of great importance for water quality and reduction of flood risk.

---

[3] Silcock P & Lovegrove C (2007) Retaining the environmental benefits of set-aside—a policy options paper. Report prepared for the Land Use Policy Group, April 2007. www.lupg.org.uk

Q6. *Is there a case for a higher level of EU financing for rural development? Do you have a view on the extension of compulsory modulation from Pillar I (direct payments) to Pillar II (rural development)?*

Rural development funding is essential for the delivery of water, climate change and biodiversity outcomes. It is one of a number of mechanisms, but is a vital part of the policy framework. Our aspiration is for an expanded RDP by 2013, including an enhanced Higher Level Stewardship Scheme. Natural England's best estimates of spending need for ES are approximately £500–700m per year. Any validation of this figure needs to ensure ES meets not only biodiversity, access and landscape objectives but also resource protection of air, land and water. The recently announced RDP budget for England, which draws on voluntary and compulsory modulation money plus domestic match funding, allocates approximately £414m per year to ES.

Due to the allocation criteria for the EU rural development budget being based on historical spend, the UK receives a disproportionately small amount of the budget. The 2003 CAP reforms introduced compulsory modulation (CM), which must be co-financed. However, even with CM, higher levels of RD funding are still needed by the UK Government to deliver its environmental commitments. As such we have supported Defra in pursuing the ability to generate additional resources via voluntary modulation (VM) and exchequer co-financing.

In the short term we support a further transfer of funding from Pillar I to Pillar II through a higher rate of compulsory modulation. However this must be combined with the continued ability to raise additional funds through voluntary modulation and a better system of allocating rural development funding, This places more emphasis on agricultural area and less on past spend.

Modulation is an ungainly device, currently favoured simply because it is the only available means of switching money from Pillar I to Pillar II. Longer term, we expect to see a detailed review of the CAP budget, resulting in a fundamental re-balancing between Pillars I and II.

Q7. *What benefits can the EU's World Trade Organisation obligations create for EU agriculture and, consequently, for the EU economy as a whole?*

We believe that the EU involvement in World Trade Organisation negotiations should be used to raise environmental standards globally. Without a level playing field of high environmental standards, or full internalisation of environmental costs into market prices, higher standards in the EU may push unsound practices to other countries, often developing countries with even more fragile environments and potentially less robust regulatory frameworks to protect them.

Q8. *To what extent has the system of cross compliance contributed to an improved level of environmental protection? How is it linking with other EU policy requirements such as the Water Framework Directive?*

Cross compliance in its present form is still relatively young, starting in January 2005. As a result only the short-term impacts are becoming evident now, and even these need to be estimated as there are no published evaluations of cross compliance yet. In the meantime there is a need for policymakers to consider the future of cross compliance, firstly to ensure that it achieves its current objectives and secondly to influence the future shape of the CAP.

With this in mind, the Environment Agency, working with the other UK countryside and environment agencies, recently commissioned some research into policy options for the future of cross compliance.[4] This found that within the common framework, Member States have implemented cross compliance in a variety of ways. There appears to be most variety in respect of GAEC.

Key factors which influence the extent to which cross compliance achieves its objectives, and hence its environmental outcomes, include:

— The standards established by Member States; ie the Statutory Management Requirements (SMRs), GAEC and permanent pasture rules which farmers must comply with.

— The information provided to farmers, including the content and comprehensiveness of information and delivery systems).

— The systems of control and payment reductions.

In broad terms, it seems likely that cross compliance will have a positive impact on specific environmental issues including water quality, soils, biodiversity, landscape and the historic environment. In addition cross compliance is likely to improve compliance with SMRs where there have been compliance issues (eg

---

[4]   Silcock P & Swales V (2007) Cross compliance—a policy options paper. Report prepared for the Land Use Policy Group, April 2007 (draft).

Groundwater and Nitrates Directives); improve compliance with other environmental regulations; establish baseline standards for land and environmental management; and improve farmer awareness of environmental issues. Cross compliance also appears to add value to agri-environment schemes by helping to reduce the gap between every-day farming systems and practices and agri-environment schemes, and enabling agri-environment schemes to focus on environmental maintenance and enhancement, as opposed to protection.

Future policy options for cross compliance will need to extend and enhance the environmental and other public benefits being delivered through the current system, and be in line with key principles underlying the future development of the CAP. These include focusing on environmental and other priorities, reducing cost, simplification, improving/maintaining competitiveness.

In the short term, there are a number of administrative improvements to improve the effectiveness of the cross compliance system, including and building on the proposals set out in the Commission's March paper.[5] We welcome many of the Commission's proposals including tolerance for minor non-compliance and harmonisation of control rates. We consider that additional changes could also be considered in the short term including:

— Adopting a risk-based approach to inspections (something we already do as a Competent Control Authority).

— Allowing Member States to retain more/all of the payment reductions to help finance the cross compliance system or fund technical assistance to farmers.

The scope of the cross compliance standards could be expanded. For example, could they be expanded by adding Directives to the existing 19 Statutory Management Requirements. Two potential candidates are selected measures from the Water Framework Directive and aspects of the forthcoming Soil Directive, both important pieces of environmental legislation that will have an impact on agricultural practices.

CAP reform to remove subsidy under Pillar I payments suggests the end for cross compliance. We consider that in future eligibility for rural development payments should be tied to undertaking certain activities or meeting certain standards, which could ultimately replace the baseline requirements of cross compliance.

Q9. *How can the CAP contribute to mitigation of, and adaptation to, climate change? What do you consider the role of biofuels to be in this regard?*

Biofuels for transport energy are governed by other European policies. There is concern that the EU is setting mandatory targets that can not be effectively serviced by land without increasing pressures on other resources, especially water quality. The Environment Agency believes there should be mandatory environmental and carbon reporting requirements to ensure that these crops do not cause or undo the benefits that will be realised by existing Pillar II funding.

It is likely that mitigating climate change through providing energy from land can be more effectively promoted by supporting the provision of infrastructure to process fuel, rather than subsidising growing bioenergy crops. Once there is a demand for biofuels and/or biomass then farmers will respond to the market by producing them. An important further area for public expenditure is the research and development of much more efficient biofuel crops and production methods. All of this should only be done in the context of significantly reducing overall energy use. There is scope to do much more in UK and some other member states to support producing energy from anaerobic digestion of crops and of manure.

Mitigation can also be improved by making better use of soil as a carbon store, moving from an overall addition of carbon to the atmosphere, the current situation in UK and probably other Member States, to an overall reduction. This is likely to prove challenging as climate change will increase the rate of loss from soils. Improving carbon capture on rural land can be done in two ways, by preventing further deterioration in peat bogs and returning them towards their previous state, and by changing agricultural practice to reduce carbon loss from farming operations. Both of these are more suited to an incentive approach rather than regulation and would be an appropriate use of rural development funding.

With regard to adaptation, agriculture and rural land use in general can provide public goods in terms of reducing the severity of the impacts of climate change on flood risk from rivers. This would be an appropriate use of rural development funding. There will also be impacts on land from the abandonment of river defences, from coastal re-alignment and managed retreat as sea levels rise. In order to maintain food production, agriculture will need to adapt now for expected climate change implications of water resources. In order to

---

[5] Report from European Commission to Council on the application of the system of cross-compliance.

provide for future water requirements sustainably, land managers will be encouraged to provide for their water resource needs, particularly by providing for winter water storage. Climate change is likely to worsen the risks and impacts of diffuse water pollution. This increases the need to address the issue.

Q10. *The Commissioner has expressed her dissatisfaction at the financing agreement reached by the Member States at the December 2005 Council. Do you consider the current budget to be sufficient? Do you consider co-financing to be a possible way forward in financing the CAP?*

The current CAP budget is significant in financial terms, representing around half of the EU budget. However, post-decoupling, the CAP lacks clear policy objectives so that it is not possible to assess whether its budget is sufficient to achieve those objectives. As subsidies are distributed to landowners in proportion to land possession, it would be fair to say that the original objectives of the CAP as in the Treaty of Rome, "to ensure a fair standard of living to farmers", is not met. This does not necessarily mean that the budget is not sufficient, but that it may not be distributed effectively to that end.

The question of whether current budget allocation would suffice for land management purposes with clear environmental outcomes is far more difficult to assess. This sort of assessment should take place as part of the discussions on the future of the CAP after the Health Check.

We are not in a position to estimate costs for achieving the Environment Agency's vision for sustainable rural land management across Europe. We know that to achieve it will have costs because land management for public goods as well as private profit will come at a price. We suggest that the current CAP budget should be secured for the delivery of public goods. Rural development is around 15% of the current budget total, so there is scope for very significant expansion of rural development spending whilst still leaving room for reduction in the overall budget spent on rural issues.

Q11. *What has been the impact on the CAP of the 2004 and 2007 enlargements and what is the likely impact of future enlargements of the EU on post-2013 CAP?*

Abandonment and intensification are the biggest threats to the farmed environment in the new Member States. Evidence already shows that farmland bird populations have started declining,[6] largely due to agricultural intensification. Farmers are taking advantage of Pillar I payments (which until 2006 were "topped up" with Pillar II money) to restructure their businesses. In addition, considerable political pressure means that rural development and agri environment funds are being used to increase productivity rather than deliver environmental protection/enhancement. There is significant investment in farm machinery and artificial inputs in arable areas whilst traditionally managed, high nature value farming systems such as low/no input grasslands are increasingly being abandoned or taken over by larger farms and managed more intensively. As a result of CAP payments, farm incomes in the new Member States are forecast to rise 42% between 2005–13.

Future enlargements of the EU will put significant pressure on the CAP budget, and are likely to lead to widespread environmental degradation in its current guise. This reinforces the need for a defendable policy that supports the delivery of public goods in exchange for public money.

Q12. *How could the CAP be further simplified and in what ways would you like to see the CAP changed in the short and/or long term?*

As identified above, in the longer-term the Environment Agency would prefer to see the CAP replaced by a single EU rural policy providing for sustainable rural land management in all economic sectors active in rural areas, not just agriculture. In the short-term, we would wish to see the CAP significantly simplified and environmental outputs enhanced, particularly in relation to cross compliance and set-aside as suggested above.

June 2007

---

6   6 RSPB (2006) Farmland birds and agri-environment schemes in the new Member States.

Examination of Witnesses

Witnesses: BARONESS YOUNG OF OLD SCONE, a Member of the House of Lords, Chief Executive, Ms AILEEN KIRMOND, Head of Land Quality, and Ms HANNAH BARTRAM, Senior Agriculture Policy Adviser, the Environment Agency, examined.

Q171 *Chairman:* Welcome and thank you very much for coming. Perhaps you would like to make an opening comment and then we can get on to questions and answers.

Baroness Young of Old Scone: We have only one flippant comment and one serious comment to make. One flippant comment is that it feels a bit like an exam. Natural England comes in and then we come in, and we hope our answers are relevant!

Q172 *Chairman:* I am going to stop you there straightaway, because when we had a look at the evidence from your two organisations, in the context of an exam, we thought that there had been a little bit of plagiarism!

Baroness Young of Old Scone: Collusion perhaps, rather than plagiarism. I think that it is true to say that, through the Land Use Policy Group, we do work very closely with Natural England and indeed with some of the NGOs on these issues, because they are so large that they can only be done by harnessing the resources of all of us. That was one point, therefore. The more serious point is that, though the Health Check is important, our slight concern is that there is quite a lot of political focus on the Health Check rather than on the longer-term review of CAP. We would be very anxious to make sure that people are clear about what the vision for the future is, and indeed what land is for in the future. I know that the Government is prompting a foresight study into what land is for, and we think that is an extremely valuable exercise, because we are asking a lot of the land these days.

Q173 *Chairman:* We are very happy to look at the longer term rather than just the immediate issues that arise in the context of the Health Check. Let us make a start. I suppose the first question is what progress do you think you have made in securing your goals through the 2003 CAP reform, and to what extent has decoupling led to a change in farmer behaviour in directions favourable to the environment? In other words, what has been the effect, from your perspective, of the 2003 reform?

Baroness Young of Old Scone: It is probably a little early to tell, because many of the provisions did not actually start in earnest until 2005; and of course many of the things that land management delivers take a bit of time to run through into environmental outcomes. They are also masked to some extent by a range of other factors, and so it is sometimes difficult to see the cause-and-effect impact—regulatory issues, consumer demands, the weather. We have had two years of drought and one year of floods, and so all of those are having an impact on outcomes. However, our belief is that some of the measures are worthwhile. Cross-compliance, we believe, has brought an increased focus on basic environmental management standards on farms. Compulsory modulation, of course, has brought additional funding; so we are pleased about that. We see decoupling as a step on the route to a longer-term future of CAP as a system of payments based on delivery of public benefits generally. At the moment, with the Single Farm Payment, other than through the cross-compliance regime, it is quite a worry that, as some of the market signals are getting stronger, particularly with the price of wheat and with the future buoyancy of biofuels, we could in fact find ourselves in the position where we have a fairly weak set of instruments to deliver the public goods, and the decoupling mechanism no longer acting as an influencer of the response to the market. Those are the sorts of issues, therefore. Generally speaking, cropping area up; livestock numbers down. There are a load of differential impacts that we could go through. More sheep in the lowlands, having come down the hill; larger dairy farms, and worries about that because of the pollution impacts of the dairy sector; block cropping and simplified crop rotations, which are not good for habitat diversity. However, there are some positive impacts: the reduced impacts on grassland; greater use of buffer strips around watercourses. I think that it is a mixed picture, and it will only be over the next few years that we will see the full outcome.

Q174 *Chairman:* You argue that a future EU rural policy replacing the CAP should provide support for rural land management in all economic sectors active in rural areas. What are the public benefits of supporting businesses because they are situated in rural areas? There is a definitional problem. How do we start defining and drawing lines on maps on what are rural areas and what are not? And I live in Banchory!

Ms Kirmond: The thing that we are arguing for is this long-term picture. Rather than constantly revisiting CAP, to argue for an upwardly funded EU rural policy that addresses issues across the whole rural economy of the UK; not just picking a bit, looking after it and trying to make it healthy at the cost of something else. I think that is quite important, because the rural environment is not just about farming; it is about the health and welfare of our rural communities. As we well know, although we have lots of problems in urban communities and we tend to focus on them, there are a lot of issues in rural communities as well, about rural poverty, unemployment, immobility, and a reduction in rural services. There are some interesting issues there about how sustainable farming supports rural communities, and that agriculture is a really important component of that healthy rural economy. A healthy rural economy has agriculture at the heart of it. However, I think that there is some very interesting work that colleagues in the Countryside Council for Wales have undertaken on what benefits flow to rural communities from investment, through things like the environment payments and so on, which means that you get more money being paid locally; local businesses are supported because people are staying on the land; they are doing something on the land; they are associated with it. There are indications out there in reality, therefore, that you can maintain people on the land; you can maintain a healthy rural economy—or you can help to maintain it—by directing funding at healthy farming, because benefits flow from it.

Baroness Young of Old Scone: Could I add to that? At the moment, we already have Axes 1 and 3 putting funding into improving competitiveness and diversification of the rural areas. We think that there is scope for more of that. I have just come from seeing a very good anaerobic digestion system for mixed pig slurry and "dead" Marks & Sparks sandwiches—

Q175 *Chairman:* That must have been a very rewarding experience!

Baroness Young of Old Scone: It was rewarding and redolent—I think the word is! There was an example of grants for anaerobic digesters for on-farm slurry disposal and processing, to produce energy for the grid and a more readily available nitrogen source for spreading on fields, and solving a food waste problem at the same time. That sort of thing is not farming *per se* but it is an extremely useful adjunct to farming.

Ms Kirmond: Certainly we are seeing rural land use diversifying and we are looking at things like bio-energy production, recreation, lots of access issues to the countryside. It is not just about paying farmers to stay on the land and spending money like that; it is looking at profitable farming providing net environmental benefit as well, because that is a very valuable commodity. It is also about building competitiveness in farming. It is enabling people to do things for themselves, rather than just being paid to do it, which is quite important. Coming back to my colleague's point about Defra's commitment to land use and a land use policy, we certainly welcome Defra's commitment to that land use strategy. We will have to take in both urban and rural; we will have to have a partnership with the CLG as well as Defra to look at the context of land use and what land is for in the future, across all our communities, not just

rural. It is a great opportunity that we have a commitment to a foresight study starting very soon, to start looking at what land could be used for in this country in the 21st century.

Q176 *Lord Plumb:* Could I ask whether you see this built into Pillar II? I think we would readily agree that there has to be a switch from Pillar I to Pillar II in terms of the use of resources. Some of the things you have suggested would have an appeal right across rural areas, but will that be an addition to what already exists in Pillar II? If I may, perhaps I could use the example you have used. I am a great believer in farmers putting in anaerobic digesters. There is methane gas coming from a lot of animals. I speak from experience when I say that we could heat the whole of the buildings, the house, the dairies and all the rest of it—or we did, before we had to give up milking cows. So there is tremendous scope for these things on farms, which need broad thinking about the whole of rural policy rather than just what exists at the moment, to assist in the development of some of those rural areas.

Baroness Young of Old Scone: The likelihood is that it will have to be Pillar II but, alas, the risk in the long-term review of the funding of agriculture under the Common Agricultural Policy and under the EU budget, is that we will continue to see pressure on Pillar II. Even if it grows, it will not grow fast enough to do everything that is needed. We think that a more fundamental review is required that produces a new rural policy and a new rural funding mechanism, rather than simply trying to force more out of Pillar I into Pillar II, because I think that will always be a bit of a struggle, quite frankly, and it does involve co-financing. It is bad enough in this country, trying to get money out of the Treasury; in other countries, it is even more difficult. I suspect that we will be stuck with trying to shoehorn it into Pillar II, but it would be nice to think that we could, in a longer-term perspective, get away from that.

Q177 *Lord Greaves:* Can I start off by referring to your comments in your written evidence that cross-compliance has been implemented in different ways in different countries? Would you like to expand on that, explain some of the differences and perhaps some of the ways in which the effectiveness of it has differed?

Ms Bartram: Helen Phillips has alluded to this already but, as you know, cross-compliance comes in two parts: the Statutory Management Requirements (SMRs), the regulatory aspects, and then Good Agricultural and Environmental Condition (GAEC). When you look at SMRs, the standards tend to reflect the status of implementation of the relevant directive in each Member State. What we have seen, through some research we funded through the Land Use Policy Group, was that defined actions taken at the farm level were more harmonised in relation to these directives than to Good Agricultural and Environmental Condition. It depends on how each SMR is being interpreted, but it is more standardised because they are very explicit. When it comes to GAEC, the details are much more at the Member States' discretion. Some have implemented a relatively large number of standards, and standards that go beyond what is in GAEC. Helen alluded to the requirement for English farmers to have a two-metre margin from the centre of their hedgerow or alongside a watercourse, for example. Farmers are also required to complete a soil protection review in England. In France, there are additional standards relating to the use of water. However, what we found was that many more Member States appear to have focused on only some of the standards or issues and that key requirements have been so loosely translated that they cannot or will not be adhered to, because of the way they have been presented. There is some evidence from Bird Life International to suggest that we are still seeing the removal of landscape features across Europe. The level of environmental protection varies therefore, according to the number and the scope of the standards that have been adopted by each Member State, which means that there is inconsistency. However, it is very important to stress that we do not want to throw the baby out with the bathwater. While we have Pillar I and Single Farm Payments, we are seeing cross-compliance beginning to encourage adherence with environmental legislation. It also sets that environmental baseline that we have been calling for for a long time. From the farmers' point of view, we feel that it provides a clear planning framework for them and they can then build the requirements of cross-compliance into their business planning, so that they have a much clearer framework that they can go forward with. Those are the advantages that we see from it, therefore.

Q178 *Lord Greaves:* You seem to be saying that we are beginning to do it reasonably well in this country but some of the other countries are not, particularly as far as the discretionary side of it is concerned—the good environmental standards.
Ms Bartram: Yes.

Q179 *Lord Greaves:* I presume that there is somewhere we can all look to, that somebody has done the research on this and we can have a look at it, and perhaps you can tell us where that is. However, where in Europe is there practice which is good practice, which we can learn from and which is perhaps better than we do here—or is there not any?

Ms Bartram: Barbara has already set out that the reforms only came into place from 2005, so cross-compliance is still very much in its infancy. It is therefore hard to see the translation of what is on paper into what is happening in the environment. On the whole, though, certainly within England—and each UK region has interpreted cross-compliance slightly differently, certainly when it comes to GAEC—we are considered to be one of the most demanding regions of the EU when it comes to cross-compliance. That is not to say that we should rest on our laurels and not look around Europe to see where good practice is being delivered.
Baroness Young of Old Scone: Even within that, however, we are not absolutely as pure as the driven snow. At the moment, there is an intense debate between this country and Brussels on Nitrate-Vulnerable Zones, where we are regarded as dragging our feet and not being sufficiently extensive in declaring Nitrate-Vulnerable Zones, or having a sufficiently tough enough set of policies that would enable them to be delivered. I think that it is therefore a pretty mixed picture, to be honest. It is always the problem with cross-European comparisons, in that some countries are good at some things and bad at others, and nobody is a kind of shining star—which makes it quite a complicated process to do the comparison.

Q180 *Lord Cameron of Dillington:* Still on cross-compliance and coming back to the UK, your paper suggests that the requirements should be simplified—you may have already answered that—and their scope extended. Could you amplify that particular point?
Ms Kirmond: As Hannah said, cross-compliance in its present form is still relatively young. It is less than three years old. The good thing is that it has raised farmers' awareness of statutory standards and made them accountable for good practice. However, there are two important points to your question. Cross-compliance is evolving and we have some experience now. The Agency is now what is called a "competent control authority" for cross-compliance. We believe that, in the first case, we can simplify some of the administrative arrangements around it. Sometimes when you put something in practice you may over-egg the pudding a bit around some of it, and we are looking at, for example, how we could look at enforcement and penalties for things like minor breaches, so that you do not use a sledgehammer to crack a nut—which is very important. This brings us back to the principle of proportionate regulation. We need to retain proportionate penalties where there is serious damage but, where there is a minor breach of something, look at how we could scale that back. In the modern world, we need a more targeted

mechanism for regulation and we really need to think about our experience and other people's experience in risk-based regulation. There is therefore quite a lot we can do around some of the administrative arrangements of cross-compliance, to make them simpler and more straightforward to deal with and not hugely expensive just to administer, which mops up quite a lot of money. The second point that you have picked up is extending cross-compliance to include some other things. Barbara and I were here earlier in the year, talking to you about the Water Framework Directive and this holistic picture. On the books, we have the Water Framework Directive and the Soil Framework Directive coming up, and they are very important pieces of environmental legislation, both of which can have significant impacts on agricultural practice, which I think is important. Taking Barbara's point, Defra's consultation on the new powers associated with the Water Framework Directive clearly targets this problem of diffuse pollution from agriculture. The Nitrates Directive will not paint the whole picture a beautiful green. That is quite clear. One of the things we would like to think about, therefore, is how we can examine implementation of the Water Framework Directive to complement the existing cross-compliance arrangements in the Nitrates Directive, and to have a look at whether we can bring in, as Hannah has said, another Statutory Management Requirement under cross-compliance to embed some of the Water Framework Directive measures in farming practices. The other thing is the Soil Framework Directive, which is in its very early stages but already, under Good Agricultural and Environmental Condition, there is an element of soil management. We are very interested in exploring how we could extend the scope of the Statutory Management Requirements to strengthen some of the soil protection issues that actually give us multiple environmental benefits around not just sediment loss but nutrient loss—coming back to the point that Natural England made about making sure the soils are in the right place, doing the right thing at the right time. There are therefore some opportunities to get some multiple benefits looking at what the basket of EU directives can give us.

Q181 Lord Cameron of Dillington: You seem to be putting quite a lot of reliance on cross-compliance to achieve your aims, and yet at the same time you are talking about moving more money from Pillar I to Pillar II, or your common rural policy that Barbara was mentioning a moment ago. In your introduction, Barbara, you mentioned the whole problem of the fact of, if that does happen, what set of instruments you are going to use.

Baroness Young of Old Scone: Could I comment on a broader issue, before Aileen comes in on this? We are riding both horses at once, because who knows what will come out in the medium to longer term. Also, quite a lot of the changes that we need to see in land management will need the whole basket of instruments that we can deploy, ranging from advice, cross-compliance, regulation, the incentive schemes, voluntary agreements—the whole suite. We are perming all of them at the moment; we cannot back the winners, because we do not know what the winners are going to be. The risk is that we see a diminution in all of them. Ken Clarke once said to me, "Thank God these levers we pull aren't attached to anything". But we would rather not be in that position! That is one of the risks—if we do not get the right sort of cross-compliance conditions. Just taking diffuse pollution from agriculture and the Water Framework Directive, my major worry is that the consultation that the Government is involved in at the moment puts in place a set of mechanisms which are pretty unpopular with farmers and probably not very effective. We will therefore have to apply advice, cross-compliance, the agri-environment schemes, voluntary agreements—the whole suite—to get that movement, because a single-bullet solution for a particular issue like diffuse pollution will not work.

Q182 Lord Cameron of Dillington: Do you see these levers as being EU-based or would you envisage some localised, Member State, UK . . . ?

Ms Kirmond: They have to be a mixture. You have to have both EU level, UK level and, as Hannah has alluded to, there will be some local issues that are most appropriate for individual administrations, because each one will have a different issue. Northern Ireland has a different agricultural picture; they have different problems with phosphates than we have. I think that we do have to look at all those levers. It is one of the things we are looking at and we are involving people like the NFU, in terms of what some of those powers will look like and what they might look like for farmers, to try to work out what the best way of applying them is, and where we can make the best benefit. As Barbara has said, however, it is a very complex picture. If, for example, you looked at the Bathing Water Directive, the best lever to pull to achieve standards in the Bathing Water Directive is to de-stock the uplands.

Baroness Young of Old Scone: We are not advocating this, by the way!

Ms Kirmond: Can we have it struck from the record that I recommended that!

Q183 *Chairman:* We will pass the letters on to you!
Ms Kirmond: It gets very complicated, and one of the things we have to bear in mind is that we have to try to hit the right thing to do in order to get the right outcomes. It is about finding the outcome, finding the levers to pull to get at it, working out whether there are any contra-indications to that, and then moving towards that. Some of the things we learned from cross-compliance was that that was not the right mechanism; there are other things we need to try. We have to be open about the fact that we are learning as we go along with this.
Baroness Young of Old Scone: One of the issues we need to draw your attention to—there are two in terms of the Water Framework Directive—is that Defra has completed something called the "preliminary cost-effectiveness assessment", which looks at which of the levers are the most powerful to deliver the Water Framework Directive outcomes. After setting teams of highly trained economists to illuminate that for three years, I think that I would probably be being kind if I said that the answer is inconclusive—which is a worry, because we do need a bit of guidance on what are the right levers to pull. However, it shows the complexity. Now the proposition is that that will be done at regional level around the River Basin Management Plan, which could be a rather complicated process. That is one issue. The second one is the consultation on diffuse pollution from agriculture and the whole concept of water protection zones being used as a means of taking a regulatory approach to diffuse pollution issues, as a backstop if necessary. That will not be a popular proposition and we do not quite know yet if it would work. We therefore have to keep stressing that we need this full basket of instruments, because we do not want to rely simply on the one.
Chairman: Let us change focus now and go on to budget matters.

Q184 *Lord Plumb:* What we are talking about now and the development that is taking place all happens before the next Budget Review. I think that you have already said to some extent, with the development of your Rural Agency, how you would see the determination and the distribution of funding. As far as we are concerned—and we would like to see the re-stocking of the hills, not the de-stocking of the hills— we want to see where we are going and therefore to what extent you might share your views with the policymakers in other member countries on the use and the investment in the various areas.
Ms Bartram: I come back to our overarching, or under-arching, principle that we want to see behind the spending of public money, namely that we think that it should be for the provision of public goods and services. We are obviously particularly interested in

clean water, robust soils, functioning flood plains, but also the wildlife/access/landscape issues. We feel that support for these goods is justified when the market does not value them, and therefore fails to deliver them at an optimal level. The EU Budget Review will closely scrutinise the CAP budget in totality. It still receives the single largest share of the EU budget, at about 43% and so, not surprisingly, they want to look at it. I think that it is probably unlikely that the Pillar I budget—that budget which feeds Single Farm Payments—will be amended before 2013. The Brussels agreement of December 2005 more or less set that in stone until the end of this financial period. Pillar II, on the other hand, is much more vulnerable. It is by no means secure—and therefore of some worry to us, I have to say. What the situation allows us to do now is to kick-start the debate on "Where next for the CAP?". If there is a clear policy position and a direction of travel, that will very much help justify public expenditure on delivering a high-quality rural environment which is also a social and economic asset. In relation to whether our opinions are supported by others, we recently held a conference in Brussels with the other UK agencies on the future of Europe's rural areas and there was a lot of consensus on this approach. Whether or not our view is shared by other policymakers in other ministries, I think that Defra is probably better placed to answer that question than us at the moment.

Q185 *Chairman:* You seem to be saying, and what you started off by saying, is that the future of the CAP ought to be to provide public goods in a context where the market fails to provide. Is that it? Is that the future of the CAP?
Ms Bartram: If you are looking at 2013 and beyond, what we would prefer to see, rather than something called the CAP, is something called the Common Rural Policy or a common policy which delivers for the rural environment and delivers sustainable land management. There may well have to be an element of some emergency food security in that, but the general thrust of that policy is all about delivering the goods that the market does not support, or is inefficiently supporting or unable to support at the moment.
Baroness Young of Old Scone: There are lots of aspirations for the future of the CAP funding and for rural policy generally. Certainly Mrs Fischer Boel, when she was responding to the outcome of some of the work that we have been doing across Europe, challenged quite hard the vision, as it were, and was clear that she also had other aspirations in terms of meeting some of the commitments that they made with the accession treaties, building a competitive agriculture in a global sense, about releasing the

economic and social potential of the rural areas. She certainly was outlining the political difficulties that we are all aware of, of moving radically to a new rural policy. The farming industry itself, of course, has some strong aspirations for what the future of CAP funding would be about, particularly when you are looking at help for bringing new entrants into farming, new methods, training, innovation, helping with the global competitiveness issue, as well as with some of the economic and social pressures in some of the more remote rural areas across Europe, which are quite different from ours. There are a lot of folk who want a lot of stuff out of it. My experience of successive CAP reforms is that we will get something, but it will fall back from whatever radically that any of us would like.

Q186 Lord Bach: I can see that you obviously have a short-term and medium to long-term view, which is very sensible of course. Your long-term view—and you have expressed it more than once—is that the CAP as we know it should go. You say that it will not happen until 2013; that is probably absolutely realistic. You would like to see it succeeded by an adequately funded European Common Rural Policy. The question I want to ask you is this. What is your thinking about what it is that farmers across Europe should actually be paid for by the taxpayer, under the new scheme that you would like to see, and whether there is not a danger that you will pay farmers for things that they do not need to be paid for and that other people in other occupations, in the same position—not in exactly the same position but in roughly the same position—would not dream of asking to be paid for? And whether there is not a danger that by giving farmers too much money under some new scheme, under the nice title of Common Rural Policy, you may in fact just be subsidising them in the same way as, arguably, they are being subsidised now? I put the question in that particularly direct way because I think that this is a fairly fundamental point.
Baroness Young of Old Scone: This is always a difficult one and I agonise about it. You can substitute the words "miners" or "the British car industry" for "farmers" and it sounds like madness. The Common Agricultural Policy sounds like total, utter madness. The reality, however, is that the difference between the farming industry and land management generally and any other economic sector is that they are *the* guardians, *the* operators over a fundamental slice of the environment, probably impacting on all three environmental media: land, air and water. They are doing something that is contextually quite different from the miners, the car manufacturers, the chemical industry, or whatever.

Q187 Lord Bach: Or a house-builder?
Baroness Young of Old Scone: Or even house-builders. House-builders have an impact on land but they are not managing the basic resource, as it were. To some extent, therefore, a product of history and the fact that you can rationalise it in that way is right. There is no doubt that in Europe there are a lot of other big pressures that people want to maintain subsidy for. You have to ask, "Would we be better going towards a completely free market approach to agricultural production, saying, 'The market will provide', and if sheep cease to exist on the hill because they are not economic, so be it?". I think that what we are saying is, as agriculture approaches the market more and there are downsides that we cannot live with environmentally, we would want to see the CAP funding move in to make sure that those downsides did not occur, and would sit alongside advice, standard-setting, regulation, and all the other mechanisms we have talked about. The market is becoming more pressing. We have made the point in our evidence about things like biofuels and what will happen if we hit £200 a tonne for wheat. We are deeply worried about set-aside going down to 0%— where I have a big bet on with Peter Kendall at the NFU as to how much land will get ploughed up, because it is too tempting if you can get that sort of money off it. I think that we are talking about market failure and the need to be protected against that. You can therefore just about get away with not substituting miners or car manufacturers for farmers whenever you talk about CAP.

Q188 Lord Greaves: How on earth can agriculture be economically successful for once—growing things and selling things that people want to buy at the price at which the farmers want to sell it—and be described as "market failure"?
Baroness Young of Old Scone: I think that it is quite patchy at the moment across the farming economy. If you are a livestock farmer, you may not feel the same way. However, I think that market failure does undoubtedly happen. You can have a very thriving farming economy in a particular sector, but you can have real downsides in environmental terms, or indeed in social terms. I live in a part of East Anglia where, quite frankly, the greater success for the farming industry is accompanied by a reduction in the number of people employed in it.
Chairman: You could have market failure in the context of a market success, because it is a failure of the market to deliver the environmental good.

Q189 Lord Greaves: Yes, the wider stuff.
Ms Kirmond: It also comes back to the point that Lord Cameron made about what the measures look like. One of the measures we are working very hard

on is catchment-sensitive farming. It is not just about a carrot and a stick and it will either work or it will not work; it is learning about how farmers can change their behaviour. Regulation is straightforward but it is a blunt instrument, and incentivisation is a different basket that costs money; but with something like catchment-sensitive farming, where you are using advice to try to raise the gain—you are not beating people up about it but you are not giving them lots of money for it—we are seeing some quite big returns in terms of how the farming community is responding to advice that helps them to help themselves to be more environmentally aware, and so on. It is also important that that third bit in the basket is there; that we need to hold market failure back by saying, "You need to be a bit more in control of your activities as well. Here are some ways in which you can do it. It helps you to be more successful and take matters more into your own hands". That then perhaps gives more opportunity for them to pull some more levers, go back into the market and say, "We are being environmentally responsible; we are producing goods that we believe you want. Where is the market price for that?".

Q190 Baroness Jones of Whitchurch: You quoted the figure of 43% of the total EU budget going on the CAP. Presumably your Common Rural Policy would not be anything like that 43%. You are talking about scaling down quite considerably here, are you not?
Baroness Young of Old Scone: If you get the finance ministers of Europe together, they will get their shovel into it somehow, but let us not give it away because, to be frank, there is not that much money in environmental protection generally—and this is the biggest single slice.

Q191 Chairman: Is this not the problem: that environmental protection is riding on the back of what has been squeezed across from Pillar I of the CAP? Is not the best thing to say, "Okay, CAP, bye-bye. Finish, end. Start again. What funding do you need to deliver environmental benefits?" and do not pretend that it has anything to do with the CAP?
Baroness Young of Old Scone: If you start with a blank sheet of paper, you can bet your bottom dollar that the amount of money in it will be a considerable amount less.

Q192 Chairman: Is that not a good thing?
Baroness Young of Old Scone: As a taxpayer, I would probably think that it is a good thing; but you also have to look at political reality. Like it or not, I cannot see the French Government believing that it can win an election if it draws a completely blank sheet and reduces the amount that is going into the rural economy by a dramatic amount. I think that we

therefore have to ride both horses at once. Also, if you look at some of the abstruse maths—I do not understand it, Hannah may—of moving money from one side to the other at the moment, we just have to make sure that we do not end up with very little, in whatever form of agri-environment or rural funding mechanism we have for the future. At the moment, if we look at all the pressures on the agri-environment schemes—and you heard Helen talk about her concerns regarding the legacy schemes—if you add together everything that we need between Natural England and ourselves, on behalf of the nation may I say, to deliver environmentally and in terms of recreation, landscape and access, it is a big, big chunk of stuff. So let us be quite wary about offering up too much of the CAP budget for sacrifice.

Q193 Viscount Brookeborough: So really we should be saying that we do not want a reduction in the overall spending; we want it changed from Pillar I to Pillar II—and we and the population would not mind.
Baroness Young of Old Scone: If you totted up everything that everybody wants out of a revised CAP or a son of CAP, or daughter of CAP—nodding to Mrs Fischer Boel—it would be a very big bill and there would not be enough to go round. I think that it will therefore be a complete political push-and-shove as to how much goes on each of those outcomes in a new rural policy. Looking at the bill, I do not think that it will fall far short of what is currently there. The finance ministers can get something out of it, but let us not encourage them to believe that it is a big chunk.
Chairman: The trouble is that there has been a total failure of finance ministers to control the CAP.

Q194 Viscount Ullswater: Can I take up what My Lord Chairman said about scrapping CAP and putting in a different policy altogether? I think that Dr Phillips in her evidence to us gave the impression that she felt that farming, up to perhaps the Second World War, was done with the environment, not making too much of an impact on it; but, subsequently, the environment has been taking quite a knock from the development of technology, sprays, large tractors, whatever it is, which can rip through the environment in a way which perhaps the old horse and cart could not. Therefore, agriculture is now likely to be acting against the environment rather than with it, and perhaps we need to move away from keeping it within agriculture and move towards a rural policy.
Baroness Young of Old Scone: I think that it is hugely variable across agriculture. Basically, what we did from about 1970 onwards was wave fivers at farmers and tell them to intensify, and they did it extremely

successfully. We have some of the most intensive and efficient farming in Europe. However, that had an impact on the environment, though many people did work hard, and some sectors in particular worked hard to keep as much environmental benefit as possible. It is therefore quite mixed across the farming community. There is no doubt that you can see quite massive changes in some of the indicators from the 1970s onwards. There are particular ones. The switch from the spring sowing of wheat to the winter sowing of wheat was like turning a switch. It had a huge impact on the environment. Little changes like that which ricochet right across the farm landscape can therefore make a huge difference. At the moment, we are seeing it in some parts of the country with the whole debate about sheep dip. You can kill people or you can kill the environment, but you cannot do both. It is our organophosphates against the synthetic pyrethroids. Which would you rather? It is a difficult one, that. Our belief is that, by a little bit of waving of fivers, a little bit of regulation, a lot of advice and support and, through the cross-compliance mechanism, a clear understanding of what is needed of farmers—farmers want to know what is needed from them—we can get some of that signal, which was very much about production, diversified into a whole load of other areas.

Q195 Lord Plumb: I was a little surprised to read that you said there was a danger that more demanding environmental standards in Europe would lead to the displacement of damaging farming techniques to other parts of the world. I have been learning from some of the WTO people over the weekend that they are concerned more about phytosanitary standards than they are about tariffs; that they believe this will be the biggest problem to trade if they are applied, because our standards will be that much higher than those countries where they are producing large quantities; like chicken from China, for instance, where the standards are very different from the level here. I was therefore a little surprised to hear that you were concerned that it had an effect there. I thought that our job was to try to encourage them to meet similar standards to the standards that are applied here, on welfare grounds. *Baroness Young of Old Scone:* I think that the business of consistent global standards is quite a difficult one. Generally speaking, in many places the impact of setting higher environmental standards is only a small part of the issue of what does competitiveness look like. Labour market costs are probably the biggest single factor in terms of a level playing field, as it were; and of course they do vary hugely across Europe and across the global economy. We therefore have to regard environmental standards as part of that, but not necessarily the single, distorting feature,

as it were. Our concern is that we do need to make sure that there is a degree of recognition in our negotiations in the UK, and in Europe's negotiations in the World Trade Organization, that environmental standards are important and that competitiveness has to take those into account, because they will have an impact both here and globally in environmental terms, and they are interconnected. We also need to make sure that, if there are specific measures coming in in European policy, they do not have unexpected consequences elsewhere. For example, the biofuels target for Europe—which clearly cannot be achieved within the European arable area, unless we put the whole area under biofuels. We are pretty sniffy about biofuels anyway, because we think that certainly first-generation biofuels are not exactly the most effective way of reducing carbon and that we need to move to second-generation biofuels; but that, even so, probably biomass for energy is a much more effective way of using the land than to provide biofuels, in terms of both cost and environmental impact per unit of carbon reduction. However, if we are to have a biofuels market globally, we do need to see some sort of accreditation process or certification scheme, because the risk is that we will simply see biofuels being grown elsewhere, on areas that should still have been under primary forest, or savannah, or whatever else that is being ploughed up for biofuel production. We have already seen a dramatic example of that in the world, which is palm oil production. The damage that palm oil has done globally is huge. We are down to the last 50, or even fewer, Sumatran tigers. I do not know about you, but I get pretty outraged when I think about a species as unique as that being driven to extinction so that you and I can have soap—which is the reality of it. I do not think that we should be repeating that with biofuels. We have to find a way of getting the benefit to climate change without screwing up the rest of the environment in the process. The timber standards through the FSC are one example of a voluntary scheme. It may not be hugely well policed globally, but the organic standard is an accredited standard and it is policed globally. I do think that we have to start pressing for some of these global certification processes.

Q196 Chairman: On that note, I think that it is time to bring in Lord Palmer.
Baroness Young of Old Scone: I could see you shaking your head, Lord Palmer!
Lord Palmer: I know that we do not always see eye to eye on biofuels, but perhaps I could go back to the question posed by Lord Bach. I am sure that the five of us around this table who are farmers would reckon that his question merited at least a three-day conference on what the future could be! You are

concerned that EU targets of biofuel production will add to the pressure on natural resources, notably water quality. If global biofuel production leads to higher food prices, can additional pressure on natural resources really be avoided? Perhaps I could add this supplementary. To what extent could mandatory environmental and carbon reporting requirements ensure compatibility between biofuel crops and Pillar II funding? Could you elaborate on what you perceive to be the environmental benefits of focusing support on the infrastructure for processing fuel rather than for growing bio-crops? I do absolutely agree with you about this ridiculous thing of cutting down the rainforest in South America and shipping ethanol halfway across the world.

Q197 *Chairman:* That is just to remove a competitor!

Baroness Young of Old Scone: What we want to see is a kind of tiered thing. We want the UK and Europe to be pretty robust in the World Trade Organization discussions about the environmental impacts of production—agriculture, food production and biofuel production. We want more informal things to happen. In development assistance, a policy, for example, where we have the ability to promote good practice, to provide training, and all of those things. In overseas aid policy, we want to see getting higher environmental standards put into agricultural production built in as part of that kind of process. We would like to see certification play a role. We believe that what we should be seeing through Pillar II funding is not necessarily funding farmers to produce a particular crop, because that seems to fly in the face of the whole trend of CAP. If we are moving away from funding production, we should not be helping fund biofuel production particularly. In our view, the carbon market ought to be the thing that funds biofuel production, by putting the right long-term price of carbon into the carbon market, which drives the right sorts of signals to people to introduce new technologies, whatever they are. Then we need these mechanisms in place to make sure that the new technologies do not have an adverse environmental infrastructure. What we are saying might happen from Pillar II is to pay support for infrastructure to produce biofuels, particularly from wastes—in the way that I described with the pig slurry and the Marks & Sparks sandwiches. Until the long-term price of carbon is right, it is actually a big leap of faith for a smallish farmer to engage, even in a consortium, in setting up an anaerobic digestion system, because it is not yet clear whether this wobbly price of carbon will ever lift off. Until that happens, it is worthwhile seeing Pillar II as a source of pump-priming of technology introduction, so that we can begin to get people using these systems—until the price of carbon

is sufficiently strong and robust for the future, so that people see just a simple return on investment in this sort of alternative fuel structure. If we were looking at the hierarchy of the most environmentally effective and least environmentally damaging ways of impacting on carbon, we would see energy from agricultural and land use wastes at the top of the hierarchy. Next, growing crops for biomass, providing all the environmental impacts are taken into account. We have a very useful tool, where you can put your biomass production methodology, what it is replacing, how it is transported, how it is grown, how it is processed, into our computer; you can turn the handle and it gives you what the environmental impact is and allows you to tweak the parameters to reduce those, and then get the best outcome possible. The hierarchy would be energy from waste; energy from biomass; and biofuels coming quite a long way down after that—unless the second-generation biofuels really start to come through.

Q198 *Baroness Jones of Whitchurch:* Sticking with the climate change issue, as you said earlier, the floods over the summer caused considerable concern around the country. You identified in your evidence that the rural development funds could be one way of addressing that issue. Going back to our earlier discussion, you could say that is quite a long way from the CAP and what was originally envisaged with all of this. However, how would you see using the rural development funds in the, rather urgent, short term to assist with some of the river-flooding issues that we are being confronted with?

Baroness Young of Old Scone: The Higher Level Stewardship scheme already has a flood management option in it. Although obviously, with the meagre amount of money that is in the Higher Level scheme, it is not doing much yet; but it is there. We therefore believe that that is an accepted proposition and could increase, but I do not think that we should hold our breath too much. There is quite a lot of loose talk about the benefits of land management for holding back floods, and I think that we need better research and evidence. There are two sorts of propositions. One is quite well tested, and that is where we pay farmers to manage their land as normal and then, once in a blue moon, we fill it up with water. In the recent floods, for example, Lincoln has two huge washlands, about which we did a deal with farmers 17 years ago. For the first 14 years they managed away like mad and had a perfectly adequate farm business. On the fifteenth year, when we had to open them up for the floodwaters, they were none too thrilled. We had to remind them that we had been paying them all this time, and so we needed to get our quid pro quo.

Q199 *Baroness Jones of Whitchurch:* Were you paying them out of the rural development fund?

Baroness Young of Old Scone: No, we were paying them from our own flood risk budget on that one. That is a proven technique, and we assess that with every flood scheme that we go to. As well as building defences, therefore, we will look at a land management option to see whether it would work. That absolutely has to be on "Will it work or not?". The second sort is a kind of generalised belief that if the land was managed in ways that made it more absorbent and to hold water back for longer, that would help reduce these peak flows down rivers, flash floods and run-off. That is true to an extent, but I do not think that it is a panacea. We therefore need much more evidence about where it will work, and that is more amenable to being built into things like the Entry Level scheme and the Higher Level scheme—particularly where you have a big flash flood issue that has been demonstrated in the past. We have just come back from seeing a farmer who grows potatoes on the top of a hill in Dorset where, every time it rains, the top of the hill runs down the road and into the river. We are worried about it on a pollution basis, as well as on a flood risk basis. There are therefore changes in cropping; changes in crop management; the increasing use of buffer strips; there is work on whether woodland is good for holding water back, though that is not yet clear. Clearly, anything that increases the absorbency and helps provide a barrier to water just running straight through will be worth thinking about in terms of flood alleviation. Therefore, if it means that we do not have to build another two feet of sheet steel further down the river, you can just do the simple cost-benefit there.

Q200 *Lord Moynihan:* In a sense, the issue of set-aside is a microcosm for some of the wider points you have been making on your journey from the CAP to CRP—though we probably need to pay more attention to the acronym! If set-aside is abolished, there will clearly be a number of environmental benefits that you want to attain—the biodiversity of soil and water protection, which you outline on page 3. What we do not have a clear picture of are some of the more specific measures, which you refer to at the bottom of your list, that might be taken to achieve this. I wonder if you could expand on that and give us some of your thoughts. You talk about new measures that are needed, but what do you have in mind?

Baroness Young of Old Scone: We have been talking to Defra and working with Natural England on the whole issue of post set-aside measures, because we are very concerned. I think that the evidence is fairly clear that it will have a huge environmental impact. Taking that amount of land and doing something

differently with it is bound to have an impact. It remains to be seen whether or not in fact lots of people do plough up their non-rotational set-aside; but I find it a bit risky, waiting to see whether that happens because, once you have ploughed it up, it is gone and it takes about another 15 years before it gets back into any sort of condition again. What we have been doing is working with Natural England, with the farming unions and also with the NGOs, to try to produce a sort of five-point plan of simple things that you can do as a farmer to mitigate the loss of your set-aside. I am hoping that Hannah knows what the five-point plan says!

Ms Bartram: The five-point plan focuses more on the permanent land that probably will not be put back into production, so the more marginal land. It is looking at things like buffer strips: having wide buffer strips along watercourses. It talks about focusing on in-field options, which are particularly important for countryside birds like the skylark, which do not like hedgerows, do not go anywhere near them and prefer the middle of the fields; so whether one can do anything along those lines. It tries to pick up the resource protection and the biodiversity in wildlife aspects of managing this land. That is the outcome of the 0% rate of set-aside, which was recently agreed by the European Union Farm Council. Then there is the longer-term issue, the abolition of set-aside as a policy through the Health Check.

Q201 *Lord Moynihan:* As this work progresses, could you let us have some further information on it and maybe a copy of the five-point plan as well?

Ms Bartram: Yes, of course.

Lord Plumb: My Lord Chairman, can I add a word—

Lord Moynihan: Lord Plumb is going to talk about skylarks!

Q202 *Lord Plumb:* Afterwards or before? I only wanted to say on set-aside that I was brought up under a father who used to tell me that we had to take ten acres of every hundred out of production every year and fallow it, and that was the way to farm. When we talk about fallow land, I think a lot of people will understand the better why that is being done in today's diversification of cropping. My other point, which is much more relevant, is are you are prepared to tell us what your bet is with Peter Kendall?

Baroness Young of Old Scone: Absolutely. It is germane to your first point, actually. I think you are right that the whole fallow issue is not one that is talked about very often, though there is a lot of fallow land as part of natural rotations. We have looked with Natural England, and they have assessed the evidence right across the rotational and the non-rotational set-aside. With rotational set-aside the monitoring that Defra has put in place to see (a) what farmers do and (b) what impact that has will, over a period of time, tell us what the impact of set-aside has been. If there are issues to do with rotational set-aside, you have the opportunity of putting them into place because, being rotational, it is not fixed to one particular set of land; you stop doing it for two or three years but then you can start doing something different that would have the same impact. The worry I have is with the non-rotational stuff. Some of it is now 15 years old and is beginning to develop the sort of biodiversity richness and the sort of ecosystem-established service which, once you have ploughed it up, has gone. That is the worry I have on the non-rotational aspect. To go on to my bet, Peter Kendall's folk did a rather modest survey of farmers as to what their intentions would be and the Defra economists—I seem to be against economists, and it is probably true—had a look at what they thought the economics of farming would drive people to do. They came to the conclusion that not everybody would plough up all of their non-rotational set-aside. So we know how much there is; we know how much the NFU survey said would not get ploughed up—

Q203 *Lord Plumb:* So do I!

Baroness Young of Old Scone: . . . and, when people make decisions in the spring about other crops rather than winter crops, we will know who was right and who was wrong. I would be delighted to let you know what the outcome is.

Q204 *Viscount Brookeborough:* Schemes such as this which, when they were brought in, we looked on as being rather more permanent have been taken away at the stroke of a pen. There are other schemes. At home, we have some grassland habitat improvement that is not going, or at least not for another ten years. Are you worried that in future they will bring in more schemes, which at the time look great and then, just because the price of products has gone up and there has been climate change, will be taken out at the stroke of a pen?

Baroness Young of Old Scone: That is why it is really important to get schemes that are focused on an accepted environmental outcome. One of the problems with set-aside was that it was always a production control mechanism that happened, because it was so large-scale, to have some good environmental benefits. So really the Health Check has to focus on getting a clear set of environmental outcomes that will be delivered through policies, because then they are less easy to move away from without saying, "Actually, we are moving away from that environmental outcome as well".

Ms Kirmond: It has to be underpinned by some evidence. Warm and rosy ideas—as long as you have evidence you have some power to retain a thing and advance it or change it over time; but—and it is something we are very interested in—we have to ensure that we have evidence-based policies.

Baroness Young of Old Scone: For the record, can I say that we want two things on set-aside? One is that, if it is not working, we do want a cross-compliance mechanism to deliver the benefits that set-aside would have delivered, starting from next season. The second is that we need Defra to press, through the CAP Health Check, for measures that will replace the impact of set-aside.

Chairman: Thank you very much indeed. It is always a delight to have you as a witness, and thank you to your colleagues as well.

WEDNESDAY 24 OCTOBER 2007

Present	Bach, L	Plumb, L
	Brookeborough, V	Sewel, L (Chairman)
	Cameron of Dillington, L	Ullswater, V
	Palmer, L	

Memorandum by the Country Land and Business Association

1. The Country Land & Business Association (CLA) is the premier organisation safeguarding the interests of those responsible for land, property and business throughout rural England and Wales. CLA members own and manage more than half the rural land in England and Wales and we are committed to the positive development of the rural economy.

2. We welcome this inquiry into the future of the CAP, which comes as we are developing our own thoughts on the issues. In the interests of brevity, we have kept our answers to the questions short but would be very happy to provide oral evidence to elaborate the points made. To provide a fuller explanation of how our thinking on this important topic is developing, we have also included a copy of a paper given by Professor Allan Buckwell. CLA Chief Economist, at the Centenary conference of the CLA, on 10 May.

What should be the long term objectives of the CAP? Does the title "Common Agricultural Policy" aptly fit your perceived objectives of the policy? What do you consider to be the main pressures on the CAP as it currently is?

3. The long term objectives of the CAP should be to enable and to incentivise land managers to produce the socially optimal quantities of high quality food and fibre, renewable energy, biodiversity, landscape, heritage, and soil, water and air management. In our view, the name "Common Agricultural Policy" is increasingly outdated; it should be understood as a land management policy, not simply an agricultural policy.

4. Currently the main pressures on the policy are the twin demands of cheap food and environmental stewardship, and ongoing efforts to address outdated problems of the 1980s—over production. In our view, the CAP should be reoriented to focus on the high priority concerns of the 21st century; global food security and environmental security. Climate change and the growing role of 1st generation bio-fuels in meeting global energy needs will aggravate these concerns.

What has been your experience so far with the reformed CAP? What has worked well and less well? And where can lessons be learned?

5. The CLA have long advocated the decoupling of payments from production and moving to an area-based payments system. We have supported the introduction of the Single Payment Scheme (SPS), but see it as a transitional scheme leading to a more permanent scheme that pays land managers for the delivery of environmental and food security public goods. Unfortunately the experience of English farmers with the introduction of the SPS has been very poor indeed. This has been well-documented and analysed elsewhere, such as the Efra Committee, and the National Audit Office.

Do you consider the Single Payment Scheme to be a good basis for the future of EU agricultural policy? What changes might be made at the EU level to the Single Payment Scheme, including to the rules governing entitlements, in the short and/or the longer-term?

6. The SPS is a good basis for the future of European agricultural policy as it increasingly relates public payments with the provision of public goods and sustainable production. In the short term the SPS could be improved by implementing many of the proposals to be considered in the "health check" in 2008. These include abolition of the supply management mechanisms such as set-aside and announcing the end of milk quota by around 2014; a reduction in the number of types of entitlement; more supportive inspections whereby

the inspectors spend more time talking through issues with farmers, and a more proportionate system of penalties.

What short and longer-term changes are required to the CAP's market mechanisms? Suggestions made by the Commission have included re-examination of certain quotas, intervention, set-aside, export refunds and private storage payments.

7. As already suggested, the market management mechanisms of the CAP, those aimed at production control—such as quotas and set-aside—have no further purpose with decoupled payments. Others, such as export refunds should no longer be needed, while intervention should be available only for extreme situations. We also believe that is important to have a balanced approach to trade policy liberalisation. At the same time as barriers to imports are being reduced, which can be expected to lower internal market prices, we should also eliminate the possible use of export restrictions that may be used when commodity prices are high. Another key element that should be on the trade liberalisation agenda is the need to ensure that sanitary and phytosanitary standards are fully maintained to ensure appropriate defences against pests and diseases.

8. More generally, we would like to see more emphasis being placed on the correction of market failures through the provision of training, R&D, and financial risk management.

What is your view on the introduction of the European Agricultural Fund for Rural Development (EAFRD)? Do you consider that it is meeting its objectives thus far? Is it suitably "strategic" in nature, meeting the needs of rural society as a whole rather than being restricted to aiding the agricultural industry? How well is it being co-ordinated with other EU and national policies on regional and rural development?

9. The RDR is a very good idea, but it needs to be developed and supported by a very much more substantial budget. In this latter regard, it is deeply regrettable that it was British tactics that led to the wholly unsatisfactory Council decision on the rural development budget for the period 2007–13, as agreed in December 2005. In England the majority of the emphasis of the RDR is on the agri-environment schemes, which is too narrow. The environmental agenda for land management is larger than that of the agri-environment schemes, which is focussed mainly on landscape and biodiversity. Resource protection and maintenance, and climate change issues, for example, need to be given a higher priority. In addition, greater emphasis should also be given to the options under axis 1 and axis 3 that provide support and assistance to improving competitiveness and profitability of rural land-based businesses.

10. Integration with other policies and the administration of the provisions are widely seen as seriously deficient.

Is there a case for a higher level of EU financing of rural development? Do you have a view on the extension of compulsory modulation from Pillar I (Direct Payments) to Pillar II (Rural Development)?

11. Yes, as just briefly explained, the scope of the RDR is very much wider and potentially influential than that that has been implemented in the England. Consequentially, we believe that there is a very good case for higher levels of funding for the RDR. With regard to the compulsory modulation mechanism, we have serious concerns about the distribution key, which provides the UK with only 80% of what is deducted from the SFP. As well, some countries have problems with the requirement to co-finance, whether because they cannot afford it or they are not inclined to do so.

What benefits can the EU's World Trade Organisation obligations create for EU agriculture and, consequently, for the EU economy as a whole?

12. The main benefit of the WTO is the provision of an international legal framework ensuring fair competition amongst nations, as well as security and legitimacy for internal programmes.

13. The liberalisation agenda of the WTO being pursued in the current Doha Development round of negotiations, will serve to accelerate the restructuring process that is happening to European agriculture and could have far-reaching—and in some cases, devastating—consequences for land usage and management. A comprehensive analysis of these effects should be undertaken but, broadly, we can expect that some farming,

such as that in areas that are less productive yet of high environmental value may be abandoned as the farms become uneconomic, while food production will be increasingly centred on fewer, larger farms. Because European farming is expected to meet simultaneously both the food needs and the environmental/animal welfare demands of the public, the implications of the WTO are uncertain.

To what extent has the system of cross-compliance contributed to an improved level of environmental protection? How is it linking with other EU policy requirements such as the Water Framework Directive?

14. There is a large and growing body of EU environmental regulation, most of which was included under cross compliance as the Statutory Management Requirements (SMRs) when the current SPS was agreed. Cross compliance has raised awareness of the increasing linkages being made between sustainable production practices and payment of public funds, and contributed to an improvement in some land management practices. Arguably it also suggests that achieving environmental changes, where those who must deliver are uncoordinated and geographically disperse, may be more efficiently done within the context of a public payments mechanism rather than by simply regulating.

How can the CAP contribute to mitigation of, and adaptation to, climate change? What do you consider the role of biofuels to be in this regard?

15. The main contributions of land managers to addressing climate change are flood control, carbon sequestration, energy substitution, particularly the supply of second generation bio-fuels, materials substitution (timber for concrete, steel and brick) and food security. None of these important activities are currently properly supported by the CAP.

The Commissioner has expressed her dissatisfaction at the financing agreement reached by the Member States at the December 2005 Council. Do you consider the current budget to be sufficient? Do you consider co-financing to be a possible way forward in financing the Common Agricultural Policy?

16. It is not possible to say with certainty, and it may be misguided to attempt to do so, whether the budgetary resources currently available will be sufficient into the future. A necessary prerequisite is greater certainty as to the future objectives of the CAP. As already stated, in our view, the future global challenges to food and environmental security are likely to demand more than is now provided in the current budget.from Budget Heading 2 "Preservation and Management of Natural Resources" that funds the CAP and environmental policy. These additional funds will mainy be required for the kinds of actions under pillar II that society demands. How we get these funds and the degree of co-financing are open questions. There is much merit in the suggestion that an EU policy—and there should be no doubt that it should be an EU policy—should be financed by an EU budget.

What has been the impact on the CAP of the 2004 and 2007 enlargements and what is the likely impact of future enlargements of the EU on the post-2013 CAP?

17. There have been few short-term consequences of the enlargement, as the current budget and policy reforms were agreed before the expansions. It is, of course, regrettable that the accession of Bulgaria and Romania was not properly provided for in the agreement on the financial perspective for the period 2007–13. This may yet lead to cuts in single farm payments under the Financial Discipline provisions of the budgetary agreement. Undoubtedly there have also been benefits from the increased labour mobility and market integration between the new members and the EU15 but the statistical evidence is not yet available to demonstrate this. Longer term, we expect that the different needs and priorities of the new members will influence the evolution of policy—with a greater emphasis on rural development and environmental stewardship—and the distribution of the budgets—with more money moving "from west to east".

How could the CAP be further simplified and in what other ways would you like to see the Common Agricultural Policy changed in the short and/or the long term?

18. Our view is that the key challenges facing land managers in the 21st century arise from the pressures of environmental deterioration, population growth, increasing production of 1st generation bio-fuels, and climate change. These pressures give rise to the twin challenges of food security and environmental security. The CAP should be refocused to address these challenges.

June 2007

Memorandum by The Scottish Rural Property and Business Association

INTRODUCTION

The Scottish Rural Property and Business Association (SRPBA) represents the interests of approximately 2,700 land based businesses in Scotland including farming, forestry and game management businesses. Our goal is a prosperous and sustainable rural sector driven by thriving land-based businesses.

Given the diversity of its membership, the Association has a broad perspective on the rural policy. Our members are land managers in the wider sense so our policy perspective is not solely focussed on farming. However, we believe that agriculture is and should remain a core rural activity upon which a thriving rural economy is built.

Our members take a proactive approach to land management. They have, through many years of continued management of land, provided a range of services and products to society—food, fuel and protection of natural resources. In the process they have created a landscape from which the public at large have benefited.

The Common Agricultural Policy has been instrumental in shaping and driving the land management activities of our members and will continue to do so. We therefore welcome the House of Lords" Inquiry into the future of the CAP and are grateful for the opportunity to contribute.

OVERVIEW

1. *What should be the long term objectives of the CAP? Does the title "Common Agricultural Policy" aptly fit your perceived objectives of the policy? What do you consider to be the main pressures on the CAP as it currently is?*

The long term objectives should be a competitive market orientated agricultural sector allied to a more profitable and sustainable countryside. However agricultural (food production) policy can no longer be considered separately from energy policy. We need to secure strategic supplies of both food and energy, and land management (including the agricultural sector) is inextricably linked with both. To this end the Common <u>Agricultural</u> Policy may no longer provide an accurate description of the policy. This is a policy for delivery of profitable and sustainable rural economy which is founded on viable and thriving land management businesses.

Pressures on the CAP stem from the fact that the CAP is expected to deliver on a whole range of social, environmental and economic objectives in an enlarging EU with a limited budget. It is no longer deemed acceptable for public funding to deliver only agriculture/food production and there are wider social and environmental pressures on funding which had historically been directed at the agricultural sector.

Land managers are stewards of the countryside who must balance the economic realities of food and energy production with the responsibility to do so in an environmentally sustainable way. A range of non-market services have historically been provided by land managers in a range of environmental and cultural landscape services. These were previously simply viewed as by-products of farming, forestry and game management activities but are now expected to be end goals in themselves. At the same time land managers are expected to be more business like in their approach which inevitably focuses their attention on outputs for which they are paid.

This sets a challenge for land managers and brings pressure on the support system. Land managers are asked to continue to innovate and produce the high quality food (and increasingly, energy) needs of Europe, and in addition to reduce pollution and increase delivery of the environmental services of biodiversity and landscape as well as free at point of use public access for health and recreation.[1]

---

[1] See "Public Goods from Private Land—why Nature needs Management" published by the European Landowners" Organisation 16 May 2006.

THE REFORMED CAP

2. *What has been your experience so far with the reformed CAP? What has worked   well and less well? And where can lessons be learned?*

The 2003 reforms have been partly successful in that they have begun to focus farmers on the market place and remove some of the distortions. The SRPBA was supportive of de-coupling production from support, although it is probably still too early to see real evidence of the restructuring of the industry that must occur as a result.

Many Scottish farmers have reacted to the reforms by using the current period of CAP to make longer term decisions and restructure their businesses. However many have not yet done so, and it remains to be seen whether reforms will need to go further in order to bring about the necessary changes in decision making.

THE SINGLE PAYMENT SCHEME

3. *Do you consider the Single Payment Scheme to be a good basis for the future of EU agricultural policy? What changes might be made at the EU level to the Single Payment Scheme, including to the rules governing entitlements, in the short and/or the longer-term?*

A first pillar of the CAP providing direct support payments remains vital to underpin most farming enterprises, at least in the medium term. The majority of businesses would simply not be profitable enough to deliver on any of the other objectives expected from farming without the single payment. This is particularly the case for upland areas where arguably employment, social fabric, social history, rural skills, landscape features, biodiversity, tourism etc become proportionately more important than simply production. Direct support is needed to keep people in these areas.

Longer term, Pillar I funding remains a good mechanism for providing a broad based payment in return for good agricultural and environmental stewardship across Europe. However, it cannot continue to be relied upon for survival.

The Single Farm Payment scheme could be simplified by ensuring adequate cross compliance obligations for the receipt of pillar one monies leaving pillar two to focus on business and agricultural development. The SFP should recompense farmers for the non market benefits that they provide through their activities. This should not necessarily rewarded on a competitive basis if a consistent level of environmental stewardship is to be achieved across the EU.

The historic basis for payment of SFP in Scotland has given time for farmers to adjust but may become problematic in the longer term. There is a particular concern about payments being allocated to "naked acres" with recipients not required to undertake any economic activity, which does not gain sympathy from either the public or the industry.

MARKET MECHANISMS

4. *What short and longer-term changes are required to the CAP's market mechanisms? Suggestions made by the Commission have included re-examination of certain quotas, intervention, set-aside, export refunds and private storage payments.*

Market interventions should be removed so that direct payments to farmers are made where there are social or other specific community, non market benefits delivered to society. This is more justifiable in the longer term. However, the facility for some emergency intervention could be required until there is a clearer strategic approach to income stabilisation. We accept that set-aside and quotas are no longer justified although consideration should be given to preserving the environmental benefits achieved through set-aside for example in water body protection. This can be done through agri-environment measures.

RURAL DEVELOPMENT

5. *What is your view on the introduction of the European Agricultural Fund for Rural Development (EAFRD)? Do you consider that it is meeting its objectives thus far? Is it suitably "strategic" in nature, meeting the needs of rural society as a whole rather than being restricted to aiding the agricultural industry? How well is it being co-ordinated with other EU and national policies on regional and rural development?*

Scotland and the UK has been disadvantaged by historic funding criteria. Without prosperous primary industries, many other objectives will not be attained, therefore the majority of funding will inevitably be directed towards them. However this does not preclude other objectives. For example more serious thought needs to be given to Natura 2000 funding. Rural development funding must be preserved for rural areas, and not small conurbations.

6. *Is there a case for a higher level of EU financing of rural development? Do you have a view on the extension of compulsory modulation from Pillar I (Direct Payments) to Pillar II (Rural Development)?*

The SRPBA has always acknowledged that Pillar I funding will be shifted to Pillar II. This should occur at the appropriate pace so that farmers are given time to adjust. Ultimately we need to retain a critical mass of profitable farming businesses if wider objectives are to be achieved. Removing too much of the direct payment too soon may jeopardise this.

Shifting of funds would be better achieved through increased compulsory modulation across the EU, rather than differing rates of voluntary modulation affecting farmers in only one or two member states.

WORLD TRADE

7. *What benefits can the EU's World Trade Organisation obligations create for EU agriculture and, consequently, for the EU economy as a whole?*

The EU's WTO obligations could possibly be beneficial for the EU economy as a whole. However producer margins are very slim and unless the market responds and the major retailers" "arm lock" is loosened then the longer term consequences for the consumer could be deleterious.

ENVIRONMENTAL PROTECTION AND CLIMATE CHANGE

8. *To what extent has the system of cross-compliance contributed to an improved level of environmental protection? How is it linking with other EU policy requirements such as the Water Framework Directive?*

Cross compliance obligations largely reflect good farming practice already in place in most cases, so may actually contribute little by way of "additionality" in environmental protection. To be a justification for direct payment, compliance should be ensured. A whole farm/estate approach could be developed that sees support being accurately and effectively cross-complied with management objectives that fit into regional biodiversity and other plans—and those objectives periodically checked and reviewed. There is insufficient joined up thinking between cross compliance and other EU policy requirements. Additional national regulation could be avoided if cross compliance was used as a tool for implementation of water framework or soils directive objectives, for example.

9. *How can the CAP contribute to mitigation of, and adaptation to, climate change? What do you consider the role of biofuels to be in this regard?*

As indicated above, it may become impossible to separate agriculture and energy policy in the EU, with agricultural businesses being expected to deliver both food and energy production. This may bring it's own challenges in relation to supply. If the CAP can deliver a more market orientated agricultural sector, then the sector would be able to pick up on the potential economic and market benefits of biofuels and respond accordingly.

There needs to be more thought given to the impacts of other policy objectives such as Water Framework Directive on agriculture and climate change. The approach at the moment appears to be "pristine water quality at all costs". The socio-economic impacts of achievement this objective must have greater priority in policy making and funding measures for rural development.

FINANCING

10. *The Commissioner has expressed her dissatisfaction at the financing agreement reached by the Member States at the December 2005 Council. Do you consider the current budget to be sufficient? Do you consider co-financing to be a possible way forward in financing the Common Agricultural Policy?*

If the Rural Development Regulation is to be the mechanism for delivering wider rural objectives, then a reduction in the budget is not feasible. However, at a time where we are competing with China and India, spending of the EU budget needs to be directed at achieving an agricultural sector that is efficient and market orientated. We need to be able to justify the budget when compared to the benefits of spending, for example, on education.

ENLARGEMENT

11. *What has been the impact on the CAP of the 2004 and 2007 enlargements and what is the likely impact of future enlargements of the EU on the post-2013 CAP?*

Digressivity to fund accession countries would be resented by other member states. In all equity the budget should have been expanded to absorb the new member states, although enlargement has been remarkably successful.

SIMPLIFICATION OF THE CAP AND OTHER ISSUES

12. *How could the CAP be further simplified and in what other ways would you like to see the Common Agricultural Policy changed in the short and/or the long term?*

SRPBA accepts that a single Commodity Market Organisation (CMO) would be a helpful administrative simplification, although as indicated above, the facility for some emergency intervention could be required until there is a clearer strategic approach to income stabilisation. Export subsidies should be reduced and export taxes phased out.

The SRPBA also supports full decoupling of payments, so remaining links to commodities should be phased out.

In principle the move to flat rate per hectare payments is a further step in decoupling, and will be expected to be accompanied by including within the single payment scheme a larger part of the total managed land area. This in turn can bring more land within the minimum standards of care defined by cross compliance obligations. If cross compliance was set at the appropriate level across the EU, then fewer competitive agri-environment measures would be needed in pillar two, so it could have a narrower focus on rural business and development.

However, there will be a significant redistribution of support if payment is removed from a historic based allocation to a regional average basis. This is likely to hurt the more intensive dairy and cattle production farms. The SRPBA therefore has supported historic payments, although with the acceptance that these will be gradually reduced over time through modulation to Pillar II.

Cross compliance could be simplified and should be consistently applied across member states to ensure fair terms of competition. The penalty regime should also be reconsidered to ensure proportionality and fairness.

The SRPBA is opposed to capping of either Pillar I or Pillar II monies. There is no objective reason for it, and it would simply penalise those farms which employ most workers. It would reverse the needed concentration and enlargement of farm businesses and set in train costly but unnecessary restructuring of businesses.[2]

11 June 2007

---

[2]   Please see European Landowners" Organisation Submission to the European Commission and Parliament on the CAP Health Check May 2007.

Examination of Witnesses

Witnesses: MR DAVID FURSDON, President, PROFESSOR ALLAN BUCKWELL, Chief Economist, Country Land & Business Association, MR ANDREW DOUGLAS, Chairman of Primary Industries and MR JOHN DON, Immediate Past Chairman, Scottish Rural Property & Business Association, examined.

Q205 Chairman: Good morning. Can I first of all welcome you and thank you for finding the time to come to talk to us? We are doing this inquiry into the health check but really looking forward as well to the new CAP. If you could just briefly introduce yourselves and then perhaps make a short general statement on your overall position, then we will go into a question and answer routine. What I do not want to do, to be quite honest, is to put a specific question to the English and then a specific question to the Scots. I think it is much better if we can have more of a general discussion. The other thing I should point out is that this is a formal session, there will be a transcript, you will have the opportunity of looking at the transcript and revising it before it is released. We are web cast and actually we do have evidence that people do listen to it. That is all I am prepared to say on that one!

Mr Fursdon: Thank you. I am David Fursdon, President of the CLA. To my left is Allan Buckwell our Chief Economist and essentially the plan was that I would give the introductory statement and I would take some of the practical questions and anything too difficult I would give to Allan to answer. Obviously we welcome this opportunity to explain our vision for EU land management and we basically see the EU policy and the budget review over the next few years as absolutely fundamental. We want to try to encourage a strategic and long term view of this. Indeed, we notice that this is what the Budget Commissioner asked for last week in Brussels, a frank debate without any preconditions or taboos on the challenges and risks for the EU going into the 21st century. That is really what motivated our paper. The UK produced its vision for the CAP in December 2005 (produced by Defra and the Treasury) but it did not seem to us to address many of the questions that we want to ask questions about and which lies behind what we are trying to produce through our policy. From our point of view, as we have said before, the EU and the world face two enormous challenges which are feeding the world—the growing population in the world—but at the same time making a significant change to the environmental impact of agriculture. We are increasing the positive externalities (in economic speak)—landscapes and habitats—but actually reducing the negative externalities—pollution of soil, water and the atmosphere. That is very complex and they are interrelated. Obviously farming affects the environment and the environment affects farming; it goes both ways. These are big enough challenges on their own but when you add climate change to that as well then we see this as really very fundamental. We

maintain that the EU is such an important zone just in terms of its population and its sheer size, economic power and so on, that it has a self-interest as well as a moral interest in looking at what are global challenges. We cannot ignore the effects of our policies on the rest of the world. Climate change and bio-diversity loss are global problems and we cannot just push them away and forget about them because they will affect us whether we like it or not. Food and environment are established core competencies of the EU and therefore as the challenges faced by these policies grow and the EU itself will grow in the years ahead, we start from the proposition that you cannot conceive of an EU budget not dealing with these issues and if it is going to deal with them we cannot see how this budget can contract as the EU expands and the problems increase. We argue that we must step out beyond the narrowly focussed discussions of things like compulsory and voluntary modulation and all that sort of thing, to look more fundamentally at our food and environmental policies and how we should tackle them. Our summary is, as we have said to you, that we need a European food and environmental security policy. Only once you get the broad objectives of that agreed can you then move on to the budgetary consequences of that.

Q206 Chairman: Thank you, that is a very impressive statement of high ideals. Would you care to make an opening comment, Mr Don?

Mr Don: Thank you. I speak as the immediate past Chairman of the SRPBA. I am a low ground farmer in Aberdeenshire.

Q207 Chairman: Whereabouts in Aberdeenshire?

Mr Don: About dead centre; half way between Inverurie and Huntly. On my right is Andrew Douglas who farms right on the top of the Scottish border with Northumberland. He is Chairman of our Primary Industries which covers agriculture and forestry and other primary industries. We do welcome this opportunity to come down to London and give our evidence to you. I think it is an especially important time because we should not interfere with the run of the 2003 reforms and they should be able to run their course. We strongly believe that agriculture and other primary industries need a period of stability following what has been a massive change. However, since we gave our evidence there have been quite a number of considerable changes, all of these changes tending to increase the effects of globalisation and liberalisation of trade. We have, for instance, seen the demand of agricultural commodities rise considerably to the point where supply and demand are much more closely balanced. This may have helped the arable sector but it has certainly not been all that helpful to the grazing livestock sector, Scotland, as you know, is a very pastoral country relative to the rest of the UK. The growing change from food production to fuel production is exerting even more pressures on both agriculture and forestry and the management of the environment. On top of this we are seeing even more clearly the effects of climate change. We have only to look at situations in other parts of the world with the all important result of water being a key resource. Yet despite these points that I make, we continue to see budgetary pressures not only on the existing CAP but also other measures covering the environment—such as Natura 2000—and minimal support for forestry. We believe that the new policy direction should recognise clearly the strategic importance of food and fuel production, and timber production. We believe that there is a need to create a core fund for primary industries that will keep farmers and foresters in production, especially when they face what might be termed natural disasters (whether they be disease, floods, storm or whatever). We also believe that policy direction should be keyed into encouraging land based initiatives in both agricultural and diversified businesses as well as supporting such issues as cooperation and the rural communities through social enterprise and related infrastructure measures. Thus this will help prepare primary industries face the increased exposure of the world market place. We also strongly believe that capping will actually have the opposite effect on that. We also believe that the way forward is for land managers to be rewarded for the non-market public goods they deliver especially with regard to the environment. Furthermore we think it is very important that there is a sound funding regime for the less favoured areas. 85% of Scotland currently sits in the less favoured area. Natura 2000 is again very applicable to us in Scotland. We believe that there should be a transition period in the system and in that transition period a core funding to ensure that primary production is kept in production. We believe that this is an unparalleled opportunity to make radical changes as long as this happens in a beneficial way, and as long as the politics of the budget and the negative dogmatic views of some do not dominate the negotiations. I have to say that we saw that (at the time of the British Presidency in 2006) which did not help the cause of rural development. There is a chance to establish, as my colleague on my left has said, a creative framework that not only supports sustainable food, fuel and timber production, but also a sustainable eco system that delivers a wide range of bio-diversity and recreational benefits. This will hopefully safeguard our security as well as our natural and cultural heritage. What we are looking for in the future is a food, forestry, fuel and environment policy for Europe.

Q208 *Chairman:* Thank you very much. I hope you do not mind if I adopt at this stage a relatively challenging tone and pick up some of the points you made in your evidence and actually appeared in your opening statements as well. The Country Land and Business Association in your evidence argue—as you argued in the opening statement—that the CAP should focus on global food and environmental security. I think the question there must be why? Why should European tax payers be expected to finance a CAP regime which has as its focus global considerations rather than European considerations? There might be a sound moral argument but that is not always a sufficiently powerful argument when we are dealing with the nuts and bolts of getting individual Member States to represent their own interests. If I can take out something from the Scottish presentation, the evidence in particular, you suggested that the objectives of the CAP should be a competitive and market orientated agriculture. What I am not clear about is what would that actually mean for Scottish agriculture? What would Scottish agriculture look like if it were viewed in terms of a competitive and market orientated agriculture? What would be the structure of agriculture in Scotland in that context? What would that do to the role of agriculture in the wider rural economy? Would that result in agriculture becoming in a way more or less important?

Mr Fursdon: We do not believe that you can separate the two, especially since climate change has come along. A lot of the effects of climate change are international and actually what we do in Europe and what we do in the world are interrelated in a way which they have not been interrelated before.

Mr Buckwell: We are not arguing that the EU should have a global food security policy; we are arguing that the EU should have at the core of its agricultural and environmental policy the objectives of food and environmental security and these things are interrelated. By European food security what we mean is protecting the long run food production capacity of the European Union. We are not talking about European self-sufficiency; we are talking about the capacity to produce. For example, a key consideration for the single payment at the moment is keeping agricultural land in good agricultural environmental condition. This seems a highly intelligent thing to do and those who are wanting to wave goodbye to the single payment had better explain how they are going to ensure that all of Europe's agricultural land is kept in good agricultural and environmental condition. We are not talking about European self-sufficiency—Europe is the world's largest food importer—but what we are saying is that if Europe insists on having higher and higher environmental standards as it is, which we support, and wants to liberalise trade and implicitly reduce its production, who does it think these additional imports are going to come from and with what environmental impacts? It is at that level we say that Europe is big enough and important enough and influential enough to want to care about the global environmental impact of its European policies as well as the local impact. European citizens care about bio-diversity loss worldwide, not just in Europe. European citizens worry about climate change which, as David says, has a worldwide impact. If we simply displaced European production and produced it somewhere else and had the same climate change impact we have gained nothing. That is why we need an integrated European food and environmental security policy.

Mr Don: It is important to recognise that, in future agriculture will have to remain competitive in Europe if it is going to survive vis-à-vis competition beyond European borders production. Therefore all measures should be designed to encourage competitiveness. In the past we have seen production subsidies which have done perhaps the opposite. I think that is really the basis of what we were arguing. The effects of this for Scottish agriculture will be a continuing pressure on individual businesses and they will tend to get larger rather than smaller. At the same time, as colleagues have said, there are a number of other pressures coming from other directives of the EU that put us to a disadvantage and that has to be recognised in future policy.

Q209 *Chairman:* Would you like to say a little bit more about how you would be disadvantaged?

Mr Don: For instance, the EU Water Framework Directive has a huge impact on land management and a considerable increase in costs as it takes effect, likewise the Nitrate Vulnerable Zone. These pressures are going to make life difficult if society wants the benefits of these directives vis-à-vis our competitors in the wider world.

Q210 *Lord Cameron of Dillington:* I would like to address the whole question of single farm payments. I have heard it said that single farm payments are environment payments in waiting and I just wondered, from the CLA's point of view, if they were converted into environmental payments what impact do you think this would have on food production and the whole question of food security? Turning to the SRPBA, in your introductory remarks, Mr Don, you said you want to keep core funding to ensure that core farming is kept in production. Actually, the

thing about the single farm payment is that it does not actually ensure that farming is kept in production. You can take the money and not do anything. I wondered, if the Scottish farmers only went for the market place where it was competitive, what changes would take place in Scotland, particularly bearing in mind that the payments are inevitably going to change to area payments in Scotland?

Mr Fursdon: I will start on the single farm payment as an environmental payment. I think one of the practical effects of the single farm payment is that it provides a steady income stream; it may be transitional but it actually enables businesses to plan and know where they are going. That component of what they get they know they are going to get. There have been some hiccups at the start of the scheme but now at least it is on stream. In terms of the environmental payments, that has been less certain particularly with some of the budgetary problems in this country we have had with environmental payments and certainly with a lack of certainty for people who are in a countryside stewardship scheme and are facing an uncertain future when those come to an end. Part of the problem is the consistency of income stream for planning for your business. It depends how you interpret your question, but if they were, if you like, in what one might call Pillar I and therefore a part of a steady income stream then that is easier to cope with perhaps, but if it is in a Pillar II environment where it is perhaps less easily accessible then I think there are some uncertainties and I think that those uncertainties, particularly in the livestock sector which are the areas where I think there are most concerns, particularly at the moment, and in disadvantaged areas, I think the effects on agriculture will depend on the way in which they turn into environmental payments and the way in which Pillar I and Pillar II interact.

Q211 *Lord Cameron of Dillington:* Are you saying that if Pillar I had had greater cross-compliance to get your environmental element in that would be something that you would welcome?

Mr Fursdon: There is already a lot of cross-compliance and it is a question of how much further you move that. I think we are saying that actually that has probably moved as far as it needs to be in order to have good agricultural condition. If you start moving it into greater environmental schemes which may well be related to climate change and others then actually you are probably moving into a different form of income. What we are trying to do is to look at what form that different income might take and not have it bound by the rules and regulations that apply to Pillar I and Pillar II at the moment. In other words, in an ideal world one would be looking for a Pillar III but we do try to live in the real world so we recognise that that may just be impossible. I think it is a question of how you work those environment payments in the future.

Mr Buckwell: The production effects of change in the single farm payment are quite well analysed now. There is plenty of analysis of this. The Scenar 2020 study commissioned by the European Commission looked at this and they show that you can change the single farm payment; you have a big impact on incomes but a much smaller impact on production. They did not analyse the environmental impacts or hardly analysed at all and that is where, if you take the UK vision of slashing the single payment and being pretty silent on what you are doing on Pillar II, you will have a big impact on incomes, you will not have such a big impact on production; the environmental impact is the one I think we would be extremely concerned about. This is why in a sense we have to get straight what is the big picture, how much resource are we prepared to put into paying for environmental services in Europe and how and where. Then it is a secondary detail in our view as to whether it is greening Pillar I or shifting to Pillar II and at the moment this gets snarled in the technicalities of co-financing which is seen very differently around the Member States of Europe.

Mr Douglas: I am a hill farmer and you did mention you were concerned about the future of the upland rural community. As you know in Scotland we are an 85% less favoured area and we have had the less favoured area payment for many years. We have always argued that that payment is a payment to keep people in the glens and valleys. When the people go the schools close which has been happening over the last few years. I am glad to say that I have employed some people recently with young children and the school buses are back running in our valley which is all good news. Those people are required to be there to carry out all the environmental changes that government and other organisations would like to see happen. I know you are arguing that we cannot have people there doing nothing so we are having people carry out environmental change. Although hill farming at the moment, sheep industry in particular, is going through a very difficult period over the last three months the likelihood is that sheep will go from the Scottish hills this autumn. There is a great future we believe for forestry in some of these Scottish hills. The Forestry Commission have told me already that Sitka spruce which we have a lot of would be acceptable even now for carbon sequestration. That is one piece of good news. Also I understand that one major retailer is planning to use Scotch blackface lambs this January instead of importing from New Zealand. They are already making enquiries through hill farmers in Scotland. If we are going to be market

orientated we need the people there to produce these lambs. If one retailer moves to Scotch rather than New Zealand we are hopeful that many others will change as well.

Mr Don: I think we would all admit that the single farm payment is not the most perfectly honed instrument, but what we are arguing for is some form of core funding, as my colleague Andrew says, to keep people in production and to keep businesses in production. If we are looking at what is going to happen to support the rural communities and the rural land management rather than just CAP in the future then I think we need a basis of core funding so that people can actually plan their businesses with a degree of security because, as I said earlier, we have all these other pressures of non-market forces on our businesses.

Q212 Chairman: Can I be absolutely brutal? Why should we keep producers in production if there is no market for the product that they are producing? The other point is, if we look at the Scottish rural economy we find that there is dependent upon agriculture but an increasing proportion of the Scottish rural population is actually employed in non-agricultural activities, so the people remain in rural Scotland for reasons other than agriculture.

Mr Don: In answer to your first question of why we should keep people in production, I think that although it is currently probably not fashionable I believe it is going to become increasingly important that we have a strategic supply of food and fuel in European production. That is the long term view and we can see the pressures on fuel for instance but also, as I said in my introduction, I see the pressures from the third world on the food supplies. It has always been an important policy to try to have a secure supply of food which does not impact heavily on the retail price index. I think there are issues around which indicate that we should support in a long term way the continuation of primary production throughout Europe.

Mr Buckwell: Can I add a flavour from England and Wales? In my view I would put a different gloss on it in addition to what John Don has said; the production of what is the question and in my view it is the production of environmental services for which we value the hills and the uplands and the point is that a great deal of those environmental services are inextricably bound in traditional livestock grazing systems. These systems have created the landscape where people want to walk every single weekend of the year; that is what they want to see. Some agricultural production goes with the provision of these services. Then when you add to that water management and carbon management and the management of upland peat (there is a lot more carbon in the peat of the United Kingdom than there is in most of the forests of western Europe), how that is managed can bring a significant contribution to this country's carbon management. We have to understand the technicalities and the incentives required to bring about that desired management.

Q213 *Viscount Ullswater:* My question really is to the SRPBA because it came out in your evidence. Whereas you accept that the existing market mechanisms should be withdrawn—production subsidies I gather from that—you do say that in the absence of a strategic approach to income stabilisation (which is obviously something which you are concerned about) that there might be a need for emergency intervention. I just wondered if you could give us a view of what criteria should be judged for emergency intervention and where it would be funded from.

Mr Don: To answer your second point first, it should be centrally funded by Europe and co-funded possibly. I think it is important to have a protection because our businesses are so long term and a disaster such as flooding or disease can have such an immediate effect (you can see how foot and mouth has decimated the Scottish sheep industry). In these circumstances we believe that Europe and our own government should protect us to keep us in business for the long term, for the strategic reasons I have already suggested.

Q214 *Viscount Ullswater:* So it would not be attached to any environmental scheme; this is really just emergency relief for the industry when it runs into a crisis.

Mr Don: I think so, which we do not really have at this point. It is not embodied in the present CAP and the present policy for land management and we would like to see that.

Q215 *Viscount Ullswater:* Does that have a reflection for England or Wales?

Mr Fursdon: I do think we have to be responsible as farmers in the first place. In terms of bio-security and disease protection and so on we cannot expect to be bailed out without doing our own bit ourselves. I think that is pretty crucial. I think there are also other mechanisms—market mechanisms or some form of protection—that need to be thought about, certainly in terms of farmers down in my part of the world in Devon. Some of them understand about how to play the futures market, some of them certainly do not. In terms of how to protect themselves against market volatility and risk we need to make sure that we are doing a bit ourselves. It may well be that in part of what we are looking for in the new policy—whatever one might call a re-run of Pillar II or something like

that—money is spent on helping the industry to help itself in crisis situations. That is important, rather than always expecting to be bailed out all the time. I think we have to stand up and be modern and forward looking in the agricultural industry and try to do it, but there will be some things which go beyond what we can do however good businessmen we are.

Mr Buckwell: To add to that, nobody has the right answers. This is a worldwide problem. The United States and Canada put a huge proportion of their farm support into stabilisation mechanisms and yet you would say that the United States has the most sophisticated risk managing capable farmers and the most sophisticated private instruments for dealing with that and yet still they feel the necessity to pump huge public resources into price stabilisation. They have not solved it, we have not solved it; we need to discuss it more. I think simply sweeping it under the carpet will not work because volatility is increasing. Animal diseases, floods, environmental disasters, market problems are going to increase with market liberalisation not diminish so this will become a bigger problem.

Q216 *Chairman:* Is the problem not the balance between the role of the state, the role of the industry and the role of the individual producer? They all have to make a contribution to deal with something like emergency impacts.

Mr Buckwell: Yes, and we have not found the mechanisms yet.

Q217 *Chairman:* There is no future in just looking towards the state.

Mr Fursdon: We are definitely looking for help in standing on our own two feet and not expecting the state to do the whole lot.

Mr Don: I totally accept that. I think it is an issue that has not been properly raised in looking forward to 2013 and beyond.

Q218 *Lord Plumb:* You refer to the producer and the state but there is another element to this of course and that is the body that is handling the product after production and support or otherwise from the state. In trying to solve the problem in this country and around the world surely all parties have to work together to try to find a solution.

Mr Fursdon: Absolutely.

Q219 *Lord Palmer:* First of all I need to remind you that I am a member of your organisation and for many years represented the SLF—as it was in those days—on the ELO. I have been very heavily involved in alternative energy for quite a long time and in your evidence you stress that future agricultural policy must be considered in the context of changes in energy policy. You also suggest that the potential of bio-fuels can best be realised within the context of market orientated agriculture. You did touch on this a little bit earlier, but what changes in land use in Scotland do you anticipate in response to demand for energy from biological sources?

Mr Douglas: We now have Set Aside coming out so there is obviously going to be more energy crops grown in Scotland, but I have a note here that we found in research that Scottish Power would like 12% of Scottish agriculture to go into bio-fuels. Whether that is going to be acceptable by the agricultural community is questionable. That would be a major change in the Scottish landscape.

Q220 *Lord Palmer:* Did you say 12%?

Mr Douglas: Yes. Scottish Power have stated their intention; they would like to put 12% of Scottish agriculture under bio-fuels. I am only quoting figures from Scottish Power; we have not discussed this but it is quite a mind blowing suggestion.

Q221 *Lord Plumb:* Have Scottish Power also said what they want to do with all these wretched wind farms which are appearing all over?

Mr Douglas: I think the problem with the wind farms, as you know, is that the infrastructure is causing more problems now than the wind farm. I looked into wind farms and of course I had no infrastructure at the top of my hills so they were not interested. I also had low flying jets which made it worse. I think wind farms would appear, certainly I think in the Borders, to have reached their limit. The wind farm companies tell me that every time a council has approached them, they have moved them onto the next council, and they moved them on again to the next one. I think wind farms have probably reached their summit mainly because of the infrastructure system.

Q222 *Lord Palmer:* I hope you are right, I have to say.

Mr Don: We think it is very important that the heat and light from biomass and bio-fuel production, using that on a community scale, will actually create huge benefits within the community where it is happening. We would like to see much more emphasis in policy directed to that rather than directed to these mega wind farm projects.

Q223 *Lord Palmer:* That is very interesting. Moving onto climate change, it has been argued that land managers' contributions to addressing climate change are not properly supported by the CAP. Do you have suggestions to offer on how policy might be changed to promote the beneficial farming practices that have been identified and in order to discourage

environmentally harmful practices which I think is a very important point, especially from the media and indeed from what the public's conception of agriculture today is all about?

Mr Buckwell: We argued in the consultation on the reform of the RDR that it was extraordinary that there was not a chapter in that on climate change; there was not and there is not. It did seem to be an extraordinary omission. What can be done? There is a debate here about whether this is a private or a public issue. If we can agree carbon accounts for land managers and the extent to which farmers and foresters are storing carbon in their soils or in their trees and we can agree the accountancy basis for that, then maybe this is an area where private action is sufficient, where there are enough companies who are wanting to offset their carbon emissions to want to do deals with land managers who are storing carbon. At the moment this has all been done through informal and non-governmentally approved and recognised offsetting schemes. We are saying that a primary task in all this is to agree the basis and the carbon accounting methodologies and technologies to unlock this potential. In a sense this is where the regulatory function can be to create the circumstances for a private market to operate but at the moment it does not. In our view that is a key step. The CLA has been working for a couple of years on this and we are hoping to launch our own version of carbon accounts for land managers (which we call CALM) as a contribution to helping this process forward. However, if the private sector is not going to pay for it and we want it done, then this may have to be part of the stewardship of the upland areas or the community's forest. We have an open mind on this but we are saying there is a challenger here that we want different behaviour and we have to find the technologies and the incentives to bring about that different behaviour.

Mr Fursdon: Can I specifically answer the question about the actual farming techniques, the way of actually doing that in an acceptable way for climate change. One of the things that we would be expecting to look at in terms of where the money should be supporting development within agriculture is things like precision farming where the precision application of nutrients does no damage. This is where the research and technology needs to be leading us and these and other methods of farming more efficiently will hopefully have a climate change benefit as well as continuing to produce the products that we need to produce.

Q224 *Chairman:* On the assumption that grain prices, if they are not going to remain at the present high level at least they are going to be at a level higher than we have seen in the relatively recent past, the

global pressure on grain price is going to remain pushing them upward, what is the future of bio-fuels?
Mr Buckwell: It may not be very long. I suspect that because policy has now determined that there will be an expansion in bio-fuels there will be an expansion in bio-fuels and we will then learn whether it is greenhouse gas saving or not, or whether it is the most effective way of achieving that. We will go through a phrase where they expand. If that drives up the food prices even more then I suspect that might be quite a brief phase. I think we have a learning process to go through. Obviously farmers welcome anything that maintains their commodity price; farmers who use them are not so thrilled.

Q225 *Viscount Brookeborough:* In the statement that you submitted to us I think you said that although grain production was going up, grain production per capita in the world was going down. Does that not argue entirely against what you have just said, especially if you are taking more land out for bio-fuel?
Mr Buckwell: I hope it does not. What I have said is that the policy on renewable energy is that bio-fuel will be a contribution. It seems to me to be perfectly sensible. Let us try it and see how far it goes and how cost effective it is in producing greenhouse gas. Let us see if it reduces any greenhouse gas emissions once people agree what the accountancy is, which they have not. This is a diversion of what could be food grain into another purpose. Given the demands from the human population one wonders how far that can go. I suspect that this will be a decade or two of experimentation until we find other forms of renewable energy that are more effective. There is a lot of land based renewable energy—it can come from biomass, particularly in the less productive areas and by the utilisation of grass and other green material—and we have a lot of technology to develop to exploit those possibilities.

Q226 *Lord Plumb:* I want to talk about modulation. In your evidence you wanted to step outside things like modulation. At the same time modulation is very much an issue, whether it is voluntary or whether it is compulsory. Natural England told us that the amount should be increased for modulation; you are saying something somewhat different. I am very interested in your comments on this because, as I read it, you said that your concern was about the distribution key which was applicable to compulsory modulation under which we receive only 80% of what is deducted from the single farm payment. How do you see the future developing on modulation? It is an issue that never seems to be resolved and therefore I think it is important that people do understand what

this is about both on a voluntary and compulsory basis.
Mr Buckwell: In a sense the UK is hoist by its decisions in the 1980s and 1990s to not make use of what we now call Pillar II, the predecessor schemes. Therefore we have a miserable share of Pillar II budget, therefore if we want to have sensible sized environment schemes and rural development schemes we have to modulate. The UK is out of line with all of the other Member States through its history of how it has developed policy over the last 20 or 30 years. Therefore that has brought up this discussion of voluntary versus compulsory modulation. English, Welsh and I suspect Scottish farmers feel that we have gone far enough at the moment by the decisions that have already been made where our modulation will be approaching 20% by the end of this financial perspective. If there is more compulsory modulation one assumes that the voluntary modulation will diminish accordingly. However, paradoxically, because with voluntary modulation all the receipts remain in the Member States that is more attractive from our perspective that compulsory modulation where 20% of it is siphoned off. This then gets us caught up into these wider issues about the distribution of the budget and co-financing which of course have to be grasped. In our feeling we have to get the big picture right first and if we are all agreed in Europe that there is going to be more funding in the things we currently do in Pillar II and if that is going to be co-financed we have to agree the keys for this so it is seen to be fair and reasonable to all Member States, whereas at the moment the UK is not being dealt with fairly on this score we feel.

Q227 *Lord Plumb:* What about Scotland?
Mr Don: In general terms we would like to see the argument on modulation disappear into a more sensible regime in 2013 which would be fairer to the UK, to England, Wales and Scotland. In the meantime we are caught in the dichotomy. Our individual member farmers are not very keen on increased voluntary modulation or modulation of any sort. With a historic payment we have always said in our organisation we see a move from the core Pillar I funding to more money going into Pillar II, to use the current terminology. What we would really like to see is a re-thought out policy in the future. As I said in my opening remarks, we see a policy for land management rather than the CAP embracing all the issues of land management rather than just agriculture.

Q228 *Lord Plumb:* Do you see the problem increasing because of the new member countries? Sitting there we had the minister from Romania telling us that the average sized holding in his country was something like three hectares. When you talk about switching money from Pillar I to Pillar II for whatever purpose or however it is done, how can you relate this to the wider scale? We talked to him about the possibility of the use of this in terms of environmentally friendly farming et cetera and he said they do not want money for that, they want money to improve their structures and that is understandable but if they improve the structure of farming surely that comes back into Pillar I. It is a dilemma I think that Europe itself is going to battle with for a very long time.

Mr Fursdon: Can I just say one thing on modulation? When it actually arrives on the paperwork that you receive and it says "Modulation" and you look at it and it takes money off, it is a pretty seminal moment as you will know. I think it emphasises the feeling amongst a number of people that it has gone from here but if I am to actually develop my business where is it going to be available to me in the future? The whole question of Pillar II and whether it is accessible is linked to this. I think the feeling about how one can actually plan an agricultural business in the changing that is going on at the moment is really quite hard and I think that is part of it. Will Pillar II and the funds that have been modulated actually provide an ability to plan forward for your business in a way that Pillar I has traditionally done? I think that modulation raises that whole question.

Q229 *Viscount Brookeborough:* I must declare an interest in that I live in Northern Ireland and Northern Ireland is not represented here today, but we do have various rural development funds at the moment which may be proportionally more than the remainder of the United Kingdom through the peace dividend and I do use some of it. For the CLA first, you indicate that more funding should be directed towards Axes 1 and 3 of the Rural Development programme. Would you like to comment a little more on this? More broadly, could you outline your views on how rural industry should be supported by this and other funds? For Scotland, we would like to know to what extent this may contribute to a moving of population from the rural area to other areas?

Mr Fursdon: Could I start by the second part of your question which is about rural industry and say that I think the Common Agricultural Policy has a bit of a role but there are a lot of other things which impact on rural industry and rural business development which probably lie outside the Common Agricultural Policy. I am thinking in terms of things like the planning system and that sort of thing which actually has the capacity to alter the ability of rural businesses to develop and diversify in a way which might allow the market to provide a solution if the template was

right and planning formed part of that template. I see it having a bit of a role but there is quite a lot of rural business development which is not impacted, I do not believe, by the CAP.

Q230 *Viscount Brookeborough:* In Northern Ireland we live close to the Republic and we would find that money that is made available to the government is far easier to get at in the Republic. We would say that if you go into an office and say, "I've got an idea for rural development in the Republic" they would say, "Brilliant, this is it, this is what you can have". If you were to say, "What are the problems?" they would say, "Oh, sort them out later". If you go into the equivalent which would be a UK type office they would say, "Oh my goodness, there are a lot of problems here; we don't know how we'll get round this". These stumbling blocks are very, very important whether it is planning or otherwise.

Mr Fursdon: I absolutely agree and I think the thing is compounded a little bit by the way in which, if you take the aspect of the CAP that might be applied to this which would be the Rural Development Regulation and you look at the fact that we are now facing a situation where everybody is trying to do it differently in all the RDAs around the country and you have different schemes being evolved and in terms of a national organisation which we are, trying to look at it strategically is increasingly difficult because you have different interpretations around the country. I reinforce what you say so that it is actually compounded by the way in which Pillar II is being dealt with in the regional development agencies.

Mr Buckwell: We do not think your colleague Lord Haskins did us a huge favour in devolving responsibilities of some of this to RDAs who do not seem to us to be the ideal organisations to deliver. Regarding the emphasis we made on more Axes 1 and 3 this was intended to be more of a European point and it was Lord Plumb's point that we are trying to devise a second pillar of the CAP that suits incredibly different countries—27 of them across the EU—and in many of the countries in the east and the south of Europe there really is a lot more need in Axes 1 and 3 to improve the infrastructure and the restructuring of marketing and quality production of food and getting farmers to work together because they are incredibly small structures and so on. There is also more of that work to be done in the United Kingdom and in England, and I can perfectly understand the Government's questioning why they should be European funded, but in the wider context of cohesion across an EU of 27 I can perfectly see that the south and the east of Europe see a tremendous use for the ideas of Axes 1 and 3, competitiveness of agriculture and diversifying the rural economy. I still think, as David said, that what really determines whether your rural economy is vibrant or not is more to do with your domestic infrastructure, service provision, planning system and tax treatment of small businesses and so on.

Q231 *Viscount Brookeborough:* Particularly, too, tourism in Scotland. We sometimes visit further north than Sutherland and the picture we get from local people there is that the hotels are not developing—if anything they may be going downhill—because there are fewer tourists going further north because there are fewer facilities and less support for the environment there.

Mr Douglas: I think you are obviously concerned about the rural de-population in Scotland (this came up earlier on) and we already have in Scotland the Land Management Contract Scheme which has run out of money at the moment but it is in place to give environmental benefits in Pillar II which are non-competitive. The main payment out of Pillar IIs the LFASS payment which I talked about earlier which is designed to keep people in these rural areas. As someone said earlier in the meeting, tourists are obviously very important to Scotland—I think it was our colleague from England who said this—but the tourists do not want to see a Scotland with no animals, so we have to keep people there farming in some way to have the hills in an attractive state for the tourists to go. I must say that the tourist problems in Scotland are not being helped by the enormous costs of getting to the north of Scotland from wherever because of transport costs. I can see that problem becoming greater over the next year or two.

Q232 *Viscount Brookeborough:* What developments could there be through funding?

Mr Douglas: The RSPB are very keen to have the wildlife explored in Scotland. They always argue when we go to LFASS meetings that they need the money to keep people there, even to show tourists the wildlife that is on the Scottish mountains.

Q233 *Viscount Brookeborough:* I do not think we have very many new ideas of what could be done if this funding became available and how it could integrate with agricultural communities.

Mr Douglas: We have discussed in our organisation that possibly some of the LFASS money would be directed to small businesses which might operate in some of the highland areas of Scotland, farmers having their small farm and having an alternative business.

Q234 *Viscount Brookeborough:* Do you have problems with planning for diversification?

Mr Douglas: Yes, we do.

Q235 *Viscount Brookeborough:* In some cases it might even be where somebody wants to change the use of a barn and not even change the appearance of it and they are told they cannot do it.

Mr Douglas: There is a major problem with planning in Scotland, yes.

Mr Don: I would add that that differs from region to region but on the whole planners are obstructive rather than constructive in more cases than not. From the reports that have been coming in centrally to us there are difficulties with planning and making changes to strategic plans, five year plans. It is a very rigid system.

Q236 *Viscount Brookeborough:* So when funds do become available there are major national stumbling blocks.

Mr Douglas: Yes.

Q237 *Viscount Ullswater:* I should say that I am involved in farming in the Lake District. From what you have been describing it sounds as if agriculture, certainly in the Borders and further north, is under severe pressure. If I was in any other business I would expect the assets to be reducing in value, ie the land would be reducing in value. However, the opposite seems to be happening. Why should we, as tax payers, be funding a business of which the asset value seems to be continuously rising? People seem to be wanting to invest in land and then, when they have invested in land (generalising of course) they say, "We can't make money out of this; we need some support" and that sort of thing. Is there an answer to that?

Mr Douglas: I accept that land prices in Scotland are holding firm but I think everyone would agree that it is non-farming money that is focussing on the land price. As you agree, when the people come there they think it is a great life coming to Scotland and buying a farm but then when they try to make any money out of it it is a different ballgame. We are finding that lifestyle people are coming to Scotland, buying the farm and then they are asking the existing farmers who are there to do the farming for them, whether it be contracting or on the new tenancy programmes that have been put in place by the Scottish Government. That is happening all the time.

Q238 *Viscount Brookeborough:* From a Northern Ireland perspective, farmers are buying land—all grass, no cultivation at all—for up to £20,000 an acre so they must see something that nobody else has seen.

Mr Douglas: If we had sat here a year ago and someone had told us that milk would be 30 pence a litre by Christmas we would say that was absolute rubbish, yet here we are, we are facing it. If anybody had said to us that wheat would be £200 a ton in a year's time nobody would have believed it. This has all happened.

Q239 Chairman: Surely the position now, because prices are so strong, is that we can remove any form of support in terms of income support and just pay for the environmental security side. The market has sorted income support.
Mr Buckwell: For how long?

Q240 Chairman: It is like all of us, we are all in jobs that sometimes the market rewards and sometimes it penalises, and if you get it wrong you move out.
Mr Don: The sheer volatility of farming and the importance of having a strategic supply of food and fuel is going to be a long term need for Europe and for this country.
Chairman: I think on that point I will hand over to Lord Bach.

Q241 Lord Bach: I want to ask about budget implications. I detect a difference of emphasis, if I may say so, putting it mildly, between Scotland and England and Wales on the issue of what subsidies should be for. I think Scotland thinks they should, in a way, be for production still, while England and Wales certainly do not feel it should be for production but for environmental goods. Am I right in detecting a slight difference of emphasis between you on that, which would be quite understandable? My next question is slightly more serious. Even if England and Wales are right and there should be payments made for environmental goods and environmental services or whatever you call them, the issue arises as to why the tax payer should fork out 43% of the EU budget to the CAP to get farmers to behave properly environmentally when in most other industries—in fact I think in all other industries—those industries get penalised when they do not behave environmentally properly? Why should it be the other way round with agriculture? Thirdly, the figure of 43% was given to us in evidence last week, the total budget of the EU being spent on agriculture and there is a hint in what you have told the Committee in written evidence that you do not think that the amount in the settlement in 2005 was enough. Would you like to expand on why 43% across Europe on agriculture is not enough?
Mr Fursdon: Can I start by giving the England and Wales view which is that while we certainly subscribe to the view that environmental payments are the way forward and that is what we would expect to see the CAP for, there are other things as well in our evidence that we suggest that money should be for. Some of that is production of food in a way which is

environmentally sustainable. There is an element of making sure that production can be done right, ie in an environmentally acceptable way which we believe is one of the objectives of the CAP. I obviously cannot speak for my Scottish colleagues but I would say that we believe in the environment but we believe that there is an interaction with production if we are going to produce food in the right sort of way. In terms of why the tax payer should pay, going back to making sure that we have the ability to produce food in an environmental way and contribute to climate change are, we believe, pretty important things. When you look at the amount of benefits provided by land managers for which there is no market reward, we believe that that is the reason why, in the industries that we are involved in, there is more of a case than there is in some other industries where there are not the same degree of public goods provided.
Mr Buckwell: The 43% of the European budget is the most phoney statistic that anyone, including the prime minister, could use. Because we decided to only give agriculture and structural policies to Europe then of course their budget share figures larger in the European budget. What matters is that the 53 billion euros per annum on budget heading two in the European Union is about 0.5% of EU GDP, it is about 1% of European total public expenditure. That is the figure that we should be looking at in relation to looking after 75% of the territory, 75% f the environment; most of the bio-diversity and the natural environment is in that 75% and not the urban part where there is little natural environment; it is dealing with 40% of the population, 5% of the working population and 3% of EU GDP. We feel that 1% of the European budget to do all that is not completely stupid. When we see that the challenges confronting us in both food and the environment in the decades that lie ahead, it does not seem to us to be completely stupid to think that we might have to spend more to get what Europeans want on those fronts rather than less and that we would rather argue about what the policy is for and how we are going to achieve it and then decide the budget, rather than do what the UK Government is hell-bent on doing which is to reduce the budget first and then ask what we are going to spend it on. That is our answer. Why should consumers pay for the environment where other businesses are paid to obey environmental laws is a very good question. It is because land managers, farmers, steward environment the way that no other business does. If you simply say to farmers, "We are liberalising your market, we will expose you to international prices, you are going to get no single payment (which is the UK vision) and we will give you a small amount of money to deliver a few environmental goodies", do you think we will get the English countryside that the public wants because I

24 October 2007   Mr David Fursdon, Professor Allan Buckwell, Mr Andrew Douglas
and Mr John Don

do not and we do not. Go and talk to the environmental organisations, they do not think so either.

Q242 *Lord Bach:* Why should farmers have to be paid, that is what I do not understand?
Mr Buckwell: Because consumers will not pay in their food. Take organic farming. Organic farming has had 30 years of massive publicity. It is a sign of quality, of looking after the environment, and still it is only about 3 or 4% of total consumption and we have to provide public subsidy otherwise we do not get enough of it. There is a clear indication that what people say they want in environmental standards they do not match in their purchases in the supermarket. If we do not provide some assistance to the deliverers of these environmental services then we will not get the services.

Q243 *Chairman:* I used to help run a medieval university and it had some medieval buildings which were quite expensive to maintain. People used to flock in droves to look at this wonderful university campus. Tourist buses used to stop. We had to spend a lot of money on maintaining it but we did not get a penny of public money to sustain that environment.
Mr Buckwell: That is why our heritage is crumbling.

Q244 *Lord Bach:* You would argue for more money, not just in agriculture but much wider than that.
Mr Buckwell: We are certainly saying that there is such a thing as rural cultural heritage which costs to be maintained and those who are bearing those costs are being exposed to unremunerative prices by the market alone so that if you take away the present support do not expect to get the same quantum of looking after of these services.

Q245 *Chairman:* Surely the argument is that you could get the environmental return through regulation but at a cost which has to then transmit itself through the price mechanism.

Mr Buckwell: I guess the argument then is: can you achieve the outcomes we were talking about by regulation, by fear, thou shalt manage your farms better. I am suggesting to you that our experience in being able to do that is not very satisfactory. In terms of achievement and results you will find that if you try to bring about the environmental standards you want by pure regulation you will not achieve it. Look at the mess we have made of the regulation of the single payment and environment schemes at their introduction. That is a really sad thing because the last four years were correct moves in policy, the farming industry in a sense was signed up to it and we made such a bad job of the administration of the introduction of the single payment and environment schemes that farmers are turned off these things.

Q246 *Lord Bach:* The 43% figure is not just used by the prime minister, it was used by the environmental groups that came last week. It was they who gave us the 43% figure. I think maybe a word in their ear.
Mr Buckwell: Thank you for the tip.

Q247 *Chairman:* I will now just give you the chance, if you think there is something you really wanted to say and have not had the opportunity, now is the time. If not, very many thanks.
Mr Buckwell: R and D and extension for agriculture, how we are going to produce the food we want in the world with the environmental standards we want in the world is a very serious issue. Again it is not all being done by the private sector and in Europe we are turning our back on some of the technologies that are on offer. This is a very serious issue.
Lord Plumb: I wonder whether the CLA and Scotland could respond a bit on trade liberalisation. The Doha Round is ahead of us and who knows what effect that is going to have on liberalisation, what effect will it have through the phytosanitary measures and so on and so forth. Are they going to be more important to us than tariffs and so on? I think if you could expand on them a bit in your notes back to us that would be very helpful.
Chairman: Thank you very much indeed.

WEDNESDAY 24 OCTOBER 2007

Present	Bach, L	Plumb, L
	Brookeborough, V	Sewel, L (Chairman)
	Cameron of Dillington, L	Ullswater, V
	Palmer, L	

Memorandum by the Campaign to Protect Rural England

1. CPRE works for a beautiful and productive countryside which is enjoyable for both present and future generations. We campaign for the more sustainable use of land and other resources. We are a leading non-governmental organisation in the field of planning and the protection of the countryside and the integration of these with land management policy. We also have considerable experience in the field of rural service provision and the management of rural development in order to retain a clear distinction between urban and rural England and tackle rural poverty.

2. CPRE has led the debate about the purpose and the future of the countryside since its foundation in 1926. We have worked with successive governments to ensure that the incomparable asset of the English countryside is retained and enhanced for future generations. To a significant extent we enjoy a countryside which is the product of over 80 years of work and policy influence by CPRE.

3. We were closely involved in the development of proposals for Natural England and the Commission for Rural Communities, which were part of the Government's response to Lord Haskins" Rural Delivery Review. We played a leading role amongst the environmental non-governmental organisations during the passage of the Natural Environment and Rural Communities Act. We have also been engaged in the development of farming and land management policy and the future of the funding of land management and rural development. We gave evidence, both written and oral, to the House of Commons EFRA Select Committee during their inquiry into the Government's CAP Vision document.

4. We draw on our insight into the protection and enhancement of landscape, its associated biodiversity, enjoyment of it by the public and the viability of rural communities from the position of a stakeholder unencumbered by the ownership of land and the particular perspectives and priorities that land ownership can generate.

5. We are grateful for the extension to the deadline for evidence that we have been granted.

6. CPRE is one of the signatories to the submission by Wildlife and Countryside Link to the Inquiry. For the sake of brevity we restrict our own response to observations additional to those made in the Wildlife and Countryside Link submission. CPRE is particularly concerned with the effects of the CAP on the management, conservation and enhancement of agricultural landscapes and their very diverse character. We are also concerned with the effects of agricultural practice on our historic and archaeological inheritance. Furthermore, we are concerned with the effects of CAP reform on agricultural communities and those whose livelihoods are closely dependent upon the future of agriculture and forestry. CPRE acknowledges the crucial role that food production plays in the management of the English countryside. We are also strongly aware of the importance of sustaining a farming community which has this expertise, together with the associated professions and businesses: veterinary practices; machinery maintenance, markets, product processors and trade support, for example.

OVERVIEW

Q1. *What should be the long term objectives of the CAP? Does the title "Common Agricultural Policy" aptly fit your perceived objectives of the policy? What do you consider to be the main pressures on the CAP as it currently is?*

7. The long term objective of the CAP, or any policy which supersedes it, should be to maximise the sustainable management of land for public benefit through encouraging agriculture, horticulture and forestry to deliver public goods. The title "Common Agricultural Policy" does not adequately describe these objectives. However, CPRE is clear that the role of agriculture in any future approach to land management will be crucial. Essentially, CPRE is calling for an Agricultural Public Benefits Fund. Developing the long term objectives of the CAP, (or a fund under any new name) should be regarded as an opportunity to re-affirm the part of farming and land management in the quality of all our lives and to take stock of the huge value of continuity

of good farming practice. It is also an opportunity to make a determined effort to move away from environmentally damaging farming processes and look for possible new ways to harness responsible land management for the public good.

8. There is an urgent need for the CAP to evolve into a system of support for land management with a range of public benefits clearly stated as objectives. This could deliver public goods through farming which would compete in world markets. The attendant public benefits of competent and responsible agriculture would be accommodated through the financial support of a land management fund. CPRE strongly believes that our farming industry is an immensely valuable national asset, with strategic, technical, environmental and societal contribution to make far beyond the short-term calculation of contribution to national prosperity from food and commodity production. Most of the landscape, access and habitats that we value require management which is intimately associated with the productive use of land. Our joint report in 2006 with the National Farmers Union, *Living Landscapes: hidden costs of managing the countryside*, illustrates this point very clearly. The report is submitted to the committee as supplementary evidence. We identified landscape management activity conservatively estimated at £412m per year, beyond that directly stimulated or required through agri-environment schemes. This figure takes no account of work dedicated to wildlife management by farmers which will not always overlap with the landscape work we recorded in our research.

9. The prospect of farmers pursuing world markets so far as they can while their actual management practices are partially directed by financial support for environmental objectives is sometimes characterised disparagingly as "park keeping". CPRE strongly rejects this slur as it misses the crucial point on two counts. First, because this view shows a failure to understand the intimate connection between landscape and habitat management on the one hand and productive farming on the other. Huge differences to landscape and habitat quality arise from different levels of intensity of farming, both in terms of margins of land left for lower productivity and also the level of production from the main areas dedicated to production. The public benefits of land management would be much harder to secure without production taking place. Second, all the activities referred to as "park keeping" are, and always have been, integral to good farming practice. It is the destructive mixture of production subsidy in the past, intense global competition and supermarket dominance which has suppressed many of these good management practices. CPRE regards a reformed CAP and a new land management fund as a means to redress the unhealthy and unwelcome dysfunction of such pressures for over-intensive farming.

10. A reformed CAP needs to prevent a substantial and disorderly collapse of farming. The significant contraction of agriculture in England and the collapse of certain parts of the industry would have far more destructive consequences than in many other countries. This is because of the intimate association over millennia of the productive use of land, wildlife habitat and the character of the landscape, by comparison with places in the world where productive agricultural land and wildlife-rich wilderness are segregated. Examples include Canada, the USA and the formerly collectivised farmland of some central European countries.

11. The serious decline of farming in England would do far more than simply reduce inputs and the area under cultivation or grazing. Networks of semi-natural landscapes (our farmland), with combinations of management to which the majority of native species have adapted, would be lost. The variation across the country, expressed in the style, scale, age and pattern of field boundaries, woodland, farm buildings, livestock, crops and soil, would be suppressed or allowed to degenerate. The three processes most likely to damage locally distinctive landscapes and habitats on a very wide scale are the abandonment of farming on less productive land, market-oriented rationalising of farming techniques to cut costs, and renewed and increased intensity of farming on better grade land. All three are very likely if farming comes under significantly greater pressure in England. Some would argue that the pace of change is already accelerating and that this is masked for the time being by the inevitable time delay consequent upon long term investment decisions and existing contracts and capacity of individual farmers.

12. Just as much of England is dependent on farming for managing and maintaining its character and wildlife habitat, so it is dependent on farming for its identity and thus its marketability for visitors and tourists. The economic interests of rural settlements and market towns would be very severely affected if they were surrounded by landscapes increasingly polarising between dereliction and intensification. The overall proposition of visiting England could suffer too and with it, the fortunes of the tourism industry. The views of Visit Britain on the value of agricultural activity to the tourism industry should be heard. Accelerating suburban and ex-urban development would also be much more likely as diversification away from farming became increasingly attractive to struggling farm businesses.

13. CPRE is clear that successful rural diversification depends on a wider context of agricultural activity, which keeps the countryside distinctive and cared for. Ironically, it is likely that if farming were to decline significantly, the proposition of rural location could become less marketable. This would not be surprising:

successful urban communities are rarely derelict or overwhelmingly dominated by commercial interests. Rural communities and businesses would become less rural and less distinctive and would suffer as a consequence.

14. Further CAP reform should not be undertaken until there is a broad consensus on the likely effects of such reform, agreement on what we value about the countryside and how we shall retain what we value in the long term. In CPRE's view, the Government is under an obligation to lead this debate, and build a new foundation for farming and environmental land management in the future.

15. A reformed CAP could be a great opportunity. But ill-judged or hasty change could help destroy the system which puts to good use the vast majority of the land surface of England and with it, much of its cultural significance, wildlife and distinctive character. We might lose the function of much farmland in England, some of our few remaining links between the wider population and the land and the ability to manage and use it productively for the widest possible public benefit.

The Reformed CAP

Q2. *What has been your experience so far with the reformed CAP? What has worked well and less well? And where can lessons can be learned?*

16. CPRE welcomes the decisive break with production linked payments, despite the considerable difficulties experienced in the transition to an area-based payments system. We were disappointed with the concession of some ground to the NFU on the question of exemptions of small arable fields from cross compliance rules concerning hedgerow protection and overall, we consider the environmental benefits from cross compliance to be meagre. Such a weak deal for the tax payer is unlikely to be defensible for very long. However, the value of the Single Payment in helping continuity of farming in very uncertain times is considerable and, we believe, sometimes underestimated.

17. The chaos and uncertainty surrounding payments of the Single Payment, Entry Level Environmental Stewardship and Higher Level Stewardship needs no further exposition, but there are important lessons to learn from the experience. For CPRE, one of the most important is the urgent need not to let farmers down if they rise to the challenge to calls to farm responsibly and imaginatively for landscape, access and habitat improvement. Farming and its associated land management practices require long term investment decisions and making changes can be onerous. It is profoundly damaging to the public interest if Governments, acting on behalf of society, disenchant the only group of people competent and numerous enough to achieve agri-environmental goals.

18. The Government's record in negotiating an agreement for agri-environment funding until 2013 over the last eighteen months has been only partly salvaged by the achievement of 14% modulation. This is still far below the 20% target which the Government itself established. The funds available, though substantial, are not enough to deliver the scale of land management improvements which are now regarded as necessary for biodiversity targets. The character and diversity of farmed landscape, which does not benefit at present from a PSA target, is more vulnerable still to this shortfall. Higher Level Stewardship is an immensely valuable scheme and remains, in our view, under-funded.

The Single Payment Scheme

Q3. *Do you consider the Single Payment Scheme to be a good basis for the future of EU agricultural policy? What changes might be made at the EU level to the Single Payment Scheme, including to the rules governing entitlements, in the short and/or the longer-term?*

19. CPRE does not anticipate a long term future for the Single Payment as its benefits to the wider public are not direct enough, or good enough value. As an interim measure, it serves a useful purpose. But the challenge is to make a transition to a new funding regime for land management without losing most of the resources which are presently devoted to the Single Payment.

20. The ending of the Single Payment is likely to have a profound impact on the profitability of some businesses, communities and families engaged in farming and land management. Some beneficial land management activities will become less easy to accommodate within farm businesses calculations. Means need to be found within an international agricultural trading system of providing sufficient incentives to ensure these continue where they are necessary. Where competitive farming is likely to bring pressure for environmentally harmful activities, resistance to these should be encouraged. Otherwise, the indirect costs to society in terms of soil and water quality and condition, as well as landscape and wildlife damage, will escalate in the long term.

21. In terms of social equity and in recognition of the advantages of economies of scale, a case can be made for refining the system through tapered payments beyond a certain threshold of income received. It would be wrong in our view to have an absolute cut off, as a large scale of farming can be beneficial and competitive; a reduction in payment per acre for very large holdings, might, however, be more equitable and might make more resources available for smaller, more hard pressed enterprises.

MARKET MECHANISMS

Q4. *What short and longer-term changes are required to the CAP's market mechanisms? Suggestions made by the Commission have included re-examination of certain quotas, intervention, set-aside, export refunds and private storage payments.*

22. One significant risk which is very likely to arise as the result of the move towards ending the Single Payment is the loss of the environmental benefits of Set Aside, both rotational and permanent. Set Aside is the Prodigal Son of agricultural policy, which has yielded significant public benefits after a very shaky start and a conception which had little environmental inspiration. But over the last 15 years, Set Aside rules have been altered to the extent that where rotational cropping has been retained when otherwise it might have been abandoned; there have been good effects on soil quality and wildlife habitat as well as the texture of arable landscapes. Permanent Set Aside has provided an attractively funded route for some farmers to re-establish important linear habitats and hunting grounds for bat and owl species and their prey. Permanent Set Aside has also allowed the protection of water courses and wetlands in intensive arable landscapes. In an unexpected way, Set Aside policy has come of age just when it is likely to be abolished. There is an urgent need to retain its benefits and its effectiveness through another mechanism which is as attractive to farmers in the longer term. The requirements of the Water Framework Directive would be more likely to be met with a management agreement available which offers returns that are competitive with intensive cropping in sensitive or vulnerable places within river catchments.

23. CPRE is seriously concerned that moves to incentivise bio-energy production could replicate the damaging mechanism of production-led subsidies for food, from which we are only now emerging. Damage to eco-systems and landscapes and possibly local food production is as potent, whether the commodity is food or energy.

24. Another significant risk lurks in the dedication of significant acreage to bio-energy production. By definition, the commitment of land for fuel must be long term. There will be far less flexibility in land use in an era when large areas of productive land are contracted to power generating companies and when society is, in turn, dependent on this land for core energy generation. The pressure on less intensively farmed land will grow, to the likely detriment of soil and water quality as well as habitats and landscape character. Expansion of bio-energy cropping should not be artificially boosted without regard for our long term food and other commodity production needs.

RURAL DEVELOPMENT

Q5. *What is your view on the introduction of the European Agricultural Fund for Rural Development (EAFRD)? Do you consider that it is meeting its objectives thus far? Is it suitably "strategic" in nature, meeting the needs of rural society as a whole rather than being restricted to aiding the agricultural industry? How well is it being co-ordinated with other EU and national policies on regional and rural development?*

25. CPRE welcomes the continued commitment by the Government to the EAFRD. However, we consider that closer integration between the three axes of the Fund would be welcome. Closer integration of funding for improving competitiveness, the better integration of farming as a way of life into communities and the measures which encourage the delivery of substantial public goods though farming would probably improve the overall effectiveness of the EAFRD. As different authorities are responsible for different axes, such integration requires particular commitment, for example by Natural England and the Regional Development Agencies.

26. In CPRE's experience, rural development which is supportive of traditional and land based industries, is vulnerable to displacement by footloose commercial activities which can generate higher returns. But such footloose businesses often have unwelcome effects such as attracting out-commuting from towns and cities, generating longer journeys to work on average and failing to offer employment to local people. The EAFRD could help redress the economic pressure in rural economies to abandon land-based businesses which in turn can make a more effective contribution to local economic and social fabric. Our research report *The Real*

Choice, How local foods can survive the supermarket onslaught published in 2006, showed conclusively how valuable local land based businesses can be both for social and economic success at a community level as well as supporting good land management practice and local landscapes and habitats. A copy of this report has been sent to the committee.

27. CPRE is well aware that farming is intimately and inextricably linked with other aspects of rural economies and community. We regard axes one and three of the EAFRD as playing important support roles in farming communities, especially where, as in uplands outside national parks, pressures on communities are very great.

28. We look for more substantial funding for the EAFRD, and in particular for the Higher Level Scheme within Environmental Stewardship. We should also welcome the expansion of the EAFRD to initiate and incentivise local food networks where these are weak or non-existent. Connections between local producers and processors on the one hand and local schools, prisons and hospitals, for example on the other, could be encouraged by expansion of EAFRD funding.

Q6. *Is there a case for a higher level of EU financing of rural development? Do you have a view on the extension of compulsory modulation from Pillar I (Direct Payments) to Pillar II (Rural Development)?*

29. CPRE considers that there is a very important case to be made for increased funding for rural development measures in the UK. Specifically, a more extensive distribution of Higher Level Stewardship schemes is needed, particularly outside the currently targeted Sites of Special Scientific Interest and nationally designated landscapes. CPRE supports the present priorities but we are aware of the demand for funding outside these targeted areas.

30. The extension of compulsory modulation would be welcome in order to present a more equitable face of agri-environment funding to English farmers than the present system of voluntary modulation allows. English farmers are put under additional competitive pressure from the present arrangements. Whether or not this is fair is less important than whether or not it is damaging to our national interests. It should not be achieved, however, at the expense of the overall level of funds available for Pillar II payments. In the longer run, should the Single Payment come to an end, we anticipate that a new land management fund might be founded in expanded resources for Pillar II.

WORLD TRADE

Q7. *What benefits can the EU's World Trade Organisation obligations create for EU agriculture and, consequently, for the EU economy as a whole?*

31. For CPRE, the reciprocal and synchronised removal of trade distorting measures both within the EU and with the rest of the world is a *sine qua non*.

32. The case is made by some for the removal of support payments for English farmers based on the moral argument that such expenditure directly harms the livelihoods of farming communities in developing countries. CPRE would welcome the decoupling of land management in England from damage to the local rural economies of developing countries as was implied in paragraph 1.11 of the CAP Vision paper which the Government published in December 2005. Should radical reform of the CAP take place, it would be possible to establish a support system for farming in England which rewarded farmers for the successful "export" of our native landscape in terms of both domestic and international tourism. This is something which is unlikely to be regarded as a priority for those intent on removing trade distortions.

33. The EU is already ensuring substantial support for developing countries through the Generalised Scheme of Preferences and the "Everything but Arms" agreement. Expenditure on export refunds is now much reduced. It would seem to be unnecessary and unwise to make further concessions in WTO talks which might damage our agricultural industry to little benefit.

34. We should not ignore the serious consequences of merely exporting environmental damage to other parts of the world, many of which have far greater biodiversity to lose than England, or the consequences of increased carbon emissions from the expansion of long distance food export. Both modes of transport and the methods of agriculture need to be carefully appraised for their carbon performance. Furthermore, the urbanisation of the developing world is proceeding very rapidly in many of the countries most able to compete in agricultural trade. It is unclear whether the decoupling of agricultural support from the damage to developing rural economies will be a lasting or effective legacy. We should not, therefore, contemplate the abandonment of much traditional English farming in the unsubstantiated hope that traditional sustainable

agriculture in poorer countries will benefit. For this argument to carry conviction, there would have to be targeting of support for small-scale farmers in developing countries, which is contrary to the likely outcome of opening up global markets.

ENVIRONMENTAL PROTECTION AND CLIMATE CHANGE

Q8. *To what extent has the system of cross-compliance contributed to an improved level of environmental protection? How is it linking with other EU policy requirements such as the Water Framework Directive?*

35. CPRE considers the system of cross compliance has played a limited role in improving environmental protection. We describe this as meagre. Anecdotal evidence suggests some improvement in the management of hedge and ditch margins in arable fields. The imminent end of Set Aside is more likely to threaten successful achievement of the standards required by the Water Framework Directive. It is also apparent from our discussions at a local level that there is considerable frustration amongst some farmers at the inconsistent and sometimes inflexible approach of Defra to minor infringements of cross compliance rules. We are unable to draw any generalised conclusion from the limited evidence available to us. It would appear wise, however, to allow as much discretion as possible for local officials to encourage confidence in the system.

Q9. *How can the CAP contribute to mitigation of, and adaptation to, climate change? What do you consider the role of biofuels to be in this regard?*

36. While there is no need to achieve maximum production from farmland in the foreseeable future, there is a need, in the view of CPRE, to keep indigenous farming systems in England viable and stable. Continued support for the farming sector to prevent a precipitous decline in the national capacity to use land effectively is vital. Such support should come in terms of Pillar II incentives rather than the Single Payment in the medium term.

37. The unpredictable effects of climate change add to the importance of protecting productive agricultural land in our relatively temperate country. The protection of productive land from development is an essential part of this process. The existing planning mechanism protecting Best and Most Versatile Land (BMV) is now weaker, since the publication of Planning Policy Statement 7, Sustainable Development in Rural Areas in 2004. The Agricultural Land Classification System on which BMV is based and which dates back to 1966, also took no account of climate change. CPRE considers that there is an urgent need for a new system which protects land from development and which includes the calculation of the potential of land to produce food, fuel and other commodities in changing climatic conditions. Such recognition of mapping and valuing the versatility of land to climate change must underpin any serious strategic discussion of how farming can play a part in both adaptation and mitigation policies.

38. CPRE is not convinced of the value of biofuels grown in the UK to the mitigation of climate change. Clearly, biofuel crops, including those presently grown on Set Aside land, are strongly attractive to farmers and to some extent this is welcome. But the environmental footprint, both in terms of carbon and landscape, water and soil impact as well as associated built plant and traffic movement, will sometimes be considerable. The development of local biomass capacity appears to be more promising and less likely to contribute to unforeseen environmental damage than, for example from the increasing of demand for unsustainably produced biofuels from former tropical forests.

39. CPRE welcomes efforts made by the farming industry and individual enterprising businesses to address the carbon footprint of agriculture through on-farm biogas schemes. This has obvious secondary benefits for local, decentralised power generation.

FINANCING

Q10. *The Commissioner has expressed her dissatisfaction at the financing agreement reached by the Member States at the December 2005 Council. Do you consider the current budget to be sufficient? Do you consider co-financing to be a possible way forward in financing the Common Agricultural Policy?*

40. CPRE considers that the UK and English shares of the budget devoted to Pillar II funding (for example, our share of the Rural Development Regulation) has not been adequate in the past and this remains the case. In the circumstances co-financing is likely to be necessary. We are clear that the domestic benefits which would derive from adequate land management funding from the Exchequer would justify such a course of action. In the longer run, there is also a need for successive governments to maintain a commitment to financial support

for land management as the benefits are so long term and securing them is so vulnerable to other economic and social trends.

41. If substantial co-financing were to be contemplated in the long term, the Treasury would be acquiring a crucial role which it has not had hitherto. It would no longer be possible for the Treasury to display a lack of regard for the effects of world trade on domestic agriculture and land management quality. The relatively high standards we maintain in England would need positive support. It is possible that the Treasury might prefer to leave this responsibility with the EU.

ENLARGEMENT

Q11. *What has been the impact on the CAP of the 2004 and 2007 enlargements and what is the likely impact of future enlargements of the EU on the post-2013 CAP?*

42. CPRE considers that the UK Government should be prepared to make a strong case for continued funding for rural development in the face of demands for a substantial reduction in the share of funds allocated to the western European states. It is likely that the land management practices we value in this country will be more vulnerable to economic displacement than in some less prosperous nations.

SIMPLIFICATION OF THE CAP AND OTHER ISSUES

Q12. *How could the CAP be further simplified and in what other ways would you like to see the Common Agricultural Policy changed in the short and/or the long term?*

43. The evolution of Pillar II funding into a new land management fund would be a welcome medium to long term simplification of a further reformed CAP.

June 2007

Examination of Witnesses

Witnesses: MR IAN WOODHURST, Senior Rural Policy Officer and MR TOM OLIVER, Head of Rural Policy, Campaign to Protect Rural England, examined.

Q248 Chairman: Thank you very much for coming. I should explain to you that this is a formal session and there will be a transcript which will be made available to you after the session so you can check for accuracy. Secondly, this is actually web cast and there is a possibility that somewhere somebody might be listening to what we are saying. We did have evidence the other week that somebody was listening. If you would like to start by making a general statement we can then get onto questions and answers. If you do not want to make a general statement we can go straight onto questions and answers.
Mr Oliver: Thank you. I will make an extremely brief statement of introduction to explain the perspective that CPRE brings to this question. CPRE has been around since long before the Second World War and its perspective on the development of agriculture has therefore been tested through a range of different circumstances since 1926. Throughout that time we have been consistently interested in the links between food production, rural businesses, the strength of rural communities and planning as well as farming. Our particular interest is in the pattern of land use where the relationship between farming, forestry and landscape is something which is millennia old. Therefore our interest in sustainable use of land

partly reflects our interest in that long term relationship between production and landscape. I think it is probably true to say that we are one of the very few non-governmental organisations with an environmental remit which is interested in the whole of the landscape, both urban and rural, and as a commentator and policy advising organisation rather than as owner organisation which does set us apart from some of the main players within the environmental NGOs. We are interested in the relationship between farm businesses and the future of the landscape and relating the national asset, that is the farmed landscape, to everybody's interests. At that stage we would be very happy to take questions on our written evidence.

Q249 Chairman: That is very interesting because you bring a perspective that other witnesses we intend to have do not necessarily bring. Your focus is a little bit different. Your evidence did express concern about the impact of modern farming practices on agricultural landscapes and on England's historic and archaeological inheritance. To what extent is that being driven by agricultural factors and farming factors and to what extent is it a product of perhaps wider changes in society and the economy? Is it fair really to focus on agriculture as being the negative factor when in fact there are much wider processes taking place, the development of non-agricultural based housing in agricultural areas, that sort of issue? *Mr Oliver:* Our commentary on the Committee's inquiry is primarily related to what happens to farmed land. It is clearly the case that as society develops and a society's needs change, some farmland ceases to be farmed and, if you like, the outcome for that farmland is part of the story of the landscape. I think it is quite important, given the remit of the present inquiry, to focus on the effects of farming and its associated activities on the management of land which could be farmed. Once land ceases to be in agriculture permanently it is subject, as you rightly say, to a huge range of other influences. In the 1920s and 1930s it was true to say that a very large influence on the east of England's agriculture land was the severe decline in cereal markets and that led to very substantial release of land for housing which might not have occurred otherwise. To some extent the pressure on land today for development produces a similar situation although under very different circumstances. Our primary focus in responding to the Committee's inquiry is on the role of farming in changing the landscape. In that respect the intensification of production since the resurgence of agriculture at the beginning of the Second World War and which has seen several phases, does play quite an important role in the condition of the landscape.

Q250 *Chairman:* Moving onto the impact of CAP and perhaps the advantages that CAP reform could offer, how do you see CAP reform as it has taken place—the 2003 reforms—and then looking forward to how it may progress in the future? What opportunities has reform produced for enhanced benefits of landscape and habitats and where is that coming from? Is it coming from the Pillar II side of the house or is it to do with the changes within the single farm payment approach? We would be fascinated to hear anything you have to say on that. *Mr Oliver:* I will start and then it may be wise to hand over to my colleague Ian Woodhurst. I think the first point is that in the short run, reform in 2003 made possible a recognition of the great value of well-targeted and thoroughly well-planned agri-environment schemes. For many years there has been a strong argument made by CPRE and others for the importance of funding very specifically to achieve agri-environment outcomes. The reform in 2003 allowed an opportunity to expand that funding and as we have heard from the CLA drawing on a low base of Rural Development Regulation funding there has been expansion with the present round of modulation and that is welcome. In the short run the

expansion of the available resources for agri-environment schemes is a very welcome part of reform. However, we are also very clearly aware of the enormous pressure on European budgets and of the political pressure on the negotiation over them and the influence of other diplomatic and economic issues at an EU level on the deal struck on the future of farming support to which we can add the accession countries' role in the debate and the progress of the Doha Round. I think the evidence you have heard from the CLA amply demonstrates a longer term opportunity to radically reform the funding of land management for environmental benefits. Our evidence to some extent recognises the fact that we are at a very early stage in the development of a new mechanism which would probably be within an EU context, for a much wider recognition of what managing land does for the public at large, whether it is landscape character, bio-diversity, protection of natural resources, or the retention of stable and responsible production. In the longer run the radical reform of the CAP further offers much wider opportunities and much larger scale benefits should those be seized and should the Government be interested in delivering those changes on the land. I think how that is achieved depends very largely on marshalling enough evidence to show what is necessary in order to achieve the outcomes that are generally agreed between environmental organisations, land owning organisations and the non-departmental public bodies (the Environment Agency and Natural England). There is a great need for evidence gathering and a great need for recognition of the common interest in a much broader approach to land management, but at the same time remembering that farmers will be the primary deliverers of this because they are, by and large, the only people who have the competence and presence to achieve very large scale landscape change. *Mr Woodhurst:* I would not have that much more to add to that except to say that the primary benefits of the last set of reforms were to draw attention to the fact that farming and environmental interests were moving much closer together. I think that has been a very welcome outcome of the last set of reforms. In the past there was perhaps a divisive position between some of the environmental organisations and the farming community. I think we are now in a very different world and there is much more common ground to be found between farmers and environmental organisations and environmental outcomes. The fundamental question, as Tom has said, is that we really do not know how much resource we need to deliver both the environmental outcomes and to sustain some of the farming systems upon which those environmental outcomes depend for delivery. Just going to a few ballpark figures for some of the bio-diversity deliverables, we are looking at estimates of shortfalls of around £300 million per year so we need a doubling of the money that is being spent on bio-diversity outcomes. Work that the CPRE and the NFU did on the amount of labour costs that farmers put into landscape feature management we estimated to be worth around £412 million per year, that is beyond what is already being received through agri-environment schemes spending. If you add in other environmental outcomes like the Water Framework Directive we are seeing implementation costs of around £400 million to £600 million a year. When you start to add up the cost of all these different outcomes that we hope to see farmers deliver, through the establishment of a different mechanism for paying for these through further CAP reform, the costs add up quite significantly.

Mr Oliver: It is important to add that there is quite a lot of overlap between those figures but how much overlap is not known. It is like Lord Lever's question about what to spend on advertising and not knowing which half he was wasting.

Q251 *Lord Cameron of Dillington:* You are proposing that that CAP should be replaced by an Agricultural Public Benefits Fund. What sort of public benefits are you talking about here? How do you measure them and how are they paid? Are they judged at a European, national, regional or parish level?

Mr Oliver: The purpose of describing the title as we set it out, as you quite accurately described it, is to draw attention to what is being asked from the mechanism. In other words, this is a primarily agricultural process which delivers other benefits beyond the agriculture. You ask which benefits would be forthcoming, they would include the present outcomes which are so welcome from Pillar II funding which include very substantial amounts of improvement in bio-diversity and habitat, improvements in landscape character and the condition of farm structures and farm systems of a semi-natural nature, increased access to this by as many people as possible because of its great value in terms of culture but also health. And also a recognition of the interrelationship between the protection of natural resources which includes the ability to make use of land productively which sometimes is forgotten when people talk about a natural resource protection within farming, with those other landscape, bio-diversity and access outcomes. The long term future of the support by the tax payer for land management must reside in recognising the comprehensive interactive quality of managing farmland. It is the fact that the farmland does many things at once and the degree to which it

achieves those outcomes is dependent on quite subtle shifts in incentive and regulation.

Q252 *Lord Cameron of Dillington:* Obviously landscape is a raison d'être of the CPRE in some ways and the landscape is, as you say, an interaction, it is a living essence. The trouble I see in handing over the management of what landscape should look like to public subsidies is that you are tending to freeze existing land patterns and I do not think that is necessarily a good thing to do.

Mr Oliver: Whether or not one passes judgment on the last point you make, it is easy to observe that since the war very substantial change has taken place in the fabric of landscape whether one looks at the length of hedges or the amount of unploughed permanent grassland or the amount of arable land in cultivation or the condition of ancient woodland, for example. There is no doubt that intervention in farming behaviour by government can have a great deal of effect on the landscape. CPRE would contend that the balance of that effect until the 1980s was to reduce the quality of habitat and extent of semi-natural landscape and the quality of the landscape with the benefit of very substantial increases in production which went with that change. The balance sheet as it stands is standing quite strongly in favour of intensification and modernisation of the farmland in England. Even if one recognised that one wished to retain that level of balance between production and the retention of semi-natural features there is a very substantial amount of work needed to be done to retain the qualities that remain of the semi-natural landscape which is farmed. As my colleague Ian has said, the amount of money needed merely to maintain what remains of traditional landscapes within their modern context and which brings very substantial benefits in terms of landscape character, tourism, bio-diversity and other benefits, would require substantial funding. Whether or not that funding would seriously impede the modernisation further of farming I think is very questionable. My answer to that is that the market will determine to some extent the degree of innovation that takes place on farmland because if markets are available within environmental regulations they will be sought by enterprising landowners. The balance of support for traditional landscapes and structures brings with it the huge value of continuity which is something which stretches back far further than the last 60 or 70 years and goes back to landscape features that are often many hundreds of years old sitting in the context of semi-natural systems which are very valuable.

Q253 *Lord Cameron of Dillington:* To take Allan Buckwell's point, do you think people really want to pay for that? Why should they pay for it, picking up

24 October 2007   Mr Ian Woodhurst and Mr Tom Oliver

Lord Bach's question to him earlier. If, for instance, you were putting this to the World Trade Organisation, to the World Trade Talks, that is support for agriculture, in inverted commas, I do not think you would be able to get away with that.

Mr Oliver: To answer the first question, I think there is very strong evidence that people do wish to spend what amounts to very modest amounts to the Exchequer on protection and enhancement of the way in which traditional landscapes are farmed and it is important to remember that this land would be productive. There are benefits deriving, for example, from local food and local identity and recreational activities which are quite intimately linked with the continued protection of hedgerows or stonewalls or ancient woodland. In terms of the World Trade context it seems that the most important thing is to focus clearly on what amounts to trade distortion. I do not think that any nation would concede that its beautiful landscapes or its attractive towns and their hinterland are in themselves anti-competitive features. Actually what we are talking about is giving those who own and manage and work on the land the opportunity to market those benign outcomes to the world not on the basis of production subsidy, not on the basis of false protection from the buffeting of world markets but actually on the basis of the quality of the outcomes they produce. That requires some funding to recognise the cost of traditional landscape features' management—not the cost of producing food or any other commodity from them but the actual cost of managing those features in their own right—that seems to me entirely reasonable and is commensurate with the protection of heritage, for example, which is not regarded as anti-competitive.

Q254 *Chairman:* Is there a market in international tourism in this respect and are there any facts to prove that?

Mr Oliver: Yes, we looked into this and the answer is that there is. To put figures on this is difficult and we made some efforts and we can do more if you would like. My colleague can give you chapter and verse but I can refer very specifically to my experience this summer where I visited rural Romania through a company called Transylvania Uncovered based in Cumbria (a very welcome piece of rural diversification for Cumbria) and which revealed an extremely keen market at a very high premium for exactly that sort of tourism from England to Romania. It has clearly had a great significance for Romania's prosperity. My colleague can give you further information.

Mr Woodhurst: We did try to look into this and I think in international terms in some of the other EU Member States there is perhaps a bigger push towards promoting agri-tourism, particularly in some parts of Spain. We found an example from

Zaragoza where a hotel offers visitors a chance to spend the day with a shepherd in the mountains learning about the environmental and cultural aspects of shepherding. I do not know whether we would actually contemplate those sorts of activities in the UK. Indeed, when you look at the *Visit Britain* website there is a lot of play made about the quality of landscapes, national parks, AONBs and it lists by region some of the landscape features which people might be able to see, and can view on their international website, such as dry stone walls. But there is actually no mention at all of what any of this has to do with farming or the fact that farming systems are producing and still maintaining these environmental assets and these landscapes. I think there is a lot to be learned from a UK perspective on how to promote some of these connections between farming and tourism and some of the tourist activities you can base around them. There is also *Farm Stay UK* which lists accommodation where you can go and stay on a farm but I think there is still a lot to be done in making those connections.

Q255 *Lord Sewel:* So the Scottish landowners need not worry, they can get people to pay them to come and help round up their sheep.

Mr Oliver: There is an important point here about the permeation of the advantages of this sort of tourism across the country and clearly places which are more peripheral physically have a harder time of it. On the other hand there is evidence, of certain initiatives for example in Herefordshire, that they emphasise the importance of high value, low volume tourism in order to benefit most from high quality fishing or high quality landscape or high quality countryside which is of course something which people seek and which is increasingly under threat. There is one figure which we can quote from a *Wildlife and Countryside Link* submission presently in draft which is that in 1998 20% of countryside visitors pursued activities such as hiking, rambling, field studies and cycling and that accounted for 26 million tourist trips which spent £2.7 billion. That is one way of looking at the way in which people use the countryside, a very specific one, and it is from nine years ago. To go back to your previous question about whether there is a willingness in society to pay for this, I think Allan Buckwell's point about the degree to which the Exchequer contributes is important. Also in 2000 a survey from the Ramblers Association indicated that 75% of survey respondents wanted the Government to legislate for greater access to the countryside which was luckily just about to happen. That was a very welcome outcome and it indicates that very large numbers of people see the value in going to the countryside and by definition I would regard that as quite good value in terms of public expenditure.

Chairman: This is no criticism, these are absolutely fascinating points that you are making, but it would be particularly helpful to us if they could be put in the context of CAP reform. We are really looking to say things on the next stage of CAP reform and how these sorts of arguments and issues feed into that would be particularly valuable.

Q256 *Viscount Brookeborough:* An interesting point on the landscape is that people tend to appreciate the landscape in this country, in England as opposed to the highlands of Scotland, because they are passing through it. It is quite difficult to get people to have the landscape as a destination, literally in itself, and therefore it is for some other reason, whether it be cycling or fishing or whatever. In the 1970s we had a lot of development with grants of guest houses and that sort of thing and it was not very well controlled as to why people would go there and there were an awful lot of guesthouses which came into being without anybody going to stay in them. The other point about tourism and farms is that there is a limited market but there is a problem with health and safety—sheep biting people or whatever they do— and it is quite a problem for a farmer to take it up, to put the expense into making his place acceptable and actually getting enough people to pay for that acceptability or standard. Your evidence discusses the pressures affecting rural communities as a whole rather than just farming and you suggest the development of local markets could play an important role in increasing the viability of traditional activities. How might this concept be developed in England through greater use of Axes 1 and 3 of the Rural Development programme? What kinds of interventions do you have in mind for such things?
Mr Oliver: The separation of delivery of Axes 1 and 3 from Axis 2 funding and the relocation of the Rural Enterprise Scheme (as was) to regional development agencies presented both an opportunity and a problem. The opportunity presents the idea of course that regional development agencies could, for the first time, really take seriously their rural responsibilities. The difficulty lay in that there was the risk of their being little, if any, connection between the initiatives which were encouraged and funded for economic developments in the countryside and those which were associated with the management of land. Work we have done since 1998 on the network of local food producers, processors and distributors in Suffolk suggests that where you encourage the local infrastructure altogether to invest in its own production capacity and its own ability to find markets, you have a very substantial increase in the number of businesses and at the same time secure the land management which otherwise

needs to be solely supported through agri-environment schemes. Our proposals in draft for how this might be taken forward would be to re-integrate where possible the economic initiatives associated with traditional farming practices, so that is primarily to do with food production but it also to do with things like harvesting wool for insulation, for example, and to bring back the relationship between those initiatives and the management of land surrounding where those businesses take place. Other work that we have done has indicated that unless there is a very clear targeting by grant structures from a future reformed CAP for those sorts of businesses which are land-based or closely related to what goes on on the land, footloose businesses are much more likely to take over the space and the available private investment because they are largely more profitable and in turn that tends to generate various other unwelcome phenomena like the reduction in local employment and an increase in commuting to the countryside from towns, and a reduction in the relationship between farms and businesses which in the long run can reduce the quality of land management. In future it would be better if there were a closer relationship between local food production and local adding of value in the countryside to that management of land which, for so many other reasons, we value. When it comes to the specific question of local food networks the opportunity to invest very substantial sums where there is private investment available in addition to improve the quality of local food networks would be a good example which would fit in with all sorts of other government objectives in terms of healthy eating, local economies and a de-centralisation of control. Going back to Lord Cameron's point about parishes, there is an interesting opportunity, if you are dealing in small scale business diversification from a land-based point of view to encourage farmers to participate in that at a much more local level.

Q257 *Viscount Brookeborough:* To what extent, if at all, would you promote supporting businesses, be they quite small businesses, which are actually unrelated to the land in the rural environment?
Mr Oliver: To a very modest extent in general terms because it is very evident that the attractiveness of that sort of investment in business development is very strong and there is a lot of evidence that there is little need to encourage that. There are a few examples where this is not the case, for example with care farms which relate to health outcomes where, as you were suggesting, some of the health and safety issues surrounding farming impinge on other aspects of health and safety obligations. In general terms encouraging private investment in diversification which is not related to the use of the land is not necessary.

Q258 Viscount Brookeborough: What about use of the buildings and the planning issue where it is very often turned down regardless of the fact that the outside of the building may be remaining the same?

Mr Oliver: Clearly the development control question of what happens to buildings is an important one and the response must vary depending on whether the building is listed, the building's rarity, its attractiveness and what other functions may be available. However, clearly there is a need for a realistic response depending on what the application is asking for and its context. Very specifically in terms of rural planning policy, there is very little evidence of a need to encourage diversification which is not land-based and quite a lot of evidence that if ill-considered, some rural diversification can actually undermine local market towns, for example, by locating retail sites far from where high streets are and this can actually have quite a severe impact on small rural towns which are actually service centres. There is evidence to suggest that there must be quite careful judgment when it comes to encouraging diffuse diversification. Clearly there are cases where opportunities for diversification should be encouraged which are not being encouraged. It is a patchy situation and it depends a lot on the way local authorities interpret PPS7 and it depends quite a lot on the quality of the applications that are made.

Q259 Viscount Brookeborough: You are largely against rural retail.

Mr Oliver: I did not say that. I am against rural retail that has no justification for being outside settlements.

Q260 Viscount Brookeborough: It might be retaining employment in the countryside. Secondly, if I wish to convert farm buildings because I have no other use for them and tourism will not fit in and I had a good business opportunity even though it did not change the outlook of that building or whatever, you would not necessarily like to see it happen.

Mr Oliver: I would not necessarily like to see it happen, but one has to regard quite carefully what, for example, planning policy guidance note 13 says about transport policy in relation to this sort of question. There is clearly a need to discourage substantial private transport dependency in rural areas which is not very sound from the point of view of carbon as well as tranquillity. The point remains that there are occasions where rural diversification, particularly where it offers local employment to people who already live locally, should be strongly encouraged. There are good examples of that in England, in Cumbria for example, where post foot and mouth, very substantial progress has been made and that is very welcome.

Q261 Lord Plumb: You say that cross-compliance does not necessarily represent good value for money for the public and you anticipate the phasing out of the single farm payment and it will decline in importance. I am sure most people are accepting that there will be a phasing out as, hopefully, there is the move from Pillar I to Pillar II, giving the advantage of course for more environmentally friendly farming, et cetera. Cross-compliance means that the occupier of that land or the farmer of that land can see clearly what goes to Pillar I and what goes to Pillar II; that is the benefit I think that he gets from it, so it is very much an exercise in itself of determining those areas. Every farmer is very conscious of it if he has applied for entry level schemes and the rest of it. Therefore, how do you see this ultimately benefiting the public? Pillar I has gone; Pillar II will be there. That surely will benefit the public. It is going to happen gradually and what you are suggesting is that there is no benefit at the moment. I would have thought there was, if you are getting more into Pillar II and therefore greater use of Pillar II which is what the public themselves surely want.

Mr Oliver: If I understand your question correctly you are asking whether the trend towards Pillar II is not so beneficial that one should not worry about the view on Pillar I.

Q262 Lord Plumb: Yes.

Mr Oliver: It is important to remember that the proportion of funds in Pillar II is still very, very substantially smaller than that in Pillar I. It is also important—I think the CLA make the point correctly—that the transition from a long inheritance of very substantial funding (now called the single farm payment) will need very careful management because most of our businesses to some extent or other have planned over the years for that level of support or something like it. It is unrealistic to expect that not to matter in the future. For all the reasons that we subscribe to in terms of protecting the ability to produce, the capacity to produce and protecting the interests of farmers in managing their land, a transition from Pillar I needs to be made carefully and predictably. Then the question arises as to whether the scale of the Pillar II increase and any new agricultural public benefits fund might come along to replace it will be adequate to deal with the scale of obligations that society would like to see farmers implement. As my colleague has pointed out, there are very substantial sums of money attached to the Water Framework Directive outcomes, to bio-diversity targets and to landscape management beyond those already funded. Should the new agricultural public benefits fund be of the same level and scale as the present single farm payment or something like it, then the question is answered in the sense that the public's benefits are paid for successfully and then one gets into the question of how one frames that fund and access to it to encourage as much as possible interest in it. The risk is that on the one hand we fail to recognise the value of the single payment in retaining continuity of farming and, as we take that away, fail to replace it with substantial enough funding within Pillar II to do other things which will carry farm businesses on and allow them to compete in world markets to the degree that they wish to. That is the problem. We would identify lack of realism on the part of the Government at the moment—and probably on the part of all political parties—as to the scale of the funding needed to do the things the public really want and the risks associated with not meeting those.

Q263 Lord Plumb: Would you accept that cross-compliance therefore should continue until such time as we see either the elimination of or lowering of the payments in Pillar I?

Mr Oliver: Indeed, and I think it is important not to take from our evidence the implication that we disapprove of cross-compliance. We approve of it, we simply take the view that it is very difficult to justify paying very large sums of money per hectare to farmers to do what amount to quite meagre environmental actions. It is entirely possible that cross-compliance could be expanded in the future, but then we reach the question which was being discussed earlier with the CLA when they were giving evidence which is: to what extent is it effective to incentivise people to do good things and to what extent is it effective to regulate them to do so? Our strong feeling is that it is much more effective to incentivise people than it is to regulate them into doing things.

Q264 Lord Plumb: I think farmers might argue with you that if the implementation of some of these schemes is not meagre. The six metre strips round every field, for instance, has changed the method of husbandry to some extent and similarly with all the hedge planting and so on that is going on which I encourage and we do ourselves is great, but it must change the attitude I think of farmers apart from the way they run their business.

Mr Oliver: I think there is an unwelcome problem which arose during the negotiations of the exact terms of cross-compliance in England which was a division that opened up between the farming lobby and the environmental lobby of whether, for example, fields of under two hectares should be exempt from the two metre rule, two metre for hedges and one metre for ditches. I think CPRE took the view that this was too assiduous a lobbying by some of the farming lobby on its own behalf, but the important thing is that the payment of £200-odd pounds per hectare is a very substantial one by

comparison with the £30 per hectare for entry level. With the best will in the world one is looking for much more substantial benefits from much more substantial sums of money.

Mr Woodhurst: I think it is important to remember that cross-compliance is supposed to be a base line through which farmers can then progress into higher tiers of environmental management. Without that base line you immediately add on quite substantial costs before you can leap into other sorts of management which might be an Environmental Stewardship scheme option. I think our view has always been that it forms a management base line for which there might be costs in a reformed system, those costs would have to be recognised as part of a new payment system, perhaps in a tiered way, so that there would be representative payments for the outputs that one required for these sorts of management.

Mr Oliver: Perhaps it would be convenient to talk about Set Aside now because it fits closely with what my colleague has just said. One of the great debates this summer has been whether the environmental benefits of Set Aside which were entirely unintended at the time (and which organisations like CPRE did not foresee and in fact CPRE opposed Set Aside in 1988—or whenever it was—when it was originally discussed) should be recognised. I think there are various lessons to be learned from this. The first is that it is very important to deal with what is going on on farms rather than what was intended. It is also very important to recognise that it is important to reconcile farm planning which is something which is a mixture of capital and management planning over very long periods of time and competence and investment with political decisions that sometimes can be imposed, if you like, at very short notice. I think it was unrealistic to expect the Government to respond to what happened so far as the Commission was concerned for this cropping year. However, we are faced with a distribution of land in fallow, either rotational or permanent, which is not related to the willingness of farmers to participate in environmental schemes and there is some value in some of the distribution of that land management which we inherit now that Set Aside is set at zero rate. The need is to recognise a transition from, if you like, an untargeted but nonetheless quite substantial area of land in Set Aside to an addition to the present entry level scheme which manages that land which is valuable environmentally from its status as Set Aside land to its status within environmental stewardship. That needs a transitional mechanism which recognises that some people did not regard themselves as environmental enthusiasts but happened to put land in Set Aside to great advantage for bio-diversity or water quality for example.

Q265 Lord Plumb: Would you see a difference between rotational Set Aside and non-rotational Set

Aside?

Mr Oliver: A great difference because the virtues and dangers of losing both are different. Interesting work by SAFFIE (Single Arable Farming for an Improved Environment) which includes sponsors such as RSPB and LEAF suggests that how you manage both rotational and permanent Set Aside makes a great difference as to whether it has public benefit or not. In fact, for example, opening up the sward of permanently Set Aside strips can greatly help their usefulness for barn owl feeding. It is important to recognise that there is more work to be done on how you manage that permanent Set Aside just as there is work to be done on where you locate the rotational Set Aside. There is interesting work by the Game Conservatory Trust as it used to be called which suggests that the exact location of rotational Set Aside makes a great deal of difference to its usefulness for some bird populations.

Q266 *Viscount Ullswater:* When Dr Phillips gave us evidence last week from Natural England the thought was that you could only rent environmental improvements from farmers by paying them some form of subsidy for agri-environmental schemes. It looks as if the test is now going to be on Set Aside as to how much environmental benefit will be left after a lot of farmers will be ploughing up rotational Set Aside in order to benefit from the prices of corn at the moment. Are there some further structures that you think should be in place in order to effectively buy into environmental improvements which are going to be permanent? We have got SSSIs, we have SPAs; is there some form of other permanent improvement which then will not be dislodged if the payments cease?

Mr Oliver: There are two ways of answering your question, one is in terms of the designation of land and the other is in terms of the scale and length of an agreement with a land manager. In terms of the scale and agreement with a land manager, as I have just said, we would argue for a mechanism to bring Set Aside—whether rotational or permanent—which is of environmental value into environmental stewardship, recognising the fact that its origins are not that and that farmers have some justification for resisting a de facto environmental status for their Set Aside land, but also recognising that some Set Aside land is of no environmental value at all because it was never meant for that purpose and is not located in the right place. There we would recommend extension of the environmental stewardship scheme. Depending on the degree to which you want outcomes you can put that into the entry level scheme or the higher tier scheme, but either of those requires expansion of the funds for that scheme, recognising that Set Aside will no longer going to be doing that job for us by mistake, as it were. In terms of designation of land,

there is something to be said for pursuing the catchment management analysis of the Environment Agency in terms of the location of cultivation and indeed intense livestock farming. There it might be that some development of the Nitrate Sensitive Zone approach might be worth looking at. I am very conscious that that system is, to some extent, disliked by farmers for its lack of targeting and lack of clear outcomes. It is very important and incumbent on the environmental movement to come up with coherent reasons why it wishes to target land which should be cultivated more carefully or with greater restraint because of water quality. There is a very strong argument for it but at the moment it is not clear that the argument is being made successfully to the farming community as a whole. That would be one area where you could have territorial designation. I think there is a third one which is whether the public benefit of land close to settlements should be subject to some form of designation for a future agricultural fund from Europe. We feel frustrated that the debate about the Green Belt, for example, often invokes the lack of enrichment and good management of land which uniquely in England is permanently protected. The idea that it should be possible to target land close to settlements for long term good management to increase its diversity and its attractiveness and its access is a strong one. Under any guise of a further form of the CAP it would be very welcome if nation states could have a greater say in why they wish to target land for particular kinds of management. The urban fringe and Green Belt is a clear candidate for that. There has also been an interesting debate about whether the Thames Gateway would be a place where that would be important because of the need to reinvigorate the vast majority of that land which will remain farmed after the development has taken place.

Q267 *Viscount Ullswater:* I take your point that this is an awful lot of land round settlements—whether it is towns or villages—which is impossible to farm because of vandalism, because of animal cruelty and all sorts of things, so that does need to be protected in a way which is better than it is protected in the moment, which is covered in tin shacks and a few ponies. I call it equi-culture rather than agriculture. I think you have a real point there which would increase the beauty of the landscape hugely.

Mr Oliver: And make it very visible to the vast majority of tax payers and their children who would be paying for it. To address the core desire to increase the focus on a future CAP fund, that is an important point. At nation state level and possibly at a more localised level than that we can do a great deal to focus the public benefit if we are given that ability. The fact that we are able to identify heathland, for example, as an important landscape and habitat but not identify the urban fringe in itself as an important landscape and habitat is a frustration where the sorts of situations prevail that we have just been describing.

Q268 *Chairman:* If my memory serves me right, the Forestry Commission either has or had an urban woodland scheme.

Mr Oliver: The Community Forests Initiative, yes. Community woodlands along with country parks which tend to be owned by local authorities have advantages, but the problem is that they are subject to budgetary vicissitudes and restraints which very often reduce their quality and reduce their attractiveness. The history recently of country parks—I am not sure if this is true of community forests—is that the local authorities seek to divest themselves of the responsibility to manage them. It seems to be much, much wiser to let farmers manage them for production within the context of providing public benefits while retaining the form of the land as a productive unit.

Q269 *Lord Cameron of Dillington:* I wondered whether, in your list of public benefits, food security played any part. Also, where do you stand in the debate we had earlier with the CLA in connection with the Government's role in managing the risk involved with all of that?

Mr Oliver: I think the CLA were right to distinguish between self-sufficiency and food security and we would subscribe to that distinction. For us the principal question is the perpetuation of the capacity to farm competently and this is whether it is livestock farming or arable farming. It relates to all the other subsidiary but crucial services that surround

farming—for example abattoirs, large animal vets and the marketing and technical support for farmers—and in a world where technical ability and development is going to be increasingly important that support is also necessary. We subscribe to the view sometimes characterised as critical mass analysis which is that there needs to be a strategic view taken by government on what farming can take before it ceases to be effective as a system overall. That requires more research into the resilience of farming to world competition. That is something we called for some time ago in our evidence to the House of Commons EFRA Select Committee and which I think we would renew now, in particular as part of that process the revising of the agricultural land classification system to take account of the resilience of land to climate change. The system we have at the moment was set up in 1966 and it takes no account of the versatility of land in response to climatic change whereas that is going to be a crucial question when it comes to food security in the future, whether land can produce even if we do not need to produce from it in the next few years. We would strongly call for the Government to review the agricultural land classification system and to recognise in planning policy the value of protecting land which has great versatility in an era of climate change as well as increasing demands for food and commodities.

Q270 *Chairman:* Thank you very much indeed. If you think there is something you want to say that you have not had the opportunity to say, now is the time to say it. If not, then that is fine.

Mr Woodhurst: I have nothing to add, thank you.

Chairman: Thank you very much indeed for your evidence.

WEDNESDAY 14 NOVEMBER 2007

Present	Arran, E	Jones of Whitchurch, B
	Brookeborough, V	Palmer, L
	Cameron of Dillington, L	Sewell, L (Chairman)
	Dundee, E	Sharp of Guildford, B

Memorandum by the New Zealand Government

SUMMARY

1. The efforts by the European Union (EU) to reform the Common Agricultural Policy (CAP) are commendable. Not only were the 2003 CAP reforms far reaching, but, more importantly, they (and current proposals) are leading the EU in the direction of greater market orientation and reducing distortions to international trade.

2. New Zealand's own policy shift towards market orientation was supported by our farmers, who saw the advantages of this change and who remain strong proponents of reform. They prefer to be reliant on markets rather than the whim of government policy for their incomes. The New Zealand agricultural sector and the wider economy has benefited from those reforms. Europe should experience similar gains from any comparable market-oriented reform.

3. As a party directly affected by the CAP (on EU and world markets), New Zealand will, therefore, continue to be vitally interested in proposed CAP changes. New Zealand will also continue to engage with European Commission and Member State colleagues on the implications of those proposed changes, in particular for their trading partners.

4. The upcoming "health check" and budget review, aside from a reduction in CAP spending and further movement towards a wholly decoupled system, should ensure that the most is made of the intended gains of reforms. The health check should also send clear signals as to the direction and speed of further reform to facilitate the agricultural sector preparing itself for the structural adjustment required.

INTRODUCTION

5. New Zealand welcomes the opportunity to comment on progress to date with the 2003 CAP reforms and to examine what further policy changes at the EU level are required in both the short-term, and beyond 2012.

6. New Zealand's reference points in making this submission include:

— a significant domestic policy shift towards market orientation in New Zealand almost two decades ago;

— New Zealand's experience as an exporter of agricultural products to the EU and the rest of the world; and

— a desire to see a minimisation of distortions in international trade and consequential resource misallocation, consistent with numerous international declarations on development and sustainability.

When making an oral submission on the topic of the future of the CAP, New Zealand can provide more detail on the policy shift that took place in the 1980s.

7. Agricultural production and exports of agriculture products are critical to New Zealand's economic and social wellbeing. The bulk of New Zealand's production of these goods is exported and accounts for more than half of our foreign goods trade receipts. As a long-time exporter of pastoral and fruit and vegetable products to the EU, and as a country forced to compete with subsidised EU products on world markets, **New Zealand has a strong interest in the evolution of the CAP**.

8. While usually thought of as a developed country, **New Zealand shares many common interests with developing countries**, which are similarly dependent upon agricultural exports, and which have experienced the negative flow-on effects of the CAP, both in their own markets and through the spill-over effects in

international markets. The views expressed by New Zealand would therefore be shared by many developing economies, for example those demonstrated by the Membership of the Cairns Group of countries that work together in the context of World Trade Organisation (WTO) agriculture negotiations.

OVERVIEW

What should the long-term objectives of the CAP be? Does the title "Common Agricultural Policy" aptly fit your perceived objectives of the policy? What do you consider to be the main pressures on the CAP as it currently is?

9. **It could be argued that the original CAP objectives have either been met or are no longer appropriate**. This is in the context of a much larger and diverse EU following its enlargement to 27 Members States, and in a substantially altered international setting, where globalisation and internationalisation have radically changed the relationships between economies. These developments have led to a greater appreciation of the negative spillover impacts of some national policies into the global domain. They have also increased awareness of the benefits of economic liberalisation for world social and economic wellbeing.

10. The EU has an opportunity to recast the mould post-2013. In this changed global environment, the United Kingdom (UK), the EU, and New Zealand are now facing largely the same pressures and challenges in agriculture, such as climate change, food safety issues, and biosecurity. It is thus sensible to expect that our policy objectives may look similar long-term, although reflecting our geographic and other differences. Therefore, we could see an **ideal set of objectives for the future CAP** as including:

— to provide for the orderly structural adjustment of the rural sector away from dependence on market support measures via subsidisation (Whether the latter be developed through price support, direct payments linked to output, inputs or price, export subsidies, or border protection);

— to provide a policy environment conducive to EU producers continuously adjusting farm scale, and methods and types of production in ways which make them internationally competitive;

— to provide frameworks for the efficient operation of markets as the key means of allocating resources used for agricultural production;

— to ensure food safety and biosecurity;

— to provide for an effective innovation system;

— to provide policy frameworks which foster the long-term sustainability of the EU's natural resource base of land, water and air, and the maintenance of biodiversity;

— to provide a legal framework for the protection of animal welfare; and

— to otherwise limit the scope of governmental regulatory intervention to clear instances of market failure.

11. Such a set of objectives would **closely mirror New Zealand's agricultural policy objectives**. While EU agriculture may have different historical roots, justifying a more extended adjustment pathway, the end-game is the same as that for New Zealand.

12. Since 1992, the **EU has achieved substantial reform of its agricultural policy**, in particular in terms of the move away from direct price support, market intervention purchasing, export subsidies for surplus disposal, and the move toward greater direct support of farmers, most latterly via the Single Farm Payment (SFP). These developments have been publicly welcomed by New Zealand and would also have been welcomed by many developing agricultural exporting countries (with the qualification that sugar and certain Mediterranean-related product sector reforms have been much delayed).

13. EU farmers still, however, receive **considerable subsidies** via the effects of high import tariffs (accompanied by export subsidies) and some continuing commodity-linked payments, which directly impact on the prices of farm products. Further, while direct payments are clearly less distorting than price support, they still deliver indirect support. This maintains resources in agricultural uses which would otherwise flow to other, more efficient uses.

14. It would be beneficial to UK farmers, the EU economy, and to those economies heavily dependent upon agricultural exports if ongoing EU reforms led to reduced use of such instruments, and focussed more on the **facilitation of structural adjustment of the EU's rural economy**. It will, of course, take time for a new market-driven focus to develop, but the EU is able to provide funding to assist farmers through difficult transitional periods. New Zealand did not have such a mechanism at the time of its reforms, aside from a write-down of farm debt for some farmers, and an exit package for those farmers who still remained deep in debt following this and who had little prospect of future viability.

The Reformed CAP

What has been your experience so far with the reformed CAP? What has worked well and less well? And where can lessons be learned?

15. New Zealand's experience with the reformed CAP has been in relation to our exports into the EU and on the world market. New Zealand welcomed the 2003 reform, which based the new support system almost entirely on decoupling payments from production (although we note that some Member States have chosen to maintain some partially coupled supports). The introduction of the "cross compliance" concept, linking the SFP to respect for environmental, food safety and animal welfare standards was also positive.

16. Agricultural subsidies and border protection negatively affect agricultural exporting countries. They tend to create an oversupply of agricultural products inside the protected market, considerably limiting the export of agricultural goods to the protected market. Subsidised exports result in unfair competition in international markets. The much-anticipated reform of EU sugar subsidies was therefore **a step forward on the path of subsidy reform**.

17. Although the reformed CAP now has greater market orientation, the benefits would have been greater if all Member States had made **full use of the scope for converting commodity-linked payments into the new SFP**. It is very important that the "health check" results in a reduction in the flexibility for Member States in implementing reforms and therefore makes the most of their intended gains.

18. The reduction in export subsidisation by the EU since 1994 has had a material positive impact in international markets benefiting both the EU budget and agricultural exporters, including New Zealand. This is a welcome policy change.

19. The EU's 2003 reforms represent a major step forward for the EU. The CAP in 2006 should, however, be seen as a work in progress, if the EU foresees a similar end-goal for the agricultural sector. Features such as ongoing partially coupled payments, intervention systems and export refunds prevent full market signals getting to producers, and do not address all of the new and emerging challenges facing agriculture. The review processes underway with the health check and budget review offer an opportunity to better orient the current CAP to address these issues.

The Single Payment Scheme

Do you consider the Single Payment Scheme to be a good basis for the future of EU agricultural policy? What changes might be made at the EU level to the Single Payment Scheme, including to the rules governing entitlements, in the short and/or longer-term?

20. While the SFP is a very good <u>transitional</u> step, **support payments should be progressively phased out**, allowing time for markets to adjust in an orderly fashion, in particular the market for land, given that historic subsidy levels have been capitalised into artificially high land prices. Sweden recently became the first EU country to take the position that all EU farm subsidies (except those related to environmental protection) should be abolished. New Zealand strongly supports this position. (New Zealand does not have any measures similar to the SFP, and nor was such a scheme a feature of our own reform process).

21. This will result in **the determination of resource allocation by way of relative prices for products**, a highly desirable outcome for European Member States, their consumers (who will benefit from wider choice and lower prices), and for the international competitiveness of their producers and the wider economy. As the SFP is based on 2000-2002 subsidy levels, individual farmers will not see any immediate difference in their income. Consequently, there may be little effect on production levels in the short-term, an expectation supported by recent research.[1]

22. The SFP is also positive in the sense that it removes disparities in assistance levels for different products. Over time it may offer an opportunity to reduce direct support to farmers, particularly those larger or higher-income farmers most readily able to cope with the economic impacts of reform. **Future policy reform should be as simple as possible without acceding to special cases** except where a "one size fits all" policy would result in grossly inequitable outcomes involving significant economic hardship.

---

[1] Farm Level Adjustment in Ireland Following Decoupling, Teagasc Rural Economy Research Centre.

MARKET MECHANISMS

What short and longer-term changes are required to the CAP's market mechanisms? Suggestions made by the Commission have included re-examination of certain quotas, intervention, set-aside, export refunds and private storage payments

23. EU "market mechanisms", including intervention purchasing and export subsidies, have been abolished or reduced in some agricultural sectors, which is a positive step. **The ideal next step would be a progressive removal of such mechanisms across the board**, full decoupling and, if the SFP is continued, making it applicable to all agricultural sub-sectors previously subject to price support. The European Commission appears to share this view, and its upcoming proposals for the "health check" could promote this process. If the EU is to achieve a truly market-orientated agricultural sector, removing remaining distortionary measures will be key to creating a "level playing field" and therefore provide incentives for farmers to take an innovative approach to their product mix.

24. In New Zealand's case, the high levels of price support were negatively reflected in **resource misallocation**. The most common example relates to the sheep sector—since the reform period New Zealand's sheep numbers have fallen dramatically, from 70 million to 40 million today, yet export revenues from these smaller numbers have risen. Also of note is that marginal and easily erodible land has been taken out of production. The sector as a whole has become leaner and more efficient.

25. We note that the EU's dairy sector remains an exception to the newly-reformed norm, but that changes are expected in the near future. The eventual elimination of dairy production quotas will be key to this, but must be done carefully. **Dairy production quotas** should remain in force until the EU has permanently ended export subsidies and reduced its currently high tariffs to very modest levels. If dairy production quotas are freed-up prior to export subsidy elimination and tariff reform, there is a great risk that the EU dairy sector may expand significantly in response to prices which could be well above international levels. This would be to the detriment of other EU sectors which have lower levels of protection, as well as non-subsidised exporters (such as New Zealand). The EU itself would then also be faced with a more difficult adjustment process when tariffs are subsequently reduced following the WTO Doha Round or other trade-liberalisation measures.

26. Proposals to remove the **set-aside of land** are encouraging, as this is a hangover policy designed to avoid some of the negative economic effects of price support measures and reduce the environmental detriments of such support mechanisms. Non subsidy-based regulatory interventions now may be more appropriate to deal with residual environmental objectives not achieved by the removal of price subsidies. Such measures might include, for example, land-use requirements and mandatory biodiversity corridors. New Zealand has not applied a concept such as set-aside, but does successfully address environmental objectives through a range of regulatory initiatives.

27. **Export refunds**, which have been a key mechanism for transferring the costs of excess EU supply to economies reliant on international markets, should be eliminated. Export refunds represent one of the most undesirable aspects of the CAP, allowing the EU to capture perceived strategic benefits in terms of domestic self-sufficiency at the direct, and large, expense of those economies which suffer from the resulting international market price volatility and depression impacts.

28. High **EU tariffs** are another market mechanism where there should be some substantial downward adjustment. Until such changes are made, the EU and the rest of the world will suffer substantial resource misallocation costs.

RURAL DEVELOPMENT

What is your view on the introduction of the European Agricultural Fund for Rural Development (EAFRD)? Do you consider that it is meeting its objectives thus far? Is it suitably "strategic" in nature, meeting the needs of rural society as a whole rather than being restricted to aiding the agricultural industry? How well is it being co-ordinated with other EU and national policies on regional and rural development?

29. Support for rural development is beneficial where it is aimed at improving the efficiency, and thus international competitiveness of, European agriculture, which should eventually enable the EU's rural economy to exist without support. The EU should be mindful, however, that the establishment of rural development funds can potentially have the same indirect effect on output as price subsidies and, to a lesser extent, direct payments. In other words, **such funds should be aimed at meeting the specific and targeted needs of rural society**, rather than acting as a channel to fund further support of the EU's agricultural sector.

WORLD TRADE

What benefits can the EU's World Trade Organisation obligations create for EU agriculture and, consequently, for the EU economy as a whole?

30. The EU's current WTO obligations have served to reinforce and "lock in" the EU's unilateral reform programme. The move from price support to direct payments has revealed more clearly the real economic costs of a high level of agriculture sector subsidisation. The fiscal impact of these "on budget" costs will serve to provide incentives to EU governments to **continue the overall reduction of farm support**.

31. While **food costs** are not a large proportion of average EU household budgets, they impact on wage costs and, through that mechanism, have an impact on international competitiveness in industrial goods and services (which are, by far, the largest contributor to the EU economy). New Zealand has one of the lowest tariff profiles in the world, including for food and beverages. This has benefited consumers who enjoy a wider range of products at lower (world) prices, and producers who benefit from the competition.

32. Overall, past reforms have benefited the EU via economic welfare gains, and from reduced environmental degradation and improved sustainability of farming and natural resources. The EU's policy goals associated with assisting the economic development of developing economies are being well served by the reduced negative impact of subsidised exports. However, there is a considerable opportunity for further gains through the *elimination of export subsidies*, and progressive **opening of the EU's borders to imports**.

ENVIRONMENTAL PROTECTION AND CLIMATE CHANGE

To what extent has the system of cross-compliance contributed to an improved level of environmental protection? How is it linking with other EU policy requirements such as the Water Framework Directive? How can the CAP contribute to mitigation of, and adaptation to, climate change? What do you consider the role of biofuels to be in this regard?

33. The introduction of cross-compliance, and refocusing of the **CAP** on environmental objectives is a useful first step to encourage farmers to act in an environmentally sustainable way. The **removal of subsidies** will reduce the incentive to increase output in a way unrelated to market demand, thereby reducing the pressure on the environment and resulting in improvements in water quality, biodiversity, and sustainability of other natural resources. A reduction in livestock intensity will promote a reduction in greenhouse gas emissions, and water in air contamination from animal effluent.

34. In terms of new policy, New Zealand has a **taxation (polluter pays) and regulatory-based approach to environmental protection**, rather than a subsidy-based approach (there is no need for a New Zealand cross-compliance system as New Zealand farmers do not receive subsidies). The key measures include:

— the fisheries quota management system (1986);

— the Resource Management Act 1991, which codifies sustainable management of natural and physical resources into legislation;

— the Biosecurity Act 1993, the purpose of which is to exclude, eradicate, or effectively manage pests and unwanted organisms;

— the Hazardous Substances and New Organisms Act 1996, which governs the protection of the environment, and the health and safety of people and communities by preventing or managing the adverse effects of hazardous substances;

— the Agricultural Compounds and Veterinary Medicines Act 1997: to prevent or manage risks from agricultural compounds to trade in primary produce, animal welfare, and agricultural security;

— the Local Government Act 2002, which gives local authorities a role in promoting social, economic, environmental, and cultural well-being of communities; and

— New Zealand's Sustainable Development Plan of Action (2003), which guides policy and decision-making by using sustainability principles as well as focusing on four key issues affecting New Zealand, including quality and allocation of fresh water, and energy.

35. The recent **inclusion of agriculture and forestry in an economy-wide emissions trading scheme** (ETS) is a critical element in the New Zealand Government's recently announced mitigation response policy package to the challenge of climate change. By making producers liable for greenhouse gas emissions while rewarding the creation of carbon sinks, the policy is expected to encourage the adoption of less greenhouse gas intensive forms of agricultural production and expand farm forestry activities.

36. At the same time, the New Zealand Government recognises that farmers currently have limited technical opportunities to reduce emissions without reducing agricultural output, and is therefore phasing in the inclusion of agricultural gases in the ETS, while making available substantial funding for research into the development of emission reduction technologies. Other complementary policies include:

— technology transfer activities (including new tools for measuring and monitoring emissions at the farm level);

— education programmes on existing opportunities to reduce emissions and emerging technologies and practices; and

— an afforestation grant scheme (providing incentives for the creation of carbon sinks) for smaller farm foresters not wishing to be part of the emissions trading scheme.

37. Climate **adaptation** is another important area for New Zealand. Significant funding is being provided for research and technology transfer activities into how best farmers can respond to the changing climate, in particular the likely increase in the occurrence of extreme weather events such as flooding and droughts.

38. New Zealand also places importance on the use of **biofuels,** and is looking to encourage uptake of fuels that are produced from sustainable sources.

FINANCING

The Commissioner has expressed her dissatisfaction at the financing agreement reached by the Member States at the December 2005 Council. Do you consider the current budget to be sufficient? Do you consider co-financing to be a possible way forward in financing the Common Agricultural Policy?

39. The recent CAP reforms have been far-reaching and are heading in a desirable direction, but, from an outsider's perspective, the **level of financial support for agriculture in the EU remains high** and continues to be linked to retention of resources in the sector. This is at the cost of EU consumers and society, as well as the EU's trading partners, notably developing countries. Any increase in the CAP budget (particularly as it accounted for 45.5% of EU expenditure in 2005, predicted to decline to 32% by 2013) would not be recommended. Even with modulation moving funds to rural development programmes, the funding remains in the agricultural sector.

40. New Zealand observes that for some Member States, the imposition of costs on national budgets may serve as an incentive to moderate expenditure. Co-financing, however, risks a trend towards re-nationalisation of agricultural policy with a loss of transparency, reduced policy cohesion, and efficiency losses.

ENLARGEMENT

What has been the impact on the CAP of the 2004 and 2007 enlargements and what is the likely impact of future enlargements of the EU on the post-2013 CAP?

41. New Zealand notes that the recent enlargements of the EU from 15 to 27 Member States have greatly changed the face of the EU, and the agricultural sector in particular. The introduction of new agricultural land, with huge potential for productivity improvements creates new challenges and opportunities, which may require new policy responses. These, and any further enlargements that might follow, are likely to reinforce the current incentives and pressures for reform along the established line. **Enlargement can provide a stimulus for greater competitiveness** in the agricultural sector.

SIMPLIFICATION OF THE CAP AND OTHER ISSUES

How could the CAP be further simplified and in what other ways would you like to see the Common Agricultural Policy changed in the short and/or the long term?

42. The ongoing simplification of the CAP will be important for the future of EU agriculture, and should enable farmers to focus more on farming than on administration. Clearly, the elimination of all subsidies and indirect supports would also make the CAP simpler, but we appreciate that such a step will take time.

43. For New Zealand, the gains from agricultural sector reform in the context of a major economy-wide reform have been substantial—and may be a useful reference tool. The critical aspects of reform have been the development of a level playing field, not only within the agricultural sector, but across the economy. This was achieved by the **removal of subsidisation and allowing markets to be the prime factor determining resource**

allocation. The New Zealand Government has abolished almost all agricultural assistance (except in the event of severe climatic disasters, outbreaks of plant or animal disease, or for the provision of innovation funding). This has resulted in a much simplified agricultural policy.

44. The New Zealand Government, in regard to agriculture, now focuses its attention on:
    — sustainability;
    — innovation;
    — food safety;
    — biosecurity;
    — multilateral trade liberalisation; and
    — other regulatory frameworks.

45. In the EU or elsewhere, national welfare is enhanced by **gains in productivity**. New Zealand found that its mid-1980's reforms had a markedly positive effect on total factor productivity in the agricultural sector. This total factor productivity averaged 2.5% a year in the post-1984 period (after a three year recovery period) compared with 1.5% beforehand. This is because the reforms enabled the sector to improve its allocation of resources and level of responsiveness to global market signals as well as to maximise cross-sectional synergies. General agricultural productivity growth since the economic liberalisation of the mid-1980's has been three times greater than in the rest of the economy.

46. More specifically, the pattern of farm output has changed:
    — *Sheep and beef*: The national flock decreased from 70 million in 1983 to around 40 million currently. (There are now 31% fewer sheep and beef farms). Lambing percentages have increased by 25% and average carcass weights have also increased by 25%. Export revenues (in value-added product) from the sheepmeat sector now exceed those generated by the former 70 million-strong flock ($2.25 billion in the year ended 31 March 2007).[2]
    — *Dairy*: The number of dairy herds fell by 17% from 16,000 in 1983 to 13,000 in 2004, but the national herd size increased from 2.3 million to 5.3 million, the average herd size increased from 150 to 330 (2006), and there has been a 75% increase in the volume of dairy production (with exports worth $8.41 billion in the year ended 31 March 2007).
    — *Deer*: New Zealand only had a very small deer industry in 1984. New Zealand's export earnings from deer are now $260 million (year ended 31 March 2007).
    — *Horticulture*: In 1983 New Zealand exported $55 million worth of kiwifruit and $185 million worth of other horticultural exports. In the year ended 31 March 2007, it is expected more than $759 million worth of kiwifruit alone, and nearly $1.12 billion worth of other horticultural products.
    — *Wine*: The reforms had a significant impact on the development of New Zealand's wine sector. It has been a growth industry: exports were worth less than $13 million in 1984 and had increased to $660 million in the year ended 31 March 2007.
    — *Farm income*: Currently approximately 705 of New Zealand farms have some form of off-farm income either via off-farm work or investments, or other initiatives such as rural tourism.

47. Agriculture is a hugely diverse sector in the EU, which has developed structural rigidities as a result of both legal structures for land tenure, and a long history of subsidisation which has prevented ongoing adjustment. We accept that these forces and the rigidities they have induced cannot sensibly be unwound in a short time frame as was done in New Zealand.

48. Therefore, the signalling of a clear medium-term policy direction is essential to the achievement of an orderly pathway of adjustment and to give producers the regulatory certainty they need to make investment decisions. This applies in particular to adjustment in the market for agricultural land, as the historical level of subsidy has become capitalised in land prices.

49. Time is required to allow the necessary correction to occur and transitional measures are required. It must be recognised, however, that when second or third-best policy approaches are applied, the chances of interventions having unwanted and negative impacts is high. The design of transitional mechanisms presents significant challenges. **Shorter adjustment pathways** are therefore preferable in order to minimise the economic costs of adjustment.

October 2007

---

[2] Note all figures in New Zealand dollars.

Examination of Witness

Witness: MR MURRAY SHERWIN, Director-General of the New Zealand Ministry of Agriculture and Fisheries, examined.

Q271 *Chairman:* Welcome and thank you very much for (a) finding the time to come and meet with us but (b) presenting us with a refreshing and interesting written piece of evidence. I do have to say it is not the usual tone of evidence we receive from some Member States and organisations. We are having an inquiry basically on the CAP health check and looking forward to CAP reform in the future. This is a formal evidence session, so there will be a transcript. You will have the opportunity later to correct it. We are also web-cast. If you want to make a few remarks of a general nature, then please do so. We will then move on to a question and answer session. We will have a conversation really.

Mr Sherwin: My Lord Chairman, thank you for the opportunity, a rare one for a colonial boy. I have a couple of colleagues with me: Ms Saffron Powell from the Ministry of Agriculture and Forestry in Wellington and Peter Kell from the High Commission here in London. By way of opening comments, let me say that I certainly would not hold myself out as an expert on the CAP, far from it. The acronyms and intricacies of it leave me totally bewildered. We do have a good deal of experience, though, of its impact on New Zealand as a trading partner in agricultural matters and we have obviously had a good deal of experience of our own agricultural system and approaches that we have taken to that. Historically, New Zealand has not had a great deal of support for its agricultural system. That changed through the Sixties, Seventies and in particular into the early Eighties, largely as a consequence, I would say, of first the oil shocks but, secondly, Britain's entry into Europe in the Seventies, which was something that obviously marked a substantial shift in our agricultural trading relationships. I am an economist by training and a member of the New Zealand Association of Economists. Through the Seventies and the Sixties there was a tradition of the Association of Economists at their annual conference for a prominent economist to speak and give a toast to *le générale* and thanks for his unstinting efforts to keep Britain out of the EEC! As I said, through the Seventies and particularly in to the early Eighties, as the impact of the closure of markets and other pressures came on our agricultural system, we attempted to offset the income losses by building support subsidies and other things. If you take the producer support estimates that the OECD uses, at our peak we got through about 10%, so still well below where Europe is now. We are currently at 1%; we moved to that very quickly post-1984. This whole mechanism of trying to protect agriculture and other parts of the economy moved apace rather spectacularly and we moved to a free trade model.

There are some reasons for that, apart from a strongly-held principle about the benefits of free trade. In a very small economy of four million people and a GDP currently of the order of magnitude of US$ 120 billion, if we attempt to provide support for any sector of the economy, but particularly for a very large sector such as agriculture in New Zealand, you have to look at where that support is coming from. In a large economy, you may be able to push the costs of that support off to your trading partners—and certainly we felt the back end of that in many areas—but in a small economy you have much less opportunity to do that. When you look around and try to understand who is going to pay for the support, there are not very many candidates putting their hands up. As we did attempt to go down a more supportive route through the Seventies and Eighties, I think all we found was that we were recycling support through bureaucracy without great effect. We tried to focus on responsiveness to markets. We tried to focus on innovation. I think one of the outcomes has been that our primary industries really are the drivers of our productivity gains over the last 15 to 20 years. I think what we found also is that at the end of the day competitive advantage and productivity wins out, and so agriculture is far from being a sunset industry for us with a growing share of GDP. It is a little mixed but certainly it is in its best state that it has been in for a long time, but continuing to evolve and in ways that we as bureaucrats I think would not necessarily have guessed and probably would not have managed through a tight regulatory environment. Let me stop there. I am happy to take questions.

Q272 *Chairman:* Thank you very much indeed. Your paper describes beautifully the process of moving away from significantly supported agriculture and relying almost entirely now on the market, is it not?

Mr Sherwin: It is about 1% in GDP terms, mostly in R and D.

Q273 *Chairman:* What about the farmers themselves? What was the initial reaction of New Zealand farmers to waking up one day and finding they did not have a nice warm support of subsidy around them and they had to face the cold wind of the market?

Mr Sherwin: Context is really important here because what was occurring in agriculture was part of a much wider reform process that was taking place in the financial sector and in the public sector and elsewhere. It was part of a comprehensive reform agenda. It was also clear that there were very few alternatives at that stage available to us. We had some serious economic problems on our doorstep that had to be dealt with. It is also true to say that farm leaders were amongst the strongest proponents of change. At the time, they had come to the conclusion that there was no future in continuing down this route of subsidies and protection. Again, context is important. Overwhelmingly, given such a small domestic market, our primary produce is exported. So they are dependent on export markets; they are price takers in export markets, except to the extent that they can influence where their products are positioned. I think it had become very obvious to them that attempts to protect the sector largely ended up with farmers themselves paying for that protection, but recycling it through other routes. Farm leadership was amongst the strongest group of supporters for reform. If you look right across, there are many farmers who went through very tough times. This was not an easy transition. From 1984 through until about 1992, farmers went through some very difficult times. There were substantial reductions in the values of properties. Not very many left the land; about 2% came off the land. The government reaction there was to provide essentially exit packages, support for farmers to leave, rather than trying to offset the impacts of the reform process, to encourage those who had come to the conclusion that there was no future for them to leave the land. There were small grants up to about $45,000 maximum. Farmers went through a tough time and some difficult adjustments.

Q274 *Chairman:* In terms of products, how did it restructure? Who were the winners and losers?

Mr Sherwin: Within the agricultural sector, initially what we saw were shifts in land use particularly away from sheep and beef and, in the more marginal hill country, in forestry. There was quite a sweep of that through the late Eighties and early Nineties. For others, it was just loss of income for a period, loss of asset value. Some concluded that this was a difficult and prolonged adjustment but that they would come out of it better by investing in larger-scale and so forth. Within the sector, there were adjustments in farm size and property holdings.

Q275 *Chairman:* Was there any concern about the mental health problems and things like that of farmers? They tend to be an isolated group.

Mr Sherwin: They do tend to be an isolated group and those can be concerns. There were certainly cases that were reported. Rural communities tend to be very supportive, though, in those circumstances. The fabric of rural society is important and was important at the time, and continues to be today.

Q276 *Chairman:* We have come across quite a lot of this wonderful phrase "the European model of agriculture", which is always used when any form of rational argument has been exhausted. At its best, it is saying really that there are non-market benefits that agriculture provides, like a landscape, environmental benefits, some social benefits. If you move to such a market-led model as you have got, this gets all pushed to one side, does it not?

Mr Sherwin: No, I do not think so. No, in fact I think our rural communities are stronger than they have been for a very long time and stronger for reasons that again many of us would not have predicted at the outset. Again, context is all important. We are a very young country. Our landscapes have been changing radically and rapidly over, say, 150 years in European settlement of New Zealand. Landscapes continue to move; land use continues to move quite a lot. I talked about the movement from sheep and beef into plantation forestry in the wake of the reforms. During this period of subsidies of course, there had been quite a move into pasture in scrub areas and even bush clearance, as encouraged by land development grants and fertiliser subsidies, and so forth, often into countryside that was not really suited for farming. We saw a pull-back from that. What we have seen more recently again is significant diversification into horticulture, grapes in particular and wine grapes, in areas that we would never have expected and never have predicted. That is still taking place. There is a good deal of experimentation. You end up with a combination in rural New Zealand of wine, food and tourism. It makes for a very vibrant rural economy. One of the great joys of getting into rural New Zealand right now is to see the way that that has evolved and has diversified the rural economy and the rural landscape. That will continue as we move into different circumstances.

Q277 *Chairman:* Has it had an effect on settlement patterns? The argument would be in, say, the north of Scotland where I live that if we moved away from less favoured area payments, that would lead to the sheep and the bests coming off the hill and ultimately to major adjustments to settlement patterns, which would be seen as a bad thing.

Mr Sherwin: Yes, of course there are adjustments there. Again, to go back to that period immediately post-reform, some of the rural communities took a real battering. There were school closures, local services closing and so forth. Some of those will be diminished pretty much for ever, one would presume, but also, if you look right now, most of our strongest growing regions are provincial centres. In the deep south, it is a shift from sheep farming largely to dairying, which is very strong right now. The horticultural industries in other rural areas have been very strong, and so we have seen shifts and patterns.

As I have said, the fastest growing populations on a proportional basis are in those rural areas.

Q278 *Viscount Brookeborough:* You mentioned forestry as being something on the increase recently. What percentage of your land is covered by forestry? Ours is about 11%, which is lower than any other nation in Europe. What proportion are you increasing by? Presumably you are not through the first rotation crops since this occurred anyway?

Mr Sherwin: About 30% of the total land area is forestry and that is predominantly indigenous forests. That is not commercially harvested a lot for the most part. Virtually all of our commercial forestry is in plantation forestry. In the region since the depression when the first plantation forests, *Pinus radiata*, got underway, a rapid growth in plantations through that post-reform period—the late Eighties and early Nineties—has fallen off substantially. In fact, we have a period of deforestation occurring now. I suspect that is going to turn around with climate change policies coming through and the re-establishing of stronger incentives into the plantation forestry area; profitability has been quite weak over the last five, six or seven years.

Q279 *Viscount Brookeborough:* But the prices are going up at the moment?

Mr Sherwin: Yes, but offset by a number of other factors.

Q280 *Earl of Dundee:* Very roughly, what is the percentage of your forestry which is publicly owned and that which is privately owned?

Mr Sherwin: In plantation forestry now, which is the guts of the commercial forestry sector, very little is publicly owned. My own ministry is responsible for probably about 15%, but that is largely government owned forests or trees on mostly Maori-owned land. The process is to establish strong commercial forests and put them back fully in Maori hands as the rotations roll through, but it is quite small. Most of it is privately owned.

Q281 *Baroness Sharp of Guildford:* I enjoyed an extended holiday in your country in the spring this year, and certainly the issue that you raised in terms of moving over to viticulture was very obvious. There are two questions at the time I thought about and I might as well raise with you now. First of all, is there not a danger of you overdoing that?

Mr Sherwin: Almost certainly.

Q282 *Baroness Sharp of Guildford:* Secondly, the whole question of irrigation, because a lot of the land requires irrigation: it struck me that at a time when we are worried about climate change whether it was really sensible to move into areas that required persistent irrigation.

Mr Sherwin: To go back to that first question, almost certainly it will be overdone. At what point is that predicted? If we look at it right now, there are areas that are expanding in viticulture—

Q283 *Baroness Sharp of Guildford:* I found it amazing that in the Canterbury Plain south of Christchurch, which was very rich arable country, you should be shifting over to viticulture there.

Mr Sherwin: Viticulture is much more profitable and even more so in parts of central Otago, in the Queenstown area, which one might never have expected to be suitable for producing grapes.

Q284 *Chairman:* We have had quite a lot of evidence on the New Zealand vine industry when we were doing our inquiry into wines. If you are overdoing it, do not be tempted by distillation subsidies!

Mr Sherwin: I think there is very little danger of that but some of these people will get it wrong. I think we have about 500 vineyards now. It has grown hugely and I think the smaller ones are feeling the squeeze; others are desperately looking for more wine because the international demand is there. We cannot predict where that is going to work out, but it will, and no doubt for those who overdo it, there will be an adjustment in asset values and it will sort its way through somewhere. Some of it will no doubt be pulled out at some stage. On the question of irrigation, we are not hugely dependent on irrigation in viticulture but in some areas certainly it is important. New Zealand typically does not have a shortage of water. It is not always in the right places at the right times. I think that will become more pronounced. In the Canterbury Plains area in particular I think we are giving a lot of thought to irrigation. It is a much bigger issue in the dairy industry than it is in viticulture; the bodies required are much larger and the impacts are much larger.

Q285 *Lord Cameron of Dillington:* Just carrying on with the New Zealand experience and bringing it up to date, you said that you do have some emergency funding for disaster, for R and D mostly, you said.

Mr Sherwin: No, not quite.

Q286 *Lord Cameron of Dillington:* I am just wondering, but certainly in particular in relation to the disaster fund, who decides when it should be paid out and what is the methodology of arriving at who should receive it?

Mr Sherwin: We can give you policy statements on that. There has been quite a lot of work done on it of late. The general principle is that we try not to get involved. The motivations to become involved are where there has been an event, whether it is floods or droughts or wind or whatever, that has gone well beyond the capacity of the local community to cope on its own. Support is typically directed for farming to uninsurable loses. If it is insurable, then that is your problem as a farmer. Then there is an insurance-type principle which is applied. We are looking largely here at, say, pasture damage which cannot be insured, some infrastructure (fences, tracks and things) but most other things can be insured and farmers are expected to insure them. The first $10,000 or 10% they wear themselves and then there is a 50% subsidy on restoration up to a cap. That is essentially triggered where, as I said, the scale of the event is too large for a local community to cope on its own. We try to keep quite tight criteria on that. In terms of allocating it to particular farmers, typically we build a rural trust and essentially it is local farmers or local community leaders making those judgments with their peers. We have found those to be very effective. Farmers are typically the toughest judges on who has taken appropriate care and who has not and all the processes run behind that. Typically, that has been very effective.

Q287 *Lord Cameron of Dillington:* I notice that there is no social safety net? It does not come out of any agricultural budget that is on the side supporting farmers in trouble?
Mr Sherwin: No. For those whose income has gone completely for a season or whatever, they may have access to the standard social welfare income support networks.

Q288 *Lord Cameron of Dillington:* Turning now to the Common Agricultural Policy, you are proposing that we should limit agricultural assistance to transitional, structural aid only. At the moment, there are huge sums of money going from various Member States into other Member States and our very own dear Treasury gets very upset about this. I was wondering how we get from here to there in your scenario?
Mr Sherwin: It is not easy. Again, as I have said, context is everything here. I would be the last one to try to set myself up as an expert on how to do this in a European context. I think the issue is around establishing long-term directions and moving towards those over whatever timeframe is judged appropriate, but with a good deal of certainty and persistence in that process so that farmers have the time to understand how their settings are going to be changing and how to adjust to that.

Q289 *Lord Cameron of Dillington:* You quite rightly say that there is a huge potential for growth and productivity in new Member States.

Mr Sherwin: And even in existing ones.

Q290 *Lord Cameron of Dillington:* Possibly, but I would not like to comment. Do you think exceptions should be made for the Member States, somewhere like Romania for instance, that will need quite a lot of extra funding to bring their agriculture up to standard?
Mr Sherwin: My understanding is that there is essentially a contract written as they join, which is well established. Again, I would not like to get into the detail of how one would do that, but there are transitions to be made. It is important that they are transitions. I think the notion that there should be permanent, ongoing subsidies is where the real damage starts to be incurred.

Q291 *Viscount Brookeborough:* You are very cautious about rural development funds and how they should be used. You indicate that they have the potential indirectly to affect output and argue that such funds should be targeted at specific needs rather than setting up a channel through which to continue supporting agriculture. How far would you accept that some of these specific needs, such as protection of landscapes, cannot be delivered without continuing farming activity? To put it another way, how would you counter the argument that continued farming activity should be supported in this way?
Mr Sherwin: I can only talk about it again in the context within which we are trying to deal with these issues at home because it is not as if we had a free market, open approach and are totally disinterested in environmental, social and other outcomes. Our point is that we need to be very clear about the outcomes we are trying to create and very clear about how we are targeting those and what polices we have available to target those. We have a great deal of interest in New Zealand in issues around water quality in particular. Our approach to that is to try to understand the externalities that are being created by decisions on land use and particular techniques applied on the land and as much as possible to find devices that will channel those externalities back into the pocket of the decision makers so that they are wearing the costs of their own decisions. There are other regulatory approaches as well but for us that is operated largely through local government but not with direct support. If there are negative consequences from decisions being taken by farmers, then farmers need to be aware what those negative consequences are and what the costs associated with those are and, as far as possible, build them into their own decision making. That is the approach that we take.

Q292 *Viscount Brookeborough:* To what extend do you support rural development financially compared with what you used to when you were supporting agriculture?
Mr Sherwin: We do not provide any support.

Q293 *Viscount Brookeborough:* You do not provide any support at all for diversification in the countryside?
Mr Sherwin: No.

Q294 *Viscount Brookeborough:* Would you say that farmers or agricultural people who wish to diversify meet problems in the planning process. Here, if you talk to people who wish to diversify, very often they are inhibited by the planning process which says that they may not use their farm buildings for an alternative use other than agriculture.
Mr Sherwin: Again, it is my understanding that is much less of an issue in New Zealand given the lower population densities, different history, different settings. Local decisions are run through local councils, local government, and under a comprehensive piece of legislation called the Resource Management Act. It is outcome based rather than prescriptive as to what people can or cannot do. My sense is that it is probably rather less intrusive, although there are plenty of people in New Zealand who would argue otherwise, in terms of the capacity for people to shift land use around. It is one of the issues that local regional government is debating with central government right now as we move into a more comprehensive climate change response policy and their concerns are that that may prompt land use changes quicker than they can adjust their planning procedures. It is just part of that process that they have to work through.

Q295 *Viscount Brookeborough:* You note in your evidence that as a result of reforms in New Zealand marginal and easily erodable land has been taken out of production. Could you tell us a little more about this process and explain how you reassure those concerned with abandoning it?
Mr Sherwin: New Zealand is a much younger country physically. Many of those hillsides have been exposed only in the last hundred years or so, having had their indigenous forest cover or scrub cover removed. It has been discovered that in fact the soils are in unstable under pasture and they need to go back into some sort of forestry cover or other use which provides the soils with more protection and in doing so protect the rivers and so forth. There has never been an issue of seeing that as abandoning the land. Some of it will go into plantation forestry and will be very successful in that form. Others in the last few years have been beginning to look at the carbon farming opportunities which exist there, but as an

issue in rural development or rural depopulation or abandoning the land, that has never been a particular issue publicly for us.

Q296 *Viscount Brookeborough:* During the wine inquiry, which we have just finished, tremendous arguments were put up by users of marginal land in Italy and Spain about erosion taking place. In actual fact when that land went out of wine production there was enough scrub and enough things growing on it that it really was not as big an issue as they said. Is that the way that you would look at it?
Mr Sherwin: Yes.

Q297 *Earl of Arran:* Just going back to forestry for a second, out of curiosity, is it mostly softwood or hardwood that you grow?
Mr Sherwin: Pinus radiata is softwood, relatively rapidly growing, about 25 to 30 year rotations, originally a native of the Monterey Peninsula but very adapted to New Zealand conditions. There has been quite a lot of genetic selection over the period that we have been working with it to produce the characteristics which will suit our needs.

Q298 *Earl of Arran:* So it is a 30 to 40 year rotation?
Mr Sherwin: It is 25 to 30 years, and at that level— and I speak with some close familiarity—you can expect internal rates of return of 7 or 8%, as a forest owner and grower.

Q299 *Earl of Arran:* I am not sure whether that is good or bad. I am told it is good.
Mr Sherwin: That does not mean to say that everyone has always received that return, but it is possible.

Q300 *Earl of Arran:* Ours is getting better, I think. My other question was on your attitude toward co-financing and the CAP; it is a little bit ambivalent. Are you able at all to elaborate on what you regard as the inherent risks of renationalising agricultural policy?
Mr Sherwin: I think our concerns in that area are largely focused on the potential to lose transparency about the nature of the support and the complexity. For those of us sitting on the outside and trying to understand what is going on, it just becomes much more difficult to keep a track of the nature of the support and the extent of the support.

Q301 *Earl of Dundee:* What do you consider to be the current obstacles following the Doha Round?
Mr Sherwin: There are 190 member countries. There are clearly some difficult balancing acts being worked through in Geneva right now between trying to achieve the sort of levels of ambition that were originally laid down in the Doha mandate versus the concerns that many countries have to protect their

own particular interests. There are no doubt trade diplomats who could talk for a very long time about exactly those issues. It seems that the key issues at present relate to access to developing country markets and also the treatment of sensitive products into developed country markets. I think the EU, the US and perhaps India and Brazil are the key partners to try to come to a conclusion on this. Our sense is that the agricultural negotiations have been moving reasonably well, but the non-agricultural market access issues and one or two of the other areas are perhaps moving a little less well, and they all have to land at the same time.

Q302 *Earl of Dundee:* Following these aspects which you identify, what further concessions therefore do you think may be required of either the European Union itself or of any other parties?
Mr Sherwin: I am reluctant to start trying to put issues on the table in this area but, as I said, I think it is still further movements on access to developed country markets and on the sensitive product areas in the more developed countries. I would be reluctant to go beyond that. There are sensitive enough discussions going on in Geneva that they do not need me muddying them.

Q303 *Earl of Dundee:* You note that the policy agendas of the European Union and of New Zealand have much in common: both of those emphasise climate change, market forces, food safety, biodiversity and so on. How will those types of issues affect future international trade negotiations?
Mr Sherwin: I think they enter the complexity of them and finding ways in which we are actually liberalizing trade yet allowing members to achieve the outcomes that they need in areas of climate change, and a number of other matters as well, is quite a balance. We strike this regularly in our negotiations with free trade arrangements in a bilateral sense. I think what we have reckoned with always is a tendency towards much greater complexity in some of these deals and the more complex they are, the harder they are to agree, but, with the right attitudes and the right will, one can bring those forward into agreements.

Q304 *Earl of Dundee:* So far with these trade agreements and your own negotiations, where do you reckon you have had your greatest success?
Mr Sherwin: The greatest success for us is typically managing to achieve greater access to markets because the key agricultural exports in New Zealand, and primary industries account for about two-thirds of our total physical exports, are very heavily protected just about everywhere, so we are trying to jump over barriers almost everywhere. In terms of free trade agreements, the best one we have by far is

with Australia, and we have had that for some time. We are in the middle of attempting to bring to closure what will be the first free trade arrangement with China at present. Again, for us it is maintaining access to markets and being able to maintain also the degrees and standards that we require on bio-security in particular. Some interesting tensions in that area emerge in some countries. Just about any one of these agreements that provides us with some reduction in the trade barriers we face is a strong positive for us. We have a very strong vested interest in that.

Q305 *Baroness Jones of Whitchurch:* If I could just follow that up, it could be argued that the only reason that you are here and putting such a strong gloss on how easy it has been in New Zealand, if you like, is all just part of a strategy to do away with the CAP and open up another market for yourself. I am just pushing you a little bit. I am using the word "gloss". I am sure you would not say anything that was inaccurate.
Mr Sherwin: I hope I did not leave any impression that all that this was easy because it certainly was not. We are asked a lot to talk about the New Zealand experience because I think many countries are facing the prospect of having to do something with their own agricultural sectors and looking at what different models exist. I am usually very careful to try to say, as I think I have been saying, that the context is important and one cannot pick up one model and place it down somewhere else and expect it all to be the same. As I said earlier in response to the last question, our agricultural sector is our major industry. As we have gone through the deregulation process, it has constantly reasserted itself in terms of competitive and comparative advantage and we face extraordinary trade barriers almost everywhere with these products. Yes, we would like to talk about the fact that they are alternatives to heavily protected and subsidised models around the world. There is no doubt in our minds that for us to be successful in persuading a few others, it is likely to be helpful to us. I think it is also likely to be helpful to a lot of other countries, including those most prone to high degrees of protection. You could even argue in some cases that to the extent that removing the subsidies and protection would make some of those economies and the agricultural sectors in those economies more competitive, we are setting ourselves up for a bigger battle, but that is the nature of the world.

Q306 *Baroness Jones of Whitchurch:* Are you going to visit France and Italy too?
Mr Sherwin: I have just had a holiday with my wife in the south of France. It was the first time in a few years that I had been there. You cannot help but be impressed with the extraordinary opportunities that exist there in agriculture: the soils, the land, the space,

the climate. But, added to that, and this is what really matters in all this, the brands that exist and can be exploited. They are all in there, and so the opportunities are immense.

Q307 *Chairman:* I am going to come in behind Baroness Jones on this because you evidence has been very strong on general direction and strategy, the importance of transparency, and obviously as a producing nation you would want that. You have been pretty cautious, though, on offering any specific policy proposals. I am really going to tempt you and ask: what are the three big things that you think CAP reform ought to attend to?

Mr Sherwin: I am reluctant to go there because, as I said at the outset, I do not hold myself out as an expert on CAP reform at all or on the particular setting in which people are trying to make their decisions. What I will say is: do not underestimate the adaptability of farm systems. I think almost inevitably when people are looking at reform propositions, they get very focused on down-sides and the up-side is completely invisible. There is huge opportunity to innovate and to change. There is a real danger that the regulatory regimes try to lock the sector into a particular point in history in terms of what it looks like and how it works and all the rest of it. Innovation is the heart of any industry. Secondly, we are all members of agencies like the WTO, IMF and OECD whose starting principles are around the benefits of trade liberalization and free trade. There are not many things that economists agree on but I think there is stronger consensus around that than just about anything else. I sometimes look around and wonder: how come these organisations have so many members because they patently do not seem to believe the principles that they a have signed up for. There really are gains to be had for welfare. Yes, there are some awkward distributional issues in those at times, but some real gains both for developed and even more particularly developing countries.

Q308 *Baroness Sharp of Guildford:* Inevitably, once you move towards open competition, prices are going to be far more volatile than under a regime of support. How far have your farmers coped with such price fluctuations? Do you think there are lessons there to be learnt by the farmers in Europe?

Mr Sherwin: They have coped. They have to cope because there is nothing else to step in. Again, we are a very small economy with an exchange rate that moves through quite a wide range. The exchange rate today NZ$ against the US$ for instance is at about 77/78 cents. It is not that many years ago that it was 40, so it is a big swing. When you are exporting overwhelmingly, and the dairy industry exports about 95% of its production, there are big impacts going through from that. The industry does cope; it

copes by the way it structures its balance sheets, understanding that it is a cyclical industry, that there will be good times when you lower the debt ratios and catch up on maintenance and do some investment, and other times when you simply tighten your belts. Again, farmers are an astonishingly resilient breed. When they need to put the chequebooks away, they certainly do so. That is important. They have opportunities to hedge their risks in various ways, and I think they are becoming more sophisticated in that in terms of balance sheet hedging and exchange rate management and other risk as well. My personal view, which I am not sure that everyone shares around my organisation, is that one of the reasons why we have very strong co-operatives in our primary industry relates to the capacity to distribute risk in a way that a more conventional limited liability company does not and that we end up with these large producer-owned co-operatives in our primary sector because of the nature of the risks and volatility that they are faced with. That is more of a hypothesis at this stage. It is something we would like to do a little bit more work on.

Q309 *Baroness Sharp of Guildford:* It is an interesting issue, is it not, of the co-operatives? The milk in particular was one that hit me when we were visiting New Zealand. We visited a dairy farm and they talked to us about the way in which they sold to the co-operative. In this country, the co-operatives have largely disappeared, have they not? Perhaps there is in that a lesson to be learnt in Europe.

Mr Sherwin: We have experiments of course running as we speak in New Zealand with non-co-operatives, conventionally structured companies, emerging in the dairy sector. It will be interesting to see how they manage through these large price cycles.

Q310 *Baroness Jones of Whitchurch:* Moving on to climate change, we are interested about the emissions trading scheme that you have. You have described in your evidence the elements of it. It seems to me quite a large concentration of that is about reforestation or capitalising on the forests. Would you like to tell us a little more about that? Do you think the forests are crucial to it?

Mr Sherwin: Forests are certainly important to it, but I think reducing emissions is also important, perhaps more so. This is all very new for all of us to try to work out how to respond effectively to climate change. What has been announced in New Zealand is the intention to go to a comprehensive emissions trading regime, which is all greenhouse gases in all sectors. The application of that to the agricultural sector in particular will be very interesting to work through. We have a little bit of time to do that, but not much. I think it is going to involve a great deal of work around how we can reduce greenhouse gas emissions from agriculture. The most promising prospects on the agenda at this stage are new products such as nitrogen emitters applied to the soil, which hold the nitrogen in the soil longer and make the nitrogen more available for pasture growth and so forth. The other area of work in agriculture is a very substantial research agenda around basically a better understanding of the physiology of the moon and how you can work with that to both improve the efficiency of conversion of feed to protein, if you like, and reduce methane emissions in particular. That science is going to be more difficult but there is a lot of collaborative work internationally with the New Zealand science institutes and counterparts offshore, including the UK. That will be the focus of a great deal of attention. Forestry is important and some complexities there relate to the way the Kyoto rules are written and the way our forestry industry is structured. It is quite tempting simply to plant trees and solve your Kyoto obligations that way. I do not think it is going to work quite like that. Tree planting will be important. Part of that will be additional plantations of our existing *Pinus radiata* species, but I think a significant part of that is likely to be regeneration of indigenous forests in areas that should never have been cleared. One of the things that we are attempting to do in the ministry is to join the dots between sustainable land use, water quality issues and climate change so that we can encourage the reforestation agenda, but on land that is otherwise erosion prone, and that is likely to help manage some of our flood risks and other risks as well. Joining those dots is going to be very important to us. We do not want just to agree a climate change policy that runs independently of the other objectives that we have in mind.

Q311 *Baroness Jones of Whitchurch:* Would you say that you were at the leading edge in terms of that sort of understanding of agricultural emissions and what needs to be done about it?
Mr Sherwin: I think we are a lot more focused on it. Whether we are at the leading edge, I am not sure. The fact is that when you look at the Kyoto accounting, 50% of our emissions are livestock derived, so it is hard for us to deal with Kyoto without paying some real attention to the livestock sector, but it will not be easy. We are under no illusions about that.

Q312 *Chairman:* How do you marry that approach, which is actually going to require intervention and regulation, with a liberal market?
Mr Sherwin: That is where the emissions trading regime comes in. Basically it is a cap in trade regime, which is again all sectors and all gases. The adjustment process will be a long one. We would expect the agriculture sector for instance to start off

with an allocation of essentially free units, which will be scaled down over a time period. A lot of technical detail goes into that. As an administrator, if you like, I get nervous about how much detail we may have to plug into that and how heavily involved we may need to be. One of the joys of my particular ministry at this stage is that we do not do a lot of regulatory work. We just are not equipped for that sort of thing. That is a new initiative for us and one that will be quite difficult.

Q313 *Viscount Brookeborough:* You live a long way from your markets, perhaps not in the middle of nowhere. How much bearing do you think in the future food miles or wine miles are going to have, accepting that there are some murmurs of people saying that over the last 40 years they have been used to having food from anywhere in the world; we have strawberries at any time; we get something whenever we like it, and perhaps we should be thinking more about eating seasonal foods.
Mr Sherwin: It is certainly something we have been focused on for a period of time. Food miles is a catchy phrase and easily catches the eye. The work that we have been doing is really trying to build the scientific base to add to the understanding of that and to ensure that this is not just about food miles but a broader greenhouse gas foot printing approach, which is much more on the full life cycle. I think people typically do not understand just how efficient modern container shipping is, certainly relative to other modes of transport. What is important to us has always been low cost production and low cost distribution. That is the hallmark of the business. The way I look at this is that if you can take a product unsubsidised and deliver it into a market at a competitive price, you are unlikely to be embodying a lot more energy than the price that you are competing against; you simply cannot afford that. We will do the number work or metrics around that. We have to be alert to it and it is one of the reasons why we spend a lot of time looking at consumer trends and what is influencing them and where the opportunities and risks are for us.

Q314 *Lord Cameron of Dillington:* You say "we". Is that the New Zealand Government that is doing that market research?
Mr Sherwin: In conjunction with our industries, yes.

Q315 *Lord Palmer:* Before I ask my two further questions on climate change, did I hear you correctly when you said that 50% of your emissions are of animal origin?

Mr Sherwin: Yes.

Q316 Lord Palmer: Could you comment on the regulatory framework through which New Zealand aims to secure environmental protection and its perceived effectiveness in doing so?

Mr Sherwin: Environmental protection is a big term. There is a core piece of legislation in New Zealand, administered by the Ministry for the Environment under the Resource Management Act. That is an effects based or outcome based piece of legislation that allows for local communities to be heavily involved in developments in their local communities and provides also, though, for overarching guidance in terms of national policy statements on things like water quality, air quality and so forth. I am sure there are learned people who could give long lectures on that. We could certainly provide you with briefing on that Act and the way it works and the way we apply that. The other and related area of work is something that we are engaging in directly with industry groups around responses to climate change, water quality and water allocation. If you wish to follow up on that, we can provide more material on it.

Q317 Lord Palmer: That would be helpful. You probably see almost every day there is something about biofuels in the papers. Even day OPEC are saying how ineffectual biofuels are going to be. Some countries have been subsidising their biofuel production, a trend which some people say actually impacts on commodity prices. Is this likely to become a new source of trade distortion? In New Zealand in particular, what role do you think that biofuels might play in your own long-term agricultural strategy and indeed perhaps energy security?

Mr Sherwin: There was a very nice article in the *Financial Times* I think last week by Martin Wolf on biofuels, which I would recommend to anybody on the economics of biofuels. He made a point which I agree with strongly that there are very few biofuel opportunities or options out there right now which are both economically and environmentally positive and that the tendency towards subsidising production of biofuels can have negative consequences both for the environment and for the consumer. Biofuels I think are certainly already influencing agriculture commodity markets. We have seen it in the dairy sector and in other sectors as well with pork and chicken, neither of which are major industries in New Zealand but we are certainly seeing those impacts on prices. For us there is a fairly modest biofuels target that has just been established by the government. My guess is that a sizeable portion of that will be met from imports. We have some obvious sources of biofuels: one is away from milk, which has already been signed up by one of the local distributors; the other is tallow for biodiesels.

Both of those products have very high value alternative uses and putting them into biofuels by themselves is not necessarily economic.

Q318 Lord Palmer: What type of uses spring to mind?

Mr Sherwin: Food ingredient uses, a whole raft of other industrial outcomes and so forth but typically biofuels would struggle to compete with them unless support prices continue to spiral, in which case all bets are off and a lot of us will be doing lots of different things because they will become economically viable Our sense is that the first generation biofuels will not make a huge difference for us, simply because we are unlikely to have competitive production possibilities in New Zeeland relative to existing land uses. Second generation with lignose digestion, or whatever the term is, looks more promising. We certainly have opportunities there. Some are looking at waste product from the forestry sector, although I think if you want to do that sort of second generation biofuel, you would not necessarily start with *Pinus radiata* as your choice of feedstock. There is other work going on, whether it is algae on sewage ponds producing biodiesels and so forth, and that is all very interesting, and may well prove to be viable, but our sense is that we may well be better off to import biofuels at this stage and continue to produce our products and, to the extent that our product markets are influenced by biofuel enthusiasms elsewhere, that is fine; we will have some price advantages from it.

Q319 Chairman: Just to finish off, unless my colleagues have any other questions, there is the problem with mindsets. When we did our recent report on the European wine regime, which is a dreadful construction across the regime, what struck us was that at least amongst some producers there was a degree of entrepreneurialism and innovation that was almost being repressed because of the nature of the regime itself. The greatest conservatism and protectionism was amongst agricultural politicians who tended to be very defensive and who basically came up with slogans which were really blaming the consumer rather than the producer, those sorts of silly things. How do you get that chain? Did you have a problem in New Zealand with your politicians? That is a risky question, is it not? Was there a protectionist element that really misread the situation?

Mr Sherwin: I think, if you look at our political and economic history, it was that 1984 transition which was so spectacular. We skipped a whole generation in our politicians. We moved on from a set of politicians under Sir Robert Muldoon as Prime Minister. These were largely men whose formative years had been through the depression and the Second World War.

They had a very deep commitment to protecting the ordinary bloke from all these nasty trends going on and had a genuinely felt need to protect what was dear and valued in New Zealand society, and eventually it became unsustainable. There were major balance of payments problems, inflation problems, fiscal deficits and all the rest of it, for the reasons we have talked about. In the incoming 1984 government the average age of the cabinet from recollection was only in its mid-thirties. We skipped a generation and went to a sort of Vietnam era generation of politicians, many of them successful professionals in their own right with no particular hankering to be long-term politicians, much more interested in the decisions and stimulated by the decisions than wanting to submit themselves for a career as politicians, and many of whom have subsequently moved back to very successful careers outside of politics. That was a strongly reforming government. I always remember the *Harvard Business Review* article on management reform, which was first: if you have not got a crisis, create one so that you can engender the energy and the drive for change. We had our own crisis and they were determined to take advantage of it in terms of moving the agenda forward. I think there are many people who look back now who were very anxious about that process and who would now concede at least that it set the platform for a much more successful economy subsequently over the past 20 years.

Q320 *Viscount Brookeborough:* What is the level of your organic food production? Has it gone up as a result of farming reforms? Secondly, you talk about these pine trees: what proportion of your temporary seed is pine trees and are you perhaps in danger of getting hooked on a single species, like we seem to be on Sitka Spruce? If they do get a disease, we have really had it?

Mr Sherwin: The proportion of our forestry coming from that one species is very high, over 90%. It is an issue. It is fine while it is successful but that will need to move on. Organics: I do not have a number; it is relatively small but growing, and again growing in response to market demands. Not only is the organic sector growing but what we are seeing, particularly in horticulture, is a move to not fully organic but zero detectible residues, and so much more attention to not limiting themselves to not using some chemicals but being very cautious about when they use them and how frequently they use them and integrated pest management, trying to build an ecology in the orchard, for instance, which recognises that there are particular pests present but in balance, if you like, rather than nuking the orchard with a bug killer and then having whatever happens to re-establish first dominate and drive a demand for continually re-spraying. They try to keep those sprays right down. As I said, the target for those producers is zero detectible residues.

Q321 *Chairman:* I will give you the opportunity if you think that there is something that we have missed that you really want to say, now is the time.

Mr Sherwin: No, that has been very comprehensive. I very much appreciate the time that you have given to us. We have enjoyed the discussion.

Q322 *Chairman:* I was going to say: now that you have seen us in the flesh, do you really want to take photographs?

Mr Sherwin: It is not often that a small boy from the colonies gets to appear at the House of Lords. It would be a pity not to have some record of it for the family album.

Chairman: Thank you very much indeed. That was very refreshing.

WEDNESDAY 21 NOVEMBER 2007

Present   Arran, E   Dundee, E
               Brookeborough, V   Jones of Whitchurch, B
               Cameron of Dillington, L   Palmer, L
                  (Chairman)   Ullswater, V

Memorandum by NFU Cymru

INTRODUCTION

1. NFU Cymru represents the majority of farmers in Wales and has some 15,000 members. We are pleased to be given the opportunity to submit written evidence for the Committee's consideration. This submission deals with the issues raised by the Committee, in chronological order, and are given from a Welsh perspective.

OVERVIEW

2. The CAP was introduced with a view to providing food security and ensuring a fair standard of living for those who derive their income from the land. The objectives of the CAP are now, in our view, much broader and complex and involve in combination, issues of food, energy and environmental security. In order to deliver on these wider facets, there is a need for a broader and more flexible approach, but which does not detract from the need for simplicity, and a common and consistent approach to its application. NFU Cymru considers a fair standard of living still to be an important objective and it is a matter of concern that profitability and viability in the livestock sectors is under severe pressure with implications for infrastructure and the wider rural economy.

3. In the longer term, provided the industry can survive the financial strain, then economic growth particularly in Asia and the growing demand for energy has the potential to strengthen the demand side of the demand: supply ratio. It is important however that during the interim, the productive capacity of the farming industry in Wales is not compromised.

4. In terms of the main pressures on the CAP, NFU Cymru considers that the budget will continue to be an issue with the ever increasing size of EU; the diversity of Member State interests and needs will be a challenge in policy terms; demands for greater subsidiarity to meet Member States diverging interests have the potential to distort competition and maintaining production levels to take advantage of expanding markets whilst respecting environmental obligations will be testing.

THE REFORMED CAP

5. NFU Cymru supported proposals to decouple payments from production during the 2003 CAP negotiations. This has now provided farmers with greater freedom to farm and made market prices more transparent but has placed the EU in a stronger negotiating position in terms of the WTO. NFU Cymru was a strong advocate of decoupled payments being made on an historic basis and applauded the Welsh Assembly Government's decision to adopt this approach, which generally has served the industry in Wales well. Single Farm Payments have been made early in the window for payment since the introduction of the SPS and most of the difficulties have arisen for cross-border claimants where the Welsh Assembly has had to resolve issues with the RPA. NFU Cymru supports the continuation of the historic approach.

6. NFU Cymru is concerned that the RPA's performance in England has exposed the UK to the risk of budgetary disallowance, the ramifications of which are bound to impact on Wales, despite the fact that the Welsh Assembly's performance in terms of making payment has not been found deficient.

7. Severing the link between production and payment means that the inadequacy of market realisations is more visible and farmers are no longer prepared to cross-subsidise low market prices with production support. There appears to be a tardy realisation amongst food processors and retailers that future supplies will be contingent upon farmers being able to make a reasonable profit on their produce that allows them to reinvest for the future.

THE SINGLE PAYMENT SCHEME

8. NFU Cymru considers the Single Farm Payment as a non trade and market distorting policy is a good basis for the future of EU agricultural policy. NFU Cymru believes agriculture as an industry to be strategically important and deserving of a dedicated common agricultural policy but acknowledging that it delivers on wider social, economic, environmental and cultural objectives.

9. Next year's CAP Health Check will be an opportunity to ensure that those Member States who are continuing to operate coupled support implement the spirit of the reform agreement. NFU Cymru also sees this as an opportunity to iron out some of the unnecessary complexities that currently surround the regime, particularly in terms of cross compliance. The Council of Agriculture Ministers in June 2007 adopted EC proposals, to allow tolerances for minor non-compliances, the closing of files without further inspections if farmers take immediate action to rectify minor breaches, scope for participation in assurance schemes to determine selection for farm inspection and abolition of the 10 month rule.

10. In the context of the 2008 Health Check, NFU Cymru is seeking:

— The abolition of set-aside which is inconsistent with the move to a decoupled system.

— An increase in the financial ceilings to provide entitlement for fruit, vegetable and potato growers now that the negative list has been removed.

— Abolition of partial decoupling.

— A consistent approach to the minimum area eligible for Single Farm Payment, Tir Mynydd (LFA) support (increased from 0.3 hectares to 6 hectares)

— To resist capping of support which ignores labour employed and would merely lead to a legal division of holdings.

— To oppose voluntary modulation which discriminates against farmers in Wales vis a vis their European counterparts.

— To have the exchange rate for the calculation of Single Farm payment into sterling based on the average for September rather than on a single day, given the vagaries of financial markets.

MARKET MECHANISMS

11. NFU Cymru considers the 10% rate of compulsory set aside should be abolished as a further move towards a market orientated CAP and as a major element of simplification given the added complexities of set aside entitlements.

12. The EC has signaled that milk quotas will not be extended beyond 2015. NFU Cymru believes that there has to be a transitional period agreed as part of the 2008 Health check during which the dairy industry can adjust to unfettered production.

13. The EU is committed within the Defra round to eliminating export refunds by 2013, whilst this is unlikely to have direct implications for producer in Wales, in terms of beef production particularly, there is the potential for the home market to become depressed, if production as a result of beef from other countries which would normally have been sold to Third Countries with export refunds, remains on the EU internal market. NFU Cymru can see the need for private storage aids to continue as a management tool and to provide short-term relief in exceptional circumstances.

RURAL DEVELOPMENT

14. The Welsh Rural Development Plan has been submitted to the EC but remains to be approved.

15. The UK's allocation, some 3.5% of the EU rural development budget, is abysmally low and is reflected in the allotted amount to Wales.

16. This budgetary deficiency is reflected in the need to raise voluntary modulation over and above that which is compulsorily levied by Brussels. Whilst we welcome a devolved approach to setting voluntary modulation, which is consistent with devolved RDP's within the UK, we are opposed in principle, to the provision for voluntary modulation which leads to the distortion of competition. NFU Cymru is firmly of the view that if the decision to raise the level of compulsory modulation at an EU level is approved, then a commensurate reduction in the level of voluntary modulation raised in Wales should be effected.

17. NFU Cymru has been concerned that increasing amounts of money modulated from Pillar I (direct support payments to farmers) have been shifted to pillar II funding (Rural development money) and which is leaching away in favour of non-agricultural activity because of the minimum spends dictated by the EU under

the various axes. Over 80% of Wales is designated Less Favoured because of the permanent physical handicaps of farming these areas. 46% of Wales is already subject to agri environment schemes/environmental designation which inevitably places a significant demand on axis 2 (land management) measures. Commitments to axes 1, 3 and 4 inevitably limit the availability of funds for land management measures.

18. Agriculture remains the core activity in rural Wales and supports the rural infrastructure. We believe allowing Pillar II resources to filter down to rural communities and businesses is a more efficient method of cascading down limited financial resources.

19. As a general point we believe that since all farmers are modulated, they should have equal and fair access to all monies delivered under the RDP without the prospect of these funds being dissipated.

20. Voluntary modulation was "sold" to the industry on the basis that there would be Treasury match funding and it is essential that Treasury continues to co-fund these receipts given the inadequacy of the UK rural development allocation.

WORLD TRADE

21. NFU Cymru believes that agriculture will end up the "sacrificial lamb" in the current round of WTO negotiations. In the process of trade liberalisation the EU is committed to eliminating export restitutions and the likelihood is that import tariffs will be further reduced thus opening up our markets to cheap imports that may not be produced to the same exacting standards. The gains to the EU economy are likely to fall outside agriculture.

ENVIRONMENTAL PROTECTION

22. Both agri-environmental schemes such as Tir Gofal and Tir Cynnal, in addition to cross-compliance measures, have contributed positively to environmental protection.

23. Some 46% of Wales is now covered by Wales" equivalent of the Countryside Stewardship Scheme, Tir Gofal and by its entry level scheme, Tir Cynnal and the Organic Farm Scheme. These measures are currently under review in the context of an evaluation of axis 2 measures in Wales. We believe that these schemes can be used to preclude further prescriptions being imposed on the industry as a result for example of the Water and Soil Framework Directives.

24. Whilst the scope in Wales for growing and harvesting energy crops for biofuel is perhaps less than in the other constituent parts of the UK, Welsh agriculture has a role to play in the mitigation of climate change and the control of green house gases. NFU Cymru believes that agriculture can contribute in terms of carbon sequestration and in terms of renewable energies such as wind turbines and combined heat and power plants on farms.

FINANCING

25. It is understood that there will be no changes to budgetary commitments agreed in the 2003 reform agreement and that the 2007–13 Financial Perspectives will not be altered. NFU Cymru is however, concerned that the need to fund the cost of Single Farm Payments in New Member States may trigger degressivity at some stage depending on the degree to which market support measures under Pillar I are utilized.

26. We have alluded previously cf paragraph 15 to our concern at the inadequacy of the funds based on historic allocations that have been distributed to the UK and subsequently cascaded down to the Welsh Assembly Government. The position has been exacerbated by the fact that the percentage allocated of some 3.5% was based on a significantly reduced EAFRD budget for the current programming period. This has resulted in Government subjecting domestic farmers to a rising plane of voluntary modulation with Welsh farmers facing the prospect of a combined rate of 11.5% modulation in 2011, placing them at a competitive disadvantage to their European colleagues who, with the exception of Portugal, are not subjected to this mechanism.

27. NFU Cymru has strong reservations about co-financing as a means of making good any EU budgetary deficiencies. It would, in our view, be difficult to get political agreement to and voluntary co-funding would result in the distortion of competition between Members States, thus undermining the whole concept of a "common" agricultural policy.

ENLARGEMENT

28. The accession of New Member States in 2004 and 2007, has had the effect of diluting the funding that is available to member states of the Enlarged Community but set against this has been the development of markets for high quality products. One of the most evident outcomes of Enlargement has been the availability of migrant workers particularly from Eastern Bloc countries.

SIMPLIFICATION

29. NFU Cymru's comments in respect of the 2008 CAP Health Check detail where the burden of regulation could be reduced and simplified.

CONCLUSION

30. We hope that the Committee finds this evidence helpful and would be pleased to present oral evidence should the Committee consider this appropriate.

12 October, 2007

Memorandum by the Farmers' Union of Wales

OVERVIEW

1. *What should be the long term objectives of the CAP? Does the title "Common Agricultural Policy" aptly fit your perceived objectives of the policy? What do you consider to be the main pressures on the CAP as it currently is?*

The long term objectives of the CAP should be to provide a policy that is adaptable to what are likely to be the rapidly changing needs of Europe and the UK. For example, as a result of concerns over climate change, agriculture has recently risen rapidly up the political agenda within Europe, and the term "sustainable agriculture", having once been used to refer to localised environmental issues, is increasingly being used in the context of what is sustainable on a global scale in terms of CO_2 emissions. Any long term objectives must take this need for flexibility into account.

As problems such as global warming, rising sea levels, the growing world population, and depletions in oil reserves begin to take effect, it is difficult to envisage an appropriate common European policy that does not in truth have agricultural production of one form or another at its heart, regardless of what that policy is called.

In terms of whether the title "Common Agricultural Policy" remains apt, members commented that the commonality even within Member States had been significantly diminished (exemplified by the differences between the Single Payment Regimes implemented in the UK devolved administrations), and that differences between Member States were significant. Thus, the commonality of the policy has been significantly diminished over recent years.

Within the UK, the most significant pressure on the CAP is the Governments apparent will to marginalise farming, agriculture representing such a low proportion of the UK's GDP. At an EU level, the most significant pressures on the CAP come from the efforts that continue to be made to reach World Trade Agreements. In the absence of significant increases in world market prices, it seems unlikely that agriculture in the UK will be able survive in its current form if further concessions are made during WTO negotiations, particularly against a background of rising production costs. This poses a significant risk to both Europe and the UK, given the predictions currently being made by scientists regarding future needs for food and bio-fuels produced from areas of land that will have been significantly depleted by rising sea levels.

The incorporation of additional Member States into the European Union also represents a significant threat to the CAP in the absence of proportionate increases in the funds necessary to accommodate new Member States.

THE REFORMED CAP

2. *What has been your experience so far with the reformed CAP? What has worked well and less well? And where can lessons be learned?*

The contrast between the regimes in England and Wales highlight Wales' wisdom in choosing an historically based Single Payment system. However, while this has certainly served to preserve the viability of more productive systems based on small areas, many feel that the system has also preserved pre-existing inequalities.

The reductions in administrative burdens that Government predicted would accompany the reformed CAP have not materialised, and the time and financial costs of bureaucracy continue to escalate for farmers and the authorities alike.

The Cross Compliance regime and the penalties that accompany it has been particularly problematic, with some farmers having lost 60 to 100% of their Single Payments due to simple misunderstandings of what are subjective rules.

Significant numbers of farmers have fallen foul of CAP rules designed to penalise fraud, despite having clearly made genuine administrative errors; for example on forms. The nature of the Single Payment Scheme has increased the probability of simple mistakes leading to draconian penalties.

The scheme, as implemented in Wales, has not benefited potential new entrants to the industry, and members feel strongly that the CAP should place more emphasis on assisting young people who wish to enter the industry.

THE SINGLE PAYMENT SCHEME

3. *Do you consider the Single Payment Scheme to be a good basis for the future of EU agricultural policy? What changes might be made at the EU level to the Single Payment Scheme, including to the rules governing entitlements, in the short and/or the longer-term?*

The Single Payment Scheme, as implemented in Wales, does appear to be a good template; however, there remain significant inequalities, and changes might be made at the EU level to allow such inequalities to be corrected—the current regulations do not allow such changes to be made.

Such inequalities often derive from unusual circumstances that occurred during the reference period; for example, where normal practices were affected by the outbreak of foot and mouth disease in 2001, or where farmers changed their methods of farming between 2002 and 2004 in a way that was not accommodated for by the National Reserve.

MARKET MECHANISMS

4. *What short and longer-term changes are required to the CAP's market mechanisms? Suggestions made by the Commission have included re-examination of certain quotas, intervention, set-aside, export refunds and private storage payments*

For the reasons already outlined above, agriculture is an industry of growing importance, both domestically and within the EU. As such, both short and long-term changes to the CAP's market mechanisms should take the importance of preserving the industry and the expertise of those involved in it into account. Concessions made in the absence of clear policies that provide mechanisms that ensure sustainable incomes for the industry will therefore have serious consequences for Europe, particularly where similar concessions are not made by other major players on the world market.

RURAL DEVELOPMENT

5. What is your view on the introduction of the European Agricultural Fund for Rural Development (EAFRD)? Do you consider that it is meeting its objectives thus far? Is it suitably "strategic" in nature, meeting the needs of rural society as a whole rather than being restricted to aiding the agricultural industry? How well is it being co-ordinated with other EU and national policies on regional and rural development?

The final Welsh Rural Development Plan has yet to be submitted to, or ratified by, the EC.

Previous experience has shown an increasing willingness by UK Governments to divert Pillar II monies away from agriculture to a far greater extent than occurs in other Member States.

Members are of the opinion that monies paid directly to farmers quickly filter down to other rural businesses while minimising unnecessary administrative costs; the financial problems experienced by many rural businesses due to the English Single Payment delays highlight this effect.

6. Is there a case for a higher level of EU financing of rural development? Do you have a view on the extension of compulsory modulation from Pillar I (Direct Payments) to Pillar II (Rural Development)?

Where there is a requirement to match-fund (£ for £) modulated monies, there should inevitably be a net return to rural areas, notwithstanding the possibility of excessive administrative costs. However, modulation, in the absence of such a requirement, diminishes this potential net benefit and allows modulation to effectively become a tax that diverts money away from agriculture and away from particular geographical areas. The UK's pursuit of the latter policy, even to the extent that the law in the UK is now very different to that on the continent (notwithstanding the position in Portugal), exemplifies the pressures put on the UK industry compared with other countries.

Even where modulated monies are targeted at agriculture, this is increasingly being done in a way that targets limited geographical areas in order to replace schemes that were previously nationally funded. The FUW believes that such displacement of national monies by Pillar II monies is detrimental to both agriculture and the wider rural community.

WORLD TRADE

7. What benefits can the EU's World Trade Organisation obligations create for EU agriculture and, consequently, for the EU economy as a whole?

Members believed that concessions made by the EU during WTO discussions would only undermine EU agriculture and, consequently, rural communities.

ENVIRONMENTAL PROTECTION AND CLIMATE CHANGE

8. To what extent has the system of cross-compliance contributed to an improved level of environmental protection? How is it linking with other EU policy requirements such as the Water Framework Directive?

Much of the environmental protection that is afforded by Cross Compliance is provided by the Statutory Management Requirements that predate Cross Compliance but have nevertheless been incorporated into Cross Compliance rules.

Thus, a significant proportion of Cross Compliance has simply sustained existing levels of environmental protection.

Other aspects of the regime provide negligible or no environmental protection, and serve only to restrict farming practices unnecessarily. This is particularly the case on extensive farming systems, where rules that are clearly based upon perceived problems that occur on intensive arable farms can result in significant and disproportionate penalties, despite there being no valid scientific reason for such rules to be applied.

Many Cross Compliance rules are subjective, and open to a wide range of interpretations, therefore causing disproportionate penalties to be imposed for practices that are not clearly recognisable as breaches.

9. *How can the CAP contribute to mitigation of, and adaptation to, climate change? What do you consider the role of biofuels to be in this regard?*

As has already been stated, the CAP is likely to play an increasingly central role in the mitigation of, and adaptation to, climate change. Scientists anticipate that the role of biofuels will become increasingly important in this regard, and ongoing research would suggest that the range of crops and bi-products that are available for biofuel production is likely to increase significantly. However, such production will significantly reduce the area available for conventional food and feed production, as is already occurring in some countries where biofuel production is becoming common, and this affect should clearly be taken account of in drawing up future changes to the CAP.

FINANCING

10. *The Commissioner has expressed her dissatisfaction at the financing agreement reached by the Member States at the December 2005 Council. Do you consider the current budget to be sufficient? Do you consider co-financing to be a possible way forward in financing the Common Agricultural Policy?*

Despite the continuing, albeit lessened, protectionism afforded to European farmers, the current market appears to offer little hope of providing farmgate prices that make up the deficit caused by reductions in CAP payments. In the absence of farmgate prices that reflect production costs and provide sustainable incomes, the current budget is currently insufficient.

Given the way in which the CAP has recently been undermined by the decision to allow the UK and Portugal alone to modulate at 20% without match funding, voluntary co-financing seems likely to further undermine the CAP and the agricultural industry in the UK.

ENLARGEMENT

11. *What has been the impact on the CAP of the 2004 and 2007 enlargements and what is the likely impact of future enlargements of the EU on the post-2013 CAP?*

The enlargement of Europe has, as expected, diluted the CAP. In the absence of budgetary changes that mitigate such dilution, the overall effect will be further dilution of the CAP.

SIMPLIFICATION OF THE CAP AND OTHER ISSUES

12. *How could the CAP be further simplified and in what other ways would you like to see the Common Agricultural Policy changed in the short and/or the long term?*

The advent of the Single Payment Scheme has resulted in less commonality across Europe, amounting to complication rather than simplification. However, it is the view of members that the most significant way in which the CAP could be simplified is by reducing the burden that the bureaucracy associated with CAP represents for the industry.

8 June 2007

Memorandum by the National Farmers' Union of Scotland

1. As the lead organisation representing farmers, crofters and growers in Scotland, NFU Scotland welcomes the opportunity to provide evidence to the House of Lords Inquiry into the future of the European Union Common Agricultural Policy (CAP). We would be happy to expand on the views in this paper by giving oral evidence.

2. At present, the price obtained from the market for production in virtually all agricultural sectors does not provide a sufficient return for long-term farm business profitability and viability. The long-term objective of the CAP should be to provide support that allows farmers to make a fair living producing food and delivering wider, non-market benefits. NFU Scotland believes that food security will become a priority in the post-2013 period and global demand for food production will continue to rise. It is therefore essential that, at that stage, our farming businesses are in a position to respond positively to an increased need for domestic and global food production, as they have done historically.

3. Our understanding of the policy development process for the future of the CAP is very similar to that of the Committee and, with that in mind, NFU Scotland has been considering the future of the CAP as follows:

— Changes required in the 2008 Health Check.

— The likely scenarios that we should be planning against for the post-2013 period.

— Against these scenarios, what should the objectives of CAP be for Scottish and European agriculture.

— What sort of CAP Regime is needed to deliver these objectives?

2008 Health Check

4. The key points to be addressed in the Health Check are:

— Energy crop scheme—too little of this direct aid actually reaches producers. If this cannot be improved the funding would be better used on measures to stimulate demand and develop the energy crop supply chain.

— Fruit, vegetable and potato production—the negative list is not effective and farmers should be able to activate entitlements on land used for fruit, vegetable and potato production. We support the Commission's proposal to decouple processing aid, but all Single Payment Scheme national ceilings should be increased to reflect the new entitlements required.

— Capping—capping of aid is a blunt instrument that may reduce CAP spending but will discriminate against larger, more efficient farms and lead to artificial splitting of farm businesses.

— Minimum area—the minimum area eligible for the Single Farm Payment should be increased from 0.3 hectares but should not exceed 3 hectares to be consistent with the eligibility requirements for LFA support.

— Intervention and set-aside—options for weakening cereals intervention should be considered, without removing the system altogether. Compulsory set-aside should be abolished but, where land in set-aside has been delivering environmental benefits, the option of transferring to agri-environment schemes should be available.

— Voluntary Modulation—we are opposed to modulation generally as we believe it is an unnecessarily bureaucratic means of transferring funds from Pillar I to Pillar II of the CAP and undermines the profitability of farming businesses, which are still heavily dependant on direct support. Scottish Executive figures suggest that across all sectors, every 5% of modulation reduces net farm incomes by 19%. We are particularly opposed to Voluntary Modulation as this discriminates against Scottish and UK farmers compared to their competitors in the rest of Europe.

— Partial decoupling—we believe that the partial decoupling option should be removed as soon as possible. However, where there are strong reasons for retaining production, eg cattle and sheep for environmental purposes, simple and effective measures should be introduced to achieve this aim under Pillar II.

— Euro exchange rate—the exchange rate for calculation of the Single Farm Payment into Sterling is currently calculated on a single day (30 September), which introduces a high level of risk of an unrepresentative rate. We believe that the exchange rate should be calculated on the average over a one-month period, as under previous schemes.

Scenarios for 2013 and Beyond

5. NFU Scotland has concluded that the most likely scenario is a continuation of the current situation where the price obtained from the market does not provide a sufficient return for long-term agricultural business profitability and viability. If anything, the situation is likely to get worse, particular if there is a WTO deal which results in reduced import tariffs and therefore increased import penetration.

FUTURE CAP OBJECTIVES

6. Direct support will therefore be vital to keep farm businesses going, justified on the basis of paying for the "non-market" goods that agriculture already delivers. These include environmental benefits, higher production standards (particularly in comparison to cheaper imports), supporting jobs in the food-processing sector, retaining rural infrastructure and the quality of life. In the longer term, NFU Scotland believes that food security will become a priority and that returns from the market will increase and it is therefore vital that the industry retains its ability to produce until then. However, NFU Scotland also recognises that CAP support has sometimes distorted the market in the past, with retailers using it as an excuse to reduce the price they pay to producers. It is therefore important that any revised system of support avoids creating or encouraging such distortion.

THE CAP REGIME NEEDED TO DELIVER THESE OBJECTIVES

7. A direct support payment in return for what farming is already delivering could straddle the existing Pillars I and II. In addition, serious consideration should be given to some sort of contingency payment that would be activated if prices fall dramatically. The European Commission has been looking at this in the context of crisis/risk management but concluded meantime that there is no EU-wide system to introduce across the board. Payments on this basis would make it difficult for retailers to use it as an excuse to reduce the price they pay. A direct support payment should be complemented by business development measures as are currently available through producer organisations and under Axis 1 of the Rural Development regulation; and diversification measures as currently available under Axis 3. Such business development measures would be aimed at helping farm businesses add value and reduce costs so that profitability becomes less dependent on direct support.

8. Turning now to the issues raised in the Committee's call for evidence, NFU Scotland's views are as follows.

OVERVIEW

9. The long-term objectives of the CAP should be to support the continuation of the European model of agriculture, so that farmers can continue to produce food and deliver wider, non-market benefits. As mentioned above, NFU Scotland believes that food security will become a priority in the post-2013 period and that global demand for food will continue to rise. It is therefore essential that our farming businesses are in a position to respond positively to an increased need for domestic food production, as they have done historically. It is also important that farmers throughout the European Union operate on a level playing-field and we therefore believe that it is vital that the CAP is common across all 27 EU Member States. Currently, the main pressures on the CAP are budgetary and opposition borne out of prejudice or ignorance. On this second point, it is crucial that decisions on policy precede decisions on the budget and that they are based on an objective view of what the CAP delivers today and can do in the future, as opposed to views on the CAP that are 20 years out of date.

THE REFORMED CAP

10. Under the reformed CAP, decoupling of support has given farmers a degree of "freedom to farm". As a result, we are beginning to see production that is market-driven as opposed to subsidy-driven. In some cases, this has resulted in a much-improved balance between supply and demand, for example malting barley. However, there are some down sides including a drift of cattle and sheep away from some of our poorest, hill and upland areas in the north and west of Scotland. If such movement were to continue or accelerate, the consequences would be detrimental in social, economic and environmental terms for some of our most fragile rural communities. We also have concerns that cross-compliance has added to the regulatory burden faced by farming businesses without delivering proportionate benefits.

THE SINGLE PAYMENTS SCHEME

11. In principle, NFU Scotland has always supported the decoupling of production-linked subsidies and amalgamation into the Single Farm Payment. In a decoupled regime, and to be compliant with WTO requirements, we believe that a Single Farm Payment is a good basis for the future of EU agricultural policy. However, as indicated above, we believe that this needs to be complemented by business development measures to help farm businesses to become more profitable in their own right. We believe that in future the Single Farm Payment should reflect the cost of delivering non-market benefits, which will vary between different farm types and regions. The system of entitlements should be simplified as far as possible—at present there are four types of entitlement and we believe that this can be rationalised. NFU Scotland also has some concerns about trading of entitlements, where this leads to leakage of support away from agriculture.

MARKET MECHANISMS

12. NFU Scotland believes that the system of milk quotas is nearing the end of its useful life and agrees with the Commission proposal to bring the regime to an end in 2015. A number of transitional measures have been suggested, of which we believe that increasing quotas on an annual basis is the only serious option. As mentioned above, we believe that options for weakening cereals intervention, without removing the system altogether, should be considered. Compulsory set-aside is incompatible with a decoupled support regime and should be abolished. The Commission would appear to be committed to abolishing export refunds by 2013. While this might not have any direct effect on much of what is produced in Scotland, there are potential knock-on effects. For example, beef that benefited from export refunds and was previously sold outwith the EU might now be marketed in Scotland or the UK, undermining domestic production. We believe that private storage aids are a useful tool for market management and should be retained.

RURAL DEVELOPMENT

13. We agree with the introduction of the European Agricultural Fund for Rural Development (EAFRD) as a means of rationalising and simplifying rural development support. Subject to comments about funding below, we believe that the second Pillar of the CAP is broadly meeting its objectives. In many rural communities in Scotland, agriculture remains central to the local economy and we therefore believe that support to the agricultural industry benefits the rest of the rural community. In addition, Axis 3 of the Rural Development Regulation is specifically aimed at improving the quality of rural life and therefore benefits all parts of rural society.

14. However, the allocation of EAFRD funding on the basis of historical spend by individual Member States discriminates severely against the UK. While this is a position partly of the UK's own making because of its historically low spend on Rural Development measures, it has placed an artificial limit on the adoption of Rural Development measures under programmes for the 2007–13 period. The Scottish Executive is to be congratulated on significantly increasing its contribution from domestic funding but one of the unwelcome consequences of the low level of European funding is the use of Voluntary Modulation in the UK, to the detriment of UK farmers in comparison to their EU competitors. As stated in our opening remarks, NFU Scotland is opposed to modulation in principle. However, if it has to be used we favour a single rate of Compulsory Modulation applied to the Single Farm Payment in all Member States with an absolute requirement by national governments to match-fund the monies so raised. Should Compulsory Modulation be increased from its current level of 5%, we also believe that there must be an absolute requirement on national or regional administrations to reduce Voluntary Modulation by the same amount.

WORLD TRADE

15. NFU Scotland believes that a successful outcome to the current round of WTO negotiations will bring benefits to the EU economy as a whole, but at the expense of agriculture. The shape of CAP support has altered dramatically as a result of the Agenda 2000 and 2003 Mid-Term Review reforms and is almost entirely compliant. The EU appears to be committed to removing export refunds by 2013, which will reduce the ability of farmers and processors to export some products outwith the EU. But the biggest impact will undoubtedly be from any further reduction in import tariffs, opening up EU markets to cheap imports, potentially not produced to the same high standards as within the EU. Ironically, the main beneficiaries will not be the poorest

third world countries but those with highly-developed agricultural industries such as Brazil. Therefore, while other industries and sectors within the EU are likely to benefit from a WTO agreement, we believe that agriculture will be the main loser.

ENVIRONMENTAL PROTECTION AND CLIMATE CHANGE

16. Cross-compliance duplicates some regulatory requirements and in fact adds to the burden of regulation, while at the same time introducing an element of double jeopardy. By this, we mean that farmers may lose a significant proportion of their Single Farm Payment in addition to prosecution under the existing regulation now also covered by cross-compliance.

17. We believe that the CAP can contribute to the mitigation of, and adaptation to, climate change. The decoupling of support has allowed farmers to make management choices based on what their farm is best able to produce and what the market wants. This has opened up numerous possibilities including the production of biomass, crops for biofuels and diversification into wind and hydro power. We consider the role of biofuels to be highly important in this regard, not least because Scotland is well-suited to growing oil seed rape for the production of biodiesel. Long daylight hours mean that the oil content of crops grown in Scotland is much higher than elsewhere.

FINANCING

18. NFU Scotland shares Commissioner Fischer Boel's dissatisfaction at the financing agreement reached by Member States at the December 2005 Council. This has resulted in an almost 25% reduction in EAFRD funding from 88.5 billion Euros to 69.5 billion Euros for the 2007—2013 programming period. In addition, support payments to farmers in the new Member States of Bulgaria and Romania have had to be found from within existing resources, which will result in further cuts to those in existing Member States. Therefore, in Pillar I and particularly in Pillar II, there are insufficient funds to deliver the full range of measures that make up the CAP as a whole. We do not consider co-financing to be a possible way forward in financing the CAP, as we believe that this will only serve to exacerbate differences between Member States. For example, we do not believe that the UK government would co-finance to the same level as existing payments or at the same level as other Member States. This would place UK farmers at a financial and competitive disadvantage compared to their counterparts elsewhere in the EU. .

ENLARGEMENT

19. The main impact of the 2004 and 2007 enlargements of the EU have been on the available funding for the CAP. In addition, the policy of cohesion means that a relatively higher proportion of funding, particularly under Pillar II, will be allocated to improve the performance of the less economically well-developed agricultural sectors in the new Member States. The net result of this has been that the EU 15 Member States suffered a disproportionately high share of the reduction in EAFRD funding referred to above.

SIMPLIFICATION OF CAP AND OTHER ISSUES

20. We believe that there are a number of obvious steps that can be taken to simplify the CAP:

— Rationalise the current system of entitlements.

— Abolish compulsory set-aside.

— Remove milk quotas by 2015.

— Scrap modulation—if funds need to be transferred from Pillar I to Pillar II this should be done at budgetary rather than individual farmer level.

— Simplify the application process for Pillar II schemes—too many require the input of consultants/advisers.

— Alter the penalty system to differentiate between deliberate intention to defraud and genuine error.

11 June 2007

Examination of Witnesses

Witnesses: MR DAI DAVIES, President, MRS MARY JAMES, Deputy Director/Head of Policy, NFU Cymru, DR NICHOLAS FENWICK, Director of Agricultural Policy, MR DEREK MORGAN, Chairman, Hill Farming and Marginal Land Committee, Farmers' Union of Wales, and MR ANDY ROBERTSON, Chief Executive, NFU Scotland, examined.

Q323 Chairman: Good morning, everybody. Thank you very much for coming. I am Lord Cameron. Our normal Chairman, Lord Sewel, is away with NATO in Budapest so I am afraid you will have to put up with a lesser model! Thank you very much for coming and for your written evidence. I am told that I have to tell you that we are being web cast and that there is a possibility that someone out there is listening and looking, but unlikely we think! Would you like to make any opening statements or do you think your evidence might come out in the questioning?

Mr Davies: Perhaps I could, my Lord Chairman. I am Dai Davies and I am President of the NFU Cymru, and on my right I have Mary James, the Deputy Director and our Head of Policy for the Union. I would like to thank the Committee for the opportunity to give evidence on this very important issue. I congratulate the Committee on the timeliness of this oral session, with the communication from the Commission to the Council and the European Parliament having taken place yesterday. NFU Cymru's written evidence was submitted in October. I would like to take this opportunity, if possible, to bring our views up-to-date, especially on the news that we had from Brussels yesterday, the communication and Mariann Fischer Boel's presentation to the Agricultural Committee of the European Parliament. The Agriculture and Rural Development Commissioner asked yesterday whether the fact that she was conducting a health check implies that the patient is sick. She went on to say certainly not, but that it is quite normal for a perfectly healthy person to visit his doctor to see if he can do anything to keep himself in good shape. I have a personal motto, "If it's not broken, why do you need to fix it?" I use this phrase in the context of the EC's suggestion that we should move away from payments based on historical receipts towards a 'flatter rate' system. Given the experience of our English colleagues and the RPA fiasco, together with our experience in Wales in terms of the redistribution of support when our Tir Mynydd (LFA) support moved from a headage payment to an area payment, there is no question that our preferred approach would be to adhere to our present payment system which seems to have served us quite well. Perhaps we should not forget the fact that the Rural Development Budget is allocated on an historical basis. Another issue which the EU's recent communication raised is that in principle we should perhaps be considering applying an upper and lower limit on decoupled payments. Whilst NFU Cymru would share Commissioner Fischer Boel's view that

we should take out of the system payments to ensure that pseudo farmers do not benefit from it, I cannot see, given the devolved approach to the Single Payment Scheme, that scaling back payments without looking at the number of labour units employed would benefit the economy in general. It may also encourage the subdivision of some of these holdings. The Commissioner's communication yesterday reaffirmed that the milk quota system was to expire in 2015. Whilst NFU Cymru accepts that this will enable those who want to expand to do so, we agree with the Commissioner that this must not be done without making sure that we do not cut the legs from under the market. We were also interested in her reference to assistance, "especially but not exclusively for mountainous areas" which have a very heavy dependency upon dairy production. In this context we would see the dairy industry in Wales as being a client for assistance and would wish to explore this further. The other issue I would like to refer to is modulation. This is an issue of some contention in Wales due to the fact that we feel we are being unfairly treated with regard to the imposition of voluntary modulation. The Commissioner is suggesting that we make an annual increase of 2% in compulsory modulation to take effect in the budget years of 2010 to 2013, an overall increase of 8%, but "it goes without saying that the increase in compulsory modulation will be matched by the reduction in voluntary modulation in those Member States which apply the voluntary modulation." This is a view I have strongly conveyed to the Commissioner and I am very pleased that this position is being tabled, though I realise we have a long wait before the Commissioner's legislative proposals and ministerial decisions are taken. My Lord Chairman, I will stop at that point for the moment.

Q324 Chairman: Thank you very much. Does anyone else want to make any comments?

Mr Robertson: I am Andy Robertson, the Chief Executive of NFU Scotland. I think the Committee has seen our submission so I am not going to repeat any of that or go into any great detail. I would like to make a few general points. Firstly, CAP support has been central to maintaining a viable agricultural industry for many years. I say that knowing that many farmers, if not all, would much rather be making their living from the marketplace and not relying on that support, but the sad fact at the moment is that, for a variety of reasons which may come out during further evidence, the market does not pay a price that reflects the full value of what is delivered by farming. That is why agriculture has been supported for many, many years, long before we ever had a CAP and long before we were ever in Europe. I think the challenge for the future and I suspect what this Committee is interested in is to try and construct a CAP that delivers food security and wider non-market benefits and at the same time, while also maintaining a viable agriculture industry in the United Kingdom, delivering value for money to the taxpayer and indeed something that is credible in the eyes of the taxpayer as well. I will follow on from Dai and just quote one piece from Mariann Fischer Boel's speech yesterday, "We expect the CAP to work very hard for the good of the European Union in many ways, a safe food supply, beautiful countryside, a competitive farming sector and lively rural communities," and she said you will find all of those things in the job description of the CAP. I think I will leave it at that.

Q325 *Chairman:* Thank you very much.
Dr Fenwick: My Lord Chairman, thank you very much for the opportunity to give evidence to you. I do not intend to reiterate what has already been said except to emphasise what Dai has already said, which is the huge impact the changes from headage (ie per head) payment to area payments had on Welsh agriculture in the late Nineties and the fact that the historical model that we have in Wales is critical in terms of stopping the total redistribution of funds amongst farm businesses.

Q326 *Chairman:* Thank you very much. I should warn you that we took evidence last week from the Director-General of MAFF in New Zealand which was very refreshing. Perhaps I can act as Devil's advocate to start with and ask you the very simple question of why should farmers get paid when there is, after all, a welfare social safety net in existence in this country? Why should farmers get paid at all through this particular channel?
Mr Robertson: If we were just talking about supporting individual farmers and their individual incomes I can understand why that might be a very valid comment and very valid criticism, in fact, but it is not just about the individuals. We are talking here about retaining agricultural businesses that are viable and actually are active. I think active is the key word in here. By supporting agriculture in the way it is currently supported we have a very active agriculture. As I think all of us hinted at in our opening comments, that is about a whole lot of things, it is about producing food and it is about delivering wider benefits. We talk about non-market benefits and the environment is a very obvious one. An awful lot of the environment is created by farm management,

certainly in Scotland where farmers manage about 80 or 85% of the land. There are other industries which are very dependent on agriculture. For example, the food processing sector in Scotland, it is the biggest manufacturing sector in the country, there are 122,000 jobs that exist either directly or on the distribution side, and it is about £7.5 billion GVA. Scottish farming supplies over a third of what goes into that sector. If you did not have an active farming industry there and if you pulled away all the subsidies and goods it seeks to produce it would not just affect farmers, it would affect an awful lot of other jobs. 122,000 jobs in the context of Scotland is a lot of jobs.
Mr Davies: I would like to support what Andy has said and perhaps go further. We need to retain the capability to produce food. In the last few years that need does not seem to have been so obvious, but going forward and with climate change and so forth, we do not know when we might have to fall back on food from our own resources. I would even go further than Andy because in a Welsh situation we have cultural issues. The majority of people involved in agriculture still speak Welsh and it is a major issue for us in Wales if we wish to retain the language and our heritage. Farming does not only produce food, it has a responsibility for the environment and the environment seems very important for tourism coming in to parts of Wales. We need to retain the beautiful countryside we have in order to generate other income for other sectors, such as tourism.

Q327 *Chairman:* What seems to be happening on the corn production side is that when prices go up the taxpayer sees that you are making lots of money from farming. Would you ever see an end to the Government support under those circumstances?
Mr Robertson: All of us sitting here probably would say that if in fact prices went up and stayed up then that would be absolute Utopia and that is where we would want to be. We would want to be in a situation where agriculture could rely solely on the marketplace. If you go back 150 years, we have seen many, many ups and downs and many false dawns. I can think back to the early 1990s when the McSharry reforms of the CAP first came in. At that stage cereal prices went up very dramatically and farmers were getting the best of both worlds; they were getting subsidy and they were getting high prices. Sadly that did not last and very quickly prices tumbled to the level they were at up until just over a year ago. If the prognosis is that world prices will go up—and there are some signs of that in cereals and on milk—and it is a sustained increase then certainly that is a different world, but it is going to take a wee while to get there and certainly we will not be there overnight. If we want to have a viable agricultural industry we need to

support that industry until we get to a stage where it can be supported by the market alone.

Dr Fenwick: I would echo those sentiments. I think it is important to look at things in an historical context and ask ourselves what might have happened had we not had a CAP or the preceding subsidies. Our headquarters shares a site with a plant breeding station and that was established to stop the depopulation of the uplands of Wales back in the 1920s and 1930s. Had it not been for the introduction of subsidies in the post-War period that rural depopulation would have been significantly accelerated and we would not be as well placed to face the challenges that we are now clearly facing in terms of carbon emissions, food supplies and meeting the biofuel requirements that are going to be growing in the next few years. I think it needs to be looked at in that historical context. I would emphasise that nobody wants to be in a situation where we do require these subsidies to exist. In terms of Welsh agriculture, the 2020 group report which was published a number of weeks ago highlighted the fact that the average Welsh farm income is £12,500, which equates to around £3 an hour in terms of the payment received by those who work on those farms and we have to look at it from that point of view. People simply will not be there to farm the land.

Chairman: So what you are saying is the CAP is a temporary state of affairs dealing with a particular problem and should eventually disappear.

Q328 *Viscount Ullswater:* I am not sure that I am really reading that message from you, what the Chairman might have just said. Am I right in thinking that you see the CAP or what might be there from the Community actually sustaining the rural communities in Wales and Scotland, not just acting as a lower tier, but really there to sustain those communities irrespective of the fortunes of farming?

Mr Robertson: I lived and worked in the Orkney Islands for six years. If you take an island as a microcosm of what goes on in communities generally, you need schools, you need shops, you need services, you need transport links and so on. We had very, very clear experience there of a small island where farmers were by and large the predominant sector. If there was any reduction in the number of farmers then you started to lose critical mass and you started to lose things like schools and shops and so on. Certainly in the remoter rural communities it is fair to say that agriculture is very central to the economic and community wellbeing in these. Until we get to a stage where farming can be supported not just temporarily but in a sustainable sense and in the long term by the price from the market then I think the CAP does do that job. I would go back to what Mariann Fischer Boel said yesterday, ie it does a

number of jobs, it supports a competitive agriculture but it also supports rural communities and it delivers a good environment and so on. We cannot really just say the CAP does one thing; it does a whole lot of things.

Mrs James: I think we have seen previously that the subsidy system that we have had has actually encouraged increased production. We have now moved to a situation where there is a Single Farm Payment and where there is a greater transparency in the marketplace and that farmers will produce provided the prices that they are securing from the marketplace make it a profitable exercise. I think what we see is the CAP being a buffer. Certainly we have traditionally had a cheap food policy in the UK. You have only got to look at the sheep sector, which is particularly important to Wales, to realise that the marketplace at the moment is only satisfying about 79% of production costs. Clearly that is an unsustainable position in the longer term. Profitability, at the end of the day, to return to the earlier question, is the relationship between market returns and costs of production. Yes, market returns may well increase, but if costs of production are rising at a similar rate then clearly the net margin is not actually changing, and certainly we have seen that in the milk sector where there has been a significant increase in the producer price but costs of production have risen substantially as well. We would see the CAP acting as a buffer whilst retail prices are not discharging full recompense.

Q329 *Baroness Jones of Whitchurch:* Is there not an argument that if you were given notice that the CAP funding was going to be withdrawn in four or five years, ten years even, you would learn to adjust to whatever you were producing? If you looked at the rural landscape in Scotland and Wales in ten years' time, you would have adjusted to the fact that those subsidies were no longer there and you might be doing different things on the land, you might be growing different things, but eventually you would be able to adjust to the market. The Chairman has already given the example that we heard last week from New Zealand that that is exactly what they did. They used to have subsidies, they put people on notice and they managed to adjust and work in a market situation. Could you not envisage that happening in your areas?

Mr Davies: Efficiency and sustainability do not fit in the same box. I accept what you say, there would be a dramatic change in the landscape if you removed the supports, you would see a dramatic change in the communities and some of those communities would disappear totally. We saw this back in the 1800s when the corn laws and things were relaxed and so forth. There would be dramatic change. You would see a dramatic change in the vegetation because those people would move and find work in other areas. Evolution, if you want to call it that, would mean that, sadly, we would not be able to sustain the same type of people or the same type of communities in those rural areas that we have now. I fear that they would become dormitories for people who had decided to retire and go down the route of the good life in peaceful areas or you would have commuters. What you would do is urbanise the rural areas and that may be what you would wish to do, but I am sure it is not what people who come to visit these areas would wish to see.

Mr Morgan: We hear about New Zealand farming all the time. New Zealand is a totally different country. I spent some time there on a scholarship. Given that 80% of Wales is LFA and we house cattle and sheep for seven months of the year, in New Zealand production costs like that are out of the window, everything could be done off grass. They have a better climate than we have. To take New Zealand as a benchmark for Welsh farming is not quite right. 96% of New Zealand's agriculture goes on exports. They are very well placed in the world to get those exports into the Middle East and what have you. It would be nice to have a New Zealand climate that we could farm in Wales, but we cannot compete on production costs with New Zealand.

Q330 Earl of Arran: I agree it is a completely different climate and a different situation et cetera. From a purely farming point of view, I am rather interested to know, in Wales particularly with so much grassland, are you beginning to adopt extensive grazing at all, like the New Zealand method?

Mr Morgan: Yes.

Q331 Earl of Arran: Is that actually working, thereby you are keeping your cows out for most of the year?

Mr Morgan: No. In the uplands you would not be able to keep them out.

Q332 Earl of Arran: On the lowlands?

Mr Morgan: There are rules within the dairy industry and Dai will know better than I about that.

Mr Davies: We farm in west Wales, Pembrokeshire and Carmarthenshire, which has a very bad climate. The way forward post the 1980s was to go down the route of New Zealand-type dairy farming where you left the cattle out for nine months of the year. They were dry during the winter and you produced the milk during the summer. There was a huge shift towards that, but if you went down there now you would see there has been a huge shift back in the other direction. As far as welfare standards are

concerned, there is a need for us to comply with cross-compliance. We are not allowed to poach the land; you are not supposed to feed the cattle out and so forth. There has been a huge move back towards conventional farming and higher standards of welfare. Picking up on the New Zealand issue and what you said about them having adopted this, we have to remember that agriculture in New Zealand is a dominant part of the economy. When they did away with their subsidies the first thing they did was devalue the New Zealand dollar by 18% so they could become very competitive. I am sure if we changed our system in the UK the powers that be would not be prepared to devalue the pound by 18% in order for us to have a better market out there.

Mr Robertson: I can remember from my time in government that about 90% of the ups and downs are caused by currency fluctuations, so that is key. None of us would want to give the impression that farmers just want to sit back and take subsidies and not adapt. All farmers are trying to adapt. One of the points of the last series of reforms in 2003 was to try and get agriculture to be more market orientated. There are examples where people actually can go into, for instance organic farming because there is a market for it, but it will not work for everybody because if everybody went into organic farming there would be no price premium. Farmers are by and large small businesses and they are price takers rather than price setters. We work in a supply chain in the United Kingdom where the balance of power sits very, very heavily at the retail end. If in fact farmers were in a position where they could actually, like most other industries, set a price and say this is what we are going to produce and sell for then that would be great, but in fact they do not set their own price. They are told very, very firmly by the rest of the supply chain what the rest of the supply chain is prepared to pay for them. At that moment that price does not in any way reflect the cost of production let alone the many wider benefits that agriculture actually delivers. Any suggestion that we should move towards a subsidy-free system, which is a perfectly valid argument to put forward, cannot go forward without accepting that there would have to be some change to the balance of power in the supply chain to allow farmers to benefit.

Q333 Chairman: I would accept that and your analogy about price takers and price setters is right, but at the same time that is in the hands of the farmers. We are very bad at cooperating as farmers. If we got together and said, "Sorry guys, you're not going to get your milk at this price, you've got to pay that," something might change, which is more or less what happened in the New Zealand situation.

Mr Robertson: There is a very important point about competition law in all of that. At the moment there are not equal principles being applied to the various parts of the supply chain. For example, the four major retailers control about 80% of the food market, and one of them, the biggest, has about 35%. There has been a number of decisions, for instance in milk, where the OFT has said they would not allow a co-operative to hold more than 25% of the market. If we want to operate in much more of a free market we have got to apply the same principles all the whole way along the supply chain.

Q334 *Chairman:* I accept that. Both of the NFUs mentioned in their written statement about production capacity, "subsidies in the meantime should maintain production capacity". Exactly what do you mean by production capacity, and at what stage does it cease to be necessary to support that particular capacity?
Mr Robertson: There is a very important point of principle here, which is the one we have been referring to, which is that if the demand for food across the world increases we need to be in a position to meet that demand. If you look at the new Member States of Eastern Europe, they have got potentially some fantastic land out there, but it is nowhere near producing to its full capacity. In the Ukraine the average depth of topsoil is around 30 feet, it is fantastic land, but they cannot produce because they have had years and years of underinvestment. The fertility levels are not high enough. I think what we mean by retaining production capacity is certainly the land retaining the inherent fertility. It would be too easy for people to take a very short-term approach, to shove on lots of nitrogen but not keep phosphate levels, potash levels and lime levels high enough, which in the long term would mean you would have serious problems. The other aspect of that certainly from a Scottish perspective is infrastructure, for instance housing. Again, if you want to keep cattle, the sad fact is that you have to house them for about six months of the year and if you do not keep buildings in good condition and if you do not keep them in a condition that meets a lot of the very new environmental and other requirements then you cannot keep cattle. There is a constant investment required in land fertility, in buildings and so on and that is what we really mean.

Q335 *Chairman:* How do you square what you have just said—I may have got it wrong—with the fact that there was a genuine feeling that cross-compliance was not a very fair or just system? It seems to me that the cross-compliance is doing just what you said, trying to keep our land in good heart and so on.

Mr Robertson: There are two aspects to cross-compliance. I think the one you are referring to is good agricultural and environmental condition. Most of the emphasis is very much on environmental condition and is very much about preventing overgrazing for instance.

Q336 *Chairman:* Summer management in particular comes into it.
Mr Robertson: Yes. On agricultural condition what they say is it should be in a condition to produce the next year, which is pretty short-term stuff.
Mrs James: On the one hand a farmer, if he is seeking to maximise his income, is going to optimise his production and optimising production is not necessarily the same as meeting good agricultural and environmental conditions, there is a conflict of interest there. I guess the other point I would want to make is the one about the length of the production cycle as far as livestock are concerned, particularly cattle and dairy cows, where you are looking at a three year production cycle which you just cannot switch on and off. I think that is particularly pertinent when, as Andy says, you have to look at investment when you are trying to get back into the production. Three years down the line the resource, given the levels of income, is not going to be there to invest and upgrade in order to go back into an enterprise. I think that would actually stymie that. The other aspect is one of infrastructure beyond the farm and it is particularly things like abattoir capacity, processing capacity. The fact is, if you lose your throughput of stock your unit costs go up and you become unviable and then you lose abattoirs. We have certainly seen that in Wales in terms of the concentration in terms of abattoir capacity with only really four major abattoirs left in Wales now.

Q337 *Lord Palmer:* Mr Robertson, it is only perhaps fair to warn you that I am one of your members! You approve of the historic basis for the Single Farm Payments used in Wales and Scotland. Do you believe that production in the 2000-2004 period will be considered a legitimate basis on which to distribute Single Farm Payments in 2014?
Mr Robertson: I think it is a very, very fair point that the further we get away from 2000-2004 the more difficult it is to justify saying somebody is getting a payment because of what they did ten years ago or whatever. I think that then raises the question as to what you would move to. Some of the suggestions are that you would move to an area payment and specifically a single area payment, which would be a single rate. The CAP up to now has very much reflected what people did in terms of production. If we are moving towards something different, which might be the cost of delivering a whole lot of wider

benefits, then quite clearly the cost of delivering those benefits will not be the same on all farms on every type of land. While an historic payment may become more and more difficult to justify, I do not think that a single area payment which simply said we are going to pay X amount per hectare regardless of where the farm is, what type of farm it is and what it would be producing is valid either. We are currently doing some work, which we have referred to in our submission, to try and say what is the cost of delivering some of these other benefits, be they environmental benefits or supporting downstream industries or so on. If we have to move away from historic to area then we should actually make sure that that area payment reflects the costs of delivering these other benefits.

Mr Davies: Accepting totally what you say, my Lord, I am a dairy farmer and I produce milk according to what I produced in 1983 and I will be producing that volume until 2015, which is quite a long period of time to be tied in to historical production. The other issue I would like to remind you of as well is as far as the Rural Development Fund is concerned, that is also based on investment and historical spend that we did. The Commissioner mentions quite often that we should be using this fund for this purpose or that purpose, but that fund, as far as the UK is concerned, is very, very restricted. There are many things which restrain us which are based on historical matters. As far as Wales is concerned, there are very marginal farms which through hard work and grafting have intensified over a period of time and without the level of support they are getting at the moment those marginal farm would not be viable. We changed the system of our support for the LFA areas in Wales in the last few years and we saw a dramatic shift of resources when we went down the route of area payments instead of headage payments. A lot of these marginal farms suffered quite badly and some even went out of business.

Dr Fenwick: I would echo those sentiments. It is an anomaly to talk about historical allocations being done away with in terms of farms but saying we are going to keep historical entitlements effectively in terms of Member States. That is a clear anomaly. To do away with one without doing away with the other does not seem appropriate.

Q338 *Chairman:* Are you advocating the total reallocation of CAP funds?

Dr Fenwick: I would not want to allocate that without looking into the figures. We should also bear in mind that while we do broadly have an historical system, the trading of entitlements has taken place, so there has been trade between farmers of entitlements which has removed at least an element of the historic system. We should also bear in mind that the impact

of reallocating monies would be extremely severe. For example, the single payments the farms have received are generally based on their productivity. A lowland farm can produce similar productivity to an upland farm. That productivity you estimate, in simple terms, based on the amount of grass that can be grown. There are climatic differences and there are soil differences. For example, a 200 acre farm, in an extreme example, could have the same productivity as a 1,500 acre farm. We might assume that those two farms could have the same single payment effectively because of that productivity. To reallocate that money and totally redistribute it from a system where perhaps a lowland farm could be receiving £350 per hectare and an upland farm £40 a hectare and to put an average figure on it, obviously it does not take a great deal of insight to realise that that lowland farm is going to go out of business, it is going to be completely unable to compete with the upland farm.

Mrs James: Certainly, from our perspective, we see that by 2013 there will be a very strong push from the European Commission and from domestic government to actually shift resources away from SFP under Pillar I to Pillar II. In a way we are actually shifting the emphasis in any case. We envisage the reliance on historic payment will actually become somewhat less over time.

Q339 *Baroness Jones of Whitchurch:* I would like to follow on that whole issue which is to do with the non-market benefits of the CAP. In various bits of your submissions and this morning you have talked about the non-market benefits and you included things like the environment and the greater quality of life issues and I am sure there are others. Why should the CAP fund those non-market benefits? Are we not stretching its purpose way beyond its original intention here?

Mr Robertson: I think the quick answer to that is that the CAP has evolved. The CAP was all about securing food supplies. If you go back to the Treaty of Rome in 1956, apart from having a common market, it was the second thing that featured and it is all about, in the wake of World War II, securing food supplies. It did it hugely effectively. In fact, it did it almost too effectively at one stage and we had the well-publicised 'wine lakes' and 'beef mountains' and all the rest of it. As a result of that there have been the successive changes to the CAP. The Agenda 2000 changes introduced the whole concept of a second Pillar and a rural development pillar which actually recognised the fact that an awful lot of what agriculture does is not just about food production but it is about its effect on the rural economy and rural communities. That is really why we have got into looking at the wider effects. What I would say is that Pillar II is still, relatively speaking, quite small

21 November 2007 Mr Dai Davies, Mrs Mary James, Dr Nicholas Fenwick,
Mr Derek Morgan and Mr Andy Robertson

compared to Pillar I. There is an awful lot of what farming does which is not in any way taken account of by Pillar II payments. There was some work done in England jointly between the NFU and the Commission for Rural England which showed that there was over £400 million-worth a year of work done on farms for environmental and landscape benefit which sat outside any CAP scheme. So there is an awful lot done by farmers which is not paid for.

Q340 *Baroness Jones of Whitchurch:* If we were going to rationalise the CAP then surely one of the things we should do is put a lot more money in Pillar II, if we listen to what you are saying about the needs in your environments. If it is about environmental protection, which I am sure we all think is very important, then there should be other sources of money that we should tap into to pay for that. It should not come out of the CAP which, as you say, over the years has grown like topsy and perhaps it has lost its core purpose.

Mr Robertson: I think the CAP has changed a lot. It is a lot smaller in total terms than it was as a percentage of EU spending. I think we can get too hung up on Pillar I versus Pillar II. One of the things I would hope we would able to do from 2013 onwards is say forget about Pillar I and Pillar II, what is it we want the CAP to do? To my mind it needs to do a number of things. One is to support that basic farming core business because there is clear evidence that by keeping farmers farming there are other benefits. The second bit is to say, if there are extra things we want farmers to do over and above which are of benefit to the environment or a benefit to local economies or whatever, then actually let us have specific measures that encourage farmers to do these things. We have perhaps got far too hung up on the fact that there is a Pillar I and a Pillar II and the whole concept of modulation, which to me is the most incredibly obtuse way of transferring money from one budget to another. If we want to put more money in a budget then we should just do it.

Mr Davies: I am very interested in this other pot of money that is floating around. Perhaps we can speak afterwards!

Q341 *Baroness Jones of Whitchurch:* For example, the Government is just announcing large sums of money around the climate change issues. There might be big potential there.

Mr Davies: Thank you. I am even more interested now! As far as the expenditure on CAP is concerned, it is falling. We now hear that it is around 50% whereas it was at 60%. As far as production is concerned, there are serious constraints on production methods in the UK. As far as the population in general is concerned, they seem to

expect certain standards from farmers. If you deny us the support then certainly hand in hand with that the constraints have to disappear as well and I am not sure if the population out there would like to see efficiency being driven into the rural areas of Wales. We have to remember that the farm structures in Wales are very similar to the time of the Enclosure Acts, the field structures are very small. If you are talking about efficiency then you will have to give us the freedom to remove some of these hedges and have vast areas we can run using mechanisation efficiency, and I am not too sure that the tourists coming into the heartland of Wales want to see that. They want to see traditional methods, traditional structures and the environment being very high on the agenda. For us to be able to do that we certainly need their support.

Q342 *Chairman:* What is the difference between the CAP Pillar I funding coming into Wales and the profits from the tourist industry in Wales?

Mr Davies: As far as Wales is concerned, if you look back over the last year, milk production contributed about a third of the GDP.

Q343 *Chairman:* That is not quite what I asked. I asked about the funding from the CAP and the returns in tourism. You are defending the CAP as supporting the Welsh tourist industry.

Mrs James: Perhaps I can come back to you with the figures.[1]

Q344 Viscount Brookeborough: I come from Northern Ireland and we have quite similar problems albeit with the weather or whatever. I was interested in what was maybe a throwaway remark when you said that the Welsh language seemed to be important to your agricultural industry and whether or not the people who were speaking Welsh spoke English as well.

Mr Davies: I did not say the Welsh language was important to the agricultural industry, I said the Welsh language seemed to be very important as far as the culture of Wales was concerned and what Welsh people want to preserve, it is the heartland of the Welsh language. The majority of people involved in agriculture—and it is the only industry—are still Welsh speakers.

---

[1] £211.9 million was released in Wales under the Single Payment Scheme in 2006. Expenditure by UK and overseas staying visitors to Wales in 2004 was over 31.8billion. Additionally, leisure day visits to Wales could account for a further 31.4billion. In 2001, tourism represented 12% of all employment in rural Wales.

Q345 Viscount Brookeborough: Welsh only?
Dr Fenwick: Bilingual in the main.

Q346 Viscount Brookeborough: I am involved in tourism. I was interested in what appeared to be a contradiction because the tourists might like to hear a bit of Welsh or Irish or Gaelic but they communicate in English.
Mr Davies: My first language is Welsh but I can struggle through with a few words of English!

Q347 Viscount Brookeborough: On rural redevelopment, I am not sure that you both seem to agree on Pillar I and Pillar II. Mr Robertson said he was not too worried about the effects because it depended on what results you were getting. In Wales, are you clinging on to Pillar I and not wanting things to be moved to Pillar II?
Mrs James: We are not advocating a shift from Pillar I to Pillar II. We see the signals emanating from Europe and from Government that seem to suggest that we are going to see a shift of emphasis away from Pillar I to Pillar II. I think it is trying to predict what we are going to see come 2013. That is not to say we are advocating that. We would certainly prefer to be getting the major resource through the SFP arrangements with them obviously cross-complied.

Q348 Viscount Brookeborough: I understand that if money goes down through Pillar I and through the farms one could consider it might cascade into the community, but it does not always necessarily work like that. There could be better ways of doing it. Mr Davies said that if it works okay then it does not need to be fixed and I accept that entirely. However, certain things are going to change and therefore perhaps one should be more forward looking as to how you would really wish them to go, accepting that fact rather than just defending the past. How do you really see that rural development might continue to go on and come out of these changes?
Mrs James: We can actually see a situation where re-diverting the resources away from primary producers causes them to become unprofitable and they leave the industry as a result of it. There are no benefits in creating alternative opportunities if on the one hand you are taking the profitability and the livelihood away from the farming industry on the one side merely to create another alternative opportunity on the other. In terms of the cascading down or the multiplier effect as we would know it, there is some independent evidence in Wales to suggest that for each farming job there are ten full-time equivalents produced in rural areas. They may be in the processing sector, the food areas, tourism, whatever, but certainly there is a very significant multiplier effect there.

Mr Robertson: Can I just re-emphasise that? In Scotland, government figures have split it into 123 industry groups and agriculture is ranked 28 out of the 123 as far as multiplying for employment and it is ranked 17 when it comes to output. It is a pretty higher multiplier effect. The money you put into agriculture is recirculated and comes out in other sectors. There is some recent work which shows it is much higher than, for instance, in the hotel and catering side and also on the retail side. Agriculture is a good multiplier. We cannot just sit there and say this is what we have always done, therefore we have got to carry on doing it. I think we can get too hung up on the fact that historically Pillar I has been the direct support and Pillar II has been the rural development. What we need to say is okay, what do we need to do to keep farming businesses viable and active? There is clearly a gap between what the market requires at the moment and what is required to make these businesses viable and active. That is the support bit. It may well be that that support has to have a different justification than it has done in the past. In the past it was always very much linked to what you produced. It may well be linked to what we deliver in the wider sense. Then you have to look at what other things can agriculture do to the benefit of the wider rural community and the wider rural economy. That is where, for instance, encouraging diversification may well be a very relevant thing to do and that may well help the farming business itself too. If in fact the core business is not sufficient to employ the whole family or the current labour force then some sort of diversified activity may well help not just the business but also the local economy and you will then get that multiplier effect.

Q349 Viscount Brookeborough: Would you like to tell us about diversification in the countryside as it affects you? We have heard about tourism and so on, but there are other things, ie where farms have not been able to support the whole family, where people have attempted to diversify and there are problems such as planning, even where a farm building may not have its appearance changed from outside. Natural England gave us evidence to say that they were largely against that sort of diversification but that tourism was all right. When we asked why they were against it they said it is things like traffic on the road, but tourists are traffic on the road. What are the issues for you in terms of diversification?
Mr Davies: You mentioned diversification and tourism. As far as tourism and agriculture are concerned, they should go hand in hand. So many farmers have gone into tourism. The huge problem we have in Wales is the fact that there is a large proportion of Wales that is National Park and it is a case of hands off, do not touch National Parks. The

21 November 2007 Mr Dai Davies, Mrs Mary James, Dr Nicholas Fenwick,
Mr Derek Morgan and Mr Andy Robertson

other huge problem we have is that Wales seems to be quite attractive as far as people from the South East wishing to retire are concerned because it is a tranquil place and a green and pleasant land. As far as the younger generation is concerned, they are not in a position to compete with these people coming in well established and having enjoyed fairly lucrative employment standards in the South East. There is severe difficulty in the fact that we cannot build affordable housing in rural Wales to support these people and to enable them to work on local farms and carry on the traditions. It is a major, major problem which needs to be addressed at some stage or other.

Dr Fenwick: In terms of the trickle down effect, we have recently seen a critical time due to the foot and mouth outbreak, with farming incomes falling through the floor and particularly lamb prices going down to very, very low levels. The number of businesses in rural Wales that have unpaid bills that they are not even going to bother to chase up until early December is phenomenal. We have come under that pressure when farmers are up against the wall. We had a similar experience during the problems that England experienced. We had businesses that are on the Welsh/English border phoning us up that had connections with agriculture but were not farming businesses to ask when English payments were going to be made because they were under such extreme pressure from their banks and so on and so forth. In terms of the contribution of farming to the environment and the link between tourism and the environment, that link is not coincidental. Tourism in Wales is a direct product of agriculture in Wales and that is something that has to be borne in mind. We cannot detach the two. In terms of diversification, the vast majority of diversification is in terms of niche markets and niche markets by their definition are niche markets. Not everyone can go into that type of business. I think we have seen the peak in terms of bed and breakfast businesses. There was a huge growth in farms that did bed and breakfast and they are very obvious when you drive along the road and you see all sorts and you might suddenly get the idea that every farm has got a bed and breakfast business, but the percentage of farms that run those sorts of businesses is very low. The numbers that would be able to be established on that type of diversification or perhaps diversification in general are very low.

Q350 *Chairman:* Nowadays with Broadband you are not restricted to bed and breakfasts, you can become a stockbroker!

Mr Robertson: Can I just pick up that point about planning because I do feel quite strongly that the planning system has not kept pace with rural development policy. The planning system is still stuck in a situation where it is almost in a bit of a

NIMBY mode which says we want to keep everything as it was. There are huge opportunities for diversification, renewable energy is one and there are all sorts of renewable energy projects, whether it be wind power, hydra power or whatever. These are all things that farmers are well placed to do, they have got the resource, they have got the land, but if in fact we are going to run into difficulties with objections to planning permission then that is going to kill us stone dead. I know wind farms are a very controversial subject and beauty is in the eye of the beholder, but that is one very clear example where there is scope for diversification, but on the other hand the planning system may prevent it.

Viscount Brookeborough: Space wise Wales is an RAF training area. The RAF complains about governance. It appears if you do not want to get attacked by this country you put up wind farms!

Q351 *Earl of Dundee:* The FUW is against further concessions if made during current WTO negotiations. They believe these would undermine UK agriculture. Do you agree with that? If so, which concessions made by the EU in the current trade talks would prove to be most damaging?

Mr Robertson: We do see there are really big potential dangers there. There are three aspects of the WTO. One is the internal support and most of the EU support has now been decoupled, it puts it into the Green Box and therefore there is not any great issue as far as CAP support is now concerned. The big issue there is whether other countries, such as the USA, are going to bring their support into line with ours. The second issue is export refunds. Export refunds are pretty unpopular. They are deemed to harm the economies of developing countries and so on. It is pretty well certain they are going to go. Mariann Fischer Boel has said they are going to go regardless of whether they have a WTO agreement or not. There is not a huge direct effect. There is an indirect effect because if a country which is currently getting an export refund, for instance, selling beef to the Middle East and it does not get that export refund then in fact there will be a knock-on effect because that beef may well come into this country and pull down the market. We have to watch that we look at the indirect as well as direct effects. The real danger is on import tariffs. There is currently a range of import tariffs. For instance, let us just take one example on beef from Brazil. Beef from Brazil is currently subject to a range of import tariffs. The EU proposal was that these tariffs would be substantially reduced. If they are substantially reduced then obviously Brazilian beef becomes much cheaper and it will drag the market price down in this country very substantially and it will do severe harm to an industry which already is being paid a price which is well below what is needed to meet their costs of production. That is where the big danger is, it is from the import tariffs. If we make too many concessions then we will end up not just cheaper but, crucially, with a product which is not produced to the same standards, whether it be animal welfare standards or whether it be environmental standards. One of the real weaknesses of the WTO is it does not take account in any way of production standards. We run the risk of tariffs being dismantled and product coming in which is inferior and undercutting us.

Q352 *Earl of Dundee:* After further credit liberalisation what different forms do you expect Scottish and Welsh agriculture to take?

Mr Davies: The other issue which concerned us was the fact that as far as the UK is concerned we are not in the Eurozone, and as far as the pound is concerned we have experienced a very strong pound for the last few years and, being involved in the dairy industry, we have found difficulty in exporting our dairy produce. We seem to be sucking in a lot of cheaper products from abroad. As far as Welsh agriculture is concerned, what we have been trying to do is capitalise on our PGI status, the product of geographical indication, and produce a branded product to try and add value to it. The ideology is fine but at the end of the day the vast majority of products sold abroad are sold on a price basis and we would face some severe difficulty. We can brand a product, we can take advantage of our high standards and capitalise on that, but at the end of the day it is only a small section of our production that we can sell in that way.

Mr Robertson: You asked what would happen. There has been some work done by the Queen's University at Belfast which has a model, I think it is called FAPRI, which models the agricultural economies across the world and has a specific model for the UK and the four distinct parts of the UK. It has modelled the effects of reducing export refunds, and indeed dismantling import tariffs, and therefore an assumption that there would be greater penetration by imports, and it is quite frightening. It shows 20-30% reductions in prices and equivalent reductions in production, so if nothing else changes this model would suggest that it would have a really decimating effect on agriculture in this country. That is why we would argue very strongly that it is irresponsible not to include production standards in WTO negotiations because we would then be left with an industry which is producing to a high standard because it is required to do so, partly by regulation and partly by consumer demand, and is being undercut by inferior products, so we really have to play hard to have production standards included in WTO negotiations.

Dr Fenwick: If I can just add examples of the differences between those production standards, Food and Veterinary Office missions to Brazil have consistently over the last four or five years found problems such as animals not being tagged until 90 days before slaughter, animals being moved from foot and mouth infected areas to foot and mouth free areas, the liberal availability of growth hormones, badly labelled drugs that do not have withdrawal periods written on them, which is very important in terms of protecting human health. The list is seemingly endless and many of those problems that they found would quite possibly land British farmers in prison and yet they are at liberty to import products that are produced to significantly lower standards and compete on a level playing field as far as the supermarkets are concerned.

Q353 *Earl of Arran:* Just on another point on the CAP, I am supposed to be objective on this Committee, and indeed I shall be and am, but I am married to a farmer in Devon in dairy and her cries at night as she tries to come to grips with the CAP bureaucracy and regulatory system could certainly compete with the barrack room. The point is, how do you think the rules might be simplified when at the same time you have to satisfy the auditor that the funds have been used for legitimate purposes? Mr Robertson, in your submission here I quite agree that to "alter the penalty system to differentiate between deliberate intention to defraud and genuine error" is a very important point. Would you expand on that, and indeed would you expand briefly on your other possibilities for simplification?

Mr Robertson: Let me give you one example of what we are talking about there. The suckler cow premium scheme in 2003 required people to keep cows for six months. If a heifer calved that heifer had to be replaced by another one, and in the vast majority of cases the farmer already had that animal on the farm so there was no question of not being able to keep the requisite number of animals. They were also required to notify the department that one animal had calved and been replaced by another one. If they failed to notify the department of that they suffered a penalty, not for not keeping the right number of animals but simply for not sending a letter and—the real irony in this—for not telling the department something they knew already because they could access the BCMS cattle database and find out that that was what had happened. The penalty for that was 50% of the entire subsidy. We would all accept there have to be checks, we would all accept that if somebody does not meet the conditions of the scheme and keep the requisite number of animals and do the right bit of environmental work or whatever, fine, they should not get the money, nobody would argue with that,

21 November 2007   Mr Dai Davies, Mrs Mary James, Dr Nicholas Fenwick,
Mr Derek Morgan and Mr Andy Robertson

but when somebody is being penalised for not writing a letter to tell the department something they knew already seems to us to be absolutely mad. That is what we mean by simplifying some of the bureaucracy. We think that there are other things that we could do. I have talked about abolishing set-aside. Set-aside to us seems to be an anachronism now. In a decoupled era there should not really need some kind of artificial restraint on the extent to which people can grow crops, nor quotas. Modulation, as I say, is a very obtuse way of transferring money from one budget to another. Here we have at EU level two big budgets running into billions of euros. Instead of shifting money from one to the other at the headline they let it all go down to individual farm level and then they take a small percentage from each farmer and transfer it across and back up into that budget. That is an incredibly bureaucratic and complicated way of doing things. If we want to move money we should just move it.

Mr Davies: Nobody wants to protect criminals, but I have the privilege or misfortune in that we have an appeals panel as far as Wales is concerned to look into discrepancies. We call it an appeals panel but as far as the bureaucracy is concerned it is either black or white; there is no grey area. In reality, of course, we deal in grey areas all the time. We had an instance the other day where a chap keeping 2,500 ewes was 16 ewes short and he lost £32,000 out of his subsidy. If that man had been a criminal he would have made sure, by borrowing a few ewes from his neighbour or whatever, that he had the count. He certainly would not have faced a £32,000 loss. As far as the bureaucracy is concerned, tagging is a major issue as far as the agriculture industry is concerned where you will have the local authority coming out this week and you will have AH coming out the following week doing a TB test. Surely common sense tells us that these inspections can be combined into one. There is a welfare issue of farmers involved here as well as the welfare issue of animals. Bureaucracy gone mad as far as I am concerned is the issue of the certificate of competence which is being introduced, or should have been introduced this January, where you expect experienced people that have been in the industry for 30 or 40 years to turn up at some institution or other to look at a computer screen and put little ticks in boxes, and by putting those ticks in the right boxes he is deemed to be a competent person in handling livestock. I would have thought a far better scheme would have been to accept farm assurance, where they visit your farm and they see the individual walking between his animals, how he handles them. That can give a far better idea to an individual how competent that person is than him looking in front of a screen and wondering to himself, "What sort of answer do they expect? In which box do I put the tick?", and that is the reality of life at the moment.

Q354 *Viscount Ullswater:* I think both Mr Davies and Mr Robertson have said that if product prices were sufficiently robust for an economic return you would rather work and farm and do your business in that situation, but probably the reality is, certainly at the moment for animal production, for sheep and cattle, that that is not the position and because of the fragility of your rural communities you need the single farm payment. Of course, you do not exactly have the freedom to farm as you used to because there are so many more environmental standards that have to be adhered to as well as the animal welfare standards. When you are looking at market mechanisms I note from your evidence that you still want to have some form of storage aid and I think the NFU in Scotland also want to have the opportunity of some contingency payments if prices fell dramatically. I am just wondering if you could elaborate on the circumstances where you felt that storage aids might be needed, especially as you have already said that you like the move from product prices to single farm payments, and with product prices I include storage aid, intervention and all those sorts of things.

Mr Robertson: I think it is a very important point that you raise, and again I would quote the Commissioner from her speech yesterday, that this sort of thing should be a genuine safety net and not used to set market prices. I think what went wrong with intervention, if you go back 20 years, is that people were producing and almost producing to put into an intervention store, and that was madness. We are talking very much about a safety net where we have a complete crash in prices. If we go back to 1996, the infamous 1996 announcement in the House of Commons about BSE, the beef price absolutely crashed. That is the kind of circumstance that we are talking about—and I suppose we could also look at what has happened to the pig sector and the sheep sector very recently in the wake of foot and mouth—that if things go really badly wrong somehow or other there is a floor, and we are talking about something well down here, not the norm; we are talking about a floor or a safety net which says that if things get absolutely awful then there is some way of dealing with that. It must not become something which can be factored in, because there is no question that in the past when there has been some sort of level of support that has been factored in by the rest of the supply chain and all that has happened is that the subsidy has been given to farmers, or an intervention price or whatever, has been used to justify paying less to the farmer, and so we must make sure that this is only a thing that is used in exceptional circumstances and not something that can be factored in by retailers or others.

Q355 *Viscount Ullswater:* The CAP is EU-wide. What it sounds like is that you are arguing very specifically for a single area like Scotland or Wales rather than the EU, so where would you think that money should come from? It sounds as if you are thinking it should come from the British Government rather than from the EU if it really is just supporting a particular thing which is happening within the country rather than within the Community.

Mr Robertson: Unfortunately, I have been around this industry long enough to remember how the old intervention system worked, and there were two tests. One was that the European price had to fall and the other was that the price had to fall within the Member State, and you had to pass both those tests for intervention to kick in. I think what we are thinking is that you still have, if you like, that double test, that if there is a local problem then it kicks in. If I am absolutely honest we have not really got through all the thinking on this. You could argue that there is an EU pot of money which then can be accessed if you get a particular problem in a particular area. It may well be that we have to think of other ways of doing that. It either could become something that is a Member State issue or it could even be something for which farmers have some sort of insurance policy. It is a difficult one. Hopefully it is not something that will kick in very much at all.

Mr Davies: The way it is set up obviously is important for us, but the ability to have that in place if we need it is probably more important. The fact is that if the ability to purchase, to go to intervention, all that is removed, what you are doing is exposing us totally to the world market, and I think that is a very dangerous route and we need some mechanism, a temporary mechanism, which can be introduced at some stage or other if or when prices collapse.

Q356 *Chairman:* This is in addition to the single farm payment, is it?

Mr Robertson: Yes.

Viscount Ullswater: That is the key.

Q357 *Lord Palmer:* One of your major concerns, and indeed I share it and I think probably most of us round the table do, is the lack of a level playing field across the European Union and the lack of commonality even across the United Kingdom. You are all particularly concerned about the impact of voluntary modulation, and indeed this was touched on earlier, and are sceptical about co-financing arrangements because you believe that the UK Government would indeed be less generous to farmers than other member governments. Therefore, which aspects of the CAP do you believe should be the same across all Member States and which provisions might more appropriately vary?

Mr Davies: One instance which I would like to quote as far as that is concerned is the blue tongue issue at the moment. There is provision in the Commission for us to source funds for purchasing vaccine, 100% for sourcing a vaccine, and 50% for carrying out vaccination. At the moment the UK Government seems reluctant to source that fund. They would rather turn to the industry to be paying for it themselves. I think probably the background is that we are net contributors to the EU budget and that we would have to send more money out to Europe than we would get back, but it does concern the industry that our Government is prepared to support European farmers but deny the same access to funds to us.

Mr Robertson: In very broad terms, to answer your question, we think that the way the CAP is financed should be the bit that is common across the EU. When it comes to the detailed implementation of rules and things I think we have to accept that we have got an enormous Union now; it is 27 Member States, and the way in which the detailed schemes are implemented must be able to take account of the different conditions in different Member States. The modulation one is an absolute classic example of this. There are only two Member States in the whole of the 27 which are applying voluntary modulation, the UK and Portugal, which means that in practice UK farmers and Portuguese farmers are having their direct support reduced to a level which is significantly below that for farmers in the rest of the EU, and, given that one of the whole points of having a single market is that people are trading on level terms, that immediately to us seems to undermine the principle of a free market.

Q358 *Earl of Arran:* I understand all the problems that you are talking about. Out of interest, how lies the situation across the board with new entrants into the farming industry?

Dr Fenwick: The Welsh Assembly Government is run by a coalition, as you know, between Plaid Cymru and the Labour Party and they have published what they call the *One Wales* document, which has declared that they will establish a new entrant scheme in Wales, and so things are looking up. The main problem facing new entrants, however, is the fact that there is not the money in the industry or the prospects within the industry to encourage people to go into it. There are people who are taking those steps. There are some very innovative and exciting young people going into the industry, but when you compare the incomes of perhaps their uncles and aunts who may be farming already with the incomes of their friends who maybe have left school and gone to work for British Telecom, that is hardly encouraging, and that is one of the major problems, raising the incomes of farms, and anything that would help that would be a bonus but the primary aim should be to raise incomes.

Q359 Earl of Arran: And Scotland?
Mr Robertson: Very much the same. We have an oft-quoted statistic that the average age of farmers is 58. I am never quite sure about that.
Earl of Arran: It is rather like the House of Lords.

Q360 Chairman: If I may say so, the thing about that statistic is that it has not changed for 30 years.
Mr Robertson: Some of us will get there eventually. The point that Nick makes about profitability is key, but we are not seeing the same number of young people going into farming. Profitability is key. Why would they go and work three times as many hours as their peers for one third of the income? That is the primary thing that we have to address. No-one is going to go into an industry unless it is profitable.

Q361 Earl of Arran: Is it worse than ever before?
Mr Robertson: Yes. The comparison is now much worse. They see their peers working nine till five, five days a week for a good income and they are not doing the same. There are other issues though, and I will briefly touch on them. Education is one. We need to think very hard about the agricultural education that is being provided. We need to think much more about

getting more business skills into agricultural education. Ongoing training and advice, clearly young people will need that kind of support. Housing is another big issue. We mentioned the planning system earlier on. So often you find that the father and mother from a business want to retire, they want to stay on the farm, but they cannot get planning permission to build a house on the farm and that in itself is a tension. There is a whole range of issues. The Scottish Government is also keen to do something to help new entrants but I have to say that simply throwing money at the problem will not help.

Q362 Chairman: Mrs James, you wanted to come back on the commonality.
Mrs James: Yes, I do. I just wanted to say to Lord Palmer that from our point of view what we are looking for is uniformity in terms of standards but the mechanisms for delivery of those standards clearly should be an issue that is devolved to Member States.
Chairman: Thank you all very much. It has been a very interesting session. I am sorry I let it drift on for too long, but there are three organisations, so it was quite difficult for you all to get your points across, which you did. Is there anything you feel has not been said that you want to draw to our attention or has not come out in the evidence to date? If not, thank you very much for coming.

Supplementary memorandum by the Farmers' Union of Wales

INTRODUCTION

1. The Farmers' Union of Wales was established in 1955 in order to protect and advance the interests of Welsh families who derive an income from agriculture. In addition to 35 Area Officers, the FUW has 11 offices distributed around Wales that provide a broad range of services to members. The FUW is a democratic organisation, with policies being formulated following consultation with its twelve County Executive Committees.

AGRICULTURE IN WALES

2. As highlighted in the Sustainable Farming and Environment: Action Towards 2020 report,[1] farming plays a fundamental part in Welsh life, industry and culture. However, despite this acknowledged role, the report states that *"average farming incomes, compared with the rest of society, continue to be unacceptably low and do not fairly reward farming's contribution of capital, skills and labour"*. This conclusion was based upon incomes prior to the 2007 FMD outbreak.

3. In the 2005–06 financial year the average net farm income in Wales was £12,500, equating to £3/hour[1]. For a lowland beef and sheep farmer the average net income was as low as £3,500.[2]

4. Around two out of every five rural businesses can be classed as being involved in the farming industry.[3] In 2006 Welsh agriculture employed 56,400 people in full time, part time, and seasonal employment.[2] This figure does not include the secondary businesses related to agriculture such as contractors and food processors.

---

[1] http://new.wales.gov.uk/topics/environmentcountryside/countryside_policy/farming/sustainablefarming2020/?lang=en
[2] http://new.wales.gov.uk/docrepos/40382/40382313/statistics/agriculture/1270792/farming-facts07-e2.pdf?lang=en
[3] http://new.wales.gov.uk/docrepos/40382/40382313/statistics/compendia/comp-2001/sb49-2001-focus-rural/sb49-2001-econ.pdf?lang=en

5. In 2007 1.6 million hectares of Welsh land were in agricultural production, equating to 81% of the surface area of Wales.[4]

6. Farming also plays a key role in the preservation of Welsh culture, particularly in terms of the Welsh language, which in many areas is primarily preserved in farming communities, having been largely displaced by the English language in towns and villages.

7. The position of Welsh agriculture prior to the adverse affects of the 2007 FMD outbreak was summarised in the 2020 report[5] as follows:

> *"Most businesses would not be able to survive on the financial returns which the Welsh agricultural industry continues to produce... If production falls below what is referred to as a critical mass the agricultural supply and processing industries will suffer irreparably as a consequence. Farming, with all its diverse effects on the landscape, the economy, communities and social structures, will only be sustainable if it returns to acceptable profitability in the short to medium term."*

8. The current position is that returns are well below the level of acceptable profitability. For example, data for lamb production in the 2006–07 financial year show that, on average, market prices cover just 79% of production costs, with the top third of producers achieving returns of 5% on their investments. A similar pattern of production costs being well above returns exists for beef enterprises.

9. As such, Welsh farming businesses are wholly reliant upon the payments they receive from the Common Agricultural Policy, and reductions in CAP market protection seem unlikely to have any affect other than to further reduce levels of income. Yet the preference of the Welsh farming community would be to be in receipt of economically viable incomes purely from the marketplace, with no need for reliance on support.

10. Single Payments on Welsh farms are currently based upon average CAP Pillar I payments received per hectare during reference years not affected by what the Welsh Assembly Government deemed were exceptional circumstances (predominately the years 2000, 2001, and 2002), and/or the amount of milk quota held on 31 March 2005.

11. CAP Pillar I Payments received during the reference period were effectively based upon the number of eligible stock held on each farm, which, in turn, can in simplistic terms be considered to be a reflection of the fertility, size, altitude, and climate of any particular farm.

12. Thus, the payment received by a smaller, fertile, lowland farm can be similar to that received by an extensive, infertile, upland farm, with both payments effectively reflecting the production capacity (but not the production) of each farm. Payments can typically vary from around £60/hectare for an extensive upland farm to upwards of £350/hectare for a small, fertile, lowland farm.

13. The Farmers' Union of Wales supported the Welsh Assembly Government's implementation of an historically based Single Payment Scheme, on the basis that a flat-rate payment per hectare would result in a complete redistribution of payments away from smaller, more fertile farms, to larger upland farms, rendering many family farms unviable.

14. The removal of direct headage payments has resulted in many farms restructuring their enterprises to more appropriately reflect market demands, as was the intention of the 2003 reforms. However, it must be borne in mind that changes in agricultural practices rely on long term breeding and management strategies, and 2007 is only the third year of the current scheme.

15. Nevertheless, the economic reality of poor returns from the marketplace has resulted in significant falls in livestock numbers, particularly in the Welsh uplands, to the extent that under-grazing is now a major concern for conservationists. Welsh Assembly Government figures show that numbers of both cattle and sheep on Welsh farms fell by 4% between 2006 and 2007.

FUW REACTION TO THE COMMUNICATION FROM THE EUROPEAN COMMISSION TO THE EUROPEAN COUNCIL AND PARLIAMENT: PREPARING FOR THE "HEALTH CHECK" OF THE CAP REFORM

16. The Farmers' Union of Wales is currently in the process of consulting with members regarding the proposals outlined in the "Health Check" document published on 20 November 2007. The following comments are therefore the initial views of the Union in light of the limited consultation that time has allowed.

---

[4]   http://new.wales.gov.uk/docrepos/40382/40382313/statistics/agriculture/1270792/sdr143-2007?lang=en

[5]   http://new.wales.gov.uk/topics/environmentcountryside/countryside_policy/farming/sustainablefarming2020/?lang=en

EU Set-Aside

17. The FUW welcomes the Commission's proposal that the mandatory EU set-aside scheme for arable crops be abolished from 2009 to 2013. The decoupling of payments in 2005 significantly diminished the perceived need for set-aside, and its continuation would constrain the arable sector's ability to meet growing market needs, and benefit from increased world market prices.

18. The FUW objects to the suggestion that Cross Compliance requirements might be stepped up in reaction to the abolition of set-aside, as such changes could negate any positive effects the removal of set-aside would bring for the sector. Rather, any moves to counter perceived adverse impacts on the environment should take the form of compensatory payments made to those who wish to take/keep land out of production.

Market Intervention

19. The FUW believes that any review of market intervention should take the possible adverse, or otherwise, impacts on rural incomes into consideration. Moreover, the FUW believes that such a review should not take place until adequate controls are put in place to ensure that produce from third countries are produced to the same standards as those required in the EC. In the context of Wales, such market intervention controls are or particular relevance in terms of import quotas and tariffs for lamb and beef, and the clear impact that further liberalisation of restrictions relating to such imports would have on what are already unsustainable Welsh livestock prices.

Capping Payments

20. The distribution of farm payments continues to be the subject of considerable discussion within the farming community, and debate within the FUW as regards capping is ongoing. Superficially, larger farms that receive high Single Payments benefit from economies of scale that are not available to smaller farms. However, such large enterprises often support extended families and/or employ a workforce, and thus it is the Union's current view that the possible impact of capping on relatives, the families of employees, and the wider community should be taken into consideration when reviewing the possible impact of capping. There is also the distinct likelihood, expressed on numerous occasions by Commissioner Fisher-Boel, that businesses would simply be broken up in order to avoid a cap, with the main beneficiaries being solicitors and lawyers.

21. Notwithstanding the above, it is the view of the FUW that there is a clear argument in favour of reviewing the possible impact of mechanisms such as tapering payments in proportion to the number of hectares owned and the number of families or individuals supported by farms.

22. The European Commission has suggested that payments might be reduced for those receiving more than €100,000 in Single Payments. Such a limit is expected to affect around 400 Welsh farms, and would therefore have a minimal impact on Welsh businesses.

Modulation

23. Wales currently operates a system of Voluntary Modulation which is match funded by the Welsh Assembly Government at a rate of 90p for every £1 deducted from Single Payments. This money is retained in Wales to fund Rural Development programmes. Under the Health Check proposals, the level of Compulsory Modulation will increase, with a commensurate decrease in Voluntary modulation.

24. Receipts from Compulsory Modulation are sent to Brussels, and 80% are returned to the Member State. Unless there is a commitment to continue co-financing modulated receipts at levels that make up the expected shortfall of at least 20% of modulated monies, the most efficient and effective method of injecting monies into Welsh rural communities will be compromised under the Health Check proposals.

25. The FUW therefore believes that increases in Compulsory Modulation could jeopardise the current level of funding available to Wales under Pillar II programmes.

26. Funds available to the UK and Wales from the European Agricultural Fund for Rural Development (EAFRD) are based upon historical claims made by the UK, and the previous failure of the UK to utilise available funds has resulted in Wales receiving an inadequate and disproportionate EAFRD allocation. This is particularly pertinent given that 80% of Wales is categorised as Less Favoured.

27. Thus, the Welsh Assembly Government has had to make up the deficit in the EAFRD allocation by implementing Voluntary Modulation on top of Compulsory Modulation, leaving Welsh farmers at a disadvantage to their European counterparts. .

28. It is notable that while the Health Check paper expresses concern over the increasing irrelevance of historically allocated Single Payments, the historical allocations received by Member States are not subject to such scrutiny.

29. Thus, increasing Compulsory Modulation will further disadvantage Welsh farmers, and further compromise the efficient distribution of monies in rural areas.

30. The FUW maintains that all those whose payments are reduced by modulation should have access to modulated monies, and, in this context, it is particularly concerning that Pillar II payments are increasingly being targeted at non- agricultural concerns, such as measures available under Axis 3 and 4 of the Rural Development Plan, in order to make up deficits in domestic funding.

DECOUPLED SUPPORT

31. The FUW supports moves to examine further ways to fully decoupling CAP aid payments from production within the Single Payment Scheme. However, there should remain a degree of flexibility within the model that takes into account the importance of maintaining livestock numbers for environmental and other reasons, particularly in the uplands.

MOVEMENT TOWARDS FLAT RATE AREA PAYMENTS

32. The European Commission argues that it will be difficult to justify future aid being based on past levels of production and differences in support, especially in the historic model, and that Member States should consequently be encouraged to move towards a flat rate system per hectare during the period 2009 to 2013.

33. For the reasons given in paragraphs 10 to 14, the FUW believes that the implementation of a flat rate area payment will result in the complete redistribution of payments, in many cases away from those whose need is greatest.

34. It is notable that Single Payments are made on eligible forage area, but that no account is taken of the quality of such forage area.

35. Since the limited trading, leasing, and transfer of Single Payment entitlements has occurred in Wales since 2005, there has been some move away from the historical system.

36. The FUW maintains that it is an anomaly to scrutinise historical allocations on a farm by farm basis, without similarly scrutinising other historically based allocations made to Member States and their regions. This is particularly the case given Wales' disproportionately low EAFRD allocation.

37. Thus, the FUW maintains that, in the absence of some form of counter-mechanism, the implementation of a flat rate area payments could have severe implications for many family businesses, and that this likely effect should be taken into account.

38. The FUW believes that movement towards a flat rate area payment is likely to have a far greater impact on Welsh businesses than any moves to cap payments. Thus, any honourable motives put forward by the Commission in relation to capping run counter to the likely outcome of requiring payments to be calculated on a flat rate basis.

39. The FUW is unaware of any significant pressures from the public to move from historically allocated to flat-rate payments, and international pressures from third countries continue to focus on aid per se, and intervention, rather than the minutiae of how individual payments are calculated.

MINIMUM AREA FOR CAP CLAIMS

40. The FUW supports propositions that the minimum area for Pillar I claims be increased in order to minimise what are clearly disproportional administrative costs for the taxpayer.

CROSS-COMPLIANCE AND RELATED ISSUES

41. For many years the FUW has, on behalf of members, fought cases where farmers have been penalised for what all parties have acknowledged were genuine errors. The rate of penalisation in such cases is often draconian, with multipliers to initial penalties being applied that result in catastrophic losses to income that are completely disproportionate to the errors made.

42. Such fines are made under a bureaucratic system based upon an assumption that almost all errors are the result of attempted fraud.

43. The FUW therefore believes that penalties should become more proportionate, and that an assumption of innocence should be made where rules have been breached, with the burden of proof being placed upon the authorities where any suspicion of genuine fraud exists.

44. The current rules can see farmers suffering numerous financial penalties for single actions that are genuine mistakes; for example, a single inadvertent or negligible action could result in prosecution and fines under domestic legislation, cuts or loss of the Single Payment under EC rules relating to Pillar I payments, and cuts or the loss of Pillar II environmental scheme payments, also under EC rules. For example, the FUW is aware of cases whereby the undertaking by a farmer of a long established and inconsequential practice has resulted in multiple penalisations totalling some £15,000.

45. The FUW believes that to subject farmers to such multiple-jeopardy is morally indefensible, and that moves should be made to bring such penalisation into line with the moral principles long recognised by the British legal system; ie that double, or multiple, ιjeopardy should not be applied.

46. The FUW welcomes the Commission's intention to simplify and examine the scope of Cross-Compliance, and would emphasise the importance of ensuring that farmers within the EU should not, as is currently the case, be expected to compete with those in third-countries who are not subject to such regulations

Milk Quota

47. The FUW maintains its belief that milk quota should be continued as a means by which to manage market supply and minimise price volatility, and therefore objects to the proposals to abolish milk quota in 2015.

48. While we accept that the world market for milk is undergoing major changes, it is the belief of the FUW that any changes to the EU milk regime made to take account of those changes should take the form of a more flexible framework, rather than the complete abolition of quotas.

49. The FUW believes that acceptable prices sustained over a prolonged period must be observed before any increase—let alone the abolition—of quotas is considered. To date, price improvements during 2007 have only seen a couple of months during which farmgate returns started to approach acceptable levels, and moves to increase the EC quota in preparation for abolition are premature.

50. This is particularly the case given that 1.9 million tonnes of EU quota have not been taken up in 2007, and that dairy imports to China, which have been one of the main driving forces behind price rises, fell by almost 20% during the first 8 months of 2007 compared with the same period during 2008. Similarly, the equivalent drop in milk powder imports to China have fallen by 34.6%.

Reductions in EU-15 Payments

51. The Commission is predicting that cuts in EU-15 Member States' Single Payments are likely to be needed from 2009 onwards in order to keep the CAP within the ceilings agreed in the 2007–13 financial perspectives. Such reductions are considered to be necessary to balance out increased spending on the Single Payment in new Member States.

52. The FUW believes that the well founded concerns over the impact that climate change and growing populations will have on food supplies, coupled with the clear central role that faming must take in mitigating the causes and impacts of global warming, highlight the importance of continuing to support economically viable farming communities.

53. The Union therefore believes that such support should continue, and that the introduction of new Member States necessitates a proportional increase in the CAP budget.

54. In the context of such budgetary reductions for the EU-15, and other changes proposed in the European Commission paper of 20 November 2007, the FUW believes that far too little attention is paid to the sustainability of agricultural incomes in all regions and sectors. The Union also believes that parallel measures, such as the provision of legislation to ensure fair returns from the marketplace, are needed to mitigate the possible adverse impacts of the proposed changes, and that such measures would also benefit third countries. We would particularly highlight the misconception, based particularly upon increases in grain prices, that *market prices today are in such good shape*, whereas rising grain prices are adversely affecting incomes in large areas of Europe that, due to environmental factors such as climate and soil types, have no choice but to rely upon incomes from the livestock sector.

13 December 2007

WEDNESDAY 28 NOVEMBER 2007

Present	Arran, E	Plumb, L
	Brookeborough, V	Sewel, L (Chairman)
	Cameron of Dillington, L	Sharp of Guildford, B
	Jones of Whitchurch, B	Ullswater, V
	Palmer, L	

Memorandum by England's Regional Development Agencies

1. RDAs were established in 1999 to foster the sustainable economic development of their respective regions. The RDAs welcome the opportunity to comment on the future of the CAP.

2. This paper sets out the RDAs views on most of the issues identified in the Call for Evidence. The paper adopts the same structure as the questions in the Call for Evidence.

Question 1 *What should be the long term objectives of the CAP? Does the title "Common Agricultural Policy" aptly fit your perceived objectives of the policy? What do you consider to be the main pressures on the CAP as it currently is?*

3. The CAP's long term objective should be to create, foster and maintain a land based industry which produces safe, high quality, wholesome products in a sustainable way. These products should be marketed effectively and the businesses which produce them should do so in a way which allows them both to be profitable and to preserve the environment. These objectives can perfectly reasonably be described as a Common Agricultural Policy.

4. The main pressures on the CAP include how to try to achieve the objectives set out above given the differences outside and within the EU. International trade obligations, budgetary pressures and the ineffectiveness of some existing support mechanisms all provide further pressure. In addition there is significant and growing environmental pressure on the CAP. The role of agriculture in contributing to climate change cannot be divorced from the various support mechanisms used in the CAP.

Question 2 *What has been your experience so far with the reformed CAP? What has worked well and less well? And where can lessons be learned?*

5. The major changes made to the CAP in 2003, were designed to break the link between subsidy and production. Thus far our assessment is that the impact has been rather limited. There are two primary reasons for this. The first is that the changes are to take place over a prolonged period of time and it is still relatively early in that time period. Secondly, farming is a long term business and rapid change is not possible in some sectors. The complexity of the reforms and the well-rehearsed problems over the administration of the Single Farm Payment means that the full effects of changes in the support system have yet to be witnessed.

Question 4 *What short and longer-term changes are required to the CAP's market mechanisms? Suggestions made by the Commission have included re-examination of certain quotas, intervention, set-aside, export refunds and private storage payments*

6. Given that many market mechanisms such as export refunds, private storage aids etc bring relatively little benefit to the farmer directly there is a case for gradually seeking to phase them out. This would also be in line with a move towards a much more market orientated philosophy. The continued use of set-aside as a policy instrument needs to be reviewed—especially if the use of land to provide resources for non-food products including energy is to be encouraged.

Question 5 *What is your view on the introduction of the European Agricultural Fund for Rural Development (EAFRD)? Do you consider that it is meeting its objectives thus far? Is it suitably strategic in nature, meeting the needs of rural society as a whole rather than being restricted to aiding the agricultural industry? How well is it being co-ordinated with other EU and national policies on regional and rural development?*

7. The RDAs consider it vital that The European Agricultural Fund for Rural Development (EAFRD) is seen as part of the wider picture on Rural Development in England's Regions. We consider that the policy background and overall priorities will allow the Fund to achieve a more strategic focus than the previous programme, and delivery partners in England have maximized this in their plans and priorities, but we have concerns that the detailed operational regulatory framework may dilute the potential to carry this focus through as practically and overtly as we would like. Further details on this are given in the subsequent paragraphs.

8. The England Rural Development Programme which ran from 2000-2006 enjoyed some measure of success. So too did the Leader + programme which ran alongside it. However the ERDP 2000–06 was not particularly strategically driven nor was it especially well integrated with other strategies and initiatives. There was some improvement towards the latter part of the programme when the Rural Development Service engaged with the Rural parts of Regional Development Agencies and RDAs became members of the Regional Appraisal Panels which determined grant applications. These panels considered applications under three of the 10 schemes operated under ERDP 2000–06. Those schemes were the Rural Enterprise Scheme, the Vocational Training Scheme and the Processing and Marketing Grant Scheme.

9. Much of the funding granted under these schemes was directed to the farming sector rather than the wider rural economy, although there were some relevant measures. Although the programme was administered by the Rural Development Service there was little evidence of creative links between the three schemes mentioned in paragraph 7 and the remaining more environmentally focused schemes

10. Whilst it is true to say that there were improved links between the RDS and other delivery bodies in the latter stages of the programme that was primarily at operational level with a view to avoiding or reducing duplication rather than at a strategic level.

11. The Rural Development Programme for England (RPDE) will cover the period from 2007–13, and is established under the EAFRD. The Objectives set at EU level for the programme should give it a much stronger position from a strategic point of view for appropriate delivery by Member states.

12. From an RDA perspective Axes 1, 3 and 4 of the new programme become key responsibilities. Axis 1 broadly deals with farming and forestry businesses. Axis 3 addresses the wider rural economy although some measures specifically relate to farm diversification so the primary beneficiaries will be industry related businesses. Axis 4 requires that at least 5% of the total EU budget is spent using the Leader methodology and RDAs have undertaken the responsibility of ensuring that this obligation is met. The EAFRD Regulation sets out the minimum spending to be undertaken against each Axis and DEFRA in discussion with RDAs has allocated amounts to each region to take account of the issues facing each region (for axis 1, 3 and 4). These amounts have subsequently been increased as a result of the use of voluntary modulation. Axis 2,which addresses environmental issues, is the responsibility of Natural England and the Forestry Commission.

13. Following the publication of the Rural Strategy 2004, the regions developed Regional Rural Delivery Frameworks (RRDFs) which provided the opportunity to draw together existing strategies (such as the Regional Economic Strategy, Sustainable Farming and Food Strategy) into a more coherent pattern with clear evidence based targeting of priorities and resources. They brought together partners operating in the economic, social and environmental sectors. The frameworks also provided the opportunity to identify links with other elements of support such as Business Link, Sector Skills Councils and the LSC. This is particularly important for the farming industry which needs to adapt to being treated much the same any other industry rather than continuing to have special solutions devised for it. The RRDFs therefore set a more coherent strategic framework for intervention in rural areas linked to a wide range of broad priorities and they have therefore provided a relevant base on which to take forward more detailed planning for investment programmes to ensure improved alignment with mainstream investment.

14. For the Rural Development Programme 2007-13 the RDAs, together with regional partners, have developed detailed Regional Implementation Plans (RIPs) which outline the key priorities and focus for the programme within the region. The key elements of the plans which underpin an improved strategic and integrated operational focus include the following:

    — The development of a single regional plan ensures that the key delivery agencies for the programme (Natural England, RDAs and Forestry Commission), are working to ensure a shared focus and improved integration across the axes.

— The plans are developed with regard to the strategic priorities outlined in the Regional Economic Strategies, Regional Spatial Strategies and with reference to the priorities identified in the RRDFs which pulled all main regional strategies together to extract their application in rural areas.

— The plans feed into the national programme plan to ensure that the different priorities which exist in different regions are appropriately reflected in the national plan. This is extremely important in recognition of the diversity which applies in the regions, and in underpinning regionally and locally appropriate delivery solutions to ensure greater impact and outcomes for the programme on the ground.

15. The National Programme Plan has been submitted to the EU for approval but we await a decision on this. The RDAs' view is that, at objective level, the RDPE 2007–13 has the ability to take a much stronger strategic focus than its predecessor, and we have worked hard, as outlined above, to ensure that we maximize that. We remain, however, extremely concerned, that the operational details pertaining to the programme will inhibit the practical delivery of a more strategic approach in some form. Whilst the EU policy has drawn together a number of previously separate funds to improve the ability to set more strategic priorities, the EU finance and audit side, through the Common Monitoring and Evaluation frameworks, for example, and the budgetary frameworks, appear to be based on the previously separate programmes, rather than following the integrated emphasis of the policy documents. The requirements for the Leader element also appear to reflect a separate programme in the main, rather than emphasizing that it is, this time, purely a delivery mechanism for the wider programme as a whole. Whilst we may be able to work with these issues to still deliver projects which are integrated and provide considerable added value, the importance of this may not be reflected in the programme evaluation since projects will be required to be funded only from one axis and through one main measure.

Question 6 *Is there a case for a higher level of EU financing of rural development? Do you have a view on the extension of compulsory modulation from Pillar I (Direct Payments) to Pillar II (Rural Development)?*

16. The switching of funds from Pillar I to Pillar II is inevitably contentious. Those who advocate it are sometimes unfairly perceived as not being sufficiently supportive of the farming industry. For the avoidance of doubt therefore it is worth stating that the RDAs have been and remain committed to a farming industry which is competitive, market driven, environmentally responsible, operating to high standards and forming a key part in the fabric of rural communities.

16. It is our view that there should be a progressive switch of funds from Pillar I to Pillar II. Support for rural development will, necessarily, include support for the farming sector but by placing farming in the context of the rural economy it will be better placed to receive support from mainstream funding. A prime example is Business Link. Farming has had a range of bespoke business advice schemes over the years which has to a large extent kept farmers remote from Business Link. Many of the problems which farmers face are relevant to any business—managing change, improved marketing, adding value, risk planning and so on. By directing farmers to existing sources of assistance, not only do they have the opportunity to access a wider range of business support mechanisms which can provide added value to them through raised awareness of their role within the broader "business" framework and business to business networks and knowledge transfer networks but funds are also freed to provide assistance to the wider rural economy too. A superficial analysis would consider switching funds from Pillar I to Pillar II to be taking money away from farmers—whereas, in fact, by engaging with mainstream providers more effectively, farming and forestry industries have the opportunity to be net beneficiaries

17. At present the use of funds under the RDPE is very heavily focused on the farming sector. Apart from some funding to the forestry sector all of Axis 1 funding is directed to the farming (and food) sector and some elements of Axis 3 funding are aimed at helping farmers to diversify. Any switch of funds from Pillar I to Pillar II needs to recognize the reality of the breadth of business interests now located on farms and the broader links to wider rural development and the funds need to ensure increased flexibility in recognition of this.

18. Although the question seeks views on compulsory modulation there is the key issue of voluntary modulation to be addressed. RDAs support the general principle of switching funding from Pillar I to Pillar II. However where that is a result of voluntary modulation there needs to be a clear recognition that such an approach may risk putting the farming industry in England at a competitive disadvantage compared with states or regions where voluntary modulation is not used or is at a lower rate.

Question 8 To what extent has the system of cross-compliance contributed to an improved level of environmental protection? How is it linking with other EU policy requirements such as the Water Framework Directive?

19. The current system of cross compliance is applied in a relatively onerous fashion. A balance needs to be struck since businesses need to be economically viable in order to respond to environmental challenges. Clear guidance on appropriate cross-compliance requirements needs to be developed to reflect this. There is generally a lack of connection between requirements such as the Water Framework Directive and cross compliance.

Question 9 How can the CAP contribute to mitigation of, and adaptation to, climate change? What do you consider the role of biofuels to be in this regard?

20. Climate Change in the context of the impact of the CAP is a relatively recent consideration. For example in the Vision for the Common Agricultural Policy published jointly by DEFRA and HM Treasury in December 2005 it is barely mentioned. There is therefore a need for the industry to be helped to understand precisely what impact it has on climate change and CAP instruments should be designed to take into account those impacts. Climate change has implications for farming systems. Farming may have the potential to adapt to and mitigate against climate change in a beneficial manner, and climate change also offers potential business opportunities for the industry. RDAs question whether the CAP can be a sufficiently sophisticated policy instrument to comprehensively address climate changes issues.

Question 10 The Commissioner has expressed her dissatisfaction at the financing agreement reached by the Member States at the December 2005 Council. Do you consider the current budget to be sufficient? Do you consider co-financing to be a possible way forward in financing the Common Agricultural Policy?

21. It seems unlikely in the current political climate that the budget would be increased significantly. It also seems unrealistic to think that co-financing would be a way forward.

Question 12 How could the CAP be further simplified and in what other ways would you like to see the Common Agricultural Policy changed in the short and/or the long term?

22. The CAP has been simplified considerably by the reforms of 2003 but could be simplified further by the progressive phasing out of some instruments of support (as mentioned in paragraph 6). A switch of funding to Pillar II would provide a greater facility to place farming in its rightful context within the rural economy. Finally a clear focus on payments under the CAP being for public benefit which the market place cannot deliver would help to secure the future for farmers.

June 2007

Examination of Witnesses

Witnesses: Ms FIONA BRYANT, President Head of Sustainable and Rural Development—East of England Development Agency and MR IAN BAKER, Head of Rural Renaissance at Advantage West Midlands (AWM), examined.

Q363 Chairman: Can I both welcome you and thank you for finding time to produce the written evidence that we have had and for coming along today and talking to us. There is a little formality that I have to go through and explain that this is a formal evidence taking session; there will be a record taken—you will get a copy of it afterwards to correct if any errors have slipped in. We are webcast so that there is a possibility that somebody might hear what you say. I usually make some crack about some sort of insomniac, but we have actually found that the odd person does—and by the use of the word "odd" it does not mean that they are strange, but the occasional person listens to these things. If you would like to make a brief opening statement that might be

helpful and then we could get on to our question and answer session around the table. Could I clarify one thing? The paper is formally in the name of the Eastern area RDA but does it represent the views of the RDAs as a whole?
Ms Bryant: Yes, it does. It was submitted by the East of England Development Agency in their lead role for this agenda, but it is on behalf of all the others.

Q364 Chairman: It is useful to have that clarified at this stage. Over to you.
Mr Baker: Just to emphasise the fact that we are here on behalf of all the RDAs. I am here for Advantage West Midlands, which is the West Midlands Regional Development Agency, and both the

original evidence and our response to the questions that you have kindly provided for us today have been consulted around the whole of the RDA network. By way of an opening statement, which I will keep brief, one of the things that we most want to see from the Common Agricultural Policy moving forward is not whether we cast it on common agricultural, or rural policy lines but that it does provide a basis for strong, sustainable farming businesses, which make their connections, locally, make their connections to the market, and to those things that society requires of the land in the wider sense. Those things will include things around environmental management, which is a strong component of the current rural development programme, increasingly elements of quality of life and new agendas which will become increasingly important such as climate change. I think particularly with climate change we have really only scratched the surface of what this measure can provide. We want to see the vision of the dynamic mechanism which can foster change within the land based sector, and the Common Agricultural Policy is that mechanism to foster that change because there is no other real way in which we can produce change. Agriculture is a private sector enterprise; regulation plays a strong part but it is not a state enterprise, so that the CAP is the major mechanism. We do see that long term change is required to get farm businesses in the land based sector closer to the market and closer to what society requires, but we need flexibility within that policy. So by way of an opening gambit that is really where we see the Common Agricultural Policy going.

Q365 Chairman: Do you want to add anything?
Ms Bryant: No, I am very happy with what Ian said. I should just perhaps say on my own behalf that actually outside of my day and evening job for the RDA I do actually farm and I am in receipt of Pillar I payments, but today I am very much here in my RDA job.

Q366 Chairman: Thank you very much. Let me start the ball rolling. Your evidence indicates that the RDAs wish to maintain a land based industry that produces—I think the words you use are safe, high quality and wholesome products in a sustainable way, and it is quite difficult to disagree with that, is it not? Could you indicate, looking forward at the industry developing along those lines, how it would differ from the agricultural industry that we have at the moment? What would it mean in terms of farm sizes, the number of people employed and the location of production? How do you see outputs changing?
Mr Baker: We see that there is potential for farm businesses to operate as much at the local level as they currently do and at the national level because a lot of

our farm businesses are feeding into national and international markets and into national and international supply chains. Sir Don Curry and the Curry Commission made it very clear that the future for a sustainable farming and food sector was one based very much on one that made far greater connections, both to the needs of the communities and society as a whole, and making those connections at a local level so that we are talking about reducing food miles and perhaps even talking about food yards in the longer term, where food can be produced in local communities and communities can make much better connections to their local farms. Where entrepreneurship in connection with the land based sector is promoted, so that the sort of opportunities we are talking about with regard to the climate change agenda, where we are looking at management of energy, management of waste, management of flooding, adaptation and mitigation, those can be addressed very largely at the local scale as well as some of the bigger national mechanisms. The farmers have that potential to operate with their local communities and to offer, for instance, energy solutions such as biomass and supply chains, which do support the local school, the local community centre and local sheltered housing. We are just scratching the surface at the moment in terms of what can be produced. In Sweden (we do some work with some other regions from around Europe and take a more farsighted approach to what the current EAFRD measure can produce) the Swedish Farmers' Union are covenanting with the government in return for the payments which are being made to provide 20,000 new jobs to meet the sorts of agendas we are talking about, so be that local energy, be that local food provision, be that services to local communities, I think that potential is here as well in a far more populous country than is the case in Sweden of course. In our region—because as well as talking on behalf of the RDAs of course Fiona and I know our own regions best—37% of our farm businesses are diversified. That percentage—and we have the lowest percentage of any English region—varies widely and so in the southeast you have 73% of all farm businesses are actually diversified. But in the West Midlands, of that 37% who diversified 90% is about hiring out buildings and letting buildings for various uses. So the potential for using land as opposed to the buildings which sit upon land is really unrealised by nine-tenths of our farm businesses in our region, and I would say that it is not far off that in other regions. So we see that the potential of the Common Agricultural Policy to foster change to the needs of society is as yet unrealised. EAFRD has the potential to move land based businesses on. Potentially the land based businesses and the land based sector we see is huge in comparison to what has already been achieved to previous attempts to diversify the sector.

We think that the EAFRD can be used in a more flexible way this time than was the case with the ERDP before. There are problems with the way that we have implemented it in this country, we feel, and we can discuss those a little later; but we do see that if we are going to meet these agendas like climate change that the Common Agricultural Policy does need to be made even more flexible than it currently is because it cannot at the European level or even at the national level produce a prescription which is going to apply in all circumstances and which is going to provide you with the best way of developing your potential at a single farm community or a community level. So we are looking for more flexibility from what comes out of the future reforms.

Ms Bryant: You added to your question a bit about the change in structure. There is an ongoing trend in terms of increase in size. We already in the UK obviously have the largest average size of farm businesses. There is a trend towards and there has been a trend towards particularly increase in size to meet economies of scale, but I think what might be changing in the future is whether that is from the sale of land or whether it is simply from a change in management procedure. We do need to ensure that within the Common Agricultural Policy there is the potential to support better progression both in and out of the industry, but we are looking at the need for businesses to collaborate together more and collaborate with other sectors more to meet market demands, and I think we will see a change in the management potential not only in individually owned businesses getting together to collaborate but in individuals managing larger tracts of land in collaboration where farmers have looked to retire but not sell, for example. In terms of location and production I think we ought to be seeing both location and investment actually on the farm, but also in joint projects with things like communities, as Ian has mentioned, so the actual investment may not be on the farm but the benefit to the industry will be the same as if it were because it will be benefiting what industry is there to look for. In terms of mix and level of output, what we would like to see is an industry which combines its contribution to the production of food, its contribution to the production of environmental products, its adaptation and mitigation to climate change, both challenge and opportunity, but also maximising its contribution to the growth of the communities and the urban areas around it and making that more explicit and making the industry be seen as a bit contributor to the actual growth and the competitiveness and the success of quality of life of those communities around it. So I think in terms of changing the way we look at outputs is actually looking at it as part of the larger areas, and I think there will be a different mix in terms of the types of crops grown, in terms of the livestock, in

terms of the market development and that type of thing. I think the industry just needs to move forward and effectively follow what Ian has said, to focus on change to meet a different market in the future. It already is but I think the progression needs to move further.

Q367 Chairman: What do you think the effects would be—and I use your phrase here—of the land based industry? Would it impact on the number of people employed, looking forward?

Ms Bryant: I think that the current trend over the last ten years has actually been quite marked in terms of things like machinery and labour efficiencies, meaning reductions in the number of people employed in farming in our region. We have seen a reduction in 10,000 jobs, something like that, over the last ten years. But I think the changing requirements, the move away not just into what might be seen as traditional diversification but actually meeting some major new opportunities in major global markets, major regional markets and local markets means in fact that there is a slowing down of that trend in that actually businesses and jobs are being created both on the farm and on the link locations to farm businesses, and the growth in job creation and the potential growth in job creation in the future and in job security is actually slowing that trend and has the opportunity to do so even more.

Chairman: Lord Plumb.

Q368 Lord Plumb: I was interested in your definition of flexibility. The farmers receive payment under Pillar I and the farmers receive payment under Pillar II with their entry level schemes and whatever it may be. Are you suggesting a mix and match between the two? Is this where you are going? And if you are I tend to agree with you.

Mr Baker: That is comforting. We said in our evidence that we do see a progressive move from Pillar I to Pillar II payments because we have seen through the flexible measures that we are able take advantage of the opportunities that might exist, for instance for creating a new biomass supply chain which will enable a local community to use the local woodlands to provide heat and power to important facilities. You cannot do that certainly through Pillar I and the degree to which we can do that through Pillar II is going to be limited because the resources are so relatively limited if we are going to do that in all the communities where there is potential; so, yes.

Q369 Chairman: Can I just go on to public benefits? You are pretty hard nosed about the focus of capital; it should be very much focused on public benefit. Briefly, what sort of public benefits do you have in mind? Secondly, is there any other justification for the support of agricultural production other than public benefit?

Ms Bryant: I think the perception of public benefit normally within this sort of arena is very much seen as the public benefit of stewardship of the land, and I have to say that the RDAs do not take that position; what we are referring to in the public benefit is much wider than that. So it could be a combination of things. It can be management of the land; it can be, for instance the wider need to address mitigation and adaptation to climate change, which obviously is of public benefit, and is not covered by environmental stewardship *per se*. It can be public benefit in terms of the potential to support local ways of addressing energy and waste management and actually reducing landfill, for example. It could be, looking at the wider amenity, quality of life, recreational ability. But it could also mean in terms of benefit to the public in terms of safe, secure production of food and access to food; it can mean the competitive and successful businesses that are out there in the countryside that are actually producing that food. So I think for us probably yes, the focus should be on public benefit but for us that public benefit can mean a very wide range of things.

Mr Baker: And that public benefit can also be about the process of change. So, the example I used of creating a biomass supply chain, we would not see the long term support of that biomass supply chain being a role for the Common Agricultural Policy, but it could be the role to put it in place and ensure that people have the right equipment and skills set to get themselves going and then you have a sustainable and viable business to take it forward.

Chairman: Baroness Sharp.

Q370 Baroness Sharp: As you have been explaining you have been focusing very much on the business aspects of rural development, indicating that the environmental issues are dealt with, as you say in your paper, by Natural England and the Forestry Commission. To what extent do you anticipate the provision of ecological services—how far will they become a new major output of the farming industry? At the same time, can I ask you if you could expand a little more on your views about the possible contribution towards climate change that you were talking about and the impact that climate change might be having on rural industries in this sense?

Ms Bryant: I would just like to clarify the wording that we submitted in our written submission, which was not intended to suggest that we were ignoring the environmental side of it. We were specifically referring then to the rural development programme for England, and simply saying that we are responsible for delivering the socioeconomic part of that and that Natural England and the Forestry Commission are responsible for delivering

specifically the environmental parts. We have worked very hard together in the regions to come up with single integrated regional plans, and certainly from the RDAs' point of view we already have and continue to recognise the opportunities of the economic potential in environmental assets. What we would like to say is that actually there is already provision of ecological services but we would like to underpin that by saying that ecological should not just mean biodiversity; it is much wider than that in terms of the efficient use of resources, the potential use of carbon capture storage and sequestration in rural development for example. So I think that moves into your supplementary question really, in that actually the rural areas are key elements in meeting and bringing solutions towards mitigating and adapting to climate change potentially in terms of adaptation of the use of land, the move towards crops which are better adapted, for example, to climate change and the ability to use land management in addressing the onset of flood risk or managing flood risk, for example; but also a huge opportunity, whether that is reducing CO_2 emissions through waste management, through addressing diffuse pollution, through providing renewable energy and a number of other areas of activity.

Q371 Baroness Sharp: Do you see the development of the whole concept of food miles, which has been entering into discussions recently, and do you see rural areas meeting local community needs in terms of food to a greater extent?

Ms Bryant: There are a number of issues around that. There is actually evidence to suggest that it may not always be the right thing to look at the food miles issue, in terms of there is evidence to suggest that there are lower carbon CO_2 emissions in a product that may have come from abroad than there necessarily are within the supply chain within the UK at the moment. So we have to be careful in that. On the other hand, I think it is important for the industry to be recognised as innovative and as providing a high quality product in a global market place. But certainly there are huge opportunities which will address not just the business sustainability of the industry but also contribute to quality of life, social inclusion and other things in maximising the potential for those local and regional markets. That is not just about food; that is about energy, it is about other products like construction materials and other products that are produced on a farm that are not necessarily seen by the public at the moment as being linked necessarily to land based industries.

Mr Baker: Why I made the comment about food yards rather than food miles earlier on, because it is possible to construct a mechanism where you consume a lot more carbon by shuffling around regional produce because you have a lots of little white vans running around, rather than by the very efficient and highly sophisticated approach to food we have at present; and why by making specific connections between farmers and their local communities—where you are not going off to a distribution centre 40 miles away and then back again—that more local connection has a potential. But it does require both parties to sign up to that, and there has to be enthusiasm on both sides. I would like to go back to something in the earlier part of the question about climate change, and about the perhaps hard nosed approach we may take. If climate change is the top priority for the government and for us as a society to address I think we do have a right to see more of a relationship between meeting that agenda and the principal environmental measures which are available to land management. We would say that the environmental stewardship schemes do not address climate change issues; they are primarily to address the biodiversity issues, and I think there is the potential to look at the entry level scheme and the high level scheme in terms of the role we can play in meeting what we see as a very key agenda. But at the moment the biodiversity focus is not really having an impact there.

Q372 Baroness Sharp of Guildford: You are thinking particularly perhaps of bio fuels there, are you?
Mr Baker: It is not so much about bio fuels but the production of biomass.

Q373 Baroness Sharp of Guildford: Biomass for bio fuels.
Mr Baker: Yes, which is more about going into local production chains rather than the bio fuels, the liquid bio fuels where much bigger global market forces come into play.

Q374 Baroness Sharp of Guildford: One final question. I come from Guildford, which is in the southeast region and would your move towards rural businesses involve substantial changes in planning law?
Mr Baker: There does seem to be a clear alignment between the sort of changes we expect to see in rural areas and the planning frames within which they exist.

Q375 Baroness Sharp of Guildford: In my part of the world the green belt is sacrosanct, as you realise, and there is a lot of feeling about developments that might take place there.
Mr Baker: The green belt is becoming a bit more of an issue for the lobby groups, is it not, and the CPRE, the National Trust are all thinking a bit harder about the roles that the green belt can play, and indeed I think Natural England is thinking hard about the role it can play. Perhaps as an asset for society it is

under-utilised in the sorts of roles it does play, and it is some of the most valuable land in the country in terms of the roles that it can play for the community, for society and yet some of the worst managed and most blighted land in the country at the same time. So we would see this as a role for much more proactive and linked-up planning in development.
Ms Bryant: In terms of examples that underpin that Ian has outlined, for instance in our region we are currently the leading region for renewables and are in line to meet our targets by 2010. But obviously in terms of meeting climate change we are currently living somewhere in the region of three planets rather than one and we have an aspirational target to reduce that by 60% by 2030 instead of the 2050 that is currently the government target. In order to do that we need to realise our potential in renewables and so far every single planning application for an onshore wind farm this year in the region has been turned down at committee. Rightly or wrongly they were all turned down not on very specific planning reasons; and rightly or wrongly wind may not be the answer to everything but we do need to ensure that the government policy driver for climate change, the use of renewables, the portfolio of energy needs to be backed up by a coherent and a live time framework. We are hoping that sub-national economic development and the development of the single regional strategies, which will have more coherence between the economic development and the spatial planning side, will help to put some of that in place, but obviously there is also work to be done on the national framework side.
Chairman: Absolutely right but I think for us today it is the CAP Health Check on which we are focused. Lord Cameron.

Q376 Lord Cameron of Dillington: Good morning to you both; it is nice to see you again. I want to talk about rural development and in particular the European Agricultural Fund for Rural Development, the EAFRD. In your evidence you repeatedly emphasise the need for a strategic approach to rural development. I would like first of all to establish exactly what you mean by that and how you see the rules of the EAFRD clashing with that strategic approach?
Mr Baker: To start with I think the strategic approach is one which is coherent with the strategic approaches which exist for other sectors and, taking the point that Baroness Sharp was making, coherent with the spatial planning which exists at the local and the regional level. So what we felt—and I think our evidence makes this clear—the previous schemes were a wee bit deficient in that they were national prescriptions which paid very little heed to what was important locally. What we are able to do with the Axis 1 and Axis 3 funds through the new Rural

Development Programme is to tie much more closely to what is important locally and what is important regionally. So, take for instance, the biomass developments in our region. We use less than half of the timber growth per annum, which actually goes into any sort of production or any energy supply chain, and through the development of biomass supply chains we see that we can take up much of the rest of that growth. That same circumstance will not exist in every other region—it will be more in some and maybe not at all in others. But we know that that is a priority and an opportunity for our region. You cannot do that from the national level, you have to drive that from the local level. If you are looking at the opportunities that a particular community might have again, for instance, a community may see that it wants to do something very proactive about climate change—and in Woking and Ashton Hayes there are two communities that really want to get hold of that agenda. You can run with the grain of what local communities want to do and it is much, much easier to put that sort of thing in place if you have flexibility and a local strategic approach which can respond to those sorts of opportunities.

Q377 *Lord Cameron of Dillington:* So your strategic approach is not a stepping back it is a moving down to more local level.

Mr Baker: It is getting closer to the things that matter.

Ms Bryant: I think it is developing solutions to follow what the required need is. It is moving away not from the ideas and innovation and entrepreneurship of individual businesses but it is setting out a very clear steer about what is required in the regions at local level, and it is actually facilitating those projects to come forward and join up, where individuals might have been looking to act before actually joining up to give them a greater benefit as well, and obviously provide better efficiencies in the public sector as well.

Q378 *Lord Cameron of Dillington:* How do you see the four Axes of the EAFRD? What change of rules there would you like to see, either in terms of European or even UK government implementation of the same? And what reforms of the EAFRD might you like to see?

Ms Bryant: If I can start on that? For us the EAFRD gave a better policy steer in terms of taking the four Axes and in terms of emphasising the need to integrate between them and to address sustainable development as a whole, whereas previously there was a much greater division of policy in terms of the environmental, economic and social. I think the RDPE—and, to an extent, this starting at the EU level—the issue has been in matching the policy or not matching the policy within a regulatory framework, which has actually taken a much greater

degree of prescriptive-ness in terms of control and implementing measures, in terms of specifying very closely not only what is allowed to happen, which obviously builds on Ian's need for flexibility, but also how it happens and how it is reported on, and that has actually done more damage to send those Axes into their silos than was intended by the policy framework. On top of that, at national level, as Ian has already described, the allocation of the funds and the use of the greater part of it in a very national prescriptive scheme rather than the ability to use the funding flexibly to meet regional needs right across the Axes has actually added to that problem. Whilst we still maintain that we will work with the delivery of these to try and integrate as far as possible it is a much more difficult job than the Rural Development Regulation intended it to be.

Mr Baker: The EAFRD, was intended to work across all four Axes. Our ability to bring forward integrated sustainable rural development solutions which do bring in the environmental, social and economic together has been undermined—and I use the word carefully—by the decision to put the vast majority of funds into the entry level scheme, where there is no flexibility. Obviously with the high level scheme there is a lot more flexibility and with the HLS you can achieve a lot more in tandem with the Axis 1 and Axis 3 measures—and obviously Axis 4 as well—but the entry level scheme does not give that opportunity. I omitted it from an earlier answer because I focused on the supply side of where we saw the strategic approach going, but it is also about being market led and those markets do operate at the regional, sub-regional level as well. For instance, in our region there is a significant market in the automotive sector and we are working with a Warwick Manufacturing Group and looking at bio composites of plant origin, which could provide a significant niche for new developments and crops going into the manufacturing sector, where they have a much higher value than just going into the commodity market. So those are the other sorts of things where a strategic approach, where we can guide more development in a way that will make a difference.

Q379 *Lord Cameron of Dillington:* Presumably both of you would prefer to see more funds going into business development, ie Axis 3—

Mr Baker: Axes 1 and 3.

Ms Bryant: There needs to be a balance, there needs to be a recognition in order to achieve not only the results desired by the UK government in terms of increasing environmental management but also the value added to that in terms of the private sector investment, and there needs to be a recognition that you need a sustainable business base to deliver those outcomes that they are looking for.

Q380 *Lord Cameron of Dillington:* This is on a primary basis presumably?

Ms Bryant: Yes. And if I may, the other point is that in terms of Axis 4, which we have sort of mentioned, the RDAs are responsible for managing and overseeing the Leader approach. We are very keen to ensure that we should be able to deliver an integrated approach and I think the decision to restrict the use of Axis 2 funding through the Leader groups is extremely unfortunate on that basis.

Chairman: Lord Palmer.

Q381 *Lord Palmer:* As a farmer I have to admit to being a little taken aback when you state that agriculture needs "to adapt to being treated much the same as any other industry rather than continuing to have special solutions devised for it". Would you not accept that agriculture has a much larger impact on the natural environment than any other sector and therefore its activities have much larger and more diffuse externalities? Of course it must not be forgotten that farmers have little control over their own destiny, and of course the right weather at the right time, if you are an arable farmer, can make a great difference, and it is totally outwith the farmer's control. Surely this means that agriculture will always have to have some special label attached to it, would you not agree?

Mr Baker: I think the answer to the question is how special? And what parts of the relationship between the state and the agricultural land based sector should be managed through a separate mechanism, and those things where, the agricultural business needs to be treated like any other business. There are many other businesses that have a whole range of externalities. We do obviously accept—and my family are farmers as well so I understand the sector reasonably well—that they have externalities on the natural environment. However, we believe that some of the potential developments within the agricultural sector are being held back by the fact that farmers have historically regarded themselves as being separate and being provided with separate support, a separate government department and separate business support. If you look at your average farm business and if you asked it to rank its top ten needs I bet you that seven or eight out of those would be the same as your average business in the wider world—it would be about how you manage people, it would be about cash flow, it would be about business management skills, for instance. Providing those through separate and special agricultural sector mechanisms is not always the best way of doing things because it means that you are not getting the cross-fertilisation of ideas that, perhaps, if you sat a farmer down in the same room as a chocolate producer, a logistics manager, a health sector provider they may start to get ideas running between

them that lead to new business opportunities. That is not to say, particularly with a natural environmental relationship, the farmers do not have a very special relationship and the country depends on them to steward that land very well and to provide a whole range of things like access to the countryside, which nobody else can provide and it has to be through their actions. So there is a need for a direct relationship with farmers as a group. So it is about getting that balance right. We feel that historically the balance has not been right and it is still too much towards that the farmer should be regarded as a special sector, and we believe that the opportunities which exist, the sorts of things around climate change adaptation will only be fully realised if farmers themselves are talking to other people in those same supply chains, and the people who essentially manage the markets where their produce is going. There are ways in which we can help farmers to work together to create bigger businesses that have more impact in those market places, so they are not always in the position of being price takers but they can actually create their own impact within the market place as well. But doing that just for the agricultural sector on their own will continue to not really achieve the opportunities that exist. That is the contention.

Ms Bryant: I think our written submission was specifically around the business support area, or in particular around the business support area, which Ian has mentioned. Certainly managing the Business Link contract, which the RDAs do now as a single portal, we have already seen the benefits of opening up opportunities to the farming industry to wider areas of support that they had not recognised before because they were used to feeding into the specific support that was there for them. On the other hand, all the RDAs have put considerable investment into the Business Links to ensure that there are people in there that recognise and understand specific issues that relate to businesses in rural areas, for example including farming. Certainly EDA have just finished or are just finalising a report which was done on CAP analysis on the specific requirements for land based industries and other rural businesses where the supply database or the supplier base has not identified a relevant delivery at the moment. The other thing is that we believe that in some cases the public perception of the industry has actually been damaged more by the explicit reference to it being a particular industry, a special industry and protected in some sort of net than it should have done. There is obviously coverage of things like FMD but I think that in some cases the public perception has actually been altered by the fact that it is referred to so much as an industry over here as opposed to the rest of the world. I actually think that that has affected it and restricted it rather than the other way around. So, as Ian said, there are both sides of the fence but we need to make sure that where it needs to be it recognises that it is part of a wider industry and has a potential to succeed.

Q382 Viscount Ullswater: I would rather like to take issue with you on this concept because over the years, in particular since the war, the farming industry has responded very much to all sorts of activities that the government has done. First of all they wanted to produce a lot of food and so they encouraged a lot of food to be produced. We were very much encouraged to really plough up the hedgerows in order to increase the most amount of good we could do. We did it. We then produced too much food or too much food in the wrong place or the cost structure was wrong. Also, now the farming, the land based industry is responding to the other constraints which are now being placed on it, whether it is through the Soil Directive or Water Directive in nitrate sensitive areas, or the environmental things which are now impacting on the farming and land based industries in a way that is very responsible. What I take issue with is the fact that you are suddenly critical of the way that the farming industry is not reacting to the stimuli which are put in its way. What I am really saying is that farming is in a way nationalised, except it is done on the private sector, but very much the stimulus comes from government—or the restraints come from government as well.

Ms Bryant: I think we are actually agreeing with you; I do not think we disagree. Certainly in terms of my job we are very well aware that the farming industry has responded very much to a national directive, if that is the right way of putting it, and is continuing to respond. I think where we agree with you in terms of, for example, the business support, is that if you have been put in the position, as the industry has been put, where you are being driven in a particular direction you tend to look for guidance from that direction, and perhaps the maximisation of the opportunities in looking outside that have not been realised as much as they should have been. I think they have been realised to a certain extent because there tends to be that top-down and possibly some bottoming up, but it is a very special relationship in that way. All of the things we have said about moving the industry to a market driven approach rather than the necessarily supportive approach will actually move out of that and allow the industry to get away from what might be seen as a restrictive policy driven approach and allow them to maximise the opportunities. There are times—and you mentioned the Water Framework Directive and the Soils Directive—where there are requirements in those that are put in place, but I think it is disappointing that they are sometimes seen as regulatory driven challenges rather than opening up opportunities to business to be seen as exemplars in providing goods and services which match or exceed

their requirements. I think sometimes the relationship between policy and business practice has actually increased the potential to see it as an issue that has to be dealt with rather than an opportunity that could help move more businesses forward.

Q383 Viscount Ullswater: I think from what you have been saying—that you have demonstrated to me anyway—is that it is still a special industry and therefore needs special treatment. If we were looking at an industrial process there is not much public benefit in an industrial process and not much public benefit in a rural industry—apart from the employment that it might give—whereas a lot of the things which you said earlier in answer to other questions, the quality of the land, the recreation, the tourism, is delivered by farming and land based industries.

Mr Baker: Our contention is that it is going to be best delivered by viable businesses and we want to ensure that appropriate support is in place. We want to ensure that farmers have their fair share of the generic support, the support that is available for all businesses because I do not believe that farmers have had that fair share because they have tended to say, "What is MAFF providing? What is Defra providing?" That support is there provided for all businesses. So if you are going to enable our land based businesses to be strong and sustainable they need to have all the tools at their disposal with which other businesses are being provided. We are saying yes, that the farming sector is a special sector because of the whole range of things that it does produce, but when you are talking about the business itself those businesses really need to see the generic support that is available for developing all those businesses, and they are in the same position as all the other businesses who are around them. In our region, in a county like Warwickshire, where less than 2% of the businesses that are in the land based sector, we cannot provide specialist support for 2%.

Q384 Viscount Ullswater: Should dairy farmers give up farming because they are not producing milk economically because they have quotas, all sorts of things which are restraints on an open, level playing field for farmers as against other industries? There seem to be a lot of things which farming does and continues to do over the years, which have actually yielded a very poor return. It is very nice that the price of wheat has gone up to £180 a tonne but it was not quite so happy when it was £60 a tonne a few years ago. It was quite difficult then to have that outlook which I think you are trying to put forward.

Ms Bryant: There are opportunities. You said that industrial priorities just do not provide public benefit but what about the management and processing of waste, for instance, to reduce landfill? That is an industrial process which can. Dairy farmers, for example, have huge opportunities in terms of not only addressing some of their particular business needs in terms of the use of slurry and making more money, making more profit out of slurry as well as milk, if you like, and maximising the use of their waste potential, but also in acting as a location for, for instance, anaerobic digestion, taking in food streams from the local food suppliers and actually dealing with that waste. That is an industrial process and farmers have a huge opportunity to do it. But it is also linked to other factors and what they need to do is to make sure that they are integrating with those sectors; they are shortening the supply chain and dealing direct with their markets. We believe that they will do that, given the opportunity to be seen as an important industry sector alongside others in the right place, rather than just being seen as a special case the whole way along.

Chairman: I am going to bring in Baroness Jones at this stage.

Q385 *Baroness Jones of Whitchurch:* I was beginning to feel a little sorry for the farmers as you have been talking. You are laying big expectations on them from what you were saying and they are already, as we have heard, a complicated market system anyway. What you have described appears as part of a continuum, so we will have secured food produced, we will have better environmental standards, we will have better waste management, we will have quality of life issues—all of that you can say is part of the continuum. On top of that you have to be responsive to the market, and I think there are more contradictions in all of that than you are really facing up to. If I could give you an example, I went to visit an anaerobic digestion unit on Monday and it is great and it does all the things you are talking about in terms of more efficient waste disposal and so on, and that is of benefit to the local farmer. But then the local community has all the lorries trundling in with the food waste from the surrounding towns. The farmer there has changed his farming practices so he has become a single type of style of producer and so that idea of a more diverse kind of farming goes out of the window and therefore your idea of food yards rather than food miles does not fit easily with that. I think there are lots of contradictions in what you are proposing. I would like to know what would be your idealised farming community in an area because I think you are being quite hard on them at the moment.

Mr Baker: We are not saying that everything has to happen everywhere at the same time and all at once, and certainly with the Rural Development Plan for England we just do not have in our hands on enough resources to facilitate that scale of change. You will see that what we are talking about is a longer term

vision for change. What we can do with the current programme period is to demonstrate what those changes might be, and there are enough resources to help us put some pretty good demonstrators in place, but certainly not to help those changes in all the places where they have the potential to take place. So we absolutely agree with you, and if what is coming over is that we want tomorrow a vision of a very different land based sector then we absolutely understand, and most of our colleagues are from a land based sector from around the country. So we do understand the speed at which it is appropriate for land based businesses to respond. So I do absolutely take your point. What we are saying, not that there is a long list of must-dos but there is a long list of opportunities and we would like to see the redevelopment programme as a mechanism to help foster those opportunities and not to be seen as a rather inflexible set of schemes which fit where they touch. I would not use the word contradictions but there are going to be some real conflicts and balances. The example of anaerobic digestion, which will mean change in an area, is a good one and we cannot give the notion that this is a no-change agenda—but that the land and the landscape will continue to change as it always has done.

Q386 *Chairman:* My understanding of your basic approach is something along the lines of when it comes to traditional agricultural products and food production then that ought to be much closer to the market, more market driven, but the public support for agriculture should be really constrained and limited to the production of public benefits. You have a wide view of public benefits and of course there is always the difficulty of knowing who decides whether it is a public benefit and how much the public is prepared to pay for the benefit. Putting that to one side, is that roughly it—that market driven food production, the state coming in to support public benefits that would not otherwise be provided? Is that a rough summary?

Mr Baker: Yes, but I think the written evidence we have given also makes it clear that we would not want to see too much market distortion with regard to the rest of Europe as well. So what we are not advocating is a go it alone approach within England, and that our farmers need to be able to compete.

Q387 *Chairman:* Before I bring in other colleagues can I take it one step further? The end of the day is not your position, at a European level, to say something like, "Okay, we will have a relatively limited amount of money swilling around Europe for CAP. We will not actually put it into Pillar II because we do not think that Pillar II delivers the type of rural development that we want and what we really want is a totally divorced rural development programme, divorced from agricultural support entirely?

Ms Bryant: I think Pillar II could deliver what we wanted if the right policy drivers were in place, though I am not sure that we would advocate that. I think with the current position the answer is what we want is the flexibility to be able to deliver full rural development, regionally and locally built solutions to meet regional and local needs.

Q388 Chairman: But if it is coming through CAP it will be tied much more closely to farming and agriculture than a broader rural development programme would.

Mr Baker: What we are not saying is that we want to have a go it alone policy for rural areas. What we are saying is—and this is substantially about the land based agricultural sector—that there is a whole set of roles it can play but there is a process of change which we feel needs to be supported. Those businesses need to be strong and sustainable. So those are the sorts of priorities we would set for new Common Agricultural Policy. If you are setting Common Rural Policy, if you look at the rural economy of our region it is pretty much the same as the economy of the whole of the rest of the region as a whole—we have roughly the same proportion of manufacturing businesses, construction businesses, administration and organisation. So we are not talking about a set of measures supporting all those other sectors but we are keen to see measures which create better connections from the agricultural sector to its markets, be they local, regional or national and beyond.

Chairman: Viscount Brookeborough.

Q389 Viscount Brookeborough: Just to go back for one second, I think you said that in the different areas between 37 and 90% of farms were diversified?

Mr Baker: 37% in our region.

Q390 Viscount Brookeborough: And the high end is about 90% in others.

Mr Baker: 73% of farm businesses have diversified in the southeast. In West Midlands 90% of our diversified businesses (ie 90% of the 73%) are focused on letting out buildings as diversification.

Q391 Viscount Brookeborough: And diversification is obviously very important in rural development?

Mr Baker: Absolutely.

Q392 Viscount Brookeborough: To what extent do you have to do something different to be considered diversified? For instance, you said that 10,000 people have gone out of farming in the last ten years and therefore presumably there is less requirement for cottages for the farming community, and if you let a

cottage on a long let to a family that were in business elsewhere that would be slightly different from letting it on a holiday let and going into diversifying into tourism. To what extend do you have to do something entirely different to be considered in those figures of diversified farmers? I find it very difficult to come to terms with exactly what those figures mean, but might it not be more important to say what percentage of income earned by farmers comes from diversified business?

Mr Baker: It comes from the June census returns; that is where the information is from.

Q393 Viscount Brookeborough: What do you have to do? Is a wind farm diversification?

Ms Bryant: Yes.

Q394 Viscount Brookeborough: Give me some examples of what people do in order to get into that diversified category in a small way?

Ms Bryant: I think in general terms there are two areas in terms of the EU definition of diversification. One would be what they euphemistically call diversification on the farm, which is looking at something like an alternative crop; so, for instance, instead of growing traditional crops where that is combinable, it would be looking at something like lavender, for example, but it is still effectively growing a crop. The second thing would be diversification, as they call it, off farm, which would be away from production of a crop or livestock, so it could be selling produce from a farm shop, it could be moving into equine and livery, it could be moving into tourism accommodation, but it is away from what might be seen as a traditional agricultural activity such as growing a crop, or livestock.

Q395 Viscount Brookeborough: That is interesting. I would have personally thought that diversification was something other than farming of any kind, whether it be tourism or whatever.

Mr Baker: It is a new enterprise. I can make the report available to the Committee so that you can see the information behind the figures.

Q396 Viscount Brookeborough: Because this gives a colossal figure of different methods of farming just because somebody changes their crop origin. You compare the EAFRD favourably with past policies in terms of the level of integration and the development strategies that it allows for. Are you satisfied that the level of integration that it makes possible will meet the diverse needs of the English regions? When you talk about integration are you concerned about integration or control by RDAs? For example, how well does the new approach enable planning decisions and the implementation of the Water Framework and Soils Directives to be incorporated into strategies for rural development? And on planning decisions, not just on wind farms, do you feel that planning is flexible enough for on farm diversification of the type that I talked about as an entirely different enterprise?

Mr Baker: How long do we have?

Ms Bryant: I think in terms of the integration we have already given our views in terms of the policy supporting integration and perhaps the implementation procedures actually restricting it. We are not precious; we happen to understand the responsibility for delivering socioeconomic elements of it. I think our interest as RDAs would be seeing the right framework in place and seeing the right framework which would support the ability to drive forward sustainable development in the countryside, and that is both on farm and that maybe support for new and efficient ways of food production as well as diversification on farm, or whatever we are talking about. And in terms of support which allows better alignment between the industry and other industries, but also with other funds.

Q397 *Viscount Brookeborough:* You talked about Leader and you did not necessarily all see eye to eye.

Ms Bryant: So we are not previous as RDAs and it is not about RDAs managing the farming sector or anything like that; this is about the wish to see sustainable, competitive businesses in the countryside, both for farming and other businesses. In terms of integration with other European funding, for example, there is an issue about the match funding and demarcation particularly. For example, we have had to put forward very detailed demarcation plans between the regional development funding in the regions and the rural development funding in the regions, and as with last time my main concern over that is that we do not want to see duplication—we want to see alignment but we do not want to see a gap. In terms of requiring a detailed demarcation without the ability to need to do that before you have actually moved in and without the flexibility to actually do that on a audit and transparent process can mean that there are issues and in certain regions the ERDF is almost taking the urban versus rural approach because the RAP is expected to do rural, and I think that is really dangerous and really unfortunate because I think the contribution of rural areas to the development of the wider areas is really important. I think the other side of it is that at the moment RDPE is still very much driven as a national programme. We have been allowed some more flexibility this time and we have had the opportunity to develop regional implementation plans, which are then fed into the national programme but it is still a very national driven programme overall, whereas ERDF is actually regional programmes, and if we were honest

we would like to see the flexibility of perhaps regionally driven programmes for RDPE in future to allow better alignment on that policy basis.

Mr Baker: Viscount Brookeborough asked a couple of supplementaries about meeting the diverse needs of regions and RDA control. The potential is there in the mechanism and I think with the sort of alignment that Fiona refers to having regional programmes for both of the mechanisms we could achieve much better alignment. Planning decisions with single regional strategies for economic development and planning, there should be greater alignment but at the moment that alignment is not great and we see problems between the economic development strategy wanting to put certain things in place which are then countered by local planning approaches. RDA control, we have a very delegated approach to delivery and virtually everything that appears within the regional economic strategies in our corporate plan is delivered by somebody outside the RDAs themselves. So whilst we are responsible for strategy and the sub-national review makes it that much clearer that is our role, that is much more about getting the priorities of things right at the regional level and then that delivery is controlled by a whole range of other people, particularly local authorities.

Chairman: Lord Plumb, modulation.

Lord Plumb: Modulation is in a sense continuing the same theme, I think. Modulation should be about re-balancing the whole industry, one from another—taking from one and giving to another, and of course you make the position absolutely clear as far as the shift of funds is concerned. You expanded on that by being specific on the sort of things that could be supported—supported financially, that is. I could suggest to Mr Baker that there is a digester not far from where he is, in Kelsall, and no encouragement has been given by the local authority to use it since there is no slurry to go into it any longer. So if he would like to work on the local authority and then come and see the farmer concerned it might help! Forgive me, Chairman for raising this! It was very interesting; therefore I took an even greater interest in your particular comments.

Q398 *Chairman:* Special pleading is not part of this Committee!

Mr Baker: I am happy to take forward your query outside the Committee!

Q399 *Lord Plumb:* Modulation—this question comes up every time we receive evidence. There are those who want more modulation, either voluntary or compulsory, and there are those who want less modulation. We would like to hear your views on that because those who have stressed the importance of this have suggested diverting resources away from the industry and others say that it may help the industry. What are your views?

Ms Bryant: If I might start on that? I think in terms of the RDA position in looking at the ability to better support longer term sustainability of the industry through Pillar II, then obviously we would see modulation as an aid to increasing the speed with transferring payment from Pillar I to Pillar II. In terms of your second point, it is very important to us that we understand the reaction of people in the industry when they have concerns about modulation moving the money away from support for them, but I think we would say that actually a lot of what is done through Pillar II provides direct benefit to farming businesses without necessarily investing directly on individual farms. If I can give some examples of that, investment in a collaborative company on a location which is not on any individual farms could provide not only costs to input on the individual farm members of that cooperative business but also opens up new market opportunities realised through the economies of scale and the collaboration which would not be realised by those individual businesses. That is not money going direct on to the farms but it is going direct into their profit lines. Money support into, for instance, training providers is not going direct on to the farms but it is providing free training and advice for those farmers, which will extend their capacity to be able to meet business requirements. The same with things like investment and food distribution hubs is opening up markets. So we would say that actually it is the targeting of the funding towards business sustainability that is important and if that is better done through Pillar II then we still feel very strongly that it is providing direct support to farming businesses, but in a way which actually maximises their opportunity to contribute to the wider economic and rural development.

Mr Baker: Can I add two points, please? Firstly, I think our presumption is always towards compulsory modulation because voluntary modulation does have a distorting effect and it is compulsory on the farmer. Secondly, I think it is beholden on those in the public sector who are making use of the modulated resources to ensure that they are making absolute best use of those resources in achieving a proper benefit and challenging themselves that they are not providing another form of income support through unchallenging measures, and we certainly have some concerns about entry level stewardship from that perspective. Before imposing further modulation we need to ensure that our house is in order in those terms.

Chairman: Viscount Ullswater, on the budget.

Q400 *Viscount Ullswater:* Just on the budget, I think you say in your paper that in the political climate you do not see any chance of the total budget being expanded and I think also you make a comment about co-financing as being unrealistic. Maybe you are being pragmatic in that sense or maybe you know something that we do not. Tell me, do you have any cooperation with organisations of a similar nature to yours around Europe, and what reaction do you get from them about the financing of either Pillar I or Pillar II? Do you see any opportunity—and I think in answer to the Chairman you mentioned that you did not feel that there was too much future in looking at social funds and regional programme funds for financing the agricultural sector?

Mr Baker: I do not think we exactly said that, no

Q401 *Viscount Ullswater:* Perhaps I read you wrong.

Mr Baker: We will clarify that in the answer to the question. Is that the full question? In terms of the overall budget, we recommend a position where progressively we are moving more funds into Pillar II. This should be based on driving the process of change with the sector. As to the overall levels of the budget we would be comfortable with, it is not our call in a sense. But we are very clear that there is not enough in the current pot to drive the process of change at the pace that we want to drive it. Looking at other regions and, in particular, at our region and the southeast, are part of a network which goes by the colourful name of PURPLE. This is about peri urban regions across Europe, comprising 13 regions from Warsaw to Dublin to Barcelona to Stockholm in the network. It is fair to say that there is a diverse set of views, but they have reached a position, which we have also signed up to, on CAP reform, which again I can make that available to the Committee. Increased modulation from Pillar I to Pillar II is agreed on by all, including the French and German regions. So I think that is quite powerful, in answer to your question. Finally, in terms of whether farm businesses should be eligible for support from mainstream funds, that is part of the point we were making; we feel that farmers have for too long not been part of that mainstream and it is very hard for us as the rural leads generically within the RDAs to argue for rural funding from the mainstream funds because they say, "You have the rural programme, so we are going to prioritise this in urban areas." Fiona said we are trying very hard to make sure that there are no gaps. I fear there probably are some gaps between the Structure Funds framework and the rural development frameworks because the urban interests and the levels of funding—I think we have something like 55 million within our region for the Rural Development Programme, and the overall funding for our Structural Funds programme is £250 million. We have 80% of our population living in the urban part of the region and it is a fairly obvious bit of maths for that to be the priority. Therefore the responsibility sits fair and square with the region to ensure that it does cover the whole of the piece. With the current approach there are too many artificial separations which undermines our argument for trying to gain resources for rural businesses and rural communities.

Q402 *Viscount Ullswater:* I heard last week from Wales and from Scotland of the farming economy fragility and also that a lot of the diversification was into bed and breakfast and there was a bed and breakfast notice practically on every farm gate, and therefore it was slightly saturated. Would you see that the CAP has to be the only fund that really supports the social fabric there, or do you think in your view there are other funds that should be touched for that social area of keeping the uplands populated, which I think was their worry?

Mr Baker: We think—and perhaps there are more uplands in the West Midlands than there are in the east of England, even so not huge—the social fabric is something that requires investment from not just European but also state and local authority funds and by far the largest proportion is available through the local authorities. What comes through the national and European resources is really the icing on the cake. Really it is the same answer as before, we want to see rural areas getting their fair piece of the action, and by having programmes which are just rural as opposed to focusing on the agricultural sector, you can undermine the provision of the right sort of support in the right places. For instance, if you have a problem with regard to retaining your upland communities—and I am sure in the Lake District, from having worked there, that is an issue—that is something that needs to be addressed through the funds which go to address the social fabric across the whole of your county or your region. Trying to get essentially an agricultural mechanism to do that job

is just pushing the thing too far, I think. I do not know if you want to add to that?

Ms Bryant: Our region is a very rural region and I think there are issues in terms of access to other farming, as I outlined, but that was more on a national basis. That is another reason for requiring the regional flexibility in that very much EDA is obviously going to be responsible for managing the ERDF programme in the region over the next seven years as well. What we have done is very much align it to try and ensure that the thematic approach we want in supporting a low carbon economy is going forward jointly between RDPE and ERDF. So, for example, we are not allowed to match them because that is regulatory rules; but what we will do is try and do joint projects where we may put in large scale infrastructure for renewable energy through the ERDF but the supply chain contracts going into that and the collaboration support and government training support for farm businesses in meeting those contracts will be done through RDPE. There are issues around the social fund and particularly skills and training, in that government requirements of LSCs are very much around NVQ levels whereas the land based sector quite frequently requires more training of a vocational type approach. But we are working to provide co-financing that supports projects that do address the farming sector. There are ways of doing it but I think the RDAs and other regional partners—not just us, anyone who is dealing with it—have to be quite canny in finding ways around the rules rather than having rules which actually provide that flexibility and provide that support in an open forum.

Chairman: Thank you very much indeed. I think we have done it fairly comprehensively and taken a very broad view of what the CAP Health Check is about. Thank you very much indeed; it has been very valuable and helpful to us.

Supplementary Memorandum by England's Regional Development Agencies (PURPLE)

The Vital Role of Peri Urban Regions

The Peri Urban Regions Platform, PURPLE, calls upon the European Union institutions and the Member States to fully recognise the importance of peri urban regions. The urban pressure felt by all peri urban regions in the European Union constitutes sufficient reason on its own to justify a special position in policy, in any policy at all levels. However, to consider peri urban regions merely as areas under urban pressure would not do justice to the vital role peri urban areas play as interfaces between the urban and the rural world; they have a crucial position in bringing these worlds together. In this sense peri urban regions can usually be characterised by their duality: on the one hand a high dynamic as a result from the pressure from the nearby cities while on the other hand representing valuable qualities of the countryside with their open spaces, attractive landscapes, bio diversity and rural communities. Agriculture also still plays a major part, on the one hand representing highly modern and efficient sectors producing for world markets, while other sectors fulfil a crucial role in maintaining the landscape and offering products and services for the nearby city population.

This duality also implies that peri urban regions more often than not are facing a continuous struggle to find a balance between the needs and wishes of the cities and preserving and reinforcing the multi-functional qualities of the countryside, its agriculture and the socio-economic vitality of its rural communities. The intermediate position therefore offers both challenges and opportunities.

A New Vision is Needed that Better Includes the Role of Peri Urban Regions

PURPLE feels that both these challenges and opportunities are insufficiently met in current policy. This is also true for the Common Agricultural Policy, considering that peri urban regions play a vital role in planning and managing the transition towards multi-functional land use and a sustainable and competitive agriculture.

In this light, PURPLE welcomes the European Union's initiative to organise a mid-term review of the latest reform of the CAP. This offers an opportunity to evaluate if and to what extent the CAP is contributing to strengthen agriculture and rural communities in peri urban areas. There is, however, reason for some caution, since the last reform is still in the process of implementation, implying that the effects of this reform will not be visible throughout.

Nonetheless, PURPLE feels, based on an internal assessment and consultation that there is a need for clearer vision on the future of European agriculture and countryside. Rather than looking back, PURPLE urges the Commission to develop a coherent long term vision for the future, now lacking, in which there will be a specific attention for peri urban regions, their challenges and their opportunities. Both the Mid Term Review and new proposals to reform the CAP post 2012 should be viewed in the light of this vision.

Basic Principles for a New Vision and a New Policy

Such a vision should be founded on a number of principles that together constitute the basis of a future CAP:

1. A Common Agricultural Policy will remain necessary and must be maintained after 2013.

2. The challenges European agriculture and European countryside are facing and the products and services, both private and public, they have to provide for are manifold and certainly not of lesser importance than those of the last decades. The budget for the CAP, Pillar I and II, should therefore be based on these challenges.

3. The future CAP should have more coherence with the Goteberg and Lisbon Agenda.

4. The CAP should set common rules for all of the EU, but should also leave enough room for specific national and regional ambitions.

5. The political and societal legitimacy of the CAP will largely depend on the way and extent in which CAP support will contribute to the realisation of goals concerning:

— the transition towards an economical, environmental and socially sustainable agriculture and towards competitive holdings;

— supporting the development of all types of agriculture respectful of the environment;

— providing the highest standards in food quality;

— respecting animal welfare;

— combating climate change and increasing the production of renewable energy;

— the improvement of public health, both through food and on farm health care.;

— the preservation of vulnerable agro-ecosystems and valuable landscapes by farmers and other land owners, working together with rural entrepreneurs and institutions;

— the protection of these agro-ecosystems, landscapes and bio diversity against urban sprawl and infrastructures;

— the support of the socio-economic vitality of rural areas;

— improving innovation in and development of new products and services that respond to the needs of the urban population such as health care and leisure; and

— the improvement of water management and encouraging a more efficient water use; the preservation of the quality of water resources through preventative measures.

6. These goals and objectives should be founded on the notion of the multifunctional role of agriculture, the multifunctional role of rural areas and specifically on the role of peri urban regions in relation to the nearby urban environment.

7. Support should not only be based on historic entitlements but also on output criteria related to the societal legitimacy and the objectives as mentioned under point 5.

CURRENT ISSUES TO BE ADDRESSED BY THE EUROPEAN COMMISSION ON SHORT TERM

Based on these principles PURPLE urges the European Commission to urgently address the following issues:

Peri urban areas indispensable for competitive urban development

For urban regions to become and/or stay competitive and innovative, awareness must be raised that an attractive peri urban environment is an indispensable amenity in urban development strategies to attract business and skilled work force. From the rural perspective this means that the CAP should offer more room to include the urban environment in rural development plans. Specifically the Leader approach should offer more opportunities to come to integrated urban-rural development strategies. This means that within the framework of Rural Development Plans and Local Action Plans investments in the urban environment are also eligible for support.

More emphasis on Pillar II

In most cases, contrary to original objectives, budget for Rural Developments has been reduced. Specifically for peri urban regions this means that they have less means to encourage rural development, to protect its qualities from urban pressure and to preserve its diversity in landscapes and bio diversity and to promote its culture and culinary diversity. It also implies that there is less budget to promote and support the agricultural sector to become more competitive. PURPLE therefore strongly urges the Commission to convince to enlarge the budgets for Pillar II, also to promote innovation and increase competitiveness of the agricultural sector.

More protection of diversity

One of the main characteristics of rural Europe is its rich diversity, both naturally and culturally. This same is true for peri urban regions. United as they are in their intermediate position between the urban and rural areas, they also represent a large variety in landscapes, culture and localised food production system. This still existing diversity should be valued more strongly and utilised as assets in developing integrated rural development strategies.

Peri urban regions can contribute to combating climate change

Large scale production of bio energy crops, generally does not offer an economically valid option for most peri urban regions, as a result of the higher land prices. Peri urban regions, however, can contribute to the goals to reduce CO_2 emissions in a numerous of other ways, by maintaining open spaces and agricultural use, by reforestation programmes, processing of bio mass and promotion of the localisation of quality production and consumption to reduce food miles.

More attention on installation of young farmers

The farming community is ageing rapidly and the number of young farmers is decreasing. Although this phenomenon can be witnessed all over Europe, this is especially critical in peri-urban areas where instalment cost are higher because of high land prices and where there is a larger offer in alternative employment. Young farmers are key for the future of agriculture and are key to make the transition towards a sustainable, multifunctional and competitive agriculture. Policy should not only be aimed at offering young farmers assistance in taking over or starting a farming business, but also at presenting farming and farm work as an attractive career opportunity. Increased support should be based however on business plans, showing the farmer's willingness and capacities to become competitive and sustainable.

More policy room for payment of green and blue agricultural services based on market prices

There is a greater need for protection and maintenance of valuable landscapes, eco systems and bio diversity, especially in peri urban areas where these qualities are under constant threat from urban pressure. There is at the same time a greater potential to organise protection and maintenance of these public goods in the form of so called green (landscape, eco systems, bio diversity) and blue (management of water quantity and quality) services offered by farmers and other land owners. Payment, both public and private, for these services should no longer be based on compensating land owners for production losses, but on real market prices.

More attention to health

Health problems, problems of overweight and obesities resulting from bad diets and poor nutrition are rapidly increasing, especially among the young. If these problems are not addressed urgently and sufficiently, they will have severe implications for public health and for public health care budgets. Since these problems are most felt in cities, peri urban regions offer excellent opportunities to help address these problems by offering local, fresh and healthy food to urban consumers. This means that the Commission should create more room for public bodies, such as schools and hospitals to cater their food locally. Healthy diets and lifestyles can also be encouraged through awareness programmes in which the urban population, especially school children can be introduced to food production. By making peri urban regions more accessible to the urban population for recreational purposes, would offer possibilities to encourage people to become more active.

More emphasis on the Leader approach

Over the last 1.5 decade the Leader approach has proven its value in rural development by encouraging private and public cooperation and cross-sectorial cooperation. The Leader approach also has shown to be a excellent tool in facilitating innovation. Originally introduced as an instrument for rural development in less favoured areas, under the Leader + programme it has also shown to have an added value in most peri urban regions. Nonetheless we feel that the Leader approach is embraced only half heartedly by Member States, spurred by the realisation that in most cases budgets for Rural Development have declined rather than increased. Raising the budget for Pillar II would offer more room to implement the Leader approach on a wider scale for those Member States and regions will to do so.

8 November 2007

WEDNESDAY 5 DECEMBER 2007

Present   Arran, E   Plumb, L
            Cameron of Dillington, L   Sewell, L (Chairman)
            Dundee, E   Ullswater, V
            Greaves, L

Examination of Witness

Witness: MR WALTER DUEBNER, Head of Agriculture Unit, German Permanent Representation, examined.

Q403 Chairman: Thank you very much indeed for finding the time and coming to talk to us and helping us with our inquiry. Can I explain what we are doing? We are a Sub-Committee of the House of Lords Select Committee on the European Union. We are carrying out an inquiry into the Health Check and also looking beyond the Health Check into the future of the CAP. Technically this is a formal evidence taking session, so there will be a transcript of the proceedings. When we get back we will give you a copy of that when it is available and you can revise it in terms of any errors or mistakes. Thank you very much for coming. The best way is if we just have a conversation across the table. We have got various questions we would like to cover, if I could start. Your minister was saying that German agriculture is "booming" but just about everybody is booming at the moment, are they not. Could you give us an idea of how Germany implemented the 2003 reforms? The boom is partly a function of world prices and a fact of what has happened to commodity prices in the world, but have those reforms and the way you implemented them enabled you to take advantage and have they contributed to the boom? Are there losers as well as winners in Germany in terms of what has happened?
Mr Duebner: Thank you, my Lord Chairman, for giving me the opportunity to highlight the German position on the Health Check and other detailed questions you will ask. In answer to your first question, I was quite impressed with how intensively you read the speech of my minister. I must say that he did not make any link with the 2003 reforms in his speech. It was at the Farmers' Day of the Farmers' Union, which is a great event in Germany every year, and he highlighted, naturally, the efficiency and great efforts of German farmers. He mentioned the reliability of the government and its performance during the German Presidency, which was the main point. The 2003 reforms were adopted when Mrs Künast, a Green minister, held office and we implemented the elements of these reforms very early starting on 1 January 2005. That means we decoupled nearly all premiums from the very beginning. We had a very complicated decoupling model. The starting point was the so-called hybrid model which you apply in Great Britain as well.

Q404 Lord Cameron of Dillington: I hope yours is more successful than ours!

Mr Duebner: I had to read it again yesterday to be able to give you some more detailed information on how we implemented it. First, the premium for arable crops was transferred to the arable areas of the regions. In total we have 13 regions. The slaughter premium for cattle and other minor premiums were transferred to the grassland regions and all other premiums in the animal sector were transferred directly to the farms on an historical basis. These entitlements were equally distributed in relation to the hectares of the farms. That means that the system leads to different payment entitlements per hectare for each farm in the starting phase. We want to abolish these different payments in the second phase from 2010–13. The aim is to establish a so-called regional model with a unit payment entitlement per hectare for arable land grassland in every region. In addition to that, the different levels of payment entitlement from one region to another will be aligned. We have some regions with very high entitlements and other regions with lower, so we want to align them.

Q405 Chairman: Is there a connection between those sorts of reforms? As you said, your minister did not make the connection but do you think there is a connection between the reforms you made and the boom in German agriculture? Were the reforms helpful for the economic development of German agriculture or completely separate?
Mr Duebner: Mostly it is separate. The minister did not say anything about that, that is my personal opinion, but the farmers got a lot more market oriented with this reform. In all sectors you have world market prices more or less, especially now in the cereals sector, and you have another production line which are the renewables, the non-food commodities. In the US, for example, a third of the maize production is used for renewables so there is an immense increase in prices on the world market in these cereals. That is the main point.

Q406 Chairman: Winners and losers?
Mr Duebner: My Minister did not talk about this. Do you want my personal opinion as to who are the winners and who are the losers?

Q407 Chairman: Just give us some idea if you can.

Mr Duebner: It is quite clear that specialised farmers in the intensive production of male bovines and cows in regions where arable land is dominating will lose money because it is put on the arable land. On the other hand, extensive production systems on grassland where there have been no premiums before will be on the winners' side. That was wanted by the former government. The timescale for the implementation of the regional model has been chosen very carefully to enable the farmers to adapt. This will have an effect only from 2010–13. At the moment farmers do not feel this decrease in premiums because that will be in the second phase.

Q408 Earl of Arran: Understandably you have got concerns about the capping of Single Farm Payments, particularly from the point of view of the former East Germany farms, et cetera, where unemployment is already high. Do you have particular worries or situations which you are sceptical towards or, indeed, positive towards?

Mr Duebner: First of all, I must say we have the impression that we are heading in the right political direction. That is what the minister said in the Council last week and we want to stick to this direction because we think the reforms will strengthen the competitiveness of the European agricultural sector. The Health Check should fulfil two main tasks. First, it offers a good opportunity to eliminate certain deficits which arose during the implementation of the agricultural reform and, second, it should be used to free farmers and the administration from further red tape. We made an attempt during our Presidency in this direction concerning cross-compliance and we want to carry on with this path. We consider the idea of capping payments based on farm size to be unacceptable. Germany would be the main country affected and the effects would be very considerable. The rates of reduction discussed would cost the larger holdings in Eastern Germany approximately €300 million in income. This would mean they would have to bear almost half of the cuts in the whole of the EU. Approximately 5,700 holdings would be affected and 96% of these are in the new Länder, the eastern part of Germany. We would endanger a large number of jobs in areas which are already structurally weak and that must not be our aim. The cuts in direct payments also go against the principle of a regionally uniform area premium and the aims of the 2003 agricultural reform, a principle which is accepted in Germany and is finding increasing acceptance throughout the EU, as I have already explained. Under these aims the area premiums should also be granted as compensation for general farming stipulations which go beyond the international standard and as

remuneration for the fulfilment of social requirements. That is the main point. These are the arguments to say that capping is a no-go for us. As I understand from David Barnes, you are thinking in the same direction.

Q409 Chairman: It is a slightly different argument but it comes to the same conclusion.

Mr Duebner: We have another problem with modulation. You are more in favour of modulation than we are. We do not want to call into question the high status of the second pillar of the CAP but we must weigh up some different considerations. On the one hand, the second pillar would profit from the modulation being increased but, on the other hand, the increase of modulation to almost three times the amount would cut funds for holdings in Germany by an additional amount of approximately €375 million. That is €300 million through capping and €375 million in addition concerning modulation. Another aspect is an increase in compulsory modulation would bind further national co-financing funds. With this in mind we reject the increase in modulation for the current fiscal period proposed by the Commission but should an increase in some form be unavoidable the funds would have to be used for agriculturally linked measures and the returns to the Member States would have to amount to 100% and we would have to be assured that the Member States will not be subjected to additional burdens arising from co-financing.

Q410 Chairman: Would it not be sensible in terms of the eastern Länder where you have still got problems of agricultural and structural reform to actually go down the second pillar route because it would give you more opportunities to fund rural development in the eastern Länder rather than putting it directly into agriculture?

Mr Duebner: We have already spent a lot of money in Eastern Germany and if the industry does not want to invest you can spend a lot of money from the taxpayer and the result will not be very satisfactory. We think that additional money will not solve the problem. It is better to keep the money on the farms because sometimes they have more employees than they would need if they had a sophisticated structure. (The answer continued off the record)

Q411 Lord Plumb: I just wonder, my Lord Chairman, on that last point, which is very interesting, if I could ask a question. In the light of the development of some of the large co-operative farms in East Germany, and you said you are against capping and I was delighted to hear you say that, you are going to retain those farms and not split them up because not capping will help those larger farms and yet see more developed. Is that the way the structure of farming is going if that is the situation? Relating that to modulation, you said that our Government was in favour of modulation but that is voluntary modulation, of course, not compulsory modulation, and there is a vast difference. Taking evidence from the people we have been taking evidence from, there are those who see this as a hindrance and those who see it as a help, particularly those who see an advantage in moving money to Pillar II, which is an issue that I think we need to discuss with you because it has been very much an issue in the evidence given. On the Single Farm Payment, you have already referred to the fact that decoupling in the medium-term is on the way and you want to see decoupling continue, and that I can well understand in connection with the reform itself. Is this the end goal, total decoupling? Do you see that as a matter that we should strive for in other countries? In that context, may I ask how you see the balance of agriculture because decoupling to the arable farmer at the moment would be entirely satisfactory because of the current price of grain but in our country it is the livestock farmer who is suffering, and suffering very badly, because of the total imbalance in the whole of agriculture which has suddenly happened.

Mr Duebner: Concerning decoupling, we want to decouple all the premiums because we need equal terms of competition for all Member States, especially in the animal sector where a lot of premiums are still coupled in other Member States. In Germany we only have a few specialised sectors, like potato starch, dried fodder and tobacco, which are partly coupled; all the other products are decoupled.

Q412 *Chairman:* Are you still doing tobacco?

Mr Duebner: Yes, there is production in Germany. We are checking with the sector as to how we can decouple these aids in the medium-term.

Q413 *Chairman:* You would like to see other Member States going in that direction as well to decouple their payments, would you?

Mr Duebner: We would like them to do that, yes, but I do not know if they really want to do it. You will have my colleague from France in front of you in one or two hours so you can ask him, but I have heard that France has very complicated systems and perhaps they want to get rid of it, I do not know. We would like to have decoupled aids all over the European Union, that is our aim because of the distortion of competition.

Q414 *Lord Plumb:* We are very interested in the fact that Germany and Britain apply not entirely the same but a similar hybrid system which caused a lot of confusion in our country. Many of us use the example

of Germany saying, "Yes, they went down the hybrid route too but at least their farmers were paid out on the day", whilst a lot of farmers from 2005 are still waiting for payment. Only a very few but, nevertheless, there has been a lot of confusion and it has caused trouble. You now say that in order to mitigate the distributional effects of moving straight to area-based payments this is a different situation. I wonder at what speed you want to see that change taking place. We fully complain and believe that if we had started with an historic system it would have been much simpler but starting where we did has now caused confusion. You, of course, had a part-historic system and part-hybrid system which was complicated but how has it worked in Germany and why has it not worked in Britain?

Mr Duebner: I cannot answer why it does not work in Britain, I do not know your system.

Q415 *Lord Plumb:* I will tell you afterwards if you like!

Mr Duebner: As I have already said, we are starting the second phase heading to the regional model in 2010 and then we will see how farmers react. Until now they have been quite satisfied. I have not heard any criticisms from the farmers and the prices are high now. What will happen in 2010 nobody knows. For example, if a farmer gets €400 per hectare and the level of the premium in the region should be €300, he will lose €100 per hectare from 2010–13 and I do not know what his reaction will be.

Chairman: He is hardly likely to say "wonderful", is he?

Q416 *Lord Cameron of Dillington:* You are changing over three years, are you? It is not 2010, it is gradual, is it?

Mr Duebner: Yes. Or he gets more, if he has grassland: starting with €200 per hectare in 2010. He will get €300 in 2013. So he will be happy.

Chairman: Are you finding that some of the farmers are now saying, "2010 is a bit too soon, can we push it back further and further?"

Q417 *Lord Plumb:* Farmers would not do that.

Mr Duebner: We took the decision that we would start in 2010. Farmers have not realised yet but when it begins to affect them it will be a different situation.

Q418 *Lord Plumb:* Does this mean that farmers may be taking more interest perhaps in using funding from Pillar II than Pillar I if, as they see it, in 2010 there is the start of a reduction on the Single Payment System? Is there a growing interest or a greater interest, therefore, in environmentally friendly farming and using various schemes that are applicable under Pillar II and not under Pillar I that farmers may pick up thinking, "Well, if the money is going there then we may be able to use it better" and perhaps change their system of farming?

Mr Duebner: We have already supported the organic farming in—

Q419 *Lord Plumb:* I am not talking about organic. It could fit into it but I am really talking about maintaining the hedgerows, cleaning the watercourses, developing some of the areas so there are areas around the arable area which are protecting wildlife and so on.

Mr Duebner: We have programmes in this area but they are managed by the Länder in Germany. Some Länder do not have enough money to co-finance these agri-environmental measures so farmers cannot apply for any support. That differs from one region to another so I cannot give you an exact overview on that. Especially in the eastern part the Länder do not have much money to co-finance these measures.

Q420 *Viscount Ullswater:* I think you have answered quite a lot of the questions about rural development because you indicated, I believe, that the position is that you would rather the payments came through the first pillar rather than the second pillar, partly because you have explained about the co-financing from the eastern Länder particularly. What are the circumstances that various Länder are using to get money through the second pillar?

Mr Duebner: The Länder have a budget in the agricultural sector and then they can co-finance these measures. We have three-fold financing; money comes from the EU, from the federal government and from the Länder. It depends on them as to how much money they want to spend and sometimes they do not have enough money to offer all the measures available in the second pillar, so they have to concentrate on whether they want to support more investment in farming or if they want to support agri-environment measures or other things, to finance development strategies, making studies and so on, or support Less Favoured Areas. This is a decision for the Länder.

Q421 *Viscount Ullswater:* Is the German Government in favour of keeping the Single Farm Payment for as long as possible and not moving the money from Pillar I to Pillar II because maybe Pillar II is not looking after the disadvantaged areas because of the problems that you have outlined?

Mr Duebner: It is rather difficult to answer your question because we have such a different structure in Germany. In southern Germany we have rich Länder, Bavaria and Baden-Württemberg, which

have their own programmes and they can do a lot, and then we have the eastern part of Germany which cannot spend so much money in this sector. They are very reluctant to have modulation or to spend even more money in the second pillar, they want to keep their money in the first pillar. That is the main point. For the time being, on the discussion about modulation the federal government says we will not change the budget for the first pillar until 2013 and that is agreed in the German Government even if some politicians say we should think about a change in this policy. For the time being that is the position of the German Government. In the next few years we will discuss whether we have a vision for 2020 as the British Government already has, but this discussion has not started in Germany yet. We are trying to finalise the consultation on the Health Check and then we will have the issue paper about the Budget Review and we will discuss what will happen after 2013.

Q422 *Earl of Dundee:* What position will Germany take on the Brussels ceiling on funds available under Pillar I until 2013?

Mr Duebner: As I said, this is very difficult to answer because we do not have a position and it has been agreed in the government not to say anything on that topic because we are very busy finding a position on the Health Check. We are commenting on the issue paper from the Commission about the Budget Review and after that we will start discussing how much money we can spend in the agricultural sector in the EU budget after 2013. Personally I think that will depend on how the world markets develop. If we have high prices, such as nowadays, the politicians and even the sector itself will be prepared to lower the premiums, but if we have market prices around the intervention price level then we will have a totally different discussion.

Q423 *Earl of Dundee:* That apart, and as the German position develops for these reasons, how consistent or otherwise do you think that will come to be with CAP reorientation? What are your views on CAP reorientation?

Mr Duebner: We have already reoriented the CAP through the 2003 reforms. That has been a big step. Now we have to have the discussion as to how much money we will spend in the second pillar in future and in the first pillar or if we follow the British vision and say that the first pillar should be abolished, and we should have a free liberal market. Or, whether we still need the money in the first pillar to keep a premium so that our farmers can cope with their competitors in third-countries. That will be the main question.

Earl of Dundee: Do you believe that after 2013 there can be a much better reallocation of resources? In what particular forms would you like such reallocation to take?

Q424 Chairman: If at all.

Mr Duebner: I can only give you my personal view on that. (The answer continued off the record)

Q425 Lord Cameron of Dillington: I have always thought that Germany is capitalist, probably one of the most free trade nations in Europe and yet you have always had this blind spot about agriculture. From what you are saying you do see that possibly eventually Germany could have free trade agriculture but paying to have higher standards or maybe higher environmental standards or the state paying only for goods that it might require, such as access or environmental goods or something of that sort. It sounds to me as though that is the sort of vision that is not totally alien to what you are saying.

Mr Duebner: It is not alien to me but perhaps to a minister. If you talk to Mrs Künast from the Greens she may agree with you.

Q426 Lord Cameron of Dillington: I have had conversations with her and I think she does.

Mr Duebner: But if you talk to a Conservative minister he would have a different approach.

Q427 Lord Greaves: Mr Seehofer suggested that we are on the verge of a new Green Revolution. Can I ask you, first of all, what are the implications, if that is true, for farm incomes and production productivity? Secondly, what contribution could that make to adapting to climate change and mitigating the effects of it?

Mr Duebner: On the first part of your question, productivity does not mean that we should use GMOs. He is quite reluctant on GMOs but, of course, you can increase productivity without GMOs too. What we have recognised in the last two years is that farmers have a new production line, and these are the renewables, so they do not depend on food production alone any longer, they have another outlet, these are the renewable resources, and that is what he meant by the Green Revolution. That is positive for agriculture because prices are rising. We do a lot to support this production of renewables in Germany. We have a programme of about €50 million to support research, demonstration and market launch of non-food commodities. At the beginning of next year we will have a biomass research centre in Leipzig. All in all, the German Government is very committed to the development of renewable resources which, as I have already

mentioned, provide new income possibilities for the farmers. That is the main point.

Q428 Chairman: In the renewables are you looking beyond biodiesel and ethanol to third and fourth generation biomass production?

Mr Duebner: Yes.

Q429 Chairman: There is a lot of scepticism basically about where we are now with the first generation and people tend to be looking a couple of steps forward. Is that what is happening in Germany?

Mr Duebner: Yes, but we need a lot of time. It is not for tomorrow but for ten or 15 years to develop the second generation of biomass. That is why we have created this centre in Leipzig to support research in this sector. Producing biodiesel from rapeseed or bioethanol from maize may have all these negative effects on the demand side with prices shooting up, for example in Mexico, where the poor people temporarily could not afford to have their maize meals.

Q430 Lord Greaves: What is the balance here? There is a reaction against biofuels and so on, is there not, from people who believe that we are heading for a new serious food shortage and this is already reflecting itself in the increased prices and taking land out of food production is not the way forward.

Mr Duebner: We have a reserve in Germany. Nowadays 13% of the arable area is used for the production of renewables and we could double this percentage without having problems with the food supply.

Q431 Lord Greaves: This is in terms of Germany's own food needs?

Mr Duebner: Yes.

Q432 Lord Greaves: Or not Europe.

Mr Duebner: Yes.

Q433 Lord Plumb: Is that based on a constant level of production or on the possibility of an expansion of production?

Mr Duebner: It is status quo.

Q434 Lord Plumb: On status quo?

Mr Duebner: Yes. On the other hand there are still a lot of production reserves in Eastern Europe, in Ukraine, Russia, where production could easily be doubled or tripled.

Q435 *Chairman:* It is called market economies.
Mr Duebner: It is a pity.

Q436 *Lord Greaves:* What about the climate change side of it? Do his comments about the Green Revolution and so on have any bearing on climate change at all?
Mr Duebner: Yes. We have a decision by the European Council to raise renewables up to 20%, so we have to fulfil this aim. This will contribute to the problems that we have with climate change in a positive way.

Q437 *Lord Greaves:* On a slightly wider issue, if the climate of Europe is changing and getting hotter, wetter or drier in different places, how is that going to affect the kind of agriculture that takes place in Germany?
Mr Duebner: As far as I know it will have a positive effect, as I have heard in Great Britain too. That is why you are advocating a higher amount of area for

wine, as I understand it. You are aiming at raising the de minimis rule from 25,000 hl to 50,000 hl.

Q438 *Lord Plumb:* We are not up to quota yet!
Mr Duebner: For Germany it will have positive effects but southern Europe will have problems, especially Spain and Italy perhaps. We probably will not have any major problems in Germany with the climate change.

Q439 *Chairman:* The interesting thing on your renewables is your energy policy, although we cannot get into this, saying no to nuclear and then a heavy dependence upon Russian gas.
Mr Duebner: It is very difficult.

Q440 *Chairman:* You have got some real energy security issues.
Mr Duebner: Yes.
Chairman: Thank you very much indeed, that is very helpful.

WEDNESDAY 5 DECEMBER 2007

Present   Arran, E   Plumb, L
           Cameron of Dillington, L   Sewell, L (Chairman)
           Dundee, E   Ullswater, V
           Greaves, L

Examination of Witness

Witness: Ms KIRSTEN HOLM SVENDSEN, Minister Counsellor, Danish Permanent Representation, examined.

Q441 *Chairman:* Many thanks for coming. Let me formally say that we are a Sub-Committee of the House of Lords Select Committee on the European Union. We are carrying out an inquiry into the Health Check and looking beyond the Health Check at the future shape of the CAP. This is a formal evidence session so there will be a note taken but clearly the opportunity arises to go off the record if you wish to. You will get a copy of the evidence so you can correct it or revise it. The best thing is if we go through and have a conversation around the questions, is that okay?
Ms Svendsen: That is fine.

Q442 *Chairman:* We are looking forward but to look forward it is always a good idea to look back a bit. Go back to the 2003 reforms and what was the impact in Denmark? What sort of changes did it make to the way your agriculture operates?
Ms Svendsen: I think the major impact in Denmark has been further concentration. A lot of farms have closed down in the period, but that was foreseen and we were already on that track. Further concentration, larger farms. This process is still going on and a lot of people have gone out of business and only the very large, professional people are able to compete now. Of course, there are still some smaller farms but they will have to specialise. The trend now is that a lot of new enterprises are popping up in the countryside, like small dairy farms with their own shops, their own dairies, specialising in organic or niche products. That is the way for small farms to survive. On a large scale, as you probably know, Denmark is a big pig farming country with a large export of pig meat. That is our bread and butter in the farming community and these farms are very big and are now so big it has become an environmental problem. We are at the point now where we have to do something about that otherwise we will not be able to allow the farms to become any bigger for environmental reasons. That is the general picture but, of course, there are exceptions. The general picture is concentration and more intensive farming going on.

Q443 *Chairman:* So you felt the pressure really of market forces, consolidation?

Ms Svendsen: Yes, certainly. It was foreseen and also the farmers knew this was going to happen. We are a very small country and are producing much more than we can use ourselves. We are dependent on trade. We knew that we had to become even more competitive at a point. The situation is the same at the moment where the government is on the liberal side in the European Community and also in the Doha Round. We do see trade liberalisation as a must for a country of our size in the globalised world. That is the broad picture.

Q444 *Chairman:* Having gone through that, what would be your attitude to capping?
Ms Svendsen: I must say here that the Danish Government has not made its position clear yet on capping. We are looking at it. From a personal point of view I would say the probability is we would not be very happy about capping. Looking at the way our policy is going and our liberal way of thinking, you encourage people to become more competitive, to extend their farms to become more competitive, and once they extend their farms you cap them. On the other hand, there is also the point of view the Commissioner has brought forward that there are economic advantages in being a large farm. I do not know whether there will be some kind of balance struck. From a strictly personal point of view I think the general attitude of the Danish Government will be to not like capping very much.
Chairman: I have strayed into Lord Arran's area.

Q445 *Earl of Arran:* In particular on the Health Check, the case-by-case move towards full decoupling, as you have yet to decouple fully what is your view on this element of the Health Check?
Ms Svendsen: I think I can say at this point that we do want full decoupling. There is only a small amount still coupled in Denmark. The effects would not be very hard at this point in time because prices are what they are. We do see decoupling as a part of the market orientation process. I think I can quite firmly say that the government's position will be that we will pursue full decoupling.

Q446 *Earl of Arran:* You mentioned a lot of farms and you were generalising when you said that many farms in your country have closed down. Are they mostly dairy or arable?

Ms Svendsen: We do not have that many arable farms.

Q447 *Earl of Arran:* It is the dairy?

Ms Svendsen: Also pig farms, the smaller pig farms. Pig farming is the majority and the smaller farms cannot survive. They are still closing down at the moment because of the cereal prices.

Q448 *Earl of Arran:* Indeed, yes.

Ms Svendsen: That is happening in our country too.

Q449 *Chairman:* I think there was a survey in Britain which found that a significant number of people, particularly young people, thought that bacon came from an animal called "Danish"!

Ms Svendsen: I would believe that.

Q450 *Viscount Ullswater:* We have not really talked much about these different pillars yet and you have not really identified what the position of the Danish Government is towards Pillar I and Pillar II, but if I could ask about Pillar II that might reflect on your views on Pillar I. Do you see that move has been successful in Denmark? Are the funds there separate and distinct enough to be able to create the encouragement you need for rural development? Perhaps in this whole area, do you support the increase in modulation in order to move those funds from Pillar I to Pillar II?

Ms Svendsen: That is a fairly broad question.

Q451 *Viscount Ullswater:* It is.

Ms Svendsen: Let me start by pointing out that there is a parliamentary decision in Denmark saying that in the long run we should abolish all direct support to farmers. This is the basis for the government's thinking. Of course it has some conditions attached to it. It has to be on an even footing with our competitors, of course, and it also links up with the WTO negotiations. That means we place great emphasis on the activities in Pillar II, but at the same time it is fair to say our thinking at this moment is the way it is construed is not efficient enough for a country in our position. Again, I have to emphasise that it is probably different from the British background because we are a very small country producing a lot of agricultural products that we have to export. We would like to spend a lot more funds on innovation, for instance, research, to make sure that all the industries in the countryside can still live there and develop. Maybe not basic farming because a lot of that technology is in place, but there is still a lot to be done. We would like to spend a lot more on

developing technology and techniques in the farming community and in the processing industry. There is also a point of view on the environment. We are working with some ideas that maybe we could use Article 69 in Regulation 17/82—I do not know if this makes sense to you—but that Article is a little bit rigid and if it was made more flexible maybe you could use that for more environmental purposes and you could spend more funds on innovation and research in this area. This is just the thinking that is going on, it is not a firm position. That is what we are working on, trying to develop more technologies and on the environmental side. For instance, in relation to the problem with climate change, which is also emphasised in the Health Check, maybe we could use technologies in the countryside to store CO_2 or develop something along those lines, broader ideas on spending the funds efficiently. I do not think I can be more specific here because it is early days to be talking about that. Those are the general ideas we are working on within the Danish Government.

Q452 *Viscount Ullswater:* Do you think with the particular environmental problems with pig farming on a big scale in Denmark that the Single Farm Payment is required in order to assist with those problems if the market price at one time or another dips or the costs of production, like the increase in grain prices, make it much more difficult to cope with the environmental problems and Pillar I payments are, in fact, an assistance to farmers to get through it or improve their environmental handling of the slurry and all that sort of thing, or could it all be done through Pillar II?

Ms Svendsen: The general position is we would rather spend the money on developing technologies to solve these environmental problems. I can safely say that is the government's position. It is also the farmers' own position that they would rather not have direct support because it does give them a political problem in Denmark to be on the receiving end of support and they would rather be free of it, but it depends on the situation and whether the competitors are on an even footing, of course. Again, that explains why we work very hard for more trade liberalisation and getting rid of support everywhere else. Coming back to your question about modulation, it is clear from what I have said, I hope, that we would be supportive of increased obligatory modulation.

Q453 *Lord Plumb:* But not voluntary?

Ms Svendsen: No, thank you. Not voluntary.

Q454 *Lord Cameron of Dillington:* What percentage of the rural economy in Denmark is agriculture? In England it is only 4% or 4.5%, even in rural England. In terms of Pillar II funding, ie is there a lot of other business and entrepreneurial activity going on in the countryside?

Ms Svendsen: Yes, there is, because agriculture is such a concentrated business. I cannot say how many farms we have, about 30,000 these days, but there is only one slaughterhouse covering the whole of Denmark. There are some very small ones but there is only one major slaughterhouse that opened just two years ago. It is really huge. It is very, very modern with robot technology and all that stuff. It does show that the concentration is what it is all about here.

Q455 Lord Cameron of Dillington: That is just agriculture but with broadband and other businesses the countryside is full of other businesses.

Ms Svendsen: It has other businesses, of course, but as in other smaller countries it tends to concentrate on the outskirts of the larger cities because that is where you have the infrastructure for it. The picture in Denmark is that the smaller communities are dying out, the villages, the smaller towns, they are losing all their shops. We have just had a reform of the whole county set-up in Denmark and all the little communes have been merged into larger communes and that has an impact on how things are done because they close the little town halls and they close the libraries. There is a need to do something in the countryside and we do see the Rural Development Programme as a tool for supporting and boosting life in the countryside.

Q456 Lord Greaves: Why should that be European level funded activity? If rural development like that is necessary in communities in Denmark, why is that not a matter for Denmark? Historically, the CAP started because Europe thought that it was necessary to support food production. It continues because it is politically impossible, or so far it has been politically impossible, not to continue it because of political pressures in some of the larger countries. If the trend is towards reducing direct subsidies all the time, and you are saying doing away with them completely, why should there be any funding left at all at the European level?

Ms Svendsen: The general view of the Danish Government is if you do want to have a Common Agricultural Policy it has to go on being common because re-nationalisation of support is not something that would be helpful to us at all. We all know the theories about state aid and competing via your Treasury but it is not a situation where we would be a winner because we are just a small country with a very small economy. We do support the view that if we do have a common policy it has to continue to be common. Then again the whole philosophy behind the switch from Pillar I to Pillar II is if you make the farms more efficient, more competitive, they have to become larger and that means there will

be some activity in the countryside that you cannot have, but that is not a structural development, that is very healthy for the economies. That is not just the case for the Danish economy, it is the same for everybody else because you have other industries in the countries, and let me just mention tourism. If there is no activity in the countryside the tourists will not come there because they need to have ice cream and have a meal or whatever, something to look at.

Q457 Lord Greaves: I understand the whole environmental side of Pillar II and why that is to do with agriculture and why that might make it necessary to keep a Common Agricultural Policy going not to support agriculture but to make sure that agriculture is doing things in the right way, but I do not understand why a Common Agricultural Policy at a European level has anything to do with keeping libraries going in towns or developing non-agricultural businesses or supporting tourism or any of this stuff. I can see lots of reasons why this should take place but I do not understand what it has got to do with a European level Common Agricultural Policy.

Ms Svendsen: I do not know whether it is out of my remit to answer that question because it is highly political, of course. This is a personal point of view. The reason I see behind it is that it is balancing the effects of removing support from agriculture. I suppose we do feel since we are doing this to agriculture we have to do something to take away the bad effects. I must say this is something that is more of a personal view because we are getting to a point where I think you should have higher level officials answering these questions.

Q458 Lord Plumb: Nevertheless, it is a very interesting point. Do you find in the process of some of the farmers leaving their farms and so on, that people are moving from industrial areas to buy those farms to convert the buildings for other use into the possibility of small businesses? We are finding that is happening in Britain.

Ms Svendsen: Yes.

Q459 Lord Plumb: It is regenerating the village in many cases. At least they are taking capital into those areas and so on. Is that happening in Denmark or not?

Ms Svendsen: Not very much. At the moment the main picture is one of abandonment.

Q460 Chairman: Straight abandonment?

Ms Svendsen: Yes, unfortunately. I will mention an example. There was a big, I will not say scandal but a television broadcast where you saw a farmer who had left his pigs to die in the pigsty and you saw the trucks taking out the dead pigs. It was really terrible.

There was an animal welfare issue. The farmer had not been able to survive the increasing prices of feed and he had just left everything, "I can't handle it", and he had a breakdown. The whole focus was on the animals and not on the person. That describes the political atmosphere that agriculture has to cope with in Denmark. The farmers are not very popular because they are people who just live off support and maltreat their animals, even let them die, and you can see that on television. Being a farmer is not a very good environment to live in. If you cannot survive being a very professional farmer, extending your farm to a competitive level, there is nothing much else to do. People have been educated as farmers and you cannot just switch to something else. Then you are dependent on your wife's income, because normally there is a spouse who has a job in the city or something like that, and if you cannot live off that you have to find something totally different and today you do not see many small industries. You see a little bit but that is in the farming business, like these small dairy farms producing their own cheeses of a specialised nature with shops. You can see a lot of shops connected with farms, especially organic products, but not totally different industries which is what you were asking, not yet, but we hope that will be possible.

Q461 Lord Plumb: Is there a planning problem in Denmark? If people were willing to move out of an industrial area, for instance, would the planners object or is that not an issue?
Ms Svendsen: No, that is not an issue. I would not say that is an issue. You are dependent on having a family living off the income and normally one of the family may be willing to move and the other one is dependent on a job in a city somewhere and that makes it very complicated to leave your security.

Q462 Lord Cameron of Dillington: Do people retire to the country at all? That is a feature of England, everyone's ambition is to earn enough money to go and retire to the countryside.
Ms Svendsen: No.
Lord Plumb: In order to spend it.

Q463 Lord Cameron of Dillington: In order to spend it, exactly, or quite often to start a small business, which is what they usually end up doing.
Ms Svendsen: What we are seeing now is younger people with families moving out further away from the city but that is also because of increasing housing prices. You would have to do an analysis of causality. You do see people stating they want to see their families, their children, grow up in the fresh air, a green environment and stuff like that. There is a consciousness that the countryside is nice but it should not be smelly and there should not be flies.

Lord Greaves: And not pig slurry.
Chairman: Certainly not pig slurry!

Q464 Earl of Arran: Has this reflected at all upon the price of agricultural land in Denmark?
Ms Svendsen: Agricultural land is still quite expensive because if you are a professional farmer and you do have a large farm you can make a very substantial amount of money, but you also need a lot of land to be able to secure a large enough area for the manure. That is why land is still quite expensive.

Q465 Lord Plumb: How expensive?
Ms Svendsen: I have not got any prices with me. Maybe it does not make any sense compared to British prices. It does take quite a substantial amount of money to start up as a farmer today and it is becoming a problem for the younger farmers because they need a lot of land.

Q466 Chairman: Can I go back to something you mentioned earlier. You say you have got a parliamentary decision basically moving away from direct support.
Ms Svendsen: Yes.

Q467 Chairman: And trade liberalisation is a key objective. Then you say, quite understandably, there are conditions attached to this and these conditions are fair competition effectively. How do you get there because your competitors in the world market, the argument is always they do not have the environmental costs, they do not have the animal welfare costs, they do not have other sort of costs that are put upon the European farmer? How do you deal with the issue of fair competition?
Ms Svendsen: You are looking at me as a representative of Denmark and I do not think Denmark can deal with that and that is why we are a participant in the European Union's negotiations in the Doha Round.

Q468 Chairman: I meant it generally, not just you individually or you as Denmark even, but we as Europe.
Ms Svendsen: The WTO is a factor there.

Q469 Chairman: The WTO has stuck fairly rigidly to saying, "We talk about trade liberalisation and these are other issues and they must be dealt with in another context". The WTO has been very reluctant to take that on.
Ms Svendsen: I know they have been very reluctant but you have to take the steps you can politically. At the moment the price situation is good for liberalisation and we have seen some steps towards it from the European Community. We have been talking about intervention and we have not been able

to abolish it altogether but the situation is in favour of doing this and we have now decided to spend import duties on grains. There are steps moving in the right direction. I understand what you are getting at, that we should fill up the gap where we have stricter rules on the environment and animal welfare but it is going to be very hard to point out how much that is worth in terms of support. Of course, looking at this aspect is also part of the Health Check and it is mentioned that we should look at the special conditions for European agriculture and the environment and climate also. We have to work with it but it is early days to say exactly how we are going to do that. From what I said before on Pillar II, our thoughts circle around doing something with the funds in Pillar II to solve some of these environmental problems in a different way, doing more research, innovation, getting rid of the pig smell, for instance. If you could do that, that would be very helpful.

Q470 *Viscount Ullswater:* How much renewable energy are you being able to get through digesters of pig slurry and things like that? Is there any work being done in that area?
Ms Svendsen: Yes, there is work being done but not a lot. Our main efforts on renewable energy at the moment are still in the windmill area but we are doing research.

Q471 *Viscount Ullswater:* Because that might get rid of the smell as well.
Ms Svendsen: We are trying to research in other areas to eliminate smell.

Q472 *Chairman:* Perfumed slurry!
Ms Svendsen: No. I do not think the cover-up strategy is a very good one.

Q473 *Viscount Ullswater:* Just to go back to something you said earlier about the position of the Danish Government wanting to move away from Single Farm Payments, is that also the position of the farming community as well?
Ms Svendsen: Yes.

Q474 *Viscount Ullswater:* You were talking about the smaller farmers. Are they under such pressure that they have to agree with that sort of thing because it is obviously putting their livelihoods at risk?
Ms Svendsen: The government's partner in the hearings here is the Danish Agricultural Council, which is the organisation that represents the farming community, and they are thinking along the same lines. In that sense it is fairly easy going if you talk about it politically, but there are other elements, for instance the environmental aspect and how much of

the Pillar II money should we be spending on the environment and it is a lot, yes.

Q475 *Earl of Arran:* If I remember right, I think you said there is only one major slaughterhouse in your country.
Ms Svendsen: Yes.

Q476 *Viscount Ullswater:* What distances, therefore, do farmers have to take their stock to this slaughterhouse?
Ms Svendsen: Not very far. In the whole country the furthest distance is about 400 kilometres and this slaughterhouse is stuck right in the middle of the country. Depending on the prices, some farmers will take their pigs to Germany to be slaughtered and there we are straight into the issue of animal transport and transport times, which I was not really expecting to be talking about! I suppose everybody knows the Danish issues, that we have stricter rules in Denmark than in the European Union as such and it is an issue for us. That is not a Ministry of Agriculture issue, it is handled by the Ministry of Justice.

Q477 *Chairman:* Can we go back to the phasing out of direct support. As you look around amongst your colleagues rather than the states, do you see any close allies on that issue?
Ms Svendsen: Maybe not quite as liberal as Denmark, we are at the far end here but, yes, we do have allies there.

Q478 *Chairman:* Who would they be? Who would you look to?
Ms Svendsen: For instance, we would look to you.

Q479 *Chairman:* Anybody else out there?
Ms Svendsen: We would also look to the Dutch and to some of the new Member States. We would look to the Czech Republic, for instance, the Baltic States, and to a certain extent to Germany. Sweden, of course, but Sweden and Finland are in a different situation. Finland is in a support situation.

Q480 *Chairman:* They need it.
Ms Svendsen: They need support to have any agriculture at all but that is another discussion altogether as to whether they should have that support. (The answer continued off the record)

Q481 *Chairman:* Let us be brutally frank here. Do you see any change in the traditional approach of the southern European countries on trade liberalisation?

Ms Svendsen: (The answer was given off the record)

Q482 *Lord Plumb:* Following what you have been saying on 2013 onwards, let us assume at that stage everybody accepts what you have said, that we are in the final stages perhaps of removing direct support on commodities. One of the reasons for commodity support, which has not been mentioned now and it rarely is, is that over the years where there has been commodity support country-by-country it has been there to try to create stability.
Ms Svendsen: Yes.

Q483 *Lord Plumb:* If we lose that entirely, and are we not witnessing a situation at the moment where grain prices are nearly three times bigger than they were this time last year, if we are going to face that in 2013 onwards, should there not be still some sort of safety net at a low level which is at least going to protect not just the farmer but the industry from those fluctuations, because the fluctuations are not just farming fluctuations, they are consumer fluctuations, and the retailer will say, of course, "Okay, we are now getting the commodity very cheap but if we pass that to the consumer we can't get the price up again" and vice versa? Do you not see ahead a problem here? I have to say I have lived long enough to live through a lot of changes in agriculture policy over the years.
Ms Svendsen: I cannot answer that question in an official capacity because I do not think we have a firm position on that point but I see what you are getting at. I would say that maybe my government's position at the moment would be fluctuation is part of the market economy. That would be the liberal answer to that. Once the consumers and the voters see what the consequence of this policy is there might be a little bit of softening. This is a purely personal view. I would not be able to say what my government's position would be.

Q484 *Lord Plumb:* I think I asked the question on a personal basis.
Ms Svendsen: It is impossible to answer because the policy does not go that far. Of course there will be fluctuations and you will see people taking out the Treaty and saying the Common Agricultural Policy is made for having stable supplies to the people of the European Union and maybe we could have a debate on that because we have never seen a debate on the Common Agricultural Policy in any way when we have talked about Treaty reforms, it has never been an issue because it is too sensitive. Maybe there will come a time when we can have a fundamental debate about what the Common Agricultural Policy is all about. Maybe that would be a good thing and also for people to understand that bacon does not come

from an animal called Danish but people are producing it. Maybe we should welcome that.

Q485 *Lord Plumb:* You will keep that commodity going through quality, there is no doubt about that, everywhere you go in the world that is so. Since my son learned his farming in Denmark I have to say that.
Ms Svendsen: Oh, I see.
Chairman: A nice, easy one to finish off on the Budget Review.

Q486 *Earl of Dundee:* What are Denmark's future priorities for agriculture and also its prescription to EU policy after 2013?
Ms Svendsen: Maybe I should start by looking back and say that normally agriculture is not a priority when we are talking budgets, not at all, it is not a priority.

Q487 *Earl of Dundee:* It may not be a priority now but how about in the future if you were to conceive of future priorities?
Ms Svendsen: As things are at the moment it is very hard for me to see that our governments would put agriculture at the head of a list of priorities when they are talking about the budget. It is difficult to say anything about that because our government has just been re-elected and we take a maximum of three priorities along to the negotiating table in Brussels and I have never seen agriculture on that list and I do not think I will see it in this government's time.

Q488 *Earl of Dundee:* Do you think that direct support payments should continue?
Ms Svendsen: No.

Q489 *Earl of Dundee:* You do not, but what is your comment on the other direction, which is that farmers be rewarded for their provision of public benefits for which there is no market?
Ms Svendsen: That is one of the lines that could be pursued with the Common Agricultural Policy and that could be a part of the policy formulation that is on the table right now. As I have said before, not just the scope of producing public benefit in the way of the environment or quality, whatever, but also there would be a very large emphasis on research and innovation in our policy here. We would want to spend more money on becoming more innovative and more efficient in our production because that is necessary for a country of our size.

Q490 *Lord Cameron of Dillington:* If agriculture does not feature as a priority in your Budget Review, what are your priorities in terms of the budget?
Ms Svendsen: The last time our main priority was research.

5 December 2007   Ms Kirsten Holm Svendsen

Q491 Lord Cameron of Dillington: That is general research?

Ms Svendsen: General research, yes, but that also spills over into agricultural policy because that is basically what makes our economy competitive in the global economy. As a small country we have to be very innovative and spend a lot on research otherwise they might as well make it and produce it in China or Brazil. We have nothing to offer if we cannot do it a bit better or a bit earlier than everybody else and that is the thinking behind our whole attitude towards the Common Agricultural Policy and also in the Budget Review.

Q492 Earl of Dundee: What is the position with forestry just now in Denmark and is there a policy on integration between farming and forestry?

Ms Svendsen: I cannot say because forestry is not an agricultural issue, it is an environmental issue. Forestry is not a big industry.

Q493 Earl of Dundee: No, but even so there will be small Danish farmers who have trees.

Ms Svendsen: They do, yes, but they do not see it as a money generator. The only industry that really does very well is Christmas trees. We do not do timber or anything like that.

Q494 Chairman: Recreational forestry?

Ms Svendsen: Recreational forestry and Christmas trees, so this is the season.

Chairman: On that festive note, thank you very much indeed.

WEDNESDAY 5 DECEMBER 2007

<table>
<tr><td>Present</td><td>Arran, E</td><td>Plumb, L</td></tr>
<tr><td></td><td>Cameron of Dillington, L</td><td>Sewell, L (Chairman)</td></tr>
<tr><td></td><td>Dundee, E</td><td>Ullswater, V</td></tr>
<tr><td></td><td>Greaves, L</td><td></td></tr>
</table>

Examination of Witness

Witness: MR YVES MADRE, Delegate for European Agricultural Affairs, French Permanent Representation, examined.

Q495 Chairman: Thank you very much for coming and meeting with us and finding time. If I can just briefly explain who we are and what we are doing. We are a Sub-Committee of the House of Lords Select Committee on the European Union. Our present inquiry is into the CAP Health Check but also looking slightly beyond that and seeing how, if you like, the architecture and geography of the CAP may evolve into the future. That is really an invitation for you to talk about the French Presidency! We will have a record because it is a formal evidence session and you will have the transcript once it is ready and you can make revisions and changes to that. The best way of proceeding is through a discussion around the questions that we have indicated. If I could start it would be to say that your government has indicated that it wants to use its Presidency to open a debate about the purpose and future of CAP. How that has influenced your attitude to the Health Check? Where do you see the Health Check leading? Looking back a bit, what has been your experience of implementing the 2003 reforms? What changes has that led to in French agriculture and how do you see the change going forward? In ten seconds!
Mr Madre: I will try. First, I have to apologise for my very poor English.

Q496 Chairman: That is not the case.
Mr Madre: It is a true pleasure to be here today because it reminds me of some years ago when I was in London. In relation to the CAP, the future of the CAP and the Health Check, I hope that things are quite clear. We think that President Sarkozy's speech, which he gave in Rennes in September, tried to be clear on the matter. We have two different topics. One is the Health Check and we have to consider what the Commission intends to do with that Health Check. It is a way to be sure that the CAP reform of 2003 will be efficient until 2013. There is another debate, and we would like to launch this debate during our Presidency, about the future of the CAP after 2013. It is not a secret that this debate will be the theme of the Informal Council in September 2008 in the Alps. The aim is not to conclude in September unless all the Member States agree with the French point of view!

Q497 Chairman: How surprising!
Mr Madre: The aim is to launch the debate, and the debate will continue, as the European Union to define the policy before defining the budget. We think that is a good rule, to say that you have to define the policy before speaking about the money. It is not that money is evil or bad but it is what we do in our own Member States and it should be the same in the European Union. Those are two different exercises. The Commission and the Commissioner say that the Health Check could be a step in order to prepare the future, and why not, but it means we all need to have clear ideas about the broad line of the future. It is not Mariann Fischer Boel's aim or the French Presidency at the time or the French Government today to have a reform during the Health Check. The Health Check is not a mid-term review of the words or the meanings.

Q498 Chairman: In that debate about the future of the CAP that you are talking about, and okay you are not going to start in September and finish in September, what do you think will be the main elements of that debate?
Mr Madre: I would be very glad to be able to tell you everything. In September 2007, just a few weeks ago, Mr Barnier launched in France what is called "Assises D'Agriculture" and we will have a lot of meetings with stakeholders, unions and other stakeholders from September to March 2008. The objective we gave to all the directors of all the groups who met, and will meet again, is first to define what they are looking for from the Health Check and what according to all the stakeholders would be a good CAP for the future after 2013. Moreover, we will have a conference during the first semester of 2008 considering the theme of research theory on agriculture. This conference will deal with not only the next CAP but longer term on what research could give to agriculture and to the European Agricultural Policy. We think that tomorrow we will need a CAP but that CAP will not be necessarily the same as the one that we have today. Objectives have to be defined first. In the work we are doing in France we will not define the CAP of the future without stakeholders or the French view of the CAP for the future without the

French stakeholders so until March 2008 we will not be very talkative.

Q499 *Chairman:* You will not be very talkative?
Mr Madre: No. Nevertheless, we think that the CAP in the future should reach some aims and one is food security for Europe and something that may look strange to the United Kingdom which is food independence.

Q500 *Chairman:* Food independence?
Mr Madre: Yes.

Q501 *Chairman:* What does that mean? It does not mean having an EU pineapple regime, does it?
Mr Madre: It means we have the same idea as our American friends on the topic. Food is a tool, a political tool and if you have a shortage of food you will be weak.

Q502 *Lord Plumb:* Does that mean re-nationalisation?
Mr Madre: I am speaking about European policy.

Q503 *Lord Plumb:* I know you are, but if you are going to have independence do you mean independence around borders?
Mr Madre: No, European.

Q504 *Lord Plumb:* Around Europe?
Mr Madre: It does not mean that we have to produce 100% of what we consume, it means we are in an open market and we will be in an even more open market tomorrow than we are today, which is normal, or we hope that it will be. We must avoid being dependent on other countries for all that we need, only for the very minimum necessary, and producing in our own European territories. We know that food production will be quite a topic in the future concerning wealth creation and growth, the growth of our wealth creation considering what they will eat in Asia tomorrow. There is one aim for a Common Agricultural Policy. A second one is to participate in the world markets, in world trade and to help the world market to be balanced. The third one could be to ensure that the balance between territories within the European Union will not be destroyed and in all regions we will keep enough people, enough agricultural activities. The last one, of course, is agriculture has a main role to play when you are thinking about climate change and the environment. We are thinking about four main aims for the CAP in the future.

Q505 *Chairman:* That is very helpful.
Mr Madre: Those are only broad outlines. After that, if you ask what kind of tools and regional quotas I will not be able to answer today.

Chairman: That is fine. That is very, very helpful indeed. Thank you very much.

Q506 *Earl of Arran:* Like your country, we have many different terrains and many different types of soil which can lead to disadvantaged areas, of which we have quite a few back home. What approach does your country favour to the problems of these disadvantaged areas and how far might their difficulties be met by Pillar II policies rather than product support?
Mr Madre: We have quite a lot of less favoured or difficult areas. That is perhaps why in 2003 we decided to keep some coupled payments. At the time we thought activities in agriculture were needed especially in these areas in order to maintain the landscape, for instance, but also to maintain jobs in those areas, to maintain the fields because in a lot of these areas we have farms producing food and without farms there are no fields and then no more jobs. In France, the whole of the agricultural sector represents 14% of the total net French employment.

Q507 *Chairman:* 14% of employment?
Mr Madre: Yes.

Q508 *Chairman:* What does it represent in terms of GDP, do you know?
Mr Madre: I do not know exactly. I know the balance for exports. The first is agricultural goods and food and after Airbus and planes, et cetera.

Q509 *Lord Plumb:* Could I just ask whether the 14% includes people involved in the whole of the food industry?
Mr Madre: It is the whole of the food sector including the food industry, from the land to the consumer.

Q510 *Lord Plumb:* I just wanted to be clear.
Mr Madre: In 2003 we decided to keep direct payments just because we thought at that time that without production there are no farmers and without farmers there is no more activity in the region, no tourism and no more beautiful landscapes. Tomorrow, what will we think about Pillar II. Pillar II is useful, but we are afraid that Pillar II is not enough. If we want to maintain agricultural activities the best tool is Pillar I and if tomorrow you tell me, and maybe you will not tell me, that direct subsidies have to decrease and we have to imagine something else or be fully decoupled, why not? If you tell me such a thing, I am afraid some of us will be even more fragile. We need to help them in a very specific way to keep the basic activities and we need Pillar I and Pillar II. There is no problem with Pillar II as we have direct payments. Pillar II benefits from Pillar I and Pillar I benefits from Pillar I and the efficiency is good.

Q511 Lord Greaves: This is a slightly different question but it relates to mountainous areas. I have got a specific interest in part of the French mountains in the Pyrenees in the PNP—the Parc National des Pyrénées—and I am fascinated to see that, as far as I can understand, some of the support which was given, for example, to the maintenance of traditional alpine-type hay meadows appear to be through very locally organised and locally administered schemes, which I assume came from CAP funds but were very much decentralised and organised at a local level, at a national park level, and perhaps even groups of communes within the national park, which is quite different from the way schemes are organised in England. Is this type of decentralisation of the administration of support typical in France or is it something that just happens in that part of the Pyrenees?
Mr Madre: It is quite specific not only to the Pyrenees but to regional parks. We have such parks in the Pyrenees and in the Alps and because they are natural specific regional parks we try to manage with very specific rules to make sure that everything is very efficient. It is very specific indeed.

Q512 Lord Greaves: So the actual schemes and the things that are supported might be quite different in different places?
Mr Madre: Yes. The other schemes we have in France that are financed by Pillar II are schemes defined at national level and some of them at regional level, but they are wider than the schemes that you have mentioned.

Q513 Chairman: President Sarkozy has proposed that the CAP should continue to stabilise markets in agricultural goods. The question that obviously follows is what form of market intervention has he in mind?
Mr Madre: That is a very, very clever question. I hope that you have the answer because I have not! When President Sarkozy suggested that today, and tomorrow as well, agricultural markets have to be stabilised and we have tools to stabilise such markets, we should be very clear that it is not a question of defining a price, saying we will define a price for the next few years of wheat or meat, no, we know because of the weather, because of world markets and world prices in the European Union prices are going up and down and it will be even higher or lower than today because of climate change. The aim is not to avoid the variations but to be sure that tomorrow farmers will be able to deal with the variations and able to avoid very, very high prices or very, very low prices because that is not good for the industry or for farmers. The aim is to be clear that we do not like the CAP we had before 1992 for instance. It means that we have to work on crisis management tools, to discuss with all

Member States and to define what kind of tools would be acceptable for European agricultures, because there is not only one. As of today everything has to be defined and that is why in September my minister asked all stakeholders to work on that topic. We know that the Commission is working on that topic and we have to share our thinking on that and our experiences. Spain has some experience and we have the experience of the United States where there are some crisis management tools which, despite the name they gave to the tool, some are efficient, some are not and some are just a way to waste money.

Q514 Chairman: We are just coming up to the decision on the wine regime and there you have a crisis management tool that has become a permanent feature, crisis distillation. That is the difficulty with crisis management.
Mr Madre: Concerning wine—

Q515 Chairman: I am just using that as an example.
Mr Madre: Today in the proposal we have very good tools but tomorrow we hope that we will have some better tools. When we are thinking of crisis management tools they must be used in a very exceptional way. You mention distillation and I hope, and France wants, if ever Member States use distillation tomorrow or in the future it will not be the same as in the past. We know in the past what the result of that was, it was not a good one and that is why we reform the CMO and tomorrow it should be a crisis management tool but not a permanent market tool for some countries.

Q516 Lord Cameron of Dillington: I wanted to ask you a couple of detailed questions on the Health Check. For instance, on milk quotas the idea is to phase them out eventually. Would you support the Commission's proposal that you do this by just increasing the amount of quota? Do you as the government support that? How do the French farmers see that? Do they also support it?
Mr Madre: One year ago French farmers would have said, "No way", and that was clear. They are still considering the question of what will be the result for the French dairy industry and considering as well what other Member States think about that. We have to consider the proposal of Mrs Fischer Boel concerning the end of the milk quota and the Presidency will be very happy to consider the positions of all the Member States and then I think we will find a solution which will not be too difficult. The proposal from Mrs Fischer Boel—

Q517 Lord Cameron of Dillington: Will your solution involve the abolition of milk quotas?

Mr Madre: I have not got a crystal ball, but I think that the abolition of milk quotas is very high on the agenda of the Commission and a lot of Member States and we are open-minded and realistic.

Q518 *Lord Cameron of Dillington:* Moving on to the idea of capping the Single Farm Payment for large receivers of Single Farm Payment, we have just heard from both Germany and Denmark that they would be against that and your President has said that he could accept it under certain conditions. I just wondered what these conditions might be.

Mr Madre: Just before answering this question concerning capping, can I comment on the last one concerning milk quotas. Mrs Fischer Boel suggests very, very progressively increasing the milk quota. We are very open-minded and we will consider that but one thing has to be underlined and that is this very, very slow, very progressive move is good and could be necessary for Member States where the values of quotas are quite high, so that means for the Netherlands and Denmark. In France the value of the quota is not so high, it is quite low. We are open to discuss this. We are open to go more progressively or less progressively, we will see. Concerning capping, as with all other subjects, there is no taboo for us and if ever capping is decided some of our farmers will be affected by this measure. We understand perfectly well that it is mainly a topic for Germany, the United Kingdom and the Czech Republic, for instance, Denmark indeed. We will act as the Presidency. That was what was meant by Mr Sarkozy on that subject, that we have no taboos and if it is not the final decision and if in order to have a compromise if the answer is no capping, we will consider this and if the answer is some capping, why not? The question is very open for us. We will be very keen to listen to all of the positions.

Q519 *Viscount Ullswater:* Could I turn your attention to rural development and ask you how France sees the split of funding in the EAFRD between perhaps the agri-food economy on the one side, the environment on the other and then the broader base of rural development. You have also said that in the future you are going to need Pillar I and Pillar II, but would you see the gradual shift of money from Pillar I to Pillar II as being the right way forward?

Mr Madre: That is very difficult. I will give you, if I may, some figures first. In France, concerning Pillar II we plan to spend around 40% in Axis 1, around 45 in the second one, that is Less Favoured Areas and agri-environment, and between 10 and 15% in the third and concerning the LEADER scheme it is 5% and no more.

Q520 *Chairman:* It does not fit the Napoleon tradition, does it?

Mr Madre: I think from the figures it is quite clear what we are focusing on in France considering the second pillar. The second point is in the European Union we have a regional policy and we hope that what concerns the regional policy will be under the regional policy and not under the CAP and what concerns Pillar II CAP will be financed by CAP funds. We have several policies in the European Union and we to have use them in the best possible way. We are not keen on financing with the CAP things that should be financed by the regional policy. The last point is modulation. Modulation, according to us, should only be a tool, but sometimes I wonder if modulation is not an aim for some people. When you define a tool you must know what its purpose is. I was in an eastern country Member State some days ago and the conclusion of the scientists was, "Considering the Commission's proposals we will have 13% of modulation plus 12% of capping, so that means 25% and that is fine. We could be in favour." The last comment was, "What will we do with this money?" and after they had no idea and that is the problem. If ever anybody suggests having more modulation, the good purposes should be defined. This is the same thing when we speak about the future of the CAP. First, we would like to define the policies and after the budget, the financial needs, not the other way around.

Q521 *Viscount Ullswater:* I think you mentioned in your first answer the regional policies that you have in France and the Pillar II policies. Do they marry up correctly or are you concerned that one is trying to cover something which should be done by regional policies and using the CAP finance to do it?

Mr Madre: Today I would say it is not so bad but regional policy could do better. Tomorrow we have to use both of them. We are just speaking about CAP and the fact that CAP within the second pillar should do a lot, and that is fair enough, but the CAP should do what the CAP is defined for. I think that in some cases we have to use the regional policy and regional funds, for instance regional funds could be used in order to increase non-agricultural activities in some remote areas, not only CAP.

Q522 *Viscount Ullswater:* So it is the social policy as well as an agricultural policy that need to work in conjunction.

Mr Madre: CAP is an agricultural policy.

Q523 *Viscount Ullswater:* Bur regional can be social?

Mr Madre: Regional can be to develop regional activities and if that is the meaning of social, why not?

Q524 *Chairman:* You would have to have a fairly radical reform of regional funds though, would you not?

Mr Madre: Regional policy has to be defined for the future.

Chairman: How eloquent.

Q525 *Lord Greaves:* Are you talking about European regional policy or French regional policy?

Mr Madre: European policy. Concerning the French regional policy, that has to be defined for the future as well.

Q526 *Earl of Dundee:* Within new EU Member States agriculture is a major contributor to employment, to the economy and much structural change is called for as a result of that. What impact do you think that structural change will have on the Common Agricultural Policy? Will it simply increase its budget or will it cause the CAP's purpose to be revised?

Mr Madre: We are not dreaming about some increase of the CAP budget. I say that considering the Health Check and the future of the CAP. We want to be realistic, open-minded and we have no trouble changing. We are used to seeing it differently, but it is a question of how people see French people, of course. We do suggest discussing the future of the CAP because things are changing and the structure of the European farm industry is changing despite the fact that it remains mainly family farms. The fact is the CAP is quite alive. From the beginning it has changed successfully quite a lot of times and the CAP from 2003 has nothing to do with the CAP at the beginning or in the 1990s. Just because we define other objectives it has to be underlined that the different CAPs' aims each time were asking for more food for Europe and the farmers, thanks to the CAP, produced more food. When we said we had to be in the world market, they did it. When we said we had to avoid surprises, today there are no more surprises. Tomorrow we have to meet other goals, other aims. This is why we think we need to discuss the future of the CAP as to what will be the next European agricultural policy. It will be a strong one but aimed at remote areas and a contribution from the good and agricultural industry to the European industry and the fact that the agriculture and food industry is part of the global industry and so should play its part in the Lisbon Agenda. Everything is on the table.

Q527 *Lord Greaves:* Could I perhaps act as devil's advocate here. Discussing things is one thing and putting things on the table, but France has a long way to go to persuade the rest of us that really your agenda is not to slow down reform as much as possible and to stop as much of it as possible because France is a great beneficiary of the system as it stands

at the moment and has been seen as, perhaps, the leading country in opposing reform. Is that really changing?

Mr Madre: France is agreeing to speed up reforms. After Mr Sarkozy's speech we felt that the general feeling and general fear maybe was what is France doing to speed up and that is strange. The fact is France is acting, and will act, like its President so we are ready to speak about everything as long as it is in the right order, so first policy and then budget. The consequences of what we choose altogether as a European agricultural policy on the budget we will not try to escape and that is very clear. All the subjects concerning policy will be on the table. We will put some papers on the table, not before March but at least for September 2008 and we wish to have a very open discussion at European level. If the result of the discussion is that we have to define what is the future very quickly, why not? If the general meaning is the European Union should take time then we will consider that.

Q528 *Lord Greaves:* If France is not going to be the state holding it all back now, which ones are?

Mr Madre: We are not trying to sit on a golden vote. The next CAP should be a policy of projects, not the policy of the past.

Q529 *Earl of Dundee:* I wonder if I could connect Lord Greaves' point to my earlier question on enlargement. As Lord Greaves said, some self-interest in France or in the United Kingdom may have held up, or may hold up, the process of reforming the CAP. If you think of the impact of enlargement as something which is a catalyst it may be an ally. I wonder if you believe that or, in other words, if you think that in spite of what we will all do or will fail to do on our volition to do with CAP reform the impact of enlargement will force it through. Do you believe that?

Mr Madre: We know what the impact of enlargement will be and we knew it in 2002 when we had this initial agreement. The fact is that the impact of enlargement from now to 2013 will be less important than we thought in 2002 because of the prices, because of what we can see in the European agricultural budget. The impact of enlargement on the agricultural budget will be a matter for mainly after 2013. Today we do receive some benefit from the CAP but we are a net contributor, quite a high one. Tomorrow we will continue to be a net contributor and we are happy to be so because it is the European Union and it is about solidarity. We will not be a net beneficiary from the CAP any more and, despite that, we do think we will need a European common policy on agriculture. It is not all about money in the budget and what we can gain or not, it is more than that, it is a question of Europe, of having common policies not only on the

5 December 2007   Mr Yves Madre

market without any common idea of what should be the aim and what we should do. Of course enlargement should be considered and the consequences of enlargement have been considered, but it is not because of enlargement that we say we have to redefine the CAP for some financial purpose, it is more because of the evolution of the open markets and the evolution of farms and evolution of society and what society are asking on the environment, on landscapes and because of the WTO as well. One day we will have a deal in Geneva and we will have to consider all of the consequences of that deal. We will speak of that first and enlargement is just another point we will have to consider. We know that we will get far less money.

Q530 *Chairman:* You have drawn our attention to what President Sarkozy has been saying and he is by far and away one of the most interesting politicians in Europe at the moment and saying some very challenging things. The difficulty is when we have this new thinking coming from Sarkozy on the one hand and then up pops the idea of Community preference. That gives to some people the idea that is really just trying to replace formal import tariff barriers with non-tariff barriers and it is back to a semi-protectionist view of European agriculture.
Mr Madre: Do you think so?

Q531 *Chairman:* Oh, yes. It has the potential.
Mr Madre: Very nice. It is not Community preference but just another way to say it is fair. The Government of the Netherlands some weeks or months ago said trade concerns have to be considered when we discuss the WTO but today they are not on the agenda, that is for tomorrow. It is a question of us being fair and if we want very strict rules on our farmers on what they produce in the European Union I have some difficulty understanding why we should allow anything to be imported within the European Union. Secondly, it is a question of food safety. We need to be sure that what is imported and what will be imported is safe. It is safe and fair, not trying to find some other rules, unwritten rules, to avoid imports of American cereals or cereals from Belarussia or something like that. If it is safe and everybody has the same rules there are no problems.
Chairman: You know those words could be said almost word-for-word by John Edwards, the most protectionist candidate for the Democratic nomination.

Q532 *Lord Plumb:* How does your statement fit into the WTO rules? This would be a fairly major problem. I can see your point on fairness. If you think of the vast amount of chickens imported from China, Brazil and a lot of places where the standards of welfare are not the same as they are in Europe then I

can understand it but WTO has to have some responsibility for making sure that they comply with those standards and, as I understand it, they are moving more in that direction now. Is that not a factor and a major factor in deciding this thinking?
Mr Madre: We will see over the next year that this topic will be very high on the agenda because of the environment and standards of living, food safety. It is just the beginning. When I listen to other countries that are quite liberal free trade countries, a lot of them are considering the topic. It is for the future and we have a lot to discuss with them.

Q533 *Chairman:* We have got a question on climate change but it is such a big topic, the relationship between agriculture and climate change, if you do not mind, if you could write to us on that it would be helpful because we are virtually at the end of our time.
Mr Madre: I appreciate that because I have to catch a train for Paris to prepare for the Presidency.

Q534 *Lord Cameron of Dillington:* You talked about food security and security policy and listening to you throughout this morning I get the impression that France is still as protectionist as ever about its agriculture industry and there has been very little change. Do you ever see the day, particularly when world food shortages seem to be coming, that you will be prepared to let your agriculture industry be like any other industry and have the risks of an entrepreneurial capitalist system and not be protected at all? Do you ever see that happening in French policy?
Mr Madre: Do you think that the European agricultural sector is a very protected one?

Q535 *Lord Cameron of Dillington:* Yes.
Mr Madre: I do not think so. They have some direct payments, but—
Lord Cameron of Dillington: It is 43% of the European budget. Huge amounts of money come from the state to industry, it does not go into any other industry, and why should it, they fare in the market. We have not got the time to discuss this.

Q536 *Chairman:* I think you have opened up a can of worms.
Mr Madre: We have a European agricultural policy with some funding, we do not have any other policies, for instance for research. If Member States decide tomorrow to have a common research policy we have no more budget and it will be much higher than for agriculture. Concerning protection or not of agriculture, we are quite happy to hear that markets should lead the decision and tomorrow that will be

the case even more than today, and that is quite normal. Agriculture is quite different from, let us say, the automotive industry. I cannot succeed in taking my land and putting my land in Brazil, it is still in Brittany and that is a fact. You cannot decide just like that to go away with your land, with your farm, as you can in other industries. Agriculture is not only agricultural goods, it is a matter of the environment, landscapes, society, and we will never succeed in applying exactly the same rules.

Chairman: Thank you very much. I think it is a great triumph and a sign of major advance that we have got through this session without any reference to the European model of agriculture. Thank you very much indeed. It has been a great performance, absolutely wonderful. Thank you.

WEDNESDAY 5 DECEMBER 2007

Present   Arran, E   Plumb, L
           Cameron of Dillington, L   Sewell, L (Chairman)
           Dundee, E   Ullswater, V
           Greaves, L

Examination of Witnesses

Witness: MR VALENTIN ALMANSA DE LARA, Agriculture Counsellor, Spanish Permanent Representation, examined.

Q537 *Chairman:* Thank you very much for finding the time to come and assist us in our inquiry. I will say a little bit about who we are and what we are doing. We are a Sub-Committee of the European Select Committee of the House of Lords. We are conducting an inquiry into the Health Check but also looking slightly beyond the Health Check at the future shape of CAP and how it is likely to evolve. This is a formal evidence session so we will be taking a note of the evidence and you will have every opportunity after the meeting to get a copy and you can make changes or revisions. The best way forward is if we have a conversation across the topics that I have outlined. The Commission's Communication on the Health Check really suggests a number of policy areas that could be improved in the light of the changes since 2003. Looking at Spain, what has been your experience of the 2003 reforms? I come from Scotland, which I have to mention in that context because Scotland has gone slightly differently from England and Wales. Are there differences in the autonomous communities in how the impact of the 2003 has gone? Basically, what has happened to Spain after 2003?
Mr Almansa de Lara: We are trying to maintain the same system in the whole country. We have 17 autonomous regions and they have full competence in agricultural matters. We try to maintain from central government a more or less similar approach in the whole country otherwise we would have problems because the trade between the regions is free but if you apply different systems in different regions you could have distortions in competitiveness or the market. We try to maintain the same system and we have done that with success up to today. Now, in Spain the system is the same for the whole of Spain in general terms. The only point where we maintain a difference is we do not allow the selling of Single Payment rights between autonomous regions. Single Payments are allocated in one region and remain in that region. This is the only limitation we put on the system. The rest of the system is the same for all. We apply the same decoupling system in all areas, the same deadlines, the same dates. The rest is the same. In relation to our experience, it is too early

for us to have made a definitive conclusion. We applied the reforms in 2006 and for the first year nothing is new because the people need more than one year to adapt to the new situation and normally farmers are very conservative so they try to change as little as they can. In the first year nothing changed in Spain and the new decisions had not been taken so people maintained their inertia. This is the second year and in this year we have had various strange market situations with these incredibly high prices for cereals, milk and other commodities. We are not able to know exactly what the impact is of the 2003 reforms. We have not had the time and now we have a very difficult situation in the market and we do not know if the situation we have now is because of the reform or the change in the market. We cannot establish any conclusions now. We may need two or three years more and a normal market situation, let me say, to see exactly what is happening. In other Member States which have applied the reforms since 2005 they have more experience than us but it is too early for us to obtain any conclusion.

Q538 *Chairman:* That must make it very difficult looking forward.
Mr Almansa de Lara: Yes, of course. The Commission has presented us with this new Communication and thinks we need to move forward and we have said okay but we do not know where we are now so we need to have more figures, more dates, more information and more time to see clearly where we are going with our reforms. We did not apply the reforms until 2006 in Spain and now we are trying to change again. In relation to the Health Check Communication we think we need to separate two questions. Some are technical arrangements and we are okay with those, we were in favour of adjusting and this so-called fine-tuning of the 2003 reforms. We have detected some problems in this application and we are open to discuss these. To touch key elements of the 2003 agreement, such as decoupling, modulation, elimination of some of the market tools, intervention tools, this transition to a regional system being more or less compulsory, we think we need

more time and more debate about it. We need an impact assessment, impact analysis. We want to know exactly what is happening and then we can discuss where we want to go. It is difficult for us to think about the future if we do not know where we are now exactly. This is the general approach we have in relation to this situation.

Chairman: I think we are going to push you a little bit on the Health Check.

Q539 Earl of Arran: I see exactly what you are saying as a new entrant in the whole organisation. This is nothing to do with the Health Check particularly because I think you have answered where you are on that, but in general—I know little about your agriculture and your farming in Spain—is it sufficiently good and the industry sufficiently buoyant to be attracting many new entrants into the agricultural market? Are the youth wanting to play their part in the agricultural market when in England it is very much on the decline, sadly?

Mr Almansa de Lara: It depends on the sectors. If you speak about livestock, in my opinion we are in a very good position to compete. In pork, our increase in the last ten or 20 years was very good. We are selling a lot in Russia and other third countries, also in the Union. It is the same for beef where we have more than doubled our production. In general in the livestock sector we have more problems with poultry but with the rest we are okay. On the agricultural side, olive oil is working well, fruit and vegetables is working well, cereals is a poor sector but the problem with cereals is the rain and there is nothing we can do to solve this problem, we have no rain so our yields are very low. It is not a problem of lack of competitiveness. We think we can compete in the market but we need to know the rules to compete and after that we can discuss the European standard quality system.

Q540 Lord Cameron of Dillington: Which proposals in the Health Check put forward by the Commissioner do you favour and which ones do you find difficult?

Mr Almansa de Lara: On the official point of view it is too early for me to say because at the last Council my minister made this clear separation between what we think are deeper reforms and technical reforms. The technical reforms we are okay with if we want to change the scope or adjust the scope of the cross-compliance that is okay, we can do it. We want to remove set-aside definitely, but we have removed now so that we can do it.

Q541 Lord Cameron of Dillington: How do you see milk quotas?

Mr Almansa de Lara: We are open to the debate but we think we need more information. In the last Council most of the Member States were more or less in favour of a debate but other Member States wondered what would happen with these difficult regions, mountain regions, the production in these regions. We are open to this debate, we are not saying we do not want it, but we need an impact analysis as to what will happen in some areas.

Q542 Lord Cameron of Dillington: What about capping of large farms, where do you stand on that?

Mr Almansa de Lara: I have no definite opinion but I do not know that we have a very big problem with this. I have no official opinion. I do not think that we have a big problem with this.

Q543 Lord Cameron of Dillington: You have got quite big farms.

Mr Almansa de Lara: Yes, but the amount is not very big. We have made some calculations and this capping will cost nothing because the money remains in the first pillar and in the country. It is something like €72 million for Spain which is not a very high quantity. The modulation is much more important for us than this. It is more important that we debate modulation.

Q544 Chairman: Modulation is more important than capping?

Mr Almansa de Lara: It is much more money. The modulation is something like €240 million for us per year. This debate is three times more important than the other in terms of money. Again, this 72 million will remain in the first pillar under Article 69 so we can manage the money. Other Member States have more problems with this than us, but I am not sure if this will be our definitive position. This is a general overview.

Q545 Viscount Ullswater: Modulation brings us on to the funding under Pillar II and it forms part of the very crucial element of the CAP and its reform. Could you comment on what Spain's experience of implementing the EAFRD is? You were talking about the autonomous communities, is there any difference in their ability to apply these funds in different axes amongst those various communities?

Mr Almansa de Lara: I am not an expert on rural development. I am more of an expert on the CAP in general because I have been involved in this kind of reform since 1992.

Lord Cameron of Dillington: Here we go again!

Q546 Chairman: You look remarkably young and youthful!

5 December 2007   Mr Valentin Almansa de Lara

Mr Almansa de Lara: I have good experience of that but that is not the case in rural development so I have checked with my colleagues. They told me that in rural development we have a system that is very similar to yours. We have 17 regions and we have 17 different regional programmes more or less. It is a very complicated exercise because we have 17 regions plus central government and then we have some regions which are competence regions and some that are not which have less money in rural development. In the beginning the exercise was very complicated to try to distribute the money between the 17 regions and central government. We succeeded in the end and obtained a framework for the distribution of money. Now we have 17 regional programmes plus one, which is the National Rural Network and they tell me it is the same in the UK, you have these national rural networks, more or less with the same competence as in the UK. We put more money in this National Rural Network because we are putting in national money in co-operation with local action groups in inter-territorial and trans-national programmes. I do not know what these programmes are but we are putting more money than you in this National Rural Network because of these inter-territorial and trans-national programmes. Then we have the national programme with six programmes which are compulsory for all the regions. All the regions are obliged to put these six programmes in place. The national funds have priority in relation to these six programmes. We spend the national funds first in these six programmes and if there is more money we distribute that around the other regional programmes. We try to maintain a national agricultural policy and it is not easy with 17 but we do our best. In the different regional programmes the distribution between axes is different and there are some figures and an average on the first axis, competitivity, could be between 50 and 55%; the second axis, environment, between 35 and 40%; the third axis, diversification, between ten and 15% more or less; and around all these axes the LEADER approach has 12% of the money. We put a lot more money at a national and regional level into rural development because we obtain less money from Brussels and we try to maintain the same level of expenditure so we put more national money in that. For this programme we have €1,800 million more than in the past framework. We have put more national and regional money into the system and we receive less money from the Union because we have these two or three big regions which have met the convergence objectives. I would like to make a comment. People say that rural development funds are very important but what we saw what happen in the last budgetary perspective, where the prime ministers took the money because the bigger reduction of the budget was made in this area. This is

a personal opinion but it seemed a strange exercise to take money from the first pillar, send the money to rural development because it is very important and then take money out from the rural development. I need to reflect about this kind of exercise. This is a personal opinion.

Q547 *Lord Plumb:* Could I follow up on this question. My impression is that Spain has done better out of the CAP than any other country in Europe and you therefore rely to a large extent on support, and now the support under the Single Payment from the old system. You are giving the regions responsibility for dealing with this, they are autonomous, and moving money from Pillar I to Pillar II which is a matter of concern for this Committee because we are hearing from all over the place that this should be done. I think we would all agree with you that you do not want it moved to Pillar II and then taken away, but take a region where you have got a lot of mountainous areas, a lot of room for development in those areas perhaps, would you not think that it is probably a good thing to move the money from Pillar I to Pillar II so that in that particular region you can use the funds better in areas of need, because it is need not just for farming those areas necessarily but for maintaining the areas, probably stocking them with whatever and making them much more interesting for the tourists, et cetera, in other words partly social?
Mr Almansa de Lara: Again, this is a personal comment. We must take account of the fact that we are speaking about regions and we need to distribute the money between regions. We are not a central government with all the power. These things could be easy with central government that has the money and decides to fix a priority on milk production in mountain areas, for example, and send the money to this and it is the same for you if it is one region or another because this is your priority. But when you have autonomous regions, and I do not know if it is the same for you in the UK, you need to distribute the money first and then speak about the programmes. The exercise to distribute the money is at the beginning so it is difficult to fix priorities. The only way we can do that is with national programmes. We can make a national programme and say it is compulsory and we will put money in, but at the end you are obliged to meet the figures and see what happens. If with these programmes there is a big distortion of the distribution of money and the other autonomous regions will complain and say, "You are making a programme for one region, not for all". This is the reason why it is so difficult. We are putting in place a national programme but we must take care that this national programme does not change the distribution of the money. A little, yes, but if this national programme produces a movement of the

money from one community to another in a big amount I am sure we will have problems.

Q548 *Lord Greaves:* Within each region is the amount that is allocated to Pillar I and Pillar II, the amount to modulation, is set at national level or can that change at regional level?
Mr Almansa de Lara: I do not know. I can ask but I do not know.

Q549 *Lord Greaves:* That seems to be crucial.
Mr Almansa de Lara: It is not possible because in the last framework we lost one of our biggest regions from convergence, Castilla y León. This was the second biggest region for money. The first was Andalusia and the second was Castilla y León. We lost the money from the Union for this region because it has met convergence criteria and we were obliged to put national money in to cover this. The distribution is not in the same way that we are receiving the money from the modulation, we redistribute the money. I am not sure about the system. It is difficult because we have to maintain a balance between the 17 regions.

Q550 *Earl of Dundee:* Rethinking priorities in agriculture forms part of the budget and in that context, therefore, what are Spain's future priorities in the field of agriculture?
Mr Almansa de Lara: For CAP or the budget?

Q551 *Earl of Dundee:* If you would like to comment in general.
Mr Almansa de Lara: We think we need to reflect on the future and we prefer to reflect first in principle and then on the budget. I heard Guy Legras a long time ago, who was Director General for Agriculture for a long time, say that a politician who does not put in place policies which explain the budget is obliged to put in place policies which the budgets allow. We are in favour of discussing the principles first and then the budget. Now the situation is different than in the past, we are facing new challenges about supply and we think we have a problem with supply. We are not sure that for political and security reasons it is good to have these problems and this level of prices because now we are dependent on third-countries for a lot of commodities. What happens if we have a big drought in Australia or South America or the United States? At the end we are rich countries so we will pay, our consumers will pay a higher price, but what happens with the poorest countries. The supply is a matter of concern for us and we need to reflect on this and change our minds perhaps because in the last 30 years we have only spoken about surplus. This was the only thing we were focused on, surplus, and this was the aim of the 1992 reform and the 2000 reform. Now we are in a different situation and have a

problem with supplies. We need to reflect on supplies first and whether the policy we have in place now is good enough to solve this problem. We want to reflect on that. We also want to reflect on this so-called quality European standard. The consumers are not prepared to pay for it and when they go to a supermarket they prefer the cheapest. It is the same whether it is from Brazil or wherever, they prefer the cheapest. It is not clear that the Europeans prefer to pay for this standard of quality. It is not clear that the WTO will take on board these concerns. We need to take a decision. We can leave this European standard or we will have to pay for it. If the consumer does not want to pay then it is the taxpayers who will have to pay. This is a crucial decision for the future and we need to have a debate about this. We cannot say that we want a very high standard of quality if nobody is prepared to pay for it. This is the second point that we think we need to reflect on. We defend the highest possible standard for Europeans. We also want to reflect on the protection of the environment. The market is the word and if you read the Communication the market alone could solve all the problems, but we have some doubts about that. First of all, we are speaking about food, we are not speaking about tables or chairs, so what happens if the market makes a mistake. We need to reflect on this to see if we need to maintain some tools to control the market. We have no final position but we need to reflect on that. In relation to the protection of the environment, we are sure that bad use of the surface produces problems but we are also sure that under-use of the surface produces also problems for the environment. We can see that in Spain or in other areas. Is the market the best tool to manage the environment? Will the market pay the farmer for his role or will ask the farmer only to produce more? It is okay because the market will lead? Another problem is the management of the territory. Can the market assure us that people will be in all the territories around all the countries in Europe or do we need some measures to help the people to be there. If we leave it to the market, who will produce 2,000 litres per year or 20,000 litres per year in the high mountains? Nobody. The market will never pay for this production. We have no definitive opinion but we think before we go ahead with this exercise we need to reflect in a different way on where we want to go and what we want to do with our policy.

Q552 *Earl of Dundee:* You have explained to us how reflection is required and you need to analyse the results of recent changes. You have also pointed out how important it is to be fair-minded between the 17 regions in your country. That apart, after 2013, taking into account the direction which your regions are already moving in, what changes do you anticipate in farming, in systems, that you would like to see that you anticipate will occur in the next ten or 15 years after 2013?

Mr Almansa de Lara: I am sorry, I do not understand.

Q553 *Earl of Dundee:* I am talking about your 17 regions. I am taking your point about how one cannot jump to conclusions too readily, you need to analyse the results from recent changes.

Mr Almansa de Lara: Yes.

Q554 *Earl of Dundee:* You have also explained to us how important it is in your country with your federal system of the 17 regions to be fair-minded and to be seen to be fair-minded among those regions. Apart from that, you and your countrymen will have some ideas of what you would like to see happening in farming after 2013 and I wonder if you would like to say a few words about that.

Mr Almansa de Lara: Of course we want to see farmers in the country, we want to see people living in the countryside. We want to have an active and profitable agriculture. If we have an active and profitable agriculture we will have farmers, we will have people managing the territory and protecting the environment, and also people making money in rural areas. Our aim is that people in rural areas have money, have benefits, and can live there with their activities. This is our task.

Q555 *Lord Cameron of Dillington:* Do you mean outside agriculture?

Mr Almansa de Lara: We think agriculture must be the engine. It is possible to have other activities. Spain is a very big country and if you travel 300 kilometres from Madrid the alternatives are tourism but that is for weekends and not the rest of the week, you know.

Q556 *Lord Cameron of Dillington:* With broadband technology you can be a stockbroker.

Mr Almansa de Lara: It is possible. We saw a big change in Ireland but Ireland is a smaller country and the distances are smaller. I do not know if that is possible in Spain.

Q557 *Lord Cameron of Dillington:* You have mentioned all the reasons why: the environment, the social implications of keeping people on the territory, and there could be lots of other reasons, but can you see a situation where agriculture is in a free market, no support, and the state buys goods such as habitats, maybe even land management, in other words the state says, "We want the land in these mountains, a poor region, maintained, therefore we will pay you just to maintain the land" but agriculture itself is in a free market? Do you see that?

Mr Almansa de Lara: It is difficult because you need to be active in a business. I do not know how to explain it really. It is like the Indians in North America who are paid to be Indians on a reserve. You need some economic activity. They need to be active in their business and their business is agriculture. Again, we can pay more or differently if they maintain rules about the environment or whatever but you are obliged to maintain economic activity otherwise I cannot see people living in the countryside.

Q558 *Lord Greaves:* I am interested in disadvantaged areas and particularly upland areas, but is it not the case that in quite a lot of Spain this battle has been lost already, that a lot of areas that used to be pastures, used to be grazing land for animals, are no longer and are being taken over by scrub and areas that used to be arable, the terraces on the hillsides and so on, again a lot of it has been abandoned and taken over by scrub. In a lot of Spain in difficult areas the farmers have gone and that process is still continuing in a lot of Spain and in practice agriculture in Spain is going to be concentrated in future in the better areas, particularly if it is going to get hotter and even drier.

Mr Almansa de Lara: We will see what happens with climate change. It is clear if the rain leaves we will have big problems because Spain has problems now with the rain and if it rains less we will have big problems. You are right, Spain is in the same general trend as other Member States and we have fewer farmers. For instance, in milk we used to have something like 250,000 farmers in 1992 and now we have less than 25,000. It is clear the decrease of arable farmers is going on. We are seeing more and more older farmers on the farms and no young people. The problem is not only agricultural, it is related to other things. In the very remote areas of Spain you will have no cinema, no hospital, no disco, no girls, and it is a real problem in parts of Spain, so young people do not want to stay there because there are no girls and they prefer to go to a city or a big village. Some co-operatives are now forming programmes to put in place employment only for girls to be sure that the girls stay on the spot and the boys stay as well. These are the kinds of problems we are facing in the rural areas. They are not typically agricultural problems but related to lack of discos, cinemas. We need to try to stop this trend and if there is economic improvement on the land and we are spending a lot of money on infrastructure, the roads in Spain today are nothing like the roads ten or 20 years ago, and now you can have the Internet in most of the country. We are spending a lot of money and building hospitals in the countryside. We are trying to provide this to allow the people to be there.

Q559 Lord Greaves: That does not make it possible for people to make money out of farming, does it? It might make it better to live in those areas so that people might go and run little businesses on the Internet and so on, or buy second homes and set up tourist things, but it is still impossible to make a living from the traditional ways of grazing their sheep or cultivating the terraces.

Mr Almansa de Lara: It is clear if we were still producing like our grandfathers we would be totally lost. Our livestock system is a very intensive one, only our suckler cows are in extensive production. All of our beef production is intensive and our pig production is intensive. The system of production must change and it must be more efficient.

Chairman: Let us go back to the relationship between agricultural support and structural funds.

Q560 Viscount Ullswater: You have talked a lot about how to maintain the community in fragile rural areas. I am wondering whether the CAP should be the driver for this or whether it is European structural funds, regional funds, of which Spain is a big recipient. Do they lie nicely closely together? Do they overlap or are there gaps between them? The more modulation takes place the more money is going to be shifted into Pillar II and I wonder how you feel those two sit together.

Mr Almansa de Lara: We are trying to avoid this overlapping. It is a very strange name in Spain, I do not know if it is okay in English. We have built what we call a National Reference Strategic Framework for all funds, so there is a framework built in Spain where all reforms are involved. We try to maintain co-ordination between the actions of all reforms inside this National Framework. This involves all structural and rural development funds. On the rural development side, every programme we build must have a part which demonstrates it has a complementary relationship with the actions of the other funds. I am not sure if we are succeeding in this exercise but we are doing our best. We build a National Framework first where all the funds are involved and then every programme for rural development is obliged to demonstrate that it is complementary with other actions of other reforms. We are trying. I am not an expert so I do not know if we are succeeding in this exercise but we are doing our best. If they start overlapping we will lose money on this issue.

Q561 Lord Plumb: I know there is growing interest in turning wheat into ethanol and there are one or two Spanish companies that are very interested in this development. Is this helped financially by government? Building the plant, of course, is quite an expensive business. Is this a development that you are going to encourage?

Mr Almansa de Lara: I am not sure but I think they have big tax advantages because if you produce ethanol you have tax advantages, but I am not sure. In Spain at this moment these plants are not working because with the price of cereals it is not profitable. We have very big plants which are closed because with these prices of cereals they cannot work. I still think in pesetas, it is difficult for me to think in euros. They need lower prices. I think it is the biggest one in Europe that opened in Salamanca last year and it closed one month later because the prices were not low enough for them.

Q562 Lord Plumb: That is why I asked the question. I have been to that plant. There is a proposal to build a plant elsewhere in Europe.

Mr Almansa de Lara: Perhaps they have based that on the prices of cereals in the past. Nobody thought in 2003 that we would have these prices for cereals. We do not know what will happen in ten years, we will see.

Q563 Chairman: Could we just finish off by looking at climate change because it does seem to me that you are part of Europe that is vulnerable to climate change and the agricultural industry may face major problems of adaptation as a result of climate change in the future, just no rain. How are you responding to that at the moment?

Mr Almansa de Lara: In agriculture?

Q564 Chairman: Yes.

Mr Almansa de Lara: The bigger problem is the water, as you know. Traditionally we have spent a lot of money on irrigation and in some parts we have very old irrigation systems and we are spending a lot of money to rebuild the irrigation systems to make better use of the water. We felt we were losing a lot of money because we made bad use of it. Now we are spending a lot of money from the Agriculture Ministry on the rebuilding of the irrigation systems. In times past they used—I do not know the term in English—the irrigation system when you only opened the water and covered the soil, which was the normal system, but it is difficult to see this kind of system now and we are going to build a good system for trees, for fruit and vegetables more and more. We are improving a lot. Our main concern at this moment is the use of water because it is our worst scenario.

Q565 Chairman: Where does the money for that come from? Is it national exchequer or coming through funds?

Mr Almansa de Lara: It is national plus Community funds. It could be under rural development but I am not sure. I can check that if you want.

Q566 Chairman: It would be interesting to know how you fund that.

Mr Almansa de Lara: I will check but I do not know. We are spending a lot of money and we have a national programme because it is a high priority for us.

Chairman: I think that is it. Thank you very much for all the help you have given us.

WEDNESDAY 5 DECEMBER 2007

Present	Arran, E	Jones of Whitchurch, B
	Cameron of Dillington, L	Plumb, L
	Dundee, E	Sewell, L (Chairman)
	Greaves, L	Ullswater, V

Examination of Witness

Witness: MR PEKKA PESONEN, Secretary-General, COPA-COGECA, examined.

Q567 *Chairman:* Good afternoon. We will try and get the best use out of the time that remains. Thank you very much for getting here. We had some concerns about your health and wellbeing but you are here. Let me explain briefly who we are and what we are doing. We are a Sub-Committee of the House of Lords Select Committee on the European Union. We are conducting an inquiry into the Health Check and looking forward to the future of the CAP as it evolves. In our terms this is a formal evidence session, so a note will be taken and a transcript will be available in a little while. You will get a copy of that so you can make any adjustments or changes that are necessary. The best way of proceeding is if we go across the table and have a conversation around some of the topics we have identified. In order to try and make the best use of the time we have linked some of the questions together, so I hope that is not too confusing. If I could start with the obvious simple question which most likely produces a very difficult answer. Looking to the Health Check and beyond the Health Check to Budget Review, what do you see should be the overarching principles and objectives that underpin the future development of the EU agriculture policy?
Mr Pesonen: First of all, thank you very much for the invitation, I am deeply honoured on behalf of my organisation, COPA-COGECA, and personally. Secondly, in answer to your question, we have formulated our first reaction vis-à-vis the Health Check and at the moment are preparing more detailed analysis and another document of a long-term nature, post-2013. However, we have already had a fairly extensive discussion amongst our member organisations, 78 of them. It is not that simple to reach a conclusion sometimes but we work hard on that. In that particular discussion we have identified two items that are of relevance so far. Especially when we talk about the Health Check it is a matter of stability. In 2003 we had reform and it has only been implemented fully in most of the Member States for perhaps one or two years and we are still in the process of adapting to reforms that go together with the 2003 reforms. By this I mean sectors like wine, cotton, and fruit and vegetables, for instance. When we talk about more long-term aspects, it is a matter of our farmers in the agriculture sector and

our farm businesses fulfilling the expectations of society and the consumers. Clearly these two issues are on the table: stability and expectations to be fulfilled.

Q568 *Chairman:* Could you say a little bit more on that. If you say stability often enough and loud enough it actually means no change.
Mr Pesonen: No.

Q569 *Chairman:* What are the farmers' expectations?
Mr Pesonen: I have to remind you that this is not a formal position but we have identified these issues. When we talk about stability it does not mean that we have to freeze everything. We see opportunities in various sectors. Coming from the market we have introduced bio-energy, for instance. It has more to do with the political framework. If the farmers were told now, two or three years after the implementation of the last reform, that we were going to have another one in another direction that would be detrimental to the agricultural continuation and motivation of the farmers to fulfil those expectations that are already there in the short-term. What it means in more precise terms is that we expect there will be some sort of safety mechanisms in place to the Common Agricultural Policy in the whole of Europe. We fully support the continuation of the Common Agricultural Policy framework. We talk about the detail of what should be there and what is necessary or perhaps not that necessary, and this is why we have a detailed analysis on the Health Check. We have identified a number of issues that are of relevance, for instance, to British farmers and not necessarily as much to Italian farmers or Swedish farmers. Sometimes we have some friction between our member organisations in terms of what highlighting means. When I say market management, for instance, that means we should maintain market management tools in the marketplace. A very good example is the recent crisis in the pig meat sector. We clearly identified the difficulty that was out of reach of the farmers themselves and it was society who decided that there had to be a level of control on imports and there had to be some requirement fulfilled to import raw materials, for instance GMO.

We do not take a stand on whether GMO is good or bad but in the reality if the European Union society at large expects that we fulfil the requirements of society, namely not using GMOs extensively and not without authority from the European institutions, this has to be reflected in terms of safety mechanisms, market management, when we talk about the cereals market and the recent experience that we had in the pig meat market. Prices stagnated, costs spiralled and farmers were suffering and going out of business to the detriment of the European consumer because the pig meat we have to import would most probably be fed with GMO feed. Clearly we feel there is room for safety mechanisms, especially market management tools in the future.

Chairman: I wonder if we could go over to Single Farm Payments.

Q570 Lord Cameron of Dillington: The Commission seems to be indicating that in the long-term Single Farm Payments based on an historical basis is going to be an untenable position and, as you know, in England they are working that way and Germany are proposing the same. What do your members feel about this? Have you got any views on the conversion of the Single Farm Payment to area payments based on a regional basis?
Mr Pesonen: First of all, this option was given as part of the package in 2003, the historical reference. Some Member States have traditionally been very much in favour of such an approach. Another thing is how long we are going to continue with this historical reference. I have had some experience of this from the Finnish Farmers' Union. Even with the conservative groups, like the dairy producers in Finland, they identified the need to have some sort of transitional period for the historical reference in Single Farm Payments, I imagine the length of this transitional period is a matter of importance.

Q571 Lord Cameron of Dillington: So you accept it has got to change eventually?
Mr Pesonen: This is up to member organisations and Member States because clearly there is a link between each individual Member State and their system and their reference. For instance, in Ireland I see their justification for the historical reference, the historical link with their strong bovine sector, and since they had economic difficulty with that particular sector in early 2000 it was clear that at the same time this was a safety net for the farmers. It is not up to COPA-COGECA to say it is wrong for you or you should change that, it is up to the Member States to decide whether or not that is relevant. That is escaping the responsibility, but this is clearly something that—

Q572 Lord Cameron of Dillington: As part of the Health Check there are going to be statements about the need to change eventually.
Mr Pesonen: This is what the Commissioner has indicated.

Q573 Viscount Ullswater: The introduction of the Single Farm Payment was quite a radical reform. I would like to hear your views on decoupling. Do you welcome complete decoupling? On capping should there be upper and lower limits in the support levels? On cross-compliance, are the arrangements working?
Mr Pesonen: First of all, in terms of decoupling I have to admit that most of the member organisations of COPA-COGECA in 2003 were rather reluctant to adopt this new approach because of the clear risks involved. I have to say on my own behalf, that is a welcome change for the agricultural sector for the better. By this I mean that the market forces will be more transparent and influencing the decisions of the farmers. However, we have identified a number of products that will suffer in relative terms if we decouple totally. We have used the expertise of our working parties and identified certain sectors, like durum wheat, rice, seeds, flax and hemp, shelled fruit and tobacco. They are minor products on the scale of the European Union but if we decoupled shelled fruit eventually that would mean that would more or less totally disappear because of the relatively high cost of production. Here again we have the expectations of society. I admit that sometimes it is difficult to interpret what the expectation is but we feel when we have diversified European agriculture to the extent we have now we should have some sort of guarantee that we have the possibility to continue with particular products. This is our first reaction but we are of the opinion that until 2013 we should maintain the possibility for Member States to keep this coupling effect. In general that only represents a minor share of the total direct payments which are well above 80%, already decoupled. The overall experience from this decoupling effect has been positive from the European farmer's point of view; not 100% but generally speaking. I know this myself from the market experiences that we have had.

Q574 Viscount Ullswater: On capping? This is really a proposal, is it not?
Mr Pesonen: We have to identify the two extremes, whether we talk about the lower level of payment for farm size or the maximum. Clearly politically these are interlinked. I would imagine that many of the Member States use this as a package in total. When we talk about capping, COPA-COGECA are not in line with the Commission in terms of introducing a strict line for maximum farm size and maximum direct payment because we feel that in many of these cases there are issues that are relevant to the

agricultural activity as such. I know, for instance, in the UK there have been references to environmental matters, that it is the hectares that are the basis for cost. In new Member States we have identified the need for the inclusion of labour intensive working methods or operation methods. Quite recently, I visited a Czech Republic private limited company that employed 200 people and they had several thousand hectares of arable land, 1,400 dairy farmers, and on average it was a joint venture for a lot of smallholdings in general. This has to be taken into account and that is why we do not share the view of the Commission that there should be a ceiling. We note that the previous approach with the single ceiling maximum limit of €200,000 per holding was abandoned and now we are talking about various thresholds and the percentages that are going to be used. At the lower end of the scale we are supportive of simplifying schemes in administration to replace the additional administrative cost that is involved with small scale farms. The Commission justification for the introduction of this lower limit is the administrative cost is overwhelming in comparison with the income to farmers through direct payments. We feel that this could be simplified in terms of using a three to five year period, for instance, where farmers commit themselves in order to get a relatively small amount of money. In certain Member States this has significance in political terms. We are looking for wider acceptance of the Common Agricultural Policy, like most of the Member States, and this is going to be one of the examples of that particular approach. When it comes to cross-compliance, generally speaking we are of the opinion that cross-compliance is a crucial element of the first pillar of the Common Agricultural Policy. Cross-compliance is a pre-condition of direct payments and, in fact, the Commission is underlining the importance of cross-compliance by possibly proposing new measures under cross-compliance as a pre-condition to first pillar payments once again. We are against this approach, we do not feel it is good for the motivation of the farmers, especially when we talk about the overall approach to the Common Agricultural Policy, that we all repeatedly include new items to the package without taking into account the fact that at some point the farmers will say, "This does not add up, I will just get out of the business", so society will lose the aspects they are looking for. It is a double-edged sword as to whether you should use it but at the same time you have to be prepared to justify inclusion of new policies.

Q575 Viscount Ullswater: Are you finding amongst your members that some of the rules of cross-compliance are a little too tough and people are getting money withdrawn for rather technical reasons?

Mr Pesonen: I do not think that farmers in general think the rules are tough but the administration is overwhelming and that makes a lot of difference. It is existing legislation and how to implement it. A very good example is this ear tag business which we think is ridiculous, that we have an obligation to have two ear tags on a bovine animal where the animal is perfectly identifiable with one tag, especially if there is documentation that goes with it. We feel there are a lot of things that we could simplify in administration in order to motivate the farmers to fulfil the legal requirements. We are not asking for alleviation of the rules themselves but the administration is overwhelming.

Q576 Viscount Ullswater: Could you just give a further comment on the discontinuation of those supply mechanisms, set-aside and, in due course, milk quotas?
Mr Pesonen: COPA-COGECA, together with some member organisations, actively proposed setting the set-aside rate on the obligation level to zero. This was proposed by the Commission and has been accepted by the Council already and we welcome that move. That will alleviate the availability of feedstuffs for next year, for instance. At this stage, however, we feel that we should not abolish the system of set-aside because it is one of the very few remaining market management tools. We see that as a supply management tool but if we do not have anything else, and originally this tool was introduced to lower the supply of cereals in the European Union market, we ask for maintaining the possibility of returning to this question and we ask for a zero rate. This is the approach of COPA-COGECA. We can come forward in terms of what to do in relation to that in the future but at this stage we recommend the continuation of the existence of the scheme. When we talk about milk, politically this is a top priority for all Member States and all member organisations in the European Union. In relation to wine, for instance, this is a totally different scale of matter. The same applies to sugar. All Member States are extremely interested in milk, it is a basic commodity, and they are really interested in how to organise that in the future. This is the background from where we started last spring to organise ourselves in terms of position-taking and we identified three things. First of all, the overall quota regime has worked in favour of the sectoral balance, generally speaking, farm income, the stability of the market and general predictability. In doing so that is most welcome but at the same time we identified two particular issues. First, the market has developed and there is more potential for the marketplace to be exploited by the dairy producers and this is clear, prices have gone up. Our fear is once they go up drastically they usually come down drastically and that is what we want to avoid.

Secondly, politically the message has been particularly clear. The Commissioner has said repeatedly very clearly that she is not going to propose any kind of continuation. Of course, you could argue that her term is coming to an end but, nevertheless, generally speaking this is the opinion of the Commission at the moment. The Commission is not proposing and most probably the Member States are not going to create a Qualified Majority in favour of the Commission's non-existent proposal. The political landscape has changed. We have identified these three items and have come to the conclusion that the most important factors to European agriculture and milk sectors are stability, predictability and regional distribution of production. That does not mean that we have to freeze that but there have to be certain elements in place so we can continue producing milk in areas like mountainous regions where you do not have any other agricultural activity that remains if you lose milk. Also, the employment factor is there and we need to have another look into that. In short, we are working on the particular approach vis-à-vis the quota regime as to whether we are in favour or against the quota continuation but at this stage it looks like our members are divided more or less into two groups. We have the more market-oriented, probably the most competitive regions in the farmers' union, and then smaller Member States in general and they are in favour of some sort of system being continued.

Q577 Lord Cameron of Dillington: In terms of the Commission's proposal to remove all intervention from arable areas apart from this safety net for bread wheat, what are your views on that?
Mr Pesonen: As I said, we would support an approach where we have some sorts of measures if we have a crisis. We have had certain turbulence and volatility in the marketplace and you know better than I do that there have been certain comments coming from consumers and citizens when we have had higher prices for foodstuffs. In fact, the price increases have been rather modest, 2 or 3% at the most, but all of a sudden in Italy we have had a strike against pasta price increases and the relevance of the price increases to their economic system. We feel that if we have a management problem, especially when we are faced with international actors like Russia, Ukraine and their active involvement in terms of introducing export tax, for instance, which clearly undermines the livelihoods of European producers through the market, and then we have the GMO issue with the Americans and a lot higher prices in South America, drought in Australia, all these aspects together, especially put into the same pot with climate change, it appears that we have a need for some sort of

mechanism to be maintained and this is what we are in favour of.

Q578 Chairman: That brings us to risk management absolutely centrally, does it not, because the Commission has drawn attention to the fact that the more you open up the market the greater the level of risk. Should the industry itself begin to accept greater ownership for the management of these risks rather than always looking towards the state and the EU?
Mr Pesonen: Yes and no. Yes because the businesses are clearly the operators and they try to take benefit out of the market changes. Of course, this is what I would do if I was selling cereals. But at the same time there has to be a certain minimum mechanism that we could use, for instance, against the Russian activities or international development or all of a sudden when there is a crisis in place. We have identified that, first of all, by definition common market organisations are risk management. They were introduced in the first place to reduce risk, reduce volatility and reduce sudden change in the marketplace. By definition they are there to alleviate the problems that we are faced with in the marketplace. Secondly, of course businesses are interested in getting involved and if they can use that as a business opportunity then why not. This depends on the sector itself. Even in cereals we have a slightly different situation with oats than with barley than with durum wheat or maize, especially when we take into account issues like GMO in importation and the risks involved in the adventitious presence of GMO substances, for instance. Thirdly, the Commissioner has been very much pushing us in the direction of having some sort of risk management measures put in place and in doing so we have to bear in mind that we have a number of tools available at a national level. Clearly what we should do is use the experiences that we have had and there I talk about crisis management, let us say covering some of the unforeseen costs or damages the farmers are faced with. They are accepted by the Commission at this stage but we should use the existing measures to assist us in terms of creating something at the European Union level. There are three players basically, the common market organisations being the main tool, opportunities are there for businesses and we should take into account what we have experienced over the last few years at a national level.

Q579 Earl of Arran: Turning briefly to rural development, what view has your organisation reached on the practical implementation of the EAFRD? What lessons do you think can be learnt both in the context of the Health Check and the long-term future of agricultural policy?

Mr Pesonen: I understand that this is more of an operational question concerning the change in the financing of rural development vis-à-vis the first pillar payments. We take a very positive view with regard to that. That is a clear financial tool for rural development and for other matters in the Common Agricultural Policy. That is the most I can say about that. When we talk about the first pillar and the second pillar in general it has always been the opinion of the European agricultural lobby that we are in favour of a strong first pillar because that is a genuine Common Agricultural Policy tool. Clearly rural development has a role and it is a fundamental part of the global picture of Common Agricultural Policy but we also have identified the difficulty of having a slightly different approach in each of the Member States, both funding and policies themselves. Of course, the European Commission has proposed, and the Council has agreed, measures that should be financed through rural development but if we identify or introduce measures that are currently under the first pillar—direct payment, cross-compliance—to the second pillar, for instance hygiene regulations, that would clearly be a distortion of the competition between Member States if we did not put something in that said Member States should implement that fully in the way that has been done before. If the only reasoning for this change is the co-financing, which is a matter of interest to finance ministers, we would question this approach quite strongly. We clearly see a role for first pillar payments. Cross-compliance has a role as a pre-condition to direct payments but when it comes to rural development the concept is far wider. We welcome business opportunities to farming communities or rural communities and in certain Member States this has a high profile role in the overall Common Agricultural Policy but it does not bring in the benefits that we expect to enjoy from the Common Agricultural Policy at large. This is the general approach. When it comes to modulation, and I had the privilege to participate in this particular work on behalf of the previous government in the Finnish Presidency, the particular calculation method applied in the UK was an eye-opener for me to see the complexity of the matter and when you involved other Member States and how they reacted to that. To my knowledge, it is only Portugal and the UK which implement the voluntary modulation scheme and in neither of these two countries farmers have welcomed this. There is a different shade of grey between the two Member States but, nevertheless, the message in some cases has been that the money has been taken out of the reach of the farmers and this is something that on a European Union level we feel should not be done. If we have modulation there should be clear rules as to how we are going to use it, not like replacing the cuts when Member State governments introduced rural development funding through the European Union budget in December 2005 in Brussels. We did not feel that was justified just because the Member States did not want to commit themselves to further rural development, which was the case. That should not be replaced by modulated funds from the first pillar which will de-motivate farmers by committing to these requirements that we have already talked about and in the end endangering the whole concept of providing society and consumers with what they want.

Q580 *Chairman:* I appreciate that it has been a bit of a rush covering the ground but I think you have successfully covered the ground we wanted to cover. If you feel that you have not had the time and opportunity to expand on the issues that you would want to expand on, if you have got anything in writing we would be very happy to receive it. Thank you very much indeed.

Mr Pesonen: I am afraid the only thing I have in writing at the moment is my President's speaking notes for tomorrow's meeting at the Commission. I certainly would like to highlight that especially after the 2003 reforms it is very clear to farmers that we have two sources of funding for the Common Agricultural Framework, which we fully support. It is either the consumers, which is our preferred choice, or it is the taxpayer. There is no free lunch any more. That has made a lot of difference for farmers.

Q581 *Lord Plumb:* My Lord Chairman, I just wonder if on the risk management you would like to expand on that in writing to us because that is an area of considerable importance as we face the changes that are ahead of us.

Mr Pesonen: I will have a look at that.

Q582 *Lord Plumb:* I am just wondering if you have got some ideas on insurance policies, for instance, which could form a sort of safety net.

Mr Pesonen: Okay.

Chairman: Thank you very much indeed.

WEDNESDAY 5 DECEMBER 2007

Present   Arran, E   Jones of Whitchurch, B
            Cameron of Dillington, L   Plumb, L
            Dundee, E   Sewell, L (Chairman)
            Greaves, L   Ullswater, V

Examination of Witness

Witness: MR REIMER BOEGE, a Member of the European Parliament, examined.

Q583 *Chairman:* First of all, can I repeat my sincere thanks to you for finding time to meet with us and help us with our inquiry. If I can say initially who we are and what we are doing. We are a Sub-Committee of the House of Lords Select Committee on the European Union, which is a scrutiny committee. We are carrying out an inquiry into the Health Check but also looking forward to the Budget Review and possibly the evolution of the CAP. For us, this is a formal evidence taking session so there is a shorthand note. The transcript will be available in due course which will be submitted to you and you can make any corrections or revisions you think necessary. I wonder if the best way is if you wish to make a brief opening comment or we go straight into questions and answers. What would you prefer?

Mr Boege: Let me say first that it is a real pleasure to be with you again. I think it is now three or three and a half years since I was in London at the European Affairs Committee in the House of Lords together with my former colleague, Terry Wynn, who was President of the Budget Committee at that time. We were talking about the Financial Perspective which we had to negotiate. There are now two or three elements on the table. We are facing the review of the Financial Perspective and I am still the rapporteur of the Budget Committee on this issue. At the same time, the Agriculture Committee is preparing an initiative report on the so-called Health Check. I think you are seeing the President of the Agriculture Committee as well, so I will not say a lot on that. We are facing real challenges on one side. On the other side, I think it is important to find a balanced approach because having a multi-annual financial agreement until 2013, which has to do with primary law of the European Union as far as the accession agreements are concerned, we have to see that European policy does not change within one month, there is a phasing in and phasing out. It will be very interesting after the ratification of the Reform Treaty to see what the Reform Treaty means also for the European budget facing new policy areas such as immigration policy, climate change and so on that come about. Do we wait for the budget implications until 2013? Does it have an impact on the review already? In the Budget Committee we will work on some working documents on the implementation of

the Reform Treaty first and the next working document will come from my side as the rapporteur before the Commission has this conference on the review at the end of May next year. These are the next steps we are preparing.

Chairman: Thank you very much. I wonder if I could open the questioning by inviting Lord Cameron to start us off.

Lord Cameron of Dillington: I wanted to start by addressing the resource allocation between Pillar I and Pillar II of the CAP. In 2004 the European Parliament indicated that they were concerned that Pillar II was pretty low and I think they used the words "a bare minimum" and—

Chairman: It has got worse!

Q584 *Lord Cameron of Dillington:* --- subsequent to that it got worse. We, on this side of the table, most of us anyway, think Pillar II is a much more sensible solution to dealing with most of the rural problems throughout Europe. I wonder what you thought (a) the implications of that decision were and (b) whether in the current budget round you feel it might be reversed?

Mr Boege: Of course, it was a political declaration knowing that between the Member States and the European Commission at the very beginning of the deal there was a pre-agreement on agriculture as far as the direct payments were concerned and there was also certain guidance that the Category 1B structural funds could not really be touched. We saw the danger from the very beginning that within this political struggle, not to spend more than 1% of GNI, there would be certain sectors that could suffer more than others. It happened like this and it was very clear that rural development could be one of the victims and the amounts in the final agreement were reduced. This was our worry in the relationship between structural funds, whatever that means, and rural development. In the talks on rural development, but also Category 4, the EU as a global partner and security and defence policy, it was not discussed sufficiently and we have a chronic deficit in those areas.

Q585 *Lord Cameron of Dillington:* Are you going to be able to reverse that? Are you going to change that?

Mr Boege: The problem today is in talking about the review, personally I think we have to talk about three pillars. Pillar I is where are the leftovers or those policy areas which are not supported sufficiently from the European budget. We just solved the problem on Galileo with a reasonable result for everybody. We know that CFSP is chronically under-financed. It is clear that within the review this will play an important role. We have just decided in the conciliation procedure to spend 70 million from the flexibility instrument otherwise the new missions will not be financed at all from the European budget. This is a permanent problem because there was an under-estimation of the real needs and costs in the long-term perspective. On the programmes, it is very difficult within the first three years to evaluate and see where the amounts are that are really spent and where we have an over-estimation of the real needs. There is always a time lag between commitments and payments, especially in structural funds and also in rural development and trans-European networks as well. I would say we need two or, even better, three budget years to see within the existing system where we can reprioritise between programmes. If structural funds are not really spent, are there other political needs not to ask for higher ceilings, or if trans-European networks are not spent as planned maybe there will be more students going abroad to be educated abroad visiting other universities. For these structural fund programmes and rural development programmes we foresee a mid-term review analysis in 2010–11. Then, of course, there will be a sort of competition and we will possibly have to adjust the figures. It is too early now, we have just started. We negotiated more than 50 European programmes in the co-decision procedure. We need these two and a half or three years.

Q586 *Lord Cameron of Dillington:* What are your three pillars that you were talking about?
Mr Boege: The first pillar was the leftovers, the second pillar the evaluation of the new programmes, because in all categories we have new programmes, structural funds and rural development, and the third pillar is the preparation of the next Financial Perspective after 2013.

Q587 *Viscount Ullswater:* Perhaps we can revert to Pillar II under the CAP. If there is insufficient money for rural development within that second pillar, to what extent might increases in the other budget lines, the European Regional Development Fund, the European Social Fund and the Cohesion Fund, be extended in order to fill in some of the gaps? Is there a possibility that might be considered?
Mr Boege: It may be possible to consider this because the financial rules foresee that if we need certain amounts for special programmes, first we have to see whether there are unspent amounts in the same budget category or in other budget categories, so to respect ceilings and make transfers between programmes or categories. To have this debate before the ratification of the Reform Treaty the political price will be too high. We all know that most of the cohesion countries were not using those amounts that were foreseen in the multi-annual programming. We have a special case with Spain and Italy, for example. This idea of spending 4% maximum of the GNI via structural funds and support from the European budget was a political dream and desire but never a reality. For me, it is not only a question of what is the amount but also what is the quality of the programmes Member States and regions are developing. Coming from Schleswig-Holstein, the northern part of Germany, I know good and bad results and how Member States are using these new three pillars in the rural development programme. On the other side it is very important to say that structural fund regulations today are more flexible than they were in the past. Member States have more flexibility to decide whether they are going to support clusters, whether they will go more to the regions or even rural areas. There is a natural competition between national ministries and administrations and there is always a danger that rural areas will not get those supports because the real problems in society today are more in the urbanised areas.

Q588 *Viscount Ullswater:* Where do you believe that the environment should be funded from? Should it be funded from agriculture or a regional or rural development fund? There seems to be a debate now as to whether agriculture should carry the environment or the environment should be considered as a separate identity.
Mr Boege: In reality we have both elements today. Within the so-called cross-compliance rules many of them have to do with hygiene and environment standards, so part of the justification why we have this decoupled system of direct payments is linked to those higher standards that some competitors are not obliged to fulfil. I believe that with these minimum pillars as foreseen in rural development, whether you go to direct investments for the farmers or spend something for environmental purposes or go to rural development and so on, to give certain space for the Member States it is a wise decision to insist on minimum standards and to include these so-called former LEADER initiatives so that people from the regions can take certain initiatives. Very often there is wonderful brainstorming that you will never get in the ministries or administrations sometimes, I am sorry to say, because people are involved. This is one of the big advantages. The situations in rural areas are so different that it was a wise decision to have

these three pillars with minimum percentages to be spent. In Germany, the south is very different from the north. In the north you need more direct investment from the farmers because there are full-time farmers and in the south you have more part-time farmers and that is connected to tourism and their rural development and other sectors are more important. This also has to do with the principle of subsidiarity that many of us support and sometimes complain that we do not follow these rules.

Q589 Chairman: In a way are we asking too much of the Common Agricultural Policy in that we are asking it to deliver not only agricultural outputs but, as Lord Ullswater indicated, to deliver environmental outputs, rural development outputs, and theoretically it is not the most efficient vehicle to deliver the non-agricultural outputs? Is there a case to say use the CAP for what we know it can do best and devise other vehicles to deliver these other outputs?
Mr Boege: Being a farmer myself I am quite convinced that direct investments in the farms based on certain standards and criteria are more often giving the chance to a mayor to build a third or fourth street for cyclists. We have had some examples like this. If farmers get these amounts they will invest them. We have this emotional debate that the contribution from the farming industry to environment and sustainability is very often under-estimated in a society which is more and more linked to big cities. This is one of the problems that we are facing, what is the best way to spend and support sustainability in the agricultural sector and the rural development as well.

Q590 Earl of Dundee: The European Parliament says that it is not bound by the Brussels ceiling; at least it said that in 2004 when considering the 2007–13 funding plans. Nevertheless, the European Parliament respects the deal struck at that time. Might then the Brussels ceiling become revisited during the forthcoming Budget Review?
Mr Boege: We said it like this within the resolution tabled by Terry Wynn in April 2004 just before the European elections to say we are not bound to certain pre-agreements knowing, of course, under the existing treaties agricultural expenditure is compulsory expenditure where Parliament is not integrated in the process of co-decision which will be different with the new Reform Treaty. This was a political declaration based on certain principles that Parliament is never happy about deals which are done beforehand by the Member States just taking away, let us say, 0.75% of the total European budget and the rest we can negotiate. Normally Parliament will stand up and not accept this whether it is agriculture or has to do with other areas of policy. What will happen now within the review is this deal

which was done to come to an agreement in December 2004 says everything and nothing. If you read the sentence the review can cover everything, including the CAP and other elements, you have to find a way in the Council to change things with unanimity. Do not forget, as far as the so-called new Member States are concerned, the integration of the new Member States up to 100% of the existing premiums in 2013 is linked with the primary law of the European Union and they can see how this will develop for them from the transfer point of view. On the other side, it is clear that we are facing a situation based on the international development of the international food markets where there will be a debate as to how support in agriculture should take place in future. We say in Germany one swallow does not make a summer. We have these two pillars again, direct payments and the market development, and there are some debates which are neglecting the European balance because if you change the guideline and the transfer to certain Member States it affects the total agreement on payments and the money Member States are getting back. This will be a very hard exercise for a review. The reality in Europe is that you always have a certain phasing in and phasing out period. In agriculture the situation is changing totally if you see the situation in France and Spain. France is becoming more and more a net contributor and for Spain the agricultural budget will become more important than cohesion policy because they are phasing out.

Q591 Earl of Dundee: During the forthcoming Budget Review, and for good reason, the European Parliament might decide to not say very much and wait for others to speak. On the other hand, you might see fit to give a clear message. Would you like to comment on that position?
Mr Boege: I think the clear message will be, "Let's concentrate on a sufficient and ambitious review", as I have just explained with the three pillars, to be realistic and to prepare as a second step the elements which are needed for the next Financial Perspective after 2013 or maybe after 2015. I say this because connected with a sufficient review to solve certain of our deficits and then to have certain decisions on time, it might be good to have a parallel between the Financial Perspective which should be five years as a minimum but to connect it also with the mandate of the European Commission and European Parliament. From the parliamentarians' point of view we are negotiating a Financial Perspective which will not enter into force within our mandate but within the mandate of the next incoming Parliament and this is a very complicated situation for us. What is coming in the Agriculture Committee now to talk about elements of modulation opens certain doors but in a modest way, an acceptable

way, not as extreme as the Commission is proposing, and this could have an impact on the agricultural guideline as well. We have to be aware that within an enlarged Union we also have to take into consideration these other elements and we should not do too much within the review otherwise there will be no review, and I know some Member States would like no review at all.

Q592 Earl of Arran: As ever, continuing with budgets, the most recent Financial Perspective made provision for a reduction in the proportion of the Community budget spent on agriculture between 2007 and 2013. Do you regard this as a trend that is likely to continue or get even worse?

Mr Boege: There is very often a misunderstanding because agricultural policy is going down from, let us say, 47% to 35% in 2013. It is the only category in absolute terms which is not growing. All those programmes linked to the Lisbon Strategy, growth and jobs and so on, are growing in some way. On the other side, we cannot compare agriculture with research, there is always a comparison that we do not spend enough in research and we spend a lot in agriculture. You have to put together those figures from the national and the European levels to come to a fair comparison. The future development in the agricultural guideline is related to the political agreement as to how much money we are ready to spend through the European budget. We will vote next week on Budget 2008, second reading, with 0.96% on payments. The ceiling is 1.06 in commitments within the multi-annual framework. It is based on budgetary discipline. If there is an agreement not to spend more than 1%, to spend a lot for structural funds to face new challenges, CFSP, foreign affairs policy, international programmes, neighbourhood pre-accession and so on, the pressure on structural policy and agricultural policy will grow. This is very clear to everybody. Then we have to talk about international development again and how our agricultural system will develop after 2013, but we should avoid having a situation where at the end there will be no direct support for European farmers and at the same time we maintain the nice standards from cross-compliance which are very high. We will face a very difficult debate in our Member States.

Q593 Earl of Arran: I think you are saying the situation is likely to worsen?

Mr Boege: Yes.

Q594 Chairman: Improve, I think, is the word you are seeking!

Mr Boege: I will give you one example. I got an offer for summer barley next year to make a contract on €25.2. There might be a certain stability for the next few years but it is not guaranteed that it will stay at the high level we have. The ups and downs will grow and this will become part of the social dimension of this question. There was a political majority to abolish the old system but now, not having this intervention price system any longer, this has an impact on farmers' prices and now they are going up. I want to see what the deal will be and if the international prices go down how the supermarkets will deal with consumer prices. The ups and downs will become more pronounced and there will be many complaints but it was the political will to have this new system.

Earl of Arran: Volatility breeds uncertainty, which is very bad for any industry of course.

Chairman: It is called the market.

Lord Cameron of Dillington: He is not a farmer.

Chairman: I am a consumer.

Q595 Lord Greaves: I am tempted to get involved in your comments just now on cross-compliance, and there is a huge contradiction at the whole heart of cross-compliance, but I am not going to. I want to go back to the budget. You just said that the proportion devoted to agriculture in 2013 will be down to 35%. The question is, is there any way of looking at this objectively? Is 35% the right level? Is it going to go down further in the future with these other pressures you have been talking about? What is the right level? If there is a right level and it is not just a matter of political negotiation, what relationship has it to the contribution of agriculture to the economy of the European Union or, indeed, to the proportion of people working and their incomes, or is it something else?

Mr Boege: It is very complicated to make fair comparisons. If you talk about the contribution of the agricultural sector as a whole it is a different perception of GNI than when talking about the basic production coming from the individual farms. If you take the whole agricultural sector and everything which is linked to this sector which needs the agricultural basic production you come to a different comparison. I always warn people not to compare the wrong figures with each other. The agricultural system is based on market prices and income for the farmers from the market and these additional amounts also have to do with the systems we were creating to guarantee, let us say, a certain quality, to guarantee stability for the consumers at reasonable prices. Of course, it costs a lot for the European budget but, on the other side, there were certain guarantees for the consumers. Now parts of these elements are leaving as far as the intervention system is concerned. It is very funny that some experts are talking about the idea that we need certain minimum stocks to be on the safe side if there is a situation where Australia, Russia and Ukraine at the same time have dry weather and the harvest will not function well. We are in a system and we should be very careful after two years of implementation in changing the system again and again. No industry will accept that after a political agreement you start to change things within the first year. Europe started with agriculture first, it was 75% of the European budget at the beginning, and then there was a certain interim period in the eighties where policy was reacting too late and this led to certain budgetary crises based on development in the agricultural markets, but this is over now and everybody should recognise the contribution of the farming industry to the whole economy because we have had a certain development in productivity. When I started farming in 1975 I could get four tonnes of rye per hectare in my area and I was producing 5,500 kilos of milk with my dairy cows but today my neighbours are producing 10,000 kilos and can take from the same hectares with the same input of fertilisers, spray and so on, not four but eight tonnes.

Q596 Lord Plumb: The cows have doubled their yield.
Mr Boege: In Germany the consumer pays 13% of their available income for food only. This means that you have a lot of room for manoeuvre for other activities, whether you go on holiday, you buy a car, a computer or whatever it is. This contribution is often under-estimated in my own country as well.

Q597 Lord Cameron of Dillington: The German consumer pays 30%?
Mr Boege: 13%.
Lord Cameron of Dillington: In England it is about eight or nine.

Q598 Lord Greaves: You are dodging my question really as to whether there is an objective ideal level.
Mr Boege: It is very difficult.

Q599 Lord Greaves: It is not worth talking about because in reality it is going down to 35 in the future and we all know there will be further pressures on it so it is going to go down further but you are saying it is a pragmatic matter really.
Mr Boege: Yes, it is. When those candidates with whom we are negotiating membership join the situation will be totally different again. If you see the figures on structural funds and agriculture as far as the involvement of Turkey is concerned, for example, the figures will be totally different.

Q600 Lord Cameron of Dillington: Lord Ullswater and I want to ask you a little bit about where the money is going to come from. I gather that the European Parliament thought with the accession of the new Member States, particularly Bulgaria and Romania, that if the needs were to outstrip the

available money some sort of compulsory co-financing was in order. I wondered what reaction you have had from the Council of Ministers and the Commission to that statement.
Mr Boege: My farmer colleagues in Germany have criticised me a lot because I proposed this, but I took it on the shoulder. There were certain elements in it. First, we wanted to stick to the political agreements which were made on agricultural policy. On the other side, co-financing has something to do with budgetary discipline because we are all more careful with money where we have to co-finance and not just taking 100% from other people's pockets. It is also one of the elements where in the future a solution could be found not only with the so-called British rebates but we have many rebates in the budget. If the expenditure side of the budget is a bit more balanced and there is a certain element of co-financing—I have not talked about the real percentage which is needed—it could help as a certain correction mechanism between Member States, especially for those so-called net payer countries. I also have the impression that the situation will change with France, as I indicated, and the position presented by Parliament in the report on own resources from Alain Lamassoure was a first step to abolish all these different sorts of correction mechanisms and rebates because there was more than ten billion and the Council was negotiating on extra conditions which are not bound by common rules. Some countries got additional amounts for rural development—Austria more than one billion and even Luxembourg got 20 million—and others got extra conditions for house building from structural funds, and so on, which were not linked to common rules. There we have to start to talk about how the system can be made more transparent within this idea of co-financing because agricultural direct payment is the only multi-annual programme without any co-financing.

Q601 Lord Cameron of Dillington: If you move to area payments across Europe then co-financing is a perfectly logical next step, is it not?
Mr Boege: I know the situation of our regional and national budget in Germany quite well and even my federal state has always had big problems in co-financing all the European programmes and the national programmes on economic development as well. As a principle that Member States feel more committed to budgetary discipline, they feel more committed to invest in the right programmes, co-financing is very helpful. It does not automatically mean that it must be 50%. It could be linked to certain pillars but as a principle, and linked to this approach that we want to stick to our agreements and the element of the budgetary discipline on the other side, there are only one or two national delegations in

Parliament resisting this idea. It is still on the cards for the future.

Q602 Viscount Ullswater: Do your thoughts about co-financing direct you to only some programmes being suitable for co-financing and is that not going to lead to re-nationalisation of the CAP payments? I can see that there are many dangers and I would like to hear from you what you see the dangers might be.
Mr Boege: Nobody is talking about re-nationalisation but regional funds which are co-financed and rural development programmes which are co-financed as well. If you go in a direction where, let us say, 50 or 60% has to be financed from the national budget then it is a step towards re-nationalisation, this is very clear. Facing all the budgetary problems on rebates and special commitments to individual Member States, it could help to find a balance. I know it is very difficult and it is linked to the question of own resources where no-one really knows, although it is foreseen we will talk about it, and Member States will accept coming to a more transparent system than the existing one. It is linked to this question.

Q603 Viscount Ullswater: Do you think it will upset the level playing field between Member States in competitive terms if there is too much co-financing or too much availability for either regions or Member States being able to co-finance in certain areas?
Mr Boege: If the co-financing rate is too high that might happen. As I explained with the example of my federal state, our former government was not able to co-finance some of the national programmes and part of those amounts foreseen for Schlewsig-Holstein later went to the federal state of Saxonia because they were prepared to take the money.

Q604 Viscount Ullswater: Are there any extensions of using co-financing that you would see that you are not talking about just now?
Mr Boege: It is mainly linked to this question of the first pillar on agricultural policy. All the other multi-annual programmes are more or less regions and Member States' national authorities are involved where we have a certain sort of co-financing. Our experience with budgetary discipline and Article 44 of the Inter-Institutional Agreement that Member States should be ready to present a summary of the available accounts done by the Court of Auditors to be given to the European level and the European Court of Auditors have a more precise evaluation of how money is spent and how reluctant many Member States are, including my own, show there is a certain need.

Q605 Baroness Jones of Whitchurch: I want to talk a little bit about enlargement and some of the tensions that might be coming from the original EU-15 and the new Member States. You have talked a lot about budgetary discipline and obviously if you follow the logic of that through one of the areas is around the Single Farm Payment that ought to then be reduced to the original EU-15. Is that still going to happen? What is the timetable for that? Is that causing tensions between the original Member States and the incoming Member States about how the money is divided?
Mr Boege: There have been debates from the very beginning and it will happen again in the context of the Commission's proposals and the idea of modulation. Some countries will reject the proposal from the Commission because their agricultural industry is affected more than others. For the same reasons there will be some countries asking for a very strict cut in payments from a certain level onwards. Again, there will be some countries questioning the historical basis because they are not so productive. We know which these countries are. With each step of these reforms, starting with the McSharry Reform, we have always had this debate. This is not news; it is just the same debate. As I said, we have found a certain balance and, therefore, the Commission should take a prudent approach. I have the impression that what is coming from the initiative report of the Agriculture Committee is to say let us take a new average, not 5,000 but 10,000 direct payments, no modulation, because the administrative burden is very high and complicated, and to have a certain higher modulation in a degressive form between 2009 and 2013 but not with those amounts the Commission is proposing that will affect the UK, Eastern Germany, France a little bit, and Spain and Italy to an enormous amount. If you look into the statistics it is interesting how much Spain and Italy will be affected by the Commission proposal which will be to find a modest way of growing modulation to shift it to Pillar II but leave it in the Member States and not redistribute it. That is very important otherwise it will affect the balance of the budget again and there will be no majority for that. It was difficult enough to get a Qualified Majority in the Council of Finance Ministers last Friday on Galileo. Everybody must know what Qualified Majority means in this context.

Q606 Baroness Jones of Whitchurch: Did I understand you were saying that you would recommend a small increase across the board before the changes start being phased in? Is that what you are saying?
Mr Boege: When we faced the enlargement Bulgaria and Romania were not really integrated, but then we said if the agricultural spending goes up to more than

200 million below the ceiling the Commission is committed to do something and that means cutting payments. Of course, market expenditures are limited in the existing budget and, therefore, our idea was to link it with co-financing to remind them you cannot start again and again in a transitional period when the farming community is just going to adopt the new systems to change things again and again. Now we have enough margin within the agricultural ceiling that there is no real need for those cuts based on the enlargement of Bulgaria and Romania. We are talking about 8.9 billion over the period, of growing importance at the end until 2013 but not so important until 2009 or 2110. What is more important in this aspect is the elements of budgetary control function well and the Commission gave a warning to one of these two new countries and we have to have a very precise look at it.

Chairman: We have saved the best until last: Lord Plumb.

Q607 *Lord Plumb:* Thank you, my Lord Chairman. You started off, interestingly, first talking about the Financial Perspective. The comments you have just made are interesting. Expenditure on the CAP got up to 75% in my day and it will be down to 35% cent in yours, so well done, it is moving in the right direction, but I note that the Parliament recalled that once the distinction between compulsory and non-compulsory expenditure has been abolished, "the ring-fencing of resources for market-related expenditure and direct payments under Heading 2 will no longer exist". You have already referred to this in the comments you have made but are there any other points you would like to make on that? The second thing is what implications are likely from the extension of Parliament's powers with respect to the budget and what they have for the process of further reforming the CAP? I heard that yesterday the President made a great speech in which he said that the European Parliament would not in any way be taking away the powers of national parliaments. It is a question of the role that the European Parliament is playing in further reforming the CAP because whilst we as a Committee are looking at 2013 we have to keep reminding each other this is a Health Check, we are not reforming the CAP, we are looking at the process at the moment, how it is working and how it is operating and, therefore, it is very much a Health Check. Looking at the future and reforming the CAP, what role do you see the European Parliament playing and how should it be directed?

Mr Boege: Let me give one small example from the ongoing budget procedure of 2008. We decided to table a certain reserve on administrative expenditure for implementation of the rural development programmes from the Commission staff because we had the impression that there was a delay in evaluation of the presented programmes and the Commission was going back to micro-management which should be in the hands of the Member States and the regions and they were trying to get certain things back that they lost during the legislative procedures. That is a very small example of how we have tried to find the right balance between Member States and the European Union in implementing these programmes. The next step will be that based on the Inter-Institutional Agreement there will be an adjustment of the existing budget agreements based on the Reform Treaty. It is very clear there is no longer any distinction between compulsory and non-compulsory expenditure which mainly has to do with agriculture but also international fishery agreements and some other aspects. Co-decision will grow and will happen in the agricultural sector as well. On the other side, the budget authority is obliged to implement those figures which were agreed within the co-decision procedures of the multi-annual programmes. It is very clear that Parliament had to insist on co-decision on those elements and on the other side, if you see it from the agricultural point of view, things will not be easier in Parliament. We cannot hide any longer and say, "It is compulsory expenditure, we can table the amendment how we like it" because now we have to take real responsibility and this is a different story. This is helpful as well. It is very important that we have two elements, we are part of the budgetary authority but also a legislative authority and those agreements that are done there have to be respected by the budget authority. If there is an agreement on a certain amount, whether it is for lifelong learning or for structural funds or the first pillar, we have to implement it within the annual budgets. We are facing new challenges in agricultural policy and it will be a very interesting time, especially not knowing what will happen in the Council until the European elections in June 2009.

Lord Plumb: Thank you very much. That is interesting because the Chairman decided that after we have decided on whatever report we produce with the findings from all the evidence we have taken the next problem we will consider is fishing, so we shall be back again looking at the fisheries policy.

Q608 *Chairman:* Can I ask you to take up the business of co-decision making in agriculture and ask you to speculate a bit. In the UK there are clearly two schools of thought about what the effect of that will be. One is very similar to what you said about the European Parliament having to move away from gesture politics effectively to accepting responsibility and facing reality, so that could well make reform easier, and the other is this is just a further opportunity for narrow protectionist interests to assert themselves in the agricultural area.

Mr Boege: I do not think so. Of course, we will have a very new structure of debate and decision-making in Parliament and also between the specific committees in the European Parliament. Having done our first reading on the agriculture budget, everything is over for us. In future, based on the Reform Treaty, there will be a co-decision procedure or conciliation procedure on the budget and after the first reading there will be a conciliation period of 21 days to find an agreement between the Council and Parliament. If not, based on the restrictions of the European budget, Parliament can vote at second reading with an absolute majority and three of five members to decide on the budget. The pressure to come to an agreement between the Council and Parliament in those areas where we have this compulsory expenditure will grow and this strengthens Parliament's role. I do not think it is a question of protectionism. There will be a lot of different approaches from special national interests and there could be protectionism as well and to find a balance for the agricultural sector, including the budget, including these elements of sustainability and food production at a level of high quality and acceptable prices, is a new challenge and real challenge for the institutions, and not only for Parliament but also the Council and the agriculture ministers to acknowledge that they have to negotiate with Parliament and not behind closed doors.

Q609 *Lord Cameron of Dillington:* If you were an MEP from a net recipient country, what motivation would you have to control your budgetary demands?
Mr Boege: I have been a Member of the European Parliament since 1989 and I come from a so-called net payer because the benefit the German industry had from enlargement was overwhelming. I do not know how our economic situation would be if we did not have this European aspect and aspect of globalisation. There must be an agreement between the leading Member States as to what we are going to do in this globalised context with the agricultural policy in the next step. Nobody knows what will happen in the Doha Round, whether there will be some development not only on tariffs but non-tariff issues, for example, which are becoming more and more important—I have certain doubts about that sometimes—and what this will mean for the agricultural budget. I am quite sure if you look at the development on the international market we will not go down to cereal prices of €8, €9 or €10 in the next few years. This may create some room for manoeuvre and to modernise the farming sector in the international context. I am quite convinced that for the young farmers today facing this globalisation, and talking about budget and how they get a reasonable income, it is a better situation than I had when I started farming.
Lord Plumb: Hear, hear!

Q610 *Lord Greaves:* When you say three out of five, it needs a 60% majority for all budget items.
Mr Boege: Yes. The absolute majority of the House plus three out of five voting members in case of rejection of a conciliation result.

Q611 *Lord Greaves:* When you said that some MEPs will have special interests, are those special interests from their state not inevitably protectionist as far as those states are concerned?
Mr Boege: Of course, in Parliament you have the same situation as in the Council because first we are obliged to fight for the interests of our constituency and then for our national interests but never to forget that we have a common interest and we have to find the right balance. This is part of the exercise and the challenge.
Chairman: Thank you very much indeed.

WEDNESDAY 5 DECEMBER 2007

Present Arran, E   Jones of Whitchurch, B
      Cameron of Dillington, L Plumb, L
      Dundee, E   Sewell, L (Chairman)
      Greaves, L   Ullswater, L

Examination of Witness

Witness: MR NEIL PARISH, a Member of the European Parliament, examined.

Q612 *Chairman:* Thank you very much for finding the time to come and talk to us and help us with our inquiry. Let me just briefly say formally who we are and what we are doing. This is a Sub-Committee of our EU Select Committee, which is a scrutiny committee of the House of Lords, carrying out an inquiry into the Health Check but really looking beyond the Health Check as well to see the view of the Financial Perspective and the future shape of the CAP generally. It is a formal evidence taking session so that means a transcript will be prepared and once that is done you will have the opportunity to look through it and make changes that you feel are necessary. Would you like to make a brief opening comment or do you want to go straight into questions and answers?

Mr Parish: I know you would like to question me more, so let me set out the parameters in as much I would suggest to you the Health Check is evolutionary rather than revolutionary. It is really carrying on the Fischler Reform. When Fischer Boel came to committee last week it was very much making sure that payments were decoupled away from production across the whole of Europe, set-aside to actually be abolished rather than be on zero because, as Lord Plumb and others know, things that remain at zero here can be resurrected again, so if you want proper reform they have got to be taken out. On milk quotas, finally an absolutely clear statement that quotas would be gone by 2015, there will be an increase in milk quota next year going into services at we reckon about 2%. I would not have thought it would have hurt to have gone to a little more than that but I suspect that is what is going to be there to create the soft landing. You have modulation of 2% in 2010, 2011, 2012 and 2013 which from our point of view is very good news because I have never been opposed to modulation but, as you know, I made a little bit of fuss about voluntary modulation because I did not particularly like our own farmers to lose it and not others necessarily. I think if you are going to have a Common Agricultural Policy there has to be a commonality to it. The clear point that the Commissioner made on modulation, and I am sure she made it partly for my benefit, was that the increase in compulsory modulation will be taken off voluntary modulation, not added to it, therefore, if

you think we are on about 5% at the moment, another 8% compulsory would bring you up to 13% and the deal we more or less had in the end on modulation was about 14/15%, so from my point of view that would bring us to a much more equal position and I welcome that. Those are really the bald points. I will answer questions. We ought to talk a little bit more about where we are going. You talked to Reimer Boege and Financial Perspectives are important. If you are going to be serious about reforming CAP you have also got to be serious about reforming the budget and, dare I say it, keep quite a strict control on the budget and also co-financing does need to be introduced so that Member States at least can then be paying for a lot of their own CAP. We have to be careful with countries like Poland, Hungary and Lithuania because having invited them into the club you cannot necessarily say, "Well, all right, chaps, now you are in we will change your rules and you can pay for your own CAP". We have got to find ways of helping them as well and we might be able to do that as we do with structural funds where if they are receiving structural funds they are receiving help with CAP payments and if they are not they are paying quite a lot towards their own CAP. I think the rule should be compulsory at a European level for the simple reason that otherwise countries like France will find innovative ways of helping their farmers and, dare I say it, the UK perhaps with not quite a generous scheme. Those would be my bullet points at this stage.

Q613 *Chairman:* That is a nice little contemporary survey, thank you very much. Looking ahead, moving away from the specifics I would invite you to say what do you see as should be the underlying general principles as we move beyond the Health Check into further reform?

Mr Parish: You have got 27 countries now and you are going to have probably 28 at least with Croatia and you are going to have a tight budget. I do not think we want to necessarily carry on with a general payment on all land, we have got to start to look to targeting this. It is difficult to predict the market but in the market as it looks at the moment, it looks like cereals are set reasonably fair. The livestock sector is always going to be under great pressure, especially in areas where land is more difficult to farm. We are going to have to find ways of targeting those resources. Because the agriculture policy, technically speaking, is no longer linked to production you cannot then start saying that the market price for cereals is higher so we will re-divert some of that money to the livestock sector. That is where you can use modulated money to some degree to help with that situation. Representing the West Country I can probably talk more about these terrible barley barons in East Anglia and the need to take some money from them and spread it across to the South West farmers who are suffering on the hills. You get my meaning. There has got to be a way of adjustment. Keep the budget tight and then move into 2013 and beyond. The whole policy now will have to be much more aligned to environmental policy as well as production but, of course, we have not to forget production because we are in a much tighter situation vis-à-vis the world supply of food, so food security is becoming an issue. It is a balance between the two. The livestock sector, the suckler beef in particular and sheep at the moment, has its problems, all of these animals are kept mainly in areas of high landscape value, not only good for agriculture production in some places but also good for tourism, so the balance has to be met. I would suggest we have got to find mechanisms of finding and targeting support. I know the Commissioner is particularly keen on the fact, and I think she is quite right, and we can argue whether the historic model of payment or the regional form of payment is right or wrong, that by the time you get to 2013 you can hardly argue that the payment you are getting on that farm is related to what you were doing in 2001 or 2002, there is not a reality to that. That is where we have got to find our way. In her mid-term review there is not a huge amount on where it is going afterwards. The gossip on the street is that Barroso is going for a second term of Presidency and he did not want anything too revolutionary in the ideas from the Commissioner. While I support very much what she is doing up until 2013, I think we do have to start looking. We have got to find ways of targeting the money better. We can hope that by then China, India and Vietnam will increase their production and economies and poor people will be getting richer and wanting more food, which is the first thing they spend their money on, and then milk powder and the dairy side will be better. I am hoping the whole thing will be better from an economic point of view so we can then balance the books.

Q614 *Lord Cameron of Dillington:* We have heard what Neil Parish thinks, which is very interesting, but I just wonder what support you might be getting from your committee on co-financing and decoupling?

Mr Parish: Not as much actually.

Q615 *Lord Cameron of Dillington:* You did not mention capping but I suspect I know where you come from on that.
Mr Parish: Probably not quite where you think.

Q616 *Lord Cameron of Dillington:* How does your committee line up on all of this?
Mr Parish: They are very conservative with a small "c". They really do not want any form of change. We are awaiting a report from Lutz Goepel, who is the German rapporteur and is dealing with the Health Check, and his proposals are going to be much more moderate, shall we say, than even the Commission's proposals. It is going to be less modulation and less of everything basically except payment. It is difficult for me because when you sit in the chair you have your own personal views, and I am sure Lord Plumb knows this, but you also have to put your European hat on on occasions and take an overall view. I will take some of the committee with me, but not all. It will be conservative. I think there is beginning to be much more of an acceptance of co-financing, but not by all countries by any means. They can see that the ceiling of spending of the 1% club is probably not going to shift very much so they see co-financing, dare I say it, as a way around that 1% ceiling. I suspect co-financing is going to find support eventually, certainly among the bigger Member States and probably amongst Germany as well which, let us face it, is a big contributor to the European budget.

Q617 *Lord Cameron of Dillington:* Where would they stand on quotas?
Mr Parish: As we stand today, I understand they are in favour of quotas going. In a way they are almost key to the whole argument. Again, the Commissioner and all of us in a way are starting to be helped by the market because we finally see an increase in dairy prices and an increase of 4% in dairy trade and milk powder is the most valuable it has been for years, so that is helping. Quotas will be increased. She is very keen to get the value. Although the value in the UK has gone from the milk quota, in the Netherlands and Denmark it is still quite valuable, so that needs to be got out of the system. Not that the Commission is that worried about it, to be honest with you, because they never created it with a value so as far as they are concerned they are inclined to say it is an artificial value anyway. In the UK it is not such a problem. If quotas do remain in until 2015 I am prepared to wager you a small bet that quotas will have some value before we get to 2015 because farmers are very good at producing milk if the price is right. This year it is difficult because of high cereal prices and low quality of feed, silage and the like. It will be

interesting, I think. It will not get a high value because quotas are going to be gone but if you are producing quite a lot of milk and you are going over quota and the country goes over quota then it will be an interesting position. She will try and increase quota to absorb that if she can, I think.

Q618 Lord Cameron of Dillington: You were going to touch on your committee's views on capping.
Mr Parish: Yes. Certainly Lutz Goepel is very conservative on that because he is East German and there, of course, you have got the very big farms, the privatised estate farms basically. My view, for what it is worth, is that a little bit of capping may not be adverse as long as the money is kept within the Member State. If you started capping the very large farms by 25% you would just get them to split and you would lose the lawyers and the accountants and it would create inefficient farming for the sake of it. To play devil's advocate, if you took 5% away from the largest farms because, let us face it, there is an economy of scale, it would not make those farms split. If you could spread that money back in Member States and not send it back to the centre then there could be an argument, but it has got to be carefully handled. My one worry about accepting capping is a bit like taxation really, once you start it where does the level go thereafter. It is one of those interesting points. There will be a split in the committee on that because basically it is Germany, ourselves and Spain—Spain has got quite large farms as well—who are most interested in capping. In some ways, although it would create perhaps a—

Q619 Lord Cameron of Dillington: Denmark too.
Mr Parish: Denmark, yes. What I have said to the Commissioner, although it would make for perhaps a little re-nationalisation of agricultural policy, is in some respects if you set a maximum level of capping that any country could go to then you could almost hand it back to the Member State and say, "If you are keeping the money it is up to you how far you go up to a certain level". It is an interesting idea and I do not know whether she will take me up on it. Then it throws it back to Member State governments and gives them the grief and not the Commission. Whether she will do that or not, I do not know.

Q620 Lord Cameron of Dillington: Co-capping!
Mr Parish: Exactly.

Q621 Viscount Ullswater: If I might add a supplementary to this. Because your committee is obviously looking at the Health Check and the situation of where you have got to after a couple of years of the reform, and you say it is a very conservative committee, are they still wholly behind decoupling?

Mr Parish: Mainly, yes.

Q622 Viscount Ullswater: Mainly.
Mr Parish: Do not forget France has only decoupled this year anyway. Just as an aside, a year ago Dan said to me, "Some French Ministry of Agriculture officials want to see you" and I thought, "What have I done now?" and they wanted to come and see what problems we had had with the Single Farm Payment in the UK to make sure they did not fall into some of the same traps. I wonder if it would have worked the other way around. That is just an aside. France is moving forward now. France has still got suckler cow premiums 75% coupled so there is still a little bit more decoupling to do. There is an argument to have a grassland payment linked to suckler cows or sheep perhaps, but it has got to be a grassland environmental payment, not a suckler cow or sheep payment. Do not forget, one of the ideas of the reform from a WTO point of view is to take it out of the production box. The Irish are coming up with some interesting plans on this. I am a quarter Irish, so I declare an interest. I am interested in what the Irish do because they are very good at that sort of thing. If we are going to move an agricultural policy towards the environment we have got to remember that agriculture is very much part of the environment and if there are environmental schemes which are good for agriculture and good for the environment we must not rule them out, we have just got to find ways. The Commissioner is keen to get all Member States decoupled and then move the whole thing forward into the modulation of 2010, 2011, 2012 and 2013. That is her role. As far as the committee is concerned, they are reasonably keen on the Single Farm Payment and decoupling, they are not very keen on modulation at all in a nutshell. That is where the committee is.
Chairman: Let us move to modulation and particularly voluntary modulation.

Q623 Lord Plumb: May I say I was interested to hear you say the committee is conservative with a small "c". You did not have Barbara Castle to deal with or else it would not have been conservative. She was on my committee a long time ago.
Mr Parish: We have New Labour now. I must not be political here.

Q624 Lord Plumb: They were happy days. One thing you said was not payment on all land and that was an interesting comment. Is that not capping? Do not answer me at the moment, wait a minute. You have made your position quite clear as far as voluntary modulation is concerned and you know, of course, the British Government favours voluntary modulation. They favour everything that is voluntary, of course. I am more interested in your views on the suggestion that has been made that in the Health Check the rural development funds can only be achieved through increased co-financed compulsory modulation involving a 2% increase annually from 2010–13. Much of the evidence we have received from so many different bodies and organisations has been, "We have got to take money from Pillar I and put it into Pillar II" and that is where rural development really lies. Our concern is how that is going to be used. If we are going to have some modulation that is going to affect cross-compliance, as of course it can and will, then how does it operate and to what extent is that money used in the rural development area?

Mr Parish: In some ways we are partly putting the cart before the horse. What I think you are saying, Lord Plumb, and I agree with you, is that in some ways we should have proved to us what that money is going to be spent on before it is taken off the Single Farm Payment. Once you get to 13 or 14% you are creating quite a large sum of money and we have got to get that targeted right. I think a lot more of this money, if not all of it, will need to be targeted towards the livestock sector in some shape or form and that is where you can look for special grassland payments. The point I made about payment being targeted, this is after 2013, I am not suggesting up to 2013, but by then we will see in some way how the market is shaping up and we can then see whether we can move that money on to targeting the mountainous areas and everything else we need to target. It is difficult to make that decision now in some ways. I went to a meeting of Polish farmers and others who said to me that the job of the Common Agricultural Policy was to keep every farmer in a farm in Europe. You and I both know that is not going to happen. The huge debate, and this is a serious debate, as we go into 2013 is, is this an agricultural environmental policy or is it a social policy. That is what we have got to watch as a country because there are a lot of the southern and eastern Member States who would like to make it a social policy. I am not against part of it being a social policy but the bulk of it has got to be agriculture environment policy and that will be our big challenge. That is why we have got to watch how this rural development money is spent. One of the comments the Commissioner made during her statement, which when I see her next week I have got to ask her about, was she talked about the amount of employment on the farms as well. You have got to be ever so careful with that because the fact that you have got a lot of employment on a farm may make you efficient or it may make you inefficient and, like I said, I do not want that to be the only criterion. There are big debates to be had out there. We would be deluding ourselves if we think when we get to 2013 we are going to have enough money to carry on in the same way we are at the moment. I think we would all

accept if we can have a good profitable agricultural food sector where farmers are getting the majority of their income from the marketplace and not from public money that would be where I would like to see us. I cannot predict what it is going to be like in 2013 but certainly from the predictions of world trade at the moment in foodstuffs it looks like we are seeing the world drying up, Australia having more difficulty and economies in the Far East improving. The need for food production is there and so I think we might be in a position to be able to be reasonably radical. I repeat, the great debate here is going to be in 2013 onwards: is it an agriculture environment policy or is it a social policy? As you know, Lord Plumb, from your past experience and now with 27 countries and with quite a number of countries coming in with very small farms, it is an even greater debate.

Q625 *Viscount Ullswater:* Perhaps I can turn to the question of how the Parliament is going to look at the current situation and in the future. As I think the Chairman explained, we are looking at the Health Check and the Budget Review so I would be very interested to hear how you feel the European Parliament tends to approach the matter. Is it going to look at the Health Check in isolation or examine both of these together?

Mr Parish: The Agriculture Committee will certainly look at the Health Check largely in isolation from the budget and then they will seek enough money to be able to pay for whatever they want. I am not being facetious, that is exactly the way they will deal with it. One point I have not raised and I probably should is there are two lines of opinion but the opinion seems to be if the Treaty is accepted, or the Constitution or whatever you want to call it, by January 2009 the Agriculture Committee will have co-decision powers. If this was off the record I would make another comment but I will not because it is on the record.

Q626 *Lord Plumb:* You can go off the record.

Mr Parish: (The answer began off the record) I think the committee will deal with the Health Check separately and it will want to negotiate as much money as it can out of the system and it will always be pressing the Council for more money. Being in the chair it is quite difficult for me to say to the Agriculture Committee that we do not necessarily need all that money, we should cut our suit of clothes according to our cloth. That is how it will play. We will play hardball through this session because we know that the Commission want to deal with it by 2008, we know that the French want to put it to bed during their Presidency and we also know that we probably will have co-decision powers by January 2009, so people have woken up to that fact. My view, now speaking as Chairman of the Agriculture Committee of the European Parliament, is that

Parliament will be best to negotiate as strong a deal as possible before we get co-decision powers because we might be able to get a better deal for the Parliament before we have co-decision powers rather than after and if we co-operate we can say, "We will co-operate but we want X, Y and Z". That is the negotiation tack I will take.

Q627 Earl of Dundee: Clearly debate over the Budget Review will be pretty intense both inside and outside the European Parliament, the policies will vary and Member States will differ. In spite of that background, what measure of agreement do you believe can still be achieved?

Mr Parish: There will always be an agreement, whether it is one that we particularly want or like, that is the way Europe works. Love or hate Europe, you have got 27 countries and at least we are all talking and trading together, so that is good news. The bad news is that it is sometimes difficult to come to an agreement but we will come to an agreement. It comes down to fairly blunt politics. In Europe you have got those countries that are paying and those countries that are receiving and the receiving countries will want to push up the budget and the paying countries will want to push down the budget but we will come to an agreement. We will put forward an argument as to what we need for agriculture, rural development, structural funds, research funds, a total budget, and we will sit down and negotiate and an agreement will be had. It will be interesting to see which position the French take this time on agriculture. It is a little bit mixed messages from Sarkozy—

Q628 Chairman: There certainly are.

Mr Parish: I do not want it publicised but I am going to Paris next Tuesday on the way to Strasbourg to see Barnier and various other French ministers to talk about agriculture and reform and various things. I could probably give you a better answer to where I think the French are coming from then. The French and Germans will still be key players, especially in agriculture, but you have 27 Member States. It was bad enough to get the 15 Member States to agree before, so getting 27 will be difficult but we will get to an agreement, I have no fear. It will be the eleventh hour and burning into three or four o'clock in the morning but an agreement will be got.

Q629 Earl of Dundee: As you have said there is bound to be some late night agreement, we would be surprised if that did not happen. However, a superficial consensus might well simply reflect some degree of horse trading between national finance ministers and that is a bit sad. How might that unwelcome outcome be prevented by the European Parliament and your own committee?

Mr Parish: I do not think we can prevent that at all, to be perfectly blunt with you. What we have got to do is sit down and we will take a view on what funding we believe will be necessary to fund Europe how we believe it should be funded. This is not a personal comment, this is how the Parliament will come to its agreement. The Parliament's aspirations will be greater than those of the Council of Ministers, you can be assured, and the Commission will be sitting somewhere in the middle of all this. There will be quite an element of horse trading but, as I said, I see no alternative. The Budget Committee of the Parliament hopefully will take a much more realistic view on life, I suspect, so there will be a slight convergence there. Eventually the Parliament will come to an agreement and, as I said, our aspirations will be greater than that of the Council. In a nutshell that is the way it is.

Q630 Lord Greaves: You have answered all the questions I was going to ask but could I ask two follow-ups. The fact that some of the focus of negotiation is now going to switch to the need to get an agreed line between the Council and the Parliament, does that process help the Council to get more of a consensus and to work together as a group or does it not work like that?

Mr Parish: I hope it might. You are all politicians, or were, and you sit in the House of Lords, not as political I know.

Q631 Lord Greaves: Don't you believe it!

Mr Parish: Many of you probably sat in the Commons before. Every institution is jealous of its powers. There is going to be an element of the fact that we as MEPs have considered over the years that we have not been treated with the importance that we believe we should have had because we are the only directly elected politicians for the whole of Europe, so to start with there is going to be an element of flexing of muscles and in agriculture nobody quite knows how this will work. It works in environment at the moment, so we will find ways. The European Parliament, rightly or wrongly, is going to believe that it has got greater powers after this Treaty is in place. From the Council of Ministers' point of view it is going to be perhaps in some ways more difficult to deal with the European Parliament but, on the other hand, they are making big overtures now with the informal councils on agriculture and the Commission services, not only the Commissioner herself, are making great overtures towards me as the Chairman of Agriculture because they see moving into co-decision. If we can work together it might help, but there is going to be some flexing of muscles on the whole thing. It will be interesting to see how it pans out.

Q632 *Lord Greaves:* Let me assure you the House of Lords is a highly political place, even if we still have loads of hereditaries who are also around the table here.

Mr Parish: You are just a bit more pleasant to each other.

Q633 *Lord Greaves:* We are very polite.

Mr Parish: You are polite as you are political, that is right.

Q634 *Lord Greaves:* The second follow-up is to ask you about the Agriculture Committee. Is the small "c" conservative nature of it built in forever on the basis that these are the people who want to be on that committee and therefore put themselves forward or is there hope that it might become a bit more progressive in the future after the next elections perhaps?

Mr Parish: (The answer began off the record) I am a farmer but I do try and take a slightly broader view. There are quite a number of members on the committee like that but there are also some who take a very narrow view, a very narrow vested view. We have got the wine reform going on at the moment and naturally you have a Spanish position, a French position, an Italian position, and even a British position where we do not want to have anything to do with it because we want to be able to carry on to increase the small amount of wine production we have got which is successful. You are going to get that position, that is the way it is.

Q635 *Chairman:* Can I come back to co-decision making. There are two arguments that have come up, not just here but in all the discussions we have had. There is one argument that says co-decision making actually stands a chance of improving reform because at the moment the European Parliament can indulge in gesture politics on agriculture because with the first reading that is it, when it comes to co-decision making it will seriously have to think about priorities and not just within the Agriculture Committee but, as you indicated, the budget considerations riding to the rescue and imposing a more rational prioritisation. That is the pro-reform argument, if you like. The other reform argument is as far as agriculture is concerned the European Parliament is just irredeemable and it means that there will be another means by which protectionist interests can slow the whole process down.

Mr Parish: Heaven forbid that we would have a protectionist instinct, but you are right in some ways that we do. There are those two lines of thought. I would say, and I will stick to my guns on this, I am glad that the reform has gone as far as it has because it would have been difficult to achieve the Fischler Reform. Although you may sit there and say this reform has not gone very far, if you talk to the French and the idea of decoupling away from production, "Non, non, non" and all of a sudden it was "Yes" and they had to go along with it. We have moved a long way with the Fischler Reform but have got further to go. By the time we get to 2009, quite a lot of the reform will be going in the right direction. By the looks of it we will have co-decision powers. Where you are right is it is a bit like when we had to rush through the decision on set-aside and the Commission was late bringing it to the Parliament and some of my parliamentarians were chuntering about this and I said, "Yes, but I am not going to block it because I don't want farmers to hang us out to dry by saying we don't know now whether they can plant on set-aside land because the European Parliament held it up". Co-decision is a mixed blessing. Yes, you will negotiate a hard deal in the Parliament but if you are seen to be the ones who are blocking it there will be a backlash on the Parliament, which we do not have at the moment because we do not have those co-decision powers. In that respect you might be proved to be right. My experience over the last eight and a half years is we would not have got to the reform that we have now. Every time the Parliament is reformed and the institutions are reformed, Europe gets on with the business. You can argue whether it does it in a great way, a slow way or any other way but in some sort of strange way it works, it gets there. I am not saying it is ideal but it actually gets there. This will work its way through and I suspect it will not be hugely helpful towards reform, but we will see.

Q636 *Chairman:* I make it clear that I was not advocating a particular line.

Mr Parish: I realise that. As you quite rightly say, some of what I am telling you is what Neil Parish thinks and believes and I have also been trying to tell you where I think the committee and the Parliament will be and those are slightly different positions as you have probably become aware.

Chairman: Thank you very much. It has been enormously useful getting your views on (a) what your committee is thinking and (b) your own analysis as well. That has been very, very helpful indeed, thank you.

THURSDAY 6 DECEMBER 2007

Present	Cameron of Dillington, L	Plumb, L
	Dundee, E	Sewell, L (Chairman)
	Greaves, L	Ullswater, V
	Jones of Whitchurch, B	

Examination of Witness

Witness: Ms DALIA GRYBAUSKAITE, European Commissioner for Financial Programming and Budget, European Commission, examined.

Q637 *Chairman:* Good morning, it is very nice to see you.
Ms Grybauskaite: You are not the first and will not be the last who are interested in our exercise on the future budget reform. Usually what comes from your country and your Parliament, the House of Lords, as reports are very good quality proposals and papers and we use them. I am very happy you are investigating into this subject and you will be preparing something for us which we will use. You will receive something from us now and we will use your paper later.

Q638 *Chairman:* Just tell us what you want us to say!
Ms Grybauskaite: Of course.

Q639 *Chairman:* Thank you very much, Commissioner, for finding time to meet with us and to help us in our inquiry. As you know, we are a Sub-Committee of the European Union Committee of the House of Lords carrying out this investigation into the Health Check and looking beyond the Health Check to the Budget Review and the future evolution of the CAP. I always have to say formal things. For us, this is a formal evidence taking session so there will be a record.
Ms Grybauskaite: I need to understand that I can only say what can be written and I will leave the rest in my pocket.

Q640 *Chairman:* That is not quite true. You are able to go off the record if you want to. Would you prefer that we go straight into questions and answers or would you like to make an initial comment?
Ms Grybauskaite: As it is so formal we can go straight into questions. I know that what you have probably received about me is not so formal, but because you are so formal I will do the best I can to be formal in my answers. I would prefer to go by questions, you ask and I will try to respond. This is my Director from the service level responsible for budget reform. This is a political person from my *Cabinet*. They will try to keep an eye on me and I will do my best to say as much as I can.

Q641 *Chairman:* Thank you very much. You mentioned at the outset of your consultation document that the Commission had been invited "to undertake a full, wide-ranging review covering all aspects of EU spending, including the CAP, and of resources, including the UK rebate". How does the Commission plan to interpret those specific references to CAP and the UK rebate and the mandate? Are they focal points of the review, are they key points, or are they just part of the context?
Ms Grybauskaite: December 2005 was very much a politically specific environment and the mandate we received covered all aspects of expenditure and revenues. The addition which you have mentioned relates purely to the political context of negotiation, that is our understanding. We will look into all aspects but not as focal points. There are no focal points for us, all budget reform is a focal point. We will look at all aspects, expenditure and revenues. That is the short answer.

Q642 *Chairman:* That is a very complete short answer. You also stress, and quite rightly, that spending must be organised in such a way that spending meets its goals. It could be argued that the CAP's original goals have very largely been achieved, while its new goal, particularly in relation to the Single Farm Payment, remains a contested area. Would the approach that you advocate demand a consensus on the future goals of EU agriculture policy before you start allocating the spending? In other words, are you looking at getting a consensus on the policy direction before you do the allocation?
Ms Grybauskaite: Because I am responsible for all budgets I will answer more generally and then specifically on your question. The main aim of the budget reform exercise is to focus our attention towards policies of the European Union. The exercise will be mainly policy driven. That means we agree first on the substance of policies and only then will we talk about monies. That is the direct answer to your question, yes we would like to agree on the objects, subjects and goals of CAP and only then talk about how to finance it and how much it will cost. It is policy driven and inclusive of CAP. We would like to

have an agreement before we talk about the allocation of resources.

Q643 *Chairman:* Inevitably the proper approach is always a policy driven approach.
Ms Grybauskaite: We have never had it before. Member States wanted us to talk about 1% or something else. For the first time in history we have a chance. This is the first time we have agreed with all Member States that we will exercise this as a wide revision of all aspects for the future European budget. We will be revising this for decades to come, it is not for the next financial framework. That is why in our paper there will be no figures, no monies. We are trying to avoid that and do not agree with Member States who are trying to talk only about how much it costs. Policy is first. The Health Check, which you are now looking into in more detail, is some kind of preparation for reform. For me it is a preparation stage, it is not reform yet. This Health Check was agreed in the reform in 2002. Moving inside the framework and the monies, which we have already agreed until 2013. For me, as in sports, it is a warming up for the real reform. I am targeting more ambitious reform for decades to come, not the Health Check. The Health Check is just a step adapting the situation to the challenges that we are facing now. In the reform we would like to look beyond the Health Check after 2013 and 2020. The short answer is for CAP the first decision is on substance, on policy, and then money and allocations.

Q644 *Chairman:* When we did our inquiry into the reform of the wine regime we kept coming across a mentality which was very much the money that is there under the wine regime, whatever happens keep it in for wine in some way or another, which is a totally disastrous approach.
Ms Grybauskaite: We will never avoid that. Now I am talking as an ex-finance minister and finance minister for the European budget. As national governments are negotiating a new budget all ministers try to keep as much as they can, no matter what the reform is about, just to keep the money inside. We will have this mentality inside and outside the house but that is exactly what reform is about. We need to look at a macro-level, at an umbrella level, at what policies will give more value added to be spent at the European level and what may be returned to Member States. That is the case especially in CAP. You said at the very beginning that CAP has reached its goal, and it has, but the goals are old ones.

Q645 *Chairman:* Yes, exactly.
Ms Grybauskaite: Today we are faced with different challenges. We usually agree the CAP for ten or 12 years and then fix the monies and we are not able to move inside. That is why the Health Check is useful, because we can move inside and adjust a little bit but it is not flexible enough. Life is changing so fast and our financial framework is so inflexible that we are not able to adjust fast enough with what is happening outside the window. Especially in agriculture with the interventions and market prices, environment challenges, diseases in the agricultural area, we are not able to react because the monies are quite inflexible inside the package. I am saying that we need to look very radically at new goals, new challenges, how much can be done at the European level, maybe something returned back to Member States which they are responsible for. We need to look very seriously at the long-term future.

Q646 *Lord Cameron of Dillington:* Taking you on and perhaps just applying what you have said in more detail to the CAP itself, in the CAP we have got Pillar I, agriculture, and Pillar II. We think that Pillar II presents a great opportunity because it is more diverse but, if you look at the goals that you were talking about just now, Pillar I's goals must be social for the people in the countryside, environmental, the landscape and so on, and a lot of those goals are probably better achieved through Pillar II money than paying for farmers as such, either through the Single Farm Payment or otherwise. My question is how do we get more money into Pillar II out of Pillar I and why do we do it through modulation, why not just allocate the money anyway?
Ms Grybauskaite: I do not want to be rude because of where this proposal came from and from whom. There are a few possibilities as to how to increase the leverage of rural development with Pillar II. The more we look into the future it is supposed to be more and more important. The direct payment scheme, no matter how we relate it to the land or the crops or whatever, we see that the results are not always what we expected or, as I said, it is too inflexible a system that is not able to react to changing market conditions. Rural development before was in structural funds and after one financial framework it came into the agricultural funds. It is not necessarily the only solution to move there via modulation but the problem is that until 2013 all monies are fixed between the pillars and there is not much flexibility. It is a rigidity in the European budget that we do not have enough leverage to redistribute. In the Health Check there is a proposal to increase by 2% each year to do a little bit more rural development, and modulation was proposed as one of the possible measures how to push towards rural development. You are right, it does not necessarily have to be modulation. If we decide that rural development is a more progressive part of the policy, why not do what we want to without any modulation. The decision is about modulation. It was discussed under the Presidency of your country in 2005 and at that time

it was a good solution politically because it was very difficult to push inside the CAP towards more rural development. The problem is modulation is not a final solution. How we look at it for the future and what goals it will solve, we need to be very careful to see what we can do in a balanced political way and what will be between the direct payments part and the rural development part. It is not the best solution but it was good in 2005. It was one of the creative approaches that we had in that rigid environment we had.

Q647 *Viscount Ullswater:* The idea of moving money from Pillar I to Pillar II also means that it has got to be co-financed when it reaches Pillar II and there are huge amounts of opportunities for spending money under Pillar II under the various axes, a whole list of things. Are we not creating a situation where we are slightly re-nationalising some of the spending because the various states, and even the regions within states, are going to spend the money very, very differently when they have it available to spend? Is that still a European policy or is it going back to the Member States to decide? Is it going to create some form of unequal playing field where people are going to be competing on slightly different terms?
Ms Grybauskaite: That is a very interesting and speculative question. If you use the word "re-nationalisation" everybody will go, "Oh". Let us look at the policies. Do we have pure common European policies without co-financing? Can you give me an example? That is very difficult to find. For example, rural development is co-financed, all structural actions are co-financed and 12 Member States' direct payments are co-financed until 2013, (until 2016 in case of Romania and Bulgaria), so practically today we have the phenomenon of co-financing. Is it re-nationalisation? We still call it the Common Agricultural Policy. It depends what we mean by the word "re-nationalisation". It depends how we use co-financing. It is not really about co-financing, it is if co-financing is voluntary that it is a problem. The richer countries will be able to do more, and so on. If it is not voluntary but mandatory then nothing will happen. If it is mandatory and you fix the exact amounts you equalise the conditions and the competition in all Member States. It depends how you do it. Co-financing is not something bad as a word but I am not saying it is the only solution because we can save or modernise CAP, not necessarily with modulation or co-financing. But co-financing is a fact today in agriculture.

Q648 *Lord Cameron of Dillington:* Would your co-financing also extend to Pillar I?
Ms Grybauskaite: Yes. Today. 12 Member States are co-financed.

Q649 *Lord Cameron of Dillington:* For instance, Spain yesterday were almost nervous about transferring money from Pillar I to Pillar II because it would leave the regions to make the decisions and they were a bit nervous about that. They preferred the money in Pillar I because it was mandatory and it was not co-financed.
Ms Grybauskaite: You are right, the problem is with the beneficiary countries who are receiving the most. The country you have mentioned is in the top five receivers on agriculture. This will be the same in Poland and new Member States and they will be asked to add something from their budgets because these monies are earmarked and it is easy, "You do nothing, you receive something". I would say it is a kind of addiction to easy money.

Q650 *Lord Cameron of Dillington:* Absolutely.
Ms Grybauskaite: They do not need to compete, to fight, to provide any nice rural development projects, they just receive it. Do we want such a budget for Europe?

Q651 *Lord Cameron of Dillington:* So co-financing in Pillar I is not outside your thinking?
Ms Grybauskaite: Co-financing is not what we are thinking at all, we are listening at this stage. I am trying to say that co-financing is an instrument which exists and if it is a mandatory instrument it does not make for any problems because if it is mandatory the same Spanish people will receive this not from the European Union but national government. We put as an idea in our budget reform that where European monies are better and give more value added they could be spent at a European level and maybe at a national level, especially in some areas of agriculture. I sometimes go to Member States and ask, "Why do you want Brussels to dictate to you what colour of apple you grow? Why do you not want to decide it on your own?" It is not an easy question but the problem in negotiations is people do not want to talk about policy, they want to talk about money, and if you talk about money there is no policy. The European budget has become a redistribution budget, you put money in and ask, "Give me money back". In the Court of Auditors I had a joke proposal from one member who said, "Why do you need a European budget at all? Why do you need a Commission at all? You could have 2,000 people, make everything into executive agencies and distribute to Member States by their size. No matter what policies or programmes they have, just redistribute". That is exactly what we are talking about. What is the goal of the European budget? It a redistribution function only or is it for policy? We agree and then we pay. Agriculture is the same, and especially agriculture because, as I said, the easy money which has been decided in the first pillar, especially now for the main beneficiaries and

new Member States, is becoming more and more addictive. This will be a serious obstacle to reform, at least in the short and medium-term. In the long-term it is another matter. Between the EU-15 agreement was possible in 2005 until 2014 because it is so difficult to change or do something with it. I am not saying that co-financing as an economic phenomenon is wrong. I am not saying we are going to propose it, there are other ways in which we can reform CAP without it, but if Member States agree there are policies which are more important than the first pillar in this amount maybe they will agree more on rural development or something else. That is what we are targeting. We do not want to talk with Member States about money and we are pushing them not to approach us with how much they will have. The problem is not how much but for what and who will pay, the European budget or national governments. In Spain they are main receivers of structural funds also, in the top five, and if you look at this country they are in the top five everywhere.

Q652 *Baroness Jones of Whitchurch:* Given what you have said about getting the policy right first, which I am sure we can all understand, I am not sure how far you are able to answer my question. Given that we have seen the CAP declining as a proportion of the total budget and is planned through to 2013, do you see that trend continuing all things being equal or is it too soon to say that? Do you think that we should aim to have agriculture as a smaller portion of the overall budget in the longer term?
Ms Grybauskaite: Again, it depends on how Member States will agree what policy priorities are supposed to be financed via the European budget. If we are talking economically we see that agriculture gives about 7 or 8% GDP maximum in Europe, it depends on country to country, but it is 40% of the European budget. The message that we send to Europeans is very clear: we are not paying for the areas where Europe is challenged as priority areas. It was an agreement on two common policies in the Treaty and we cannot avoid it, we cannot cut it or change it. It is about policies that Member States will agree in the future, how fast we will phase in new ones and how fast partially phase out old ones, how much we reform the old ones inside and what budget we will have finally. If the budget is 1% of GNI different proportions will be one way for each policy and a larger budget will be in different proportions for the policies. It is very speculative to say today. Historically we have seen in absolute figures the trend is diminishing for CAP but I do not want to speculate for the future, everything depends on what policies Member States agree. We have seen in the future Lisbon Treaty that some new policies are already mentioned: energy, immigration, climate change. These will be future trends and more attention will be

given to these policies. Research and innovation is a trend, yes. We cannot simply cut agriculture because in the CAP today in the first and second pillars, especially in the second one, a lot of resources are given to fight problems on the environment in agriculture. For example, in December in Parliament in the 2008 budget we proposed, and it is on the way to being confirmed, about 11% will be given to environmental problems. Diseases which you cannot stop, cow diseases or bird flu or whatever, on the border means Europe has to tackle it together and some amounts will be given. It is very clear that the CAP as we see it will be shaped differently in the medium and long-term. We are trying to compare it with the CAP today but such a CAP will not exist tomorrow and I would be happy if it changed faster. It depends how we will be able to negotiate.

Q653 *Baroness Jones of Whitchurch:* Do you see that the big environmental agenda, and if you extend it towards climate change it gets even bigger, being funded through the CAP? Is that a mechanism for carrying on in that way?
Ms Grybauskaite: I would say very partially via for example biodiversity which can be supported by the CAP but all of these policies are under negotiation because we need to avoid duplication. We have these elements in separate policies and they all fight, "I need to do it", because they want to keep their portfolio. There is this enthusiasm sometimes, or what I call environmental populism in finances, and we will need to look at this very carefully and avoid duplication as to which policy will take the lead and where monies need to be transferred.

Q654 *Baroness Jones of Whitchurch:* Could you envisage having a separate environmental pot from which people would make separate bids, a separate strand of financing?
Ms Grybauskaite: We will see. As I said, first we need to agree what policies we will take as common future priorities and then mechanically structure how to do it and via what mechanisms, which is a secondary question. It is too early to say.

Q655 *Lord Greaves:* Can I move on to another aspect of which finance and which policy is used for what. The new states, particularly the newest entrant states, obviously need a great deal of structural change in agriculture and the question is how much of the cost of that structural change should come from agricultural funds from the CAP and how much should come from other structural funds.
Ms Grybauskaite: If we had equal positions between the EU-15 and EU-12 it would be a different answer. The problem is in both policies, in structural or regional policies and in agriculture, new members are only phased in. New members will be full participants

6 December 2007   Ms Dalia Grybauskaite

of the CAP only in 2013 and the next two, Romania and Bulgaria, only in 2016. Today the figures are so small that your question will be more relevant to the situation after 2014. I can say in 2006 we looked at execution, so for EU-10, because 2006 was before enlargement to 27, only 6% of European CAP was given to them and 94% went to the EU-15. What more can we do? Today your question is not very relevant but in the future these countries will not be new after ten years. After the Health Check the CAP will be changed and moved a little more towards rural development and market development and after 2013 the EU-25 will be more or less equalised in the policy approach, there will be no possibility of distinguishing what can be done via rural development or structural funds because it will be a discussion about rural development still. I am not speculating but the question is open to leave it in agriculture or somewhere else.

Q656 Lord Greaves: They may not be new in 2015 and beyond but the needs are still going to be there. The contrast between the old farming systems and the rest of Europe is going to remain and probably get even greater. Where is the resource going to come from to tackle this problem? Until this problem is tackled there cannot be a proper level playing field in terms of agricultural trade and agricultural production within the Union, can there?
Ms Grybauskaite: You are absolutely right to say the differences in the quality of agriculture between EU-15 and EU-12 or EU-10 are still very large. Today's CAP is not managing to reduce these differences. The problem is the monies which are agreed in the packages are agreed and fixed until 2013 and we have no choice, we are not able to move from one to another pocket. (The answer continued off the record)

Q657 Lord Greaves: Your answer to my question is major unfinished business.
Ms Grybauskaite: My answer to your question is until 2013 we are fixed and whether or not this is good or not is up to you to decide. We are not able to move more radically. Modulation was one of the chances within this rigidity to try to move to rural development. It is not the best solution but it was a good solution in 2005. I think your country and one more uses it but nobody else. Portugal uses it. Under lobbying, governments are not able to do it because direct payments are such easy money, addiction is so fast and the lobby is so huge. It is very difficult to come out from there. To reform CAP and agriculture is very difficult politically. For new members it is a specific situation.

Q658 Lord Plumb: Looking at the future, if there was more flexibility in the use of funds from the rural fund or from the funding of Pillar II, would this not start to solve the problem that you have because we can all see very clearly that problem? For instance, take a country like Romania where the average sized holding is three hectares or whatever, we talk about two metre strips around a field which has to deal with the environmental interests and that is impossible for a country like that. If there was greater flexibility and the money was either switched or funding was found for the rural policy, that being as flexible as possible to deal with some of the structural problems as well as the environmental problems, without breaking the system would that not help to start to find a solution to the problem that you so rightly raise?
Ms Grybauskaite: Theoretically and academically, yes, but on the ground and in the concrete environment, no. All governments are under pressure to give the same treatment to their farmers and if governments are going to be more strategic they will think about strategic changes but farmers do not care, they want exactly the same payment their neighbour has, and that is the problem. If any policy has too much flexibility or a voluntary mechanism governments will not be able to stand against the pressures. If we have something common it is supposed to be not voluntary but obligatory. Do we need to have so much to regulate in this area, that is the question and it is very fundamental. Maybe we need to return some functions of regulation to Member States fully and to reduce this common policy to a smaller amount. If you have something and you go for voluntary this will not work. We proposed modulation and we gave the chance to Member States but only two use it.

Q659 Lord Plumb: Taking the report we had from the Spanish representative yesterday, the problem there seems to be within regions not the national part, it was the arguments they had within regions, which you can well understand because they have mountainous regions in need of help and so on and other areas are developing still further.
Ms Grybauskaite: You are absolutely right. Europe is so diverse and Member States so diverse, there is diversity in the environment, in territory and in government structures also. We have small countries which are centralised and we have confederations and so on. Can we afford to have a Common Agricultural Policy with such diversity between and inside Member States? That is a very fundamental question we need to ask. What is possible and can be done at a European level should be done at a European level, the rest should be given back.

Q660 Chairman: You are coming forward with some really radical, mind challenging propositions.

Ms Grybauskaite: I am not radical, I am a pragmatist.

Q661 Lord Cameron of Dillington: We strongly approve.
Ms Grybauskaite: I come from a region which for 70 years was under reforms, reforms and radical reforms and we were not afraid to scrap that and start from zero and create something new and we looked to the best practices but then we were approached with some policies from the European Union which we are supposed to take.

Q662 Chairman: To put it crudely, what support do you think you have got?
Ms Grybauskaite: For that?

Q663 Chairman: Yes.
Ms Grybauskaite: Time and only time. If we propose change from 2014 I know what will happen: nothing. I am going for options between radical options and time. In the short and medium-term we will have the Health Check, some small shifts of phasing in and phasing out, but I want Member States to look and decide what trend for European future finances we need to have and for each financial framework to take some pieces on which it is possible to get agreement, because there is still unanimity, and then we will really start to talk about programmes, financial frameworks and monies.

Q664 Lord Greaves: Can I go back to my original question. There is certainly a lot of agreement amongst us and elsewhere obviously that the future financing of farming and of farmers in Europe has to come mainly through the market and direct support to farmers generally for pretty well everything they produce is going to reduce further and ought to reduce further and perhaps ought to be eliminated, but there are then certain things, such as environmental needs and support in difficult areas, mountainous areas, et cetera. It seems to me one of the greatest of them all is what we are talking about, which is the need to finance structural reform in many of the new countries at some stage which will require huge investment. Where is that investment going to come from if it cannot come from the CAP up to 2015 and perhaps after then? Where is it going to come from? Does it come from the private sector in some way and how does that happen?
Ms Grybauskaite: It is coming also from structural actions. If you talk about road infrastructure, services for farmers, it is coming already, it is coming from rural development. Because rural and structural funds are co-financed it will be private. Between 30 and 40% of co-financing is necessary for any structural or rural development programme, it depends on the complete design. There are three sources now and in the future it will be more or less

the same plus governments if they are asked on some agreed common basis to help. Here again, we need to agree altogether that this is more important than the first pillar. These policies have to be accepted by all Member States because, as I said, especially the newer ones are less and less interested in the second pillar because it is more difficult to absorb, it is easier to go for the first pilla. Rural development is more difficult, the same as structural funds, you need to prepare programmes, you need to have improvements, it is a lot of control.

Q665 Lord Greaves: Is there understanding in some of these countries at a national level that there has to be change which is not going to be necessarily financed from European funds?
Ms Grybauskaite: That is not the case yet. Easy money spoils everything, not only understanding. As you know yourself, the problem is governments live from election to election and strategically to be able to think about it only those institutions which are more or less independent can do that. It was good that it was given to the Commission because we are not so dependent on elections. Of course, we are dependent on the European Parliament and criticism of some Member States, but usually what the Commission can propose is more strategic, more long-term. From this point of view it is optimal that the proposal is here but the decisions will be made by governments. The reform of the Common Agricultural Policy showed this exactly. They started negotiating in 1999 and finished in 2002 under the pressure of future enlargements. Of course, the proposals were made quite soft and moderate but agreement was only possible because the governments deciding knew that they would not be in office after 2015. I am counting on that myself.
Chairman: That is a very good defence of the House of Lords, if I may say so.
Lord Greaves: We understand the question of not having to be elected.

Q666 Lord Plumb: First, I think you are right to say that farmers jealously care about what they are getting and what their neighbours are getting and, therefore, will always demand fair play. You pointed out very clearly that financial discipline is a very difficult business and it becomes more difficult because of the expansion of Europe, 27 countries, possibly to be expanded further with a different situation in each of the countries. It is very difficult to ask you the question of how you see this proceeding because you have already answered it to a very large extent. Do you anticipate a discipline mechanism which does reduce the Single Payment, or should reduce and I believe will reduce the Single Payment, over a period of time, probably down to 35%, which may continue further? A lot will depend on its use and

where it is going. We are seeing a situation in farming at the moment, and I speak as a farmer, where the imbalance in farming is worse than I have seen for many years, meaning the arable sector is doing extremely well and the livestock sector is doing very badly. That is speaking for the UK but it also speaks generally for many countries in Europe. That is a worrying situation because the livestock have to consume the cereals that are grown, cereals which are now at a very high price. That may be exacerbated further, of course, as we see the use of cereals for energy production and so on and so forth. In all of this I think the question on financial discipline is how do you see this mechanism working, accepting that there should be a reduction in the expenditure in Pillar I, and how will it be used? Do you expect the operation to be received by the Member States in different ways? From what you have just been saying, in my opinion it would go down quite well if we were to start talking about radical reform in the future rather than tinkering around with what may be a slight adjustment even after 2013. I speak as a farmer and I know that I can speak for many who are saying, "It has not worked in the past as perhaps it should have done". If radical thoughts come forward I honestly believe that there would be more political acceptance than perhaps you imagine at the moment.
Ms Grybauskaite: Thank you very much. Please help us. You know how I will be battling inside the house.

Q667 *Lord Plumb:* We have got a pretty good idea!
Ms Grybauskaite: We need the support. If you can come with some proposals it would be very, very useful politically. You are a very solid institution with very solid recommendations, at least as I hear from other people. You are right, the Health Check that is on the table is less radical but already some Member States have called it too radical and others not radical enough. On the triggering of the financial discipline mechanism, Mrs Fischer Boel will give you a more detailed prognosis but in my understanding, because of the changing situation in market conditions and prices, the mechanism will be postponed. That is my perception. For example, this year we have a margin that is not used for agriculture because of this, about 2.5 billion at a European level and next year 3.5 billion. We did not envisage that during the 2005 negotiations, it was unexpected. We are still not able to use the margin. Before it was expected in 2009 or 2010 the discipline margin may be triggered but now I am hearing 2010 or 2011 and it is pushed further. Everything will depend on market conditions and at this stage until 2015 it is very difficult to say. Mrs Fischer Boel will tell you more precisely but in my understanding it will be later than was thought before and maybe not at all in this financial framework.

Q668 *Lord Plumb:* I wager that if I were to ask the question through the farming papers in Britain, "Would you prefer to get money from the market or from Brussels?" 80% would say from the market.
Ms Grybauskaite: That is very good, but I am sure that is the case only in your country and maybe two or three others. If you tell new Member States we are calling for budget reform and saying that CAP is old fashioned, the reaction in Poland and my country also is, "What do you mean old-fashioned? You don't want us to receive fixed, clear, guaranteed monies?" That is the question.
Chairman: It is quite interesting because when we have been going around on various inquiries, to be frank we have been surprised by the willingness of producers to move away from direct subsidies and the conservatism comes from the politicians.
Lord Plumb: Even on wine.

Q669 *Lord Cameron of Dillington:* Particularly on wine.
Ms Grybauskaite: Did you visit some new members?

Q670 *Chairman:* No, we have not visited new members.
Ms Grybauskaite: Please go to new members because that is where the largest obstacle will be, not the old ones, in the future reform battle.

Q671 *Chairman:* It was interesting in France generally, for example, where the producers are more up for change than many of their formal spokespeople.
Ms Grybauskaite: We have started to feel that changes are coming in France and Germany in the more conservative parts and that is very, very good, but new obstacles are growing in new Member States, especially in Poland.

Q672 *Chairman:* I heard the strongest defence for a protectionist agriculture policy from a Polish minister.
Ms Grybauskaite: It is probably explanation and understanding and what can happen in the future. In most cases the new members calculate exactly how much they will get in their pocket, they do not care about policy. Politicians understand it is not the best investment in the quality of their country's growth. After a night's discussion on politics if you are told you will not receive it, imagine the politician who has to do that. It is easier for me to do that from far away. I am an ex-finance minister, so for me it is easier to look at the macro-economic impact from a distance.

Q673 *Lord Plumb:* Is it partly because a lot of people in the new member countries were led to believe there was a pot of gold in Brussels?

Ms Grybauskaite: You are partly right because in some advertisements for membership and arguments politicians used this element that there are economic and financial benefits from membership, not only political.

Q674 *Lord Greaves:* It comes back to the question of structural change then, does it not? If you are going to rely on the market you have got to be efficient and you have got to be able to compete and if you do not think you are going to be able to compete you are not going to be confident of relying on the market, you are going to continue to believe that the only answer is direct subsidisation. The two should go hand-in-hand surely.
Ms Grybauskaite: I would be happy to hear such questions from my parliament members but I have never heard that.

Q675 *Viscount Ullswater:* You said that it was going to be driven by policy before the budget, so agree on the policy and then work out how the budget is to be disbursed, but I think I am picking up a couple of policies which slightly worry me, and that is food security for the EU, which means that is a little bit of protectionism for the EU farmers, and the other one is the non-financial tariffs, ie a higher standard of animal welfare within the European Union, which means we cannot import chicken from China because their welfare standards are not high enough. Are those legitimate policies that you are going to have to address or are you going to find that they are rather protectionist?
Ms Grybauskaite: There will be a lot of proposals, and creative ones, as to how to keep money in the agricultural pocket. If we are changing something under the reform, an animal welfare is not such a bad policy but whether the chicken was raised with or without music is not quite so good. These creative ideas will arrive in all areas and that is why I am saying it will not be easy to clarify and streamline and say what is better done at the European level or at home. That is a challenge but not only in the agricultural area, for all policies. The creative minds in this house and outside are working very hard to keep things in the same pockets.

Q676 *Chairman:* Do you think that a co-decision making CAP will make your life easier?
Ms Grybauskaite: Do you mean the Commission's life? The Commission's life is not easy anyway. We are always caught between two pressures, between the Council and Parliament. The extension of co-decision elements will make the Council's life more difficult.

Q677 *Lord Plumb:* That is good!
Ms Grybauskaite: For the Commission it will be the same more or less. We need to battle with both and sometimes we are a facilitator for both, sometimes battling both, it depends on the situation. I think it will be more difficult for the Council now but the decision making process will be shorter, only one reading in the annual budget.

Q678 *Chairman:* Do you think reform will be more or less likely, easier or more difficult?
Ms Grybauskaite: Budget reform is taken away from the budgetary procedures really, it is a more political exercise. It is in consultation with the European Parliament and national parliaments but the final decisions will be made by governments. These exercises do not involve a co-decision element.

Q679 *Earl of Dundee:* I wonder if I could refer to the switch from production-based subsidies to area-based payments. Media coverage of the EU Court of Auditors' recent report suggests that one consequence of this is that funds earmarked for agriculture are ending up in the coffers of golf and riding clubs. How exaggerated is that allegation? That apart, what are your own views on the way in which the CAP budget is currently managed?
Ms Grybauskaite: It is very difficult to comment on the press headlines because if you look at the Court of Auditors' report the agricultural area spending was evaluated as one of the best in recent years. The report on agricultural spending found possible errors at about the materiality level, 2%, while in the structural fund it was more difficult. You are referring to press headings because nobody is paying for golf. There was no error or illegal payments to anybody. I do not want to comment on press headings, but the Court of Auditors' report on agriculture is very positive.

Q680 *Earl of Dundee:* As you say, we learned that in 2006 about 2% of the total farm and development budget was not properly justified. If so, how might the balance between decentralisation and effective supervision be further improved?
Ms Grybauskaite: We agreed that by 15 February each year each Member State will present their declarations of assurance as to how all European financial resources are spent. For the first time in history, this year we pushed and with the support of the European Parliament we were able to have an agreement with Member States that they agreed to transparently present all beneficiaries of structural funds in 2008 and in 2009 all agricultural beneficiaries, who receives what and why. This information has never been public until now. This will mean huge pressure on governments from the media and the public on how it is used. It is good for

me because it will be the largest pressure to reform agricultural policy more than any political discussion, I am sure about that. If somebody asks in Germany why 80% of resources were received only by 15% of farmers, or not by farmers but by owners, or not by owners but by industry, that will be perfect pressure for CAP reform. We are introducing these elements step-by-step in Member States and for the first time they have to present this assurance on 15 February next year. It was agreed between the Court of Auditors and Parliament and we pushed and we have got it in the financial regulations now which came into force from May of this year. Of course, 80% of all of the European budget is spent by Member States and the Court of Auditors is pressing for this. In the Lisbon Treaty one good thing is today the Commission is responsible for final management results. We are not doing anything on the land but we are responsible. In the new Treaty it will be Member States and the Commission, equal responsibility, so Member States will not be able to avoid it by claiming that the Commission was not sufficient enough, the methodology was not enough, these kinds of things. The responsibility will be equally shared. This will put pressure on governments to make control more efficient and more reliable.

Q681 Earl of Dundee: It is really good to hear what you said about transparency, but on knowing what people are getting up to and being clear about it, is that nicely across the board throughout Europe or are there anomalies and differences between clear results from, say, the newer countries compared to the older ones, or is that not so?
Ms Grybauskaite: In agriculture especially you mean?

Q682 Earl of Dundee: Yes.
Ms Grybauskaite: As I said, and the next Commissioner will explain a lot more, during one year in the agricultural area on controls she did a lot and her Directorate did a lot and this was acknowledged by the Court of Auditors. That was the largest improvement in the largest spending portfolio. That was not exactly the case in structural funds. One of the outcomes of this is that we are very seriously thinking about some restrictions on direct payment decisions for Romania because they are still not fulfilling their requirements for this year. We are looking very carefully into new Member States. For the EU-10 it is less problematic. I recently heard there were some problems in Greece but in the EU-10 we do not hear of any large problems. There are problems in Romania and we may still decide to cut as set out that under the membership treaty of

Romania by 25% of direct payments. The final decision has not yet been made and Commissioner Fischer Boel will be able to answer in detail. We are trying to be hard.

Q683 Chairman: We have talked around this in a way but could you clarify for us what you consider to be the practical implications of the abolition of the distinction between compulsory and non-compulsory expenditure.
Ms Grybauskaite: This is only in the Treaty very generally. During 2010 we will be negotiating between the Parliament, the Council and us on procedures and how decisions will be made. We need to change all of the procedures on budget and on the financial framework. Before the financial framework was not in the treaties at all, it was a gentleman's agreement, it was only necessary to agree on the annual budget. Now the multi-annual budget is in the Treaty and that means it is obligatory. On the cycle of negotiations we will have for seven or five or whatever we will have in the future, a seven year budget is about a three and a half year cycle. During this cycle we still negotiate on the annual budget each year and the largest impact of this distinction which is disappearing between compulsory and non-compulsory will be on annual budgets. It will only be one reading and that means more scrutiny efforts will need to be taken by all institutions, the Council, the Parliament and the Commission. All budgets will be co-decided. If on agriculture Member States were able to keep some autonomy, that autonomy will now disappear. It will be an equal balance between the Parliament and the Council on all parts of the budget. This depends on procedures and goodwill from both institutions, it can be easier or it can be more complicated. Each year I negotiate the annual budget, and I have already negotiated four, and after each year I think, this was the most difficult one, the next will be easier", but no, every year there is something new that pops up, new complications, new people, new tensions and Presidencies. It very much depends on the Presidency's capability to deliver, what the country is, who the people are doing the job. Your Presidency was efficient. It was difficult as a partner to negotiate and deal with but it was very efficient. After the very stiff and conflicting relations, especially for me it was not easy and I was critical about the Presidency and the Presidency was critical about the Commission, we finished with respect for each other. If the Presidency is able to deliver and treats you with respect you have good results and that is important. (There followed a short discussion off the record)
Chairman: Thank you very much indeed.

THURSDAY 6 DECEMBER 2007

Present   Cameron of Dillington, L   Plumb, L
              Dundee, E   Sewell, L (Chairman)
              Greaves, L   Ullswater, V
              Jones of Whitchurch, B

Examination of Witnesses

Witnesses: MRS MARIANN FISCHER BOEL, European Commissioner for Agriculture, and MR POUL SKYTTE CHRISTOFFERSEN, Head of Cabinet, European Commission, examined.

Q684 Chairman: Good morning.

Mrs Fischer Boel: I am very pleased to see you here on the day when we have started the conference on the Health Check with representatives from all the different stakeholders. It was a very lively, very frank and open debate. It is a good way to kick off the discussion. Your visit is very timely and I would like to tell you what intentions we have in the Health Check.

Q685 Chairman: First of all, Commissioner, thank you very much indeed for finding time to see us. It is always a delight to come and talk with you because it is very helpful for us in preparing our reports to take evidence directly from you. I have to go through a little rigmarole saying this is a formal evidence session of the Sub-Committee, so a note will be taken, but if you would like to go off the record please say so. Obviously a transcript will be available shortly and you will be able to revise it. Would you like to make an opening statement and then we will get on to questions and answers after that?

Mrs Fischer Boel: I think it would be useful just to give you the headlines of the Health Check. First of all, I continue saying that the Health Check is not a new reform but it is more than just fine-tuning. The reason for this Health Check is because of the fact that the world has changed since 2003. We now have 27 Member States, 12 new customers. We have a changing globalised world. Throughout the last six or 12 months we have seen that agriculture has changed from being a surplus production with intervention stocks with too high production to a situation where at this stage there is even a shortage in some areas, but it is a much more balanced market. I think it is a very positive situation for agriculture, it makes it much more positive and it is much more fun for farmers to see that they can respond to the market. In the Health Check we would like to look at the market tools. Do we need export refunds? Do we need intervention systems? What about the set-aside that we have abolished for one year because of the shortage of cereals? The whole quota system is now to be discussed. I have sent some very clear messages on dairy, that we need to increase from April 2008 by 2% so that we do not spoil the market. There is a

shortage in some countries, not in the UK because you do not produce up to 100% of your quota. The Single Payment Scheme has been implemented in many different ways in many different Member States and personally I think we should work towards a more flat rate system, a less complicated system, where you have a payment of the same value, or entitlements of the same value, linked to the area. Within the regions in the UK it would be England, Wales and Scotland where you could diversify but it would be the same payment. From a psychological point of view, I think we will face difficulties in 2013 or 2018, just to mention a year, explaining why two neighbouring farmers get different payments with the same conditions for production because the former owner had dairy production in 2002. That is going to be difficult to explain to taxpayers. We need to move towards a more flat rate. We need more decoupling. There is no reason for maintaining a partial coupling in the cereal sector. Cross-compliance should be simplified but maintained. I have introduced the idea of a progressive reduction of the payments and a discussion on the very small farms. I do not think 0.3 hectares is a farm, by the way. I can guarantee that golf courses have never been eligible for payments and they never will be eligible for payments, just to make it crystal clear.

Q686 Chairman: That is one question out of the way then.

Mrs Fischer Boel: We know that we will have to respond from agriculture to climate change. We know that we need some sort of risk management and water preservation, bio-energy and biodiversity. We need solutions to all of these new challenges and solutions require money. That is why we have suggested increasing the compulsory modulation which will mean if we can agree with those countries that have introduced the voluntary modulation they should reduce when we increase the compulsory modulation. We have proposed an increase of 2% which means 8% before the end of this financial period. Then a reopening of Article 69. This Article gives Member States the possibility to take up to 10% of the direct payment without co-financing and use it for different new challenges. I am open to discuss how. It already exists but it is very narrow. Today, if you want to use Article 69 you can take it from the dairy but then you have to use it in the dairy sector, so it is very complicated. I consider the Health Check to be a stepping stone for discussions on what is going to happen after 2013. That was a very short introduction.

Q687 *Chairman:* Thank you very much. There are a number of detailed points that you have raised that we have got questions on and we will come back to those. Can I start by looking beyond the Health Check, as you indicated in your last sentence virtually. Your Communication praised the degree to which the combination of the 2003 reforms have made EU agriculture much more market-oriented and, as you say, makes it more fun to be a farmer engaging more directly with the market. The success of 2003 linked with what has been happening on world markets and the boom in agriculture really does create an environment where is it not worth trying to be even more ambitious in terms of reform. *Mrs Fischer Boel:* In the Health Check?

Q688 *Chairman:* No, looking beyond the Health Check. At least setting a medium-term policy objective that is more radical than we are used to thinking about. *Mrs Fischer Boel:* When you look at the budget available for agriculture, it was decided by Heads of State in 2002 to put a limit on the expenditure. It is a decreasing trend because the budget is only regulated by an inflation rate of 1%, which means in the real world it is going down. Secondly, we are now financing the accession of Romania and Bulgaria under the same ceiling and, therefore, we have a budgetary discipline which means when we hit the ceiling, minus 300 million, then we have to reduce the direct payments to the farmers. We already have a decreasing scale plus we have introduced the modulation into the direct payment. The discussion on what our policies are going to look like after 2013 is part of the mid-term review of the Financial Perspectives that takes place in the Commission in parallel. In our first discussions internally here in the *Cabinet*, we would have liked to have had the Health Check and a mid-term budgetary review in parallel. We had already created the headline, "One Vision, Two Steps". We did not manage to convince the 13ᵗʰ floor that this would be an idea to pursue. We have had to concentrate on our Health Check and now there is a Communication from the Commission on the mid-term review of the Financial Perspectives but in much broader language where they introduce the idea of co-financing, not specifically linked to agriculture but in general. My personal view on co-financing of the first pillar is that it is the first step to a total re-nationalisation of the Common Agricultural Policy. Could you imagine if we decided that Member States had to pay 40 or 50% of the value of the first pillar. It would be very, very difficult to get agreement in the Council. If it was voluntary for Member States to co-finance I know two countries that would be very hesitant, the UK and Denmark, to co-finance one single cent. Then you would have no level playing field for European farmers any more.

Q689 *Chairman:* I will try something else on you. What about actually saying now that really our ultimate objective is the abolition of direct payments and what we will concentrate on is dealing with issues like the environment and rural development, and even if necessary take them out of the CAP and have completely new mechanisms to deal with those issues? *Mrs Fischer Boel:* That is exactly what I am trying to do in the Health Check, to say we need more money for the environment, for animal welfare, for competitiveness, for rural infrastructure, for the Internet, for everything in the rural areas. We need more money and, therefore, we want to increase the budget for rural development by reducing the direct payments.

Q690 *Chairman:* Just abolish it! *Mrs Fischer Boel:* But that will be over my dead body. We need a common policy in agriculture. I am totally on the same line as you. The budget for agriculture will not remain at the same level that we see today after 2013. We need a common policy because we need to respond to the demands of the consumers and taxpayers. We need to be able to say to our farmers that we have certain requirements on environment, on animal welfare, on high standards of production, and we know that we have higher costs of production in Europe than in South America. If we reduce completely without any security net in the market tools then I fear it will end in a situation where we will see a very, very industrialised agricultural sector. By the way, this was one of the ideas in a programme that Gordon Brown launched when he was Chancellor. I do not want an industrialised agricultural sector in Europe. I want to see a diversified sector where there is room for the small ones, for those who want to specialise in fruit and vegetables, organic or whatever, and the big competitive ones as well. If you take away all the direct payments we have no way of securing that we can maintain diversification.

Q691 *Chairman:* What we are saying is that the role of direct payments in the future is going to be much more as a form of compensation, which is the wrong word but nearly the right word, to pay for the enhanced standards that we require of European agriculture so that it is not disadvantaged in the world market.

Mrs Fischer Boel: Then we should try to encourage quality and quantity. We are presenting a Green Paper on quality next year. If you look at the competitiveness of the European agricultural sector we will never be able to compete with Brazil on certain production and, therefore, we need to find some niches where we can be strong, where we can take our share of the markets when we look eastwards at the new emerging markets in India and China, and we can only do so because we can do something else. We have a very, very high level of food safety in Europe. We have spent hundreds of millions of euros to win the battle on salmonella, just to mention one. We have specific strict rules on imports of product from hormones, SPS issues, where our consumers do not want to have hormone beef. From my point of view, we should try to keep the European model of agriculture which is a diversified agricultural sector with lots of small producers in niche production and lots of competitive bigger farms. I would like to keep it like this without preventing the sector being dynamic to meet the new challenges. On climate change we need to contribute as well. By the way, agriculture has been reducing the CO_2 emissions since 1990, mainly because of the fact that we have reduced our production, but we need to encourage more innovation and more research in the second generation of biofuels because the first generation is a step on the way to the second generation. If not it is clear that in the future this competition between feed, fuel and food will not be sustainable. Where we can use surplus from our forest sector, where we can use straw, grass, slurry, slaughterhouse waste, that will be the future. Innovation should be at the top of our list. I hope you do not consider me a very conservative Agriculture Commissioner, I try to move things and sometimes I feel agriculture is a super tanker and you do not turn it around just like that, but I think we have been moving.

Q692 *Chairman:* You certainly have.

Mrs Fischer Boel: I have 27 customers sitting around the table in the Council and they have very, very different views on the agriculture sector and I need a majority.

Q693 *Viscount Ullswater:* Commissioner, can I get back rather more to the detail particularly about the Single Farm Payment. In your very interesting paper you appear to regard the decoupled payment as a success, quite a substantial reform that was introduced in 2003, and yet there is a little hesitancy in it in that some areas, and I think you mentioned suckler cow premiums and perhaps durum wheat, need intervention of some sort or another. I would be

interested to know how you propose to identify those particular circumstances which might need this sort of support. Might it not be easier to cope with these problems under the Pillar II way of financing so that you can manipulate that a little bit more according to the market needs over this longer period rather than deal with it in Pillar I?

Mrs Fischer Boel: I completely agree with you. First of all, I do not think there is any reason to maintain coupled payments in the cereal sector. On the other hand, I do not underestimate the difficulties that some regions of Europe with suckler cows, which you mentioned, would face with totally decoupled payments.

Q694 *Viscount Ullswater:* You mentioned suckler cows.

Mrs Fischer Boel: Then they would disappear. We have no interest in the disappearance of those. It could be sheep, by the way, as well because lawnmowers are much more expensive to manage and there is a shortage of labour as well. We need something. This could be solved in the best way in the rural development policy. There is no difference of opinion on this.

Mr Christoffersen: One of the reasons why we might need some kind of coupling in particular cases, which have to be examined region by region and it has to be very much a regional approach, is that we want to keep Pillar II green in the WTO context. That means we cannot introduce coupled payments into Pillar II because we would destroy the green value of Pillar II. That is why if we want to preserve, for instance, animals or cows in a particular region we have to seek another solution.

Chairman: Upland pasture payments.

Q695 *Viscount Ullswater:* An extensive farming payment or whatever.

Mr Christoffersen: We do not want to pollute Pillar II.

Q696 *Chairman:* You cannot say beef or sheep but you can say maintenance of pastures, can you not, environmental pastures?

Mrs Fischer Boel: You can make agri-environmental schemes—

Mr Christoffersen: But not one linked to a particular production.

Mrs Fischer Boel: No. We will be open to ideas.

Mr Christoffersen: It is the only way forward to preserve those objectives.

Q697 *Viscount Ullswater:* Can I develop that a little further. At the moment with the change, and we are still pretty early in this reform and some countries have only just introduced decoupled payments, I would anticipate that most farmers think the Pillar I payment is part of their income from farming, they would just consider that is due to them for having given up coupled payments, but that is probably the wrong way for farmers to approach that. I know there is cross-compliance, but in the arable sector you have now got the rewards from the marketplace being much more substantial and that means people have ploughed up their set-aside in order to gain that financial advantage. Do you think we ought to move quicker in shifting the money from Pillar I into Pillar II and rewarding farmers for the public benefit that they do through Pillar II rather than just giving them a blanket payment and saying "Carry on farming, please"?

Mrs Fischer Boel: The rural development policy is where the music will be playing in the future and that is the reason why we have to continue from the 5% modulation we have today, plus what the UK and Portugal has introduced. We have to do it in a way that means we will get support from Member States. I know there are some stakeholders who would like to see a 20% modulation. We have to try to find a solution.

Q698 *Lord Cameron of Dillington:* A happy medium.

Mrs Fischer Boel: Yes.

Q699 *Chairman:* 17½%?

Mrs Fischer Boel: With the plus 8% and a possibility to reopen Article 69, which is very attractive for Member States because that is not co-financed whereas rural development is co-financed. If we manage to get through with plus eight then it would be one of the greatest victories we have ever had. It will be extremely difficult. In the 2003 reforms it was 20% as the first proposal and it ended up at five. I could have re-launched 20 but then Member States would have said, "She's crazy". We saw last time it didn't fly so we might end up with almost nothing. This is credible. I would like you to come and join a Council meeting because then you will get an impression of the huge differences between 27 Member States. I was the Minister for Agriculture in Demark when we were 15 and I would not say it was easier but it was more manageable than with 27. There are such huge differences. Romania is a good example of a country where their farming is a big strong sector but they are lagging behind now.

Q700 *Chairman:* Is there not the danger that as they become more and more integrated into the benefits of the CAP, and certainly on direct payments, you get direct payment dependency amongst those agricultures?

Mrs Fischer Boel: Yes, but imagine if you took in new members and excluded the direct payments, that would not work. You saw the difficulties with the phasing in from 25%. We see this very clearly today

in Poland, that you capitalise the value of the direct payment and, therefore, it is going to be very difficult to cut the direct payment because it has been part of the business. On the other hand, it is a disadvantage for young farmers because the land is so expensive that it is very difficult to start from scratch without any ancestors or a rich uncle.

Q701 *Lord Greaves:* Can I take you to the question of capping the Single Farm Payment which you have been suggesting should take place. Can you give the justification for this? What are the reasons why you think it is a good idea? What is your answer to people who say it is going to be penalising more efficient, successful farms and farmers or, in some places, those which employ a large number of people relatively and would therefore have social costs if it affected that employment?

Mrs Fischer Boel: First of all, it is not a capping. It is not as in the previous 2003 reforms that when you had received €300,000 then you got nothing more. This is a progressive reduction which means even if you are very big you will only be reduced by 45%, so you will continue to get payments until the very end. It is a completely different set-up from the previous one where you were really punished after 300,000. You can explain that there is an advantage of economies of scale in agriculture. To meet the reduction requirements in fertilisers you need to have the machinery that is modern technology to place the fertilisers in the drill to have the optimal use of your inputs and this is possible only if you have a certain size. After this, you can explain that there is an economy of scale in the bigger farms. I know it is a very controversial discussion and, therefore, at the other end of the scale I have introduced the idea to see whether it is possible to reduce or get rid of support to the very small farms. In the UK you had so many new beneficiaries that it killed your system actually.

Q702 *Lord Cameron of Dillington:* Yes.

Mrs Fischer Boel: We will see whether this 0.3 hectare is really a farm or we can find another level. With 0.3 it is more expensive administratively to pay the direct payment than the money you would receive. It is controversial in some new Member States, Romania among others, where they have very small plots and they have not yet been through the changes in their agriculture sector. I have also clearly said that if the result of this progressive reduction is only that we make a better living for lawyers then I will take that into consideration, of course.

Q703 *Lord Greaves:* Can I divert from that question a little bit and pick up on what you said about Romania. In our previous meeting we had some interesting discussion about the need for structural change, and Romania is a classic example, although there are very many of the other new entrants where this is the case. It is difficult to see, whether or not there is a Common Agricultural Policy in 20 years' time as we would recognise it or not, how the agricultural market within Europe can function properly while there is such a huge disparity in the types of farms and systems. The need for structural change in a country like Romania is glaringly obvious but how on earth is it going to be achieved and where is the investment, the funding, going to come from?

Mrs Fischer Boel: When we look at the results of the enlargement in 2004 with ten former Central European countries, it has been working extremely well both to the benefit of the new Member States and the agricultural sector in those new Member States and the old EU-15. It has been a win-win situation. Lots of investments are taking place in the new Member States, not always investments from the country itself but from people coming from other countries, not buying the land but renting the land with the present domestic legislation bringing new know-how. In general I think it has been a huge success. Romania is a very big agricultural country and we had our doubts as to whether they would be able to manage the payment and, therefore, we introduced a safeguard. As we have not got evidence that everything is working well we still have the safeguard in place and the possibility to reduce the direct payment by 25%. We are aware of the difficulties in Romania. When I visited Poland in 2002 and when I go there now it is a completely different atmosphere, a much more dynamic country and Poland has these very, very small farms. They have now been through the structural changes necessary, as you say. I do not underestimate the difficulties with Romania but I am sure that we will manage.

Q704 *Lord Greaves:* When you say they have been through the changes, it is certainly true, as I understand it, that changes are taking place but there is a huge amount of change still necessary. Are you really saying that is going to happen without any very significant intervention at a European level or at a national level from the government, it is simply happening because the markets are taking care of it? Are you really saying that is the case?

Mrs Fischer Boel: We started paying the support funding to the ten new Member States but also to Bulgaria and Romania to make them able to fulfil their requirements within the agricultural sector. We know that new Member States have to apply to the same rule on SPS issues, sanitary and phytosanitary, and therefore there are dairies and slaughterhouses in new Member States that are not able to sell into the market from the very beginning but have the possibility to invest with this support. I do not

remember how much money we have spent in Romania to improve their sector but it is significant. There is a willingness in most of the new Member States to improve the quality of their internal production. With the experiences that we have had since 2004 it has been more positive than we could have expected. I was on the Budget Control Committee and we are finding more difficulties with Greece than with some of the new Member States. They have been doing well because of the fact that eight of them introduced this simplified system, the SAPS system, which is a flat rate system. That was the reason for not facing too many difficulties.

Q705 *Lord Plumb:* I think you rehearsed a very good speech for the Oxford Conference, if I may say so. A lot of what you have said is important. I would like to pick up one point if I may, first, which just concerned me a little. You said in relation to globalisation, and we are seeing Peter Mandelson later on so we will be talking more about WTO and so on, that we are in a situation where there is a much better balance at the moment. We heard from the Danish representative yesterday of the desperate situation in the pig industry in Denmark and the fact that a number of places are closing and so on and so forth. I know I am bringing this a bit more local.

Mrs Fischer Boel: No, that is fine.

Q706 *Lord Plumb:* We have got the same situation in Britain and it is happening in other countries too because of the surprising take-off of grain prices which is affecting the red meat industry in a very big way and the words are "fuel, fibre and feed" and arable farmers are doing exceptionally well but for the livestock farmer, particularly with foot and mouth, bluetongue, TB and so on, it has made it difficult. It worried me a little when you said the balance is better. My colleague reminded me that in the old days we used to talk about horn and corn and up a bit on one and down a bit on the other, and it must be very difficult to get it back. My question is more on managing the market and milk quotas. I know you announced your decision realising the ending of milk quotas presumably by 2015 at the latest and you are announcing an increase of 2% which, as you said earlier, will affect more countries than the United Kingdom for obvious reasons. I would have expected you to put it up a bit more actually to make a softer landing when you do decide to remove it. How do you see that working? Do you see a take-up by farmers and what effect do you think it will have on the whole of the milk industry?

Mrs Fischer Boel: First of all, the discussion on dairy quotas was part of the 2003 reforms and it was decided to abolish the quota system by 31 March 2015, so this decision has already been taken, this is not a new thing. I said more than a year ago that we need to find a soft landing otherwise we will see a situation where in some Member States the price of the quota will remain very high until the very last moment because there will be people out there saying, "Ah, don't believe in this quota ending, it has been prolonged before so it will probably b prolonged again". I have a certain weakness for young farmers and they would pay a very high price and then there would be zero. That was the reason for introducing this soft landing. For me, a soft landing is to increase slightly the quotas without destroying the market. Then I got a strong signal from the Council in September as to whether it would be possible to increase before 2009, which was our initial idea, 2009–13, the gap that the Health Check is covering. We made an impact assessment and we could clearly see an increase of 2%, which was the idea in 2003, would not destroy the market and we will present to the Council in December a proposal to increase by 2%. Further discussions on the quota system for dairy will be part of the Health Check. If we look at the whole period up to 2013 we need a further increase but we will have to be careful to find the right balance because if we increase too much we will see these cycles. Predictability for farmers is extremely important, that they know when they invest more or less—there are always risks—what the political level will be deciding and what their future could look like. To abolish the quota system before 2015 will probably be legally impossible because there might be some farmers who would say that they had legitimate expectations and, therefore, we would probably face difficulties. That is the idea in the dairy sector. We have invited all stakeholders to a conference in Brussels on 11 January only to discuss dairy because there are many ideas floating around to get rid of the super-levy and other interesting and strange ideas.

Q707 Lord Plumb: From all countries?
Mrs Fischer Boel: The UK does not produce up to their quota.

Q708 Lord Plumb: I am sorry, at the stakeholders' meeting.
Mrs Fischer Boel: From all over Europe, yes. This morning there were representatives from all countries via the COPA membership.

Q709 Chairman: Could we just go back a little bit on intervention. You said no intervention on cereals but you have made an exception about bread wheat. Why have interventions on bread wheat?
Mrs Fischer Boel: Because there are some anxieties in the public outside that bread is a fundamental product in agriculture or is a daily need for consumers. That was the reason for maintaining the possibility of an intervention system.

Q710 Viscount Ullswater: So it is strategic?
Mrs Fischer Boel: Yes, exclusively. It is not to manage the market because those days are gone completely. We do not want to use the intervention system to manage price levels in the cereal sector, no way.

Q711 Lord Cameron of Dillington: So the more expensive bread gets the more you put into intervention logically. If it is strategic, if food is getting too expensive, you put more into intervention.
Mrs Fischer Boel: That would be very difficult because when we talk about intervention you would maintain a certain amount for intervention in bread wheat. In the other sectors it will be zero intervention but in wheat, if necessary, we would buy wheat. It is obvious in a market where prices are high that people would never sell for intervention because the price would be much lower than they would normally be able to get in the free market.

Q712 Chairman: But if prices were to go down and you had intervention that would really produce a distortion, would it not?
Mrs Fischer Boel: If?

Q713 Chairman: If cereal prices generally were to go down and you kept intervention for bread wheat, people would flock into bread wheat for the intervention price and that would produce an enormous distortion.
Mrs Fischer Boel: No.

Q714 Chairman: You do not think it would?
Mrs Fischer Boel: No.

Q715 Lord Plumb: The yield is so much lower anyway.
Mrs Fischer Boel: You have to take into account that bread wheat requires a special way of producing it. It is more difficult to produce bread wheat than other wheat because of the contents of the starch. The starch part has to be high and with the present reduction that we have in the country and the use of fertilisers because of the Nitrate Directive it makes it very difficult to produce bread wheat. It is not that easy, therefore I do not think it will happen that everybody will go into bread wheat.

Q716 Chairman: It is a food security issue.
Mrs Fischer Boel: The yields are lower in bread.

Q717 Lord Cameron of Dillington: I have two questions, one a detailed question and one more forward looking. The detailed one is on set-aside. We totally approve of zero set-aside and, in fact, the abolition of set-aside, but you did say in your Communication that you felt there were other ways of dealing with the environmental problems that come along with the abolition of set-aside. Have you got any solutions to dealing with these environmental problems?

Mrs Fischer Boel: We had a discussion this morning. I said that set-aside has never been an environmental measure.

Q718 *Lord Cameron of Dillington:* No, but it has turned out that way.

Mrs Fischer Boel: There were lots of people from Birdlife International.

Q719 *Chairman:* We know them.

Mrs Fischer Boel: They reacted immediately. It is not a total abolition of the set-aside, it is simply we do not have any compulsory set-aside so farmers can still maintain areas, and I know they are going to do so. If you are a farmer and you have a forest you would never plant close to the forest because nothing grows there anyway, so why not keep it? A lot of farmers would like to go hunting as well, so it could be nice in some areas. I do not consider zero set-aside as the outcome. We have to find solutions in the agri-environmental schemes if we can make it interesting for farmers to say, "Yes, we would like to take this scheme up". The problem is if we make it compulsory then we cannot use rural development. We have to make an attractive agri-environmental scheme that can take over the environmental benefits that there have been from set-aside.

Q720 *Lord Cameron of Dillington:* So that is more money to Pillar II again, very good. We approve.

Mrs Fischer Boel: That is why we need more money in Pillar II.

Q721 *Lord Cameron of Dillington:* My longer term question is I have seen particularly the Single Farm Payment at a flat rate, decoupled, as being a step to much more market orientation, possibly even complete market orientation, and yet one of the problems you have to deal with is the ups and downs of food production in the marketplace, for weather, for financial reasons, even in Australia or wherever it might be. All businesses have to cope with risk and you have a big chapter on risk in your Communication, which is good. Would it not be better if we could put more of that risk into the hands of the farmers? Instead of having the Single Farm Payment to support farmers—I am talking long-term, 2015 onwards—would it not be better if the EU paid half an insurance premium for farmers to cope with the risk and then it withdrew, it is the farmer's insurance policy? The Single Farm Payment seems very unsatisfactory and I am thinking of ways of giving more responsibility to the farmers to pay.

Mrs Fischer Boel: The ideas on risk and crisis management will always leave the responsibility to the farmer to tackle the normal risks that are in every business.

Q722 *Lord Cameron of Dillington:* Not in the wine sector it does not.

Mrs Fischer Boel: Wait and see what is coming up. I hope it will be positively received. We do not want a European scheme for crisis management, we want Member States to create schemes, but we would be open to look at the possibility of co-financing the premium via the rural development scheme.

Chairman: That is all right. That is good.

Q723 *Lord Cameron of Dillington:* Good.

Mrs Fischer Boel: That could be a possibility. We cannot prevent farmers from taking certain risks, that has always been the case. I am not going to try to translate what President Sarkozy means.

Q724 *Lord Cameron of Dillington:* Nor is he, I doubt.

Mrs Fischer Boel: If there should be any expectations of an income safety net, forget it. This would be a countercyclical payment, exactly what we are accusing the Americans of using as the most trade distorting measure. If you hear this idea, please kill it. It is not "green box" when we discuss the WTO terms, it is the most trade distorting ever. That simply will not fly. I think the majority of Member States would not accept this step back.

Lord Cameron of Dillington: I agree.

Q725 *Viscount Ullswater:* There is one thing that bothers me about this shift from Pillar I to Pillar II because in all our discussions it has been, "Oh, let's move that into Pillar II" and there seems to be an endless series of things which qualify for Pillar II, whether it is co-financing or financing. I was very taken by what you said about these small farms getting Single Farm Payments and the cost of the bureaucracy of giving them monies is greater than the monies they receive. When I look at all the axes and all the things which are available under Axis 1, Axis 2, Axis 3 and Axis 4, are we not running into that sort of danger again, that the bureaucracy of administering these schemes in Member States is going to be so great that most of the financing is going to go on the administration? Tell me I am wrong.

Mrs Fischer Boel: In this Commission we have a headline saying "Simplification" and in agriculture I think we are the winner of the day on simplification. It might be because there are lots of possibilities to simplify. What we have done on set-aside, on the reform in fruit and vegetables where we reduced the number of entitlements and previously we had an entitlement for fruit and vegetables and for set-aside, and this can all go I hope. That is the reason why I am looking forward to a flat rate system because then it will be a simple system. Cross-compliance has been accused of being very, very complicated. We had a report the day before yesterday which shows it is much, much less complicated than it is now labelled. I must say when I look at the results—it is six different Member States we have been looking at—they are very different, which means that there are some Member States that are over-implementing—

Q726 Lord Plumb: We can name one.

Mrs Fischer Boel: --- which means adding national things on top of what was the intention. I am really going to look into this because I am constantly accused by Germany and it turns out that Germany is a country that made it much more complicated for their farmers than anyone else. Member States need to help to simplify things.

Mr Christoffersen: Just on your particular question, I heard a suspicion that by saying there are a number of new challenges which we see and have to solve through rural development that means we will add a number of new instruments in the rural development field. But on our analysis thus far shows that we can use some of the existing possibilities in the rural development scheme to respond to most of the new challenges. The question is only to reinforce those particular possibilities financially. We talked about compensating for the disappearance of set-aside, but we have plenty of possibilities inside the present rural development scheme for supporting activities that could do that. Do not assume that by saying that we have new challenges to respond to that this means adding new additional possibilities in the scheme, it could just be about reinforcing the use of some of those that already existed.

Q727 Baroness Jones of Whitchurch: That fits very neatly into the question I was going to ask because you have talked about climate change and indicated that could be dealt with effectively through elements of Pillar II. Given the broad spectrum of issues around climate change, not only about drought, flooding and so on but the need to reduce CO_2 emissions and so on, how would you realistically manage those issues? How could you do that within the current Pillar II requirements?

Mrs Fischer Boel: First of all, the paper on energy and transport from the Commission on 10 January this year gives some clear signals on the reduction of CO_2: 20% by 2020 and 30% if we get others on board hopefully at the Bali meeting. Secondly, by 2020 10% of our energy demand should come from renewable energies and here agriculture can contribute. In fact, it is the only one that can contribute in the transport sector. That is the reason for the clear signals from the agricultural sector that we will be able to deliver

on the reduction of CO_2 emissions via bioethanol or biodiesel but we require that the production takes place in a sustainable way, which does not mean we will accept that pastures are ploughed up or forests are cut. We will put the same requirements on imported energy, be it oil or fuel, biodiesel or ethanol. We can deliver our part. We can do quite a lot more within the primary production reducing emissions from a manure tax to ensure that you do not blow the manure up into the air but place it on the soil directly, you do not bring it out in the autumn where the snow absorbs it. There is quite a lot that can be done. I have flagged up the idea in the Communication that we do not need the energy scheme that we have at present. We have the possibility to pay farmers €45 per hectare on up to two million hectares for growing energy plants, but today we have a well-functioning market so I hope we can agree this will disappear and then maybe spend the money in innovation or the possibilities of developing the second generation of biofuels instead.

Mr Christoffersen: As the Commissioner has said, one very typical example of where we need to do more is on manure because the greenhouse problem from agriculture is not so much CO_2 as the other types of greenhouse gases.

Mrs Fischer Boel: Methane.

Mr Christoffersen: This is a very important point. We have possibilities in the rural development scheme but we need to reinforce the use of those possibilities. Another important part of climate change is the whole water management and water conservation policy and that is one area where we need to do more.

Q728 Baroness Jones of Whitchurch: We heard this morning from your finance colleague that because everybody can see that the environment is a key policy issue coming up everybody is suddenly adding the environment on to their list of responsibilities and in the budget round they will be a factor, they will all be saying, "We can solve your environment problem out of our budget and our responsibilities". Do you think there is going to be an inevitable level of duplication because some of the areas you are talking about do not fit naturally with the existing farming regime as it stands? We are talking about quite a big shift.

Mrs Fischer Boel: In which area would you solve it?

Q729 Baroness Jones of Whitchurch: By having an almost separate function that deals with the environment issues rather than trying to fund it out of the existing budgets.

Mrs Fischer Boel: Normally I have a very good imagination. You might create a new fund to finance investment in agriculture via the addition of a different budget. I will not kill any ideas from the beginning but it sounds a bit difficult.

Mr Christoffersen: In general today if you look at the instruments which the Commission has at its disposal they can legislate and force Member States to undertake certain environmental measures but agriculture is the main instrument for the Commission to do things directly for the environment. The second pillar, cross-compliance. If you are looking at measures inside the Commission today which have a direct bearing on the environment most of them are under your responsibility.

Mrs Fischer Boel: They are coming from agriculture. I think it would be difficult to find another financial donor.

Mr Christoffersen: We are actually saying we are prepared to finance this by moving more money into the second pillar.

Q730 *Baroness Jones of Whitchurch:* But presumably by increasing. You are not saying you are going to do it on a—

Mrs Fischer Boel: Not increasing.

Q731 *Baroness Jones of Whitchurch:* You are going to do all the climate change stuff within the existing budget?

Mrs Fischer Boel: The budget for agriculture will not be increasing after 2013. We will have lots of different challenges but we have not asked for more money. We will simply try to reallocate within our budget from the more traditional direct payment into the rural development policy.

Q732 *Earl of Dundee:* You mentioned that there will not be an increase in funds to the CAP from the EU budget and you also suggested that compulsory modulation should be accompanied by decoupling. Is this not a recipe for distorting competition within the Single Market given that there really is so much variation in different EU States in their political priorities as well as in the relative strengths of their farm lobbies?

Mrs Fischer Boel: First of all, I think the discussion on financing for agriculture will be negotiated together with the British rebate. It is always a French/English discussion.

Q733 *Lord Cameron of Dillington:* And the other rebates.

Mrs Fischer Boel: You get the biggest ones. That is the reason for not expecting any higher budget in the future. Personally, I know those of you who are close to farming society know that farmers would love to make their income from their production instead of from payments. If this is what we can see on the

horizon and hopefully this is where we are heading, higher prices, I am very happy to see the price increases in agriculture because for 15 years we have been in a decreasing situation. Those who are complaining about milk prices, as long as they never complain about buying a litre of Coke, which is sometimes more expensive than a litre of milk, I could not care less.

Q734 *Lord Greaves:* Water, never mind Coke.

Mrs Fischer Boel: I have carefully looked into the prices of water and unless you are going for a very special one it is still cheaper than milk, but Coke is a different matter.

Q735 *Chairman:* Finally, I think something that has underpinned a lot of our discussion is to identify what aspects of the CAP it is essential to keep common across all Member States and what aspects you can allow to have greater variability in the context of particular problems of Member States. Have you got a thought on that, what is absolutely essential to keep hold of across the board?

Mrs Fischer Boel: I want to keep a certain level of direct payment co-financed exclusively from the Commission. We all know going from the northern part of Finland down to Sicily that there is a huge difference and that is the reason why we have introduced the possibility in the rural development policy for Member States to make their own programmes tailor made for the challenges they face in their specific regions. This must continue because you can never make a one-size-fits-all programme in rural development. Those are two huge differences between the direct payment and the rural development policy. I am sure we will have a discussion raised by the new Member States as to why their direct payment is lower than that of the old Member States because of the history of the direct payment which originally was a compensation for the drop in prices in the McSharry Reform. As this can no longer be the only explanation I am sure you will see a queue of new Member States saying, "We need a flat rate but this has to cover the whole of the European Union". That is going to be a very, very difficult discussion. If this happens then you will see a severe or huge reduction in the old Member States and an increase in the new Member States because the levels are completely different. This is for the discussion that will take place. It is a fantastic job I am in, you can imagine.

Q736 *Lord Cameron of Dillington:* Article 69, which seems to be pretty important, do you have support for your desire to relax the rules in Article 69?

Mrs Fischer Boel: I do not know yet because we have not started the discussion.

Q737 *Lord Cameron of Dillington:* That is going to be quite important, is it not, particularly all this talk about more rural development?
Mrs Fischer Boel: Why should Member States be against it?

Q738 *Lord Cameron of Dillington:* I do not know, but I never understand what Member States do.

Mrs Fischer Boel: If it is voluntary why they should they block the possibility for those who want to use it to make it much less complicated.

Q739 *Chairman:* Thank you very much indeed. We look forward to the outcome on wine.
Mrs Fischer Boel: Really. The most important request from the UK is to increase the de minimis.
Chairman: Thank you very much indeed.

THURSDAY 6 DECEMBER 2007

Present   Cameron of Dillington, L.   Plumb, L.
             Dundee, E.   Sewell, L. (Chairman)
             Greaves, L.   Ullswater, V.
             Jones of Whitchurch, B.

Examination of Witness

Witness: MR PETER MANDELSON, Commissioner for Trade, European Commission, examined.

Q740 *Chairman:* Good afternoon.

Mr Mandelson: I am the Trade Commissioner, not the Agriculture Commissioner by the way. I just thought I would enter that caveat.

Q741 *Lord Plumb:* Agriculture relies on trade.

Mr Mandelson: Yes, and we are doing rather well on that basis in Europe. I think we are probably the biggest agricultural exporter in the world, just about. Why is that? It is because we have become more efficient, more market-oriented with a rather useful and beneficial reform process that needs to continue, and I suspect will.

Q742 *Chairman:* We have got very high hopes that it will with a degree of acceleration.

Mr Mandelson: You were kind enough to indicate the areas of questions you wanted to put to me. I have got wonderful answers for you here. I am not at all sure whether it would not be better for us to have a political conversation and I simply leave you with the answers. They are quite interesting answers and they are very full.

Q743 *Chairman:* They are going to take a long time for you to read out.

Mr Mandelson: Yes.

Q744 *Lord Cameron of Dillington:* That is a good idea.

Mr Mandelson: I honestly do not see why not. It does not make too many disparaging remarks about our Member States, I hope, the less reform-minded of them! Anyway, how would you like to play this?

Q745 *Chairman:* I think it might be useful to have a general discussion.

Mr Mandelson: Bearing in mind that you must throw me out by twenty past three because I have got to receive somebody at half past.

Q746 *Chairman:* It would be useful if we could have the formal answers and spend the time on a discussion.

Mr Mandelson: Do you want to know in the first instance what is going on in the Doha Round?

Q747 *Chairman:* I think that would be a useful start. That was the first question in any case.

Mr Mandelson: The agriculture negotiations are the most complex, the most detailed and most advanced. It does not say a great deal for the other sectors in the negotiation, but they are. They are now text driven. We had the chairman's text before the summer. On domestic support, I would say that we are close to an agreement for the final language that we want to see and can agree on the "green box" which allows us to continue with the Single Farm Payment scheme to allow the transfer of entitlements and to assure the continuation of our rural development programme. It is very important for us to be able to protect the "green box" because that "green box" represents, and is the vehicle for, the non-production linked rural development driven basis of our reform policies. We are well ahead of the United States in our reforms, as you know, because they are nowhere on their reforms, they have not agreed any reforms, and the Farm Bill which has now been agreed in Congress is certainly not reform driven. It is marginally different but in its overall effect just as bad as the 2002 Farm Bill. They are not yet signed up finally either to the reforms of their trade distortion programmes in their "amber box" and their "blue box" or to the overall ceiling on their trade distorting subsidies. The US will come on board at the last moment in the endgame, if we ever get to the endgame in these ovetly negotiated negotiations. On market access we have got the proposed ranges of the tiered formula for tariff reductions which are a perfectly acceptable basis for a political agreement in my view. The chairman is not proposing in the range that he has tabled anything that we cannot live with, assuming that we are coming somewhere in the mid or upper end of the range which is not the most extreme. There you get into a lot of very detailed fine-tuning of our offer: what sensitive products are agreed within the overall tariff reduction formula that is in place; the treatment of our sensitive products. They cannot ask us to do everything, they cannot ask us to have the most ambitious tariff reduction overall and the most generous treatment of our sensitive products, generous from an exporter's point of view rather than our own, with the most extreme consumption data used as the basis for this treatment of sensitive products. They cannot have everything. With due swings and roundabouts we can get to a point where we are certainly arriving at an ambitious and generous outcome in this negotiation, but we have to have flexibility in how we arrive at that generosity and that ambition. I think they understand this. This is the most sensitive area for our Member States, right down to the last cut of beef. This is the most sensitive for our Member States and the most difficult for us to handle internally within the EU and, therefore, in negotiations we are undertaking with our partners. At this stage we have not declared any final list of sensitive products and ultimately that designation will depend on the treatment that is agreed within these negotiations of those sensitive products, what the outcome is on the special safeguard measure that currently exists and we want maintained. We have not reached that stage yet but our negotiating partners and those who have the most ambitious designs on our agricultural markets—the US, Australia, New Zealand, Brazil, Argentina—know pretty well what we can do in the final endgame of this negotiation. That depends not only on what we can and will do, it depends on what others are prepared to do both within agriculture and other sectors of the negotiation. We are not going to be taken to the cleaners and back whilst everyone else is sitting in roadside cafes having their third cappuccino, thank you very much. They have got to make efforts of their own. This is particularly the case in export subsidies. We have given a commitment, as you no doubt know, to phase out all our export subsidies by 2013 and to frontload a lot of their removal two or three years before that, but the United States has got obligations and Australia and New Zealand have got obligations. You asked me a question about New Zealand and if you look at the small print of what they do and get up to, New Zealand has rather carefully maintained export arrangements that favour their producers and exporters. They are not completely pure, the New Zealanders, and they have got to step up to the table and deal with the export subsidising aspects of their own policies in their own machinery. On geographical indications, those are very, very important for our southern Member States. We do not have many friends on geographical indications in these negotiations. They say it is a matter of legality and economic interest, but I think it is more a question of ignorance, prejudice and cultural misunderstanding on their part. Anyway, we continue to fight for a reasonable outcome on geographical indications. We will know where we are finally when we have the revised chairman's negotiating text and that is due to appear at the end of January. That will reflect all the detailed negotiation that has taken place since the previous chairman's text. It is very, very important, not only

for its own agricultural sake but also because it is the key to the negotiations in other parts of this round. Brazil will say to you, "Well, we will see what we can do on industrial tariffs or services when we see how much of the lemon we have been successful in squeezing every last drop from" and that will be reflected in the chairman's next revised text. The end of January, beginning of February will be a very crucial time for these negotiations. If you are ask me what I think the chances are of agreement being made in 2008, I would have to say no more than 50/50, and perhaps I am being my usual optimistic, sunny self in saying that. These are hard. If we do not manage to get a breakthrough in 2008, and early in 2008 because it will then take six months to do the detailed negotiating, we will have a change of administration in the United States and even an incoming US President who was keen and interested and committed to taking up where President Bush left off would need a good six to nine months to see themselves into the negotiation. As we have already learned from Mrs Clinton in her interview in the *Financial Times*, she is not going to take up where President Bush left off. She is sceptical about trade, she says. Whether this is simply for the purposes of winning votes in primaries or whether she would carry that view into office should she be elected, it is very difficult to say. We will certainly strive for a balanced deal in 2008. This is the only way in which we can make the maximum use of the CAP reform of 2003 is to get that bound into the WTO and made irreversible in international trade terms. We need this agreement and our trading partners need this agreement from us.

Q748 Chairman: Some ten years ago we had an EU which was pretty reluctant to reform its agricultural policies and we had the threat of the WTO there to sort of prod CAP reform on. Is it right to say that the emphasis has changed a bit now, that the 2003 reforms have set the direction of reform of European agriculture and really it is not that WTO has ceased to be a prod but we are not as far off the game as we were ten years ago?
Mr Mandelson: I think the main drivers of reform have been internal considerations, not external pressure. I am not saying the external pressure has been non-existent or unimportant, it has been present and we in Europe are good boy scouts and girl guides and if we see an international negotiation coming along we prepare properly for it, we carry out our reforms so that we can then use those reforms as the basis of tabling a generous offer in a multilateral trade round. We are the first, second and third multilateralists in the world. We believe in, and also benefit from, a rules-based international trading

system with a strong WTO at its heart. For us, seeing the success of the world trade round is very, very important. When it was launched in 2001 we knew that agriculture would be a dominant issue, quite rightly. Agricultural reform internationally negotiated and multilaterally driven did not take place in the previous Uruguay Round and we took on commitments but, frankly, we were pretty evasive about implementing them. There was no real reform in Europe driven by the outcome of the Uruguay Round. Is that too strong a statement? I do not think so. We knew that the time would come with this round, should it be launched, when we had to step up to the table and be instrumental in bringing about a fundamental restructuring of agricultural trade which requires a very substantial reform of our internal arrangements. The United States tends to do it differently. Rather than reform first, table second and then negotiate a satisfactory outcome, the United States has chosen to negotiate first and then reform afterwards should the negotiation be successful. The problem with that approach is it has left a lot of open-ended question marks about where the US will end up, what they will be prepared to do, what they are negotiating into this round and it has bedevilled us in these negotiations that those who have met the demands of the United States have never been clear, and are not clear even now, what the US at the end of the day will be prepared to sign up to and do, whereas in the case of the European Union they know full well, they have taken us further beyond what we initially envisaged doing but, nonetheless, we had a solid base of reform which provided the mandate in the negotiating envelope for me on the trade side. I would maintain my view that although we have chosen to approach these negotiations in that way we have nonetheless seen reform being driven more by an internal recognition and desire to reform for its own sake than to provide us with a basis for negotiation in a world trade round, and that is what I think will remain the case.

Q749 Chairman: Can you help us solve the riddle of Mr Sarkozy, on the one hand saying things which are fairly liberal—
Mr Mandelson: Really, what were those?

Q750 Chairman: Every now and then there is a word but basically there is still a lot of semi-protectionist stuff coming out.
Mr Mandelson: If you look at the small print of what President Sarkozy said in his CAP speech, which was before the summer, he said that we must continue reform but what he actually has in mind is reforming the CAP back towards the original state that it found itself in before the 2003 reforms kicked in.

Q751 Chairman: Community preference.
Mr Mandelson: Just be guarded slightly that when he talks of reform he may be talking about reform that takes the CAP backwards to what it was rather than forwards to what it may become.

Q752 Lord Cameron of Dillington: Apologies, I have to go, I have a formal dinner in Taunton at eight o'clock tonight.
Mr Mandelson: Have a good time.

Q753 Lord Cameron of Dillington: I must go in a minute. My question is about the integration of the Health Check and your negotiations. Is there anything that really stands out that you would like to see further and more in the Health Check that might help you? My second question is on the question of risk management. The Commission have put forward a proposal in the Health Check that there is a possibility in the future, which we strongly support, for the CAP to be reformed or even abolished. We feel that farmers should be able to take on more risk management and perhaps there could be a role for the EU to subsidise that, part-fund it maybe through insurance premiums or something like that. There is clearly a risk and talking to Mariann Fischer Boel we heard that might impinge on the "green box" in the WTO talks.
Mr Mandelson: I would be a bit nervous of reform moving in that direction because we are starting to become close to the sorts of trade distorting programmes that the United States like to operate. I would be a bit wary of that, without anticipating where Mariann wants to take the reform process. The straight answer to your original question is there is nothing happening in the Health Check that I would either want or expect to impinge on the offers we are making in this trade round. Frankly, in Mr Sarkozy's view, we are taking our offers beyond what we can afford.

Q754 Lord Cameron of Dillington: Can it go further?
Mr Mandelson: I would say up to the limit of what we can afford, but there is room for disagreement and there is a very strong view that I am stepping outside the mandate, I am stretching the 2003 reforms to breaking point, that a combination of domestic support reduction plus the tariffs that we are dramatically reducing, plus the progressive phasing out of export subsidies, is going to leave European agriculture in an extremely vulnerable state. I do not accept that. Our agricultural sector in Europe is both shrinking and becoming more efficient and competitive as it becomes more market-oriented. Our demand for agricultural produce and food is outgrowing our ability and the capacity of our shrinking farm sector to provide for that. We need to import more because demand is growing. Frankly,

we will be importing more of what we cannot compete with on efficiency and cost and price terms through domestic production. That does not mean to say that the agricultural sector in Europe is disappearing, it is becoming more lean, more specialist and more competitive, driving growth in agricultural good and processed good exports. It is doing very well but it is changing, it is not the same as it was, and it does not have the same mass commodity production that it once had. Why? Because we can get things cheaper from elsewhere and in the meantime produce those things that we are best at and good at exporting and see ourselves in premier place in the export league tables. We are sustaining whilst changing. Our competitiveness and export capacity is growing whilst our demand for food is also growing and, therefore, our imports are increasing. We are also coming out of certain international markets as we grow in others. There is a lot of change. The end that we will see is a more market-oriented, more competitive and, therefore, more sustainable agricultural sector in Europe than the one we have seen in recent decades. Do we have to do more to take European agriculture in that direction through the Health Check or the ensuing reforms in order to meet our commitments in the world trade talks? No, we do not and I would say that we are at the outer limit of what we can offer in those trade talks and I would not ask for or expect any Health Check to deliver a better offer which is more within our means in the agricultural part of those negotiations.

Q755 Viscount Ullswater: I think you explained that the reforms of 2003, the introduction of the Single Farm Payment, had allowed you to negotiate on the fact that we were not supporting farmers with national aids which might contradict your negotiating position. The marketplace has improved the situation for the arable side but there has been a certain amount of comment about whether the beef and sheep sectors can manage just with the Single Farm Payment. You touched on it a moment ago saying that we will be importing a huge amount of sheep and beef from South America and other parts of the world. That might severely damage the European beef and sheep markets. Is it possible that things introduced under Pillar II in rural development can be undertaken to support these sectors without running up against your problems with trade?
Mr Mandelson: They can, but without re-coupling payments to production. At the end of the day they have to produce the sort of quality at the sort of price that people want to buy and are prepared to pay for in Europe and elsewhere. That is the bottom line. Of course, the Single Farm Payment scheme, which necessarily provides fully decoupled payments to

farmers, can sustain a local production capacity and quality of life and integration of the rural economy and rural way of life which would support beef and sheep farming. In my view, a condition for that cannot and will not be a reversion to the sort of production linked subsidies that have had such an impact on world markets in the past.

Q756 Chairman: One of the moans that we frequently get from our producers is that on the one hand they have been urged to become more market-oriented, which they have undoubtedly become, yet on the other hand they are being landed with increasing costs, specific costs on the environmental side, animal welfare and stuff like this, and saying, "We are trying to be more market-oriented but we are having these costs put on us which significantly disadvantage us in the global marketplace". What is the response to that moan?
Mr Mandelson: I suppose the response I would make is the obligations that we are placing on them, the standards that we require of them, are designed to make them competitive. In a sense, we are going where the market is heading in any case and we are going to produce quality products which people can absolutely rely on in health and other terms which will correspond to the sorts of high standards that European consumers, and people like European consumers, want to pay for. We are at that end of the market and, frankly, in that sense agriculture is no different from any other production sector in Europe. We are competing in a very, very tough global economy with premium products, added value, high standards, whether it be high technology linked manufactured goods or agricultural produce and foodstuffs.

Q757 Lord Greaves: I agree with all that but at the moment the farmers who are holding their heads above water, or some doing very well perhaps, are being subsidised to do that and if you take away the subsidy can they still survive in that market?
Mr Mandelson: If it is non-trade distorting and if we can reflect this in the payments that we make in a continuing progressive move towards a "green box" from the most to the more trade distorting forms of expenditure, yes, we can maintain that. Look at what they are getting back. What they are getting back when they have to operate high animal health standards is protection from the sudden and savage economic impact of an outbreak of animal disease, whether it be BSE, avian flu or bluetongue disease. They might think, "Thank you very much for helping us save us from ourselves, as it were, but you had better continue to support us otherwise it is just going to become so onerous for us to operate and maintain these standards when others in the world are failing to do so", and my answer to that is we cannot in this

sector, animal originated goods, see a race to the bottom. Our task is to drive standards up. If people cannot meet our standards then they will not get their products into our market. I face another pressure on me from developing countries who then say that this is just protectionism by another name or by another means.

Viscount Ullswater: Non-financial tariffs.

Q758 Chairman: Mr Sarkozy.

Mr Mandelson: "What you are doing is saying with one hand you are getting rid of your trade distorting subsidies but, on the other hand, you are setting the bar so high in the standards you require that you know we could not possibly compete with you and that is how you are favouring your domestic producers". It does not happen quite like that, although we will face a difficult decision possibly in the next week. Perhaps I should not discuss the success with which Brazilian beef is now—

Q759 Chairman: That was what I was going to raise.

Mr Mandelson: —meeting our SPS standards. Let us not anticipate the discussion that I am going to have to have with one or two other Commissioners in the coming week, but Brazil needs to know that if it is producing safely and supplying meat that corresponds to our standards there will be no penalisation of their produce by our trade distorting subsidies and no artificially high SPS standards which will be a bar which is impossible for them to get over. They need to know that, but at the same time they need to put in place operational arrangements, which at the moment they are not doing entirely and fully, and if they choose to step in line in ways that we are entitled to expect and ask them to do then there will be no barrier to their products, however painful it is for us to take in so much of their meat.

Q760 Lord Plumb: You would not expect me to use the word "moan" like my Lord Chairman as far as producers are concerned.

Mr Mandelson: Never. You are not a moaning farmer, Lord Plumb.

Q761 Lord Plumb: But let me give my impression of the reaction of farmers, not just in Britain but in some of the other parts where production is taking place. They have two things in mind at the moment. One, we are going to lose subsidies within a very short time, and they are anticipating that and are prepared for it. Two, if we are going to compete in this market we have got to produce the best possible product, be it from grain or the livestock that we can produce, and we are prepared to face that. I was particularly pleased that you mentioned the two extremes, if you like, of America and New Zealand in the context of what they are doing because the Americans are being

terribly dishonest in my opinion in not facing up to the reality that they have to face up to under the Doha Round. New Zealand do to a large extent but when you said they are not always honest, and I was there last year—

Mr Mandelson: I do not think I said honest, I think it was "pure". I am not accusing them of dishonesty.

Q762 Lord Plumb: I know what you were saying. If we take the Doha Round, which I favour and I favour free trade, the possibility of opening up markets throughout the world, and you made a speech a little while ago in which you said that we are now importing more products from the ACP countries than any other part of the world and that is fine, that is the sort of thing we should be talking about, we should also be taking advantage of exports, and the difficulties we have there we know only too well are related to disease problems and so on which blot the market from time to time. I want to give one example. We have had difficulty, certainly in Britain, this last year with lamb, partly because the lamb is up on the hills and you cannot get it down and there is foot and mouth. It was only two or three months ago now, just as British lamb was coming on to the market when 10,000 tonnes of New Zealand lamb landed, and the reason for that was the Canterbury Plains were going dry, the lambs were losing condition and, therefore, they were being slaughtered and sent over in carcass form. I know that for a fact from my contacts in New Zealand. They are now criticising themselves because they realised that there was an element of dumping at that time but, nevertheless, in legal terms what they were doing was committing the amount that they could send in because they had not met their commitments of lamb for a long time. I said to New Zealanders only last year, "Britain did two things for you that were always good for New Zealand, that was for Britain to join Europe because we opened the door to 40 different countries and, secondly, I go back and tell all the farmers in Europe that we will get rid of the subsidies tomorrow night if we have the same import controls that you have got" and they say, "We don't have any import controls", and of course they do not because they do not have to because nobody is exporting to them, other than motorcars and this sort of thing. If we are going to have a market under Doha, and a freer market, then we have got to have some pretty tough regulations on some of these countries, whether it is Brazilian beef, New Zealand lamb or American products that are coming here. Another aspect of that is the whole question of soya. We are bringing in so much soya from these countries, 98% of which is genetically modified. Is that coming on to the market and declaring itself not to be genetically modified?

Mr Mandelson: I hope and assume not.

Q763 Lord Plumb: If we are going to really have a free market then it has got to be a fair market on the basis of the regulations that they will adhere to in the same way that we are in Europe.
Mr Mandelson: Do you want to have a discussion about whether we should be more prepared to embrace genetic modification?
Lord Plumb: I would be very happy to but I do not want to do that now.

Q764 Chairman: Not today.
Mr Mandelson: And whether we can maintain our productivity and our competitiveness without doing so, because I am not too sure.

Q765 Lord Plumb: That is not my argument. My argument is that people unknowingly are consuming a product which is so much cheaper believing, of course, that it is just as good as it might be from elsewhere.
Mr Mandelson: It may be cheaper but is it lower quality?

Q766 Lord Plumb: Not necessarily.
Mr Mandelson: If it meets our SPS standards and fulfils the terms of our SPS agreement then that is our—I hesitate to use the words—"ultimate defence", that sounds a bit beleaguered, but as tariffs go down and our markets open then other goods will come towards our markets, that is absolutely true, but they do not just pass freely into our markets because they have to get over the hurdle of our SPS agreement. In a sense, the more we reform internally and the more, assuming the Doha Round ever finishes in a successful conclusion, our border protection comes down, the more important our SPS agreement becomes.

Q767 Lord Plumb: Exactly.
Mr Mandelson: That is what we rely on to ensure that we do not just get well-priced products but that we get safe products. It is going to become much more important in the future even than it is now.

Q768 Viscount Ullswater: Are you undertaking any analysis of these two things, the reduction of export subsidies and—
Mr Mandelson: We model all the time. It is a combination of the three things. I get very impatient and slightly frustrated with our negotiating partners who choose just to talk to me at one moment about domestic support and is it going far enough, is it a genuine reduction, are you not just tabling what you have already decided to do. We did decide to do it, partly because we wanted to do it and partly because we knew we would have to provide a basis for the

offer that we table in these negotiations, so do not doubly punish us for being good people coming in at the outset with a good offer which you then pocket or discount and say, "Where is your real offer?" This has been the American fear which has inhibited them from coming forward before now. That is an approach I have rejected. I have said, "You can take it as a given that what we are tabling we do in good faith. We will sustain that offer and will maintain that flexibility but do not come back to me and say that if I am going to get anything in return I have got to do twice or three times what I have already tabled because that is when the negotiation will stop. I am not playing that sort of game". It has enabled me to be on the front foot as a negotiator, always knowing what I could table, always putting in a good offer and knowing how far I can go in subsequent negotiations but also knowing my limits and taking it up to that point and not going beyond it, whereas some would say that approach is simply naïve. I think that was the term President Sarkozy used repeatedly about me during his election campaign when he referred to this, " . . . fonctionnaire who goes round the world giving things away to America and to developing countries. We need to have the negotiations taken out of the hands of this fonctionnaire and put back into the hands of somebody who is less naïve". I must say, I have never been called naïve in my political career so it stung me somewhat when it came from his lips. The point is this: I have always been conscious, because we have computer modelled it, of what the overall impact will be of all the changes that we are prepared to take on and the offers that we are prepared to table. I do accept that in the case of tariffs, the reduction of border protection, it is not an exact science. I know that Mariann and her Director-General who provide the material when we try and negotiate that cannot say with precision that this reduction in border protection coupled with this price effect will have that impact on domestic markets and producers, but they have a pretty fair idea and, frankly, they approach this in a pretty prudent way. DG Agriculture in the European Commission has not been operating agricultural protectionism for 50 years without learning a trick or two about how to protect European farmers.

Q769 Earl of Dundee: I wonder if I could touch on long-term CAP for a second. You have pointed out that all the players and sides have different journeys to travel and that may be a fact that we cannot get away with. Nevertheless, how do you think it will affect some degree of protectionism after 2013 and maybe continuing for quite some years after that?
Mr Mandelson: First of all I reject the term "protectionism". I might go as far as prudent protection with you, but not "protectionism". What will the argument be about after 2013? I suspect it will

be more about the difference between or the balance between Community expenditure and national expenditure on agriculture, to be honest. I think that there is quite a strong appetite for reducing the agricultural share of the Community budget. If some of our Member States, within the terms of the international agreements that we have signed up to, want to exercise some national preference as opposed to Community preference within limits it may well be that they are either encouraged to do so or will choose to do so themselves.

Q770 *Chairman:* Would you see the development of co-financing as part of that as well?

Mr Mandelson: Yes, I think so. I am now getting way out of my remit and depth, particularly my depth. These are the sorts of things to talk to Mariann about. I always feel with Mariann, and have you met her Director-General, Mr Dumartin?

Q771 *Lord Plumb:* Yes.

Mr Mandelson: A very shrewd Frenchman. I always have the feeling with those guys that they know exactly what they want to do and where they are going to end up, it is just a question of managing the Member States adequately to come in behind them in the direction they have chosen, but you are never quite sure what that destination is. You know there is a destination but you are never going to be privy to the full picture with these guys. That is the way they treat me as a trade negotiator. They say, "Absolutely not. You cannot go below this. You cannot table that. To go beyond that, the roof of the Common Agricultural Policy would fall in" and, blow me down, three months later I pick up a briefing paper and exactly what I was told was unimaginable before has suddenly become not even my bottom line. They are skilled, I was going to say manipulators but that is too tough. They are skilled manoeuvrers. They are taken by surprise by market developments.

Q772 *Chairman:* That is good.

Mr Mandelson: You also fine-tune your computer model and find that what comes out is affected by the assumptions that you put in and you put in different assumptions.

Q773 *Chairman:* You said that you undertake the modelling on the impact of eliminating export subsidies and import tariff reductions but you avoided telling us what the model showed.

Mr Mandelson: The impact on domestic production?

Q774 *Chairman:* Yes.

Mr Mandelson: Smaller production obviously.

Q775 *Chairman:* In which particular areas?

Mr Mandelson: Look, if you were from the Irish Parliament would I be saying to you that there is a question mark over the future of the Irish beef industry? No, I would not be saying it to them, but since you are not from Ireland, you are from Britain, I can say there is a question mark over the future of the Irish beef industry, they know it and they are very worried about it and very angry with me, and I am routinely denounced where effigies are burnt.

Q776 *Viscount Ullswater:* They will get round it some way, will they not?

Mr Mandelson: I think they will get round it but they have got to change their production model. That is the same in every other economic sector. Think of the areas of production where we face Chinese competition on a scale hitherto unimaginable which is not going to go away in any short time. I have just been in China crossing swords with them over their dirty products and their filthy food. I do not mean all of it. They are not fair traders. I am not saying they are completely unfair traders either but our job, my job, is to keep them on their toes. Yes, they have a set of comparative advantages which are unquestionable. Secondly, they have a number of other distortions of price and competition which add to their natural comparative advantages which naturally I strongly object to. Do they open their markets in the same way to us as we do to them? No, they do not. Do they give us legal protection once we are in their markets with our goods and services? No, they do not. We are prudent, precautionary, sometimes offering protection where it is needed and justified, but just as we have been serial offenders when it comes to trade distorting farm subsidies in the world, we have subsidised, we have dumped, we have now become the most active and successful serial reformers. That is what people sometimes do not understand or accept in the country I know best. They rage against the Common Agricultural Policy as if it is in the same form that existed in the 1960s, 1970s and 1980s, they have no idea how much it has changed and how much reform has kicked in. Compare and contrast the United States. I know they do not subsidise on the scale that we do, or have done, but they have got a long way to go to catch up with us when it comes to reform.

Chairman: Thank you very much.

THURSDAY 6 December 2007

Present   Dundee, E   Plumb, L
             Greaves, L   Sewell, L (Chairman)
             Jones of Whitchurch, B Ullswater, V

Examination of Witnesses

Witness: MR BENIAMIN GAWLIK, First Secretary (Agriculture), Polish Permanent Mission, examined.

Q777 Chairman: Thank you very much indeed for coming and helping us with our inquiry. We are very grateful to you for finding the time.
Mr Gawlik: I hope it will be a great pleasure for me. It is the first time I have spoken before such an honourable audience. I hope I will be able to answer all of your questions. I must admit I might have some problems with answering questions concerning rural development. Unfortunately, I am not a specialist in this area but I have some handouts from my colleagues from the capital so I will try to use them from time to time.

Q778 Chairman: We are a Sub-Committee of our European Union Committee and for us this is a formal evidence session, so a record will be taken. If you want to say anything off the record just tell us. The other thing is you will get a copy of the transcript as soon as it is ready so you can make any revisions. I suppose a good starting point is to ask you what has been the experience of Polish agriculture since Poland joined the EU and what effect has joining the EU had on your agriculture?
Mr Gawlik: From our perspective, and that of our farmers, the CAP is a marvellous tool. Just before accession farmers were the most euro-sceptical part of our society and according to the polls only 20% of farmers were in favour of joining the EU and accession. After accession that figure has changed dramatically and 70% of farmers are euro enthusiasts. From the farmers' perspective it was a good thing and they have profited from accession and for the part of the economic sector concerning agri-food it has been a positive thing. From accession our export to the European market has increased to both old and so-called new Member States. The overall net balance of trade has risen by five times during the first two years. It has been quite positive. Our sector, especially the processing sector, has made quite good progress if you take into account that before accession in 2000 or 2001 there were only 100 processing establishments which could sell to the European market and after accession there are more than 2,000 establishments in the sector of meat processing and dairy processing which sell to the European market. It is true that at the beginning some of the processing plants had transitional periods to adjust and there were close to 700 such

establishments which were listed in an annex to our Act of accession. Right now the end of the transitional period is approaching and I asked my colleagues in the capital and it seems a couple of them will not adjust in time. It is also worthwhile mentioning that many of them had adjusted even before the end of the agreed period for adjustment. Some of them have adjusted totally but for some of them, if they were involved in a different type of business, let us say a meat processing plant which also had a slaughterhouse, to adjust the slaughterhouse was very costly so they just closed the slaughterhouse and invested in the rest of the business.

Q779 Chairman: The benefit to Polish agriculture has been more the access to European markets, that has been the main thing, rather than CAP payments, is that right?
Mr Gawlik: CAP payments, yes, and all the instruments which are connected to the CAP. Most of the farmers feel that there is still unequal treatment on the European market, at least in the case of farmers because they started from 25% of the direct payments. Definitely the introduction of the CAP led to a more stable market for the farmers and direct payments have led to an increase in their ability to modernise. On the other side there was also part of the rural development support even before accession, the so-called SAPARD[1] programme, which was used quite efficiently by our processing industry. Maybe less by the farmers but definitely by the processing industry. After 2004 farmers had access to the second pillar as well.

Q780 Lord Plumb: So market prices have risen by what sort of percentage?
Mr Gawlik: It varies from market to market. In the case of sugar beet the rise in prices was close to 50% and there was also similar rise in the sugar prices for the final consumers. After accession sugar beet production became one of the most profitable types of agricultural activity in Poland. A growth of producer prices that was also the case for beef production and pork production. In certain types of production, like pork or poultry, there was an

---

[1] SAPARD (Special Accession Programme for Agriculture and Rural Development) established in June 1999 by the Council of the European Union to help countries of Central and Eastern Europe deal with the problems of the structural.

increase in prices immediately after accession but in the case of poultry, for example, there was a drop back to the levels before accession just after these problems with avian influenza at the end of 2005, beginning of 2006. The market for pork is very volatile. Prices rose just after accession but then they dropped once again to the levels noted before accession. In the case of milk there was a rise in prices but that is more a European-wide phenomenon, not only connected with our accession, the increase in demand for milk and milk products on the European and international markets.

Q781 *Chairman:* Looking at the Health Check, various elements within the Health Check, do some cause you concern or do some give you optimism? What is your view on the various elements of the Health Check?

Mr Gawlik: Our concern is the possible implementation of the intervention measures. That is the biggest concern. We think that will lead to a further decrease in prices. There is no space for discussion about diminishing the direct support because right now it seems there will be no additional compensation for the price drop. That is probably the most important concern. There are a couple of things which seem to be positive. For example, the Commission seems to see that our simplified system of direct payments, so-called SAPS,[2] is quite efficient. It is appreciated by the farmers. It is also quite easy to manage for the administration. The Commission considers that it is worthwhile to discuss the prolongation of this type of system of direct payments up to 2013. It is quite a positive signal for us but we are rather disappointed that the Commission would like to leave it for discussion in the mainstream Health Check discussion and then we could expect a decision about the prolongation of SAPS at the end of 2008. Right now, this is a good occasion to discuss the prolongation of the system because there is a proposal concerning the simplification of the cross-compliance discussed in the Council and within the framework of this discussion on simplification we presented our request to prolong the system. It is hard to understand why the Commission cannot agree to our request. It is not only a Polish request but a request from many of the new Member States who apply this system. Why should we wait for the end of 2008 to possibly have a positive result from the Health Check discussion on the prolongation of SAPS? As a positive signal we see the possibility to discuss the so-called "fatter" rate payment in the case of direct payments. We apply flat rate payments and, in fact, we have only a couple of markets where we have higher and differentiated support but mostly due to the so-called complementary direct payments from the national

budget. It is just for a couple of products where in the past support in the EU was quite high and it would be discriminatory. for our farmers if they were not paid at a level a little closer to their colleagues from the EU-15 can get for tobacco production, hops or potato starch production. We think the Commission could be more ambitious because, as it is presented in the document, it will be a possibility to have a "flatter" rate payment but only at the Member State level. We think we might be more ambitious and start to discuss "flatter" rate payments within the European Union.

Q782 *Chairman:* The philosophy behind much of the reform recently, and even going forward into the Health Check, is very much to get European agriculture more market-oriented moving away from product subsidies, direct subsidies generally, and the farmer getting a greater return from the market and if that means structural change in agricultural industries then so be it. Is Poland comfortable with that approach or is Poland really looking to defend its direct income?

Mr Gawlik: We would definitely like to retain the direct income support if there is any change in the price level. For us, there is no room for discussion about the level of direct payments, especially as we are still waiting to get full direct payments. At the time when we reach this full direct payment level, for us it might be the time to be on a level playing field with everybody else within the EU. In relation to your question, at least in the case of Poland, and probably in the case of many new Member States, when we apply this simplified system, and there is single support or a single rate of support for one hectare of arable land we think it leaves farmers with the possibility to adjust to market signals.

Q783 *Viscount Ullswater:* The 2003 reform made the receipt of SAPS, in your case, dependent upon cross-compliance. I am wondering how that cross-compliance was implemented in Poland. The Commission in the Health Check are proposing some amendments to that, and you have mentioned those already and said you are in favour of them, but could you say what changes particularly you would welcome and the arrangements around cross-compliance.

Mr Gawlik: In the case of Poland and the simplified payment system, right now we apply good agricultural and environmental condition,[3] It is implemented now and respected by the farmers and controlled during the checks connected with the direct payments. In relation to cross-compliance, the provisions on which cross-compliance is based are fully implemented in Poland but cross-compliance as

---

[2] Single Area Payment scheme

[3] According to the Article 5 of the Regulation (EC) 1782/2003 with later amendments

6 December 2007   Mr Beniamin Gawlik

such will start to be implemented from 1 January 2009.[4] Right now there is discussion in the Council on the proposal from the Commission to implement this cross-compliance in new Member States in three stages, as in the case of the old Member States, starting from 2009 with a part A of these cross-compliance requirements from Regulation 17/82/2003.[5] These are environmental requirements. From 2010 these are health and sanitary requirements which should be respected and from 2011 animal welfare requirements. We agree with starting the implementation of the environmental requirements from 2009 but we think the new Member States should have the possibility to implement cross-compliance in the longer term. We agree with the three steps approach the Commission has proposed but we propose two year-intervals between each step so full cross-compliance will be implemented from 1 January 2013. It will be the time when our farmers will receive full direct payments. Why would we like to see such a longer period for the implementation of cross-compliance? First, it will be quite a task for our administration to implement this. Most of the administrations, even in the old Member States, have had problems with the implementation of this. As far as I remember from discussions at the Council level there was the issue of the 1% of farms which should be checked for the cross-compliance and different requirements are controlled within the Member States by different inspection bodies, so there is this problem of co-ordination. Even old Member States have problems with that. We will have to control 15,000 farms as far as the environmental requirements are concerned.

Viscount Ullswater: Quite a vet!

Q784 Chairman: Would it be a good thing to have fewer farms?
Mr Gawlik: I thought that might be your next question! As far as the animal welfare requirements are concerned we think that even though the law is implemented it might be the hardest part for the farmers to adjust to fulfil these requirements.

Q785 Viscount Ullswater: Will that be because of investment?
Mr Gawlik: Exactly.

Q786 Viscount Ullswater: Investment rather than cultural?
Mr Gawlik: If you take into account that right now there are about 600,000 pig producers and they will have to adjust to the stock density requirements, or a certain number of these farmers will have to adjust, especially those who are smaller but are still

producing for the market, they have to adjust and there will not be enough money from the rural development sources for them. Of course, due to the lower direct payments they will not have as much possibility to invest due to their lower incomes.

Q787 Lord Plumb: It is the next question. We are well aware that there are a lot of hard working and quite efficient smaller farmers in Poland but there are big farmers too. What is your view on, in effect, what is called the capping of the upper and lower level holding back payments at a certain level possibly? What is happening structurally? Are changes rapidly or gradually taking place in structural reform? To what extent is investment taking place from foreign investment and is that permissible, legally can people just come in and buy land, and are they doing so? I will ask my other question at the same time and you can answer altogether, if you like. The other question is on the whole question of milk quotas. The Commission, as you well know, have proposed the elimination ultimately of milk quotas. They are in being at the moment and the proposal now is to increase the milk quota by 2% making a softer landing when they are eventually eliminated. Does that commend itself to Polish farmers?
Mr Gawlik: I will be quite brief here because we are still analysing the issue of the upper limit. In our case, in relation to the lower limit, an agricultural holding is considered as a farm when it has at least one hectare of arable land. The signals from the Commission are that there will be quite a large degree of flexibility for the Member States to state what they would consider as a farm. Right now we think we will have no problem with the lower limit, if there is any.

Q788 Chairman: Do you want to keep a lot of farms of the size of one hectare?
Mr Gawlik: In our case if we keep them away from the business that will be a couple of thousand farms or hundreds of thousands of farmers and there will be no real alternative for those people. They have to have something to earn their living.

Q789 Lord Plumb: You said there are 600,000 pig farmers.
Mr Gawlik: Yes.

Q790 Lord Plumb: What is the average number of pigs per holding?
Mr Gawlik: I am afraid I do not know.

Q791 Lord Plumb: I am talking very generally.
Mr Gawlik: I would be pleased to provide you with that information.[6]

---

[4] Accordingto the current legal framework
[5] Point A of the Annex III to the Regulation (EC) 1782/2003 with later amendments

[6] According to the EUROSTAT data for 2005 the average pig number per holding was 31.3 animals

Q792 Lord Plumb: I think it would be very interesting to look at this and see what is happening.
Mr Gawlik: What concerns the pig farming, and it is connected with your first question, my Lord Chairman, is that there is quite a big change in the concentration of production, so middle and medium-sized farms are more important in production for the market than small farms. Concentration is quite visible. Those farms which produce for the market and are the most efficient are of a bigger size.

Q793 Lord Greaves: Are the very small farms mainly producing for themselves, for their families, or do they sell at markets in the villages and so on?
Mr Gawlik: It depends on what type of production they have. They produce mainly for themselves and partially to sell to neighbours and at local markets.

Q794 Lord Plumb: Do they add value? Do they kill pigs and make products from the pig meat and sell them? Is it something that is developing in the rural areas?
Mr Gawlik: I am not aware of that because then you have to fulfil quite strict sanitary and veterinary rules if you run this type of production.

Q795 Lord Plumb: Milk quotas?
Mr Gawlik: We welcome this discussion about the soft landing and milk quotas as such. You might be aware of the fact that two months ago we presented our proposal to the Council to increase milk quotas from the next marketing year by 5%. (The answer continued off the record) It is welcomed by us that the Commission sees a possibility to increase milk quotas immediately from the next marketing year because there is room on the international market and the EU market to produce and sell more milk products. It would be wise to give our farmers, at least those who would like to use this possibility, the chance to produce more for the market. In relation to milk quotas, we think it is not the best time to make a final decision about the abolition and dismantling of the quota system totally. It is quite a favourable situation in the market at the moment. It seems that everybody is quite enthusiastic and sees the possibility to dismantle the system. It would probably be less painful right now but nobody can question that the system as such has some stabilising value. Before the analysis we are not sure whether we should dismantle system totally.

Q796 Earl of Dundee: A theme of growing importance since 2003 has been the need to safeguard the natural environment and, of course, Poland has some of the most valuable areas of natural habitat and landscape. Through Pillar II and EAFRD are enough funds available just now to look after these assets?

Mr Gawlik: This is part of the question which I am not best prepared to answer but I will do it with the help of the notes from my colleagues. Within this rural development plan for the next Financial Perspective there are a couple of activities which concern the most endangered species of birds and most vulnerable habitats which are outside the Natura 2000 areas. To answer the question whether this money is enough or not it is hard to answer right now, we will have to wait and assess whether those actions are efficient. In the discussion about the Health Check we think that it would be worthwhile to start discussions about possible support for the farmers who operate on so-called vulnerable zones under the Nitrate Directive. As I understand it, they are excluded from the agri-environmental programmes right now which is connected with the principle of "polluter pays". It might be worthwhile to start discussions about whether these farmers could be supported within the EAFRD.

Q797 Earl of Dundee: What efforts, if any, so far have been made, or maybe it is too soon, to exclude such farmers from the agri-environment programme?
Mr Gawlik: I am afraid I cannot answer your question precisely. If you are interested in obtaining this information I could provide you with it in written form.[7]
Earl of Dundee: That is very kind of you.

Q798 Baroness Jones of Whitchurch: Could I just ask a quick supplementary and, similarly, you may not be able to answer it but it is a more general point. Do the Polish farmers understand the need to protect the environment or do they see themselves just as farmers or do they understand why in the EU we might want the farmers to have a broader environmental responsibility as well? Do they understand that or do they think we are slightly odd for expecting that?
Mr Gawlik: They definitely understand it because they are working closely in relation to the environment so they rely on the environment.

Q799 Baroness Jones of Whitchurch: Would they understand if we made a case for stronger biodiversity or maintaining semi-wild habitats and things like that?
Mr Gawlik: In our case during the 1990s there were quite negative changes in agriculture and after the transition agriculture has been less intensive so it will not be so hard for them to adjust to the higher environmental requirements.

Q800 Lord Greaves: I have got a couple of technical questions on what I might call the rural development side of the rural development funds as opposed to the

---

[7] This information is provided in the form of additional note to this transaction

environmental side. Before asking them, I wonder if I can ask something else. I have been thinking about these hundreds of thousands of people on very tiny farms of perhaps one, two or three hectares, which in many ways are for their subsistence and so on, on a typical Polish farm of a very small size like this, will there be people who are not earning their income from the farm but who have other jobs? Would it be typical that if there is a couple, a man and a woman, that one of them might have another job and perhaps their children might have jobs? Would that be typical or would they all rely on the farm?

Mr Gawlik: In many cases it works like that. On those smaller farms, the farm is not the only source of income for them. In the past and for a certain period of time after transition[8] it was even more common for them to be more small farmers who relied not only on their farms and later, due to economic changes, they were forced to rely on what they earned as farmers.

Q801 *Lord Greaves:* Because the other jobs had gone?

Mr Gawlik: Yes.

Q802 *Lord Greaves:* What sort of other jobs? We are talking about rural villages here, not next to towns where people can perhaps go into the town and have a job but out in the sticks, as we would say, what sort of jobs would they have?

Mr Gawlik: You mean in the future?

Q803 *Lord Greaves:* No, now. What sort of jobs might be available out in the countryside which are not farming?

Mr Gawlik: It depends on the region. If there is the agricultural processing sector in the region it might be those kinds of jobs. Sometimes it is not permanent jobs but seasonal jobs within processing. Sometimes it might be jobs within services, for example in communication and transport companies, wholesale and retail trade, construction sector.

Q804 *Lord Greaves:* It is jobs which are providing services for the agricultural community and agricultural economy of the area?

Mr Gawlik: For the agricultural community but not only for that, for the general public as well.

Q805 *Lord Greaves:* That is very helpful. I must say I do not know how many of these people would come to this country and get similar jobs in similar industries nowadays, but we will not pursue that. Certainly quite a few perhaps, and presumably they will send the money back home and help to subsidise these little farms. Are those rural development funds integrated adequately with other European structural funds and, indeed, with Polish national

programmes, whatever they may be? Has the presence of the rural development funds so far helped farmers in any significant way to improve their competitive position by improving their efficiency, perhaps by the amalgamation of farms, et cetera?

Mr Gawlik: I will have to take a look at my notes. Taking into account our experience from 2004-06, when we implemented these rural development measures under the old policy and when it was divided into two parts and partially financed by the structural funds, we can see it is quite positive that those funds have been integrated into one single rural development fund. It is also the case that the rural development programme should be quite efficiently integrated with other policies under the structural funds. Taking into account our experience it is quite obvious that support from the rural development funds, and only support from the rural development funds, for the rural areas is not enough. To solve problems like hidden and register unemployment deficiencies in infrastructure and services we definitely need more support from the structural funds in rural areas as well.

Q806 *Lord Greaves:* Does the Polish Government itself have programmes of development in the rural areas to help with this?

Mr Gawlik: I know that there was intense co-operation between two ministries, one dealing with regional development policy and the second one the Agriculture Ministry in this process of preparation of a rural development programme to integrate it with programmes run within regional policy. Unfortunately, I cannot provide you with the result of that discussion. It was one of the requirements by the Commission to integrate both types of programmes. I assume our rural development plan was accepted by the Commission, so the Commission is satisfied with the result of this discussion between the two ministries.

Lord Greaves: It is still very early days. Thank you.

Q807 *Viscount Ullswater:* The Commission's Communication envisages two quite substantial changes, the end of export subsidies and also greater access to the EU markets for third-country suppliers. How far is Polish agriculture prepared for such a competitive environment in the future? Is there a good supply chain from the grower to the market already established? What changes do you see are either needed to react to this new competitive climate or just to improve the efficiency of the sector?

Mr Gawlik: For the European products a possibility for equal competition with products from the third countries is, let us say, hampered a little bit by all these strict and quite high standards which should be fulfilled by our farmers and our processing sector. In this respect, when the imports come from the

[8] It is after economic and political transition in 1989

countries where these standards are not respected or lower, our European industry is in a worse position. If we open our markets to imports from third-countries the possibility for sales of our products might be hampered and diminished. It could have some negative consequences for the consumers and generally for food security as such. There is a need to protect European agriculture in such a way as to secure food supply. The situation could be comparable to that of fuel security as well.

Q808 *Chairman:* But there will be continuing pressure, will there not? The commitment to abolish export subsidies is there and there will be continuing pressure to decrease tariff barriers, so there will be pressure to improve efficiency.

Mr Gawlik: Before accession, our agricultural sector as such was quite efficient and competitive, in many cases without any export refunds. Taking into account the fact that the processing side of the sector has adjusted enormously from just before accession to right now, they will have room for manoeuvre and the possibility to adjust to a new situation. But on the other hand after implementation of the CAP and after some years of activity under the CAP umbrella there might be some problems with a more open market for third-country imports as well.

Q809 *Viscount Ullswater:* Do you see then the output of the farming industry dropping in the next 10 years, a retraction of the whole sector?

Mr Gawlik: Right now it is hard to assess whether it will drop or not because we have no agreement at an international level[9] about how far our protection will drop. Going back to your question about concentration and co-operation within the agriculture chain, I must say that the situation varies between different sectors because in the poultry sector, for example, this sector is quite concentrated on the production of the raw materials is quite concentrated and there is a strong vertical concentration and co-operation with the processing industry as well. On the contrary sectors like pig production and pork processing or the fruit and veg sector, and the processing industry for fruit and veg, there is definitely a need for adjustment and for actions to support vertical co-operation between the raw material producers and the processors.

Q810 *Baroness Jones of Whitchurch:* As you probably know, the whole issue of climate change is moving up the political agenda at the moment. In

---

[9]It means the Doha Round negotiations in the WTO have been not finalized

Poland are the farmers already experiencing the effects of climate change? Is there a debate going on in Poland about what would need to happen to mitigate the impact of climate change in the future?

Mr Gawlik: As you have mentioned, our farmers are experiencing something which could be connected with climate change. For example, this year there was a strong frost at the beginning of spring which affected fruit production in many regions of Poland. As far as more general issues are concerned, the decoupling of support is helping in a way to cope with climate change because right now there is no link between how intensive production is and how big the support is for farms, so definitely less intensive farming will lead to mitigating negative effects of farming on the climate. The second pillar of the CAP gives some possibilities to implement actions which might cope with the negative effects of climate change. Within the Commission's Communication document water management was mentioned and within the second pillar it is possible to support these actions which are connected with the retention of water or flood control measures.

Baroness Jones of Whitchurch: What about trying to cut down on the agricultural impact on CO_2 emissions?

Chairman: Greenhouse gases generally, I think.

Baroness Jones of Whitchurch: Yes.

Q811 *Chairman:* There are a lot of pig farmers.

Mr Gawlik: What about the dairy farming or cattle farming? In our case, the intensity of this type of production is definitely lower than in certain other Member States so, of course, support for extensification of production will be more welcome, especially in the second pillar. There is quite a big issue on biofuels or renewable resources of energy where agriculture might have quite a big influence. This is still an area for discussion, especially in the case where there are obligatory targets for the use of biofuels and we think we should start to discuss equal conditions for the production of raw materials for biofuels or bio-energy within the European Union. It seems that in new Member States there has been quite a positive response from farmers and increase of energy crop production but there is still not equal treatment for farmers in the old Member States and those in the new Member States in the level of support for this type of production. In the old Member States they can use land for which they receive 100% of direct payments plus this energy premium whereas in the case of new Member States they will receive the energy premium and lower direct payment due to the phasing in mechanism.

Chairman: Thank you very much indeed for your time and your patience with us. Thank you very much for helping us with our inquiry.

Answer to the question Q797—additional information

This additional information shall be read in relation to the answer to the question Q796.

Farmers operating in vulnerable zones under the Nitrate Directive (Nitrate Vulnerable Zones) are in fact excluded from the agri-environment programmes, which is stated in the answer to the question Q796. This exclusion relates to all the packages consisting of farmers' commitments corresponding to requirements defined for the programmes drawn up for the purpose of the Nitrate Directive. In Poland agri-environment programmes consist of the so-called packages which set out farmer's commitments for which he/she receives a flat rate payment.

In practice agricultural holdings operating in the Nitrate Vulnerable Zones are excluded from the possibility of receiving support under the package "sustainable agriculture", which requires the drawing up of a nutrient management plan. This exclusion results from the rules of the agri-environment programme, which provide that only commitments going beyond mandatory standards and requirements established by the EU or national law can be eligible for payments.

However, in Poland's opinion this problem is broader and certain forms of assistance for farmers in Nitrate Vulnerable Zones should be envisaged to encourage them to take action for the benefit of the environment under Pillar II of the CAP. Taking into account that water management and water protection are very important elements in the discussion on the future of CAP it would be worthwhile to consider some measures of diverse nature supporting local initiatives for the benefit of the environment, including water protection. This might take the form of aid for the creation of conditions and infrastructure for biogas production (purchase of equipment for slurry transport, construction of fermentation tanks and systems for electricity production), support for purchase of special machines for slurry disposal, construction of small sewage treatment plants.

WEDNESDAY 12 DECEMBER 2007

Present   Arran, E of   Palmer, L
               Cameron of Dillington, L   Plumb, L
               Greaves, L   Sewel, L (Chairman)
               Jones of Whitchurch, B   Ullswater, V

Memorandum by the Food and Drink Federation

The Food and Drink Federation (FDF) represents the UK's food and drink manufacturing industry, the largest manufacturing sector in the country with a turnover in excess of £70 billion. Our industry employs more than 500,000 people or 14% of the manufacturing workforce. We are committed customers of UK farmers, purchasing around two-thirds of the country's agricultural produce. To supplement our raw material supply base, we also import around £7 billion worth of ingredients for further processing. The UK is the world's fifth largest exporter of value-added food and drink products, exporting almost £10 billion worth in 2006.

1. *What should be the long term objectives of the CAP? Does the title "Common Agricultural Policy" aptly fit your perceived objectives of the policy? What do you consider to be the main pressures on the CAP as it currently is?*

FDF member companies operate in an increasingly open and competitive international market place. To succeed in this environment, the industry must be able to access a steady supply of raw materials that are safe, of high quality and competitively priced. The CAP must underpin the competitiveness of the EU food and drink industry by ensuring that adequate supplies of agricultural raw materials at competitive prices are available for food production. FDF believes the CAP's long-term objective should be a prosperous and sustainable domestic agricultural sector that responds to market signals and not state subsidies. Successive rounds of CAP reform are shifting European agriculture in the appropriate direction, but still further reform is needed to achieve greater market orientation.

The use of the word "Common" as in the "Common Agricultural Policy" is key for food manufacturers, as it is crucial that a level playing field exists amongst EU Member States in terms of the various support payments made to farmers to avoid market distortions for agricultural raw materials sold to food manufacturers.

In FDF's view, the main pressures on the CAP are finding the budget savings necessary to fund recent European Union (EU) enlargements; and the need for a more efficient allocation of resources, including land. A possible deal on the WTO Doha Development Agenda (DDA) and the commitment to eliminate export refunds will put further pressures on the CAP.

2. *What has been your experience so far with the reformed CAP? What has worked well and less well? And where can lessons be learned?*

FDF welcomed the 2003 CAP reform as it resulted in: the decoupling of direct payments from production for cereals, beef and dairy; reducing or abolishing intervention prices; Single Farm Payments; and a greater focus on rural development with payments subject to cross-compliance. FDF members are just now experiencing the positive effects of the 2003 CAP reform. However that said, continued reform is needed in order to move towards greater market orientation.

It is fair to suggest that the EU's reform of the sugar regime has not worked well. FDF's sugar processors are concerned that if the current proposals to modify the Restructuring Scheme do not succeed, there will be an across the board compulsory quota cut hitting efficient and inefficient alike.

3. *Do you consider the Single Payment Scheme to be a good basis for the future of the EU agricultural policy? What changes might be made at the EU level to the Single Payment Scheme, including to the rules governing entitlements, in the short and/or longer-term?*

The Single Payment Scheme is a good basis for future EU agricultural policy because it moves towards greater market orientation and it is WTO-compatible.

4. *What short and longer-term changes are required to the CAP's market mechanisms? Suggestions made by the Commission have included re-examination of certain quotas, intervention, set-aside, export refunds and private storage payments*

The CAP's market price support systems, when combined with high EU import tariffs, mean that UK food and drink manufacturers can pay comparatively high prices for key raw materials. Raw material costs represent between 30 and 75% of our industry's total operating costs.[1] With the average food and drink manufacturer's profit margin rarely exceeding 7%,[2] it is clear that raw material prices can determine whether a company makes a profit or a loss. Without further reform of the CAP and the realisation of more competitive prices for key agricultural raw materials, our industry may continue to downsize and move offshore. A proliferation of bilateral trade agreements, which provide nothing more than greater access to the EU market for processed food and drink products from third countries, would further exacerbate this trend. FDF has examined a number of CAP market mechanisms which need further modification:

— **Decoupling direct payments** from production is essential because it brings farmers closer to the market, freeing them to produce agricultural products in line with demand. The current system of allowing Member States to decide the extent to which they decouple certain payments undermines the European Single Market principle. Full decoupling would provide the following economic benefits: encouraging a more efficient allocation of resources; reducing administrative costs; increasing opportunities for farmers to respond to new market opportunities; and helping achieve necessary budget savings.

— FDF is opposed to the notion of **capping direct payments** for large farmers, as it would discourage the process of consolidation, so disadvantaging many of the UK's large, efficient farmers by providing them with a lower rate of per hectare support than their Continental competitors. A reduction in payments to larger farmers could result in an inequitable decrease in local production and a corresponding increase in prices.

— FDF believes that the existing **intervention systems**—particularly for dairy and cereals—should be phased-out as part of the 2008 "Health Check" as they inhibit market fluidity and contribute to the maintenance of uncompetitive commodity prices in the EU. As the European Commission withdraws from market intervention, the likelihood of increased agricultural price volatility could be limited through market based risk management tools, for example futures markets and farmer-based risk insurance systems.

— **Production limiting programmes** such as EU milk quotas, lead to an inefficient allocation of resources. FDF therefore favours an agreement to phase-out dairy production quotas as these are preventing necessary industry restructuring.

— So long as the EU maintains systems which produce artificially high prices for key raw materials, it should continue to provide **export refunds for processed or Non-Annex One (NA1) products**. These refunds are critical to maintaining the competitiveness of the food and drink manufacturing industry. NA1 export refunds provide compensation for high domestic raw material prices and, therefore, the EU must ensure that it continues to provide NA1 export refunds, so long as there is a difference between EU and world market prices for key raw materials, notably sugar and dairy products.

— FDF agrees that there is no place for compulsory **set-aside** in a market-oriented environment where payments to farmers are fully decoupled. Set-aside, in our view, inhibits the efficient allocation of resources, discourages farm consolidation and provides only questionable environmental benefits. It is also inappropriate given the EU has agreed mandatory targets to develop a large scale biofuels industry which will lead to a significant increase in the demand for land to grow crops for renewable energy in direct competition with crops for food.

---

[1] *Source*: estimate from the Conf€d€ration des Industries Agro-alimentaires (CIAA).
[2] *Source*: CIAA.

5. *What is your view on the introduction of the European Agricultural Fund for the Rural Development (EAFRD)? Do you consider that it is meeting its objectives thus far? Is it suitably "strategic" in nature, meeting the needs of rural society as a whole rather than being restricted to aiding the agricultural industry? How well is it being co-ordinated with other EU and national policies on regional and rural development?*

N/A

6. *Is there a case for a higher level of EU financing of rural development? Do you have a view on the extension of compulsory modulation from Pillar I (direct payments) to Pillar II (rural development)?*

FDF supports compulsory, as opposed to voluntary, modulation as this avoids competitive distortions between Member States. However, any extension of compulsory modulation must be linked to a review of Second Pillar measures to ensure their effectiveness and to maintain food supply chain competitiveness. Consistency across Member States is essential to avoid market distortions.

7. *What benefits can the EU's World Trade Organisation obligations create for EU agriculture and, consequently, for the EU economy as a whole?*

EU food manufacturers can benefit from WTO negotiations through further trade liberalisation and a fairer and clearer set of multilateral trading rules. The effect of the CAP and EU import tariffs is that UK food and drink manufacturers pay comparatively high prices for key raw materials. FDF members feel that the CAP can benefit from WTO obligations by accepting ambitious tariffs cuts as part of the Doha Development Agenda, in order to put downward pressure on these raw material prices to safeguard the competitive position of EU food manufacturers. FDF's sugar processors would like sugar to be treated as a Sensitive Product in the negotiations, although our sugar users would not as they are looking for lower domestic prices.

Increased access to third country markets is a continuing key goal for food manufacturers given its potential benefits, even though many FDF members have already invested in production key third country markets. Providing WTO obligations are not damaging to the EU food and drink industry, FDF welcomes them as they can help our members remain competitive.

WTO obligations should be adhered to, as trade disputes can lead to the imposition of retaliatory sanctions that create "innocent victims". Irrespective of whether the EU wins or loses a WTO case, the domestic food and drink industry frequently suffers as the target of retaliatory sanctions. These sanctions either increase raw material prices or reduce export competitiveness.

FDF members however do not support WTO Panels rewriting understandings, implicit within existing WTO agreement texts, in dispute settlement cases.

8. *To what extent has the system of cross-compliance contributed to an improved level of environmental protection? How is it linking with other EU policy requirements such as the Water Framework Directive?*

FDF supports cross-compliance principles aimed at promoting specified standards as it reinforces consumer confidence in agricultural production and environmental protection.

9. *How can the CAP contribute to mitigation of, and adaptation to, climate change? What do you consider the role of biofuels to be in this regard?*

FDF believes that the 2008 "Health Check" should consider the impact of agriculture on climate change. CAP subsidies encourage certain production methods that contribute to carbon emissions. The UK food industry is currently working with the Carbon Trust on carbon footprinting. Farmers should therefore consider their own carbon footprint to help mitigate climate change.

FDF supports the role that renewable energy from agricultural sources can play in tackling climate change. However, ready accessibility to agricultural raw materials is essential for UK food and drink manufacturers to meet consumer demands for food. As such, it is also a priority to ensure that EU and national policies formulated to increase renewable energy are managed in a way that avoids distorting the availability of agricultural raw materials for food and animal feed. Existing renewable energy policies have already had a significant knock on effect on the availability and costs of some agricultural commodities, which carry implications for consumer prices. FDF's current priority, therefore, is to ensure that robust economic analyses and feasibility studies are undertaken of land use, which is a critical factor, and the increased demands being placed on it to avoid unforeseen or adverse implications for food and feed supply and consumer prices. As stated above, FDF agrees that compulsory set-aside is inappropriate; given the EU has agreed to mandatory targets to develop a large scale biofuels industry, which will lead to a significant increase in the demand for land to grow crops for renewable energy in direct competition with growing crops for food.

10. *The Commissioner has expressed her dissatisfaction at the financing agreement reached by Member States at the December 2005 Council. Do you consider the current budget to be sufficient? Do you consider co-financing to be a possible way forward in financing the Common Agricultural Policy?*

Clearly the budget needs to be sufficient for the goals that the Council has set for the EU's agricultural policy. FDF supports CAP reform in line with market orientation, which implies a continuation of the trend of reduction already set for the CAP budget overall. Our principal concern is to ensure that, as CAP reform continues, the budget for essential elements such as export refunds, which are needed to overcome the disadvantages of market distortions, remains sufficient to allow international trade to continue on a competitive basis.

11. *What has been the impact on the CAP of the 2004 and 2007 enlargements and what is the likely impact of future enlargements of the EU on the post-2013 CAP?*

An impact of EU enlargement on the CAP is further pressure on the EU's budget. More money is required for Pillar 1 payments and this could cause payments to be moved away from Pillar II (as happened with the Budget settlement for 2007-2013). This is a complicated issue and FDF broadly supports EU enlargement because of the increased single market and new market access which benefits FDF's members. However, it can be a difficult transition with new Member States starting from different stages of development. New Member States have also impacted upon EU levels of self-sufficiency and the availability of raw materials in a complex set of ways with differing impacts upon the internal market.

12. *How could the CAP be further simplified and what other ways would you like to see the Common Agricultural Policy changed in the short and/or the long-term?*

FDF supports the UK Government and the EU's respective policy goals to reduce red tape and, in particular, unnecessary burdens on business. Simplification of the CAP is essential to reduce costs to operators and should continue to be a main objective during the upcoming "Health Check". FDF would like to see a suspension of the current bureaucratic system for allocating NA1 export refunds, as this is unnecessary given the current ample availability of funds in the budget. The NA1 export refund certificate system is burdensome and complex for operators. Given that there is no risk of exceeding the WTO commitment of €415 million for spending on export subsidies, the existing export refund certificate system should be removed. Monitoring of the situation would be sufficient.

FDF disagrees with the European Commission using its tendering system for Annex 1 products as a management tool to determine the value of NA1 export refunds. Export refunds should be paid to exporters of goods from the EU to third countries in order to compensate for the difference between EU and world prices. This is not happening, however, as the refunds are not compensating for the difference in world and EU prices.

June 2007

Examination of Witnesses

Witnesses: MR CALLTON YOUNG, Director of Sustainability and Competitiveness, Ms RUTH RAWLING, Vice President Public Affairs, Cargill, and Chairman of Trade Policy and CAP Committee, MR TIM INNOCENT, Head of Purchasing, Nestlé and MR SIMON HARRIS, Senior Adviser, British Sugar, examined.

Q812 Chairman: Can I start off by thanking you all for finding the time to come and see us and to help us with our inquiry. We have received, obviously, written evidence which has been enormously helpful in any case but it is always nice to have that amplified through a chat across the table. A couple of formal things; we are technically being webcast, so what we are saying here is possibly being heard by some person somewhere—we have never actually been able to find out whether anybody does, but never mind, I will pass on quickly. Secondly, it is a formal evidence-gathering session so a record will be taken and you will get the typescript as soon as possible, and you can check it and make any adjustments that you feel necessary. I wonder whether any of you would like to make a brief opening, orientating statement, or would you prefer to go on to questions and answers?

Ms Rawling: If I may, My Lord Chairman, I would like to just introduce my colleagues and make a brief statement. Thank you very much for inviting us to this hearing this morning; we do appreciate that and we do appreciate the fact that you are taking the time to look into this important area of work. I would like to introduce the team I have brought with me here: on my left is Simon Harris, who is an adviser to ABF and British Sugar; next to me here is Tim Innocent who is from Nestlé, the purchasing manager for all their food direct materials. He is also chair of the UK Industrial Sugar Users Group. On my right is Callton Young who is the director of sustainability and competitiveness at the Food and Drink Federation. I myself am the vice-president of corporate affairs for Cargill in Europe and also I chair the FDF's Trade Policy and CAP Committee. You have seen our written paper but, as you well know, the FDF is the voice of the food and drink manufacturing industry in the UK, the largest manufacturing sector in our country. We focus really on three key areas for our business: food safety and science, health and well-being and sustainability and competitiveness. The area we are in today, as far as our members are concerned, is the sustainability and competitiveness area. I would just like to stress two key things which run through our evidence; one is how important access to raw materials is for our members and how important it is that we have a level playing field within the EU in order for our industry to remain competitive in the UK. Secondly, it is very important that within the EU overall it remains competitive on a global level, with the rest of the world, because we are competing, particularly in high value added products, with food industries in other parts of the world and we need to keep the competitiveness issue in front of us to enable the manufacturing industry here to remain here. That is all I would like to say to start with.

Q813 *Chairman:* Thank you very much, that is helpful. I will kick off with a couple of questions: the note in your evidence was that the food and drink manufacturing industry must obviously be able to access a steady supply of raw materials that are safe—a fundamental requirement—are of high quality and competitively priced, and that the CAP should help to achieve this. Is there a tension lurking somewhere between your calls for competitively priced agricultural raw materials and your request

that these be safe and of high quality? It is a tension that we hear from time to time, that sourcing on price leaves open the difficulty of safety and high quality. If there is a tension there, which of those considerations do you consider to be the more important?

Ms Rawling: Thank you, My Lord Chairman. All of us would absolutely stress that food safety is non-negotiable, so wherever you source your food and drink materials from, whether within the EU, the UK or outside, safety has to be the paramount consideration. Beyond that there is of course a balance to be struck between quality and price, but I would say that there are many examples of our members being able to source high quality products which are competitively priced and we want that to continue. I suppose the one issue we have is that sometimes if a number of standards are imposed on farmers in the EU which their global competitors do not face, then that is an issue which could over time affect the competitiveness of EU agriculture, and there is a balance here between how many constraints you put on in the interests of quality in different kinds of areas.

Q814 *Chairman:* Is that a real concern at the moment? Are you suggesting that that is now something that is almost coming to a sort of tipping point, or is it something that you see as a danger that may be in the mid-term or long-term?

Ms Rawling: It is an issue which we live with constantly, that there is always an issue with. I would not say it is something that is coming to a tipping point; in fact I actually think that there is greater recognition today than perhaps there has been in the past about the issue of the constraints imposed on EU farmers vis-à-vis the rest of the world, and it is a difficult issue to deal with but it is something that actually is understood better than perhaps it has been in the past. I do not know if any of my colleagues would like to comment on this.

Mr Harris: If I might, I would just like to make the point that actually this is not just an issue for farmers it is also an issue for the food manufacturing industry itself; particularly in the sectors that I am involved with you could find that the regulatory conditions that you are required to meet in different countries around the globe vary very substantially and this can affect your cost-effectiveness.

Q815 *Chairman:* Can we move on to the next one which is you mentioned the continued downsizing of the food and drink manufacturing industry and the tendency for companies to move offshore due to, basically, price pressures. What is the evidence for that in the UK and is that the same experience in other EU Member States? I suppose, to finish off that little bit, have the CAP reforms of 2003 improved the competitive position of British food and drink manufacturers or even adversely impacted on the competitive position?

Ms Rawling: Thank you. I would say on this point that this is not a point we want to labour too much, we do not want to make very heavy weather of it. There is some research done by Defra which was published in 2006 and it did conclude that the evidence of offshoring is actually quite limited and really, perhaps, had only occurred in the confectionery sector, and that was what we had in mind when we wrote our evidence to you, but we would not want to over-emphasise this point. Our concern is that things like export refunds which enable our members to export processed goods and be compensated for higher priced raw materials, if those for example were to disappear before we have a level playing field on access to raw materials, that kind of thing would be a consideration to take into account in terms of moving plant, but there are a lot of very complicated issues that come in as well, it is not just the raw material prices here. I do not know, Callton, if you want to add to that.

Mr Young: That covers it pretty fully from our perspective. It is a very complicated area, one we need to keep an eye on as CAP reform goes ahead. Export refunds are really the main issue for exporters and if you have companies which cannot export competitively you can leave them little choice but to move that production closer to the markets to which they are exporting.

Q816 *Chairman:* You mean they cannot export competitively because of the regulatory burdens placed on them here, is that the argument?

Mr Young: Yes, that is the argument—and also the issue is about export refunds. Unless the export refunds are linked in with CAP reform, i.e. export refunds are not removed before CAP is reformed, then there are potential problems for the future.

Chairman: Thank you, I will pass on to Lord Plumb.

Q817 *Lord Plumb:* Two questions related to market mechanisms, and it becomes a bit of a cliché to say that we are moving towards a much more market-led food industry, everybody accepts that, and many would say that is a good thing. You emphasise the need for full decoupling, the end of intervention in the dairy and cereals markets and the end of set-aside, but you oppose capping which is interesting—and this question comes up before many people at the moment. We asked Mrs Fischer Boel this question the other day; which changes should, in your judgment, be given priority in the health check which we are looking at at the moment, recognising of

course that 2015 will be starting off almost a new world.

Ms Rawling: Yes, thank you. Obviously, the 2003 reforms did very much push in the direction of market orientation, and we welcome that. It is quite difficult to single out particular measures from this health check package as to which would be preferable because they all form part of a piece, but what we are looking for is market orientation which allows farmers to respond to market signals from the food industry and obviously, ultimately, from consumers and also which allows them to be efficient, which is why we do not think capping is a good idea. To the extent that capping would impact on the efficiency of farmers, trying to respond as best they can to market signals, it seems to go against some of the other things that the abolition of set-aside and further decoupling are really aiming for. I hope that helps answer that question.

Q818 *Lord Plumb:* Thank you, can I then ask my second question which is perhaps of greater concern in the longer term. You say in your paper that there is a likelihood of increased agricultural price volatility. We have already seen that this year, particularly of course between grain and livestock but you say that could be limited through market-based risk management tools such as the futures market and farmer-based risk insurance schemes. We could have a debate on that if you have views, but it is the most important question, frankly, looking to the future because in the past producers have grown accustomed to stability and would like the stability of the way things have been stabilised under the old system, because at least we had that stability which is not going to be there as we move into a much more market-led food industry.

Ms Rawling: Thank you. There are two key points I would make to this. One is that there are already market-based types of systems which help farmers cope with price volatility such as the futures market and various kinds of contracts. The biggest obstacle to market-based risk management systems of this kind actually is government policy because the one thing that futures markets cannot predict is sudden shifts in policy and that is going to be the real dilemma in how far are you going to be sure that government policy does not suddenly take a turn, so I really think that is one of the biggest obstacles. The other point I would make is that because of the market orientation and the fact that farmers these days have quite a lot of other considerations to take into account when they are producing certain qualities et cetera, quite a lot of the management of price is done through long term contracts, which give you a certain stability if you like in your pricing. I think, therefore, that we should not have the idea that the entire market is going to be dependent on things like futures markets because an awful lot of the market these days does actually go through contracts and that does provide a certain amount of stability for farmers. I do not know if my colleagues would like to add something. Tim.

Mr Innocent: We buy a lot of materials that are commoditised and are subject to price risks, et cetera. As organisations we are able to cope with that, but as Ruth has accurately said if we get to a position where on Thursday we have one set of rules and on Friday another set of rules it is very difficult for us to move forward in that framework. We are, as I say, used to it; you are quite right in what you say, Lord Plumb, that this year has been a difficult year and I think sometimes in private we say slightly different words to "difficult year".

Q819 *Lord Plumb:* I could join you.

Mr Innocent: But we have got through that, and we have to put mechanisms in place and talk to our customers about the things that are going on, but it is when we have fundamental changes that we cannot price the risk or the difficulty.

Q820 *Lord Plumb:* I was particularly interested in your suggestion that there could be farmer-based risk insurance systems; that is not something that has applied necessarily in the past, but if I was to use more the futures market there are those who said we relied on the futures market last year when they decided to offer their grain on the futures market and lost half the value of the grain because of it and they feel that perhaps once they have been bitten they are a bit shy. Nevertheless, it is a system, I accept, that obviously is going to perhaps be used more in the future, but the insurance risk, do you think that is something that will grow?

Ms Rawling: I am no expert on this, but when they did the fruit and vegetable reform recently apparently there are some conditions in there which allow producer co-operatives to offer certain types of group insurance schemes of this kind to their members, and that kind of idea is one of the things the Commission is thinking about on a broader basis behind this. If you look at the US, for example, they do have some quite considerable farmer-based insurance schemes, but I understand that the Commission is not thinking so much of those types of systems, partly because they are extremely expensive.

Q821 *Lord Plumb:* That might encourage farmers then to co-operate more.

Ms Rawling: Yes, indeed.

Q822 *Lord Plumb:* Which you would welcome as a food industry.

Ms Rawling: I think if that is one of the ways that farmers feel more comfortable in managing risk in the future, that should be encouraged, but there should always be alternatives including the more market-based systems for farmers as well.

Mr Innocent: The danger that we could see with these types of systems is that we may go back to an intervention or protectionist type scheme by default really, we might move ourselves in that direction by the back door, and that is something that we want to prevent, so we need to understand more about how these schemes are going to work before we could make a fuller comment on it.

Mr Harris: If you look at the US experience it is quite interesting in this. They had, almost like the EU but more formalised in the US, a system of disaster relief, and in the US you always have a major climatic event somewhere every year. Colin Peterson, who is the current chairman of the House Ag Committee, his idea now is that they want to maintain disaster relief on a formalised basis rather than on an ad hoc basis responding to each year's disasters, but only on condition that farmers themselves take out risk insurance first, so the federal government is not going to pick up the entire tab for climatic variation and the risks that go with it, but they are there as it were as the last resort when your insurance-based system will only cover you to X per cent.

Chairman: Let us move on to modulation; Viscount Ullswater.

Q823 *Viscount Ullswater:* I note that the FDF supports compulsory modulation rather than voluntary modulation because of the risk of distorting the marketplace between Member States. Do you actually support an increase in compulsory modulation? I note from your evidence that you suggest that if there was to be any increase in moving funds from Pillar I to Pillar II the Pillar II scheme should be reviewed, but could you give us an indication of what you have in mind with this?

Ms Rawling: Our real concern here goes back to our fundamental themes; it is all about maintaining the competitiveness of the farmers we source from and not putting in place schemes that can put them at a disadvantage vis-à-vis farmers in other Member States. For that reason it seems a better idea that there should be one rate of compulsory modulation across the EU; however, I would not want to exaggerate this too much because some of these measures have really rather little impact on actual production and therefore probably do not really impact competitiveness that much, so I think that is the key point for us. We know that people are balancing other objectives with these schemes— Callton, I do not know if you want to add something to that.

Mr Young: That is true; reading the Defra impact assessment of the UK voluntary modulation package it concludes that actually there will be very negligible impacts on production and price, and we have to accept that, but one of the real issues with a lot of impact assessments prepared by government is that there are lots of negligible impacts and the cumulative effect of all those negligible impacts do add up over time. We do not want to make heavy weather of this. Our main point is that a level playing field with compulsory modulation across the EU Member States would be preferable paid at one level. We would not object to that at all because it is a level playing field. The real issue we have is where you get significant variations from which all the negligible impacts are then cumulative in their effect.

Q824 *Lord Cameron of Dillington:* You indicated your general support for the WTO but you call for retention of export refunds for processed and Non-Annex-One products. If, in the Doha Round, tariffs on agricultural imports fall to a level no higher than those on other manufactured products, could you still argue that export refunds are justifiable?
Ms Rawling: Thank you very much; this is quite a tricky question actually, if I may say so, and therefore a difficult one to answer because it is always an issue of where are the EU prices versus the world prices and just what are the tariffs on manufactured products. We have always stipulated that export refunds should not be phased out until we have a level playing field.

Q825 *Lord Cameron of Dillington:* But are you ever going to get a level playing field?
Ms Rawling: I do not know, but it is an ambition we have to strive for in order to keep our competitiveness and keep the price of our finished goods competitive on a broad basis. Tim, I do not know if you want to add to this.
Mr Innocent: For us, particularly in confectionery, where we are exporting a lot of confectionery product, then one of our key raw materials is sugar—and I know we have a question on that later. Essentially, even under the reform of the sugar regime the price will not arrive at the world price level so there will always be a discrepancy and, therefore, to make us competitive with our confectionery products to export to the free market, to the world market, we do need to continue to see some form of export refund for processed products.

Q826 *Chairman:* They are not flavour of the month though, are they?
Mr Innocent: No.

Q827 *Lord Cameron of Dillington:* I was wondering is it in the spirit of your general support of WTO?
Mr Innocent: What we are supporting really is alignment of prices. As I think we said in the previous answer, we are able to cope with the volatility within markets by different mechanisms or different types of contract with suppliers, farmers and so on, but when there is a structural difference in pricing it is very difficult, and that is really the government intervention point that we made. Whether we will ever get to a completely level playing field I do not know, but if we were at that point then clearly export refunds would not be needed.
Ms Rawling: If I may just add something, it is very interesting that just recently of course the Commission has proposed to eliminate or suspend the import duties on grain, given the way the world markets have gone this year, and of course we are in something of an exceptional situation. But as an experiment, if you like, in terms of what does it look like if you actually do have a level playing field, this year is actually quite interesting and may help people see that in fact there is no need to be quite as scared of some of this reduction of tariffs as might have been thought to be the case. Obviously this year will not continue forever but that is an interesting example of the kind of level playing field that you might eventually get to, and of course in the grains sector with very low tariffs within certain import quotas we are much closer to it than we were even five years ago.

Q828 *Lord Cameron of Dillington:* I must say if you have access to agricultural imports from all over the world without tariffs then there cannot be any justification for export refunds it would seem to me.
Ms Rawling: We would agree with that, it is simply the discrepancy in the raw material prices that we are facing that we need export refunds for; that is the reason for them and once we are able to buy raw materials at the same price as everybody else then we do not need them.

Q829 *Lord Plumb:* Just adding to your sensitivity on this question, who has benefited most from export refunds in the past?
Ms Rawling: I do not know if Tim wants to take that question.
Mr Innocent: In terms of manufacturers, do you mean, or named companies? I am just trying to get a sense of the question.

Q830 *Lord Plumb:* All I am really saying is the criticism of export refunds, which comes mostly from the Americans, has always been that the farmers benefit in this country from export refunds, but you are now calling for the retention of export refunds in certain parts. I am just asking the question, are you now saying we should retain export refunds when in fact the farmers are accepting that they are going to go.

Mr Innocent: It is to maintain the balance, and it is a jobs issue and an economics issue, is it not really, in terms of if we have comparable costs then we have efficient operations and we can therefore produce the products and export them, but if we do not have comparable costs it is difficult for us to do that so the notional amount that we produce as an export can be very beneficial to factories in terms of overhead absorption et cetera. The benefit may not be per se to farmers, but the benefit is in terms of the general jobs argument within the UK and retaining a sound UK feed manufacturing business.

Mr Young: We are not arguing to retain all the export refunds, it is for processed products.

Mr Innocent: It is where there is a discrepancy only between the world price and the institutionalised EU price.

Lord Plumb: My question was really related to the principle of the system.

Q831 *Lord Cameron of Dillington:* Can I move on to sugar now, probably a question for Mr Harris. Why should sugar be regarded as a sensitive product?

Ms Rawling: If I may take this question first.

Q832 *Chairman:* That is the deal is it?

Mr Harris: She is the leader.

Ms Rawling: As chairman of the committee there are some things I have to do. The European sugar industry, as you know, has undergone recently a radical reform for us with a 40% cut in production and a 36% cut in support prices, and this is envisaged to go through until 2015. The WTO negotiations—and of course we do not know where those are going to come out—are looking at something like a 70% cut in the import tariff applied to third country sugar imports and quite such a large cut was not really envisaged at the time of the reform negotiations, so there is a possibility that it could undercut the European market at the time when that market was beginning to stabilise. Our sugar processors view this development as extremely damaging for the remaining European producers and also for those developing countries who will have unrestricted access to the EU market from 2009, and therefore they would like to see sugar treated as a sensitive product as a way of redressing this potential imbalance and preventing any possible collapse of the market and avoiding that a WTO agreement could undermine the sugar reforms. Our sugar users, on the other hand, would be unhappy if sugar were treated as a sensitive product and they would like the implementation of sugar reform to move forward as they feel we will need imports to ensure we have

sufficient sugar in the EU, and imposing tariff restrictions on sugar is not generally in line with our general call for liberalised markets. I would be very happy if my colleagues want to add to that.

Mr Innocent: We debate this, as you I am sure can tell, on a number of occasions. We have another question later about sugar, but we have a common viewpoint that we would like to see efficient industries and, clearly, we have another common viewpoint which is that it is a key raw material for us and therefore we need it to manufacture our products. Our call on the non-sensitive issue is to make sure that we have ready access to that very vital raw material and if the only way that we can do that is by having imports at the world price with no restrictions, then that will be what we need to do to maintain our manufacturing base. I maybe do not agree but I can understand where Simon's point is, the industry is going through some very significant changes and we are probably, jointly, not happy with some of the ways that the quotas have been cut on a cumulative basis for the very efficient manufacturers.

Mr Harris: We would both jointly like to emphasise the large area of common agreement between us, apart from when we are arguing about price. Leaving that to one side, as Tim said our interest is in having an efficient industry. Our concern as a sugar processor would be that the industry is already going through a very traumatic restructuring process. You are talking about taking out 40% of production capacity. That is a hell of a lot and because it is such a capital-intensive industry we are having to use a standard, industrial type restructuring scheme to do it, which is going to cost of the order of €6 billion to buy out that redundant capacity that is having to go. With that sugar regime reform, the second strand of it was the stick which was a 36% price cut. That was based on an implied WTO agreement on a cut in the topmost tier of import tax, which is where sugar falls, of no more than 60%. We are now looking at, probably, a cut of 70%; that is over the tipping point and the effect would be, with low world prices—particularly with the US dollar weakening all the time—that the EU market could be undercut by third country supplies even on an import duty paying basis unless sugar is either treated as a sensitive product and/or the special safeguard clause which currently exists is maintained. We should recognise that sugar is sensitive in virtually all countries where there are sugar industries in the world, Australia being the exception, and even there they are finding that their espousal with trade liberalisation is not serving them so well as they thought it would do. The point here, as I have already said, is that there is so much capital invested in this industry, in particular on the cane side—the cane industries are development polled for

12 December 2007   Mr Callton Young, Ms Ruth Rawling, Mr Tim Innocent
and Mr Simon Harris

the countries in question—so that governments willy-nilly are involved with these industries.

Q833 Chairman: Could I just check where we are with sugar reform because you are speaking as though it is going ahead full steam and everything that we seem to hear is that basically the Member States are trying their best to subvert the sugar reform.

Ms Rawling: My understanding is that there was an agreement in the Council in September for further cuts in capacity, but this is actually not happening until the beginning of next year.

Mr Harris: If I may, the original reform had one fatal error in the text when it said that the compensations to be paid to growers should be at least 10% of the total compensation payable. That phrase "at least" meant it became an area of negotiation and, once it became an area of negotiation between farmers and processors, governments got drawn in and once governments are drawn in then that delays everything and it all gets into a big mess. At the same time, in Eastern Europe in particular a lot of governments are saying we did not join the European Union in order to lose our sugar industries, which was in effect what they were faced with, because they only joined in 2005, so they walked straight into sugar regime reform as it were. The third issue is that everyone had under-estimated the unwillingness of the co-operative sector to rationalise and, off the top of my head, over half the sugar industry capacity is now owned by co-operatives, but not the more traditional, small farmer co-operatives, these are big companies who just happen to be owned by farmers to an extent. We have been led into the need for a second reform therefore, the reform of the reform, to address these issues and, in particular, they have introduced the right of grower initiative so that growers can demand to renounce quota irrespective of their processor, whether private or co-operatively owned, and irrespective of their government. At the same time, the amount of compensation going to growers was vastly increased so that for one year they will give an amount of €300 per tonne of sugar equivalent as compensation, which is a huge amount of money—it is more than ten times profit, more than ten years worth of profit, particularly in Eastern Europe where their costs are generally lower, and this will break the logjam. At the same time, processors have been offered an inducement in terms of being persuaded to renounce quota, which we are going to come onto in a subsequent question.

Chairman: Let us move on to biofuels. Lord Palmer.

Q834 Lord Palmer: As you are no doubt aware, there has been tremendous, in my view ill-informed, press speculation, and you do indeed express a certain amount of anxiety about the consequences of the expansion of biofuel production on the prices of food and indeed feed. Have you undertaken any research to identify what impact might be expected? Would the economic analysis you call for examine the net emissions savings from differing strategies for fuel production—and of course we are all aware that ABF have just opened the first bioethanol plant last week?

Ms Rawling: Thank you. First of all I would say that our members do support the idea that renewable energy from agricultural sources does have a role in tackling climate change and food security, but of course our primary concern is that we do have access to the raw materials for our food and drink manufacturing. We would like the policies around renewable energy to be formulated in such a way that they avoid distorting the availability of raw materials for food and feed. We have not undertaken our own research, I do not think we are actually equipped to do it because it is actually quite complex to do, but we have called for some really thorough impact assessments to be done in this area which look at the market, not just of the UK and the EU together, but also how it fits into the global market, because one of the things that really has happened and caused the past volatility this year is that biofuels mandates and things were introduced at a time when stocks of arable raw materials were at their lowest for a generation on a worldwide basis. That confluence has not helped to keep our raw material prices for the food and drink manufacturers accessible. There are other factors that come in—a confluence of various climatic factors and things as well—but we do think this is an area where it is complex, you need lots of different parts of government doing some joined-up thinking about how different areas of policy interact with each other in order that you do not get unintended consequences happening in different sectors. We notice that there has been other research done, in particular there is a recent study by the OECD which is quite relevant to this, but we do think that this requires quite a lot of underlying work to be done and, on the emissions point finally, it is clear that one of the reasons for promoting biofuels is to help climate change and, therefore, you do need to measure the emissions here. It is a complex thing to do; I have not really understood yet that anybody has a really good methodology for measuring greenhouse gas emissions on agricultural supply chains, so let us be aware that this is a very complex area. Of course, for the food manufacturers more emphasis on second generation biofuels would actually be the way we would like to see things going and we would very much be behind the Council conclusions back in the spring which said that the EU biofuels target is subject to two very significant caveats: one, that second generation biofuels are available and, two, that sustainability criteria are fully worked through. We would very much endorse that; we are just worried that people have been rushing into this a bit without thinking it all through properly.

Q835 Lord Palmer: It presumably has not helped that food today is the cheapest it has ever been in real terms for the last hundred years; particularly with such a tiny percentage of the weekly wage going on food it does add to the complexity of this very difficult subject, would you not agree?

Ms Rawling: Absolutely, and it is true that food is now a small part of expenditure of families in countries like the UK, but that is not true in some of the countries in Europe, those who have recently joined the EU, like Romania or the Czech Republic where it is still around 30% and of course in other parts of the world. You do have to look at the balance here because there are knock-on effects from this really being felt in many different places.

Mr Young: I agree, I was just looking at the summary I had of the OECD's report of September which concluded that "Increased biofuels production at target levels assumed by the EU, the US and Brazil [this is the global picture] and others would lead to upward pressure on agricultural feedstock prices. The rapid growth of the biofuels industry is likely to keep these prices high and rising throughout at least the next decade between 20 and 50% by 2016." That is significant, and I would agree with the observation that in the UK food prices are relatively low compared to income, but the impact, particularly in urban communities in less developed countries, would be very significant as a result of EU biofuels policies, US biofuels policies, and that is why a joined-up approach, a global thinking-through of the impacts of these policies, is really essential.

Chairman: Sugar regime. Lord Greaves?

Q836 Lord Greaves: Back to sugar! You think you have dealt with it, do you?

Ms Rawling: I am sure there are always additional things to say about sugar!

Chairman: I think we have discussed it this side of the table.

Q837 Lord Greaves: I think we have established so far that the position is difficult. The existing reforms have not reduced production by as much as expected and some of your members anyway are not happy about across-the-board quota reductions to tackle the problem further. What are the answers?

Ms Rawling: I think, as has already been mentioned, an efficient industry is in all our interests, and these across-the-board reductions tend to cut the most efficient as well as the least efficient, and that is why I

do not like them, but I would allow my colleagues to add to that.

Mr Innocent: From the point of view of sugar users the thing that we worked on with the Commission through CIUS, our European organisation, was that, yes, there needed to be some change but we wanted to see the efficient industries remain. I think that the recent across-the-board cuts that we have seen are quite counter-intuitive really to the initial premise of the sugar reform. Essentially, we do need the supply of that raw material, as I think we have already said, and in many ways we would be happy for there to be no quota and to allow the most efficient to produce in the most efficient place. We know that was not in the reform but it was certainly the position that we put forward and I think that the UK Government was of that view as well.

Q838 Lord Palmer: Could I ask a quick supplementary. I ought to know, but roughly what percentage of UK sugar usage is actually imported at the moment?

Mr Innocent: What percentage for industrial use?

Q839 Lord Palmer: Well, for food use?

Mr Innocent: For food use. In terms of industrial usage by companies like ourselves, about 70% of EU sugar manufacture is used in industrial products. The remaining 20-something per cent will be used in domestic. There is some industrial usage but I think that is predominantly outside those quotas, is it not Simon?

Mr Harris: Yes.

Mr Innocent: For a lot of the industrial usage. A significant proportion is in edible food I would say.

Ms Rawling: I think perhaps just to be clear here when you talk about industrial use you mean use within the food manufacturing sector.

Mr Innocent: Sorry, yes.

Ms Rawling: Just in case there was any confusion there.

Mr Innocent: The EU classifies it as industrial use, which means for making food but it is not industrial use when it is for making paper and citric acid and other things, so it is a strange anomaly and I seem to be using their language as well!

Q840 Viscount Ullswater: The sugar regime was a very false regime anyway, from some way back, of maintaining prices which were not equivalent to world prices. Are there any other sectors which have slipped into this position which we ought to be taking note of?

Ms Rawling: I think the sugar regime has always been somewhat unique.

Q841 *Chairman:* I do not want to distort our discussion actually because we have done quite a bit on sugar in the past, so I do not think we ought to spend too much time on it. I appreciate its importance and I think if there are general comments that you want to make on sugar, fair enough, let us hear them now and then finish it for sugar.

Mr Innocent: I think the more general comment would be that should the reform go through in the way that is envisaged then there would be a shortfall of sugar at the European Union level, and therefore imports of sugar and ready access is very important, so in all of the reform we should keep our eye on that and make sure that that access is maintained.

Ms Rawling: Simon, one last word?

Mr Harris: Two points. I would like to agree very much with what Tim has said about the way the reform of the reform has changed the original premise. The original premise was that you were going to take out the least efficient capacity. That has turned out not to be working properly for a whole host of reasons. The reform of the reform in effect means that everyone has to share the pain of adjustment, which means some of your most efficient capacity is going to have to come out. We are going to have to give up some capacity. We are the lowest cost processor in Europe and we are going to have to give up some, which is perverse, so that is one issue. That leads into the second issue which is that the Commission has set this up to provide scope for increased imports from developing countries, and here we are talking not only the least developed countries, of which we know of about 50 on the United Nations classification, but also now the whole of the ACP, that is the rest of the African Caribbean and Pacific countries which are not LDCs, so the effect is you are going to have quota free and duty free access from a very large chunk of the developing world, including virtually the entire African sub-continent plus parts of the Caribbean and the Pacific and Asia. The question then becomes whether they are actually going to be able to take this up or whether the European Commission has been rather too gung-ho in saying we need to cut back on quota.

Chairman: Fine, let us move on to the environment and Baroness Jones.

Q842 *Baroness Jones of Whitchurch:* We have touched on the whole issue of the environment already and the impact that the pressure that we are under to switch money from Pillar I to Pillar II is having. I understand your argument for compulsory modulation and a level playing field and so on, but do you have some sympathy with the argument that we should be giving more of the CAP money to Pillar II to have those wider environmental concerns taken

into account, perhaps moving away from just a concentration on food security and price?

Ms Rawling: Yes, I think overall our members believe that for the market in food and agriculture to operate efficiently you need the market determining what farmers produce and what the food industry is producing for consumers and what government money is there for is public goods and where the market is failing. Therefore we certainly are fully behind the overall move from supporting prices (which is market distortion) into supporting other public goods such as the environment, which is clearly becoming a concern for all of us. I think on a broad level, yes indeed, that is not a concern to our members. What is a concern is whether for example UK farmers will have to face a lot more environmental constraints than farmers in other parts of Europe, and indeed farmers globally. Our overall preference—and again this is something that is going to take some time to get there—is to see environmental externalities taken into account internationally. That would be our ultimate aim here so that not only UK farmers but if there are environmental concerns these are taken into account broadly. It is the level playing field argument for us and our competition as manufacturers vis-à-vis other manufacturers as well.

Q843 *Baroness Jones of Whitchurch:* But do you feel you are having pressure from consumers on the organisations you represent almost to be one step ahead, to champion some of these issues? It seems that there is an increasing consumer concern out there. People who are buying your products would want you to have a strong environmental or at least an environmental bent. Do you do that?

Ms Rawling: Absolutely. In fact, very recently, in October this year, the FDF launched its environmental ambition, which is the ambition of our members to focus on particular areas of the environment in the next few years and reduce emissions, reduce resource use, et cetera. Callton, I do not know if you just want to explain a bit more in detail about that.

Mr Young: We launched our five-fold environmental ambition on 25 October. Those are ambitions to reduce our CO_2 footprint by an absolute reduction of 20% by 2010, to aspire to a 30% reduction by 2020. If we achieve the 30% reduction that is equivalent to saving 1.5 million tonnes of CO_2 per year or taking 350,000 cars off the road per annum, so it is quite a significant commitment. We have also made similar commitments in relation to our water use and in relation to producing fewer and friendlier transport miles. To answer the question, you are really saying is the drive coming from consumers. I have quickly flicked to some IGD research which shows how consumers react, and this was also done by Defra in the context of sustainable consumption and production, which shows that price is king. It always has been in the sense that consumers put that at the very top. Then it is taste, then it is sell-by date, then it is brand, then it is healthy, then it is appearance, convenience, and it gets down to country of origin and quality marks. If you ask the consumer in the street is the environment important they would say yes but whether that translates into behaviour remains to be seen. What we at FDF are doing is making sure that we behave as good corporate citizens and so we have got our five-fold ambitions. We are going to be more resource efficient and there will be a degree of choice in this. We are making sure that our products are environmentally friendly and that is what the consumers would expect of us, even though they would not necessarily be prepared to put it at the top of their list.

Q844 Chairman: I know it is undeliverable but if there was an environmental requirement built into WTO would you support it?
Mr Young: It depends what the requirement is, I guess.

Q845 Chairman: That would give you a level playing field, would it not?
Mr Young: Exactly, and on that basis, yes, because our 30% aspiration on CO_2 reduction really is a recognition that at the moment many UK food manufacturers operate internationally and want to lead by example by going for that much tougher target in advance of the Climate Change Bill, in advance of anything being proposed by government for our sector, because we think it is right and proper and because climate change really is the biggest issue facing this planet. If you galvanise that at WTO level then I think it has got to be something we would consider very seriously and want to support.
Chairman: Last question.

Q846 Earl of Arron: Two very simple questions to end up with. Under the subject of enlargement I would imagine that your companies would be able to extend their marketing activities into the new Member States. Is it probable that some will wish to relocate to areas where labour costs currently will be lower and markets for processed foods seem likely to grow reasonably rapidly?
Ms Rawling: I think, as I mentioned before, this whole shifting of manufacturing locations issue is not something we really want to make a great play of. At the time of enlargement there was a limited amount of relocation into the countries which were newly joining the EU, but it was limited, as I said before, mostly to the confectionary sector. I think today already the conditions in those countries are changing such that it would be less advantageous than it was a few years ago to move, and since we only saw limited movement then I think we are not likely to see a great movement in the next few years. Labour costs of course are significant but they are only one factor in the whole range of factors that go into a food manufacturing facility. If we have a level playing field on raw material prices, across the EU at least, raw material prices being a significant part of our cost, then that would be something mitigating against moving a facility. There are lots of things that come into it here and labour costs are only one of them.

Q847 Earl of Arron: You mentioned changing conditions in your first answer. Where are the conditions changing?
Ms Rawling: What has happened as these countries have joined the EU and joined the various EU systems and schemes—and I do not have data in front of me and I do not know if Callton you do— what you see then is rising wage levels, you see rising prices, et cetera, from the levels they were at just before they joined the EU for example, and I am sure that can be documented.
Mr Young: Yes.

Q848 Chairman: Right, I think that is it. Thank you very much indeed all of you, you have been most helpful.
Ms Rawling: Thank you very much for inviting us, Lord Chairman.

Examination of Witnesses

Witnesses: Ms HEATHER JENKINS, Head of Buying, and MR DUNCAN SINCLAIR, Agricultural Manager, Waitrose, examined.

Q849 Chairman: Hello and thank you very much for coming along and helping us with our inquiry. We are having a look at CAP reform and the future of the Common Agricultural Policy. Let us just say a few things to begin with. Firstly, we are webcast so there

is a possibility that somewhere someone may be listening. We have never actually found out whether anybody is; we have our doubts! Secondly, this is a formal evidence session and so a note will be taken and you will get the transcript and be able to have a look and correct any errors that have crept in. As I say, thank you very much for coming. The only slight difficulty is that I come from the north of Scotland and the name Waitrose means nothing to me unfortunately! What would you like to do? Would you like to start and make a brief opening statement and then go on to questions and answers, would that be suitable to you?

Ms Jenkins: Yes, that will be fine.

Q850 *Chairman:* Away you go.

Ms Jenkins: I am Heather Jenkins and I am the Head of Buying for meat, poultry, fish, dairy, frozen products at Waitrose. We are the food shops of the John Lewis Partnership; we are employee-owned; and our shares are held in a trust and therefore we are not answerable to the City. In terms of the discussions today and CAP reform, we have taken a long-term approach to our supply arrangements many of which have been in situ for 15 years or more. We have an established producer group structure representing in excess of 30 livestock schemes. The principles are based on cost reduction, continuous improvement and reward for quality and consistency. We also have a communication structure in place to motivate those livestock schemes and provide clear understanding of the role of each sector and how it makes up the supply chain. Lastly we take a practical approach to running our schemes, supporting farmers, but we also take a stick and carrot approach to achieve the performance and the focus that we need to serve our customers.

Q851 *Chairman:* Okay fine, and your colleague, Duncan Sinclair, who are you?

Mr Sinclair: I am the Agricultural Manager at Waitrose so I manage the 30-odd livestock schemes right across the piece, from the meat side to fish and dairy. Approximately we have 2,500 farmers supplying us feeding their product into the various supply chains.

Q852 *Chairman:* I wonder if I could kick off with an opening general question. Being the House of Lords, in order to look forward we always look back. The European Commission initiated a "health check" with the intention really of building on the 2003 reforms. Did you notice any impact from what happened in 2003? Has it had any impact on your company's operations? Then I suppose looking forward, what do you see are the long-term objectives of the Common Agricultural Policy and did 2003 head in the right direction?

Ms Jenkins: There has been significant impact, and given the background the producers involved in our schemes had a headstart in understanding more about getting returns from the market-place. As a result of the 2005 deadline, we upped the focus on

what that actually meant, so what decoupling actually meant from a market position. That included instigating benchmarking and sharing best practice and trying to create awareness, first of all, of the realities of getting a return from the market-place and the realities of getting farmers to focus on performance. I guess from a retailer perspective it would be very easy for us to be seen as dictating to farmers, but I think that as a result of our work we do not have any contracts, it is all based on trust, sharing best practice and information and dealing with difficult issues as well as celebrating the successes. Fundamentally, what we were trying to do was to interpret what the CAP policy meant, and from our perspective it was absolutely right that there was no subsidy on production because what that was doing was focusing on volume and not the cost of getting there nor indeed the consistency of the quality. Those have been some of the impacts and they continue because there is different understanding in different sectors of what the best way forward is. One of the things that we have been able to do (because we do have a joined-up approach) is to show farmers what happens at the processing stage and what happens at the retail stage. Once they leave the farm gate many people think that retailers have a propensity to take advantage with little understanding of what happens to an animal once it has left the farm gate, so we have undertaken to take them through the processing stages in many forms, including literally taking them through factories and showing them what actually happens, but also to drive home the importance of not having any waste. In the 30 livestock schemes that make up our supply chain, it is absolutely crucial that we use every piece of those animals that are reared exclusively for us, and in doing so our challenge is to add value, not to devalue it, because if we devalue it from a retail perspective then that reduces the amount of profit available to go back down the supply chain. We are probably unique in the way that we approach balancing carcasses whereas our competitors are probably cherry-picking the bits that they want and leaving the rest available to market forces.

Q853 *Chairman:* And 2003 helped you in that direction, did it, with your suppliers to make them more conscious?

Ms Jenkins: I would say that 2003 created awareness. It also created a significant amount of work and a huge amount of focus and intensity, and farmers needed leadership because a lot were like rabbits in the headlights.

Q854 *Chairman:* What you have described seems to me to be absolutely distinctive. Are there other supermarkets, either in the UK or the EU, that have gone down that road and, if not, why not?

Mr Sinclair: I cannot really speak about Europe. I do not know the European retail sector that well. I am not aware that that model is replicated anywhere. I think that Marks & Spencer's do a fair amount but I am not aware really that any other retailer is involved to the extent that we are. Part of that is to do with the type of business that we have, being a partnership, but the other part of that is about looking ahead and wanting to have those supply lines in place to serve our customers in 10 or 15 or 20 years' time. That is very much how we approach our supply strategy, hence the reason that it has been evolving over time.
Baroness Jones of Whitchurch: Could I just pursue this uniqueness for one second because we have just heard from the Food and Drink Federation that the key thing that drives consumers, whatever they say, is the price. Price is the thing that really determines where they shop and so on. Obviously that does not apply in Waitrose. Are you resigned to being a niche supplier or do you think the principles that you are now espousing --
Chairman: That is why they avoid Aberdeen!

Q855 *Baroness Jones of Whitchurch:* --- could roll out across a much wider consumer base?
Ms Jenkins: I think if we were resigned to being a niche we would not have a future because at the end of the day price is very important to everybody, and whether you are a Waitrose customer or another retailer's customer price is still important. Customers enjoy a bargain, value for money; they do not enjoy being ripped off, they do not enjoy being misled, so I would say that the model is achievable by anybody, but you need to take a long-term view and understand the supply chain. We are in a different supply and demand situation today than we were in 2005 or even 2000, there is an awareness now in terms of shortages of commodities that perhaps could focus others' minds. I think it is disappointing that we need to see industries disappear before action is taken, notwithstanding the fact that there are performance issues out there in every sector. One of the key things that we have driven through benchmarking is to get farmers to think in the same way as any other business about performance and what is good and what is bad and how it could be improved and how there can be a benefit for them as a result.

Q856 *Lord Palmer:* Could I ask a very quick supplementary. Can you just remind us what percentage of the UK grocery trade Waitrose claims to have now?
Ms Jenkins: As a multiple retailer we represent 4% of the market. In the area that I am responsible for, it is anything between 4 and 10%, so in the primary agricultural sectors, from beef through to chicken and fish, so we generally out punch our weight in those sectors.

Mr Sinclair: On the organic sector we have a market share of something like 18%, so that is significantly higher than the overall market share.

Q857 *Chairman:* That tells us something about your customers, does it not?
Ms Jenkins: It does but, if I might add, we feel it is really important and right that in terms of the policy going forward that all of us should get our return from the market-place, but there is a role for the market-place to play in terms of transition and acknowledgement that we have to get from A to B before we can actually make that happen.
Chairman: Lord Plumb on the environment and animal welfare.

Q858 *Lord Plumb:* There are three questions to this but I would like to put them into one, if I may. Environmentally of course everybody says they want everything produced in an environmentally friendly way yet of course the market-place determines the price at the end of the day. How many of your customers therefore will say yes they will pay more if the product is produced under environmental terms which are acceptable than they might do otherwise? Customer behaviour, in other words, is really the question I am asking about and whether that reflects the concern both on environmental issues and on animal welfare. People talk a lot about the importance of making sure the animal is well looked after and we would like to know what proportion of your customers or consumers generally are prepared to pay that premium. Then, thirdly, the extent to which consumers are willing to pay a premium, could this in your view provide a way of rewarding farmers monetarily for the public benefits that they provide? Do you anticipate that there will always be a residual role for the government in this area, be it through subsidies or other instruments? Might I just add to that, since you mentioned the organic production and the sale of organic goods, what is your concern in this field—because I accept and I am with you all way on your initiative, I think it is excellent that people are demanding more organic goods—how many people in this country are consuming a vast amount of soya, for example, that is produced in America that is not necessarily organic and certainly 98% of it is genetically modified, and yet they are against that sort of thing and it is a totally different base that the product is coming from? I think those are areas of concern—the environment, animal welfare and how the consumer reacts.
Mr Sinclair: Taking the first point, in terms of the environment I think one of the key drivers for us is to make sure that our own farmers involved in our various livestock supply chains are fully engaged in the various schemes that are available out there in the industry. We have developed a specific scheme on

select farm milk producers, which I think is probably a leading standard in terms of where commercial farm and habitat and agri-environment can actually work hand-in-hand together. We set them a target to have 10% of the farm area devoted to wildlife and habitat and when we did an audit in spring this year we found something like just over 20% of the farm area was actually devoted to habitat and agri-environmental features. We have other supply chains which do not appear to be fully engaged in the agri-environmental schemes as we would like. I understand the Red Meat Industry Forum have just done a survey of livestock farmers in the West Midlands and found that out of a group of 150, only 10% of them for example had actually signed up to an entry level scheme. When challenged, the reaction appeared to be apathy at the farm level in terms of they did not want to have to fill out another form to prod out that funding. In the post-decoupled era I think it is important that farmers are business focused and that they actually sign up for the agri-environmental menu of options as well. We are using resources to produce food and I think we have a responsibility collectively to actually deliver some of the environmental benefits back for the general public. It is certainly something that we are working on at the moment to get all our various supply chains engaged, and certainly in England signing up to the entry level scheme, or the equivalent in Scotland or Wales, because we feel that is a very important thing.

Q859 Lord Plumb: And the consumer will pay a premium for that product?
Mr Sinclair: At the moment it is difficult to know from the market research that we have seen. There was some IGD work that was done in spring this year which definitely showed that things like price and brand were leading drivers of consumer patterns and at a much lower level were agri-environmental and environmental issues. That may well have changed because of the high profile that the environment and climate change has taken on through the course of the year. Things like animal welfare and organic production were much lower in the pecking order as well. For us our position in the retail market-place out there is such that from a brand perspective our customers expect us to be doing a lot of these things, actually taking responsibility and being able to deliver the agri-environmental benefits to take a proactive stance to ensure that we have high standards of animal welfare and care for the animals through their lifetime. We have done a significant amount of research, in conjunction with some of our suppliers, looking at how we can actually raise the animal welfare situation within our various supply chains and in time, as more of that information becomes available and we have projects complete, we will be incorporating that into our production

protocols. We are continually looking to raise the level of animal welfare credentials, as it were, moving forward. We have got to be practical and it helps if there is good scientific evidence to justify that, but there is an expectation from our customers that we are working to make sure that animals have been treated with respect, et cetera, through their lifetime. There is a relatively small proportion of the public who may well look for these high welfare products, but I think it is part of an overall bundle of expectations, and I think at the moment in terms of some of the ethical drivers but some diet and health and healthier options, as it were, are at the moment some of the main drivers and they are taking a higher priority in terms of driving purchasing decisions than maybe just environment or welfare, but for us it needs to be the entire package. We have done work right across the board so it feeds in in terms of the various different strands that make up our production protocols, and we need to make sure that we are delivering a consistent, good-quality product that tastes good and that is produced to high standards with environmental credentials as well as animal welfare credentials.

Q860 Lord Plumb: I think what we are getting at is if you walk into a supermarket and you see a whole lot of chicken, it may be branded and it may have the country of origin (although occasionally it has not had in the past) but supposing that they are Brazilian and Chinese chickens and they are half the price of the chicken you offer of the standard that you are describing, what is the consumer going to take?
Mr Sinclair: For us certainly in our fresh meat offering the vast majority of that is sourced from within the United Kingdom.

Q861 Lord Plumb: So you do not have the problem, you do not import Chinese chickens?
Mr Sinclair: Certainly not on the fresh side.

Q862 Chairman: Can I put what you are saying in a different way. Do you think that your customers are prepared to pay almost a general premium to shop at Waitrose because they are buying into something that is a package that is quality, environment, animal welfare, and it is all wrapped up in the total ethos of what Waitrose is?
Ms Jenkins: Not necessarily.

Q863 Chairman: Well, I have got it wrong!
Ms Jenkins: I think, our customers expect us to have considered all these issues on their behalf and so they would expect us to deliver on the environmental strategy although they probably would not understand it because it is quite difficult from a consumer to understand how farmers are spending their money so, as Duncan said, it is a package of

credentials that is delivering the Waitrose brand. If we look at milk for example, we have Select Farm milk produced to the highest animal welfare standards and we have been paying as close to the cost of production since 1999 rewarding for the quality standards, which is completely against what the rest of the market have been doing, and we have been selling it at the same price as everybody else, so there is a combination of things that we would do because it is the right thing to do for our brand and it is the right thing to do for our customer. Whether it is CAP policy, whether it is UK strategy, whether it is legal requirements, we are interpreting those all of the time and translating them into whatever livestock scheme we are offering, and therefore what it looks like in terms of an assortment of choice to a customer. We are in a position where we can add value and we are creating the choice, so the entry level, if you like, the British standard meat offer that you see at Waitrose (because we do not sell anything else except New Zealand lamb in season) is our entry level and that will have high welfare credentials. We will not necessarily charge any more money for it because it might not be accepted by the customer or it just might not be competitive. Coming back to the niche market discussion, we cannot afford to trade in a vacuum. You could say maybe ten years ago that Waitrose customers were Waitrose customers, indeed they were and they are today, but they are more promiscuous and everybody wants to trade in the premium end of the market so going back to where do customers pay more for environmental credentials, the evidence that we have got is that the customers believe that your credentials should be throughout your business not just an emblem or a logo on a pack in amongst Chinese chicken or whatever else imported meat might be in there, I think they have a very cynical view from that point of view. It does not necessarily follow that just because you are serving Waitrose that we can pay a premium, because we have to trade in the open market like everybody else, and what we try and do, as I said, about trying to balance a carcass and find differentiation, we try and add value. There are challenges associated with that but if you are able to take a long-term view and be innovative, then there is a long-term benefit for everybody involved in the chain. The most important thing for customers, whilst we talk about animal welfare and environmental credentials and what we do on the farm, is that it tastes good.

Chairman: Can we move on to risk management and Lord Cameron.

Q864 Lord Cameron of Dillington: With falling intervention in the EU and falling tariffs, the Commission has, quite rightly in my view, put forward the proposal that risk management is

something that ought to be looked at and that the farmers ought to take their share on that. I should declare an interest before I ask the question, namely a) I am a supplier of organic milk to Waitrose and b) I am a supplier of non-organic potatoes to Tesco's.
Baroness Jones of Whitchurch: Promiscuous!

Q865 Lord Cameron of Dillington: Promiscuous, yes! I was wondering what role the supermarkets for instance could play in this in terms of supplying their suppliers with very good market information, perhaps their own forward analysis of the market-place and, more importantly, and this is the thing I have struggled to achieve both with potatoes and milk, some form of long-term contract so that they are sharing the risk? Let us avoid milk and take potatoes, for instance, where prices go from £40 a tonne one year to £200 a tonne the next, as a farmer one would really long to have some sort of consistency of price but it is almost impossible to achieve.
Ms Jenkins: I do not think it is impossible but I think there has to be equal risk taken. The two examples I would give today is the activity that we have had in the beef and the sheep sector this year in particular. I did say that we do not have any formal contracts—I think milk is slightly different—but in the sheep sector, for example, there was no way that they were going to get the right return for producing sheep meat so we underpinned the market. We have done that all season and again we were the only retailer to actually do it in the way that you are referring to. We have also taken a stance on beef prices and given a structured approach to the next 18 months. That is quite a risk for one retailer to stick their neck out when there is no sign at the moment that the market is going to follow suit. Coming back to why we can do it and others cannot, I think that fundamentally others do need to look at the base commodities with some sort of sense of "what is this worth and where are these people going to be?" otherwise they are not going to be there in the future. So I think that contracts can be developed. It is a bit like a marriage; there are good times and there are bad times and you need to go into it with your eyes open. I think in the past what we have seen is that farmers can be fair weather friends and when the market changes they walk away, so it has equal responsibility in risk-taking because at the end of the day we are trying to provide the customer with a consistent quality and a consistent price.

Q866 Lord Cameron of Dillington: I accept that but again reverting to potatoes, the cost of producing a potato with cold storage and all the rest of it is about £150 a tonne. To have a contract for £125 a tonne would be quite good over a five-year period, but it is almost impossible and supermarkets have got to learn to share the risk and not just go entirely on spot price.

Ms Jenkins: I think so. It is also about reducing the variables so it is about having clarity as to what the exposure is. You would not be the first person to talk to me about Tesco potato contracts I cannot believe that the UK cannot provide all the potatoes that every retailer wants. We do not need to be going abroad to get our potatoes. I think that there is an opportunity there but again I would also say, as I say to our own producers, that working together is far more powerful than trying to do it on an individual basis.

Q867 Lord Cameron of Dillington: I agree with that.
Mr Sinclair: One area where we have actually through our suppliers been working as a group is on the organic cereals side because we have got a significant share of the organic pig meat supply in the UK, and one of the biggest challenges we have there is having enough organic cereals. We started some work in the summer time, long before the cereal prices reached the high level that they actually did, because we were concerned that with a poor harvest in the UK and elsewhere in Europe whether we would have enough organic cereals to be able to maintain our various livestock supply chains moving forward. Essentially we took a stand at two organic cereals events in the summer and we got 35-odd leads to follow up with farmers to discuss a two or three-year contract price for organic cereals to provide them with something that they could actually plan for their future, in the same way as our livestock farmers could plan with some certainty for the future. The biggest challenge we have had is because the cereal price increased markedly is trying to say what would be a level that would be acceptable on a two or three-year period and that little exercise has essentially been much more difficult in the way in which the cereal market has actually evolved. We were taking the view from the integrity of our supply chain that to have to rely on Eastern European supply, Kazakhstan supply of organic cereals is something that we would prefer not to have to rely on. We would much rather that that product was grown in the UK and we would have much more faith in the quality of the raw material. That is an example where we have through our suppliers tried to look at a contract scenario, but it has proven to be a very challenging exercise.
Chairman: We must move on to biofuels and climate change.

Q868 Lord Palmer: Both my questions are fairly topical with the Renewable Transport Fuel Obligation, et cetera. What is Waitrose's view on the food miles debate? Are there alternative strategies for reducing the impact of the food chain on the emission of greenhouse gases that should, in your view, receive

greater attention? I find this very difficult because I live next door to one of the largest potato packing plants in the country. I am told potatoes get shipped from Lord Cameron's part of the world, all the way to the Scottish borders, get washed, get packaged and then shipped all the way back to Lord Cameron's part of the world. Quite a lot of our witnesses have also expressed great concern about the impact of policies to encourage bioenergy and renewable energy. How do you think this might have an effect on the supply and indeed the price of food and are you worried about this long term?

Mr Sinclair: I think the extra demand for renewable energy is something that has certainly been one of the major driving forces behind a significant increase in cereal prices that has occurred this year, allied to the poor summer weather and so on, and it has had a major impact. I think the obligations that set out the aspirations of the EU Commission for different Member States to achieve different level is going to be a factor that could mean that we are facing a scenario where livestock production costs, particularly in the pig and poultry sectors, are going to be much higher in the future than maybe they have been for the last five to ten years, so it could be a fundamental difference in the cost structures of these particular sectors. It is something that we have had to respond to but we have found it extremely difficult in the current economic climate to be able to recoup these extra costs at the retail end of the supply chain. I think one of the big issues for the industry is how we balance the discussion between land for providing and producing feed to supply the domestic industry versus using the land to meet some of these renewable energy targets that the Government have to meet moving forward. It is a discussion that is going to intensify in the next couple of years but it could mean that we are looking at significantly different cost structures, particularly in those two sectors here and across Europe, and the fact that set aside may well disappear as part of the CAP health check, I think it is going to be an interesting scenario to see when that land is released and cereals are grown at one end, does that product end up as animal feed or does it move into the biofuels supply scenarios. I think some work I have seen that some folk in the EU Commission are suggesting is that to meet some of the renewable obligations by 2020 we could be looking at something like 15% of the EU arable land would have to be used for production on biofuels versus the current ratio of 3% of the EU arable area. It is a difficult thing to assess moving forward but I think it could be fundamentally different cost structures we are looking at in some sectors.
Lord Palmer: Thank you.
Earl of Arron: You have not really answered the food miles question.

Q869 *Lord Palmer:* You have not, no.

Mr Sinclair: I think the food miles is at least part of the concept. For us it has to be looking at it more on the entire picture of the carbon life cycle. You start with your inputs and then the production system. I think one of the things that might help is if we could have some standard methodology for assessing the carbon footprint. I understand in spring there is going to be a BSI standard published. An amalgam of the BSI, the Carbon Trust and Defra have been working to develop this one methodology. I think that will actually help the discussion. For us in working with our supply chain, we have through the main agricultural commodities virtually plugged our figures into the Cranfield model to give us an idea on the various livestock sectors, where are some of the hot spots, where are some of the big issues in terms of carbon footprint and equally so with the major processors that we use. They have done a carbon audit of their processing facilities which I guess is possibly easier than making assumptions at a farm level with a view again to looking at where the hot spots are. What are the things that you can do to try and adapt and mitigate the effect and reduce these factors moving forward. We have begun the process but I think there is more we could actually do.

Q870 *Lord Palmer:* And this will be in your long-term plans, will it?

Mr Sinclair: Yes, it will be.

Q871 *Chairman:* Can I ask on cross-compliance, obviously farmers in receipt of Single Farm Payments have to observe some basic cross-compliance conditions. In your judgment, does that improve the quality or safety of UK-produced farm goods and would you like to see changes in the requirements incorporated in cross-compliance, so where are we with cross-compliance and how useful is it?

Mr Sinclair: I think it was a concept that many farmers were very nervous about in terms of when it was discussed, when it was agreed, exactly how that would affect how they do things on the farm. What I detect is that it has not been as intrusive as they maybe felt it would have been. It was originally perceived that it might not to be able to do not a lot of the general activities that they actually did. I think it has been positive in terms of it certainly raised the awareness of environmental issues on farm. On things like increased legislation in this area, it has probably encouraged people to think about best practice, the sort of things like the new legislation that is about to come in and extend potentially nitrate-vulnerable zones and extra Framework Directive legislation probably and because we have raised the awareness then I think it will probably help in possibly being able to achieve some of these things

moving forward. It is difficult sitting here to know whether the way in which we have been able to address some of the measures here in the UK are the least cost options and is there any work being done across Europe on other ways in which to address some of these issues in other Member States and could we learn from that, because I think we have got to make sure that from a competitive point of view we do not saddle our industry with an extra burden of cost relative to our European counterparts. I think that is an important part that we are able to deliver against the EU frameworks but we have got to have some flexibility in there and I think at some point we have got to take stock to make sure that the measures we have got are actually delivering what was expected of them.

Chairman: Trade liberalisation and Baroness Jones.

Q872 *Lord Palmer:* So if the outcome of the Doha negotiations is that it opens up markets so that there are more imports coming here from third countries, would you envisage taking up that opportunity to import more is or is your ethos committed to British products at all costs?

Ms Jenkins: We have been involved in developing British production schemes for many, many years and our belief at the moment is that providing the UK can provide the indigenous resources to do it effectively, then that is where we will continue to place our emphasis. It is true to say that part of the reforms is creating awareness with farmer suppliers in terms of if you see that you cannot produce what we need you to produce at the prices that we can retrieve from the market-place, then we are going to seriously have to think about where else we go in the world, and certainly our specifications are transferable; we have no issue with that. For us it is about if we can produce it indigenously then we should, in the interests of everything, whether it is animal welfare or environment or food miles or all of these things taken into consideration, and if we cannot, then we have to look elsewhere like any other buyer, but that is certainly our strategy.

Q873 *Baroness Jones of Whitchurch:* And are there opportunities for you in terms of greater exports, the quid pro quo of opening up some of these markets. I do not know what proportion of your product you export, presumably a relatively small amount?

Ms Jenkins: We have an interesting export business. We do not have any bricks and mortar but we do have a developing export business and, yes, we are looking at all those opportunities to grow that in the future.

Q874 *Baroness Jones of Whitchurch:* So then lastly you have talked very persuasively about the health and animal welfare standards that you have—and you are probably a leading example of it—do you look forward to extending those principles out beyond the EU to wider international levels? Do you think that they should be taken up as part of the Doha negotiations or beyond?

Mr Sinclair: I think it would be a very difficult issue to try and achieve an agreement, and certainly when this was discussed the last time around in the context of the Uruguay Round they ended up being cast aside to actually achieve that Framework Agreement. I think the big issue moving forward is the mechanism and if we cannot actually see them include it in the Doha Agreement, whenever that may come, I think the challenge will be does the EU try to differentiate EU-produced product versus non-EU produced product out there in the market-place. I think that is an important thing and I think the animal welfare aspect, as Heather mentioned, is one aspect because our experience has been essentially to translate our UK production standards into other European Member States and also to non-EU Member States, so they are virtual equivalents across the world in terms of where we are actually sourcing. I think we are probably unique in that, but I think the challenge will be if we cannot see that incorporated into the next agreement can the EU try in some way to differentiate. I know there has been some discussion about an EU project looking at welfare labelling. That may be a potential mechanism to try and differentiate in consumers' minds between product produced in the EU meeting the EU's standards versus imported third country product that does not. I think that is one of the confusing issues out there at the moment. I think many consumers expect imported product to reach the exact same standards as we would have within the European Union and in a whole range of different sectors that is not the case.

Chairman: What is quite interesting is in the defence and security world how some of those people are now talking in terms of building environmental requirements into trade negotiations because they see environmental issues as being real security threats, and that is one way of dealing with it. I think it is impossible to deliver them, but never mind. Thank you very much indeed. It has been of very great help.

WEDNESDAY 23 JANUARY 2008

Present   Arran, E   Palmer, L
               Brookeborough, V   Plumb, L
               Brooke of Alverthorpe, L   Sewel, L (Chairman)
               Dundee, E   Sharp of Guildford, B
               Jones of Whitchurch, B   Ullswater, V

Examination of Witnesses

Witnesses: LORD ROOKER, a Member of the House, Minister for Sustainable Farming and Food, and Animal Welfare, and Ms SONIA PHIPPARD, Director, CAP Reform and EU Strategy Programme, Food and Farming Group, Defra, examined.

Q875 Chairman: Good morning. Having finished wine, we are now on the CAP reform: the health check and looking forward. Use your opportunity now, if you want to say a few general things to begin with.

Lord Rooker: I would like to, actually. I am conscious that the last couple of times I have been here I have not, because there has not been the need or I have not come prepared with a statement. However, given the nature of your inquiry and, in a way, the position of flux that the Government and the UK are in, it is a fairly short statement but it would set the scene for the other remarks that I am probably able to give in answer to your questions. Obviously, we very much welcome the inquiry. Given the nature of what you might want to know about today, there is a lot that I will not be able to comment on until we have seen the full legislative proposals in May and here we are, in January. At that point, we will consult our stakeholders of course, and there will be a full consultation; but obviously there is a good chance today to comment on the overall direction of travel. As you know, the Secretary of State set out a clear vision for farming at a conference last November, just across the river, outlining what we would like to see for farming and from farming. The industry earns its rewards from the market for quality, safety, environmental and animal welfare standards. We want it to be profitable and competitive, domestically and internationally; an industry that works together to meet the challenges it faces and to manage its risks; one that embraces environmental responsibilities, because those who own, manage and work on the land are at the front end of dealing with climate change; and certainly we have to manage the water and the soil better than we have probably done in the past. We see all those as issues which are essential for long-term economic success. We want an industry that is valued and rewarded by society for the environmental goods that it provides. We think that the Common Agricultural Policy reform is a key element in achieving the vision for UK and European Union farming. The CAP as it stands is expensive, wasteful and inefficient in providing ongoing support for farmers. It definitely distorts global markets, weighs farmers down with regulation—and I suspect most of you know that—and it certainly acts as a disincentive to farmers to maximise their competitiveness. Our long-term vision is to see the elimination of Pillar I of the CAP altogether, leaving public subsidy targeted at specific public benefits, such as the environmental enhancement through Pillar II. The health check is an important step in the process. You appreciate that it will not touch the overall size of the CAP budget, but it does offer scope to revise some of the distortions in the Common Agricultural Policy. We therefore very much welcome the Commission's health check paper, in so far as it is in line with our own vision. It has the potential to bring benefits for farmers and to improve the delivery of the environmental benefits, and we have to make sure that the proposals in May are ambitious in that regard. In order to bring such benefits, we believe that the health check legislative proposals should be underpinned by the following principles and aims: to reduce the regulatory burdens; give farmers greater control over business decisions; to cut further the trade and market-distorting nature of the CAP; to direct policy and public spending towards delivery of targeted public benefits. This will be a process of negotiation between ourselves, the Commission, other Member States and the European Parliament; and we hope that the Committee appreciates the need for caution in revealing what are our red lines and end-game tactics at this particular stage, in January 2008. There is no secret about what our feelings are on many aspects of the CAP. For example, we want to see an end to coupled payments in all Member States to create a more level playing field and give farmers full autonomy over their production decisions, so that they can compete in a global market. We would like to see the phase-out of export subsidies and intervention, the abolition of milk quotas, and the abolition of set-aside. We obviously have to ensure that we mitigate the environmental effects of aspects of set-aside. These measures have distorted trade, increased costs to consumers, and inhibited farm competitiveness. We would further like to see modulation of funds from Pillar I to Pillar II towards targeted rural development schemes. Beyond the health check, the Budget review—which will come much later, of course—provides the important opportunity for the European Union as a whole to examine the CAP closely and to consider how that policy should be shaped post-2013, to make sure that it is fit for purpose, delivering, we think, a greater benefit for European Union taxpayers, in line with our vision. In particular, the CAP continues to cost European taxpayers substantial amounts of money. In 2005, Pillar I of the CAP cost the European Union Budget more than €42 billion and placed an additional burden on consumers. We will engage with other Member States, the Commission and the stakeholders in the coming years to ensure that negotiations on the next Financial Perspectives address these concerns. I hope that statement gives a flavour of how we wish to proceed, in somewhat general terms but also with some specifics; because the timetable we are involved in is such that—while the health check document was in November last year—it will not be until May this year that we get the legislative proposals. We intend to get political agreement by, say, November; and I understand that it is agreed that there should be a conclusion of the health check exercise during the French presidency, which will end on 31 December.

Q876 Chairman: Thank you very much indeed, Minister. As you have said, we are here talking in January, waiting for legislative proposals in May, and I recognise the difficulty that creates. This is a public, on-the-record session. Would it be helpful if we were perhaps slightly more informal and stopped the public record for a ten-minute review at the end of the session?

Lord Rooker: I have no objection to that, if we are in a position to be able to assist the Committee. That is what we are here for. We are from the Government. We have come to help.

Q877 Chairman: That is very worrying! Two of the specifics that you have mentioned—the abolition of milk quotas and set-aside—we have almost subconsciously ticked the boxes on those and seen them as having been achieved, in the bag, as it is. That is the general impression we have had from everybody we have spoken to. There is that assumption around. Perhaps I could go beyond that and look at the extent to which there is a shared vision at a UK level. We have taken evidence not just from the English but from the Welsh, the Irish and the Scots—a delightful experience!—and what I am asking you really is the extent to which you think that, in approaching CAP reform and the health check, the devolved administrations are signed up to

the type of vision of the Common Agricultural Policy that was in your 2005 document, and is clearly still driving policy with Defra ministers. I suppose the specific question is whether the devolved administrations are equally keen to get rid of Pillar I direct payments as you are.

Lord Rooker: It would be daft for me to sit here and say that we are all 100% in agreement, bearing in mind there have been political changes in all three of the devolved administrations since the *Vision* document. A year ago, the administrations were completely different. There was still direct rule in Northern Ireland, so there was a government direct-rule minister. In Wales there was a slightly different coalition arrangement, as indeed there was in Scotland. In fact, therefore, the agricultural ministers in the four countries that make up the United Kingdom are all from different political parties. That does bring a slightly different perspective. Generally speaking, though, in terms of reform, we are rowing in the same direction; indeed the new administrations are looking at their views. I am not saying that they would be exactly with us on all the minutiae of the detail, but in terms of wanting to get reform, better value for the taxpayer, I do not think there is a major difference. There clearly will be differences, maybe with the speed of process, say, to abolish Pillar I and moving to Pillar II, and the issue of the use of national envelopes, which Scotland uses now in one respect but nobody else does. There is the issue of modulation. There will probably be different views on that. However, I am not aware, from my daily existence or the discussions I have had with them relating to other matters—essentially, disease control in food animals—that we have major fundamental differences that will inhibit our negotiating as a UK Government with the other Member States.

Q878 Chairman: Do you think that you will be able to incorporate it in the UK, with the Scots' emphasis on national envelopes and their concern to maintain something like the beef calf scheme and things like this?

Lord Rooker: Certainly as far as reform is concerned, whether it is the national envelopes or looking at other aspects, what we do not want through the back door are a load of new schemes which are all there as support mechanisms, putting back the worst of the CAP. We are on guard for that. Quite clearly, in the present situation, with what occurred during the summer of last year in the meat industry, I fully understand why the Scots and the Welsh were taking a slightly different view about support mechanisms, particularly with what happened on the hills. They are quite entitled to do that, as long as they pay for it. We do not rule differences out but what we will be very mindful about and watchful of—and this also applies to other Member States—is that we do not want to rebuild support mechanisms: production subsidies being put in through the back door, really.

Q879 *Viscount Brookeborough:* In your *Vision*—and you have just made it clear again that you would like to see the end of Pillar I, namely no direct payments and no market management—if there is to be a compromise in the future or as part of a transition process, and there were to be a residual level of Pillar I expenditure, what in your view should it and could it be spent on?

Lord Rooker: Our objective is to see the end of Pillar I. Going back to the old-fashioned way of running the Common Agricultural Policy, Pillar I is money straight into the bank for no particular purpose whatsoever. Unlike the Pillar II programmes of environmental goods, environmental benefits, it simply distorts the market; it distorts businesses; and shields people from the realities of competition. Our objective, therefore, is to do that. We are some years down the road; we are not talking about this in respect of the health check. This is for the future. We are talking about 2015-2020. That is some considerable way away. By and large, the general view—and we have always made this clear, there is no secret about this—is that we do not see a long-term future, for the foreseeable future. I cannot really speculate on what they might be used for. Obviously, moving from where we are now to, let us say, the abolition of Pillar I, there would be substantial transition periods. No one is talking about turning this off overnight. That would be catastrophic for some businesses; for others it would not make any difference, because they are getting such a tiny amount. From the public's point of view, however, there is more and more exposure as to what their tax money is being spent on. If we can show as a government, and indeed the farming industry can show, good environmental benefits—mitigating climate change, the way we are looking after the soil, keeping the water clean—these are all good things that can be pointed out; whereas at the moment for Pillar I you cannot directly show any public benefit for what is, for England, £1½ billion. It is not an insubstantial amount of money.

Q880 *Viscount Brookeborough:* One could say that it is all very well for Defra, settled in London, and that most of England is an entirely different type of countryside to those areas on the periphery, the devolved areas—being Scotland, Northern Ireland and Wales. To what extent do you think that the environment should continue to be appreciated, as a result of some grazing or some farming in those areas? If that is so, can a future Pillar II in lieu of Pillar I sustain it? Or are you saying—which is undoubtedly true—that animals produced on the Isle

of Skye, the Hebrides or the hills, cannot be produced in England?

Lord Rooker: First of all, if you take the situation regarding, let us say, Northern Ireland, they have a land border with another Member State; obviously, the consequence is vastly different schemes. I think that the thrust will be towards eliminating the subsidies for which they are paid for no particular purpose.

Q881 *Viscount Brookeborough:* But there is a purpose where sometimes the environment requires some of this marginal land to be grazed, rather than simply left.

Lord Rooker: In that case it ought to be part of a scheme to do it and based, for England's purposes— it is slightly different in Northern Ireland, Scotland and Wales—on some kind of scheme, some kind of arrangement with an end output, so that you have something you can measure; as opposed to now: simply saying, "I've got an area of land that is farmed, in good agricultural condition, and I demand my money". That is not quite the long-term vision that we have. In Pillar II and also through the RDAs, we have lots of arrangements for environmental works and stewardship of the environment. I freely admit that, in the hills, there is very little you can do. The sheep do a really good job for us to make sure the landscape is maintained, as man-made. The city-dwellers like it. They will be the first to complain if we allow it to be covered in bracken. Therefore, there is an environmental benefit to farming the hills, and by and large done with sheep. However, that is something you can measure and I think that is a much better purpose. I think that farmers are much more comfortable in having the money flow when there is an output, because the output is there. It may not be the output in terms of tonnes of sheep meat to market, but we measure it in a different way and it is much more acceptable to the public as well.

Q882 *Lord Plumb:* May I ask a supplementary? If the Lisbon Treaty goes through, qualified majority voting will include agriculture, which it has not done in the past. A lot of these countries, structurally, are beginning to think in terms of development and therefore using the Pillar I fund for structural development. In fact, it should not be available for Pillar II use. Will there not be a difference of opinion here at the end of the day, when you get around the table before May and other countries say, "We must continue this fund for a considerable amount of time, in order to make our structural improvements effective"?

Lord Rooker: I might be wrong, and I will take advice from Sonia, but I do not think that the May issue is relevant. It is long-term, abolishing reliance on Pillar I to Pillar II. That is part of the budget post-2013;

that is not relevant to the health check, which we will be looking at from May to the end of this year. It is a much longer period for discussion with the 15 Member States plus the new entrants to the EU. It varies, particularly with some of the new Members; the structure of their farming is completely different. However, if they all joined on the basis that there is a load of money out of Pillar I, then they will be sadly disabused because there will be a different arrangement. It is best that they share the lessons we have learnt, in a way, from running the CAP the way we have done, which has been anticompetitive and not beneficial. However, this is a long-term discussion, after the health check and then into the Budget, which will be post-2013. We are therefore talking about 2015-2020 for that kind of arrangement, and I suspect there will be a phasing-in and a phasing-out. It is not something that we are under pressure for to deal with this year. It is useful to let the landscape be painted, though, so that people know where the UK is coming from. We are not alone in this. At the end of the day, we will have to face the World Trade Organization and other matters, keeping our farmers and food producers competitive and able to compete on a global scale. At the present time, we are not able to do that.

Q883 Lord Palmer: You virtually answered my question in your opening remarks and in replying to Lord Brookeborough but, in your opinion, what proportion of Pillar I spending should be transferred to Pillar II and what proportion should disappear altogether? I think I understood you to say that basically 100% should go almost at once.
Lord Rooker: No, I have not implied that at all. I do not carry around all the figures for the UK in my head but, in terms of England, as I have said, it is just over £1½ billion. I am not proposing that overnight we withdraw £1½ billion from what is, in effect, support to farmers in England. No, this requires long-term change. I do not have a figure and the reason, as you will appreciate, is that there is an objective to reduce the proportion of the EU Budget spent on the CAP. It is around 45% or something of that order. It is a phenomenal amount of money. There will be a view amongst Member States, I suspect, that we have seen Pillar I go, and " ... Right, we'll have that money" and that gets moved to Pillar II and maybe other schemes. There will be some countries, and treasuries in some countries, that will say, "Hang on a minute. Perhaps we don't need to raise taxes as much. We'll have that money and take it off the budget". There will be all kinds of negotiating arrangements. At the present time, I understand that Pillar II—if you take all the various schemes—is about 20% of the CAP funding. The single farm, direct, inefficient payments form 80%. What we want to do is get rid of those. I am not in a position to say how much of that we

would like to see go over the Pillar II and how much we would like to see wiped off the budget altogether; but there will be discussions about this, because there will be an attempt to reduce the overall size of agriculture in the EU Budget. That is not a very precise answer, I am afraid, but it is the one I can give you with some safety for my own skin!

Q884 Chairman: We did invite the Treasury to come along and talk to us but, they did not seem to be particularly keen to do so.
Lord Rooker: I had a chat earlier about that. For all practical purposes, I am the Government and I speak for the Government. I have a standard phrase here, and you read it in a letter that you have had from the Economic Secretary, that "No decisions have been taken on how the Government intends to approach the Budget review or the Commission's process". I cannot go any further than that.

Q885 Viscount Brookeborough: You seem to be quite optimistic, Minister, that maybe there would be a reduction in the total budget, but what we have seen in other sectors—be it the wine sector—is that actually the deal in the end was that there would be no reduction in the budget; it would merely be used in different ways, be it a different Pillar.
Lord Rooker: Yes.

Q886 Viscount Brookeborough: Do you have good grounds, from discussions with other countries, for feeling that we will succeed?
Lord Rooker: No, we just have our vision and our attempt. The opportunity does not come along very often to have a look at the fundamentals of the EU Budget. The last one was dealt with and this will be dealt with at, let us say, a much higher political level than my humble position. You are quite right: it will probably be the result of trade-offs on other issues when the time comes.
Chairman: Let us move on to rural development.

Q887 Baroness Jones of Whitchurch: You have emphasised several times now the importance that you see in Pillar II in the future, and you have talked in particular about the increasing environmental responsibilities that you see being carried out under Pillar II. In fact, we were talking before you arrived about what Pillar II really meant and what rural development really meant, and of course it is much broader than just the environmental aspects. There is the economic aspect, the cultural aspects, and others as well. Do you think that we are in danger of overloading Pillar II with a whole lot of new responsibilities, way beyond what it was originally intended for, and really way beyond agriculture in the way that we had originally envisaged it?

Lord Rooker: In some ways, the way Pillar II operates—the concept and the operation, as I understand it—is flexible enough and broad enough for us to deal with virtually all the objectives that we would want to deal with. We look at it through, on the one hand, the stewardship schemes that are funded through Natural England and the rules there relating to the work that is done by farmers in respect of the environment; but also money is channelled through Pillar II, through the Regional Development Agencies, through various organisations that would not be related to the environment but related to rural life in general. There is a host of schemes out there. In fact, they are so complicated that people set up businesses to explain the schemes to people. In some ways, I do not see that as a criticism; it shows that we think Pillar II is broad enough and flexible enough certainly to be able to cope with the Rural Development Programmes that we would wish to operate. Indeed, we have a very substantial Pillar II Rural Development Programme over the next five to seven years, running into nearly £4 billion, reaching all kinds of activities. We do not see a threat of it being overloaded. I do not deny that, if Pillar I goes—and we are obviously talking about a decade ahead—and Pillar II changes substantially, then certain Member States, and we would be no different, would start to look at delivery mechanisms. As we are now, do we have the machinery of government right for delivering these programmes? Obviously, if we have a different system we will have a look at it; but, at the present time, it is flexible enough and broad enough to achieve our objectives. However, I am not saying that would be the case if, for example, half of Pillar I was saved for the taxpayer and the other half went over the Pillar II. That would be a substantial amount of money—I am just thinking aloud on that—and you would start to look at how you deliver such programmes. Would the present arrangements be sufficient, and also what would the programmes be? At the present time, however, we do not have a problem with it.

Q888 Baroness Jones of Whitchurch: Could a lot more of that be done by individual Member States? Why do it at a European level anyway?
Lord Rooker: That is part of the other issue. Looking at the budget, I keep seeing this word "subsidiarity" and occasionally I ask, "What have we got back? What do we do now that was done for us by the EU some years ago?". Examples are given, but there is a lot more that we ought to be able to do that does not distort competition, and actually makes it fit for purpose in the individual states. We see that here. Given the fact that it is a devolved issue in the UK, we have enough experience of dealing with different programmes in Wales, Scotland and Northern Ireland, and we can build on that. It can be dealt with

at a local level, therefore. I absolutely agree with that. There is no reason at all why Brussels should be dictating the details of Rural Development Programmes—as long as you have a programme, and the big picture is bought into, that we want the European Union to be concerned about the economy, if you like, and quality of life in rural areas.

Q889 Chairman: Several decades ago, when I had a professional interest in rural development, my conclusion was that, if you were serious about rural development in a broad sense, the last thing you should do was to put money into it through farmers or agriculture. Surely the problem with Pillar II is that it does not give you that broader flexibility to put money and support into the rural economy beyond the farming/agricultural route?
Lord Rooker: That may be true, but the experience we have through the RDAs anyway, outside of Pillar II work, is in creating and sustaining rural business and innovation, to make sure that all our towns and villages do not look like chocolate box lids, where people commute in and out and there is no vibrancy of life. That is exactly the opposite of what we are trying to do, but we are not necessarily using Pillar II for that. However, if in the EU context rural development became bigger then, as I have said, we would look at how we would deliver that; but we are not relying exclusively on Pillar II for the work that goes on there. You are absolutely right. I have forgotten what the figure is now, but it is confined to 1 or 2% of people involved directly in agriculture—who live in the rural areas. I think it is 25% of people who live in rural areas, although the definition can be argued about. So there are lots of other issues that have to be dealt with. The social infrastructure in those areas has to be maintained and enhanced. That is important, and it does not necessarily come through Pillar II.

Q890 Viscount Ullswater: You have almost answered the question I was going to ask, which was basically, if you are going to get rid of Pillar I, why not just have a Rural Development Programme and scrap CAP altogether? Perhaps I can phrase it in a slightly different way, however. If this is the trend—and in your *Vision* I think that is the direction in which you are looking—what sort of percentage of Pillar II, however it is funded, would go back into agriculture under the sort of scheme Lord Brookeborough was mentioning, namely access to marketplace for cows from the Orkneys, grazing the uplands, or the public benefit of keeping the landscape and the environment? What sort of percentage of that do you think would go back into agriculture, back into the farming side of things?

Lord Rooker: I cannot give a percentage, but I do not envisage reductions in that area. Obviously, the public good that the public will pay for in terms of the landscape, looking after the water, the soil, and the visual amenity, if you like—there is a case for doing more on that. That can really only be delivered through the farmers in that sense, when you are looking at that aspect of it. I do not envisage less, therefore; but I am not in a position to put a percentage on it. We have something of the order of half the farmers in England signed up to stewardship schemes now. We are getting a lot of benefit from it and it has been a good experience for them to be in those schemes. In fact, for the High Level scheme— mainly because of financial restrictions—we had a queue that we could not accommodate, because of the budget problems that arose last year. Do not get me wrong: I am not seeking to come here and say that we want to chop off this source of funding. There is a public good argument. There will always be people— I suspect those who control the overall budgets—who might start to question, "What is the public good of looking after this?" and I think it is the job of everybody else who is involved in this to put a price on protecting the landscape. However, the effects of climate change and mitigation are upfront for everyone to see. All this is very much tied in with that: making sure that we grow the right crops, look after the soil, protect the water—where water will be a serious problem long-term. I cannot put a percentage on it, but I do not see any less than that. However, I am not in a position to play with any figures, because I have no information in that respect.

Q891 Lord Brooke of Alverthorpe: Perhaps I may refer to *A Vision for the Common Agricultural Policy*, the 2005 document. Following this through, understandably you cannot put figures on it, but in Chapter 3 you did in fact pose a whole series of questions. The first range of them was on the topic we have just been covering. You go on to say, "Indeed, the rural economy could benefit significantly from shifts away from general agricultural support towards more targeted rural development". We are now nearly three years on since that was first written. I am wondering, therefore, if you are in a position to put a little bit more flesh on the bones there. While you cannot give figures, can you give some views on the targeted topics you would want to go for, beyond the ones you have just mentioned—because they were essentially of farming?
Lord Rooker: Actually, I do not think I can help. I do not think that I have come with a list on that, unless I have misread my notes. The fact is that we have only just announced the new programme. I think there was a delay in the Rural Development Programme because of the problems in Europe about getting the budget agreed. The €3.9 billion programme was only

announced—that is for England, by the way, which would double the size of the previous programme— and I think this is probably the first year that we are involved in that. I am not in a position to give a report back on that. Obviously, there will have to be a report back because it is a large programme. This was announced just before David Milliband would have left the Department, if I remember rightly. I cannot give you a list now, unfortunately, because we are in the first year of that programme, which, as I say, is twice the size of what we have done previously.

Q892 Lord Brooke of Alverthorpe: I am coming new to the subject and I have been reading—
Lord Rooker: I am brand-new to the subject, by the way!
Lord Brooke of Alverthorpe: I mean in Europe. I am just wondering when, on the Chapter 3 questions, the Government will have reached the stage where it will start to answer some of the questions.
Chairman: Let us move quickly on!

Q893 Lord Plumb: I am not brand-new to the subject! I was quite impressed by your comment about the stewardship scheme and the fact that farmers have responded very well. I think it is encouraging that there was a queue of farmers wanting to come in, who found it difficult to get in. However, last year on the Entry Level scheme there was a decision to stop the management tools, and a lot of people who applied to get into the Entry Level scheme this year have been denied the opportunity to follow it through. The Entry Level scheme, of course, is seen to be the second pillar, if you like, of the stewardship scheme as a whole. I think that a lot are beginning to find the benefits of that—and I do speak from a bit of experience of it—and are disappointed that they cannot get into the scheme because the management tools have gone. Why?
Lord Rooker: I do not know. I will have to find out and write on that. It is one that I cannot give a direct answer to. I just plead guilty. Even though I am farming Minister, it is not part of my day job, in terms of Natural England. This was a policy that was not decided by the UK Government in the first place.

Q894 Lord Plumb: I do know that.
Lord Rooker: It was something we had next to no control over, really.

Q895 Lord Plumb: As I understand it, it was a decision taken in Brussels.
Lord Rooker: In Brussels by the Commission, yes.

Q896 Lord Plumb: I have asked the question there and I have not had an answer. I just wonder where this was blocked. It seems strange to me, because it was such a good scheme.

Lord Rooker: I do not know the background to the Commission decision, but I will certainly make it my business to find out and report back to the Committee with an answer.

Q897 *Chairman:* I have to say that if Lord Plumb cannot get it out of the Commission—
Lord Rooker: I was going to say that, but I decided against it!
Lord Plumb: That is not for the record!

Q898 *Baroness Sharp of Guildford:* If we are looking at the current budget envelope, in a sense the division between the monies in Pillar I and Pillar II are important—as we can see from what you have already been saying—because to some extent the current spending under Pillar II does help to effect the transition from Pillar I to Pillar II here. How do you respond to the accusations that have been made that the UK Government is partly responsible for insufficient funding being available under Pillar II, because it pushed cuts through in the last budget deal under the UK presidency, which meant that in effect there was not really enough funding there under Pillar II?
Lord Rooker: First of all, in reality we ended up, as far as our own programme was concerned, with double the size of the programme in England. We had the presidency at the time and it was a question of trying to get compromises in order to get the decisions through. I do not accept that we therefore have to take any blame for that; on the other hand, we do take responsibility for being in the chair at the time. We had 25 Member States and we had to try to find a workable solution. That was our responsibility. However, the reality is that David Milliband announced a programme that was double the previous programme in respect of England. I do not think it is a question of blame and responsibility. We had responsibility because we had the presidency and our job was basically to bring the 25 to the table and get as good a deal, where people were as content as possible. That means give and take, at the end of the day.

Q899 *Baroness Sharp of Guildford:* Making trade-offs and that sort of thing.
Lord Rooker: It does.

Q900 *Baroness Sharp of Guildford:* Perhaps that explains why the Commission feel they do not have enough funds to carry this one through as they would wish to.
Lord Rooker: Yes.

Q901 *Viscount Ullswater:* Perhaps I could turn to what might come up in May with Article 69. The Commission look as if they wish to reopen this particular argument, where you can via 10% spent on these various sectors for direct payments, as long as the money is kept within the sector. Do you suspect that in May the Commission might come forward and say, "Actually, you can spend this on other sectors" and are you in favour of that? What is the view of the Government on that particular matter? It could become quite wide, could it not?
Lord Rooker: We want to understand more about the Commission's views on this. We are not particularly clear ourselves. As I said in my opening statement, whatever they do seek to clarify, in terms of where the national envelopes might be used, we would be very keen to make sure that they are not used as a back-door method of production support. It would be so easy to make a case, in different parts of different Member States, for all kinds of schemes which, when looked at, are basically supporting something that is inefficient and which perhaps should not be going on. We do not want new distortions, therefore. I understand the national envelopes might be used to address different activities, whether it is water management, climate change or biodiversity. There is a range of issues but, until we know more about their thinking, I am not in a position to give a view. As I say, we are not against it but we will be very watchful. 10% is a lot of money, because you are dealing with big budgets here. Scotland has taken advantage of the current arrangements, but—

Q902 *Viscount Ullswater:* Which I take it they would not like to give up?
Lord Rooker: No, I am absolutely certain they would not like to give up. However, we are watchful. First of all, we want to know more about the Commission's thinking. Secondly, we would not want it to be used as a back-door method of production subsidies.

Q903 *Chairman:* Does not a lot of it, in the southern states, go into olive oil producers? The argument being that, if you do not support the people to produce olives, you will get desertification. That is the old argument—but it is a straightforward production subsidy.
Lord Rooker: It is, but then you have to see whether it is a production subsidy in that sense or—and I do not know the issue in detail—would it be part of an environmental benefit? I do not know whether or not southern Europe will become a desert under climate change, but these are issues that will have to be dealt with in the future in terms of the environment. However, that is our general principle on this. First of all, we do need to watch this, to be careful about the way they could be misused; but we are not saying that they do not have a purpose.

Q904 *Baroness Sharp of Guildford:* The same argument could be levelled at hill farmers, could it not? If you are going to have to pay to keep the olives in the landscape—
Lord Rooker: Precisely. The economics in the hills particularly—a really severe disadvantage in any definition of farming—isolated communities; but without millions of sheep on the hills the landscape will be transformed. As I keep saying, the first people to complain about that will be the city-dwellers, who use it as their playground and their green lung. When they say, "Where's it all gone?" we say, "You didn't buy the lamb. The industry collapsed", and therefore there is an argument for maintaining it; but how do you do it? Do you subsidise it as meat production or do you subsidise the pure environmental goods or the individual families in those areas? It is a very difficult decision, but the principle is exactly the same.

Q905 *Lord Plumb:* Voluntary modulation has not been very popular with producers here, believing that there is competitive disadvantage with their competitors from other parts of Europe. We understand, of course, that if that is reduced it does not necessarily follow that compulsory modulation will be increased—although we know that the Commission are bidding for an increase. Would it mean that, if it is increased, you would reduce the amount of voluntary modulation to make up the difference? Also, we understand that environment organisations say, and have told us, they rely on some of these funds for many of their activities. We wonder, in that event, whether the reduction in voluntary modulation accordingly would help in the overall use of funds.
Lord Rooker: I have to say that I find modulation an incredibly complicated issue to get my head round. The long and short of it is that, first of all, there is only us and the Portuguese making use of voluntary modulation. You say it is unpopular. Without it, though, we would have far less money for our Rural Development Programme. There is an historical element to this as to why we need voluntary modulation, simply because we had very small programmes in the past. Also, I understand that there is a mechanism where we swap from voluntary modulation to relying on compulsory modulation. At the present time, we get far more bang for our buck out of voluntary modulation than we would do if we swapped over. Pound for pound, we would lose 20% to start with, because there is some mechanism with the compulsory modulation. There is no mention of voluntary modulation in the health check document. We are not really certain, therefore. There is obviously a discussion to be had there. We think that it is good value for money, but I understand that it is unpopular amongst the farmers who are seeing their single farm payment top-sliced, as it were. There

is a benefit to the rural economy, and there is no question about that. At the moment, there is a greater benefit from voluntary modulation than the straightforward compulsory. We get a bigger bang for our buck, as it were.

Q906 *Lord Plumb:* It is very difficult to explain that to farmers who have just had a 17% reduction in their single payments through modulation.
Lord Rooker: Yes, it is to an individual farmer, directly. It is not easy to paint the greater good of the rural community, because obviously they are seeing it in the bank balance. On the other hand, people have to make connections—with families and networks in rural areas. In the rural economy, not everybody depends on farming. Members of families work in different businesses and are involved in different kinds of organisations, some of which are supported through Rural Development Programme measures. But they see it directly, and I fully accept that. They see it on the cheque that comes in. It is not as though it is a surprise to them. We discussed this thing fully before we did it, and we have ended up, as I say, with a large programme for rural development. We think that is for the greater good and, basically, the farmers have to be encouraged, and they are being encouraged, to get closer to the market and be more competitive.

Q907 *Lord Plumb:* It is difficult to explain it to them on Sunday mornings.
Lord Rooker: It certainly is. I find it not easy to explain when I am up a six-mile, cul-de-sac valley, where there is no end; where there are a couple of farmhouses; when they are looking at whether the offspring want to stay in farming, and what the future of the hamlet is. It is incredibly difficult. I fully accept that. I have been there. It is true, and I grieve for your difficulties on Sunday mornings—but they are nothing as compared to mine!

Q908 *Chairman:* Is not the root of the problem in the need to rely on voluntary modulation to fund a Rural Development Programme the historic low level of funding?
Lord Rooker: Yes.

Q909 *Chairman:* Is there a way of tackling that historic low-level base?
Lord Rooker: We made the case in Brussels. We have 12% of the viable land of the 15 Member States and we get 3½% of the money. I think that is the reality. However, I freely admit that there is a historical issue here of the UK—and this goes back under both governments—not paying sufficient attention to rural programmes. So when it came into Brussels and someone had the bright idea of doing this, they had to look at the historical cut-off point of what Member

States were doing and then apportion the money based on what had happened in the past. We were actually at an incredibly low level. It was in 1990, or something like that. That is a long time ago. We ought now to be saying, "Let's look at, say, even the last five years. Let's reapportion this amount of money". We would end up getting a lot more than $3\frac{1}{2}\%$.

Q910 *Chairman:* That is a live issue now.
Lord Rooker: It is a live issue, yes.

Q911 *Earl of Arran:* My Lord Chairman has already touched upon this, and I am suspicious of what the answer might be. So far, the Treasury have felt disinclined to come and talk to us about how the CAP will feature in their policy on the forthcoming EU Budget, saying that their policy was still being formulated. I suspect that is the answer you might give, Minister, but I would be interested to hear what your answer is.
Lord Rooker: I have not come here to cause problems between myself and the Treasury! The fact is that the size of the CAP as a percentage of the EU Budget is enormous, and it will be a really big issue. There is no question about that. The Treasury is in the position of formulating what the response is going to be. No decisions have been taken, and that is why the Treasury were obviously quite content for me to come here and say that rather than a Treasury minister. Your Lordships' House does not have a Treasury minister, as you know. I cannot recall whether there has ever been one, but it is not as though you have a captive member of the House who is a member of the Treasury team. I have no explanation, other than what you have had in the letter from the Economic Secretary.

Q912 *Earl of Arran:* Would you hope that, when indeed they have formulated their policy, they might come to talk to us?
Lord Rooker: I think that when people have really good policies that they are proud of, they ought to take every opportunity of coming to Parliament to boast about them. That is my view.
Chairman: Then we look forward to seeing you again, Minister!

Q913 *Earl of Dundee:* We note that you were concerned about the possible introduction of new EU risk management measures. We also know that these reservations are shared by the EU Trade Commissioner, Peter Mandelson. Why do you take this view and where do you see risks?
Lord Rooker: Our view is that farmers and those working on the land, looking after the landscape, are really businesses. Let us not put too fine a point on this. There is the odd hobby farmer, and I suppose

there are others who do not do it themselves. However, they are all businesses, and all businesses are duty-bound to take cognisance of the risks that are involved in the business they are running. I am not quite sure where the issue of risk management comes in. It could be potentially—and I only say "potentially"—another area where back-door subsidies will be the order of the day. Other businesses—non-farming, non-agricultural—have to take account of the risks of running their business, whether it is manufacturing, petrochemicals, woodworking, whatever. They are duty-bound to do that as part of running the business. We see it as no different for farms; so we are a bit suspicious of the concept of, let us say, a new scheme of risk management—because anything with the word "scheme" in usually has a pound sign or a euro sign at the end of it. In other, narrower areas, particularly in disease control, we are having discussions and have just published a consultation paper, where those who look after food production animals have to be fully aware of the risks involved in that and take account of it. We are not certain that every animal-keeper is fully aware of the risks that are involved. We know that from the recent outbreaks, frankly. Therefore, we try to bear down on making sure that companies are taking account of the risks. We do not have a great push for this. Getting insurance, I fully understand, is not easy. Crops in the ground cannot be insured. I have talked to insurance companies about insuring food animals. It is not easy; though it can be done at the margins. In terms of bearing down on managing the risks, we see that as a matter for the industry, not for Brussels to come along and impose some scheme or some regime of risk management—when other industries cope with it perfectly well, and from professional point of view as well. This is not us, by the way, saying that we are not interested or saying that it is not our responsibility. We are clearly saying it is the responsibility of the industry.

Q914 *Earl of Dundee:* On your suspicions and caveats here, how much solidarity do you expect to get from various of our EU partners, such as the German Government perhaps?
Lord Rooker: I do not know about particular governments. Maybe very little. We are trying to modernise and trying to avoid mistakes of the past. It may be, in trying to explain to some of the accession states, we say, "Actually, we did it this way in the past and it didn't work. It is best that you don't spend 20 years creating the same kinds of problems that we had with the CAP to start with". I am not certain about individual countries, however. This is something that will have to be discussed. I am just giving the UK Government's view on this: that this is one where we do not want issues brought in to distort

trade, distort competition, and to be used as a back-door method of further subsidies. Sonia can provide the German position. You asked about Germany, so something must be known about Germany.

Ms Phippard: It is simply to confirm what the Germans said at the Agriculture Council on Monday, which was that they can see that Member States might want to use Pillar II mechanisms to encourage risk management provisions where they are not there at the moment; but they are completely opposed to using Pillar I for risk management, which is where the French, for instance, are coming from.

Q915 *Chairman:* The Pillar II approach would be to help the industry set up its own mutual insurance scheme, would it not?

Ms Phippard: Yes.

Q916 *Lord Plumb:* Which Germany has at the moment. They have an insurance scheme; they have a stock insurance scheme, which started years ago.

Ms Phippard: They do in certain parts of Germany. In Bavaria, I believe.

Q917 *Viscount Ullswater:* Perhaps I could go back to your risk assessment analysis, Minister. If it is a single business, if it is your own business, you can comprehensively understand the sort of risk that you are likely to take; but sometimes you are overwhelmed by things, particularly like foot-and-mouth, which is not of your own choosing, or bluetongue, which is a new risk that I do not think people could have taken into account. Although that particular disease might not have struck you personally, it can destroy the marketplace for your animals, because of movement restrictions or whatever it is. Is there a way that the industry could be encouraged, with government's backing, to set up insurance schemes, if there is not to be any form of direct replacement values given by the Government?

Lord Rooker: In some ways that is the very issue we want to discuss with the consultation document that we put out in December on cost and responsibility-sharing. That is the very issue. There are some practical difficulties, but we are consulting on the issue and not on a policy, because we then want to formulate a policy. Europe itself is discussing these issues, particularly regarding disease in animals, to formulate a policy. But you are quite right, because I discovered during the foot-and-mouth outbreak that, where it first started, the three farmers who were first affected—the two who had foot-and-mouth and the other one where we slaughtered on suspicion—were model farmers. They were doing everything that the UK Government would expect from farmers. They had diversified; they were running other businesses; they were getting value-added. They were model farmers. One of them was even insured for

interruption of business. Unfortunately, the small print made it clear that it did not work when it was foot-and-mouth. The interruption of his business was his farm shop. If it had burnt down or a lorry had gone into it or it had been flooded, he was covered for loss of his goods and stock and interruption of the business while it was put right. Because it was foot-and-mouth, he was not covered. I think that is outrageous, in a way. It was not as though it was his animals. He may have been a farmer and not affected; he could have been the next-door farmer. That is the very issue that we want to discuss with the consultation on cost and responsibility-sharing. Only about 15% of animal and crop farmers in the UK carry any kind of insurance, some of which is there only to top up—in other words, it is fixed in with the government compensation for slaughter of animals. Obviously we pay compensation where we slaughter compulsorily. Bluetongue is a different issue. The issue of bluetongue for later this year, which we fully expect to come back, will be serious. Once we classed bluetongue as being there, we did not slaughter. Because we do not slaughter, we do not compensate. That is a thorny issue, and we are in ongoing discussions with the industry regarding bluetongue over this very issue of what farmers do. I was at a farm in Lincolnshire post-floods, to have a look at the consequence of flooding. The destruction of the crop in the fields was terrible to see. One of the farmers had an ancillary business of potatoes. He had a large factory, preparing, scrubbing and washing, and all kinds of things. As he said, if his factory had been struck by lightning or had burnt down, he was fully insured; all his risks were covered for that. The crop in the field—nobody will insure him for that. He wanted to cover the risk but could not; there is no mechanism for that. As you can well appreciate, the cost of disease control can be enormous. This is something we have to discuss with the industry, therefore. That is what we are doing now. It is a narrow part of it, in terms of animals; but, with climate change, new diseases coming and, I might say, endemic diseases—we still have the issue of bovine TB—with the exotic diseases, where we have different policies for operating, we want to share the risks and the responsibility with animal-keepers. That work is ongoing now, quite separate to the health check, quite separate to this analysis. However, our experience will form part of our discussions in Brussels, as and when a proposal has come forward from the Commission.

Q918 *Lord Palmer:* Before we leave risk, you would accept, would you not, that farming is completely different to any other sort of business when it comes to risk, in that you have this problem of the weather? For a purely arable farmer, the right weather at the right time can make an entire difference in yield—

which, particularly with wheat at £160 a tonne, can mean an enormous amount of money. You would accept that, would you not?

Lord Rooker: I accept that agriculture is different to many other businesses and industries. When you have a factory that is stable in one location—goods in and goods out, people turning up at the same place—it is also quite different to, let us say, the construction industry, where you have a peripatetic workforce and you never know where you will be working. There are differences there. The weather affects a lot of businesses. It is difficult to mitigate it because the landscape is not covered, for a start. I have met farmers who quite rightly say to me, "Jeff, we expect this land to flood in the winter. We take account of it with what crop we put on there. We are now in the middle of July and it is under three feet of water. We don't normally expect it to flood in the growing season. This is a bit of a problem for us, you must appreciate"—and I certainly do. Because in this country the primary producers do not, as in other countries, have a big enough stake in the rest of the chain—by co-operative marketing and advance preparation—they are extremely vulnerable, both to the weather and also to the market. We have seen that in the summer. To that extent, I do accept that it is completely different to any other industry, yes.

Q919 *Lord Palmer:* Could you expand on your reservations about capping? Do you think in reality that these proposals will continue, bearing in mind the strong opposition that they face, not only from our own Government but also from the German Government?

Lord Rooker: We are very opposed to upper limits. All that will happen—and we are beginning to see this anyway in the threat of capping of the single farm payment—is that people will spend money on lawyers, dividing up their businesses. For some it will be very difficult. I do not want to go into individual details but, for the largest farmer in the country, it is almost impossible but not completely out of bounds, and actions are being taken. This is not a good use of resources. It is barmy. We are opposed to it, and therefore we hope that it will not see the light of day. I have not come with a figure of the distribution. There are some incredibly large payments. Everybody knows; the figures are all published anyway. The largest recipient of the single farm payment is the Co-op—the largest farmer in the country, almost by definition. There are very few large ones. There is a big bloc in the middle and, of course, there is this huge tail. We are certainly opposed to capping at the upper limit but we certainly want to have a bigger *de minimis* at the lower level, if you like—to chop out a few tens of thousands of recipients, which I consider to be a complete and absolute waste of money, of resources of my department, in the structures that we have had to set up to make those payments. Hopefully, the penny will drop that simply capping will not have the effect that those who propose it may think. All it will do is cause land parcels to be divided up; and the only people gaining out of that, as far as I can tell, will be the lawyers, preparing the necessary documentation.

Chairman: It may now be an appropriate time to move into a more off-the-record, informal session, Minister.

Written Evidence

Memorandum by the Agricultural Law Association

This is the response of the Agricultural Law Association to the Committee's Call for Evidence published on 30th April 2007 in respect of its inquiry into the future policy direction of the Common Agricultural Policy (CAP).

ALA is the UK's premier independent cross-disciplinary organisation dealing on an agenda-free, non-partisan, non-political basis with all matters arising in connection with rural business. Our membership of over 1,000 across the UK includes solicitors, barristers, surveyors, valuers, accountants and other professionals, whose common characteristic is a commitment to rural affairs and the rural community.

The CAP is, by definition, at the core of the business of ALA and our Members and we are pleased to have this opportunity to contribute to the debate.

We retain the Committee's headings for ease of reference.

OVERVIEW

The legal starting point for any discussion of the CAP is Art 33 of the Treaty, whose objects, paraphrased, are:

— to increase agricultural productivity by technical progress and optimum use of the factors of production, and thus to ensure a fair standard of living for the agricultural community;

— to stabilise markets, assure stability of supplies and to ensure that those supplies reach consumers at reasonable prices.

Those objects were fixed in 1957. There are those who say that the modern rural world fits uncomfortably with agricultural drivers of that era and they would be correct. However, if one changes the emphasis of "agriculture" from "farming" to "rural business", the objectives still have much merit.

For example, previously, increases of production of agricultural products might have been obtained through intensification; nowadays, increases of economic prosperity—production of another sort—in rural communities may be obtained through encouragement of diversification. Support for the standard of living of those communities is increasingly provided through funding of rural business projects rather than direct market support, and so-called public goods—in short, a clean and attractive countryside—are encouraged through the various agri-environment schemes.

We support the trend away from market support and towards the development of rural business in the wider sense. However, there are two other issues of present times which the policy ought to look to protect—food security and energy security.

In our view, there was an opportunity lost, in the formulation of the Treaty for a European Constitution, to revisit Art 33 and Title II in general. However, even if that opportunity cannot be regained, there is enough in the current legal requirements for the policy to support the current public agenda for a policy providing an adequate supply of affordable food and a pollution-free environment, which includes measures necessary to manage the effects of climate change. The emphasis must be on changing the substance of the Policy; a change of label by comparison is decoration.

THE REFORMED CAP

The Single Payment Scheme (SPS) has the capability to be a smooth, elegant and streamlined mechanism for the support of rural business. The Reports of the House of Commons EFRA Committee of 21 March 2007 and of the National Audit Office dated 18 October 2006 have dealt with the shortcomings of the process of implementation in England and we shall not comment further.

However, in terms of the reform on an EU-wide basis, the present system results in anything but a common policy. The system proposed by the Commission in 2003 involved a fully decoupled single payment calculated on the basis of a historical reference period or of area, at the option of the Member State. What resulted from the Council agreement of June 2003 was a hotch-potch of historical, area and hybrid systems, partial decoupling and national envelopes, which mean that farmers across the EU are not competing on the same basis. Any environment in which one producer receives production subsidy at a greater rate than another will lead to unfairness.

Indications are that those who campaigned for derogations are not taking advantage of them. Had that been so, one might have expected to see around 50% of payments remaining decoupled to some extent; in reality, according to the figures published in Regulation 1156/2006, that applies to only just over 10%, and that mainly in France and Spain. We suggest that the system, if it is to continue, should become fully decoupled and those derogations should be abandoned.

The overriding objective should be to ensure that the same framework applies across the Union, with only such limited local discretion as is justifiable on the basis of geographical, climactic or economic conditions.

SINGLE PAYMENT SCHEME

Much of what we have to say is covered above. In general, the foundations of the scheme are sound. However, it should be implemented as simply and with as light an administrative touch as possible, subject only to those measures necessary for the authorities to comply with their obligations to the EAFRD. The difficulties being experienced in England arise not from the scheme itself but from the vertiginous complexity of the chosen method of implementation and the overbearing and inconsiderate way in which it is administered, to the detriment of the scheme's beneficiaries.

There is much that could be said about the attitude of compliance officers, which ignores the fact that, for the vast majority of farmers, their farm is their livelihood and they do not therefore deliberately devalue it by neglect. A starting premise of "good farm/bad farm", with a tolerance permitted where the overall standard is good and a more rational approach to the application of reductions, would be a more acceptable method of proceeding. However, we accept that technical discussion of those issues is outwith the scope of this inquiry.

The fundamental concept of paying farmers to comply with Statutory Management Requirements and keeping land in good agricultural and environmental condition is sound. However, a decoupled system must be allowed to function in free market conditions, and, both as a matter of policy and of enforcement, cross compliance should not be a barrier to that.

MARKET MECHANISMS

The concept of the SPS proposed by the Commission, as indicated above, involved full decoupling of support from production. Farmers were to be allowed access to a free market and were to be expected to operate and develop their businesses accordingly. We have said that coupled support should be withdrawn; so should all production control measures.

Intervention buying, private storage aid and export refunds distort the market. What were designed as safety nets have been so ingrained into consciousness that some now perceive them as a legitimate outlet for produce. Yet they have no place in a decoupled system. The provisional agreement to abolish export refunds by 2013 should inspire their reduction to nil by that date.

Similar comments apply to set-aside. It is unreasonable to expect farmers to respond effectively to market conditions and at the same time to require them to take part of their production capacity out of service regardless of the market. We are aware there are those who have suggested the retention of set-aside on the grounds that it has had a beneficial effect on wildlife and that its abolition would be detrimental to it. With respect, we do not consider that the mechanism of set-aside is the correct vehicle to deal with that issue. If it is accepted as policy to encourage wildlife and biodiversity, it should be achieved by encouraging farmers, through agri-environment and similar schemes, to take land out of production, not by penalising them for putting it into production.

We take the view that all of the above—intervention, PSA, export refunds, set-aside—together with milk quotas, which fall into the same category and have no longer any useful function, should be abolished as soon as possible. Allowance may have to be given for a phasing out period (or, in the case of milk quotas, for the fact that they are by regulation in place until 2015) but that should not detract from the need for abolition.

RURAL DEVELOPMENT

The public consciousness more easily accepts the support of rural businessmen from the public purse for the delivery of a clean and attractive countryside than it does for product and income support. This drift has been apparent at political level also in the discussions in Council over several years.

We view the distinction between what are presently known as Pillar 1 (market support) and Pillar 2 (rural development) to be unhelpful, since it presents them as alternatives to one another rather than as parts of a composite whole that is the CAP. However, we will continue to use those terms since they are most readily understood.

The balance between Pillar 1 and Pillar 2 must be resolved. The financing arrangements are presently muddled. The introduction of the EAFRD was a positive move, providing a common fund from which all payments may come.

However, the fixing of Pillar 1 payments under the budgetary accord of 2002 has led to Pillar 2 suffering the full weight of budgetary cuts in 2006. Modulation is an artificial mechanism to restore the balance, although it does so to nothing like the required extent; it should not be necessary in circumstances where the Member States can freely make a decision on the balance of funding. It is to be hoped that in the budget discussions of 2008/09 this can be addressed.

Voluntary modulation is emphatically not the solution. It distorts the market and militates against the commonality of the CAP, which should be applied in as uniform a way as possible across the whole Union. To have a situation where different rates of modulation apply in different Member States—and even in different regions of the same Member State, viz UK—puts farmers at a competitive disadvantage with their counterparts in other Member States. Worse, in this country, they are disadvantaged as between themselves. That is counterproductive.

Access to rural development funding in England should be simplified. Under the former RDP, the conditions required to be fulfilled before an application for certain grants—eg Processing and Marketing or Rural Enterprise Scheme—could be entertained were time-consuming and expensive. Whilst it is, of course, quite reasonable to expect a rural businessman to be prepared to invest time and money in his project, many saw that as an unacceptable gamble and, as a result, many perfectly good schemes to improve the lot of both the businessman and his community did not get off the ground. It is to be hoped that mistake will not be repeated in the next RDP.

Attention should also be given to a greater uniformity of approach across the regions of England. It is reasonable, of course, that each region should have a discretion to apply those elements of policy best suited to its circumstances, but the service received from RDAs and Rural Hubs depends too much on the ability and enthusiasm of the persons involved and not enough on common standards and shared experiences. There should be greater inter-region communication and exchange of ideas.

WORLD TRADE

Development of the CAP is irrevocably bound in with the development of WTO's international rules of governance. The pressure to ensure a fair competitive environment for all nations is bound to influence policy development at a supra-national level.

The greatest single benefit that will ensue, in our view, is the independence of rural businessmen to make those decisions best suited to their place in the market. The resultant restructuring is bound to have consequences: for example, less productive areas will be vulnerable to abandonment; food production may become concentrated upon fewer but larger farms. It is the moral duty of any community to mitigate so far as possible the impacts of such changes and this can be achieved through the CAP with proper focus of funding, eg the use of retirement support for those leaving the industry.

ENVIRONMENTAL PROTECTION AND CLIMATE CHANGE

We doubt that cross compliance has made any contribution to improvements in the level of environmental protection. Cross compliance does no more than increase the penalty for non-compliance with pre-existing legal requirements by reducing the transgressor's level of single farm payment. It is the underlying legislation that improves environmental protection, not cross compliance.

It is important to maintain a proper perspective on climate change. Climate change is a reality and under the control of the planet, not of mankind. The behaviour of man may have influenced its degree and may assist in its management, but to suggest that even global, still less local, policy can somehow prevent or control it is hubris. The focus must be on managing its effects, for example helping farmers cope with changes in weather systems, crop types and growing cycles to ensure adequate food supply.

Biofuels provide one tool in the management of climate change—they are not a cure-all; they may not even be the best alternative to fossil fuels. If growers are to be left to the market, they will produce biofuels according to demand. If, as a policy decision, greater production of biofuels is required, that may entail interference with the market to achieve the result. CAP might be used to that end to provide the necessary financial incentives. Such a move, however, would go against the prevailing trend to reduce market interference.

A balance must be struck between food and energy security, both of which have implications wider than the CAP. Both are necessary, but finite availability of land and competition for its use, amongst other issues, will influence how far policy can and should go to regulate either.

Whilst reduction of output of greenhouse gases—not merely CO_2—is important, it must be integrated with proper management of the land and the ability of the Union to feed its citizens. In that connection, we believe that too much credit is given for the ability to import foodstuffs in the assessment of the Union's food security. The guiding principle in judging the contribution of imports ought to be the carbon footprint of doing so as opposed to producing at home. Account should also be taken of the effect on the ability to import of potential reductions in availability of transport fuels at economic prices.

FINANCING

Any policy will benefit from further funding provided such funding is properly applied. As indicated above, we believe the greatest difficulty to be in the mismatch between the stated political rhetoric in respect of wider application of funding to rural communities and the actual budgetary agreement which restricts the width of that application in favour of outdated and outmoded support measures. For that reason, as much as for its overall level of funding allocation, we agree that the December 2005 agreement was unsatisfactory.

ENLARGEMENT

Simplistically, enlargement has altered the cohesion balance between Member States and therefore the position of the EU-15 in relation to the average of the EU–25/27. This has led to a redistribution of funds amongst Member States and can be expected to lead to further redistributions in future.

SIMPLIFICATION AND OTHER ISSUES

The Commission's current proposal to amalgamate 21 common market organisations into one is an example of what can be achieved in terms of operational, or technical, simplification. The introduction of the Single Payment Scheme—in spite of the disasters that have befallen our country by reason of maladministration—is an example of the same philosophy in action in a political sense.

However, there is a danger—which applies in every policy area and not just to the CAP—that constant tinkering with the rules of engagement leads to an inability properly to assess the performance of the policy in the medium to long term.

What is needed above all else at the present time is a period of stability. We have just witnessed, and have still to come to terms with, the most radical reform of the CAP in its 50-year history. Time must be given for that reform properly to establish itself and for its effect on the market and on rural communities to be properly assessed before further significant changes are contemplated.

The so-called Health Check in 2008 provides an opportunity, in effect, to complete the 2003 reforms by doing what should have been done at that time—the various measures which we have mentioned in this response. It should emphatically not be used as a platform for further upheaval.

The House of Commons EFRA Committee, in its report of 16th May, suggested that the government should "grasp the fresh opportunity presented by the CAP 'health checks' and make it the time for the UK to direct the debate towards scrapping the existing CAP and replacing it with a 'Rural Policy for the European Union'". We see that as being in keeping with the application of a sledgehammer to a nut and we do not, for reasons which will be clear from the above comments, believe that it will be remotely necessary.

We will be pleased to offer further assistance to the Committee should it be asked of us.

11 June 2007

Memorandum by the Australian Government

INTRODUCTION

1. Australia has a deep interest in the evolution of the European Union (EU), especially its Common Agricultural Policy (CAP). We welcome the reforms that have taken place in the way production linked payments and market interventions, such as export subsidies, are being progressively eliminated. While these market orientated reforms will inevitably bring about positive change, a notable and significant gap in the reforms to date has been a failure to adequately integrate European agriculture into the increasingly globalised market for food and agricultural products. The forthcoming CAP "Health Check Review", the Financial Perspectives Review and the Doha Round provide the opportunity to enhance the competitiveness of European agriculture, reduce long term dependency on farm income support, and to build long term sustainability.

2. Australia readily acknowledges that the shift away from production linked farm payments is a significant positive step forward in European agricultural policy. A key concern remains with the quantum of payments delivered to European farmers that acts to distort agricultural production through risk and wealth effects. These distortionary effects are exacerbated by tying of farm payments to land units (thereby capitalising the payments into land values), and where payments are constrained to certain agricultural activities and/or there are limited alternative agricultural land enterprises. In view of these distortionary effects, we would therefore encourage a shift from income support payments to policy aimed at promoting innovation, capacity building and sustainable rural development, such as that envisaged under Pillar Two of the CAP.

3. At the same time, CAP reform to date has not resulted in any substantial change to market access barriers—even though these barriers constitute a form of producer support through the maintenance of higher than normal price levels. In Australia's case, with the exception of wine and some comparatively minor access for a small number of other agricultural products, this means Australian products are effectively locked out of the European market. As with other forms of producer support however, a policy of restricting market access leads directly to higher producer and consumer costs. For producers, these costs accrue though delayed or distorted investment decisions, while for consumers, higher food costs prevail.

4. In contrast, the Australian experience has shown that reducing support measures (including tariff protection) has produced a highly efficient and equitable farming sector (over 95% of farms in Australia are family owned) and an agricultural sector able to adapt to changing markets and to resist major shocks, such as periods of droughts and depressed prices. Australian farmers now compete effectively in the market place without the need for costly and inefficient support measures.

5. The policy experiences of the Australian agricultural sector are therefore directly relevant to the European sector. In particular, Australian experience has shown that, by providing an environment wherein competition is encouraged (through more open markets and reduced support measures), farmers will adjust their farm businesses to suit the market by adopting new farming practices, changing product mixes and generally seeking new ways to meet changing consumer demands. Australian government policy has sought to facilitate the shift to this market orientated environment through programmes that promote business adjustment, capacity building, innovation, while, at the same time, eliminating market management measures and tariff barriers to imported product. The Australian dairy industry provides a tangible example of this approach having seen the industry move from a highly supported and regulatory constrained sector to a sector now fully deregulated and exposed to the international trading environment. This has seen, despite the presence of persistent drought, the growth in the Australian dairy industry to the point where it is now a major influence on world dairy markets.

LEVELS OF AGRICULTURAL SUPPORT

6. Levels of EU agricultural support have changed little since the late 1980s (figure 1). The EU has been making positive changes in its agricultural support policies through changing away from price support toward less market distorting decoupled payments, and limiting budgetary expenditure on agriculture. It has been willing to change forms of support for its agriculture but it has done little to reduce levels of support. Figure 1 also shows that EU support levels are higher than the OECD average.

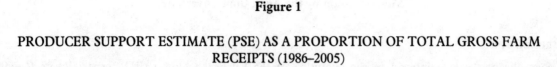

Figure 1

PRODUCER SUPPORT ESTIMATE (PSE) AS A PROPORTION OF TOTAL GROSS FARM
RECEIPTS (1986–2005)

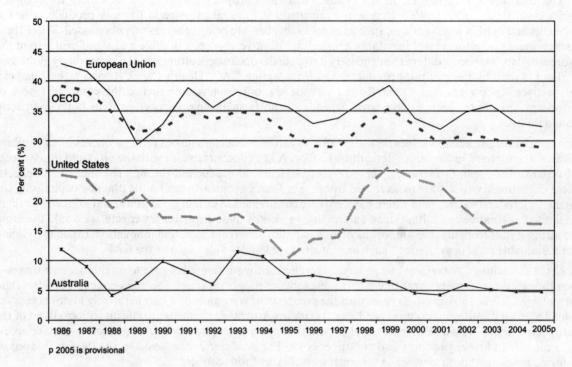

p 2005 is provisional

Source: OECD 2006.

STRENGTHS AND WEAKNESSES OF DECOUPLED PAYMENTS

7. The EU has retained substantial levels of support and protection through tariffs and tariff quotas while member states have also retained some coupled payments. It has framed the rationale for changing toward decoupled payments in terms of decoupled support being minimally market distorting, as is stated in the Uruguay Round Agreement on Agriculture. If the payments are truly decoupled in an economic sense, they should have the same impacts on production, consumption and trade as would the complete removal of the payments.

8. The extent to which the changes actually reduce market distortions depends critically on whether the decoupled payments are in fact minimally market distorting, not just considered to be; the level of support provided and the effects of other forms of support. To be minimally distorting to production, consumption, trade and prices, changing from current coupled payments or price support to decoupled support should be almost identical in its effects to complete removal of the coupled payments. Changing from highly distorting price support toward decoupled payments reduces market distortions because prices faced by consumers are closer to world prices. Because of this the EU change toward decoupled payments along with lower price support means less market distortion than maintaining the same levels of price support.

9. There are many reasons however why changing to decoupled payments reduces production distortions by far less than eliminating the support. These include:

— income and wealth effects from the payments affect credit availability and adoption of technology, thereby affecting production;

— the payments are being made in conjunction with forms of clearly distorting support, including tariffs and tariff quotas that affect prices and mean that even if the payments themselves were properly decoupled, the support system would still distort market prices, production, consumption and trade;

— expectations by producers that payment bases and/or rates can be changed by current planting or production decisions and political pressure can affect current production decisions. The EU Single Payment Scheme (SPS) may reduce but not eliminate this factor;

— importantly, ongoing payments enable producers to continue to produce products that have been revealed as their preferred products without the costs or risks of making substantial changes that would be required in the absence of support. As such they lock in existing production patterns and levels—levels that have been highly distorted by decades of production stimulating support arrangements;

— the payments support agricultural land prices. The higher prices help maintain land in agriculture rather than have it transfer to non-agricultural uses. They also make it more difficult for new farmers to enter the agricultural sector; and

— whole farm payments such as the SPS are a subsidy to farming and farmers. As such they are likely to maintain resources in farming that would flow to non-farm activities if that subsidy were removed.

10. Because of these factors, the economic benefits from changing from coupled to decoupled payments are likely to be overstated, with the change to decoupled payments being only a partial substitute for reducing levels of support.

11. Overall, the EU is making progress toward an agriculture that is less costly to its economy and less distorting to world markets than the very distorting, open-ended price support policies that formerly applied. However support levels remain high and many remain considerably market distorting. The move to decoupling is helping reduce distortions but can only go part of the way. There are several areas where distortions could be reduced further, especially through reducing tariffs and other barriers to market access.

REORIENTATION OF SUPPORT MORE TOWARD RURAL DEVELOPMENT

12. Until recently about 90% of EU budget outlays for agriculture have been from Pillar One of the CAP. The remaining 10% has been under Pillar Two that covers rural development expenditure.

13. The extent to which such investment is well spent in rural development depends on the returns obtained, both in terms of profitability of activities and social outcomes relative to such returns from alternatives. If modulation results in reduced direct support for agricultural production and helps remove obstacles to rural adjustment it should help reduce market distortions arising from support. However, market distortions may be perpetuated if projects for rural development amount to little more than state financing of activities for private profit. Examples could be government financing of pollution abatement by farmers where to obtain efficient outcomes the costs should be internalised under the "producer pays" principle, or state provision or subsidisation of improved planting material which would be effectively a production subsidy.

14. Australia supports the European Commission's (EC) move to create a single instrument to finance the rural development policy: the European Agricultural Fund for Rural Development (EAFRD). Australia encourages the EC to shift Pillar One spending to the EAFRD (Pillar Two). The objectives of the EAFRD align closely with the objectives of the Agriculture Advancing Australia (AAA) package. The AAA package is an integrated package of Australian Government programmes that help primary producers in agriculture, fishing and forestry be more competitive, sustainable and profitable.

15. A project administered under the AAA package may provide:

— funding for business and natural resource management training and education;

— support for industries undergoing change;

— financial management tools;

— financial information and referral;

— funding for professional advice, skills development and training;

— assistance for farm families in serious financial difficulty; or

— improved access to markets.

16. Projects under the AAA programme allow industries to identify challenges and opportunities, and address them by developing and implementing industry-led strategies. Australia has seen the positive results these programmes deliver to rural communities, while not distorting trade. It is for these reasons Australia supports EC instruments such as the EARFD and encourages the EC to shift funding from direct support towards rural development programmes.

AUSTRALIAN REFORM EXPERIENCE

17. Australia's agricultural sector was never highly protected, but it was more structured and burdened by statutory regulation throughout the 1970s and early 1980s. This resulted in many industries experiencing poor export performance and high costs of production, effectively burdening producers and consumers alike.

18. There have been significant structural and macroeconomic reforms in Australia since the 1980s, for example, the floating of the exchange rate in the early 1980s. These reforms have been aimed at reducing, or removing, distortions to competition in order to improve the functioning and flexibility of markets. The resulting rise in Australia's productivity and improved competitiveness in world markets has enabled real GDP to grow at an average annual rate of about 3.5% during the past 15 years, which has raised per capita income to 8th place among OECD countries. Reform has also made the economy more flexible and resilient to external shocks, like the Asian Financial Crisis in the late 1990s and, more recently, the drought.

19. Australian farmers now compete and win in the market place. There may well be lessons for European countries in the processes Australia has been through over the last two decades to reduce regulation successfully and remain competitive in the world market.

20. The Australian dairy industry provides an example of agriculture's response to structural change following the removal of price-distorting support. The removal of regulated support policies and the introduction of competition have led to positive industry adjustment and expansion. The Australian experience has shown that farmers, given clear market signals, can adjust well to the removal of market support mechanisms. Despite preliminary concerns among some advisors that deregulation would result in widespread and permanent reductions in income and in industry contraction, this was by no means an observed impact.

21. The Australian dairy industry went through a 15-year deregulation process, beginning in 1986. Policy reforms by the Australian Government during the late 1980s and the 1990s largely deregulated the manufacturing segment of the industry. These reforms led to a build-up of pressures within the dairy industry during the late 1990s for the complete removal of all remaining manufacturing and fluid milk price supports at federal and state levels. The industry, recognising the pressures for this final step in deregulation, took a reform proposal to the Australian Government. It then worked cooperatively with the Government to develop a restructure package that gave dairy farmers the opportunity to adjust over time to a completely deregulated market place.

22. This reform package, which did not substantively increase the overall level of assistance to Australian agriculture, saw all existing price supports for dairy products removed on 1 July 2000. The package provided an eight-year stream of direct payments to farmers, based on historical production but unrelated to current or future production levels.

23. Since the reform, farmers in Australia have used the adjustment assistance to restructure their operations and improve their productivity to offset the loss of price support. Some farmers used the payments to effectively invest off-farm and, in some cases, to withdraw from agriculture altogether.

24. The impacts of deregulation have varied between dairy enterprises and regions. Many farmers reacted to the change in the market environment by increasing their farm output. They expanded herds and changed the way they used secondary inputs such as feed. More efficient use of pastures, fertilisers and irrigation increased farm-carrying capacity, enabling farmers to utilise land more intensively in the production mix. Overall, since deregulation, dairy production in Australia has moved towards more efficient dairying options, with more effective pasture and supplementary feeding management contributing to improved productivity across the entire dairy sector.

25. Dairy farm numbers have almost halved in the last 20 years—a period that included deregulation. Milk production however, has doubled and the value of exports has increased from $A331 million in 1983 to $A2.42 billion in 2005.

Conclusions

26. New European agricultural policy moving towards increased use of Pillar Two mechanisms (such as EAFRD) will lead to European farmers being increasingly competitive in international markets. The positive experiences of other nations reflect possibilities for EU farmers, as shown by the success of the Australian export-focused dairy industry and Australia's AAA programme. The EU is well placed to show leadership by removing trade distortionary expenditure to the benefit of its farm sector and the global market.

27. Overall, Australia welcomes EU progress toward an agriculture that is less costly to its economy and less distorting to world markets. Support levels remain high however and many remain considerably market distorting. The move to decoupling is helping reduce distortions but can only go part of the way. There are several areas where distortions could be reduced further, especially through reducing tariffs and other barriers to market access.

28. True reform cannot be undertaken with continuing high tariffs and interventionist policy. In order to be globally competitive, the regulatory burden must be reduced and policies must encourage self-reliance. The factors contributing to the success of Australian agriculture, through self-determination, capacity building and adjustment assistance are equally applicable to the European situation.

FURTHER REFERENCES

The following reference materials are included for further information:

Harris, David. Australian dairy market deregulation: *Coping with policy change*. 2006.

Rural Industries Research and Development Corporation. *Coping with change—farm level adjustment and policy reform*. 2006.

Australian Government information brochures:

— *Farm Success without production subsidies*;

— *Helping farmers through exceptional circumstances*;

— *Dairy reform: Creating a profitable, export-oriented dairy industry*; and

— *Managing Risk: Australia's farm management deposits scheme*.

15 June 2007

Memorandum by Berkley Hill, Professor Emeritus of Policy Analysis, University of London (Imperial College London)

This communication relates to only selected Issues identified in Call for Evidence, issued 30 April, 2007. It is submitted in a private capacity.

ISSUE ONE—OVERVIEW

What should be the long term objectives of the CAP? Does the title "Common Agricultural Policy" aptly fit your perceived objectives of the policy? What do you consider to be the main pressures on the CAP as it currently is?

1. The official objectives of the CAP, as agreed by EU15 Member States, are set out in Agenda 2000 in a list that was developed from the objectives appearing in Article 39 of the 1957 Treaty of Rome and which, in effect, replace those of the Treaty. *The Agenda 2000* formulation was as follows:

— increase competitiveness internally and externally in order to ensure that Union producers take full advantage of positive world market developments;

— food safety and food quality, which are both fundamental obligations towards consumers;

— ensuring a fair standard of living for the agricultural community and contributing to the stability of farm incomes;

— the integration of environmental goals into the CAP;

— promotion of sustainable agriculture;

— the creation of alternative job and income opportunities for farmers and their families; and

— simplification of Union legislation.

2. Commentators have concluded that, in practice, the aim of ensuring a fair standard of living (the "income objective") of the CAP has dominated spending under the CAP.[1] Even after modulation, Pillar One (which supports income, primarily now in the form of the Single Farm Payment) is still about four times larger than Pillar Two (which includes agri-environment, less-favoured area and other rural development spending).

---

[1] See review in: Hill, B, (2000) *Farm Incomes, Wealth and Agricultural Policy*, 3rd Edition. Aldershot; Avebury. ISBN 0-7546-1132-9. 375 pp.

3. Despite its prominence, the "income objective" has never been set out clearly, for example by defining what is meant by a fair standard of living, or who forms the agricultural community (a conclusion supported in a 2004 report by the EU Court of Auditors).[2] Furthermore, CAP decision makers have never had access to statistical evidence on the household incomes of farm operators and other indicators of living standards in a form that would enable them to assess the number and location of those whose living standards were less than "fair". Only in 2007 has Eurostat commissioned a feasibility study of how this sort of information could be made available (a study in which the writer was part of the research team).[3] Only when such information is to hand could the CAP focus on the cases most in need.

4. At present Pillar One support is given to farm operators and their families in a blanket way, related primarily to past levels of production and subsidy. The OECD[4] (and others) have concluded that this represents a very inefficient use of public funds, most support going to farms whose operators have levels of income and wealth that compare very favourably with those of the rest of society.

5. The majority of farm operators have incomes that include rewards from non-farm activities; this takes many forms but the most significant is income from off-farm jobs and businesses. Diversification is a long-established feature of European agriculture, and many small farms would be unviable without it.

6. Given that economic and technical pressures will continue, changes in the structure of agriculture are inevitable. Rather than cushion agricultural producers from these pressures (which is the approach of Pillar One), the long-term and sustainable objective of policy should be to enable them to adapt in a way that produces an industry that is competitive and yet at the same time meets the environmental and social aims of society. This will need a further reform of the CAP in the direction started in the 2003 Mid-term Review, with the phasing out of Pillar One support (including the Single Farm Payment).

7. A recent review of historical situations in which farmers have been subject to policy reforms[5] suggests adjustment is part of normal practice, and it is easy to underestimate the ability of farm families to make changes to their businesses (such as by shifting balance between enterprises or reduce inputs). Where more radical steps are needed, such as changes in farm sizes or setting up a diversified activity, these are facilitated by two factors; first, a working land market (in owner-occupied and/or rented land) that enables transfers to take place between those wanting more land and those wishing to release it and, second, an adequately educated and trained labour force (including the self-employed). Of course, in some circumstances there may be environmental or social reasons why changes in current practice should be prevented (for example, to maintain present land-uses for landscape reasons). However, it is easy to make ill-founded assumptions, for example that conserving the appearance of the countryside is dependent on keeping the existing number and sizes of farms, whereas the key factor is more likely to be the type of farming system employed.

8. In short, the aims of the CAP should be to facilitate the development of an industry that is competitive and innovative. This is likely to lead to further reductions in the numbers of people who depend primarily on farming for their livelihood, though the development of pluriactivity will mean that in many parts of the EU families will continue to live on farms and form part of the rural community. At the same time measures must be in place to protect the environmental features that society wishes to conserve, using agriculture as a vehicle where this is appropriate.

9. ISSUE 3—THE SINGLE FARM PAYMENT

10. Various factors suggest that The Single Farm Payment is not a sustainable instrument of the CAP. These include the following:

— *Lack of economic rationale.* The direct payments introduced as part of the 1992 MacSharry CAP reforms were a compensation for the reduction of market support and a political expedient to achieve those reforms. The SFP is a reformulation of this compensation, not directly related to present production levels but linked to the occupation of land. With the passage of time the equity (compensation) and political economy (facilitating CAP reform) justifications recede into history. Beyond this, there is very little, if any, economic rationale for the continuation of the SFP as part of EU policy towards agriculture.

[2] Court of Auditors (2004) Special Report on the measurement of farm incomes by the Commission Article 33(1)(b) of the EC Treaty, together with the Commission's replies. 2004/C 45/01.
[3] Agra CEAS Consulting (2007) *Feasibility Study on the Implementation of Income of Agricultural Households Sector* (IAHS) Statistics, Eurostat, The Commission, Luxembourg.
[4] OECD (2002) *The incidence and transfer efficiency of farm support measures.* AGR/CA/APM(2001)24/FINAL. Paris. OECD (2003) *Farm Household Income: Issues and Policy Responses.* Organisation for Economic Co-operation and Development, Paris.
[5] Hill, B and Blandford, D, (2006). *Policy Reform and Adjustment in the Agricultural Sectors of Developed Countries.* CAB Publishing, Wallingford. ISBN 1845930339.

— *High transparency and political vulnerability.* Related to the above, the transparency with which transfers are made (direct payments) without any obvious supply of services in return from beneficiaries has already attracted media attention and makes them vulnerable to political criticism and erosion.

— *Impediment to structural change.* The link to land occupancy hampers the level of structural change compared with that to be expected if the SFP were purely a financial asset unlinked with occupancy. A case can be made that the SFP is therefore imposing an economic cost on society though, on the other hand, there may be some environmental implications of rapid transfers of land from one group of owners to others.

— *Policy prospect.* The Agriculture Commissioner has already signalled that the SFPs are unlikely to survive beyond 2013.

ISSUE 5—RURAL DEVELOPMENT—THE EUROPEAN AGRICULTURAL FUND FOR RURAL DEVELOPMENT (EAFRD), ITS OPERATION AND FOCUS ON AGRICULTURE, AND ITS CO-ORDINATION

11. The present writer has experience as an evaluator working with the England Rural Development Programme 2000–06 (carrying out the baseline study) and as part of a team considering the Welsh Rural Development Plans 2000–06 and 2007–13.[6] In theory the process by which these are drawn up allows local issues to be addressed; a SWOT analysis forms part of the process by which the European Commission approves spending in support of proposed schemes that are designed and administered are the national (or sub-national) level.

12. The complexity of the funding stream in the 2000–06 period severely handicapped the ability to assess the performance of these RDPs. For example, in Objective 1 parts of Wales certain schemes were financed from the Guidance part of the old EAGGF that in other areas were financed from Guarantee, while some were funded from other Structural Funds. Because evaluation has to be carried out linked to budgetary lines, there was no formal way in which an overall view could be taken. By bringing rural development funding under a single instrument (EAFRD), in future it should be much more straightforward to assess the performance of interventions.

13. There is little doubt that the focus on agriculture in EU policy on rural development is misplaced, though history (especially CAP reform) makes this imbalance understandable. Agriculture, as an economic activity, contributes only a very small share to total incomes and employment in most rural areas. According to the European Commission,[7] even in areas classified as Predominantly Rural at NUTS3 level in EU25 the primary sector (agriculture, forestry and fishing) only accounted for 5.5% of GVA in 2003, and was only more than 10% in four countries (Estonia, Greece, Latvia, Lithuania, and Portugal). Even in the rural parts of Wales, most of it classified as Less Favoured Areas, farming occupies less than 5% of the resident population. Thus support to agricultural development (diversification, training, marketing, modernisation etc.) is unlikely to be a suitable way of influencing the broader economy of these areas in a significant manner. A case can be made that support to other industries and sectors (such as support to village post offices, schools, other small businesses in rural areas etc) could achieve economic and social aims much more effectively and efficiently. On the other hand, farming and forestry are very important to issues that involve landscape and the natural environment. Agriculture and forestry represent 78% of land use in the EU-25, ranging from 50% in Malta to 95% in Poland.

14. Even within current agri-centric Rural Development Programmes, for the period 2000–06 there is no certainty that the balance between spending on investment in farming and forestry, in training and development of human capital, in agri-environment and support of hill farming, in organics, and in marketing improvement, has been optimal. Allocation was heavily influenced by previous commitments to agri-environmental payments, so that there was only limited ability to reflect broader needs in the RDPs. Though there was some provision for support to the broader quality of life in rural communities in the 2000–06 RDPs,

---

[6] Hill, B, (2002) with Victoria Schoen, Alan Rogers, Angela Edwards and Kate Murray, *Baseline Study for the ERDP Mid-term Evaluation*. ICON Consultants for the Department for Environment, Food and Rural Affairs, London. 97 pp plus Annexes. (Publiished on Defra website).
Agra CEAS Consultants (2003) *The Mid-term Evaluation of the Wales Rural Development Plan*. Main volume (151 pp) and 12 separate appendices. Welsh Assembly Government (available from the www.wales.gov.uk website).
Agra CEAS Consultants (2006) *Ex-Ante Evaluation of the Wales 2007–13 Rural Development Plan*. Welsh Assembly Government, Cardiff.
[7] European Commission (2006) *Rural Development in the European Union: Statistical and Economic Information*—Report 2006. DG-Agri, Brussels.

in England and Wales spending has been small (though this is not necessarily the case in all other Member States). Because of the mix of environmental and economic aims, the balance of resources has to be a matter of political judgement rather than value-for-money estimation. Programmes for the 2007–13 period have been subject to minimum spending levels for each of four Axes (including on using the LEADER-type approach towards bottom-up development), though there is no guarantee that this will give a mix that meets needs in an appropriate way.

15. Unlike Pillar One support to agriculture, public policies for rural development are a mix of EU, national and sub-national interventions. Attention in this Evidence focuses on the EU level, since this provides a consistent framework for most of the spending explicitly directed at rural areas in Member States, and national measures have to be consistent with EU policies. However, the significance of purely national interventions (land use planning, social security payments etc) to many aspects of conditions in rural areas should not be underestimated.

ISSUE 6—RURAL DEVELOPMENT—THE CASE FOR A HIGHER LEVEL OF EU FUNDING

16. It is difficult to give a categorical answer on whether a higher level of EU funding for rural development is justified. Any case for adjusting the level of EU funding for rural development must reflect the coverage of the programmes involved, which in turn depends on the provisions in the Rural Development Regulations that underpin them.

17. On the one hand, there is some evidence that more funds would enable the level of activity under the present provisions to be expanded; for example, the designs of the Welsh Rural Development Plans for 2000–06 and (especially) for 2007–13 were constrained by long-term agri-environmental commitments entered into under previous schemes, leaving relatively little available for initiatives, in particular for increasing the amount of support provided for the non-agricultural parts of the rural economy. Axis 3 within the Rural Development Regulation that covers the programming period 2007–13 provides for enhancing the quality of life in rural areas and diversification of the rural economy by measures such as support for the creation and development of micro-enterprises with a view to promoting entrepreneurship and developing the economic fabric, encouragement of tourism activities, basic services for the economy and rural population, village renewal and development, and conservation and upgrading of the rural heritage. A minimum of 10% of EU spending has to be on this Axis, though in theory it could be far higher before feeling the constraints of minimum spending on the other Axes. On the other hand, at scheme level it is clear that uptake can reach capacity (for example in diversification on farms, or afforestation possibilities), and that situations can arise where using more resources would not be effective. The possibility of absorbing more resources has to be judged on a scheme-by-scheme basis.

18. However, the list of what may be tackled under EU-supported Rural Development Programmes does not cover many of the economic and social problems found in rural areas, at least those encountered in England and Wales.[8] These are often generic and also seen in non-rural areas (deprivation of various kinds, low income and employment opportunities, lack of affordable housing, poor access to services etc). The causes of these problems are not particularly linked to the characteristics of rural areas, such as land use or low population density, though conditions there can add a particular dimension (income deprivation can be a different experience if suffered in an otherwise prosperous countryside from that in an urban area where it is a shared feature of certain communities). At a general level, economic conditions in rural areas are likely to reflect those in the country as a whole due to the close links and interdependency between all parts of the economy, conditions that in practice are outside the influence of any rural development policy.

19. Meeting the full range of economic, social and environmental needs in rural areas could only be tackled by Rural Development Programmes if the coverage of their underpinning Regulations were to be widened considerably. But the generic nature of the needs raises the issue of whether policy interventions that are unique to rural areas are appropriate (either because of their causes or because of delivery mechanism). Rather, they might be better tackled by general policies (on transport, education, health, housing, alleviation of poverty, taxation etc.) that may contain special provisions for any peculiarities of rural situations. This would leave Rural Development Programmes to concentrate largely on environmental issues, with responsibility for economic and social issues only where specifically rural dimensions were encountered, though these might well stretch beyond agriculture and forestry.

June 2007

[8] Hill, B, *et al* (2005) *The New Rural Economy—Change, Dynamism and Government Policy*. Institute of Economic Affairs, London. Evidence is taken also from Countryside Agency (2004) *The State of the Countryside 2004*. Cheltenham.

Memorandum by the Biscuit Cake Chocolate and Confectionary Association

INTRODUCTION

1. The Biscuit, Cake, Chocolate and Confectionery Association (BCCCA) represents all the leading and many smaller manufacturers of biscuits, cakes, chocolate and confectionery in the UK. In all, the Association represents more than 70 British businesses. The sector as a whole employs some 56,000 people (though this number is falling—see below) and has annual consumer sales of around £7 billion.

2. We have used the "specific issues" headings in the call for evidence, dated 30 April 2007.

OVERVIEW

3. We support the objectives of the 2003 reform of the CAP:
   — to promote more market orientated and sustainable agriculture;
   — to strengthen rural development; and
   — to enhance the competitiveness of EU agriculture.

4. We continue to favour supply driven by demand; the shift from product to producer support through decoupled single farm payments; and clear rules regarding environment, animal welfare and food safety in accordance with consumers' expectations for a sustainable model for agriculture.

5. With regard to rural development, the strengthening of Pillar 2 (Rural Development) has reinforced EU credibility in the context of WTO negotiations. Premiums for farmers who commit themselves to quality assurance programmes and to meeting standards (for environment; public, animal and plant health; animal welfare; occupational safety) are very useful in the promotion of a new culture of consumers' expectations.

6. We support the scaling back of intervention measures in the general drive for competitiveness of EU agriculture. The intervention price must be seen as a safety net to be used exceptionally and should not cover the full cost nor ensure a profit margin; its clear role is to prevent a complete loss.

THE REFORMED CAP

7. Our experience of the reformed CAP has been mixed, but overall generally disappointing.

8. Dairy reform was not sufficiently radical in that the support price reduction programme was too little and too slow, whereas the possible phase-out of quotas has been far too long.

9. The sugar reform package, although not part of the 2003 CAP reform package, has proved disappointing since its adoption in July 2006. The most significant obstacle to competition has been the retention of national quotas, whereas the attempts to reduce the hugely over-supplied domestic market have failed through the implementation of an insufficiently rigorous restructuring programme, compounded by preventive withdrawals of quota which merely exacerbate existing impediments to a competitive supply chain.

10. Measures to reform the cereals CMO were initially successful, but latterly the Commission has hindered the good work by allowing "biofuels policy" to intrude. For example, a proposal last year by the Commission to authorise the sale of cereals intervention stocks to the biofuels industry at prices significantly discounted to market prices for cereals raised a potential huge problem for cereals users such as our sector. Fortunately, the Commission has only passed enabling legislation and will not allow such sales without significant justification. However, this is a prime example of how the Commission is allowing the in vogue attraction of biofuels to impact on the availability of raw materials for the food manufacturing sector.

MARKET MECHANISMS

11. The European Commission has long employed market mechanisms so as to manage the various CAP commodity regimes, but with only limited success.

12. Quotas must be abolished as soon as possible in that they distort markets and the supply chain. Real market forces mean that prices will find their true level, but quotas prevent this from happening.

13. Intervention is no longer necessary, but if retained, stocks must be available to principal users, who have been subject to the regime's support price levels eg the food industry before being released (often at discounted prices) to the non-food industry eg chemicals and biofuels.

14. The requirement for set-aside is no longer appropriate, given the increased demand for agricultural land triggered by the promotion of biofuels.

15. The EU has already called time within the context of the WTO Doha agriculture negotiations on export refunds, but they must be retained so long as differentials exist between EU and world raw material prices. They are essential to allowing the EU food manufacturing industry to remain competitive in third country export markets. However, export refunds should only be preserved to bridge the differential between EU and world raw material prices and should not be used as a market management tool by the Commission on the domestic raw material supply chain.

Milk Products

16. As already stated, there is virtually universal acceptance that quotas restrict supply and should be abolished. However, the Commission does not want to bring forward the scheduled end date of milk quotas from 2015, but sees the need to work towards this date with a phased soft landing transition. We do not think that the market can wait for such proposals under the CAP Health Check in 2008. Action must be taken now to increase quotas so as to generate more liquid milk, which will reward efficient producers and help ease the extreme tightness in the current supply market.

17. The 2003 CAP reform package included a combination of small increases to milk quotas, coupled with progressive cuts to support prices (butter and skimmed milk powder), but the programme of quota expansion has been too small, whilst the phased cuts in support prices have been implemented too slowly. Nevertheless, combined with the introduction of a ceiling on butter intervention, overall intervention stocks have fallen rapidly in recent times. Indeed, EU intervention stocks for milk powders and butter are currently at zero, whilst private storage is well below normal levels. There is a supply shortfall at world level of 20%. These pressures have pushed milk product prices through the roof ie doubling in the last six months.

18. Whilst it may be argued that market mechanisms have been justified in the current milk products regime, this perception owes more to the impact of climate throughout the world as reflected in milk product supply shortages and the inexorable rise of prices at world level. Quotas distort the supply chain, giving rise to bottlenecks in some parts of the chain, which are not incentivised because real market prices do not move along the whole chain ie prices are artificially held up/forced down in certain parts of the chain. It is perverse that in such a current tight supply market UK dairy farmers are exiting and not even fulfilling the UK dairy quota. Bottlenecks in the distribution chain do not allow for the current demand for dairy products to be satisfactorily met. It is only in very recent weeks that UK farmers have been offered a price for liquid milk to encourage and incentivise them to meet quota. However, there is the possibility of a two tier system developing ie liquid milk and industrial use. Quotas will not work in such a system as farmers will seek to maximize their production (quota) to the higher price areas (liquid milk), but leave food manufacturers short of milk products.

19. Over the past years export refunds and the reduced price butter scheme have been used as the lesser of evils in EU taxpayers' expenditure as a way of easing the previously over-supplied milk products sector. These measures are no longer necessary and have been virtually phased out, but they are merely indicative of an inappropriate supply chain market.

20. The inadequacies of the market can by and large be laid at the door of national quotas. If the Commission is not prepared to bring forward the end date of milk quotas from 2015, then at the very least quota trading between member states must be introduced during the transition period. This would help to match supply with demand and would be particularly valuable to the UK so that farmers could fulfil quota and meet the demands of the food manufacturing industry for dairy products.

Sugar

21. The EU sugar reform package, which was introduced in July 2006, retained the national quota system, which will remain in place until 2015. We reiterate that the quota system stifles competition by isolating each national sugar market, thus allowing the few large processing companies that dominate to collude and raise prices.

22. The BCCCA commissioned a report by Agra CEAS Consulting in 2005 and the report pinpointed that the national quota system was responsible for the reduction in manufacturing of biscuits, cakes, chocolate and confectionery in the UK. The report highlighted the loss of jobs; reduction in volume of production; movement of production out of the UK; and the erosion in the balance of trade situation over a five-year period to 2004. The report found that in that five-year period up to 16,000 jobs were lost in the BCCCA sector

(a fall in employment of more than 20%), whilst there was a fall in production of BCCCA products in the UK (sugar confectionery − 11.6%; biscuits − 6%; chocolate − 4.5%).

23. The fall in the level of production has continued (currently running at a rate of 5% per annum), whilst the trend towards concentration in the BCCCA sector through merger and acquisition and towards divestment of production facilities out of the UK persists. BCCCA member companies are more readily able to produce for the UK market in another EU member state where it is more economic to do so (eg where the costs of sugar for industrial use is cheaper). This has led to a series of divestments with production being moved outside the UK, further reducing employment in the sector.

24. The Agra CEAS Consulting report identified the existence of the production quota system as one of the key contributory factors to this deteriorating situation *("... the only reform options which allow an improvement in the competitive nature of the sugar supply chain are those that result in the elimination of production quotas.")*. The House of Commons EFRA Select Committee identified the iniquities of the quota system in its 12th Report of 2003–04: *Competition will be increased more by abolishing quotas than through any other policy change.*

25. The Commission's communication of July 2004 on sugar reform proposals suggested that quota transfer should be permitted across member state boundaries as a reasonable second best to outright abolition, but this modest proposal was not included in the finalised reform package. We maintain that quota transfer would help to halt the flight of manufacturing jobs out of the EU.

26. On implementation of the reformed EU sugar regime in July 2006, the Commission recognised that the market was hugely over-supplied and, as such, there was a need to remove four million tonnes. The reform package included a restructuring programme, which offered a juicy carrot for inefficient sugar beet processors/ growers to leave the sector. However, although the financial incentive was very generous, the take-up has been very slow (just over two million tonnes in two years).

27. There are various theories as to why this financial inducement has proved insufficient, but it is almost certainly the case that the Commission underestimated the profit margins being made by sugar processors, who have preferred to remain in the game, even though the support price has been reduced. Equally, national governments have undoubtedly put pressure on sugar processors to remain in business by threatening to cut back on the theoretical proportion of compensation (90%) for the processor. (In the case of Ireland and Finland, some 34% and around 20% respectively of the compensation package have been directed to farmers and other stakeholders.) These uncertainties have meant that some sugar beet processors, who would have opted to leave the business, have not done so.

28. The Commission is currently changing the provisions of the restructuring plan so as to encourage further leavers. This may happen, but overall we have a situation whereby a levy has been imposed on the price of sugar for use in manufacture since July 2006 that has fallen on food manufacturers, but no benefit has been derived through a restructured/improved supply market. Indeed, in the event that sugar processors do not take up the restructuring programme this year, the Commission should withdraw the requirement to pay the restructuring levy next year.

29. Owing to the inadequacies of the restructuring programme, the Commission has attempted further to reduce the over-supply by withdrawals from national quota, but this is virtually an across the board quota cut, which merely holds up market prices and therefore conveys no benefit to sugar users, upon whom the restructuring levy has fallen. The Commission is also looking at the method of quota withdrawal, but seems to be obsessed with merely driving down the production volume and has lost sight of the original reform package intention of developing a streamlined, smaller, efficient, competitive supply chain ie having shaken out inefficient processors/growers.

30. We maintain that restructuring will be driven most effectively by price reduction. The reform package is designed to cut support prices by 36% in four years, but this programme is proving to be insufficiently radical. Market prices have not fallen so there is no price pressure on sugar producers. Price pressure is needed for farmers and sugar processors to review the future validity of whether to stay in the sugar supply market. We can only conclude that the reformed regime has set the reference prices too high, because in an over-supplied market and with a juicy carrot to leave the sector farmers and less competitive processors ("inefficients") are not moving out.

31. The Commission's attempts at market management within the new regime are far from satisfactory. Export refunds have been retained, but are used as a tool to manage supply and price levels, rather than as true compensation for exporters to meet the differential between EU and world prices. The Commission has also introduced a system of price reporting, but whilst the first published price is currently awaited (June 2007), it is unlikely that a single EU price (based on data several months old) published every six months will prove

of much value. Even if the price shows a significant discrepancy to the EU reference price, it is unlikely that any action by the Commission, even taken immediately, such as the opening of a limited tariff-free quota to non-EU imports, would have much effect on either the retrospective or current market situation.

RURAL DEVELOPMENT

32. Compulsory modulation is preferable to voluntary in that it maintains a level playing field across all member states.

WORLD TRADE

33. The benefits of the WTO obligations/negotiations are more likely to be seen for the EU economy as a whole rather than agriculture. However, for the food manufacturing industry and our sector in particular, we seriously value the potential for increased market access to raw materials and increased export opportunities for finished products, although the latter is becoming increasingly harder competitively to fulfil.

ENVIRONMENTAL PROTECTION AND CLIMATE CHANGE

34. Measures such as cross compliance are good in theory, but we are not qualified to judge how successful they have been in practice.

35. At EU Council/Summit level (and probably WTO level) there is a need to decide the order of priority between the troika of factors impacting on climate change policy viz environment protection; fuel security; food security. Only when this debate has been resolved can the EU determine how the CAP should be appropriately framed. Biofuels policy will be very important in this context, but the specific nature of biofuels policy must be dependent on the previous decision.

FINANCING

36. Given that there are concerns that the current budget for the CAP may prove insufficient, co-financing does appear attractive as a way forward. However, whilst it is not possible to gauge at the present time, co-financing could give rise to future distortions for EU member states' internal competition.

ENLARGEMENT

37. The new entrants under the 2004 and 2007 enlargements have been heavily biased towards agriculture and this trend is likely to continue in the future. This means that the EU supply base for agricultural raw materials has been significantly increased, although the domestic market, by and large, is already saturated. Until EU raw material prices align with world prices, there will continue to be a financial strain on the CAP.

SIMPLIFICATION OF THE CAP

38. The proposed single CMO may seem good in principle on the grounds that simplification of the CAP is desirable. However, there are concerns that the adoption of a Single Management Committee could give rise to the loss of both Commission and member state administration expertise. This could result in slower and possibly poorer quality decisions.

11 June 2007

Memorandum by Mr Andrew Brown

I would like to give evidence to your Committee regarding the future of the CAP.

The long term objectives of the CAP should be to provide the residents of the EU with a sustainable, affordable, secure and if necessary self sufficient food supply. This can only happen if we stop the haemorrhaging of agricultural land and labour away form the industry and into the hands of wealthy city folk, who see the countryside as a playground rather than a place to provide food.

The 2003 reforms have meant that many farmers have effectively been able to mothball or retire completely from farming, but still collect large amounts of EU money. This means we are losing critical mass and there will be a point fairly soon where it will take many years to get back up to speed. We still see the largest land owners receiving the greatest amount of money and the smaller family farms, which are the back bone of local communities being squeezed. The market place does not give a big enough return to make the vast majority of farms viable, we therefore see 90% of farmers using their SFP to subsidise their businesses. As the historic element of the SFP diminishes we will see the livestock sector virtually disappear in the UK and the face of Britain will change dramatically.

The Single Payment System need radically overhauling so that it gets the money and support to the small and medium sized farms which make up the majority of the sector. The average being around 100 Ha. All payments across the EU need to be made within the same month or there is no level playing field. England is currently running 5-6 months behind all other countries with payments. How can we compete if our neighbours can restock and reinvest so much earlier?

To combat climate change the CAP can help by incentivising farmers to grow energy crops, but not allowing the processors to cream off large parts of the subsidy as is currently the case. For example the 45 Euro/Ha energy crops payment is halved by the processors taking 22.5 Euros in an administration charge, this cannot be right.

Farmers who farm in an environmentally friendly and carbon neutral way should be rewarded with either an extra payment or those who don't should be penalised.

Farmers and land managers are the key to the climate change problem and need to be rewarded or incentivised for mitigating carbon emissions.

EU enlargement has seen several almost third World countries join, whose agricultural systems are 50 years behind ours. This will take many years and vast sums of money to redress, and with such a leviathan as the CAP the opportunities for corruption and abuse are enormous. We may see huge black holes appear which will devour massive sums of EU money to fund Eastern European gangs.

Any level of EU modulation must be the same across all countries or it is not fair. National modulation should not be allowed, as it distorts the process. Rural development is all well and good but it needs very close monitoring or we will see money that is meant for agriculture going to projects completely unrelated to it. Such as rethatching bus shelters. This money may also fall into the hands of very wealthy hobby farmers who have no need for it. I think there is a case for means testing to be brought in for this money.

These are a few of my thoughts on this matter, if you wish me to enlighten the Committee further please do not hesitate to contact me.

Memorandum by the Countryside Council for Wales

OVERVIEW

1. *What should be the long-term objectives of the CAP? Does the title "Common Agricultural Policy" aptly fit your perceived objectives of the policy? What do you consider to be the main pressures on the CAP as it currently is?*

The EU has invested considerable effort over the years in attempting to re-position farm payments in the light of WTO negotiations. The Macsharry reforms involved shifting a considerable proportion of CAP spending into the Blue Box, whilst the more recent Fischler reforms, based around the creation of the Single Payment Scheme (SPS) appear to have shifted the bulk of spending into the Green Box. Much of Pillar 1 (the SPS) and Pillar 2 (rural development) are now justified on the bais of the multifunctional nature of European farming.

In CCW's opinion it is now time to convert rhetoric into reality by establishing a "Common Rural Policy" equipped to support multi-functional and sustainable farming. This should ensure that farmers and other land managers are equipped to deal with the challenges posed by climate change; reverse the loss of biodiversity and maintain both quality and quantity of water supplies whilst supporting both the social and economic health of rural communities.

THE REFORMED CAP

2. *What has been your experience so far with the reformed CAP? What has worked well and less well? And where can lessons be learned?*

The 2003 CAP reforms introduced the concept of "decoupled" payments so that the majority of agricultural subsidies could be paid independent of the volume of production. The new Single Farm Payment (SFP) constitutes an income support which is linked, via cross compliance, to environment, food safety and animal welfare standards as well as the requirement to keep all farmland in good agricultural and environmental condition (GAEC).

The application of decoupling has not been uniform across Europe. The only countries to have discontinued all coupled payments are: Germany (from 2009), Ireland, Luxemburg, England, Wales and Northern Ireland. The countries continuing with highest level of coupled payments are Austria, France, Portugal and Spain.

CCW is primarily concerned with the environmental impacts of CAP reform. However, these are not easy to predict and are likely be both negative as well as positive. Changes in land management appear to be taking place relatively slowly and the resulting environmental impacts will take even longer to emerge. In addition, a wide range of drivers besides the CAP have an influence on land management decisions. These drivers include world trade patterns, climate change, regulation and consumer demands as well as the various "flanking measures" that accompanied decoupling such as cross compliance and agri-environment schemes.

Within Wales, work commissioned by CCW and the Welsh Assembly Government has focused on the need to develop indicators capable of assessing change at regional/ local levels as well as at the national scale. This is because the CAP reforms are likely to result in different changes in different parts of Wales according to the type of farming systems that are present. Gathering data at the national scale alone presents considerable risks as any changes at the regional level may cancel each other out and hence will not be picked up. Existing national data sets such as those based on the Breeding Bird Survey need to be expanded to ensure that statistically valid data on environmental change is available on a regional basis.

In addition, the work carried out in Wales has identified the need to use both "top-down" national level approaches to monitoring (combining remote sensing and Countryside Survey techniques) along with "bottom-up" approaches where environmental change at the farm (or even part farm level) can be matched against farm management change. Such bottom up approaches should allow for economic drivers to be matched to changes in farm management and hence to environmental impacts.

THE SINGLE PAYMENT SCHEME

3. *Do you consider the Single Payment Scheme to be a good basis for the future of EU agricultural policy? What changes might be made at the EU level to the Single Payment Scheme, including to the rules governing entitlements, in the short and/or the longer-term?*

The SPS is an income support measure which may have only a limited lifespan bearing in mind the pressures likely to arise from additional EU expansion, financial discipline, EU budget reviews and any further review of the WTO Green Box. Indeed, there is already debate at EU Council level over the possibility of introducing mandatory farm insurance schemes. These would in turn bear down on the capacity to fund the SPS at current levels. With this in mind, CCW is of the view that it would be more appropriate to devote scarce and declining resources to assisting the industry to adopt the challenges that lie ahead, in particular climate change and the need to meet evolving market demands. Transferring an increasing proportion of funds from Pillar 1 to Pillar 2 (either through modulation or budgetary review) represents the most effective way of funding this process of adaptation.

MARKET MECHANISMS

4. *What short and longer-term changes are required to the CAP's market mechanisms? Suggestions made by the Commission have included re-examination of certain quotas, intervention, set-aside, export refunds and private storage payments*

CCW wishes to comment only on the issues surrounding Set Aside. As part of the CAP Health Check, Commissioner Fischer-Boel has questioned the logic of supply side policies in the post-reform decoupled era (where farmers should be more market orientated) as well as emphasising the need to simplify the administration of CAP.

Whilst Set Aside was originally introduced as a market measure, it has now been shown to have incidental environmental benefits. The available evidence suggests that these benefits are likely to be substantial, especially since large areas of Northern Europe are occupied by Set Aside. This often occurs in areas where relatively little semi-natural habitat still remains, and a proportion of this land is now managed specifically to provide environmental benefits.

Birds appear to be one of the main beneficiaries of the policy. Winter stubbles provide food sources whilst regenerating cover provides enhanced habitat during the breeding season. In addition, well situated Set Aside strips also have the potential to contribute to reductions in diffuse pollution, by intercepting soil particles, pesticides, herbicides, fungicides and fertilisers before they can reach watercourses.

If Set Aside were to be abolished, we feel that the environmental benefits currently delivered by this policy would need to be provided by other means. One possibility would be to increase the level of cross compliance requirements under the Single Payment Scheme, perhaps by requiring that a minimum percentage of each holding was managed for wildlife (as in Switzerland). However, the value of the SPS is likely to drop over time due to EU budgetary constraints—so substantially increasing the level of cross compliance whilst at the same time reducing the value of SPS entitlements could be problematical. Alternatively, the environmental benefits provided by Set Aside could be replicated using an expanded agri-environment programme. Thus the environmental benefits of what is now part of Pillar 1 could in future be provided by Pillar 2. As a result, we contend that the additional agri-environment funding required should be sourced via an increase in the rate of compulsory modulation. In the final analysis, however, the environmental benefits provided by Set Aside may best be replicated using a combination of simple cross compliance measures coupled with rather more sophisticated agri-environment prescriptions.

RURAL DEVELOPMENT

5. *What is your view on the introduction of the European Agricultural Fund for Rural Development (EAFRD)? Do you consider that it is meeting its objectives thus far? Is it suitably "strategic" in nature, meeting the needs of rural society as a whole rather than being restricted to aiding the agricultural industry? How well is it being co-ordinated with other EU and national policies on regional and rural development?*

The final text of the new Rural Development Regulation represents a substantial achievement in bringing together a wide range of existing rural development measures under a common programming framework. The establishment of a single fund for rural development (EAFRD) reflects the response to the demands for a simpler and more coherent approach to rural development programming which resulted from experience with the previous mix of Guidance and Guarantee funding under the EAGGF.

The previous round of Rural Development Plans (RDP) exhibited marked differences between individual Member States with richer parts of the EU prioritising environmental land management and poorer regions placing a much greater emphasis on the modernisation of agriculture. As a result, it is unsurprising that the Commission has attempted to ensure the production of a more balanced set of RDPs through the introduction of Axis 1 (improved competitiveness), Axis 2 (land management) and Axis 3 (social and economic rural development) together with a cross-cutting Leader Axis. However, it is still to early to say whether this approach will be more effective in delivering EU priorities than the previous system.

Examination of those RDP's already notified to the Commission reveals that Axis 3 & 4 programmes account for about 19% of planned spending, whilst Axis 1 accounts for 35% and Axis 2 for the remaining 46% *(Agra-Europe 30 May 2007)*. It is likely that in those member states with large numbers of very small subsistence holdings, more traditional farm based approaches to rural development will prove ineffective. However, there is little available evidence to assess the environmental impact of switching substantial resources into more traditional economic rural development measures.

Prior to the establishment of the EAFRD, the Welsh RDP was based on a mixture of EAGGF Guarantee and Objective 1 funding. From 2007, there is now a much clearer separation between the role of EAFRD and Cohesion funding, with the WRDP providing support for on-farm activity and the Objective 1 programme addressing rural issues at a more strategic level. However, since both of the new Welsh programmes have yet to start, it is not possible to comment on the degree of complementarity achieved in practice.

6. *Is there a case for a higher level of EU financing of rural development? Do you have a view on the extension of compulsory modulation from Pillar 1 (Direct Payments) to Pillar 2 (Rural Development)?*

The Community Strategic Guidelines for Rural Development set out three priority areas under Axis 2 viz: biodiversity and the preservation of high nature value farming and forestry systems, water and climate change. Bearing in mind that Axis 2 accounts for only 46% of spending within those RDP's so far submitted to the Commission, we believe that there is very strong case, based on readily identifiable needs, for an increase in the level of Pillar 2 funding. Additional EU funding is especially necessary in the case of the UK, which currently receives only 3.7% of EAFRD funding, despite having a large area of agricultural land.

Modulation is currently the only available means of switching money from Pillar 1 to Pillar 2. During 2008/09 we hope to see a profound review of the CAP budget, resulting at the very least in a fundamental re-balancing between Pillars 1 and 2 after 2013.

Under the terms of the EU-level agreement reached on 19th March 2007, UK administrations now have the capacity to use voluntary modulation (VM) to substantially increase Pillar 2 budgets.

Compulsory modulation has the advantage of creating a level playing field across the EU. However, 20% of receipts have to be returned to the Commission, match funding is compulsory and the application of the franchise means that any given modulation rate produces rather less funds than expected. By contrast, VM can be applied at a higher rate, 100% of receipts are retained in the member state and match funding can be at a lower level than with CM. However, VM creates significant regional disparities by reducing the level of SFP in some locations but not others. VM is also a more complicated tool than CM, and the present arrangement leads to the perception among farmers that they are being unfairly penalised, especially if access to Pillar 2 schemes is subsequently rationed.

At the present time, both VM and CM require match funding (at least within the UK). Whilst the major disadvantage of CM is that that 20% of the receipts have to be returned to the Commission, we believe that the balance of advantage now appears to lie with an expansion of CM.

However, we believe that the UK must guard against trading in VM for CM only to discover that the latter is set at a rate insufficient to meet environmental needs. The Commissioner was recently quoted *(Agra Europe 25th May 2007)* as favouring a 10% compulsory modulation rate by 2013. This is considerably less than the rate of 19% (both VM + CM combined) now applicable in England (the Welsh rate is still to be established following the recent Assembly elections).

In view of the above, CCW's support for an increased rate of CM is conditional on (i) the retention of VM for the foreseeable future (ii) a better system of allocating rural development funding at EU level—with more emphasis on agricultural area and rather less on past spend. It would also be preferable if the CM arrangements could allow for all of the money collected at member state level to be returned to the country of origin.

WORLD TRADE

7. *What benefits can the EU's World Trade Organisation obligations create for EU agriculture and, consequently, for the EU economy as a whole?*

A successful Doha round should benefit the EU economy overall by expanding international trade across a wide range of goods and services. From an agricultural perspective, WTO negotiations have proved to be a driver for decoupling and may well result in further reductions in Pillar 1 and a progressive growth in Pillar 2. However, reductions in tariff barriers are likely to increase imports of both beef and dairy products, with consequent downward pressure on internal market prices. The environmental impacts of this are not clear-cut as they will vary from region to region depending on farming practice. In CCW's opinion, it will be important for EU negotiators to use both the sensitive product and special product (PGI, PDO etc) mechanisms to ensure the protection of environmentally benign extensive farming systems, in particular within the beef sector.

ENVIRONMENTAL PROTECTION AND CLIMATE CHANGE

8. *To what extent has the system of cross-compliance contributed to an improved level of environmental protection? How is it linking with other EU policy requirements such as the Water Framework Directive?*

Cross compliance as a mechanism for ensuring basic environmental protection for land in receipt of Single Farm Payment was introduced in January 2005. Given its relatively recent introduction, evidence of its environmental impacts is still very limited.

Information on rates of non-compliance is also rather limited, but the most common breaches of the Statutory Management Requirements (SMR) at both UK and EU level are related to animal identification and registration. Regarding the environmental SMR's, breaches of the Nitrates Directive have also been identified as significant. Regarding Good Agricultural and Environmental Condition (GAEC), the most common breaches involve requirements for a minimum level of land maintenance and standards on soil erosion.

Cross compliance seems to function largely as a means of encouraging compliance with EU and UK legislative standards—by preventing those in receipt of income support from carrying out damaging activity. By contrast, encouraging positive land management activity is more properly regarded as the role of Pillar 2.

CCW's view on the evolution of the cross compliance is that it would be better to extend the "horizontal reach" of the policy over time by adding additional simple controls across a wider range of topics (water protection, waste, air quality, climate change) rather than seek to "raise the bar" by setting more demanding standards on existing topics. However, the pace of evolution may be dictated in large part by the changing value of SPS entitlements. Given that the SPS may very well have ceased to exist by 2020, then cross compliance is a time limited tool. In such a scenario it is perhaps best viewed as a policy lever for encouraging farmers to develop a better understanding of evolving market requirements.

9. *How can the CAP contribute to mitigation of, and adaptation to, climate change? What do you consider the role of biofuels to be in this regard?*

We believe that a revitalised CAP can help land managers play a major role in helping to meet the challenges posed by climate change. Areas to focus on include reductions in the emissions of greenhouse gases; soil management techniques designed to reduce and possibly reverse CO_2 emissions; management of water supplies in the light of reduced summer rainfall; reduction in the risks posed by flooding and adoption of both energy saving and energy generation measures.

The potential contribution of biofuels in relation to tackling climate change is complex. While replacement of fossil fuels with biofuel would seem to offer benefits by reducing CO_2 emissions the reality is more complex. Current technologies tend to concentrate on conventional crops such as oilseed rape and cereals as feedstocks. Grown using conventional techniques to maximise yields and then processed the resulting biofuels require considerable inputs of energy. Thus the overall benefits in terms of reduced greenhouse gas emissions can be marginal.

Using land for biofuels may also result in a wide range of indirect effects. In particular, by competing with land used to grow both human and animal feed, such crops are already starting to drive up commodity prices. There is the possibility of using Set Aside land, but this will have an environmental impact. Relying on imports from countries with lower environmental safeguards may lead to a global loss of biodiversity and a substantial increase in overall CO_2 emissions depending on where such crops are grown. The development of second-generation biofuels may involve lower environmental impacts, but the present generation seems likely to result in an intensification of land use and more pressure on biodiversity. From a Welsh perspective, the area of high quality arable is relatively small, so first generation biofuels are unlikely to be taken up on a significant scale. However, they may still exert a substantial indirect impact by increasing the price of animal feeds.

FINANCING

10. *The Commissioner has expressed her dissatisfaction at the financing agreement reached by the Member States at the December 2005 Council. Do you consider the current budget to be sufficient? Do you consider co-financing to be a possible way forward in financing the Common Agricultural Policy?*

In relation to co-financing, the European Parliament has shown itself to be strongly opposed to any apparent re-nationalisation of the CAP. In particular, during the recent debate over the draft voluntary modulation regulation, Parliament applied a 20% reserve to the EU rural development budget until such time as it was satisfied that the regulation would be applied in a way that respected the common policy framework. As a result, the Commission now appears to have little appetite for engaging in similar debates in the near future.

Co-financing has the advantage of instilling a greater sense of discipline in those involved in the delivery of spending programmes. However, it is less popular amongst those member states who are net beneficiaries of the current system. Whilst Pillar1 is entirely EU-funded at present, Pillar 2 spending is already co-financed. One way of introducing a greater measure of co-financing into the CAP would be to use compulsory modulation to transfer funds from Pillar 1 to Pillar 2. This would attract support from within the Commission and possibly also from sections of the European Parliament.

ENLARGEMENT

11. *What has been the impact on the CAP of the 2004 and 2007 enlargements and what is the likely impact of future enlargements of the EU on the post-2013 CAP?*

The recent accession of countries such as Romania has resulted in the addition of large numbers of very small peasant farms which it is probably impossible to support using traditional farmbased Pillar 1 or 2 measures. Should Turkey accede to the EU, this problem would be magnified to an even greater extent. The solution would appear to reside in an expansion of economic rural development measures using a combination of Axis 3 (EARFD) and Structural Funds. The environmental implications of such a policy switch are difficult to predict and are likely to vary from one location to another depending on the measures used and the nature of the rural areas concerned.

SIMPLIFICATION OF THE CAP AND OTHER ISSUES

12. *How could the CAP be further simplified and in what other ways would you like to see the Common Agricultural Policy changed in the short and/or the long term?*

The Commission's current proposals appear primarily to affect traders rather than producers. CCW does not envisage any significant environmental impacts arising from the technical simplifications currently proposed. From a general persective, CCW also supports a streamlined and simplified approach, provided this can be achieved without any damaging environmental side effects.

8 June 2007

Memorandum by Dairy UK

1. Dairy UK is the trade association that represents the interests of the United Kingdom's dairy farmers, milk producer co-operatives, manufacturers of dairy products and processors and distributors of liquid milk. Between them, Dairy UKs members handle 90% of the milk produced in the United Kingdom.

GENERAL

2. In the long term the UK dairy industry aspires to operating entirely free from the support and constraints of the CAP. The industry possesses natural climatic advantages along with efficient farmers and processors which would allow it to compete successfully in a liberalised market. As part of the process of liberalisation Dairy UK supports the abolition of dairy quotas when their current legal basis expires in 2015.

3. In respect of the CAP Dairy UKs primary concern is that the EU should maintain an EU wide policy framework in place for agriculture that recognises the specific peculiarities of the sector, safeguards its productive potential and minimises the potential for competitive distortions created by the discretion given to Member States for the implementation of the CAP within their territory. Within these broad parameters the policy should over time move away from direct responsibility for market management, whilst still providing a minimum of residual safeguards against market shocks, and assist the industry in developing its own strategies and tools for adapting to a more liberalised framework.

4. The continuing issues of transition from the current policy framework also need to be recognised. In particular the operation of the CAP has generated profound distortions in the pattern of milk production in the EU and the EU's relationship with the world market. These distortions will take some time to unwind and this will create a requirement for adequate transitional measures.

5. In the present commercial environment of high world prices, these distortions would not necessarily create an issue for the industry. However, whilst the supply/demand balance is expected to be in the industry's favour for next 12 months at least, it is unclear whether they will last in the medium term. This may mean that in the transition to the abolition of quotas the renewed engagement of the EU in certain aspects of market management may be required.

What should be the long term objectives of the CAP?

6. The EU still needs a common policy targeted specifically towards agriculture. A common rural policy is not a substitute. Agriculture, as a sector of the economy, has specific needs distinct from other economic sectors and these still need to be addressed. In particular the inherently fragmented nature of primary agricultural production needs to be recognised and the vulnerability of small agricultural enterprises to external shocks needs be acknowledged along with the dependency of farming on technology developed by external centralised research establishments.

7. Within the current framework the main pressure is from the tension between maintaining a common EU policy and the greater opportunity for competitive distortions created by the increased discretion given to Member States in implementing the CAP in their national territory. This could undermine the operation of the single market for agricultural goods which is one of the greatest achievements of the CAP.

8. In the longer term the main pressure facing the CAP is the need to adapt its strategic focus. At present the CAP lacks a clear unambiguous justification from which it can legitimately sustain its claims on the budgetary resources of the EU. The justifications advanced for the CAP have evolved from fear of scarcity, through addressing an embarrassment of over supply, to a situation were the rationale for continued support is now notionally the provision of environmental benefits to the public in exchange for direct payments. This

justification rests on the value the public wishes to give to these benefits when there is no clear way of calculating such a value.

9. Newer drivers such as energy and food security and climate change have yet to be fully incorporated into the policy because the necessity to do so has not been felt by experience. As suggested by the NFU this points to the need for a CAP that at least addresses the maintenance of productive potential, as opposed to product output.

THE REFORMED CAP

10. The impact on the dairy sector of the reformed CAP is difficult to determine. Dairy farmers did not receive any form of direct payment prior to the reform. By providing an income stream decoupled from production obligations the single payment may have given dairy farmers greater liberty of action in determining how to take their businesses forward and this may have accelerated the restructuring of the industry.

11. The failure of the RPA is well known and lessons on its performance belong to the debate on change management and the introduction of complex software projects in Government agencies.

12. A handicap for English dairy farmers is the distortion created by the different ways the single payment was implemented in the UK as a result of the various options open to the constituent countries of the UK. This has created an uneven commercial environment which parallels the distortions created at the EU level.

THE SINGLE PAYMENT SCHEME

13. On its own the single payment scheme is not a sufficient basis for a Common Agricultural Policy for the EU. It helps to support individual farmers and is a means by which changes in farming practices and the provision of public goods can be obtained from the sector. However it only addresses issues at the level of the farm and does not address some of the wider strategic issues that need to be incorporated into the CAP.

14. These would include the orientation of long term technological research that would provide the EU agricultural sector with the range of tools that would allow it to respond to the changing demands that will be placed on it. Whilst this is particularly important in the area of climate change mitigation the issue of seeking continued improvements in productive efficiency will also still need to be addressed. The volatility of markets that can be expected in a fully liberalised framework and the need to address the risks that this will create for farms also has to be acknowledged in some way.

15. Changes that should be made to the single payment at the EU level should seek to create a common and simplified framework for all of EU agriculture to ensure the minimisation of trade distortions and unnecessary restraints on production. This would include abolishing the remaining coupled payments and abolishing set-aside.

MARKET MECHANISMS

16. Dairy UK supports the abolition of the quota regime as a necessary and inevitable step towards the creation of a market based industry free from public support.

17. Elimination should ultimately be achieved by a gradual increase in quota volumes. The international transferability of quota should not be permitted as this would create the risk of quotas within the UK acquiring value. This would impose an unnecessary cost burden on dairy farmers remaining in the industry that wish to expand their business.

18. The logic of quota abolition also necessitates the prior withdrawal of export refunds to ensure the EU is not exposed to an unlimited expenditure liability when production constraints are lifted. The debate on how export refunds should be lifted has recently been complicated by the sudden and unexpected rise in world prices which has allowed all export refunds to be currently set at zero.

19. Whilst there may already exist a long term convergence between EU and world prices for milk powders, the current convergence between the EU and world prices for butterfat maybe of a more temporary nature. If world prices fall back again then in order to avoid the build up of intervention stocks the EU needs to be prepared to revive export refunds until such time as the price differential between the EU and world market is addressed over an appropriate transition period.

20. Quota abolition does not necessitate the abolition of all market management tools. Private Storage Aid could continue to provide a useful role in minimising seasonal market volatility. The development of private sector risk management tools could also be assisted by the EU, eg the development of futures markets for dairy products.

21. In the absence of market support the primary tool available to the industry to deal with the risks of price volatility that can be expected from a liberalised market is scale of operation, either through consolidation of processing operations or through merger of co-operatives. The necessity of this process has to be recognised by EU and UK competition authorities.

RURAL DEVELOPMENT

22. Dairy UK is concerned that the implementation of the Rural Development Regulation in other Member States should not create significant trade distortions. This requires a clear and unambiguous legal framework and close scrutiny by the UK and the EU of the schemes operated in other Member States.

23. Implementation of Axis 1 and Axis 3 under the Rural Development Regulation in England has been devolved to the Regional Development Agencies. The regional administration of these funds could create inconsistency and a fragmentation of effort. We look to Defra to monitor the situation closely.

24. English dairy farmers are disproportionately affected by voluntary modulation used to fund the Rural Development Plan in England. This is a reflection of the UK's historic failure to obtain a proportionate share of the pillar II budget. Dairy UK would therefore support a greater use of compulsory modulation as this would create a more equitable environment and allow a reduction in the use of voluntary modulation.

WORLD TRADE

25. In the current market environment the benefits of a WTO trade deal may be academic. Export refunds are already at zero, no conceivable reduction in import tariffs would make the EU market an attractive destination for importers and expenditure on domestic support is minimal in relation to any prospective obligations that could be imposed on the EU.

26. However, assuming a more normal relationship between the EU and the world market, then the abolition of export refunds would have serious implications on the ability of the EU to manage its internal market. This is why it is important that the EU obtains from any WTO agreement a flexible framework for phasing out export refunds consistent with its obligation to eliminate them.

27. Abolition of export refunds would also place the EU under strong pressure for a further round of intervention support price cuts for the dairy sector, particularly for butter, to bring its internal price into greater alignment with the world market. The impact these cuts would depend on their intensity, period of implementation and the situation in world market.

28. In the long term the effect of the WTO deal is to open the gateway for the abolition of the quota regime as this can only be achieved once export refunds have been eliminated. Once the quota regime is abolished this will allow the EU dairy industry to fully participate in the growth in the world market. Previously EU exports have been restricted by limits on the use of export refunds imposed under the GATT Uruguay Round. This should benefit consumers outside the EU as the growth in world demand for dairy products cannot be met without the supply contribution from the EU.

ENVIRONMENTAL PROTECTION AND CLIMATE CHANGE

29. Cross compliance and agri-environment schemes have made a positive contribution to environmental protection. The full extent of the improvement is yet to be quantified, but the existence of these measures and the improvement they are generating would justify a moratorium on new prescriptive legislation such as may be proposed for the Water Framework Directive.

30. Agriculture can play a significant role in mitigating climate change. There are several EU policy initiatives to support the production and use of biofuels. However these policies need to be subject to constant scrutiny to ensure that they do not generate unintended or unacceptable side effects.

31. In the UK the enhanced Renewable Obligations Certificates proposed in the May Energy White Paper should provide an important stimulus to the development of on farm anaerobic digestion plants which could allow dairy farmers to become energy exporters. Opportunities also exist for Centralised Anaerobic Digestion plants which would utilise waste streams from both dairy processing plants and dairy farms.

32. On the other hand the decision to increase the Renewable Transport Fuel Obligation will create a distortion in the demand for arable crops. This, along with similar initiatives at the EU level, will increase the cost of animal feed to the dairy sector. Cost increases induced by biofuel initiatives can logically only result in an increases in the price of milk to recover these costs that will ultimately be passed on to the consumer, or an intensification of the pressures on industry profitability.

FINANCING

33. Over the past few years the CAP budget as always been regarded as under pressure. Forecasts arising from the recent and previous round of accession indicate that this pressure is set to continue. However, CAP budgets regularly come in under-spent, and the recent improvement in the market situation should help to alleviate this pressure.

34. Co-financing would not be a solution to the financial problems of the CAP. Mandatory co-financing could imply a fundamental re-distribution in the contribution made by Member States to the EU which would probably lead to significant resistance to such a proposal from a number of EU members.

35. Voluntary co-financing would probably significantly disadvantage UK agriculture. To a degree voluntary co-financing has already existed for the UK under the Fontainebleau Refund negotiated by Margaret Thatcher. Under this formula 70% of any savings in CAP expenditure in the UK is passed back to the UK Treasury. This has provided a strong incentive for the UK Government to minimise discretionary expenditure under the CAP. Explicit voluntary co-financing would accentuate this process to the disadvantage of UK agriculture. The competitive distortions this may create would be inflated by the active support given to agriculture that could be expected in some other Member States.

ENLARGEMENT

36. The 2004 enlargement has worked to the benefit of the dairy industry. Essentially the quota deals negotiated by the Commission with the accession countries ensured that the old Member States benefited from the growth in consumer demand in the new members. This has acted to improve the EUs internal supply/demand balance and prevent EU prices being pulled down by any sudden rise in production in the new Member States in response to the higher support prices provided by the EU.

37. So far there as been no discernible impact from the 2007 enlargement.

38. EU enforcement of hygiene regulations has meant that advent of the new members within the EU single market has not in any way undermined consumer confidence in the safety of dairy products.

39. In the long term however the quotas restraint imposed on the new members have ensured that they are very largely opposed to the continuation of the quota regime as it is apparent that the quota system is imposing expansion costs on their efficient farmers and preventing their industries from realising their competitive advantage and meeting the growth in demand in their domestic markets.

40. It is difficult to forecast what impact the further enlargement of the EU would have after 2013. Assuming the quota regime is abolished in 2015 then further enlargement would increase the agricultural area in the EU that is potentially suited to dairy farming, which could be destabilising to the market balance at the time, but it is not clear how long it would take to realise this potential.

SIMPLIFICATION OF THE CAP AND OTHER ISSUES

41. The European Commission is currently undertaking a 'simplification' of the CAP by creating a single regulation covering all market support regimes. The exercise is of questionable value as the majority of market support measures are in line for abolition. In reality the exercise is no more than a codification whose primary benefit will be to simplify the process of the Health Check and increase the discretion given to the Commission.

42. The real opportunities for simplification are in the implementation and enforcement by UK authorities. There still exists duplication in many inspection agencies and opportunities for greater co-ordination and co-operation between Government inspection agencies should be exploited. This would be strongly welcomed by farmers.

July 2007

Memorandum by EuroChoices

OBJECTIVES OF THE CAP

1. The objectives of the CAP as stated in Article 33 of the Consolidated Treaty need to be overhauled and modernised. They reflect the priorities of a different era and are no longer appropriate targets of public policy, if they ever were. The competitiveness of EU agriculture has not been well served by this policy framework. Higher productivity, fair standards of living, reasonable and stable prices can be delivered in a more effective, efficient and sustainable way by allowing EU agri-food and rural resource markets to operate more freely and trade more openly on world markets, with less intervention by the state.

2. The CAP of the future will need to have a much greater focus on issues that are more legitimate targets of public policy in the 21st Century. It will also need to reflect more explicitly the rural dimension that is now *de facto* a major element of CAP expenditure. Fundamentally, policy will need to be orientated more towards correcting the market failures and missing markets associated with land utilisation and food and fibre production. This would encompass not just environmental issues but would extend to landscape management, biosecurity, food safety, animal welfare, bioenergy and climate change issues.

3. Such a radical revision of policy objectives seems called for when one considers the likely nature of future policy priorities. It also points to the need for a change of name for the policy programme to reflect these changed priorities. Various suggestions have been made ranging from quite modest changes to include "Rural" in the name, to more radical options that seek to encompass notions of "Land Use, Food, Energy and Environmental Security". There are important questions, moreover, about whether the policy can or ought any longer to be described as "common", given the highly diverse nature of the agri-food and rural sector in the EU-27.

THE REFORMED CAP AND THE SINGLE FARM PAYMENT

4. At the centre of CAP Reform in June 2003 was the decoupling from production of various direct payments (DPs) to farmers and the introduction of a consolidated Single Farm Payment (SFP) attached to land and based on DPs claimed in 2000–02. From an economic standpoint this was and remains an attractive concept as it is likely to increase the influence of the market on production and trade. It signalled the break with the previous coupled system of support which had the ludicrous effect of providing incentives to farmers to operate enterprises at commercially unprofitable levels of output simply to collect the production linked subsidies. The political sustainability of this system of direct aid linked to historical levels of production, however, is very much open to question.

5. Formal economic analysis of the impact of this reform on UK agriculture has been carried out. In the UK beef sector, for example, the projected effects relative to the baseline pre-reform situation are shown in Figures 1 and 2. The introduction of the SFP results in a 17% drop in UK beef production by the end of the projection period. There is, however, a marked increase of 9% in projected beef prices: this is driven by an EU-wide reduction in beef production and subsequent increase in EU beef prices. The evidence suggests that the impact of the policy on overall market receipts (excluding DPs) is likely to be broadly neutral. It is worth noting, however, that the beef and sheep production sector in much of the UK is in a rather parlous state: underlying profitability is very poor and this is likely to accelerate the trend to part-time farming in this sector.

Figure 1

UK SUCKLER COWS

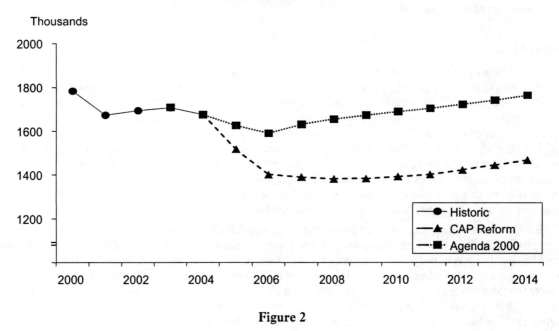

Figure 2

UK CATTLE REFERENCE PRICE

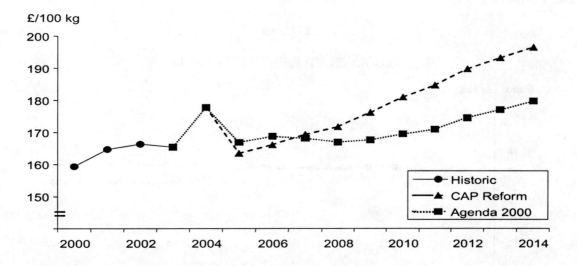

Source: FAPRI-UK.

6. Experiences with the implementation of the 2003 CAP Reform illustrate the lack of a "common" approach to policy implementation in the EU-27 and the way in which this can hinder desired policy outcomes. There are now significantly different levels of decoupling or recoupling of payments throughout the EU. The basis on which these payments are made differ quite markedly: some are paid according to an historic entitlement formula, others have an area basis, and there are static or dynamic hybrids of these two approaches. This uneven pattern has important implications for the prices of agricultural commodities. The fact, for example,

that certain member states have opted for recoupled payments means that overall EU production of certain commodities is greater than if they had implemented full decoupling. This tends to keep the EU price of the relevant commodities lower than if payments had been uniformly decoupled, thus penalizing members who have implemented decoupling in full.

MARKET MECHANISMS

7. As part of the CAP Reform process and WTO commitments the EU is reducing the intensity of traditional market management instruments, particularly intervention purchases and the use of export subsidies. This should remove the need for production limitation measures such as set aside and milk production quotas. Evidence suggests that elimination of export subsidies would impact significantly on the UK dairy and beef sectors. The negative price effect in the dairy sector is likely to be felt most severely in the butter market, implying that intervention prices for butter would need to be reduced to avoid the costly build up of intervention stocks following the elimination of export subsidies. As a result there would be downward pressure on producer milk prices and production. UK beef prices and production would also be negatively affected relative to a baseline scenario where export subsidies remain in use. The impact on the sheep sector would be minimal as it is not heavily dependent on this form of protection.

8. The EU Commissioner has signalled her intention to abolish EU milk quotas when the current legislative basis runs out in 2014. Evidence suggests that abolition of quotas coupled with export subsidy elimination would have either a relatively neutral or only mildly positive impact on production at the EU-25 level; there would be some downward pressure on EU producer milk prices. Within the UK dairy sector, however, the impacts would be more significant whether under Uruguay or Doha Round trade rules. The UK producer price of milk is projected ultimately to be 9% to 11% lower compared to a baseline without these policy changes (Figure 3). This leads to a fall in UK milk production of between 14% and 16% (Figure 4). Market receipts for the dairy sector decrease by between 26% and 29%, the substantial decline reflecting the combined impact of production and price falls. Dairy cow numbers are projected to fall by about 15% with knock on effects on supply to the beef sector.

Figure 3

PRODUCER MILK PRICE (ENGLAND)

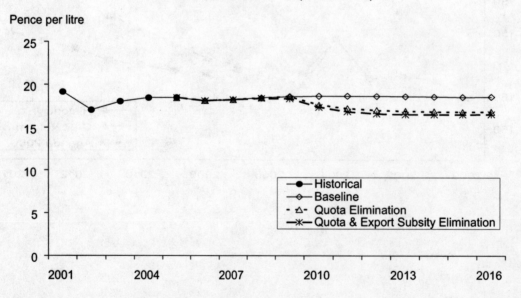

Figure 4

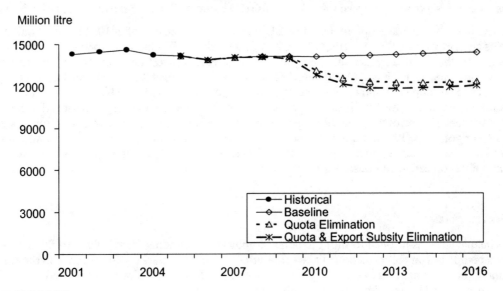

UK MILK PRODUCTION

Source: FAPRI-UK.

ENVIRONMENTAL PROTECTION AND CLIMATE CHANGE

9. The projected reduction in EU cattle and sheep numbers as a result of the 2003 CAP Reform and WTO commitments will result in significant reductions in methane emissions from both enteric fermentation and manure management. In areas of the EU where livestock production predominates it is estimated, in Carbon Dioxide equivalent terms, that the reductions from agriculture would be 15–20% by 2015 compared to the pre-CAP Reform period. The extent of the reductions, however, can be influenced by the management systems followed. Further thought, therefore, may need to be given to the potential of the CAP to capture the full benefits of projected reductions in livestock numbers.

10. Another means of reducing Carbon Dioxide levels in the atmosphere is carbon sequestration into agricultural soils ie the creation of carbon sinks. Agricultural producers can increase the carbon content of the soil by changing production practices, such as the adoption of minimum tillage. This practice, potentially, could complement wider efforts to reduce emissions from the burning of fossil fuels. The science surrounding sequestration is disputed but the United Nations Framework Convention on Climate Change (UNFCCC) is slowly developing the rules and modalities governing all aspects, including inventories, measurement of additional stocks and the unintentional release of stocks.

11. A central plank in the EU's strategy to reduce Greenhouse Gas Emissions (GHG) is the Emissions Trading Scheme (ETS), which began operation in 2005. The ETS, however, does not trade credits generated by sequestration, reflecting a general EU reluctance to adopt this practice and ongoing opposition from environmental groups to reliance on carbon sinks that might dilute the commitment to emissions reductions. This will limit the potential for agricultural producers to earn income from this activity, in contrast to the position in the USA where its use is being encouraged in a modest way. The CAP Second Pillar, however, could be a possible avenue to compensate producers for sequestration activities. A recent evaluation by the Commission has estimated that agricultural soils could sequester up to 20% of the total EU commitment to reduce emissions.

12. Bioenergy has the potential to contribute to a new energy paradigm, not as a replacement for oil but as one element in a portfolio of renewable sources of energy that can diversify energy supplies and reduce strategic dependence on imported fossil fuels. Biofuels such as ethanol and bio-diesel could offer an important low-carbon alternative to petroleum, depending on the production technologies adopted. Ethanol produced in industrialized countries from corn, for example, may reduce life-cycle GHG only 10–30% compared to oil, whereas ethanol produced from sugar cane or cellulose may reduce it by 90% or more. In both cases, the

greenhouse gas reductions increase significantly if agricultural practices are adopted that enhance soil carbon sequestration and are less intensive in their use of petroleum-based fertilizers and fuels. This is especially significant in the case of bioenergy-dedicated crops like grasses and trees, as their production is characterized by relatively low use of fertilizer and other petroleum-based products. If, however, areas which are currently acting as a carbon sinks are disrupted the release of GHG could well cause an overall negative impact.

13. The EU has a biofuel target of about 6% of EU fuel supply by the end of 2010. The potential market for biodiesel is currently larger than for ethanol as 60% of fuel is diesel. Production capacities for biodiesel in the EU tripled over the last three years and there have been increasing investments in ethanol production. If the EU follows an appropriately regulated, market-based approach then there will probably be significant opportunities to develop sustainably the production of biodiesel and bioethanol feedstocks, resulting in a very significant increase in land use for bioenergy production. In the USA the bioenergy sector is developing apace and in the process is transforming agricultural markets. Ethanol production and consumption has grown by about 23% per year since 1998 and now represents 20% of maize demand. Rising prices for maize have all but eliminated the need for government supports. If the EU sector moves ahead in similar fashion we can expect significant effects on cereal and oilseed markets.

RURAL DEVELOPMENT

14. In principle it seems justified to shift the policy emphasis and funding from Pillar I to Pillar II measures, with greater emphasis on the correction of market failures and missing markets, for example in the area of agri-environment interactions. This has been signalled as a goal by the Commissioner but is likely to be politically unattractive at an EU level. Any move in this direction raises both conceptual and practical problems. Conceptually, for example, work needs to be done to clarify and perhaps reach a consensus on where the balance of public interest lies in a number of areas. We need, for example, more comprehensive and robust evidence of public preferences and values for socio-cultural landscapes that reflect different types and intensities of farming, in both lowlands and LFAs. Practically, will member states be able positively to pay farmers for production of valued public goods rather than just compensate for income forgone? Will there be adequate flexibility to reflect regional preferences? Pillar II is currently co-financed at 50% thus creating a built-in disincentive to make the switch to Pillar II, so will we need changes in the co-financing rules? We know that the administrative costs of agri-environment-type programmes can be high, so can all of this be accomplished with the minimum of bureaucracy and cost?

15. Rural development policy in the future might place a more strategic emphasis on the situation in farm households rather than focusing narrowly on the farm holding. Indeed this would be consistent with the ethos of the so-called European Model of agriculture. This is essentially a multifunctional model reliant on family labour but where farmers and their spouses are increasingly finding ways to combine on-farm and off-farm employment. Farm households, therefore, are now more directly affected by a range of other policies, pointing to the need for greater integration and complementary between rural development and mainstream policies. From a farm household perspective policy should facilitate the development of a more diversified rural economy, human capital formation and enhanced quality of life. Future rural policy, therefore, could focus more on the adjustment process of labour moving out of primary agriculture and look at measures which support diversification and entrepreneurial activities such as market access, value-adding (organic/local produce), knowledge transfer, education, retraining and social networking. The role of rural policy in contributing to social and civic goals and the structures through which these are addressed perhaps needs to be reconsidered.

WORLD TRADE

16. The EU's WTO obligations, if implemented, will have differential effects on EU agriculture. Dairy sector simulations of the impact of reducing EU tariffs agreed under the URAA by 60% (currently the EU offer in Doha) indicate only minor price and production impacts beyond what can be expected from the elimination of export subsidies (paragraph 7). The reason is that internal price reductions due to export subsidy elimination enhance the effectiveness of import tariffs in protecting the EU market. Thus, even when import tariffs are reduced by 60% they still stem the flow of imports from third countries into the EU.

17. In the beef sector the impact of a 60% tariff reduction is more significant; this seems to be about the level where beef tariff reductions begin to bite. Prices ultimately fall a further 4% beyond what would be anticipated from eliminating export subsidies. In the arable sector tariff reductions, in addition to eliminating export subsidies, had little impact on prices and production as they were still effective in stemming crop imports.

18. The details of an eventual WTO trade agreement are crucial. The chairman of the WTO negotiating group on agriculture, Crawford Falconer, has stated that the EU will likely have to make tariff cuts of more than 60% in order to obtain an agreement. This would undoubtedly result in substantial third country imports and downward pressure on EU market prices for certain commodities. Lower food prices, of course, will benefit consumers, especially the lower income groups that spend a relatively high proportion of their budget on food. This should lead to a net gain in economic welfare in the EU as a whole.

8 June 2007

FURTHER READING

Buckwell, A, (2007). *Next Steps in CAP Reform.* EuroChoices 6 (2), Special Issue on the Doha Trade Talks. Forthcoming.

Burgess, D and Hutchinson WG, (2005). *Do People Value the Welfare of Farm Animals?* EuroChoices 4 (3), 36–43.

Davis, J, (2007). *Whither the World Trade Talks?* Editorial. EuroChoices 6 (2), Special Issue on the Doha Trade Talks. Forthcoming.

Davis, J, Caskie, P, and Wallace, M, (2007). *How Effective are Farmer Early Retirement Schemes?* EuroChoices 6 (3). Forthcoming.

Donellan, T and Hanrahan, K, (2007). *It's the Environment Stupid! To What Extent Can WTO Trade Reform Lead to Environmental Rather Than Economic Benefits?* (www.webmeets.com/files/papers/ERE/WC3/352/donnellanhanrahan.pdf).

Häberli, C, (2007). *How to Conclude the Doha Development Agenda.* EuroChoices 6 (2), Special Issue on the Doha Trade Talks. Forthcoming.

Henning, C and Latacz-Lohmann, U, (2004). *Will Enlargement Gridlock CAP Reforms?* A Political Economy Perspective. EuroChoices 3 (1), 38–43.

Moss, J, McErlean, S, Patton, M, Kostov, P, Westhoff, P and Binfield, J, (2003). *The Impact of Decoupling on UK Agriculture.* EuroChoices 2 (2), 24–25.

Moss, J, Binfield, J, Patton, M, Kostov, P, Zhang, L, and Westhoff, P, (2006). *The Impact of Trade Liberalisation on Agriculture in the UK.* EuroChoices 5 (2), 28–29.

Moss, J, Binfield, J, Patton, M, Kostov, P, Zhang, L, and Westhoff, P, (2007). *Analysis of the Impact of the Abolition of Milk Quotas, Increased Modulation and Reductions in the Single Farm Payment on UK Agriculture.* FAPRI-UK Report, Agricultural and Food Economics, QUB-AFBI, Belfast. pp 23.

Shortall, S, (2004). *Time to Re-think Rural Development?* EuroChoices 3 (2), 34–39.

Ugarte De La Torre, D, (2005). *The Contribution of Bioenergy to a New Energy Paradigm.* EuroChoices 4 (3), 6–13.

Westhoff, P, Thompson, W, Kruse, J, and Meyer, S, (2007). *Ethanol Transforms Agricultural Markets in the USA.* EuroChoices 6 (1), 14–21.

Young, LM, Weersink, A, Fulton, M and Deaton, BJ, (2007). *Carbon Sequestration in Agriculture: EU and US Perspectives.* EuroChoices 6 (1), 32–37.

Memorandum by Jean-Luc Demarty, Director General for Agriculture and Rural Development, European Commission

Thank you for your letter dated 3 May 2007, addressed to Commissioners Dimas, Grybauskaite, Mandelson, Michel and Fischer Boel, in which you invite the Commission to submit evidence to the House of Lords Inquiry into the Future of the Common Agricultural Policy (CAP). Mrs Fischer Boel has asked me to answer on the Commissioners' behalf.

It is the intention of the Commission to adopt, towards the end of 2007, a Communication assessing the evolution of the CAP, in particular those issues relating to the 2003 Reform *Health Check.*

Since this Communication will address most, if not all, of the topics you have identified, and will reflect the collegiate views of the Commission, we would ask you to consider that Communication as the written contribution from the Commission. Furthermore, the CAP will be part of the review covering all aspects of EU spending on which the Commission will report in 2008–09.

June 2007

Memorandum by The Family Farmers' Association

The Family Farmers Association is a self supporting group of farmers and other people interested in farming and the countryside. We do not have any resident economists and thus our opinions are based on common sense and the observations and experience of practical farmers rather than theoretical economics. Herewith our comments on the future of the CAP.

1. After the last war the government supported farmers so that they maintained food production and received a reasonable reward for so doing. This was the basic objective of the Common Agricultural Policy when we first joined the EEC, as it was then. As modern methods developed, farming became both more productive and more profitable. Taxpayers complained that too much money was going to farmers, and the CAP started to encompass other rural activities. In the course of time Governments lost interest in food production, finding that food could be bought more cheaply from abroad and a "Pillar 2" of the CAP gradually claimed an increasing share of available money for various rural and social objectives. The long term object should be to support and encourage the type of dual purpose farming which both produces food **and** cares for the countryside. If this can be made profitable again, rural communities will flourish.

2. There have been a series of "reforms" of the CAP, introducing various new systems for rewarding farmers. The objectives and logic of the changes were not always entirely clear. Whatever the intentions, the result has been a diminishing number of farmers, and apparently no change to the unfortunate statistic that 20% of farmers receive 80% of the subsidies. Since the latest "reform", food production receives little or no direct support and producing food is no longer a profitable activity. However some of the CAP money has been very useful in funding, via the ERDP, environmental schemes and providing grants to entrepreneurial farmers wishing to add value to their products.

3. The Single Farm Payment does not appear to be a particularly sensible scheme, and it is hard to see the point of it. It perpetuates the fact that the largest farmers get the most support. We have long advocated that as Entitlements (to SPS) become larger, they should be scaled down. How long taxpayers will be happy that, just because you own 1,000 ha of land you receive a cheque for something like £225,000 each year is a moot point. Payments would be more acceptable if Entitlements of over £25,000 were reduced by a small percentage, which increased for larger Entitlements. A ceiling at half a million pounds might be a good idea. (Marian Fisher-Boel has suggested a ceiling of 300,000 euros, which is a bit drastic, but we think a sliding scale, starting lower, would be more likely to be accepted. There must be some means of rewarding farmers for cross compliance.) The money saved from this reduction should be kept in the agricultural budget, perhaps used to make more generous environmental payments. (Just now there is talk about the millions, or even billions, of pounds, spent on bribes to keep the arms industry alive. Agriculture is by no means the only recipient of government finance.)

It is very difficult to determine how farming can best be supported. Environmental schemes seem to be the most useful approach and there should be a study of what aspects of the countryside are most valued and worthy of financial encouragement. Having small fields and small woods or copses should be added to the list of things to be rewarded. Also maintaining variety in cropping and stocking. There should be help for young people starting out in farming, especially if this can somehow be combined with helping older farmers to retire with dignity.

4. Some market mechanisms can be helpful. Milk quotas were very helpful in discouraging those with capital to throw around from expanding their dairies, to the detriment of those who needed to be able to make a living from smallish dairy herds. It is acknowledged by "experts" that ending quotas will reduce the already very low price of milk still further. It is time the NFU came to grips with reality on this issue. Dairy UK says British farmers want quota to end, but this is based on a "survey" of 51 important figures in the milk business. And they are the ones who admit the price would drop! Set-aside seems to be pointless now there is a requirement for biofuels. Quotas on imports, or some means of limiting them, would be very helpful. If both export refunds and production quotas should end, what can we do with the resulting surpluses?

5. It is unfortunate that the whole of rural development has become tied up with the CAP. The CAP should concern food and farming. This, if profitable, will benefit the whole rural community. Grants for village halls, for instance, should not be classed as agricultural expenditure. It gives a false impression.

6. It is wrong that different member states should be allowed to have different levels of modulation. Those receiving more subsidy will be able to sell their produce more cheaply. It is all very well to say that those who lose money through modulation can regain it through environmental schemes. But farmers who are already environmentally orientated will already have money from this source. Also they may well be the farmers most in need of support.

7. We have always been opposed to the inclusion of agriculture in the edicts of the WTO. When the WTO started, as the General Agreement on Tariffs and Trade (GATT), agriculture was not included. It was later brought in, under an Agreement on Agriculture (AoA). This seems to serve very little useful purpose, if any, but benefits the most powerful food exporting nations and multinational traders. Many people think we would be better off without the AoA. We believe in food sovereignty, that is the right of nations to protect their farmers from cheap imports. It should apply to us and even more strongly to developing countries which are trying to expand their own food production capability and are seriously hampered by the WTO.

8. It is too early to tell if cross compliance has been helpful. It surely must have been, but it will be difficult to measure to what degree.

9. There is so much argument re climate change we have not been able to form opinions on it.

10 and 11. The budget was not very adequate before enlargement, and was mainly settled without reference as to how much more would be needed after it. It seems the original sum is now to be spread more thinly over more countries. As, contrary to government hopes, the Single Farm Payment is probably all that many farmers will have to live on, smaller farmers will inevitably not receive enough to support them. Our high rate of modulation will mean we are worse off than the rest of Europe—but then we are quite used to that! It would be wonderful if that situation could be improved!

12. The CAP and the economics of food production have now become so complicated that it is hard to see how the present economic structure could become disentangled, especially if we are expected to conform to the rules of the WTO. Consumers of our products have become used to buying them at bargain prices, often below the cost of production. They will complain if they can no longer. So will the government if consumers have to spend even a fraction more on food, leaving less to spend on manufactured goods. (And in the new casinos?)

Certainly the EU seems hell bent on regulating every detail of life, especially on the farm. Waste regulations, especially on carcass disposal, are shining examples of pointless rules causing extra expense. Set-aside should be abandoned now there is a need for biofuels. The EU should recognise the importance of food production and base its rules of trade on the fact that food is a vital product, and to be encouraged, not regulated into the ground. But food production at home should not be detrimental to other nations, who also have the right to food sovereignty.

June 2007

Memorandum submitted by Dr Tom MacMillan on behalf of the Food Ethics Council

1. The Food Ethics Council is a charity that works as an independent think tank and advisory body. The organisation promotes ethical decision-making that leads to better food and farming. The Council is chaired by a farmer and its members include consumer advocates and leading academic researchers.

2. The Council welcomes the Committee's inquiry and this opportunity to comment, and would be glad to provide further evidence on request.

3. This short response draws on research for a discussion paper that the Food Ethics Council published in December 2006, which fed into a policy workshop organised by the Sustainable Development Commission. Copies of that discussion paper and a report of the workshop have been submitted with this memorandum [not printed].

4. We respond below to three of the questions posed in the Committee's call for evidence.

Question 1: *Objectives of the CAP*

5. Many areas of the economy and public life are subject to special policies, including health provision and the defence industry. While the founding rationale of the CAP has weakened, agriculture needs a distinctive policy framework into the future because:

— Agricultural supply is less elastic and more insulated from changes in consumer demand than other sectors due to its dependence on ecological processes and the structure of the supply chain.

— Food production has a major impact on public health.

— Agriculture has a disproportionate impact on land use, the environment and animal welfare compared with other economic activities.

— Agricultural trade has an exceptional impact on the wellbeing of people in developing countries who depend on farming for a livelihood.

6. A common policy framework for the EU is essential because only a common approach can:

— Redress the harmful legacies of previous CAPs.

— Command the resources needed to safeguard the common environmental, social and cultural heritage in EU agriculture.

— Enable member states to be a progressive influence within international negotiations on agriculture.

7. The CAP of the future should help to make EU agriculture sustainable and the sum of its products healthier. It should:

— Promote public access to safe and nutritious food.

— Enable viable, diverse and dignified rural livelihoods.

— Respect the biological limits of natural resources, combat climate change and be a net contributor to the environment.

— Achieve consistently high standards of animal health and welfare.

8. It should pursue these aims:

— Now, yet also sustain the social, economic and natural resource base into the future.

— Within member states and for all third countries that the CAP affects.

— Recognising that agriculture supports and depends on other aspects of rural development.

9. Interventions under the CAP are only justified when the market would not otherwise meet these aims, and if they comply with the following principles:

— Public spending may only be made to reward the provision of public goods.

— Public goods are rewarded at best value to the taxpayer, taking into account that agricultural systems are ecologically and socially complex.

— Public investment must reduce the need for such payments in future.

— Price and trade interventions (market mechanisms) must counteract the dumping of agricultural produce internationally.

Question 4: *Market mechanisms*

10. Reform of the CAP's market mechanisms is necessary in the interests of EU consumers and taxpayers, and in the interests of international development.

11. Broad consensus exists about the need for some of the specific reforms that have been proposed, for example in HM Government's *Vision for the CAP*. Principal among these is the proposal to eliminate export subsidies.

12. The advantages to international development and to EU citizens of altogether eliminating other market mechanisms, including import tariffs, are less clear. While it is expected that the removal of many current mechanisms would yield widespread benefits, it does not follow that having few or no market mechanisms at all offers the best outcome.

13. The claim that eliminating market mechanisms is to the best advantage of people in poor countries, which is the most persuasive rationale for pursuing such an approach, may rest on at least three questionable assumptions:

— That less market intervention is best for international development—The World Bank view that eliminating market mechanisms in the US would help to raise world prices has been challenged by researchers at the University of Tennessee, commissioned by Oxfam USA.[9] According to their models of US agricultural reform, market management, where some market interventions are maintained, offers the best deal for poor countries. The US analysis does not translate to the EU, of course, but in the absence of similar research on the CAP it raises the question of whether proposals to date have considered a sufficiently broad range of plausible policy scenarios.

— That other conditions will be met—As the *Vision for the CAP* notes, major benefits to poor countries from EU liberalisation depend fundamentally on additional conditions being met, including investment in the infrastructure needed to trade, help with adjusting to "preference erosion" and protection for poor countries from forced liberalisation.[10] These conditions are not being met and

---

[9] Ray, D, De La Torre Ugarte, D and Tiller, K 2003. *Rethinking US agricultural policy: changing course to secure farmer livelihoods worldwide*. Agricultural Policy Analysis Centre, Univeristy of Tennessee, Knoxville, TN.

[10] HM Treasury and DEFRA 2005. *A vision for the Common Agricultural Policy*. HMSO, London, December: 7, 56.

it is questionable whether they will be, since they are not integral and enforceable components of the agricultural trade framework. In making informed comparisons of the pros and cons of different CAP reform packages for international development it is important to consider their effects under scenarios where these accompanying conditions are not fully met.

— That rising GDP trickles down to the poorest people within poor countries—It is widely accepted that eliminating market mechanisms in the EU would lead to pronounced winners and losers among poor countries. So, too, within them. Where poor countries benefit economically from liberalisation of the CAP, a substantial portion of those rewards may fall to large landowners and international companies. Corporate concentration in the food supply chain creates its own market distortions and puts producers in a weak position to benefit from increased access to EU markets.[11] Indeed, EU market access is irrelevant to many small-scale producers who will continue to depend on local and regional trade, including the half of the world's 852 million hungry who live in remote rural areas.[12] If the effects of CAP reform on international development were modelled in broader terms, with a greater focus on distributional issues compared with GDP, the optimal reform package might not be wholesale liberalisation. It is unclear how far current analyses of the effects of alternative CAP reform packages rely on GDP as a proxy for international development, compared with broader concepts of wellbeing in keeping with the principles of sustainable development.

14. By questioning these assumptions we do not mean to imply that introducing new mechanisms is necessarily preferable to eliminating them in the manner that HM Government proposes. However, it would seem prudent to explore, for example through economic models, the possible effects of a broader range of CAP reform scenarios, beyond simply dismantling current market mechanisms.

15. Alternative reform scenarios might consider, for example, the effects of mechanisms that reduce imports of animal feeds or the effects of market mechanisms designed to offset any indirect subsidy to production from CAP payments to EU farmers under Pillar 2.

16. In evaluating the possible effects of different packages of market mechanisms, it is crucial to ensure that the criteria used correspond to the objectives of CAP reform. If a major objective is to promote sustainable development internationally, in keeping with Defra's notion of "one planet farming", then evaluation criteria need to consider likely environmental impacts beyond the EU, for example to biodiversity or climate change. If an objective is to promote international development and combat poverty, then evaluation must go further than simply considering the effects on the GDP of poorer countries.

Question 9: *the CAP and climate change*

17. The CAP can contribute to the mitigation of, and adaptation to, climate change because it is an important factor affecting land use across the EU. It can include incentives and penalties that encourage land uses that result in lowered emissions of greenhouse gases or act as carbon sinks. It can also speed up changes in land use to adapt to a changing climate.

18. A wide array of instruments under the CAP might contribute to these ends. In designing and implementing such instruments, it is crucial to consider that:

— The UK and the EU's food will come from somewhere and climate change is a global problem. Hence, measures that lower the climate change impact of land uses within the EU, for example by reducing agricultural production, may result in a net increase in greenhouse gas emissions from our land use and from the food we eat. If we produce less food domestically then we will transport more from further away often, though not always, having a bigger impact on the climate.

— There is more to climate change than carbon and more to the environment than climate change. In "greening" the CAP, we must look for win-wins that mitigate and adapt to climate change, that bring other environmental benefits, for example to biodiversity, that are good for public health, and that contribute to vibrant rural communities and economies.

— In order to identify such win-wins, it is important to have a well thought-through vision of what "one planet farming" might look like in practice. At the moment, there is welcome direction of travel towards a lower impact food system, but little analysis of whether the trajectory we are moving along could result in EU land uses and a food system that could be sustained within its share of the planet's resources. For example, a "one planet" farming and food system for the EU might require major shifts towards low-input agriculture and curtailing food transport by road between EU member states—the CAP is one package of instruments that could help us rise to that challenge.

[11] Murphy, S, 2006. *Concentrated market power and agricultural trade.* IATP, Minneapolis, MN, August.
[12] UNDP and FAO estimates cited in Windfuhr, M and Jonsen, J, 2005. *Food sovereignty: towards democracy in localised food systems.* ITDG Publishing, Bourton-on-Dunsmore, March.

— Even if we recognise that climate change is a major problem, it does not follow that farming and our food system should make no net contribution to climate change. The UK or the EU could make a political decision that food and agriculture could be net contributors to climate change, offset by greater savings in other areas, or net sinks, potentially allowing for greater emissions from other activities. A precautionary approach would suggest that it is most rational, given the complexity of climate change and severity of its impacts, to err on the side of reducing greenhouse gas emissions more than might seem essential across most activities, including agriculture and food production— this is the approach taken by Government, in saying that agriculture should make a net positive contribution to the environment, and it is an approach that we endorse. However, the political issues this raises have not been fully resolved. For example, some reductions in climate change impacts may come at a disproportionately high social or wider environmental cost. The current debate over cutting back the air-freight of produce to the UK from poor countries is a case in point—at issue is not only the climate change impact, but how sustainable the export of fresh produce is as a development model.[13] Such issues warrant more direct policy and public debate.

— Biofuels development, mooted as one way of mitigating and adapting to climate change, covers a broad range of activities. At one end of the spectrum, agricultural waste can be used on farm as fuel, creating a relatively closed system with a low environmental impact. At the other, energy-inefficient industrial biofuels production, subsidised at the expense of EU taxpayers, promises to repeat the economic, social and environmental mistakes that sustainable development sets out to avoid.

29 May 2007

Memorandum by Professor David Harvey, Newcastle University

1. OVERVIEW

What should be the long-term objectives of the CAP? I see no reason to quarrel with the most recent expression from the European Commission (with the changes as indicated below)

— A competitive agriculture sector which can face up to the world market without being subsidised, since this is *not* acceptable internationally *nor coherent or sensible domestically*;

— Production methods which are sound and environmentally friendly, able to supply quality products of the kind the public wants;

— Diverse forms of agriculture, rich in tradition, which are not just output-oriented but seek to maintain the visual amenity of our countrysides as well as vibrant and active rural communities, generating and maintaining employment;

— A simpler, more understandable agricultural policy which establishes a clear dividing line between the decisions that have to be taken jointly and those which should stay in the hands of the Member States;

— An agricultural policy which makes clear that the expenditure it involves is justified by the services which society at large expects farmers to provide.

European Commission, Explanatory Memorandum, *The future for European Agriculture Agenda 2000*, Agricultural Proposals, June, 1998

Does the title "Common Agricultural Policy" aptly fit your perceived objectives of the policy?

No. A better title would be Healthy Agricultural Trade (HAT). The general objectives do not imply a specific policy for agriculture as such, other than assisting and encouraging competitiveness and responsiveness to market opportunities and demands. Specific policies are necessary for ensuring fair competition between member states, and for ensuring adequate provisions for public goods and for dealing with externalities, especially with reference to the environment.

---

[13] MacGregor, J and Vorley, B, 2006. *Are air miles fair miles?* Food Ethics 1(4): 13. Dalmeny, K, 2007 *Low-carb diet*. Food Ethics 2(2): 9.

What do you consider to be the main pressures on the CAP as it currently is?

The main forces appear to be: (1) public legitimacy, rational coherence, and fiscal balance of support/payments to farmers *versus* industry dependence on support, and capacity to accept and adopt further reform and adjustment; (2) the enlargement of the EU to include even more economies in transition, coupled with the shift of emphasis towards payments for environmental goods and services, implies widely differentiated and targeted policies, undermining the traditional logic of a common policy, commonly financed. These points are elaborated below.

2. THE REFORMED CAP

(a) *What has been your experience so far with the reformed CAP?*

Merely as a disinterested analyst/commentator.

(b) *What has worked well and less well?*

No comment, not elsewhere specified (nes).

(c) *And where can lessons be learned?*

No comment, nes.

3. THE SINGLE PAYMENT SCHEME

(a) *Do you consider the Single Payment Scheme to be a good basis for the future of EU agricultural policy?*

Yes, but only as a stepping-stone to elimination of all strictly agriculturally-related public payments and towards the development of appropriate mechanisms for the payment for environmental goods and services.

(b) *What changes might be made at the EU level to the Single Payment Scheme, including to the rules governing entitlements, in the short and/or the longer-term?*

In the long term, universal entitlements to SFP should be phased out, or the payments themselves phased out. In the short term, the co-responsibility for provision of environmental goods and services could be made more stringent and explicit, though the implied bureaucracy and possibilities for political failure should not be underestimated and suggest that phasing out is sufficient.

4. MARKET MECHANISMS

(a) *What short and longer-term changes are required to the CAP's market mechanisms? Suggestions made by the Commission have included re-examination of certain quotas, intervention, set-aside, export refunds and private storage payments*

The logic of coupled support, plus the clear international (WTO) aspirations to reduce (eliminate) coupled support (ie market intervention) both strongly suggest that all commodity market mechanisms should be eliminated in the long run. Short-term changes should be designed with this long run goal in mind. Arguments for government-sponsored stabilisation and insurance schemes need critical examination, though US style loan rate instruments, at safety-net levels, could be sensible as short-term facilitating measures in some underdeveloped market conditions (in some economies in transition).

5. RURAL DEVELOPMENT

(a) *What is your view on the introduction of the European Agricultural Fund for Rural Development (EAFRD)?*

A sensible political initiative, though of limited real value: (a) development involves more than agriculture, and depends on non-agricultural activity, involving the release of resources and labour from farming *per se*; (b) sustainable development is "bottom up", not "top down"; (c) what passes for development assistance is frequently confused with redistribution from the rich to the poor—and the EU budget, even with fiscal co-financing, is too small for sensible re-distribution policies.

(b) *Do you consider that it is meeting its objectives thus far?*

Probably meeting political objectives; too soon to tell whether it is making any real difference.

(c) *Is it suitably "strategic" in nature, meeting the needs of rural society as a whole rather than being restricted to aiding the agricultural industry?*

No—see above.

(d) *How well is it being co-ordinated with other EU and national policies on regional and rural development?*

Not at all well, as far as I can see.

6. IS THERE A CASE FOR A HIGHER LEVEL OF EU FINANCING OF RURAL DEVELOPMENT?

(a) *Do you have a view on the extension of compulsory modulation from Pillar 1 (Direct Payments) to Pillar 2 (Rural Development)?*

A good idea in principle, since it requires member states to be more explicit about their objectives and appropriate instruments.

7. WORLD TRADE

(a) *What benefits can the EU's World Trade Organisation obligations create for EU agriculture and, consequently, for the EU economy as a whole?*

An important added pressure for further internationally responsible reform of traditional farm policies, and an important "blame-shift" mechanism for domestic (EU) politicians to use in making necessary, but initially unpopular reforms. Free(r) trade is demonstrably one necessary (but not sufficient) condition for sustainable development.

8. ENVIRONMENTAL PROTECTION AND CLIMATE CHANGE

(a) *To what extent has the system of cross-compliance contributed to an improved level of environmental protection?*

Too early to say, except in certain very restricted conditions and circumstances.

(b) *How is it linking with other EU policy requirements such as the Water Framework Directive?*

Rather accidentally, so far as I can see, with exceptions of such initiatives as Nitrate Sensitive Areas.

9. HOW CAN THE CAP CONTRIBUTE TO MITIGATION OF, AND ADAPTATION TO, CLIMATE CHANGE?

In its present form, hardly at all, other than through a (likely spurious) shifting emphasis of commodity support towards bio-fuels (see below). Rather, the apparent (and superficial) connection between animal products and food miles with greater (unsustainable?) carbon footprints could precipitate inappropriate policy developments with substantial unintended consequences.

(a) *What do you consider the role of biofuels to be in this regard?*

Mostly spurious: at present fossil fuel prices, nearly all bio-fuels make no economic sense. At sensible fossil fuel and carbon prices, some limited bio-fuel production may make sense in some circumstances, though on a wide scale must be at the expense of either forest and natural vegetation carbon sinks, or world food production potential.

10. FINANCING

The Commissioner has expressed her dissatisfaction at the financing agreement reached by the Member States at the December 2005 Council.

(a) *Do you consider the current budget to be sufficient?*

For agriculture, more than sufficient; for the environment and rural development, possibly inadequate, though there is no solid evidence to decide; for any real redistribution from the rich to the poor, totally inadequate.

(b) *Do you consider co-financing to be a possible way forward in financing the Common Agricultural Policy?*

Definitely.

11. ENLARGEMENT

What has been the impact on the CAP of the 2004 and 2007 enlargements?

Too soon to tell what the effects of the recent enlargements on the CAP might be, though I am of the firm opinion that the unification of Germany (preceding and generating the recent enlargements) was fundamental in changing the political economy of the CAP reform process.

(a) *what is the likely impact of future enlargements of the EU on the post-2013 CAP?*

Increased pressure on the existing CAP, since the policy needs of the new member states (and some—Mediterranean—members) are quite different from those of the founding and more developed members (an argument developed in part B of this submission below).

12. SIMPLIFICATION OF THE CAP AND OTHER ISSUES

How could the CAP be further simplified?

Elimination of all commodity market mechanisms would constitute a major simplification, offset (potentially, and already in practice) by increasing complexities associated with (mostly misguided) attempts to target payments to environmental and rural development objectives (see below), and with common rules on different applications of policy, and co-financing, amongst an increasing number of member states.

(a) *In what other ways would you like to see the Common Agricultural Policy changed in the short and/or the long term?*

No comment, nes.

B: ONE VISION—WHAT STEPS? AN ASSESSMENT

The recent report of the House of Commons Environment, Food and Rural Affairs Committee on The UK Government's *Vision for the Common Agricultural Policy* (HC 546-1) presents a reasoned and well supported critique of the apparent present position of the UK government on both the CAP Health Check and EU Budgetary Review. In concluding my own submission to the HoC Committee (Ev 161), I said:

> "We need to reform and develop appropriate policies to improve the match between those trying to make a living from and those trying to have a life in the countryside. We need to remove the existing policies which are not helping and which are costing more than they deliver. The reforms, however, need to work with market forces, and not seek to replace or repeal them. The 'vision' presumes that the market will work for food and farming, but ignores the transition, which in practice is what much of the policy division is about. It assumes that government intervention will continue to be necessary

for the environment and rural development, but fails to explore the sorts of intervention that might work. 60 years ago, policy makers assumed that government intervention was necessary to secure food supplies and domestic farming. We are now picking up the pieces of that assumption. We should be careful that we are not sowing the seeds for yet another policy rescue problem in the future."

We argue that there are three major policy problems embedded in the present CAP:[14]

— Engineering and assisting the transition from a predominantly agrarian to a commercial/industrial economy—why did (and do) farmers need support?

— Developing appropriate institutions and mechanisms for the delivery of public (environmental or *care*) goods and resolving (internalising) externalities—how can we ensure a sustainable and socially desirable countryside?

— Designing and implementing (rural) development policies—how can we foster effective and sustainable development?

1. *Why did (and do) farmers need support?*

All developed countries have, until now, found it politically necessary to support and protect their farmers in one way or another. A simple explanation of this fact is that the development process involves fewer people earning a full time living from farming—people stop farming and do something else. The economic signals for this structural change are falling incomes in farming and rising incomes in other sectors of the economy. These signals reflect the economic forces of development and result in a falling share of people's total spending being spent on food, with the inevitable consequence that fewer people can earn their livings (at levels commensurate with the rest of the economy) from producing food. Other things being equal, farmers become relatively poorer during the transition process. In addition, those who move tend to be those who are better able, or less dedicated to farming as a way of life. Farming becomes the domain of the less able, and the most committed.

In democracies, especially, the richer and more fortunate tend to want their governments to do something for the less fortunate. This feeling is re-inforced in the case of farming by both peoples' general beliefs about the importance of farming and food security, and by their (possibly romantic) understanding of farming as a (traditional) way of life—after all many of them have memories of farming and relations still engaged in the business. Protection and support become 'natural' consequences—and the support mechanisms chosen are the most obvious—support food prices (without, if possible, compromising the urban poor), with import duties, export subsidies, deficiency payments etc.

Many economies in transition (with proportions of populations engaged in farming at or above 25%) find themselves in exactly this position—with a strong political pressure to support farming. These member states need some policy which provides convincing and plausible support to their farmers as farmers. The present CAP, and its evolutionary trends, does not easily fit this prescription.

Problem 1: *A single common policy for farming is no longer appropriate for an enlarged and diverse Union*

However, history also shows us that traditional support and protection does not help farmers much in the longer run. The poorer and smaller farmers do not get much from commodity related support. The industry as a whole, being competitive, tends to spend the additional (support) income on extra inputs, driving up costs and increasing intensity, often at the expense of the environment, and driving up the value of land and fixed assets in farming (livestock and machinery etc.) The first and most obvious difficulty with immediate elimination of support is that it would bankrupt a substantial fraction of the present farming businesses, perhaps as many as 50%. These people have paid prices for the land and capital (live and deadstock) which presumes a continuation of support. Remove the support and capital and land values (based on farming) collapse. The present farmers see their pension funds, and their capacity to weather commercial difficulties or develop their businesses, evaporate. They can be expected to make every effort to resist such a prospect—

---

[14] Overlaying these fundamental problems are partisan political issues associated with protecting and defending established vested interests and dependencies—farmers' organisations defending their "rights" to support; bureaucracies defending and seeking to expand their areas of competence (and authority); member states defending their historic benefits from the EU, and seeking to establish greater benefits; constituencies arguing for some or greater government support/protection. Finally, the real political issues of developing a 'Community' or 'Political Union' amongst or from an increasingly large collection of diverse member states also permeate any discussion of the future of EU policies, and the politics through which such discussions occur. This assessment does not deal with these issues.

which provides the current CAP support with its most resilient defence. Never mind that the most indebted ones would probably survive quite well—banks are unlikely to foreclose on half or more of their farming clients when the realisable value of their assets has just collapsed, so they would take steps to minimise their losses, often writing off debts and helping existing farmers stay in business (the New Zealand experience). The farmers who would really suffer are those without debts, whose wealth would be severely reduced (the real point of the Defra/Treasury 'Vision' observations on the effects of support).

Problem 2: *It is politically impossible, as well as being morally questionable, to eliminate Pillar 1 quickly or easily, even in the more developed member states, without some form of compensation.*

The implicit compensation offered in the 'Vision' document is simply continuation of single farm payments and other support for a finite, limited time (10 or 15 years), presumably gradually reducing each over this period. This is of little comfort or help to farmers. They would be better served with a lump sum, once-and-for-all payment—to protect their investment value and provide them with the capacity to adjust, either by changing their business systems or by leaving and letting someone else do it. Furthermore, they need to know what the new unsupported market will look like as soon as possible. Gradual change is much more likely to generate the boiling frog syndrome—drop a frog into a pot of boiling water and it will jump out; put it in cold water and bring it slowly to the boil and the frog will die. Sudden, but reliable change will induce rapid and viable responses; gradual change is much more likely to produce mal-adaptations and responses. This is even more likely when there is strong political resistance to the changes anyway, and every effort being made to slow them down or reverse them. Even assuming that we could persuade the EU to agree to elimination in the first place.

Resolution (1) of Problems 1 and 2: *Devolve CAP responsibilities to Member States. Four central facts strongly suggest a solution to the present European impasse on CAP and its funding.*[15]

Fact 1: The CAP is the only European policy that is both mandatory and 100% funded from the EU budget. All other policies are subject to member state contributions. When the CAP was invented, this made sense, but not now.

Fact 2: Decoupled single farm payments, with environmental compliance, are a radical change from the traditional CAP, with much lower social costs and market distortion. Neither the values of environmental care, nor the costs of providing for it, are uniform across the Union—there is no logic other than historical precedent requiring payments to be the same, or that they be commonly financed. The historical legacy of mandatory spending, exclusively financed from the EU budget, is no longer either legitimate or sensible.

Fact 3: The Central European countries, with large farming populations and low incomes, have joined the CAP on very unequal terms—their farmers are only paid 25% of the payment rates to their richer and more fortunate western cousins, though this proportion is set to rise in the future. There is neither logic nor justice in this glaring inequity.

Fact 4: The British rebate is only justified (if at all) on the grounds that Britain contributes a lot to EU funds (being a large economy), but gets relatively little back through the CAP (being a densely populated and small agricultural country). Other, less glaring, budgetary inequities will persist so long as the EU maintains its present CAP financing system, which absorbs 40% of an already pitifully small European budget for the support of farmers.

An answer can be distilled from these facts: let the EU budget pay only a fraction (say 25%) of the costs of the current CAP, instead of the present 100%. Make member states separately responsible for the balance for their own farmers, as they so wish, up to the budgetary ceiling already agreed. Member states would then be free to decide whether and how to make these payments, subject to European and international competition and trade laws and agreements, and subject to the European freedom of movement of (farm) labour and capital. If we wanted to provide limited lump sum compensation, we could. How can France sustain objection? If she wants to continue the CAP, she can (but at her own rather than our expense). Some policy competition between member states would be a good thing—to test different options. At the very least, such a solution might provide some relief from the otherwise destructive British political battle about the EU, giving the UK (and other member states) more discretion and control over their own local policies, in the true spirit of subsidiarity.

---

[15] These arguments are elaborated in Harvey, 2006.

2. *How can we ensure a sustainable and socially desirable countryside?*[16]

Pastoralists, however, complain (with some justification) that the free market (eliminating the traditional CAP entirely) will not provide the right levels of environmental conservation. They often argue that biodiversity, landscape quality, and environmental amenity need government intervention, regulation and support. Continued single farm payments, or something like them, with cross-compliance conditions about conserving the environment and natural resource, seem like a practical and effective way of providing the proper level of *care* (conservation, amenity, recreation and environmental) goods and services.

Problem 3:   *The free market will fail to provide sustainable and socially desirable countrysides.*

Markets for conservation, amenity, recreation and environment (*care*) goods and services fail because the people responsible for providing them (farmers) cannot get their necessary reward from the people who are willing to pay for them (pastoralists). The transaction and negotiation costs are too high. In addition, many of these countryside care goods are "public" rather than private—once we have a pretty landscape or diverse wildlife for one person, it is available for all, regardless of whether or not they pay for it. We end up with less care than we are actually prepared to pay for, because it is in peoples' self-interest to free-ride on other peoples' contributions. An obvious answer is to force people to pay (through the tax system) and for government to be responsible for the care of the countryside.

But this is not a sustainable answer—governments, especially national (still more multinational—EU) governments are not competent to mediate or organise the provision of *care* goods and services. *Care* goods and services are inherently <u>different</u>, depending on the geography and farming systems, and who wants and provides them. The costs, and ways, of providing them are widely and deeply heterogeneous, and the social values are also very different, depending on where they are and who is providing them. There can be no single market, nor any single policy menu or framework, which can take care of them. Furthermore, there is no sound reason to believe that bureaucratic organisations of disinterested and largely disconnected people, working according to rigid legislation and necessarily inflexible rules and protocols, are constitutionally capable of organising the appropriate production and delivery of these care goods and services.

Problem 4:   *Governments will also fail to provide sustainable and socially desirable countrysides*

The essential point of the market failure is the difficulty of getting the beneficiaries of the countryside care to put their money where their mouths are, and of getting these payments, and their associated care requirements and demands, to the people responsible for managing the countryside (the farmers and land users). The care markets don't work because the effort required is not worthwhile. But, as we get richer, so the benefits of getting care markets to work increase, and they do emerge. Voluntary contributions to the RSPB, the National Trust and wildlife trusts pay land users to do the right things with their land. But there are free riders. There would be more and greater voluntary contributions if we could each be sure that everyone who valued the countryside was making their full contribution to its care and maintenance.

Resolution (2) of Problems 3 and 4:   *Encourage and foster Care Markets*

We could encourage this by (a) allowing such voluntary contributions to be deductible (within limits) from tax bills (rather than simply allowable against tax); (b) making *ex gratia* payments from the Treasury to the care trusts to make good the free-rider shortfall on a *pro rata* £ for £ basis at some centrally agreed rate. The trusts would then be responsible for reflecting the demands and requirements of their members directly to the land users. Variety and diversity of demands and supplies would be catered for through the diversity of trusts. If a trust is doing a good job, it will be supported. If not, its donation flow will dry up. The consumers/users/ enjoyers of the countryside will be directly connected to the people needed to provide and sustain it.

The alternative of government intervention, regulation and payments to farmers separates the people willing to pay from the people who need payment to provide the care by a maze of procedures, rules, forms and disinterested bystanders and bureaucrats, which is neither effective nor efficient, and does nothing to integrate society. It fails for the same reason that all central planning fails—it is not capable of reflecting the real diversity of the market and it is too rigid to adapt and adjust to changing and differing circumstances. It fails because it fails to address the fundamental problems associated with externalities and public goods. In the end, it threatens to undermine peoples' faith in government itself.

---

[16]   These arguments are spelt out in more detail in Harvey, 2003.

On the other hand, especially if pursued within the framework of a devolved policy as advocated under Resolution 1, member states would be more free to develop and invent different ways of solving the countryside problems—and more and different solutions would provide increasing experience of what works and what does not, helping us all to evolve better and more effective ways of dealing with the problems.

3. *How can we foster effective and sustainable (rural) development?*

A major lesson to be drawn from the collapse of the Soviet Union is that sustainable development cannot be generated from the top down—it is not a command and control process. Development is an evolutionary process, which can be civilised, and needs to be cultivated and grown from the bottom up, with as free a flow of goods, services, ideas and investment as possible. Under-development is fundamentally a result of insufficient resources (physical, human, social and natural capitals) or inadequate mobilisation of the available resources to generate sustainable livelihoods (eg DfID, 1999). Hence, support for health, education, communications and transport systems are generic recipes for assisting development, coupled with sound finance, secure and honest government, all of which promote mobilisation of resources, or (in the case of education and health) improve the quality and quantity of local resources. Rural development is, in this sense, no different. However, history and geography also show us that peripheries and marginal areas tend to be less developed than the nodes and centres. In other words, the "spatial" capital of localities is also important—the less well linked the locality with other more developed regions, the less development can be expected. Of course, lack of spatial connection can be ameliorated by better communication and transportation—though these will generally be uneconomic and ineffective unless people really want to go on living in the remote locality, and can persuade others to spend enough on their products and services to allow them to do so. If not, attempting to promote peripheral development is pushing water up hill—it makes no real sense.

However, one of the consequences of traditional agricultural support has been to increase the value of assets, and the accumulation of incomes and capital in rural areas. This has almost certainly spilled over, to a greater or lesser extent, into the local economies. This augmentation of rural capital has encouraged and facilitated more general rural development. If socio-economic development is thought of as cultivation and domestication of a biological evolutionary system, then agricultural support (which generally pumps more income than otherwise into rural areas, at least in the first instance) is like fertilising a natural ecology (and protecting it from climatic extremes, as a hothouse does)—some "plants" and associated 'animals' will thrive and prosper, at the expense of others. Farms get bigger and more "luxuriant", while traditional crafts and livelihoods cannot compete. Typically, much agricultural support is dissipated to urban and offshore areas as the agricultural sector increases its use of purchased inputs and physical capital produced (and earning incomes) outside the rurality, though needing supply chains, which may generate some local incomes. However, it also makes the supported "plants"—the farms—more luxuriant (in terms of capital value) and more capable of reproduction of other forms of activity, as well as farming. The ecology (economy) changes shape to reflect the "cultivation".

Removal, or substantial alteration, in the "cultivation" practices—by removing the protective glasshouse, and eliminating (or dramatically altering) the fertiliser regime—will lead to consequent alterations in the ecological (economic) development trajectory. In those localities which are rich enough in desirable and otherwise useful resources, the change will not (probably) be especially dramatic—the local fauna and flora will adapt and adjust to the changed circumstances. But in the more remote and resource-poor areas, the policy reform (or the absence of suitable policy) could be extensive. The result of the Highland clearances on the local economies of the Scottish highlands is an obvious historic example. However, this example also illustrates the major difficulties of re-creating the traditional patterns and structures of socio-economic activity—in many ways, these historic patterns have become unviable.

Problem 5: *Rural development is either no different from non-rural development, or is impossibly difficult.*

Changing the CAP to deliver payments for environmental (care) rather than agricultural production *per se* will alter the "socio-economic cultivation" of rural areas and the agricultural sector in particular. Even if payments for environmental care substitute exactly for the traditional support, the incentives and subsequent opportunities for local growth and development will change substantially, as activities associated with both the production and consumption/enjoyment of *care* goods and services are encouraged at the expense of traditional agricultural activities. However, there is no reason in principle (other than defence of vested interest) why environmental payments should substitute exactly for traditional agricultural support, either in aggregate or at the farm level. The effects of this change will depend critically on both the capacity of the locality to produce *care* goods and services, and, more importantly, on the effective demand for these goods and services by the rest of the population. Those localities which are both capable and wanted can be expected to grow—otherwise they can be expected to decline, at least in relative terms.

So, how do we support and assist the declining areas? Pursuing the cultivation analogy, by using general "fertilisers" (which improve the "soil" fertility) and risk loosing those fauna and flora which cannot tolerate richer environments (often the traditional cultures and practices), and by encouraging cross-breeding and hybridisation, and other forms of "mutations" to exploit new niches and develop new capacities—the bottom-up development processes. While "seeding" new and exotic varieties and species into these declining areas (the top-down approach) might work on occasion, it seems likely to be by accident rather than design, and the successful "invasions" are likely to happen naturally in any event, providing the local conditions are appropriate.

Problem 6: *Successful and sustainable development is a process beyond the competence of Government to manage, and is not amenable to "policy", but only to careful socio-economic strategy (or "cultivation")*

The use of the "cultivation" analogy needs careful interpretation. Our history as people has depended on cultivation of specific species at the expense of their natural cousins and predators—we can and do exploit and encourage specific "civilised" and "domestic" species to our own advantage. But what we are talking about here is not the protection and support of specific species (eg cereals, or modern agriculture), but the enrichment of the whole "natural" ecology (socio-economy). The critical difference between natural evolution and socio-economic evolution is that the former relies on natural (exogenous) selection; the latter relies on self-selection—we make the rules about who survives, thrives and prospers and who deteriorates and declines (or dies). Our rules include social conventions, economic patronage and investment, personal attributions and expectations, as well as the complete apparatus of formal government. We cannot (yet, if ever) manage this process, we can only manage with it. Development is necessarily holistic and bottom up—it needs a socio-economic culture and commitment. It will respond to the socio-economic environment and the political climate, often in ways, which cannot be predicted (managed), and in ways which were not intended.

Nevertheless, some policies and government activities are likely to be more conducive to sensible and sustainable development than others. We argue above (Resolutions 1 and 2) for more appropriate CAP related policies than we have at present.

Resolution (3) of Problems 5 & 6: Foster development strategies (not policies), and scale limited EU resources to favour the less-developed.

However, given that sensible policy will continue to promote and encourage mobilisation of existing resources (education, communication, transport etc), at root under-development remains a consequence of inadequate resources. Either these existing resources must move to more developed, and development capable regions and localities, or they must be augmented by re-distribution (explicit grants-in-aid) from the richer localities. If "rural development" means developing presently under-developed areas <u>without</u> requiring or expecting the population to move out, then the only remaining strategy is to supplement their resources (with fungible and flexible assets—money). The EU budget, restricted to less than 1.4% of EU GDP, is clearly far too small to achieve very much genuine re-distribution. However, it could, with appropriate reform of the EU finance system (as under Resolution 1 above), focus these very scarce resources on the less-developed countries and regions, by scaling the ratios of EU to member state co-financing to favour the less developed regions.

References

DfID, 1999, *Sustainable Livelihoods Guidance Sheets*, Department for International Development, (eg at http://www.livelihoods.org/info/info—guidancesheets.html£1)

Harvey, D R, 2006, *The European Budget and the CAP: an agenda for reform?* EuroChoices, 5 (1) Spring, 22 127.

Harvey, D R, 2003, *Agri-environmental relationships and multi-functionality: further considerations*, The World Economy, 26 (5), 705—725, which examines single farm payments as a means of providing countryside care, and explains the alternative of trusts, with appropriate references, Available at: http://www.staff.ncl.ac.uk/david.harvey/DRHRootFolder/DRH—research.html

17 July 2007

Memorandum by the Institute of Agricultural Management and Bidwells

OVERVIEW

The long term objectives of the CAP should be the creation of, and maintenance of, a vibrant and sustainable rural economy built around the principles of food, fuel and environmental security. The language CAP is probably unhelpful as it presents a picture of market intervention and protectionism which is still (wrongly) used around the world to deride European Agricultural Policy, especially in World Trade talks. Language such as Integrated Food, Energy and Environmental Security Policy might be more relevant for the 21st century.

THE REFORMED CAP

It is important that UK adopts a stance which is persuasive in the Council of Ministers, and starts by recognising that the 2003 reforms, implemented over the last two years, represent a substantial move forward which has yet to be fully implemented in some other member states—and that the implementation of these reforms leaves much to be desired in the UK also.

The UK must continue to push the rest of the EU to implement full decoupling as soon as practical. The complex array of partially coupled systems together with various historical and hybrid implementation measures have led to unnecessary complexity and distortions across the EU. It also weakens our WTO negotiating position when in reality about 10% of single payment aids remain coupled. A move to a totally area based payment for Pillar 1 across EU 27 would seem most logical, given that England, Germany and the New Member States adopting SAPS will effectively have this system in place by 2012.

Even an area based single payment in pillar 1 is probably not sustainable as we get further into the 21st century. Having evolved out of a complex mixture of market instruments and direct payments it is trying to be an "income support", a "compensation payment" and a "land management" payment all in one. It is a blunt and non-targeted policy instrument which, in trying to achieve a lot of things at once, will probably achieve none very well, if at all. Yet it is providing a useful transition from the direct aids of the 1990s under MacSharry to more targeted policy instruments likely to be developed as pillar 2.

The CAP should increasingly focus on securing the benefits which the market alone cannot secure ie it must identify where market failure is occurring and seek to remedy these issues. Over the last few years, the scope of the second pillar of the CAP has been widened to include a wide array of rural development issues as well as "agri-environment" objectives, but it is now crucial that it should be adapted to steer farmers and land managers to help mitigate climate change. The Commission has recognised this and declared its intention to publish outline proposals shortly.

Farmers and land managers are perhaps more directly impacted by climate change than almost any other sector, and can do more to mitigate its effects by the way they manage the land:

— agricultural practices can be adapted so as to reduce emissions of nitrous oxides and methane in particular;

— forestry and soil management practices can be adapted to optimise the extent to which carbon is sequestered or stored in growing crops, trees and particularly in the soil; and

— farmers and land managers are ideally placed to provide alternative and renewable sources of energy, thus helping to substitute mineral sources.

If the CAP is to be an effective instrument in guiding these changes, we believe this is much more likely to happen as a result of effective incentive mechanisms under an expanded pillar 2 than under cross compliance (pillar 1) or other regulatory mechanisms. What is needed from land managers is a new and positive land management practice, not grudging compliance with rules designed to support pillar 1 payments. It is accepted, however, that pillar 1 payments will remain in a much reduced form, since the Commission recognises that there have been positive benefits to cross compliance in its current form which would be lost if there was no pillar 1.

If UK is to make a persuasive case for such an approach, certain conditions need to be met:

— UK needs to be committed to, and seen to be committed to a broad definition of rural development going well beyond agri-environment schemes. A dispute with the European Commission as to whether 20% of its rural development expenditure is or is not expended on other aspects of the regulation (ie. Axes 1 and 3 of the rural development regulation) will not form a sound basis for such discussions.

— UK needs to secure a larger share of EU rural development funds—the EAFRD—based on objective criteria rather than historically low uptake.

— UK should push for higher rates of compulsory modulation across the EU—and ensure that all of these are retained by the member state—thus allowing country specific levels of Voluntary modulation to be reduced.

Defra and its agencies need to show that they understand how to use incentive rather than regulatory mechanisms to secure the delivery by the private sector of the range of objectives set out in regional as well as national strategies. Unless these objectives and the related incentives are taken into account by land managers in planning their future strategies, they will not be secured from the land management sector.

The wider debate is then whether we need a common policy, how common does the policy need to be, and how should this be funded. Once support is fully decoupled from production and the market there is less of a solid case for a "common policy"—what we really want are common *outcomes* (ie an entrepreneurial and thriving rural economy with market focussed farmers) not necessarily common policy instruments. Thus policies can be (or maybe even *have to be*) increasingly uncommon, differentiated and tailored to specific regional and national differences, to achieve this.

However, the case for at least a common framework remains. EU directives for biodiversity, habitats and species, nitrates, water, soil and no doubt in time greenhouse gases apply across the Union. The transboundary nature of most of these environmental issues—including the fact that citizens in one EU state do not only care about biodiversity on their doorstep but on a much wider scale—would suggest an element of baseline commonality with any 21st century food and environmental security policy.

I hope that these few thoughts are of interest. If you would be interested in a further submission, including oral evidence, then we would be pleased to follow this up.

June 2007

Memorandum by the Institute for European Environmental Policy (IEEP)

INTRODUCTION

1. The Institute for European Environmental Policy (IEEP) is an independent centre for the analysis and development of policies affecting the environment in Europe and beyond. We undertake research and consultancy work on the development, implementation and evaluation of environmental and environment related policies in Europe. IEEP seeks to engage directly in relevant policy debates and works closely with the full range of policy actors from international agencies, and the EU institutions, to national government departments, NGOs and academics.

2. IEEP has an established track record of policy research and analysis on the CAP. Recent work for the European Commission includes: an evaluation of the Less Favoured Area measure in the EU-25; the environmental impacts of the CAP beef and dairy regime; and, an evaluation of cross compliance in the EU-25. Work for Defra includes work on: trade liberalisation and the CAP; the environmental impacts of the 2003 CAP reform; and, the environmental benefits of Pillar I of the CAP. Our research puts us in a position to make an informed response to the questions raised by the Committee's Inquiry into the future of the CAP and gives us some familiarity with the effects of agricultural and environmental policy across the EU-27 Member States.

3. The 2003 CAP reform introduced some notable changes to the agriculture policy framework, including decoupling and compulsory cross compliance. The impacts of these changes are not yet fully apparent at farm level but a picture is beginning to emerge of the extent to which the reforms have met their intended objectives. As noted by the Committee, the forthcoming "Health Check" of the CAP in 2008 is expected to lead to short term "adjustments" with limited changes in overall policy objectives. The budgetary review in 2008–09 is likely to result in longer term reflections—and possibly decisions—on the future shape of expenditure, potentially anticipating changes to the CAP beyond 2013. There is a case, however, that more fundamental agriculture policy discussions should take place first, in advance of the budget review, if future agriculture policy is not to be steered unduly by politically contentious decisions about the size of the future EU budget. With this in mind, we offer our thoughts on both the short and longer term prospects for CAP reform.

EAFRD, for example, capable of addressing some of the most significant environmental issues facing Europe such as climate change or water management? How effectively does EAFRD address the development needs of rural areas as a whole rather than just those needs closely allied to the agriculture sector? This final question is particularly pertinent since figures for planned expenditure for 2007–13 rural development programmes indicate that Axis 3—the Axis most able to target rural development activities beyond the farm gate—will receive the lowest share of the rural development budget in many Member States.

19. Concerns have also been raised about the use of some rural development funds in certain Member States. For example, some countries such as Spain have used rural development funds for capital investments and infrastructure projects that have caused environmental damage. Similarly, some Member States with high shares of internationally important habitats and species have allocated very low shares of their budgets to environmental measures. The in-built subsidiarity of the regulations allows Member States to make such choices but the Commission, in approving plans, must ensure such conflicts are avoided as far as possible.

WORLD TRADE

Trade liberalisation may result in both benefits and threats to the environment as agriculture restructures in response. A Doha agreement is likely to require, and may encourage, further reform of the CAP.

20. Our past work on the effects of agricultural trade liberalisation on EU agriculture has focused primarily on the environmental impacts. With the WTO Doha trade negotiations entering what may be their concluding phase, although this is by no means certain, it is important to understand what the land use and environmental implications of an agreement might be and thus to begin to assess the degree of compatibility of an increasingly market-exposed agriculture with broader rural sustainability objectives.

21. Various studies[20, 21, 22] suggest that, in a European farming context, the effects of trade liberalisation will be mixed and some will not, on balance be beneficial to the environment. The form and rate of liberalisation, as well as the ability to apply any flanking measures under WTO rules, are critical in determining the restructuring process that inevitably flows from exposing a previously protected agriculture sector to market forces. The exact nature and specificity of any Doha agreement will therefore determine the impacts that flow from it. The picture is complex and there is insufficient space here to explore all the possible outcomes of a trade agreement. However, assuming an agreement is reached, based on the current inbuilt agenda, further reform of the CAP is likely to be necessary. It is unlikely, for example, that on the current scale, partial decoupling (as applied by some Member States) would be likely to survive following a Doha agreement. The extent to which EU policy makers then choose to further rebalance EU agriculture, steering it away from the production of commodities for world markets and expanding the production of quality products for domestic and international markets, is uncertain. This choice is likely to be determined in part by whether the EU is able to extract concessions on non-trade concerns such as Geographical Indications and the protection of multifunctionality.

ENVIRONMENTAL PROTECTION AND CLIMATE CHANGE

Cross compliance

Cross compliance has resulted in environmental protection but implementation could be improved. The policy could be further strengthened and its environmental outputs enhanced under various policy options.

22. IEEP is currently undertaking three European Commission funded projects looking at different aspects of cross compliance and has a wide knowledge of the implementation of this policy across the EU. Our research suggests that cross compliance is resulting in an improved level of environmental protection as a result of the following:

— The establishment of environmentally relevant obligations (Statutory Management Requirements (SMRs) and Good Agricultural and Environmental Conditions (GAECs)) with which farmers, throughout the EU must comply.

— The provision of information to farmers which has increased awareness of their obligations although not necessarily their understanding of them.

[20] Potter, et al (1997) *Agricultural liberalisation and its environmental effects*, English Nature Research Report, English Nature, Peterborough.
[21] IEEP/GHK (2005) *The environmental impact of trade liberalisation and potential flanking measures*, IEEP, London.
[22] Kaditi, E and Swinnen J (eds) *Trade Agreements, Multifunctionality and EU Agriculture*. CEPS Brussels 2006.

OVERVIEW

The CAP should continue to evolve into a more broadly based policy concerned with sustainable rural development and resource management designed to secure the provision of a range of public goods and services. The objectives of the CAP should be revised and a new title agreed that better represents what the policy does.

4. The founding objectives of the CAP, as set down in the 1957 Treaty of Rome, emphasise goals such as food security and fair incomes for farmers. Successive reforms have, without revision to the original Treaty, progressively moved the CAP towards a policy designed to promote sustainable agriculture[17] and rural development. Decoupling, the introduction of initially voluntary, and now, compulsory cross compliance measures and the Rural Development Regulation, now the European Agricultural Fund for Rural Development (EAFRD), are examples of how the architecture of the CAP has changed since the late 1980s.

5. EU policy reforms have been accompanied by a repositioning of agriculture as a more explicitly "multifunctional" activity that provides a range of public goods,[18] including the protection of natural resources, the maintenance of cultural and historic landscapes and the provision of recreational opportunities. More recently, environmental goods have been discussed in terms of "ecosystem services". The UN Millennium Ecosystem Assessment defines four categories of services:

— Provisioning Services (eg food, fuel and building materials).

— Regulating Services (water purification and climate regulation).

— Supporting Services (necessary for production of other ecosystem services).

— Cultural Services (recreation, spiritual, aesthetics and sense of well-being).

Greater clarity about farming's long term role in providing these services in Europe should underpin both the goals and mechanisms of agricultural policy.

6. Looking ahead to a world in which containing climate change is a central challenge, agriculture's role in supplying renewable resources of energy and raw materials, sequestering carbon and reducing greenhouse gas emissions will be increasingly critical.

A longer term and more integrated perspective on resource management is required. This implies greater linkages between agricultural and energy policy and breaching some of the traditional divides, for example, between agriculture and forestry. Commodity production will continue to be important but in a different context from the 1960s when the CAP was put in place. With the advent of decoupling and modulation, the mechanisms of the CAP have moved on from their original commodity production logic but with no corresponding shift in the formal objectives in the Treaty. Leaving aside the political feasibility of agreeing appropriate new objectives for the CAP, it is clearly desirable to anchor a new vision and sense of direction in an amended Treaty. On this foundation, intervention measures could be based on a new and forward looking logic rather than the historically rooted compensation rationale that underpins the present direct payments.

7. A more integrated agricultural policy will need to address:

— The longer term resource management and ecosystem services agendas alluded to earlier, with the focus on public goods.

— Reasonable stability in food and raw material supplies.

— The economic and social viability of the agriculture sector at a time of continuous change in an enlarging Europe.

— A complex rural development agenda exhibiting considerable variation within Europe.

— Sustainable and equitable trade relationships.

[17] The Council of the European Union, in its conclusions from the Gteborg Council on the European Union's Strategy for Sustainable Development in 2001, stressed the need for the EU to integrate environmental objectives into its internal policies and to improve the sustainable management of natural resources.
[18] Public goods are defined as non-rival and non-excludable, ie consumption of the good by one individual does not reduce the amount of the good available for consumption by others; and no one can be effectively excluded from using that good. Insufficient provision of public goods is an example of market failure. Production of public goods results in positive externalities which are not remunerated. Because no private organisation can reap all the benefits of a public good which they have produced, there will be insufficient incentives to produce it voluntarily. Consumers can take advantage of public goods without contributing to their creation.

THE REFORMED CAP

The 2003 CAP reform introduced a complicated package of measures which gave Member States many implementation options. Such options give rise to variable economic, social and environmental impacts which are not always easy to anticipate when policy is agreed. Any future CAP reforms should be preceded by full (economic, social and environmental) impact assessments.

8. The 2003 reform sought to simplify the CAP, but following a range of concessions to national governments, resulted in one of the most complicated packages to date due to the range of options it provided Member States. For example, there are three different options for the design and calculation of the Single Payment Scheme, options for partial decoupling and for "additional payments" (referred to as national envelopes). A simpler and different system is in place for the Member States that joined the EU in 2004 and 2007 at least for some years. As a compromise deal, it highlights the increasing difficulty of securing agreement on a common policy in an enlarged Union. The way in which Member States approach implementation of variable options can give rise to very different economic, social and environmental effects; this is confirmed from the evidence collected for a number of policy evaluations we have undertaken for DG Agriculture of the European Commission.

9. One consequence of such differences may be undesirable impacts on competitiveness within the internal market. From an environmental perspective, however, national discretion and subsidiarity may have some benefits, allowing Member States to design and target policy to reflect national or regional circumstances and conditions, as can occur with cross compliance obligations. This underlines the value of undertaking full impact assessments during the policy development phase in order to determine the likely effects of any possible reforms. Such assessments should include consideration of how implementation may differ from Member State to Member State and farmers' likely responses to policy proposals.

10. On specific aspects of the 2003 reform, we offer detailed comments on cross compliance in paragraphs 22–24 of our submission.

THE SINGLE PAYMENT SCHEME

The future of the SPS is open to question if the objective of policy is the delivery of public goods. The 2008 Health Check is an opportunity to increase rates of modulation. From 2013, more fundamental reforms to Pillar I of the CAP are required and various options should be explored.

11. The Single Payment Scheme is the central policy instrument of Pillar I of the CAP. Payment allocations do not reflect environmental and rural development needs but rather historic production patterns. Payments are based on a compensation logic, replacing support that was previously linked to production. This is not an appropriate long term basis for agricultural and rural policy which needs to have a stronger focus on the provision of public goods and services, with some flexibility regarding the variety of conditions and challenges in the EU.

12. Commissioner Fischer Boel has already hinted at likely components of the 2008 Health Check including a move to the full decoupling of aid (with options for partial decoupling removed) and an increase in the rate of compulsory modulation to shift a greater proportion of funding into Pillar II. We consider these would be important first steps in a more fundamental reform of the CAP which should continue beyond 2008.

13. The arguments for strengthening Pillar II are powerful:

— It has much clearer objectives than Pillar I and these address long term concerns and the provision of public goods.

— It is subject to planning and an analysis of needs, programming, monitoring and evaluation. These disciplines allow the policy to respond to changing requirements compared to blanket payments in Pillar I.

— There is more flexibility to match local conditions.

— Co-funding provides some incentive for Member States to seek value for money.

Given these characteristics, Pillar II provides a potentially more effective mechanism for a sustainable rural policy than a reliance on a compensatory payment such as the SPS or some of the alternatives to it in Pillar I, such as bonds. Consequently, the principle of modulation is attractive, with certain provisos:

— There have been few empirical studies of the full consequences of modulation in practice and so the impact of the measure in different settings is not yet established.

— Pillar II measures need to be well designed and sufficiently simple in administrative terms to avoid large transaction costs.

— Some of the principal environmental benefits associated with agriculture in Europe arise from "Hi Nature Value" farming, much of which comprises low intensity livestock grazing systems generati relatively limited commercial returns. Pillar II measures on their own are not sufficient to maint these systems under current circumstances and this is an issue where direct payments can contrib to the provision of wider benefits. A means of providing support for appropriate management o and above the compensation logic of agri-environment measures will continue to be required. T amounts to "recoupling" to clearer objectives not simply decoupling.

— Sufficient funding needs to be available for Pillar II on a secure footing to provide confidence t this is a long term strategic measure for Europe. This would contrast with recent experience, suc the sharp cuts in the Commission proposals for Pillar II expenditure made at the December 2 Council.

— The allocation of funding between Member States needs to be put on a more rational basis rel clearly to the objectives and the needs identified.

14. In the longer term (2013 and beyond), there are different variants of Pillar II and modulation that c be envisaged. With a decline or demise in Pillar I, various policy tools could be used to help protect incomes from the vagaries of the market, for example, crop insurance, futures contracts, tax and social sec measures. Funding for Pillar II would be increased from present levels with the final allocation based o assessment of needs. The measures contained within Pillar II should be reviewed and revised, if necessar ensure they are suited to meeting the desired objectives.

15. In evaluating the options, some key questions to consider include: which option is most likely to und the continuation of those farming activities which are critical to the delivery of many public goods? Wh the administrative and technical requirements of the different options and which are likely to be more eff in terms of the use of public money? What would be the wider effects on trade, food security, the food and rural communities of the different options?

MARKET MECHANISMS

Many market mechanisms are no longer required as a result of past reforms and could be phased ou aside has provided environmental benefits and alternative ways of capturing these should be examine

16. The CAP is already on a trajectory of reduced market intervention, illustrated by progressive re which have cut price support, reduced intervention and, latterly, decoupled support from productic farming is brought closer to the market, the need for mechanisms such as quotas, set-aside and private s decline. However, the outright abolition of such measures would be likely to result in various consequ which need to be thoroughly examined before action is taken. Changes often need to be phased in ove

17. Set-aside is of particular interest to us because, although essentially a supply control measure whic no longer be needed, some proportion of this land has proved to be of environmental value, providing v habitat within otherwise denuded areas. As part of any future reforms, we suggest that ways of "capt the benefits of set-aside be considered rather urgently. Establishing an obligation to maintain or es Ecological Priority Areas[19] could be one means of retaining non-cropped areas.

RURAL DEVELOPMENT

The measures within EAFRD should be reviewed and, if necessary, revised, to ensure that a sufficientl range of environmental and rural development needs are met. EAFRD should not be allowed t environmentally damaging activities.

18. The European Agricultural Fund for Rural Development (EAFRD) is, for the most part, a prog of earlier rural development policy (Regulation 1257/99). This earlier Regulation was an umbrella unde a range of pre-existing measures such as the agri-environment and forestry measures, first introduced i were brought together. The extent to which the EAFRD constitutes a coherent package designed to public goods, rather than an assembly of previously relevant measures growing incrementally, is the key question. The EAFRD has now been strengthened by the requirement for an EU strategy and N Strategic Plans, in addition to Rural Development Plans, which set out the priorities and justification f development expenditure. There is an argument however for a fundamental review of the option EAFRD and their implementation if, as is possible, budgetary allocations to Pillar II increase in fu

---

[19] Lessons can be drawn from the Swiss system where farmers are required to take a proportion of land receiving suppo production for ecological reasons and to manage it accordingly. Existing features such as hedgerows and copses could be i this area. Those farmers who have retained such features in the past would easily meet the requirements of the scheme w farmers would have to take specific action.

— The recent introduction of Farm Advisory Systems which should help to improve farmers' understanding of their obligations.

— More systematic systems of control which are more likely to detect non-compliances.

— The threat of payment reductions, which farmers are very aware of, and which encourage compliance.

23. It is early days, however, in the implementation of the policy and there is clearly room for improvement across the Member States. The Commission has recently proposed some revisions to the policy which should facilitate its effectiveness and help to improve the acceptability of the policy. For example, the Commission has proposed that for minor non-compliances, Member States should be allowed not to apply payment reductions but rather to "warn" farmers that they are non-compliant and that they must take action to remedy this.

24. The cross compliance policy could be further strengthened and its environmental outputs enhanced. IEEP, along with a network of European Institutes[23] recently presented a range of options for the development of cross compliance at a policy seminar held in Brussels on 26 April 2007. These options move from relatively minor fine tuning of cross compliance to a more fundamental policy reform of Pillars I and II, in line with our earlier comments. The second option considers whether new legislation such as the Water Framework Directive should be included in the SMRs or relevant aspects included in GAEC, since there is currently no direct link between this legislation and the cross compliance policy.

Climate change

The process of absorbing climate change objectives in the CAP is in its infancy. Pillar II measures could contribute to the mitigation of, and adaptation to, climate change and could support second generation fuel production.

25. At the present time, climate concerns are barely reflected in the policy measures of the CAP. The principal focus has been on incentives for growing energy crops. Here the objectives have been wider than the mitigation of greenhouse gas emissions, reflecting a concern to diversify farm incomes, for example. There has been little attention given to mitigation or carbon sequestration as priorities for agricultural policy. In the second Pillar of the CAP, concerned broadly with rural development, there are no dedicated measures responding to the climate challenge. There is, on the other hand, a clear instruction to the Member States in the Strategic Guidelines that their rural development programmes should address Community priorities, one of which is climate change. In this sense, the process of absorbing a new climate dimension into the CAP is in its infancy.

26. There are numerous ways in which the CAP could contribute to the mitigation of, and adaptation to, climate change. Possible options include:

— Using Pillar II to provide incentives to farm businesses eg for technical measures to reduce greenhouse gas emissions and improve energy efficiency.

— Using legislation and incentives to achieve "joint" climate and environmental objectives eg reducing nitrous oxide emissions and water pollution by improving management of manure and livestock wastes or re-flooding oxidising peat soils in selected locations to contribute to soil conservation, climate change and biodiversity goals.

— Using Pillar II incentives to help adaptation to climate change and respond to issues such as pressure on biodiversity, landscape change, flood management and reductions in water supplies.

27. The current focus on providing incentives to grow conventional agricultural crops for bioenergy purposes is difficult to defend in many cases given their carbon and environmental profile. Nonetheless, there may be political pressure to increase incentives for growing energy crops to stimulate supply, especially if market set aside is abolished. This does not appear good value for money in the light of the buoyant market and limited increase in carbon efficiency achieved by substituting first generation biofuels for fossil fuels. As second generation fuels become more readily available, the case for incentivising appropriate crop production on a limited scale to pump prime new technology becomes stronger especially if the efficiency of conversion processes can be improved. This could be tackled through a range of measures,, focusing on innovation, the development of sustainable production and processing technologies, the creation of suitable infrastructure and local scale initiatives.

28. Imported biofuels come from a wide variety of sources and there is clearly a role for developing countries in this market, which should not be stifled by protectionism. Concerns about unsustainable or environmentally damaging crop production are, however, legitimate, especially since biofuels are being sold as

[23] http://www.ieep.eu/publications/pdfs/crosscompliance/future_policy_options_for_cc.pdf

a "green" fuel. A code of EU standards for bioenergy crop production which would apply to both domestically produced and imported crops would help to eliminate the least sustainable practices and set standards on a non-discriminatory basis. This can build on existing cross compliance.

Whilst some farming interests regard this as duplication, the need for a transparent and balanced approach in the early stages of the industry's development is clear.

FINANCING

A greater proportion of CAP funding should be shifted from Pillar I to Pillar II and co-financing of Pillar I should be considered.

29. The financing agreement reached by Member States at the December 2005 Council resulted in a very poor allocation of resources to Pillar II of the CAP, much less than the Commission's original proposal. As indicated earlier, we support further compulsory modulation, shifting resources from Pillar I to Pillar II of the CAP. In the future, the possibility of co-financing Pillar I should be considered both for budgetary reasons and to focus more on the benefits derived from such payments.

11 June 2007

Memorandum by Mrs Sonia Kurta

In order to ensure food security the CAP was devised to enable farmers to plan ahead knowing that they could expect a reasonable return for their produce, so that agriculture would not become as run down as it had been prior to 1939.

Within 10 years a state of surplus had been reached. Unlike the UK system of deficiency payments (which were given up as being too costly to administer when the UK joined the Common Market) which enabled consumers to benefit from cheaper imports, the method of ensuring farm gate prices high enough to give reasonable farm incomes led to ever growing European surpluses. In order to balance supply with demand to get the required farm gate prices these surpluses were removed by using complicated intervention schemes, export subsidies, set aside and quotas. Unpopular with consumers, importers and countries which were having their production undercut, these schemes were largely unsuccessful.

Concluding that food security was no longer important, the Single Farm Payment, de-coupled from food production, was introduced.

However, it is beginning to be recognised that world food supplies may not be so plentiful in the not too distant future. Therefore the long term aim of the CAP should be to ensure food security whilst enabling food to be sourced from where the consumer will get the greatest benefit.

De-coupling and the Single Farm Payment is not what is needed. Due to low and/or fluctuating prices this payment is being used to bolster food production, which is not what it was intended for. Logically farmers would be expected to do the minimum required to get this payment and cease food production until they knew they would get a fair return and could therefore plan ahead.

Due to enlargement the EU now has countries with very diverse agriculture. It may well be that it would be more satisfactory if each country was allocated a share of the CAP payments to use as deemed fit, but not to be diverted from farming.

A simple deficiency payment system could be implemented for the UK, if not thought suitable for the whole EU. This would be based on average yields and prices, no individual records to be kept. Farmers registering would simply have to guarantee to, say, grow a given minimum acreage of wheat (or any other crop or type of livestock required). They would sell this on the open market, plus as much more as they cared to grow, only the agreed minimum amount being covered by the scheme. This scheme would give farmers a stable price for sufficient produce to give food security, whilst being flexible to enable them to take advantage of higher market prices when these occurred. Each individual would be encouraged to produce for the market by getting the best price he could. World prices would not be affected. The scheme would be easy to administer as each person registered would receive a cheque for a similar amount at the end of the year, based on the difference between average costs plus an agreed amount, and the average returns received for the commodity.

Further details of this system can be given if required.

June 2007

Memorandum by W H Locker

I will confine my remarks to the SFP, others will have better opinions on the rest.

The reforms of 2003 have resulted in more regulation and inspections than when the livestock schedules were in operation.

That SFP was sold to our industry on the basis that; provided the environment was not spoiled, farmers could get on, farm and produce what the market wanted.

That was a deception.

Sheep market has collapsed. Flocks are being dispersed. Milk is a disaster and the Auctioneers have waiting lists, months long, to dispose of dairy herds. Locally the numbers of suckler cows and beef stores are just not there. Traditional sales of + 1,000 are down to 300 and some sales are cancelled because of the lack of trade. Unless this decline is reversed the nation's food supply will be seriously diminished.

What concerns the industry most is that the staff (DEFRA/SEERAD) previously employed to administer the schemes have all been retained and now duplicate the inspections of Env Agency Trading Standards heritage: BDMS, Farm Assurance etc . . . etc . . . all in the name of cross compliance. A volume has been produced—complete with penalties. They now inspect everything in sight and impose penalties. For example, the borders were blitzed recently. Teams from SEERAD inspected for days at a time. Passports/ear tags/records. Another team are counting sheep against records. Substantial numbers of farmers lost 1% SFP for minute paper errors or the odd tag that had come out.

That achieved nothing to assist agriculture or food production or for the environment. There is a report in the Press one man spent four weeks measuring up strips around arable fields on one farm and measured the wave of the plough to justify a penalty. Near here 1% deduction; he had a water trough 6' x 3' between two arable fields, when his map showed a straight line.

That duplication is needlessly costing the public purse and achieving nothing except artificially retaining civil service jobs.

Once those penalties are imposed (by junior staff) there is no way you can successfully appeal. SEERAD run the appeals, at every stage—including the selection of those "independents"—who, if they found in favour of a farmer, would not be selected again. So much for an independent system!

That body still has not arranged independent appeals for over 2,000 farmers in respect of their SFP and that is four years on.

To improve the situation is not difficult but vital in terms of feeding the nation. The Press records at great length RPA failures.

Having gone for a complicated system is grand for staff retention, but hopeless for delivering (reports that 3 x payments are being made to staff to do the job they were engaged to do).

It makes no sense to consult those who set it up in the first place and who clearly cannot deliver.

1. Simplify the whole system—one single payment per acre based on deeds or IACS maps 2003 and paid only where the land is owner-occupied or bone fide tenanted, but FARMED. Special provision will be necessary to protect the hill farming and the environmental contribution they provide for the upland landscape.

   That cuts out all the previous "arrangements'" which in the past produced subsidy payments. It cuts the bureaucracy and produces massive savings to the taxpayer (it costs something like £6.50 to administer £2.70 SFP).

2. The "Env Schemes" are few, difficult to access and achieve little. There is a high DEFRA/SEERAD staff involvement on top of Nat Heritage staff.

   Farmers always have provided the landscape loved by the public. That will continue just as soon as there is an upturn in income without the bureaucracy.

3. The Assurance Schemes take care of animal welfare issues and do not need RPA involvement.

4. The RPA will continue for some time. A core will be meaningfully engaged. However, those who have presided and arranged the present discredited system need to be held to account. The public would expect them to be treated in exactly the same way as those who fail in the workplace. It sends out the wrong signal to treat those who failed to deliver.

5.   Disputes will arise. The present appeals system run by the civil service and controlled by them at every stage has failed. It encourages needless penalties which those penalized cannot address. It cannot be within the British Constitution that those imposing penalties also sit in judgement.

A single completely independent scheme must be available to both sides or all matters should got to a Court—it cannot be more costly.

Yours committee has a great responsibility for the future of farming, our nation's food and the environment. Its duty is to ensure the public has value for its taxes.

All we in the field can do is point out the issues.

I will look forward to your report in the Press.

June 2007

Memorandum by The Meat and Livestock Commission

The Meat and Livestock Commission is an executive Non Departmental Public Body set up under the 1967 Agriculture Act. Its remit is to work with the British meat and livestock industry (cattle, sheep and pigs) to improve its efficiency and competitive position; and to maintain and stimulate markets for red meat at home and British meat abroad, with due regard for the consumer. It is funded through the collection of levies on sheep, pigs and cattle slaughtered for human consumption or exported live.

The bodies that comprise federal MLC are: British Pig Executive (BPEX), English Beef and Lamb Executive (EBLEX), Hybu Cig Cymru-Meat Promotion Wales (HCC) and Quality Meat Scotland (QMS).

GENERAL COMMENTS

1. The Meat and Livestock Commission (MLC) welcomes the opportunity to respond to the Sub-Committee's Inquiry into the future of the CAP.

2. Our perspective on the CAP—whether the current CAP as reformed under the 2003 agreement or a post-2013 CAP—is conditioned by our assessment of the extent to which it enables the British meat and livestock industry to meet the challenges that face the industry now and into the future.

3. Our vision is a modern livestock and processing industry that is both competitive and sustainable, and which produces consistent quality products that meet exacting market requirements, while at the same time caring for and protecting our natural resources. It is only with economic success that our producers and processors can deliver true sustainable development.

4. The British livestock industry has only recently emerged from a decade of hardship brought about by animal disease and poor profitability. CAP reform has posed, and continues to pose, a huge challenge to what are essentially small- and medium-sized businesses. This is particularly the case for beef and sheep producers in adapting to the ending of production-linked subsidies and to a free market business environment. Global competition from lower cost producers—who are often unhindered by the level of regulation and the high labour, environmental and animal welfare standards that exist in this country—is increasing. Such global competition will intensify with the further trade liberalisation that would follow a WTO agreement in the Doha Round were an agreement to be reached.

5. On the demand side, red meat consumption and demand are robust, yet the British industry is unable to meet this demand, largely due to the historic decline in production during the second half of the 1990s and early 2000s due to BSE and FMD in the cattle and sheep sectors, the impact of milk quotas and financial pressures on milk producers, investment in high welfare production systems and disease problems in the pig sector, and, for all three species, poor returns and low business confidence leading to inadequate investment and training. The result has been growing import penetration, sometimes involving the importation of meat—notably pig meat—that is produced under welfare conditions that would be illegal in this country.[24]

6. In passing, we should also like to register our welcome for the Competition Commission's market investigation into the supply of groceries by retailers in the UK. The operations and practices of the large multiple retailers directly affect the competitiveness of our livestock producers and the extent to which efficient, sustainable and fair supply chains can be built.

7. As we discuss below, the Common Agricultural Policy is now very far from "common". This has led to the differential treatment of producers across the EU, with consequences for competitiveness across the EU. This issue needs to be addressed by policy makers.

---

[24] The British Pig Executive estimates that of total pig meat imports into the UK 70% would be illegal to produce in this country on the grounds of pig welfare.

CAP REFORM

8. Under the classical form of the CAP (ie pre-2005) production-linked subsidies tended to incentivise farmers to produce indiscriminately without adequate regard to the real quantitative and quality needs of the marketplace. Within the livestock industry this was particularly notable in the beef and sheep sectors. Subsidy receipts came to account for a substantial proportion of most producers' incomes. Indeed, for the poorer performing producers, without subsidies, their net margins would be negative.[25] As a result, many producers came to regard themselves as independent primary producers, rather than as food producers or as partners with other producers, processors and retailers in a food supply chain seeking to meet the needs of modern consumers.[26]

9. CAP reform was, therefore, a radical paradigm shift to a "real" world, and took place in a way that gave what are relatively small businesses comparatively little time to adapt to an entirely new business environment.

10. As stated earlier, the reformed CAP is now, of course, far from "common". In the livestock sector, the 2003 agreement provided considerable scope for member states to retain a variety of production-linked measures. Indeed a number of member states have chosen to maintain partial decoupling, while the UK Government opted for total decoupling. In our view, these inconsistencies and anomalies distort or have the potential to distort competition across the EU. We therefore welcome EU Commissioner Fischer Boel's commitment to review the existing derogations from full decoupling as part of the European Commission's forthcoming "Health Check" exercise.

11. We also welcome the Commissioner's statements on the need to simplify CAP legislation, and to review the practicality of some aspects of the cross-compliance requirements.

12. A further consequence of the less than common nature of the reformed CAP arises from the current rules regarding modulation. These rules allow member states to implement "voluntary modulation"—top slicing from the Single Payment and its transfer into rural development funding—over and above the 5% rate of compulsory modulation that all member states are required to implement. Only the UK and Portugal are applying voluntary modulation. In the UK, the rates of voluntary modulation will vary across the home countries.[27] UK farmers will therefore face cuts in their Single Payment that (a) they may or may not recoup in payments under the new rural development programmes, and (b) they will be disadvantaged vis-à-vis farmers in other EU countries who will receive higher levels of direct payments. It remains to be seen to what extent UK livestock producers are able to offset some of the loss of Single Payment by participating in the agri-environment schemes under the UK's four new rural development programmes. In this connection, there is some concern that livestock producers may not be the main beneficiaries of these schemes and, that, therefore, they will face a net loss in payments.

13. The most recent survey of the costs of production in a range of production systems on cattle and sheep farms in England shows that, in respect of 2005–06, only the top third performing "intensive cattle finishers" and the top third of "store lamb finishers" made a profit after all costs and excluding all support payments.[28] This picture is broadly similar in other parts of the UK. In reality, many cattle and sheep producers have relied on production-linked subsidies to bolster farm incomes.

14. While it is not unreasonable for these producers to use the Single Payment as a cushion and to contribute to investment as they seek to adjust during the transitional period from production-based subsidies to the decoupled world, this is not a viable long term approach. Ultimately, cattle and sheep producers must secure their incomes from the marketplace, as is already the reality for pig producers.

15. It is often difficult to identify clear direct economic causes and effects in the agriculture industry. Nevertheless, it is clear to us that in the grazing livestock sector, CAP reform is leading to a contraction of the cattle breeding herd and the sheep breeding flock and, thus, to an overall decrease in the size of the industry as producers either choose to retain fewer animals or to leave the industry. At the same time, it should be said that many of those livestock producers that have a long term commitment to the industry will seek to exploit the considerable scope for technical and business improvement and for building more effective supply chains in response to market signals.[29]

---

[25] While pig producers have not received direct production subsidies, the CAP provides a measure of protection from third-country imports.

[26] Many producers have not been attuned or fully receptive to the technical knowledge and advances that are available—much of these through MLC—to secure the husbandry and business improvements that might raise their returns and incomes, and reduce their reliance on subsidy receipts.

[27] In England voluntary modulation rates will rise from 12% to 14% over the period 2007 to 2012 and in Northern Ireland from 7% to 10%. At the time of writing, the rates in Wales and Scotland have yet to be announced.

[28] "Business Pointers for Livestock Enterprises", Cattle and Sheep Business Costings, November 2006, English Beef and Lamb Executive. Published by *Farmers Weekly*.

[29] Much of the activity of MLC and its constituent federal bodies and of the Red Meat Industry Forum is targeted at improving the livestock industry's performance through genetic and feeding improvements, disease control, knowledge transfer, training and business improvement, including benchmarking.

16. In summary, full decoupling in the UK as a result of CAP was implemented—in agricultural policy terms—quickly. The process of adjustment is far from easy, involving both positive and negative consequences.

THE SINGLE PAYMENT SCHEME

17. Whatever the merits or otherwise of the Single Payment system, it is vital that while it exists it is administered efficiently. It is clear that in respect of England its administration has been unacceptably inefficient, with profound adverse consequences and hardship for many farmers.

18. We have already highlighted the desirability of harmonising what are uncommon rules regarding voluntary modulation.

19. Cross-compliance is a reasonable condition for receipt of the Single Payment. At the same time, cross-compliance should be implemented in a way that encourages good farming practice. It should not be used as a heavy-handed punitive weapon. Breaches of cross-compliance rules can result in serious penalties for farmers, often arising from innocent or unintended infractions, and give rise to great personal anxiety.

MARKET MECHANISMS

20. The forthcoming Health Check provides a valuable opportunity to review and, if necessary, simplify, amend or end existing rules on a wide range of market mechanisms. In this connection our only comment is to restate a view that we have put to Defra in the course of a recent consultation on the European Commission's proposals for a single Common Market Organisation for Agricultural Products; that is, any proposals that alter the scope and substance of existing measures or change the way decisions are made should be clear and transparent in order to allow proper scrutiny and discussion, and to maintain confidence in both the institutions involved and in procedures.

RURAL DEVELOPMENT

21. In principle the creation of the European Agricultural Fund for Rural Development (EAFRD) is a useful exercise in simplifying funding streams and their administration.

22. We have commented earlier on the undesirability of uncommon rules regarding voluntary modulation, and the possible impact on producers.

23. With regard to compulsory modulation, we would not be in favour of changes that raised the level of compulsory modulation while leaving, as now, member states with discretion in respect of voluntary modulation. Rather, we would favour a common, perhaps higher, level of compulsory modulation and the ending of voluntary modulation.

24. The ending of production-linked support and the need for farmers to become market-focussed highlights the important role that the competitiveness axis (axis 1) of the new rural development programmes can play in supporting information, training and supply chain initiatives aimed at improving the technical and business skills of producers.[30]

WORLD TRADE

25. MLC strongly supports the maintenance and strengthening of a multilateral international trade system and rules under the auspices of the WTO. This is conducive to transparent, consistent and orderly behaviour by and treatment of trading nations on a global basis. It is also likely to maximise the economic and social benefits of freer global trade. A complex and opaque system of regional and bilateral arrangements is, in principle, undesirable.

26. At this stage, the prospects for an agreement on the Doha Round of trade negotiations are unclear. On agriculture, the 2003 CAP reform agreement, by dismantling trade-distorting production-linked support (so-called "amber box" support), ensured that the EU would have little or no difficulty in meeting the likely terms

---

[30] In implementing the new Rural Development Programme for England with respect to the competitiveness axis through the Regional Development Agencies, we would urge greater cooperation and sharing of best practice experience amongst RDAs where activity clearly does or can cross regional boundaries.

of a WTO agreement in respect of cuts in domestic support. On export assistance, developed countries have agreed to phase out export subsidies by 2013, with a "substantial part" of this to be achieved by the mid-point of the implementation period. The challenge for the EU relates to market access since EU levels of import protection are comparatively high. Indeed, they are very high in some key products (eg fresh and chilled boneless beef cuts).

27. For the UK livestock industry, it is the possible challenge in respect of certain key meat cuts that is a cause of concern. For example, in practice, Brazil is currently able to export its high value fresh and chilled boneless cuts to the EU, pay the full import tariff and duty and still undercut the internal EU price for the product. In this situation, even if the EU were to achieve lower cuts in import tariffs through any agreed "sensitive product" provisions, it is difficult to see that this would afford significant import protection against such low price imports. And any cuts in tariffs would be expected to put increased downward pressure on the prices of the equivalent EU products. With the EU's deficit in beef production already widening, further pressures would merely "export" the Union's remaining production capacity and increase its reliance on imports from third countries, where production standards are sometimes lower than those of the EU and where animal disease outbreaks (eg FMD in Brazil) can interrupt their supplies.

28. For the EU, therefore, while the possibility of designating some products as "sensitive" provides some potential scope to cushion the impact of greater market access, careful judgements will need to be made as to the balance of advantage between, on the one hand, accepting whatever normal tariff cuts would apply under a final agreement and, on the other hand, seeking to designate products as sensitive, recognising that market access would still be increased through a combination of tariff cuts (albeit lower than they would otherwise be) and expanded tariff rate quotas.

29. From time to time during the WTO negotiations, the EU has raised its "non-trade concerns", including the use of geographical indications on a range of speciality products, and animal welfare and other standards. We accept that such "non-trade concerns" should not be used as a vehicle for raising non-tariff barriers. Equally, they touch on the legitimate concern to prevent products produced to lower labour, environmental and animal welfare standards from undermining EU production or misleading EU consumers. The EU has a right to refuse entry to products not produced to EU standards of food safety. A similar mechanism should be considered with respect to other standards of production, most notably animal welfare.

ENVIRONMENTAL ISSUES

30. Globally, agriculture accounts for about 20% of the projected human-induced greenhouse effect, about 9% of total human-related carbon dioxide emissions, about 35–40% of the methane emissions, and about 70% of the nitrous oxide emissions. In the UK, farming is the biggest source of two important GHG. Grazing animals, notably cows, release about 35% of total UK methane emissions. Soils and fertiliser account for two-thirds of the UK's nitrous oxide emissions. But the Environment Agency notes that GHG emissions from UK farming have fallen by 12% over the last 10 years—methane emissions by 11% and nitrous oxide emissions by 13% over the same period —as a result, for example, of more efficient uses of fertilisers, minimum tillage techniques and fewer livestock.

31. In our view, the CAP can play a role in the mitigation of, and adaptation to, climate change through Pillar 2 of the CAP. In principle, as noted earlier, the EU Rural Development Regulation provides scope for a wide range of information and training activity under axis 1 (competitiveness) of the Regulation, much of which relates to agricultural practices that can contribute to strategies to mitigate and adapt to climate change impacts and also help to improve the competitiveness of the agricultural industry.

32. In the livestock sector, for example, a wide range of R&D and knowledge transfer activity serves to increase the efficiency of production through nutritional and management strategies covering the composition, manipulation and conversion of animal feed, manure management, as well as the genetic merit of stock. Such strategies can both increase productivity and profitability and contribute to reducing greenhouse gas emissions.

33. In the pig sector, a positive contribution can be made through the use of co-products in feeding, rather than resorting to landfill, as well as in aspects of energy generation.[31]

---

[31] The recently published BPEX discussion document on a Pig Industry Environment Strategy (PIES) explores a range of environmental activity and initiatives. A greater level of financial support and incentives in this area would be helpful.

FINANCING

34. We have some reservations about the concept of co-financing. As the example of the new Rural Development Programme for England shows, co-financing can be a useful tool for topping up otherwise inadequate EU funding (in this case because of the low allocation of EU rural development funds to the UK). On the other hand, co-financing carries the inherent risk of different EU member states setting differential levels of co-financing, which can tilt the "playing field" and lead to distortions amongst member states. Much depends on the rules around co-financing arrangements.

ENLARGEMENT

35. In respect of the livestock sector, the 2004 and 2007 enlargements have had a limited impact on the UK to date. The new member states are largely engaged in modernisation programmes in their agricultural sectors. In time, these countries offer both competitive challenges and market opportunities.[32]

OTHER ISSUES

36. This inquiry focuses on the future of the CAP. However, we would like to register our view that from the point of view of producers seeking to adapt to and compete in a radically new business environment, it is important that a wide range of EU policies—including agriculture, rural development, food safety, labelling, environmental, animal health and welfare, and competition—should operate in a way that: enables markets to function openly, efficiently and fairly; allow producers to deal on a more equitable basis with large retailers, make an adequate return and allow for investment; ensure efficient and proportionate regulation; and, provide consumers with accurate and meaningful information about the provenance and quality of food.

June 2007

Memorandum by The Rt Revd John Oliver

OVERVIEW

Q1. The long-term objectives of the CAP should be to guarantee an adequate level of food production in the member states of the EU; to sustain a viable rural economy (in social and cultural as well as economic terms); and to safeguard the environment with due regard to the conservation of the landscape and of biodiversity. These objectives have to be pursued in a world of increasing population, mounting pressure on water resources, and the uncertain threat of climate change. The title Common Agricultural Policy is an apt one, although recent enlargement of the EU has made it more difficult to maintain in practice the same degree of commonality as has prevailed in the past.

THE REFORMED CAP

Q2. The 2003 reforms were welcome and necessary, and the principle of de-coupling is right. Farmers are taking time to adjust to the new agreements, and to work out what changes in production are advisable. The degree of continuity in the UK is in some ways surprising, but farmers are by nature fairly conservative and prefer to stick with what they know they can do well. Fluctuations in commodity prices are difficult to predict, and radical change will come only slowly. But there can be no doubt that, in the European context, financial support for agriculture is right and proper, and should continue, subject to periodic review.

THE SINGLE PAYMENT SCHEME

Q3. The SPS is a good basis for the future of agricultural policy, but its implementation has varied widely within the EU; some member states have handled it well, others—notably England—very badly indeed. This has caused very considerable and totally unnecessary anxiety and distress. But even if the administration of the scheme were to be faultless, there are ways in which, in the UK, it should be changed. There should be a minimum area below which no entitlement should exist, unless a strong case can be made on the grounds of the use to which small parcels of land are put: eg some horticultural enterprises occupying a small area may be entitled to receive the Single Payment.

---

[32] In the pig sector, some concern has been expressed about the use by the Polish authorities of what in effect is intervention buying as a means to support internal prices.

The most important change which the Family Farmers' Association wishes to see is the introduction of a system of tapering benefits, which would ensure that adequate help was given to small and medium-size farms, but very large payments would not be made to those farming very large areas. This system will become increasingly important as the entitlement to SPS moves progressively in England towards an area basis.

In all EU member states the rules governing entitlement should be kept under review, and each member state should retain some flexibility in matters of detail.

MARKET MECHANISMS

Q4. The suggestions made by the Commission should be followed up. In particular, set-aside is much resented, and in a world where food and fuel-crop production is likely to be increasingly competing for limited areas of fertile land, it makes little sense to maintain restrictive rules over set-aside, unless such land is earmarked for specific environmental projects.

RURAL DEVELOPMENT

Q5. It is in principle right that Rural Development is seen in wider terms than agriculture. Small rural businesses of a non-agricultural nature, some forms of tourism, rural infrastructure (notably schools and transport) need strategic support. Farming in Europe is inextricably connected with other social, economic and cultural aspects of rural life, and with the maintenance of an attractive, semi-natural physical environment, which must itself be regarded as a common good.

Q6. Higher levels of EU financing of rural development are probably not necessary; in the past such expenditure has actually damaged the physical environment, which in most European countries is fragile and under threat from too much development, or development of an inappropriate nature. Insofar as there is modulation from Pillar I to Pillar 2, it should be at the same level for each member state, and should be compulsory. Voluntary modulation imposed by particular member states puts their farmers in an unfavourable position, as UK farmers are presently discovering.

WORLD TRADE

Q7. There is a common perception that the CAP represents an expensive—and some would say immoral—form of protection for EU agriculture, and that in any present or future WTO negotiations the EU should be willing to reduce significantly the level of support which it offers to its farmers. This view should be resisted; the 2003 reforms represent the limit to which EU negotiators should go, and the present arrangements are entirely defensible in terms of preserving the high standards of animal welfare, food hygiene and environmental protection which EU producers and consumers demand, and which are not achieved by many competitors on the world stage.

It is a sweeping and simplistic criticism to allege that the CAP damages developing countries. Under the Generalized Scheme of Preferences, the agreement with the ACP countries, and the "Everything but Arms" agreement, the EU is already offering substantial trade preferences. It can rightly be said that the EU could be doing more to help developing countries to build their capacity to take advantage of these existing trade preferences.

Expenditure on export refunds is now at an historically low level and continuing to fall, and no further concessions in WTO negotiations are necessary or desirable at this stage.

ENVIRONMENTAL PROTECTION AND CLIMATE CHANGE

Q8. The system of cross-compliance is a blunt instrument, and of fairly limited environmental benefit unless it is accompanied by Entry Level or Higher Level Stewardship (or the equivalents in the devolved UK administrations), but it is beginning to yield some results. Farmers are in many cases finding it quite burdensome, and resent yet another round of paperwork and inspections. It needs to be allowed to bed in, but it is certainly the case that it should in due course be more closely integrated with other EU policy requirements.

Q9. There is a potential for the CAP to contribute towards the mitigation of climate change by encouraging a reduction in CO_2 emissions from agriculture. On-farm bio-gas schemes offer a simple and relatively cheap means of reducing methane emissions and the need for electricity from the grid, usually from fossil fuel sources.

High hopes have increasingly been placed in recent months in the potential of bio-fuels to help in the mitigation of climate change. Caution is needed, and the environmental equation may be more complex than is generally understood. Bio-diesel produced from eg oil-seed rape does offer possibilities, provided manufacturing plants are not too far from the point of growth of the crop. Co-firing of certain energy crops, such as miscanthus or coppiced willow, in conventional power-stations is also possible (in place of imported wood pellets). But there are issues of economic viability, of the cost and CO_2 emissions of long-distance transport of bulky energy crops and food crops, all of which need careful consideration.

Practice varies widely between member states of the EU, and it is important that there is no large-scale development of bio-fuel plants in Europe which depend on imported energy crops grown in places which as a result suffer from deforestation and severe environmental degradation.

FINANCING

Q10. There are very great uncertainties about the post-2013 budget. At present with levels of support as they are, the budget is just adequate. But if newer EU members are to receive equitable treatment, the budget will have to be increased. The most important point to be made in response to this question is that, despite widespread criticism that the CAP budget is excessive in relation to other EU expenditure, it is in fact the only common policy, and in view of the enormous importance of food production, and of the wider issues mentioned in the answer to Q5, there should be no reluctance to mount a robust defence of present budget levels, and of any further necessary increases in the future.

Co-financing should be resisted; the CAP should remain a common policy, UK farmers, and small farmers in particular, are very reluctant to place any trust in the wisdom and benevolence of the Treasury in relation to the support of agriculture.

15 May 2007

Memorandum by the Royal Agricultural Society of England

BACKGROUND INFORMATION—ROYAL AGRICULTURAL SOCIETY OF ENGLAND

The Royal Agricultural Society of England (the Society, the RASE) is the leading independent voice for the agricultural industry and rural England. The Society has, since 1838, played a leading role in the development of British agriculture and a vibrant rural economy through the uptake and communication of good science, the promotion of best practice and a co-ordinated, impartial approach to wide-ranging rural issues. Today its work includes: support for business through communication, demonstration and facilitation; social welfare in rural communities; education; and its significant events management role, notably with the Royal Show and specialist Technical Events. It undertakes the activities above with its partner organisations the Arthur Rank Centre, Farming & Countryside Education (FACE), the International Agriculture & Technology Centre (IATC) and the Warwickshire Rural Hub, all of which are now effective, practical delivery mechanisms in their own right.

In this Submission, the Society has sought to take a long-term, impartial, a-political viewpoint which it believes to be in the best interests of agriculture and the rural economy in the UK and Europe. This is in line with the terms of its Charter and charitable status. The Society has not, therefore, directly answered the questions raised in the "Invitation to Submit", but has outlined key issues arising from an exciting vision for a much-changed agriculture over the next few years: in particular its strong belief in the growing importance of agriculture and the rural economy as a means of solving many of the world's pressing problems. The Society believes that the Common Agricultural Policy should help agriculture to change and to take advantage of the many opportunities open to it. Such change holds the hope that rural economies will in future be thriving and viable without the need for EU support.

1. WHAT CAN THE RURAL SECTOR OFFER?

EU agriculture can:

— Feed people in developed and developing nations.

— Fuel our homes and our industries.

— Produce the feedstock for sustainable materials for industry, for medical purposes, for construction, to name but a few.

— Manage a beautiful, accessible environmentally sustainable countryside.

1.1 The RASE would argue that, in order to meet the challenges which the world faces, agriculture should be given the opportunity to achieve all of the above. The pace of change will only increase, and it could be argued that recent reform of the CAP is already out of date in its emphasis on environment. It is becoming clear that the available land will need to be used very wisely indeed if it is to do all that is asked of it. Only recently, the United Nations expressed its concern about the headlong rush to use land for the production of biofuels and the need for the world to be able to feed its fast-growing population.

1.2 For the sake of its peoples, the EU's reformed CAP will need to take a view on both future food and fuel security. In the light of factors such as an increasing world population, possible greater migration as a result of climate change, a shortage of water and the uncertainty of fuel supplies, the Society would argue strongly that the CAP will need to take a robust view in order to safeguard both community food and fuel supplies.

2. CLIMATE CHANGE

Global warming and climate change are proving to be the defining issues of the era. For agriculture, the key considerations are perhaps:

— The effects of climate change on weather conditions and water availability.

— The opportunities which this may bring, crucial amongst which is the ability of farmers to solve/mitigate the problems associated with climate change, and their ability to grow crops new to the EU climates.

— The fact that agriculture (particularly livestock farming) is a significant contributor to global warming and will need to find ways to put its house in order.

— The need for sustainable supply chains not just in food but in a range of non-food uses.

2.1 In short, farmers will be capable of helping to solve many of the world's most pressing problems, and in addition will be at the forefront of a "plant-based" revolution rather than an oil revolution.

3. SUSTAINABILITY

How developed countries deal with waste and "end-of-life" issues is becoming increasingly important. The development of plant-based sustainable supply chains for a range of industries and products will contribute significantly to the ability of that industry to recycle or safely dispose of its waste in more efficient ways. Farming will be at the very heart of this "plant-based" revolution and the Royal Agricultural Society of England believes that sustainability should be a key theme of the CAP in future. We say this not least because we believe that the development of sustainable supply chains has the potential to provide significant new market opportunities for the land-based sector, with the potential to free it from financial support in the medium term. But, if these chains are to be successfully developed, the encouragement of engagement between agriculture, research and development, companies in other industries and recycling/disposal interests will be vital.

4. CHANGE MANAGEMENT

Land-based businesses will need to change further if they are to fulfil the objectives outlined above. This requires the following:

— The establishment of improved, accessible and understandable links between research bodies and rural SMEs (the Society is well-placed to do this).

— The expansion of delivery mechanisms which can work at grassroots level to bring about change through the provision of information, sharing of best practice, mentoring and facilitation of new, often collaborative, enterprises.

— Improved access to training in a form and at a time when farmers can make use of it.

5. EUROPE-WIDE POLICIES

It has often been questioned whether the CAP can be relevant and appropriate for farming and political circumstances in countries which differ widely, and indeed implement the Policy differently. It is well-known that British farmers have often felt themselves to be at a disadvantage and they place great store on the utopian vision of the "level playing field". There is another aspect to this: if agriculture is to fulfil its potential in contributing to solutions on climate change and if new market opportunities for farmers are to be linked to sustainable solutions, then Governments will need to work in partnership to provide support, commitment and continuity through, for example, fiscal policy. Already embryonic markets (eg bio-energy) in some states are struggling because of the differing environmental incentives/tax policy between their Governments and others, such as Sweden, with more advantageous policies.

6. AN AGRICULTURAL POLICY OR A RURAL POLICY

Whilst agriculture (in the UK at least) is not currently such a powerful driver of the rural economy or a major employer or contributor to GDP, its ability to contribute significantly to environmental solutions will make it an important industry again.

6.1 The effects of Foot & Mouth Disease proved conclusively that, when agriculture suffers, key parts of the rural economy such as the allied supply trade, rural tourism and market towns are drastically hit also. There are relatively few farmers now who have not diversified in some way and are earning income from other sources in addition to farming.

6.2 The Common Agricultural Policy has always reflected the broader rural economy and rural community issues and the Royal Agricultural Society of England believes that it should continue to do so. It should also increasingly include climate change solutions, sustainable supply chains and energy. The Society is relaxed about the name of the policy so long as it continues to relate to both farming and the broader rural economy. However, to abandon farming altogether in favour of a purely rural policy at a time when farming has so much to offer to the world would seem the height of perversity.

7. CONCLUSION

The Royal Agricultural Society of England believes that the opportunities outlined above are exciting for the land-based sector and at the same time offer the chance of a future when the sector will be able to support itself and make a significant contribution to the overall economy of member states. The Society believes that, above all, farmers want to make an economic and environmental contribution provided that this makes them profitable and sustainable. But they will require help to reach this stage.

8 June 2007

Memorandum by the Royal Society for the Prevention of Cruelty to Animals

OVERVIEW

1. The RSPCA has been advocating reform of the CAP for two main reasons, notably:

— The lack of synergy between various parts of the European Union on its direction for animal welfare standards. Whilst DG Sanco and its predecessors have been encouraging a move away from intensive agriculture through raising legislative standards in the sectors of pigs (Directive 2001/88), laying hens (Directive 1999/74) and calves (Directive 19997/2), DG Agriculture, in charge of CAP policies, could be said to be encouraging farmers to proceed in the opposite direction. Pillar I payments ever since the 2003 agreement as part of the Mid Term Review, are either not fully de-coupled in all Member States or are based on historical payments, such as in Wales and Scotland and still have a link to pre-2005 Pillar I payments.

— The failure of CAP policies to account for rapid changes in globalisation. Whilst it could be argued that the 2003 Mid Term Review prepared the European Union well for any Doha Development Round agreement, by decoupling Pillar I payments and moving them from the Blue to Green Box, this has still to be tested at the WTO and there are economists who believe that they would fail this test.[33] In other areas the DDA talks have driven EU policy such as the agreement to phase out export subsidies for live animals.

2. Symptomatic of the lack of agreement at an EU wide level of long term objectives for the CAP can be found not in the tortuous negotiations in the Mid Term Review or even in the almost 50–50 split within the EU on the Commission's mandate for the agricultural negotiations under the DDA, but in the failure of the EU-25 in 2004 to agree a new Article 33 under the negotiations to agree the European Union Constitution. The CAP still has a mandate to "increase agricultural productivity by promoting technical progress and the optimum utilisation of the factors of production". This is despite it being written 50 years ago, and related to a much different European Economic Community of six Member States 12 years after the end of the Second World War where European food security was a real and valid issue. We now have a European Union of 27 countries

---

[33] Swinbank A & Tranter R. *2005 Decoupling EU farm support{: does the new single payment scheme fit within the Green Box?*

operating in a global marketplace and general agreement that the EU cannot, nor should it be self sufficient in all food sectors. Even the Agriculture Commissioner is mystified as to why it proves so difficult to find more modern language for Article 33.[34]

3. The RSPCA believes that the long term objective of the CAP should be to maximise sustainable management of the landscape and farm animals to public benefit using the land productively and taking into account public desires.

4. This would send a clear message to producers that they are being paid to act as guardians of the landscape and animals on that land. It also sets the framework that farm practices and standards should take into account the welfare of the animal, reflecting that which already exists in some farm assurance schemes. The CAP would develop away from direct payments into payments that reward farmers producing higher welfare standards or managing the environment and landscape in a sustainable manner. It would mean a move from Pillar I payments (which accounts for 77% of CAP monies at present) into Pillar II payments which reward good farming and environmental practises. It was Pillar II payments that came out worst from the European Council agreement in 2005 that saw the agreed budget for the period up to 2013 take a 22% cut from the Commission's proposed budget, equating to a loss of some €19 billion over the budgetary period that will now not be available for rural development issues.

5. The RSPCA agrees with the premise of the UK Government's paper Vision for the Common Agricultural Policy that radical change is required to deliver support to farmers more efficiently and reduce the negative impact on the environment and animal welfare.

6. A number of important developments are now occurring. The agreement on the first EU Animal Welfare Strategy in January 2006 lays down the direction for the EU on animal welfare in the 2007–13 period. The Commission's Welfare Quality programme will see objective mechanisms developed to measure on farm welfare of animals giving direct comparisons between farming methods. Measurements on animal welfare have also improved. In 2006 Defra developed through the England Implementation Group (EIG) the first SMART indicators for farm animal welfare. The RSPCA released their own farm welfare indicators in 2006 and the Commission is also set to develop their own goals. This gives a real opportunity to align the rural development incentives for farmers and producers with high level strategic goals and ensure goals are built into programmes to improve the welfare of farm animals.

7. The RSPCA agrees that agriculture should be a sustainable industry and rewarded for its outputs by the taxpayer where these are producing societal benefits that cannot be delivered in the market place. The RSPCA would include animal welfare in these benefits. However the two goals of producing high welfare standards and being internationally competitive without subsidy or protection are incompatible. In some sectors, of which eggs is the clearest, there is a causal relationship between raising animal welfare standards and the risk of being undermined by imports from third countries where standards are at a lower level. This can cause the industry to become uncompetitive in its own market place let alone the export market.

8. The objectives laid out in paragraph 4 would allow funding to producers to improve standards for farm animal welfare and not be disadvantaged from imports from third countries. These mechanisms already exist in Pillar II but are being used rarely due to funding starvation and a lack of clarity for Member States on the future direction of the CAP. The objective would reinstate a direct link between the public and the CAP, a link that has been completely lost. It is the European taxpayer that funds the CAP, although most are completely ignorant of the fact that nearly half the EU's budget goes into agriculture, which in the UK accounts for nationally under 1% of GDP and 2% of employment and even in rural areas 3% in both. The Commission has been a strong advocate of understanding what the European public think, undertaking in the past three years alone two Eurobarometers into animal welfare and one into the CAP. These find that the public consistently wants better farm standards, better information and labelling on farm products and more money diverted into rural development and improving animal welfare standards. These are not desires limited to northern European countries but include majorities of the public in countries that are amongst the most opposed to CAP reform.

9. It is true that as the CAP develops into these new areas and loses production payments it becomes less of a common policy and more of rural and social policy. This reflects the vastly different landscapes, climates and farming methods in the EU-27. Payments will become more varied both within and between Member States. The present position with Pillar I payments reflects this with at least five different funding mechanisms being adopted in the EU. Pillar II payments are also likewise being highly varied. The Commission is expecting 94 different rural development programmes to be adopted by the 27 Member States for the 2007–13 period giving a huge potential for varied funding and varied goals and targets. If monies are transferred at a greater rate from Pillar I to II the potential for increased financial variation will be vastly different to the present

---

[34] EFRA 4th report of session 2006–07 *The UK Government's vision for the Common Agricultural Policy* EV89 Q 248.

position and the only common theme of the Common Agricultural Policy will be the objectives as laid out in Article 33, which are outdated.

10. The RSPCA consider that the main pressures on the CAP will be from external drivers. Climate change will require farmers to change farming practices and also react to different needs of the EU such as biofuels. Globalisation, with or without a DDA agreement will see pressure for reduced tariffs, decoupled payments and a need to reward farmers for producing to higher welfare standards and therefore remaining competitive. There will be an increased desire from the public to be better informed on the food they are buying, leading to more mandatory labelling from the egg sector into other sectors such as pork, beef, dairy and poultrymeat. The enlargement of the EU from 27 to possibly 30 countries in the next few years and any membership of Turkey will require a massive budgetary change in the way EU funds are directed and the composition and direction of CAP funds.

The Reformed CAP

11. The agreement in 2005 to decouple Pillar I payments was a positive step as it broke the link with production but it was only a partial success as full decoupling did not occur. Mandatory decoupling should be completed as part of the Health Check.

12. New rural assistance measures were agreed by the EU in June 2005 under Regulation 1698/2005. This allocated seven new animal welfare measures for inclusion in the RDPs (six in Axis 1: membership of food quality schemes, food quality promotion, training, farm advisory, investment agricultural holdings, meeting Community animal welfare standards; one in Axis 2: payment for higher standards).

13. However two problems remained. Member States were not obliged to include any of the animal welfare measures in their RDP, although this was originally proposed by the Commission. This has meant that there has not been a large take up of the animal welfare measures. In the period 2003–05 Scotland, France and Germany have schemes that were directly aimed at or had side effects that benefited animal welfare. Secondly, the agreement on Regulation 1698/2005 allocated minimum financial spend in each of the four Axes but it is likely that many Member States will allocate the majority of their funding to Axis 2, which contains the environmental measures but only one of the seven animal welfare ones. Certainly the English RDP will follow this pattern and is proposing to spend 84% of Pillar II budget on Axis 2 measures. To date only Finland, Ireland, Italy (Emilia-Romania and Toscana), and two German Länders have submitted schemes that are directly aimed at improving animal welfare under Axis 2.

14. The lack of clear definitions in the animal welfare schemes in Regulation 1998/2005 has hampered the original aim to raise animal welfare standards. For instance, payments can be given under Pillar II for membership of assurance schemes, despite the fact these may only be delivering baseline standards. The RSPCA argued that these should be limited only to schemes such as Freedom Food which is recognised by the EU funded welfare quality project as the only dedicated assurance scheme for farm animal welfare in Europe, and which aims to deliver standards above the legal minimum. Also, payments are allowed under Axis 2 for farmers producing at standards that go beyond mandatory legal EU or national standards. The payments will cover additional costs and income foregone and are for a period of 5–7 years. The RSPCA called for a definition of "beyond mandatory standards" as it farmers could be paid for up to seven years for farming at just above minimum standards.

15. This fear has been proved correct. The Commission has to date given negative advice on the RDPs of two Member States as their proposed standards were not high enough. The RSPCA would prefer to see a stricter definition of these issues as part of the Health Check, and has produced their own guidelines for the Commission. Producing clear European standards of what constitutes farming beyond minimum standards would not only improve transparency, it would give clearer harmonisation between Member States and act as a clear standard for any proposed labelling on farm products.

16. Regulation 1998/2005 also brought in cross-compliance measures for the first time for three animal welfare laws. Again it is too early to tell the effectiveness of this improvement as cross compliance was only introduced in January 2007. However it is worrying that some Member States are already proposing cutting back on cross compliance measures that have been in place for longer under the Health Check. These calls should be resisted.

The Single Payment Scheme

17. The RSPCA advocates a vastly enlarged rural development scheme and sees the transfer of payments from Pillar I to Pillar II to be an essential step in this development. It is true that the Single Farm Payment (SFP) scheme is an improvement on the previous myriad of payments as it simplifies the CAP and carries on the reform programme of moving away from production payments and quotas. The final pieces of this jigsaw such as removal of milk quotas should also be completed at the end of the present budget period.

18. However the EU is now paying farmers under the SFP but with no real definition as to why it is paying them. As this represents 77% of CAP payments, it is essential that Member States agree what the payment is for. Whether it is a reward for managing the landscape, environment and animals or is a social payment, it is much better represented under Pillar II where there are definitive goals and targets. The long-term plan should be for farmers to get paid for managing the environment and its animals and incentivised to go further than baseline standards.

Market Mechanisms

19. The RSPCA supports the removal of quotas, although in the dairy industry more economic scoping needs to be done on any effects on increased animal/stockperson ratio and increased production. Both could be negative for animal welfare. We support the phase out of export subsides under the DDA and see this as being done by 2013 for all subsidies and by 2010 for live animal subsidies. The Commission has tried in the past to ensure that export subsidies are only paid to farmers that have abided by European standards on live transport and slaughter. But this has proven impossible to enforce as some of the journey(s) and the slaughter of the animal often occurs in another sovereign state. As only three countries get export subsides for the live export of cattle, eliminating this measure would not be financially burdensome but give a clear signal that the EU is moving to a different type of CAP.

Rural Development

20. As detailed in paragraphs 15, 16 and 17, the RSPCA sees the Rural Development Fund as being the most important area for the future of the CAP. The Mid Term Reform in 2004 saw great opportunities for improving the welfare of animals under the EAFRD but there are limits to how its use can be maximised. This needs to be rectified under the CAP Health Check in 2008.

21. Animal welfare measures are not compulsory and suffer from a lack of objective definitions where they are mentioned. The lack of funding has resulted in few measures being proposed by Member States under Axis 2, where the majority of budget is to be allocated.

22. It is true that many more measures are being proposed under national RDPS under Axis I with the intention of improving animal welfare. In the period 2003–05 Scotland, France and Germany had schemes that were directly aimed at or had side effects that benefited animal welfare. The Scottish RDP 2007–13 has three budget lines for encouraging animal welfare including membership of an assurance scheme, completing a Veterinary Health Plan and for training purposes. The response on the animal welfare measures in Scotland in 2005 was extremely positive, the second most popular of all incentives given under the SRDP. The 2003-7 Welsh RDP had measures to encourage animal welfare and the proposed 2007–13 WRDP gives incentives for farmers entering into agreements committing to higher welfare standards than baseline ones under the agri-environment scheme. In Germany the present RDP provides incentives of grants for investment costs in nine sectors providing certain higher welfare standards are met.

23. More Member States including those from the 10 new members have proposed further schemes under Axis 1. But all schemes will inevitably suffer from lack of funding and it is difficult to forecast the degree of success they will have in promoting better farm welfare due to this limitation.

24. The 94 expected RDP schemes show that any harmonisation between plans amongst the EU-27 will be difficult. The introduction of better measurement indicators for animal welfare should facilitate the capture of data to show the effectiveness of schemes in achieving their objectives of improving farm welfare. But the measurement of outcomes against schemes is not specifically mentioned in the EAFRD. The opportunities afforded by the many schemes and any assessment of the effectiveness of certain schemes against others may then be unfortunately lost. This will mean that any analysis work undertaken by the Commission in the period leading up to the end of the current RDP in 2013 will be difficult and assessments on improvements and best schemes to take forward in the next budget period frustratingly elusive.

25. Until there is a clearer direction for the CAP, the RSPCA recommends using compulsory modulation to achieve the transfer of funds from Pillar I to II. This could best be achieved through compulsory modulation in the CAP Health Check, but until this time, the RSPCA supports the use of voluntary modulation.

WORLD TRADE

26. If tariffs are reduced in certain sectors, such as eggs (particularly dried eggs) there is a risk of European farmers being undermined by imports from third countries where standards are at a lower level. The Rural Development Programmes could play an important role in filling this gap and reward farmers for producing at standards above baseline. Indeed it could be argued that the Single Farm Payment, which is now given for the farm rather than the sector, has opened up the CAP to include sectors previously not covered by payments and obligations such as the laying hens and pigs sectors. Mixed farms with these animals that also receive CAP Pillar I payments would have to meet cross compliance measures for all animals and could also be eligible for payments such as ones paying one-off capitol costs or improvements to competitiveness.

27. Some consequences of raising farm standards have already been modelled. In the egg sector, there will be an economic cost of raising welfare standards under Directive 1999/74 that is 9p/dozen eggs moving to a multi-tier system or 18p/dozen eggs moving to a free range system.[35] The main exporting countries hold a competitive advantage in dried eggs before any changes in the DDA occur. Switzerland provides an interesting case study. Following the prohibition of battery cages in 1991 Swiss egg producers were rewarded through rural payment programmes for producing above baseline standards. This coupled with an aggressive marketing campaign to buy Swiss eggs has resulted in a vibrant Swiss egg sector that has not been disadvantaged, despite it being surrounded by countries using lower standards.

FINANCING

28. The problem with the financing of the CAP has already been mentioned. This is particularly relevant for the UK, which has historically received a much smaller allocation of rural development funds (some 3.5%) than other Member States. The Government intention to modulate up to 20% releases further monies that would not otherwise be available but it underlines the need within the Health Check to begin the discussion on a new financial division of CAP funds, both between Pillars I and II and between the Member States. The RSPCA would see this including a start at reducing the separation of funds between Pillars I and II with the eventual allocation of the majority of funding into a Rural Development Pillar II type fund.

29. The UK already has a number of targets that could be set or financed from Pillar II payments, either in the form of PSAs or encapsulated in existing strategies such as the Animal Health and Welfare Strategy. The RSPCA is not aware of any financial modelling and predictions that have been run by the UK Government on the cost implications of meeting these targets, and how this matches to present Pillar II funding. The lack of prioritisation with these targets has meant a skewering of the level playing field of division of funding from the Rural Development Programme in the England. For instance Natural England has a PSA target of getting 95% of SSSIs into a favourable or recovering state by 2010, much of which would be expected to be funded from Pillar II payments. It therefore lobbies Defra for schemes to meet this target from the RDP. This obviously reduces the amount of money that is available for other schemes such as improving animal welfare. The RSPCA believes that the Government could have competing targets and strategies already in existence that have yet to be or cannot be costed. These are competing against each other for a pot of money that is not likely to get any bigger until at least new negotiations start on the post 2013 budget. It is essential to have these prioritised.

SIMPLIFICATION OF THE CAP

30. The CAP has been simplified over previous reforms. There should be a long term objective to simplify payments into one rural development scheme but with flexibility to allow Member States options on choosing which of the budget lines they wish to use, depending on their own national interests and landscape. This could be set as part of the Health Check and phased in by 2013, so giving farmers the stability they ask for but a direction in which they are required to hear. For this to occur there needs to be a European agreement on what the CAP is for either in a set of guiding principles or, as part of the renegotiations on the Constitution, to agree a revision of Article 33. However at present there does not appear to be the appetite for such discussions let alone agreement.

---

[35] RSPCA *Hard Boiled Reality* 2005; RSPCA *Ecomomic consequences of egg production* 2005.

31. Pillar I, could be simplified further in the Health Check by agreeing one system for payments. In the absence of this, the CAP will continue to be reformed in a piece meal manner, responding to outside pressures such as WTO demands and globalisation rather than setting the agenda itself. It has started to progress along a route to being a Rural Policy but needs greater clarity to provide a rural programme that can respond to new pressures such as climate change and changing consumer demands.

June 2007

Memorandum by the Scottish Crofting Foundation

1. OVERVIEW

The objectives of the Common Agricultural Policy should relate to retaining rural communities, who are actively involved in sustainable land management and producing high quality goods for the market. The current design of the CAP does not achieve this.

With differing implementation across Member States and individual farmers within member states paid vastly different amounts for merely maintaining a minimum standard of husbandry, the policy can scarcely be described as "common". Likewise, with entitlement to Single Farm Payment being widely traded in financial markets, it can scarcely be described as "agricultural".

2. REFORMED CAP AND THE SINGLE FARM PAYMENT SCHEME

As expected and widely predicted, the reforms to the CAP have accelerated the trend of loss of agricultural activity in more marginal and peripheral areas.

We said in 2004 "Decoupling creates risks for agriculture in more remote and upland areas and for smaller agricultural units. It is imperative that a decoupled system of support payments is combined with measures which properly recognise the additional costs and difficulties associated with agricultural activities in least favoured areas and recognise and retain agricultural systems which contribute to the high environmental value of the north and west of Scotland".

Now that only maintenance of GAEC is required in order to access SFP, the disparity between payment levels across Scotland (varying from £2/Ha in the parish of Kintail to £639/Ha in the parish of Perth) has slanted the playing field even more against the interests of peripheral areas and the areas relatively more disadvantaged by land capability. In these areas, in spite of small levels of support payment, agricultural enterprises have continued to make a "go" of it, producing some very good quality livestock. However, against similar enterprises now taking place in other parts of the country, but subsidised to a far greater extent, these hill and upland businesses are now at a competitive disadvantage.

As we move further from the historic reference period which defines payment the system becomes less and less justifiable to the taxpaying public. In order for the CAP to be able to stand public scrutiny and justify support in the longer term, it is imperative that the policy is increasingly targeted at supporting and maintaining multifunctional agriculture, including High Nature Value farming systems.

Single Farm Payments, being based in Scotland on historic receipts are very unevenly distributed, with the more intensive systems in receipt of the largest support payments, while the more extensive receive less. This system, as would be expected, currently bears no relation to the delivery of public goods.

We do not believe that the British public wants to see and contribute to a countryside dominated by a handful of large, intensive, industrial units of agricultural production. Small farming and crofting enterprises and those managing less productive ground or land in more remote areas provide public goods in terms of high environmental value, are important for rural development, for the social economy and for the maintenance of a culture and a way of life. Future policy should seek to ensure that the CAP, supports and maintains valuable systems that deliver numerous public goods in addition to marketable commodities.

11 June 2007

Memorandum by the Tenant Farmers Association

Introduction

The Tenant Farmers Association (TFA) welcomes the opportunity of providing written evidence to their Lordships as part of the Sub-Committee's Inquiry into the future of the Common Agricultural Policy (CAP). As far as possible, this evidence is presented in accordance with the issues set out in the sub-committee's call for evidence where the TFA believes it is able to assist their Lordships with there deliberations.

Overview

In the TFA's view, the long-term policy objectives for the CAP should be as follows:

1. To ensure that farmers and growers receive a fair standard of living.
2. To ensure that Europe achieves food security.
3. To protect animal welfare and the environment.
4. To ensure a common framework of rules and incentives across the whole of the EU.
5. To minimise market distortions from policy intervention.
6. To contribute to Europe's energy security.

These objectives are expanded below:

1. *To ensure that farmers and growers receive a fair standard of living*

The objective of ensuring a fair standard of living for farmers and growers is a key part of the current CAP and should continue to be so. There are two principal reasons for holding this view. Firstly, farmers are both price-takers with regard to their production and on the purchase of their inputs. Experience over recent years has shown that reductions in farm gate prices do not lead to commensurate reductions in input prices. Many of the inputs used by agriculture are oil or chemical based and the prices of those inputs reflect more what is happening in global oil and chemical markets than they do markets for agricultural commodities. Other costs including those for labour and land also show little correlation with the profitability of agriculture. Taken together with the increasing concentration of processing and retailing capacity, farmers are unable to pass increasing costs to consumers and are therefore stuck in a cost-price squeeze.

Secondly, economic theory clearly expresses the general position that as economies develop and incomes grow, consumers spend a decreasing proportion of their growing income on food and food products. This means that producers of food see a declining proportion of national income being spent on their production and they are therefore unable to keep pace with economic growth which necessitates transfer payments from those who are able to gain from economic growth to those who are not.

2. *To ensure that Europe achieves food security*

Food security is becoming a major issue for all countries of the world. Against the back-drop of exponential growth in world population, global terrorism and climate change, it seems sensible that Europe should have a long-term policy which seeks to provide food from its own resources. The Government however seems unconcerned by issues of food security as evidenced by their "Vision for the Common Agricultural Policy" produced at the end of 2005. Although the UK provides some three quarters of its domestic food needs in temperate products, it is declining. The Government has made no announcement about the level at which it would begin to get concerned about self-sufficiency. The TFA does not rule out the benefits of international trade but we do not believe that we should become complacent in accepting that our ability to trade globally today will necessarily continue into the long term.

3. *To protect animal welfare and the environment*

Animal welfare and environmental issues are of importance in agricultural policy. However, they need to be balanced against other demands and objectives. The TFA is concerned that the dominance of animal welfare and environmental objectives in existing policy frameworks is unhelpful and self-defeating. High levels of regulation and cost faced by domestic producers for environmental and animal welfare purposes can and do drive domestic producers out of business when they face competition from imported commodities which are not produced to the same high animal welfare and environmental standards. Within the framework of the CAP, there needs to be recognition that we should not be exporting our animal welfare and environmental problems.

4. *To ensure a common framework of rules and incentives across the whole of the EU*

A common approach across all Member States of the EU is vital given the doctrine of free trade that exists within the EU. It is unfair that one part of the EU is afforded greater incentives or fewer regulations in comparison to another in the context of a free trade environment. This is most aptly viewed through the policy on voluntary modulation where producers in the UK face markedly higher rates of modulation than any other producer in the EU, and even within the UK differential rates apply which will distort the economic advantage internally. Problems of a distorted policy framework can also be viewed through the different mechanisms that are employed to implement the Single Payment Scheme across the EU. The ability to maintain an element of coupled support and the ability to choose different methods for implementing decoupled payments cause economic distortion and should be avoided in future policy.

5. *To minimise market distortions from policy intervention*

A major criticism of the CAP in the past has been the extent to which it has distorted both domestic and international markets. It will be important to ensure that future CAP policy seeks to minimise those distortions. With this in mind, the TFA would support a move towards a fully decoupled bond scheme to support producers. Greater emphasis needs to be given to how this might be integrated with the CAP at its next fundamental review.

6. *To contribute to Europe's energy security*

Energy policy is becoming increasingly important particularly with the experience of global destabilisation in gas and oil markets. Whilst the TFA is sceptical about the impact of reducing our dependence on fossil fuels on stemming inevitable climate change, from a pure energy security viewpoint, it would be important that the CAP is used to encourage farmers to produce fuel crops which can replace a proportion of our fossil fuel demand.

THE REFORMED CAP

The basis of the European Commission proposals which led to the eventual CAP reform agreement of June 2003 was sound. The TFA supported the concept of a move away from coupled support payments towards a decoupled payment on a historic basis. It seemed sensible to be breaking the link between subsidy and production decisions whilst ensuring that farmers maintained a fair standard of living. However, the TFA feels that the process of negotiation which led to the June 2003 agreement significantly undermined the potential benefit of the CAP reform agreement in a number of ways. Firstly, it allowed Member States to maintain coupled payments for differing periods and at differing rates depending upon the sector. This has led, inevitably, to efficiency distortions across the EU and allowed some producers in some Member States to compete with others on an unfair basis. The TFA believes that Member States should not have been given the option of maintaining coupled payments. Secondly, the TFA believes that the introduction of various models for decoupling has led to significant problems. The UK is a good example of those problems as we now have two parts of the United Kingdom (Wales and Scotland) using the historical model only, one part (England) using a dynamic hybrid and another part (Northern Ireland) using a static hybrid. This has led to administrative and economic problems.

The TFA however, is not naïve in thinking that a CAP reform without those distortions would have been easy to achieve in June 2003; but we do believe that the distortion significantly undermined the benefit of what was agreed and that more time and effort should have gone into creating a package with fewer distortions.

In that many of the compromises were added to the text of the final agreement at a very late stage and therefore were not given much thought, the full implications of their impact were not thought through properly. For example, the allowance of a dynamic hybrid scheme which combined historic and area payments with a minimum application size of 0.3 hectares caused a major influx of new applicants particularly in England with people who were previously unconnected with the agricultural industry. This has, in turn, had knock-on effects for the ability of the Rural Payments Agency (RPA) to administer payments under the Single Payment Scheme on an efficient basis.

One of the areas within the Commission's original package of proposals which remained as part of the final package which the TFA did question was the retention of set-aside within the Single Payment Scheme framework. We used the analogy of a car by asking why we had to keep one foot on the break when we had removed our other foot from the accelerator.

THE SINGLE PAYMENT SCHEME

Whether or not the Single Payment Scheme is a good basis for the future of EU agricultural policy is immaterial to an extent that it is the current policy and it will be from here that any new policy will have to be developed. The TFA believes that it would be difficult and costly to unravel the Single Payment Scheme before 2013. That does not mean that changes could be made to make it work more efficiently. Some examples are given below:

Firstly, whilst it was necessary to go through the process of creating fruit, vegetable and potato (FVP) authorised entitlements to ensure that historic receipts were not spread over large areas of new land and to people who had not received payments in the past, the TFA is pleased to note that the Commission has now decided to bring FVP entitlements to an end and we hope that the UK Government will make the necessary changes as quickly as possible.

Secondly, given our thoughts about set-aside set out above, we do not see any future for set-aside within the Single Payment Scheme and we are therefore pleased that the European Commission proposes to abolish set-aside as part of its health-check proposals for the CAP reform in 2008–09.

Thirdly, the TFA believes that there should be a higher minimum area for applications under the Single Payment Scheme. The current 0.3 hectare limit provision has allowed too many very small "pony paddock" type claims to come into the Single Payment Scheme and the TFA believes that the Commission's proposal to have a 3 hectare minimum size limit is sensible. At the same time, the Commission should look again at the possibility of introducing a maximum ceiling on payments so long as the excess funds can be retained within the Member State concerned and used for rural development spending.

Fourthly, in the longer term, the TFA believes that the EU should investigate how the SPS could be turned into a bond scheme, fully decoupled from land.

MARKET MECHANISMS

We have already noted the wish to see the end of set-aside and we would also be happy to see the end of milk quotas so long as there was a robust economic analysis which showed that the negative impact of their demise, particularly in small producers, was minimised.

The TFA believes that the EU should maintain its suite of other market measures to protect it against international dumping of cheap products on EU markets and to allow it to sustain its objectives for food security and maintaining high animal health, animal welfare, phytosanitary and environmental standards within the global context. The TFA believes that the EU should not shy from using market mechanisms to keep out products which fail to meet the high standards required of producers internally.

RURAL DEVELOPMENT

The concept of a rural development policy for the EU is sound although we fear that the way in which it is being implemented in the UK is causing problems.

Firstly, the decision to allow implementation through regional bodies has led to confusion, complication and administrative burden. The TFA believes that the policy should be controlled centrally with regional or local options as necessary to ensure that there is proper co-ordination, consistency of treatment and accountability. We are too small a country to be trying to administer the rural development plan through regional governance structures.

Secondly, there are significant barriers to entry to schemes; particularly the HLS which requires a costly evaluation before applications can be made. The uncertainty over funding does not sit well with a scheme which requires individuals to invest so much upfront.

Thirdly, because the UK's share of EU funding for agri-environment and rural development programmes is relatively low, it argues that it needs to take a greater degree of money from the SPS through voluntary modulation. This is "sold" to the farming community on the basis that the money will be coming back through ERDP schemes. However, this is not the case. Many participants in schemes are finding that the cost of being in the schemes outweighs the benefits on a financial basis and this is therefore causing confidence in voluntary modulation and the schemes it seeks to support to be undermined.

The TFA believes that there should be one level of modulation applied across the whole of the EU together with a fundamental review of how agri-environment funding takes place across the whole of the EU to provide a thorough basis for all concerned. Member States should not be permitted to go beyond the compulsory level of modulation set within the EU rules.

Environmental Protection and Climate Change

The TFA believes that the regulatory framework within which environmental protection decisions take place in the UK and in the wider EU produces some of the most potent benefits to animal welfare and environment anywhere on the globe. Cross-compliance has certainly contributed towards this even though it is much maligned by the environmental community as being no more than adherence to existing legislative standards. The vast majority of farmers are acutely aware of their responsibilities towards animal welfare and the environment and seek to deliver significant output in both these areas in the context of making a sustainable economic return from their businesses—this is not always straightforward. However, the EU needs to be extremely careful about adding further, uncompensated restrictions upon farmers and growers through, for example, the Nitrates Directive, Water Framework Directive and Habitats Directive. The TFA believes that there is a real danger that the extra costs associated with such regulations could cause major economic problems for the farming community across the EU.

As far as climate change is concerned, there is no doubt that our climate is changing. Farmers know this better than anyone. However, the climate has always changed and will always change. That change will not always be in the same direction. However, our response should be in focusing our resources on investments, research and development which give us the flexibility to deal with any change in climate, whatever its ultimate direction, rather than attempting vainly to mitigate climate change through carbon reduction projects and programmes.

There is a building, scientific momentum questioning the perceived wisdom that reducing the amount of human induced carbon in the atmosphere will make a measurable difference to climate change into the long-term. Increasing evidence seems to suggest that solar activity, ocean-atmosphere cycles, volcanoes and the earth's tilt all contribute more to climate change than carbon induced from human activity. Indeed recent data from ice-core samples indicates that, in periods of warming, temperature rises as a prequel to concentrations of atmospheric carbon.

The TFA therefore believes that we should be putting our efforts into policies which allow us to adapt to the climate rather than attempting to change climate ourselves. This is why the TFA is concerned about long-term food security and, connected with that, the number of farmers who are currently leaving the industry across Western Europe. The CAP should be contributing to providing research and development into new crop varieties which can cope with the outcomes of a changing climate and new techniques for cultivation which do likewise. The efficient use and storage of water will become key as we head into the future.

Conclusion

The current debate about the future of the CAP takes place within the context of provision of "public goods". The TFA would argue that we must be careful not to confuse what we might consider "public goods" today against what might be considered "public goods" in the future. Within the European context there has been a very significant change in the definition of "public good" within a very short period of years and who is to say that it will not change back again—particularly in the context of climate change, global instability and a growing world population. We need to be sure that we are not restricting ourselves from meeting our long-term policy aims by pursuing short-term options.

The TFA believes that the CAP should be maintained within the suite of EU policies, that it needs to take a proper, long-term risk based approach and be allowed to be free from what might be considered "politically correct" in today's terms only.

Much criticism is placed at the cost of the CAP but given that it is central to helping meet objectives as diverse as feeding our people and managing and maintaining our countryside, it is not unreasonable to expect that it is funded properly.

June 2007

Memorandum by Kenneth J Thomson and Sophia M Davidova, respectively Professor Emeritus, University of Aberdeen and Reader, Kent Business School, University of Kent at Wye College

1. *What should be the long-term objectives of the CAP? Does the title "Common Agricultural Policy" aptly fit your perceived objectives of the policy? What do you consider to be the main pressures on the CAP as it currently is?*

1.1 There is a continued need for the EU to have a Common Agricultural Policy—though with new objectives (see 1.2 below), given:

(a) the long-established tendency for all governments to intervene in agriculture;

(b) the need to maintain the Single Market without unnecessary barriers to internal (or external) trade;

(c) the extensive positive and negative externalities of agriculture; and

(d) the difficulty of extending mainstream policies for industry and business (eg taxation, pollution control) to the often small-scale and family-oriented aspects of farming.

1.2 The objectives of such a CAP should be to ensure that:

(i) the provisions of EU competition policy apply fully to agriculture, particularly in terms of the control of state aids and the maintenance of the Single Market;

(ii) there is an adequate supply of safe food to citizens of the EU;

(iii) environmentally friendly farming practices provide an adequate supply of public goods, ie agricultural "multifunctionality";

(iv) farming is subject to the polluter pays principle;

(v) farming suffering from structural disadvantages is offered assistance towards commercial and environmental sustainability; and

(vi) farming exposed to unfavourable weather conditions, pest and diseases is offered assistance serving as a safety net (only).

1.3 Such a policy would still be suitably entitled the "Common Agricultural Policy" rather than eg the "Common Rural Policy", but it would lose most of the current CAP objectives, some of which date back to the 1950s and are defined with a productivist mind-set. Instead, it focuses on the provision of public goods (and avoidance of "public bads").

2. *What has been your experience so far with the reformed CAP? What has worked well and less well? And where can lessons be learned?*

2.1 The reformed CAP has involved (a) conversion of most but not all commodity-linked direct payments to "decoupled" Single Farm Payments (SFPs) based on historical and/or area "entitlements" in the 15 "old" Member States and in Slovenia and Malta, and (b) the introduction of Single Area Payments (SAPs) based on registered farm areas in the 10 other New Member States (NMSs).

2.2 In the UK, the flexibility allowed to different regions has been exploited via the four different SFP systems applied in England, Wales, Scotland and Northern Ireland. This has allowed a welcome but limited degree of subsidiarity in agricultural policy decision-making. In England, the well-known problems of the Rural Payments Agency in calculating and making SFPs have damaged expected farm income flows.

2.3 In the NMSs, the changes in payment systems were more profound. Pre-accession national support programmes provided farmers with advance payments, mainly used for working capital. Many NMS farmers have apparently treated the new Single Area Payments (SAPs) in the same way, planning to use them to cover their operating expenses. The new time schedule of payment disbursement (called *ex post* by some commentators, Bozik and Blaas, 2005) has created cash-flow problems. These early experiences suggest that, irrespective of the policy-makers' intentions, as long as such payments exist, farmers will include them in their farm management decisions and that simply enable farmers to continue farming as in the past possibly with less intensive systems, since SAPs do not depend on yields.

3. *Do you consider the Single Payment Scheme to be a good basis for the future of EU agricultural policy? What changes might be made at the EU level to the Single Payment Scheme, including to the rules governing entitlements, in the short and/or the longer-term?*

3.1 The Single Payment Schemes should be used as a basis for the future of EU agricultural policy only if they are subject to further and deeper cuts due to compulsory modulation or capping at the EU level, since:

    (i)   they have no clear and defensible foundation except the continuation (sometimes in modified form) of past support to agriculture;

    (ii) they have established, and are consolidating, a powerful interest group in favour of their continuation, regardless of their merits or deficiencies; and

    (iii) the cross-compliance conditions are weak, and their monitoring and observance are uncertain particularly in view of the different administrative capacities across the EU.

3.2 In their present form and level, the SFPs do not stimulate structural change. A study (EU- FP6 project "Impact of Decoupling and Modulation in the Enlarged Union", IDEMA) of farmers' intentions indicates that: (a) the introduction of decoupled payments in England is affecting farmers' management plans only marginally; few farmers plan to modify their exit or growth decisions; and (b) some more farmers intend to adjust the output mix and to expand (slightly) their diversification into off-farm activities.

3.3 In the NMSs, SAPs mean higher and more predictable payments. As a result, farmers plan to stay longer in agriculture, would like to increase their land area and do not intend to diversify to non-agricultural acytivities. The majority of farmers are pessimistic about their ability to make sufficient profits without policy support. This reliance on support and the focus on farming activities may strengthen further the anti-liberalisation lobby in the EU.

3.4 In view of the above, in the short term, efforts should continue to extend the compulsory modulation of SFPs from Pillar I income support into Pillar II "rural development" support. In the longer term, the level of SFPs should be reduced and a time limit should be imposed on their continuation, and/or they should be converted to a "bond" in line with proposals made by LUFPIG, Swinbank and Tangermann, and others.

4. *What short and longer-term changes are required to the CAP's market mechanisms? Suggestions made by the Commission have included re-examination of certain quotas, intervention, set-aside, export refunds and private storage payments*

4.1 No comments, due to length constraints.

5. *What is your view on the introduction of the European Agricultural Fund for Rural Development (EAFRD)? Do you consider that it is meeting its objectives thus far? Is it suitably "strategic" in nature, meeting the needs of rural society as a whole rather than being restricted to aiding the agricultural industry? How well is it being co-ordinated with other EU and national policies on regional and rural development?*

5.1 The EAFRD is largely restricted to aiding the agricultural industry and population, and does little for the rest of rural society. Its establishment marked a de-coordination of agricultural and regional/rural development, in that DG Agriculture and Rural Development has become responsible, via the EAFRD, for most smaller-scale regional/rural development. Also, due to the "80% rule", there is also little coordination of Pillar II spending with the objectives of the EU's Cohesion policy, under which attempts should be made to bring poorer regions more up to the standards of the EU as a whole.

6. *Is there a case for a higher level of EU financing of rural development? Do you have a view on the extension of compulsory modulation from Pillar 1 (Direct Payments) to Pillar 2 (Rural Development)?*

6.1 Non-agricultural (or even agricultural) rural development, ie investment, restructuring, modernisation, which can be promoted banks and other private agents, seems in little need of substantial assistance in the more advanced EU Member States, especially assistance over and above that offered by mainstream state support for public infrastructure, business development advice etc. However, there is a need to fund agricultural and non-agricultural rural development in the NMSs.

6.2 Irrespective of the need for EU financing of rural development, looking more broadly at the future of CAP, compulsory modulation is a practical and politically feasible way to put pressure for the decrease of SFP (SAP). The current rate of modulation does not exert any pressure to decrease farmers' reliance of support. Iraizoz *et al* (2004) studied 369 commercial farms in Navarra, Spain, and found that after the application of the franchise, only 201 farms would be subject to modulation, with a mean reduction in payments of only about €600 per annum. The franchise of course excludes the many smaller farms from modulation completely.

6.3 Another option is to leave SFPs "exposed" with no clear justification and to hope that budget pressures and/or reasoned argument will force down the rates in a straightforward way. Unfortunately, current high world prices make financial discipline rather irrelevant—though of course it should be easier to undertake CAP reform during an "easy" period (such as the present time) than in the midst of a crisis.

7. *What benefits can the EU's World Trade Organisation obligations create for EU agriculture and, consequently, for the EU economy as a whole?*

7.1 Given the flexibility (eg on "tariffication", the "green box") and weaknesses (eg the Peace Clause) of the current WTO obligations on EU export subsidies, market access and domestic support for agriculture, and the present climate of high world market prices for agricultural products, these obligations have only patchy effects, eg for sugar and banana regime reform, via the Dispute Settlement Mechanism.

7.2 With its border protection substantially unaltered, EU agriculture is still supported by the CAP, albeit in a substantially different way, with single payments. Implementation of current or future WTO proposals would further push EU agriculture towards a more dynamic competitive situation where it must focus more on local (including EU) and differentiated products.

8. *To what extent has the system of cross-compliance contributed to an improved level of environmental protection? How is it linking with other EU policy requirements such as the Water Framework Directive?*

8.1 No comments, due to length constraints.

9. *How can the CAP contribute to mitigation of, and adaptation to, climate change? What do you consider the role of biofuels to be in this regard?*

9.1 We consider that the CAP has only a small role to play in mitigating and adapting to climate change, especially if other environmental concerns such as those for landscape and biodiversity inhibit the large-scale adoption of biomass cropping in Europe. The economic and technical efficiency of agriculture in replacing fossil fuels is as yet unproven: at a recent conference of the UK Agricultural Economics Society, it was concluded that "*biofuel production in the EU might only be profitable in the EU with oil prices over $90 per barrel, and a 10% share of biofuel in overall fuel consumed in the EU-15* [ie the Commission's proposals of January 2007] *would require an area equivalent to 50% of the current arable land area*" (AES Newsletter, May 2007). A recent Commission estimate (Summa, 2007) is that a 14% bio-fuel share by 2020 would require about 18 million ha of land in the EU-25, out of a total of just over 100 million ha. Most of this land would be used for growing cereals for biofuel (about double the present area of 4 million ha) or woody material (7 million ha). There would be a significant but not huge effect on cereal and vegetable oil prices, but meal prices would decline.

9.2 Recently there are some—probably overoptimistic—expectations about the potential for biocrops in the NMSs ("*Biofuels in Central and Eastern Europe*", conference organised by Agra Informa, Prague 17-18 April). One factors is that oilseed yields in the NMSs are still low, at 50 to 60% of the EU-15 average (AgraFood East Europe, May 2007). The potential for oilseeds in the last two entrants, Romania and Bulgaria, is assessed to be high.

9.3 Unless it is considered that biofuels are likely to have a major role in reducing the EU's dependence on external sources of energy, so far there is no clear argument as to why agriculture needs special assistance from the taxpayer in coping with the gradual shifts in temperature/rainfall involved with climate change.

10. *The Commissioner has expressed her dissatisfaction at the financing agreement reached by the Member States at the December 2005 Council. Do you consider the current budget to be sufficient? Do you consider co-financing to be a possible way forward in financing the Common Agricultural Policy?*

10.1 The current budget for Pillar I of the CAP was determined (before modulation) by the October 2002 European Council, and is certainly more than "sufficient", especially as the purpose of and "need" for single payments are undefined.

10.2 The budget for Pillar II was reduced by about 20% during the 2005–06 negotiations. We see no great justification for seeking an increase even in this part of the overall EAFRD budget, and would prefer to see development assistance channelled through the Regional and Social Funds, primarily to New Member States.

10.3 Co-financing has been an integral part of EU budgeting for development assistance. The "opt-out" ("*Sums transferred to support rural development measures pursuant to such arrangements* [for voluntary modulation up to 20%] *shall not be subject to the national co-financing and minimum spending per axes rules set out in the Rural Development Regulation*" (European Council, December 2005) came as something of a surprise, and does not appear to be taken up in the recent UK proposals for Rural Development Plans.

11. *What has been the impact on the CAP of the 2004 and 2007 enlargements and what is the likely impact of future enlargements of the EU on the post-2013 CAP?*

11.1 The 2004 and 2007 enlargements have not yet had a major impact on the CAP, largely because the current framework of the policy was determined by the October 2002 CAP budget agreement and the 2003 Luxembourg agreement on CAP reform. The first ten New Member States did not play a large part in the 2006 negotiations over the budget for 2007–13, except to insist on retaining the commitments made to them in the accession agreements, eg transition from 25% to 100% of the EU-15 single payment rates. The entry of Romania and Bulgaria in 2007 was expected by some (but not all—see Davidova and Thomson 2005 to lead to a reduction in these rates in order not to violate the budget ceiling for the CAP, but with high world prices (and hence lower export subsidy payments) this now seems unlikely.

11.2 However, the enlargements (2004 and 2007) changed the political economy of the decision-making, strengthening the group opposing policy liberalisation. The previously mentioned IDEMA study indicated that the strongest opposition to policy liberalisation comes from farmers in the NMSs. Newcomers to farming in NMSs tend to reject policy liberalisation and endorse notions that farmers should concentrate on agriculture. These views are likely to have important implications for the decision-making processes surrounding agricultural policy reform in the EU. The new entrants to the Union do strengthen the political opposition to further agricultural policy reform, and most probably to co-financing. The difficulties to liberalise the policy are likely to increase with future enlargements.

12. *How could the CAP be further simplified and in what other ways would you like to see the Common Agricultural Policy changed in the short and/or the long term?*

12.1 The Commissioner, Ms Marianne Fischer Boel, has distinguished between "technical" and "political" (or "policy") simplification (speech in Brussels, 3 October 2006). The first "*is about the detailed implementation of policy, and sometimes about form*", for example "*revising a legal document to make it clearer, or streamlining administrative procedures*". "*Political simplification is about changing underlying policies in ways which make them simpler. For example, some say we should abolish production quota systems*". She intends to pursue both types of simplification and has proposed a single Common Market Organisation for all or most agricultural products, replacing 21 individual CMOs. She also proposes an Action Plan, with "*20 proposals for practical changes which can make life easier for farmers, businesses and national administrations without changing fundamental policy*".

12.2 On the policy side, she has proposed reforms for commodity regimes, such as those for sugar, wine, bananas, and fruit and vegetables, and relaxing the conditions for receiving certain commodity subsidies. The "health check" may suggest certain adjustments in the new single payment system, eg ending "*the many exceptions to the principle of full decoupling*", a single type of entitlement, and an end to set-aside. Finally, the budget review may question the very existence of certain market instruments in the long term, ie a new role for direct payments, and a "single model for decoupling", after 2013. In her speech, the Commissioner was firm on the principle of cross-compliance, ie payments for "*the delivery of public goods and services*", as a means of winning "*broader support for our policy in the future*".

12.3 We support all these proposals for simplification, with caution over fraud from reduced paperwork. However, with the possible exception of the vague hope of "a new role for direct payments", they will not change the nature of the current CAP, ie still significant market protection via border taxes, and generous payments to farmers for little obvious social or economic (or environmental) purpose or efficiency.

June 2007

Memorandum by the Ulster Farmers' Union

Position paper from the National Farmers' Union, England and Wales (NFU), the National Farmers' Union Scotland (NFUS) and the Ulster Farmers' Union (UFU) on Simplification and Better Regulation of the CAP

INTRODUCTION

1. The UK NFUs welcome this opportunity to submit views on the simplification and better regulation of the CAP. As Commissioner Fischer-Boel has pointed out, this is an ongoing process and it is likely that further comments will be submitted in due course, both directly and indirectly through other forums.

2. We particularly welcome the fact that this simplification round takes place within the framework of the "Better Regulation for Growth and Jobs" initiative. Better regulation is something we are pressing for with our own administrations; in our view, its scope is wider than simply simplifying the rule book. It is about ensuring consistency of approach and legal certainty. It addresses the need for farmers to know exactly what rules they must observe and when, to what extent they can be penalised if they do not comply and, importantly, what the rule is there to achieve.

3. Bearing that wider aspect in mind, we would like to make comments covering the following issues:
   — Single Payment Scheme.
   — Single CMO.
   — DG Agri's Simplification Action Plan.

SINGLE PAYMENT SCHEME

Ten-month rule (Council Reg 1782/2003 Art 44(3))

4. Of all the candidates for "technical" simplification, this rule must be on the short list. It is not even clear what the current reasoning behind it is. As a measure to ensure that it is easier to identify who is responsible for cross-compliance, it does not do the job adequately and leads to confusion; cross-compliance responsibilities apply across a calendar year whereas the 10-month occupation period can potentially extend from up to three months before the calendar year to two months after it. As a rule to ensure that there is only one claimant who matches a hectare of land against an entitlement, it is unnecessary. We note that the 10-month rule does not appear to apply under the Simplified Area Payment Scheme, currently operating in eight of the new member states.

5. Once you have an area-based system, the approach adopted under the old Arable Area Payments Scheme is surely sufficient; whoever is in control of the parcel on the latest date for including that parcel in an SPS application is entitled to use that parcel to match against their entitlements. That is no more nor less disruptive to the cross-compliance regime if the basic principle is that SPS claimants can be held responsible for breaches of cross-compliance where at the time of determination they are in charge of the holding, the area, the production unit or the animal concerned (as per Article 65.2 of Reg. 796/2004).

6. The need for a claimant to have land at his disposal for a minimum of 10 months within a defined period and the possibility of only two start dates per holding has created heavy administrative burdens for our members, particularly in sectors where land is taken for short periods from other farmers for field vegetable and potato production. In order to ensure the rule is respected and payment can be claimed, complex leasing, licensing and contracting arrangements have had to be used which make a mockery of the notion that the SPS is a simpler system.

7. Having said that, we acknowledge the need for an anti-avoidance provision of some kind, to prevent a farmer using land he is controlling on the latest date to apply for payment and then transferring the parcel to a non SPS claimant who is, in effect, free from the risk of cross-compliance deductions.

Penalties

8. The level of penalties imposed on farmers for small, administrative mistakes are hugely disproportionate. There is little distinction between penalties resulting from genuine, unintentional errors and those involving intentional misinformation. What we need is a flexible penalty system that recognises the differences between these types of errors, why they occur and only applies a penalty that is proportionate to the error that is found.

Decoupling

9. We recognise that further decoupling involves policy rather than technical simplification. Nonetheless, as farmer organisations whose administrations have opted for full decoupling, we can believe that the simplification heralded by the 2003 reforms cannot be realised unless and until partial de-coupling options are dispensed with.

10. We do not believe that a non-distorting and level playing field in Europe is attainable as long as some farmers are still encouraged to produce, not in response to market forces but in order to maximise support payments.

Cross-Compliance

11. We have submitted a separate paper to the Commission on cross-compliance. Here, we would like to make just a few comments on how—in our view—principles of simplification and better regulation can be applied to the regime.

Breach at time of determination or at time of commission?

12. This point ties in with what we have said in paragraph 5 above. Article 6 of Council Regulation 1782/2003 states that where statutory management requirements or GAEC standards are not complied with as a result of an action or omission of the farmer, the total amount of payments to be granted *in the calendar year in which the non-compliance occurs* shall be reduced or cancelled. This contrasts with the provisions of Article 65.2 of the implementing regulation 796/2004; this refers to the time of *determination*, rather than the time of occurrence. The two are not, in our view, totally compatible. The breach may occur in one scheme year, but be determined in the following year. Which year's payment should be subject to deduction in this instance? In the interest of certainty, the position needs to be clarified.

For whose breaches can a farmer be penalised?

13. The risk of deductions for non-compliance threatens to impinge on public infrastructure works which previously took place by agreement with the owner or occupier. Now, we are in the ridiculous position where if a farmer co-operates willingly to allow a statutory undertaker access to carry out necessary works, he could be in breach of cross-compliance if the work involves the statutory undertaker committing a non-compliance whereas if he insists on statutory notices of entry being served, his position is protected. To be on the safe side we are forced to advise our members to opt for the more legalistic second option. There surely must be scope for clarity here. Any acts by statutory undertakers who have the right to enter land to carry out works should not be considered acts or omissions of the farmer, whether they enter by agreement or not. This needs to be set out clearly in the regulations.

Principle of legal certainty

14. What we are asking for is, in effect, that it should be clear at any point in time who can be held liable for what as far as cross-compliance breaches are concerned and what deduction could potentially be applied to which year's payment. That is a principle of good regulation. A farmer should know on 31 December of a scheme year that if there has been no determination of a breach ahead of that date, he can be sure that no deduction for non-compliance will be made to that year's SPS payment.

Payment window

15. Leaving aside the disastrous first year delivery of payments in England, we believe it would make sense to have 16 October as the start date from which payments may be made. In the same way, we would wish to see the legal deadline as 31 March. These dates have a certain familiarity, derived from previous support schemes. Payments could then be made from the start of the Commission's own budget year and the need for formal requests to make advances following summer droughts etc. would be reduced. Payments for the previous scheme year would in turn be completed well ahead of farmers submitting their SPS application forms for the next year, avoiding the overlap that is currently a feature of the regime.

Simplified Area Payment Scheme—the future model for flat-rate systems?

16. Once a member state or region has adopted a flat-rate and fully decoupled approach, with virtually every hectare of eligible agricultural land matched by a payment entitlement and the same payment per hectare applied, the payment entitlements themselves become redundant. They will be nothing more than an additional layer of bureaucracy, adding cost and risk to the process of administering direct payments (for the paying agency) and claiming them (for the farmer).

17. Whatever future direction of direct payment models is mapped out during the Health Check, we would urge the Commission to consider whether entitlements themselves can be justified where transitional phasing-in periods are complete and the management of a hectare of land delivers the same rate of payment. In effect, under the flat-rate approach, payment entitlements will have served to "convert" headage/quota/contract tonneage entitlement etc into an area payment; that done, they serve no useful purpose.

Fruit, vegetable and potato (FVP) restrictions

18. The issue of whether restrictions on FVP production should remain is principally a policy one and we have already submitted our views in other papers and forums[1]. Suffice to say here that in terms of simplification and better regulation a regulatory framework that allows FVP production to be supported in three completely different ways depending on the direct payment model selected is nonsense. A three-speed CAP is a CAP in reverse and this inconsistency must be rectified at the earliest possible opportunity.

December 2006

Memorandum by Wildlife and Countryside Link

1. Wildlife and Countryside Link (Link) brings together voluntary organisations concerned with the conservation, enjoyment and protection of wildlife, countryside and the marine environment. Our members practice and advocate environmentally sensitive land management and food production practices and encourage respect for and enjoyment of natural landscapes and features, the historic environment and biodiversity. Taken together, our members have the support of over eight million people in the UK and manage over 476,000 hectares of land. This submission is supported by:

— Bat Conservation Trust.

— Buglife—the Invertebrate Conservation Trust.

— Butterfly Conservation.

— Campaign to Protect Rural England.

— Council for British Archaeology.

— Plantlife International.

— Royal Society for the Prevention of Cruelty to Animals.

— Royal Society for the Protection of Birds.

— The Wildlife Trusts.

— The Woodland Trust.

Q1. *What should be the long term objectives of the CAP? Does the title "Common Agricultural Policy" aptly fit your perceived objectives of the policy? What do you consider to be the main pressures on the CAP as it currently is?*

2. Wildlife and Countryside Link (Link) has led the call for the reform of the Common Agricultural Policy (CAP) from the 1980s onwards and we welcomed many of the reforms to the CAP from the Mid Term Review. Since then a debate has begun on whether the CAP should exist at all and if not how could sustainable land management be supported. The recent UK Government *Vision for the CAP* set out how sustainable land management might be delivered in a post CAP Europe. However, Link believes the Government's Vision failed adequately to consider how the delivery of environmental public goods would be assured as the global agricultural trading system becomes increasingly liberalised. In addition to economic pressures creating additional demands on land for food and bioenergy the demand for provision of environmental public goods is also increasing.

3. The challenges Link believes the CAP is facing include:

— Changing land and soil management practices to tackle the causes of climate change.

— Adapting land to the effects of climate change.

— Ensuring water quality and quantity is maintained.

— Creating healthy functioning ecosystems rich in biodiversity.

— Protecting and conserving the irreplaceable archaeological resource.

— Conserving and enhancing important productive landscapes and their character.

— Improving farm animal standards without leaving European producers at a competitive disadvantage.

— Reconnecting people with the environment and understanding what it provides for them.

— Producing food, timber and energy in more sustainable ways.

4. We believe it is time to begin the process of developing a new policy framework with adequate funding to create a European Sustainable Land Management Policy in the EU that will deliver the environmental public benefits and ecosystem services that society needs. The ending of the CAP will almost certainly require new terminology. The terms Pillar I and II have become associated with a variety of preconceptions in terms of environmental damage, intensive farming, market distortions and agricultural purpose. We should seek to develop a single funding and policy instrument that will enable farmers and other land managers to deliver sustainable land management and high quality countryside as well as improved animal welfare standards.

5. While policy mechanisms such as the CAP have encouraged damage to the environment, it should be remembered that the CAP was originally designed to encourage food production. A new, fully funded European Sustainable Land Management Policy that combined funding from both pillars of the CAP could prevent agricultural practices damaging the environment and instead pay for a greater range and quality of environmental public goods over a far wider area while also improving animal welfare standards. If the CAP were to be abolished we believe the free market is unlikely to be able to deliver environmental public benefits without the existence of regulatory mechanisms that are combined with adequate funded policies to deliver these public benefits through agriculture and other land management activities. Such a fund could play a useful secondary role in ensuring a critical mass of farm businesses continue to exist.

6. We believe that the environmental challenges facing Europe in the 21st Century means that reform of agricultural policy will require concerted European intervention. Many of the detailed solutions to these challenges will need to be developed at a more local level but must recognise the crucial role of sustainable farming in managing our wildlife, the character of our landscapes, our woodlands and our soil and water resources.

7. While it could be argued that the commercial aspects of agricultural production could be treated like any other industry and should, therefore, not receive public funding, the fact remains that the production processes of commercial agriculture have a direct bearing on the quality of the countryside and its wildlife habitats. Making production processes more sustainable in order to maintain high quality countryside and achieve higher animal welfare standards, will have economic consequences for farmers. The internalisation of these costs will inevitably have limits, particularly with a lack of transparency on labelling. In the opinion of Link, sufficient public money should be made available to farmers and other land managers to underpin the delivery of public goods such as landscapes and wildlife habitats that are dependent on farming systems.

THE REFORMED CAP

Q2. *What has been your experience so far with the reformed CAP? What has worked well and less well? And where can lessons be learned?*

8. Link believes that the recent reforms have moved the CAP in the right direction. The establishment of a second "rural development" pillar for the CAP under Agenda 2000, and the decoupling of most direct commodity supports from 2005, have begun to rectify the negative effects of the pre-reform CAP of the past. The introduction of cross compliance measures means that public funding for agriculture is now linked to basic environmental and animal welfare standards. However, Pillar I of the CAP, representing the largest part of the CAP budget (and a substantial portion of the EU budget as a whole), is now a fund without a clear policy objective.

THE SINGLE PAYMENT SCHEME

Q3. *Do you consider the Single Payment Scheme to be a good basis for the future of EU agricultural policy? What changes might be made at the EU level to the Single Payment Scheme, including to the rules governing entitlements, in the short and/or the longer-term?*

9. Link believes that the new decoupled Single Payment even when it eventually becomes tied solely to the area of land for which it is paid, will be at best an inefficient policy to secure sustainable land management. Therefore, as we have set out above Link believes new approaches must be developed to achieve wider environmental policy objectives. This will continue to require public intervention to ensure the delivery of a wide range of public goods from the countryside, alongside the sustainable production of food and energy, in a way that can be built into viable farming and rural businesses.

10. The decoupling of farm payments will also have a profound impact on the profitability of businesses engaged in farming and land management. Some beneficial land management activities will become less profitable, and means need to be found within an international agricultural trading system of providing sufficient incentives to ensure these continue where they are necessary. Other environmentally harmful activities should become less attractive, and the rational move away from these should be encouraged.

11. The inefficiencies of the current system in achieving sustainable land management, and the need for a new approach is exemplified by the case of GAEC 12 in England. The new reformed CAP aims to be more environmentally aware and through agri-environment and the England Woodland Grant Scheme provides for an expansion of the tree and woodland resource in England. However even where it is beneficial to wildlife and woodland to do so, GAEC 12 prevents the growth of trees and scrub on land not in agricultural production. A derogation may be applied to allow for natural regeneration where appropriate. The bureaucracy presently involved could render this a significant disincentive.

12. Ongoing provision of public goods should be secured in different ways around the EU, but to a common framework. This will involve burden sharing both in setting objectives and in resourcing the delivery of a new European Sustainable Land Management Policy that will need to allow flexibility to deliver the different local approaches that will be needed. Any policy for sustainable land management must be compatible with the sustainable provision of high-quality food and renewable energy.

MARKET MECHANISMS

Q4. *What short and longer-term changes are required to the CAP's market mechanisms? Suggestions made by the Commission have included re-examination of certain quotas, intervention, set-aside, export refunds and private storage payments*

13. Link's main concerns in relation to short term changes to the CAP's market mechanisms are on the abolition of set-aside and bioenergy crop measures. We will shortly be publishing our positions on both set-aside and bioenergy.

14. Link accepts that following decoupling there is limited market rationale for set-aside and as a result set-aside is now a redundant concept in the eyes of many and therefore it is likely to be abolished as a result of the forthcoming CAP "Healthcheck" in 2008. Link believes that before abolishing set-aside a comprehensive stock take of both rotational and permanent set-aside must be undertaken so we know what environmental benefits it is providing and where it is providing these environmental benefits. In this way these benefits can be protected for the future rather than simply lost.

15. Link recognises that there is a need to maintain the current environmental benefits from set aside for example through the existence of a permanent network of habitats in relation to water courses, steep slopes and edge habitats for key species such as bats and barn owls. Proposals to eliminate set-aside should therefore be accompanied with mechanisms to retain the existing environmental benefits either through cross-compliance or through agri-environment schemes or a combination of both of these. The benefits of improved set aside rules since its inception should not be lost in any new regime.

16. A case may be made for short or long term changes to the CAP to secure other public goods and address other market failures in agriculture and rural development. We suggest they might include supporting local food networks, improving competitiveness, addressing peripherality, securing structural change, cohesion objectives and income support. A European Sustainable Land Management Policy could contribute to some of these objectives. The case for any further intervention in these areas needs to be clear about the need for EU intervention, respect for the single market, efficiency of intervention, and avoiding environmental damage.

17. In particular, it is essential that any support to secure food, timber and fuel security, or to address the effects of climate change, does not undermine the objectives of sustainable land management. We have a particular concern that there is a danger of this occurring as a result of support through the CAP for bioenergy crops. Receipt of payment for these crops should be conditional on production methods meeting the standards set out in an accreditation system that ensures that real greenhouse gas savings are provided by crops grown for biofuel or biomass and which do not damage habitats, landscape, archaeological sites or historic landscapes, or require unsustainable use of soil and water resources.

RURAL DEVELOPMENT

Q5. What is your view on the introduction of the European Agricultural Fund for Rural Development (EAFRD)? Do you consider that it is meeting its objectives thus far? Is it suitably "strategic" in nature, meeting the needs of rural society as a whole rather than being restricted to aiding the agricultural industry? How well is it being co-ordinated with other EU and national policies on regional and rural development?

18. Link's key principles for the EAFRD are that it should deliver public benefits through integrating environmental, economic and social measures for sustainable outcomes and that the agri-environment measures of the EAFRD should be adequately funded. We supported the UK's Government view that allocation of EU Rural Development funds should move away from the basis of historical spend and instead be based on evidence of need.

19. We were concerned that although the EAFRD regulations allowed member states a degree of flexibility in developing rural development measures an opportunity to provide greater integration between measures has been lost through the creation of separate axes. The Mid Term Evaluation of the Rural Development Regulation made a recommendation that greater integration between measures was needed. We continue to seek greater guidance on strategic co-ordination of measures across the three axes of the EAFRD provided by the Commission and the UK Government.

20. We are aware of only two member states who have so far had their programmes approved by the European Commission so it is difficult to comment on whether the EAFRD is meeting its objectives across Europe. However, Link has carefully monitored the development of the Rural Development Programme for England and provided input to the process where requested. We support the decision to allocate the majority of funding to agri-environment measures. We were relieved that the UK Government was partially successful in negotiating for the levels of voluntary modulation it needed to meet the commitment it had made to the Environmental Stewardship Scheme. We are concerned that Higher Level Stewardship will require greater levels of funding if it is to achieve its aims.

21. We also have some concerns over the extent to which Structural Funds and EAFRD funds will be integrated. Link believes it is crucial that both sets of funding reinforce each others objectives. EAFRD social and economic funding allocations will be limited in the UK and is therefore likely to support small scale enterprises. The sums available through the Structural Funds are proportionately much greater than EAFRD funding for economic and social measures. Structural Fund support should not undermine the smaller scale economic and social activities being supported by EAFRD measures.

Q6. Is there a case for a higher level of EU financing of rural development? Do you have a view on the extension of compulsory modulation from Pillar 1 (Direct Payments) to Pillar 2 (Rural Development)?

22. Link strongly believes that rural development measures should receive significantly higher levels of funding. We were disappointed with the EAFRD budget that was agreed in December 2005 which cut the amount of funding allocated to the EAFRD. We also believe that the competitive nature of negotiations for the division of funding between Pillar I and Pillar II from the overall EU budget is counter productive to the aim of making agriculture more sustainable. Link takes the view that funding negotiations take place without the existence of adequate analysis and evidence on the amount of funding needed to maintain agricultural landscapes, deliver targets for biodiversity and conservation of the historic environment, and improve animal welfare. There is an urgent need to examine the cost and range of policy tools for delivering the wide range of environmental and animal welfare benefits that arise through the management activities provided by various farming sectors which are supported through a combination of Pillar I funding and by the sustainable land management measures that are derived from Pillar II.

23. We also believe further research is needed into more sustainable systems of paying for public goods that is not reliant on the "income forgone" from often uneconomic farming systems and enterprises. Traditional farming systems themselves are responsible for many of the landscapes in marginal areas which are most valued by the public (and, paradoxically, most designated as areas of great "natural" beauty).

24. The recent disagreement between the European Commission and the European Parliament over the percentage of voluntary modulation the UK would be allowed to introduce also demonstrated the difficulty of trying to fund two sets of policy objectives that essentially both now claim to deliver sustainable land management. Establishing a single fund for a new European Sustainable Land Management Policy would end debate over re-nationalisation of agricultural policy providing that the need to maintain flexibility over the different measures required for sustainable land management delivery in each member state was recognised.

WORLD TRADE

Q7. What benefits can the EU's World Trade Organisation obligations create for EU agriculture and, consequently, for the EU economy as a whole?

25. Link does not hold a view on the extent of the benefits of the EU's WTO obligations to EU agriculture or subsequently the EU economy as a whole. However, global sustainability must lie at the heart of agricultural policies across the globe. The export of environmental and animal welfare problems as result of WTO obligations or EU measures would be both counter-productive and unethical. One area that could prove beneficial to the continuance of traditional farming practices is the securing of regional food identity exemption under WTO rules; Link would strongly support UK Government efforts to secure this.

ENVIRONMENTAL PROTECTION AND CLIMATE CHANGE

Q8. To what extent has the system of cross-compliance contributed to an improved level of environmental protection? How is it linking with other EU policy requirements such as the Water Framework Directive?

26. There is a view that following the 2003 CAP reforms and the introduction of cross compliance measures for receipt of the Single Payment, the CAP has become a "green payment". However, others consider the basic standards required for compliance as being too low for this label to be truly justified. There is a need for public support to ensure that a baseline of environmental measures are established and maintained. This should be based on maintaining land in Good Agricultural and Environmental Condition. Complying with Regulations and Directives should not in itself qualify for receipt of public support as is the case with other industries. However, as we have stated previously farming is unlikely to be able to internalise all of the costs associated with full compliance. Given that the purpose of many of these Regulations and Directives is to deliver environmental public goods is could be argued that funding is justified to help with the transition and adaptation of farming businesses to meet these requirements. Equally, it is important that measures proposed for resource protection should be adequately assessed for possible negative impacts on other areas of environmental protection (for example, the impact on buried archaeological deposits of subsoiling to reduce runoff).

27. The UK Government, in their 2005 *Vision for the CAP*, gave a great deal of consideration to the impacts of agriculture on Diffuse Water Pollution from Agriculture (DWPA). Link believes that the pressure for profit driven production derived from the liberalised trading system set out in the Government's Vision could result in very different land management pressures than under the current CAP. If these were to require different regulatory measures to be developed to maintain the benefits of the WFD than intervention through publicly funded measures could be required to ensure that the aims of the WFD were secured.

Q9. *How can the CAP contribute to mitigation of, and adaptation to, climate change? What do you consider the role of biofuels to be in this regard?*

28. Link believes that further reform of the CAP is needed to ensure land management practices can be adapted so that the sustainable production of food and energy alongside the conservation of biodiversity, the historic environment, landscape character, and soil and water resources can be secured. Link believes that the CAP even with its 2003 reforms will face difficulties in meeting this requirement.

29. Link finds that continuing direct support for production for biofuel crops is incongruous with decoupling CAP funding from production of other crops. We are also concerned that such support could result in intensification of production and could feasibly add to green house gas emissions, for example through increased use of artificial fertilisers. Biofuel production is already putting additional pressure on the historic environment, since the cultivation needed for many biofuel crops is more damaging than that for conventional cereals and grass. It is essential that biofuels are properly certified both for their carbon savings and to avoid damage to habitats, landscape, the historic environment and soil and water resources.

FINANCING

Q10. *The Commissioner has expressed her dissatisfaction at the financing agreement reached by the Member States at the December 2005 Council. Do you consider the current budget to be sufficient? Do you consider co-financing to be a possible way forward in financing the Common Agricultural Policy?*

30. Link believes that the 2005 EU budget deal represented a disappointing outcome for the environment and for sustainable rural development measures and the current budget is therefore not sufficient. We believe it is imperative that agri-environment schemes across Europe receive the levels of funding required. This is essential to achieve UK Government stated objectives for landscape, public access and biodiversity. We believe that the amount of funding needed to deliver biodiversity targets, maintain the character of our landscapes, protect our historic environment and secure our soil and water resources for the future is greatly underestimated.

31. Link believes that it is right that the cost of protecting and enhancing our environment should be shared by the EU and national governments but allocations to member states must be made using an equitable, needs based approach.

ENLARGEMENT

Q11. *What has been the impact on the CAP of the 2004 and 2007 enlargements and what is the likely impact of future enlargements of the EU on the post-2013 CAP?*

32. Link is concerned that the CAP should not encourage damaging agricultural practices in member states that have recently joined the EU These member states often retain non intensive farming practices that create diverse landscapes, conserve the historic environment and provide important habitats for wildlife. Evidence from WWF engagement in the Carpathian mountains[36] also indicates the damage to traditional farming practices of ill informed standards in food production and processing. Unless addressed such food standard's rules could single handedly destroy many valuable traditional farming practices.

---

[36] See http://ec.europa.eu/agriculture/events/youngfarmers/kazakova_en.pdf

SIMPLIFICATION OF THE CAP AND OTHER ISSUES

Q12. *How could the CAP be further simplified and in what other ways would you like to see the Common Agricultural Policy changed in the short and/or the long term?*

33. Link believes that the time has come to assess whether efforts to further adapt and reform the CAP to meet the challenges we have outlined above would be more fruitful if they were to be focused on establishing a new European Sustainable Land Management Policy. If such a decision was taken and such a policy created it is essential that there is a carefully planned transition from the CAP to the new policy. It is vital that during the transition period agriculture in Europe is supported in its land management functions that maintain and enhance the environmental public goods it delivers.

15 June 2007

Memorandum by Woodland Trust

The Woodland Trust welcomes the opportunity to respond to this consultation. The Trust is the UK's leading woodland conservation charity. We have four main aims: no further loss of ancient woodland, restoring and improving woodland biodiversity, increasing new native woodland and increasing people's understanding and enjoyment of woodland. We own over 1,000 sites across the UK, covering around 20,000 hectares (50,000 acres) and we have 300,000 members and supporters.

OVERVIEW

Q1. *What should be the long term objectives of the CAP? Does the title "Common Agricultural Policy" aptly fit your perceived objectives of the policy? What do you consider to be the main pressures on the CAP as it currently is?*

5. The Woodland Trust believes that in the long term the objectives of the CAP need to be significantly reformed into a single sustainable land management fund. As such the title of Common Agricultural Policy does not fit our objectives for the policy and should be altered to reflect a new emphasis on sustainable land management.

6. The challenges the Woodland Trust believes the CAP is facing include:

— Maintaining ecosystem services such as healthy functioning ecosystems, water quality, soil quality etc.

— Adapting land to the effects of climate change.

— Protecting and conserving the irreplaceable habitats such as ancient woodland.

— Conserving and enhancing important landscapes and their character.

— Reconnecting people with the environment and understanding what it provides for them.

— Producing food, timber and energy in more sustainable ways.

7. We believe it is time to begin the process of developing a new policy framework with adequate funding to create a single Sustainable Land Management Policy in the EU that will deliver the environmental public benefits and ecosystem services that society needs.

8. Indeed, given the proposal in the Treasury vision for the CAP whereby Pillar 1 is to go before 2020, perhaps now is the right time to consider terminology for sustainable land management funding post Pillar 1. The terms Pillar 1 and 2 come with all sorts of weighted views in terms of environmental damage, market distortion, food mountains, compulsory modulation etc. If we are to move towards a single support mechanism for public benefit delivery in the countryside, we should no longer talk about pillar 2, but simply about a sustainable land management fund.

9. In this way public money would be delivering public goods and services.

10. This will continue to require public intervention to ensure the delivery as the cost of delivering public goods and services cannot solely be internalised by agricultural businesses.

11. However, we are concerned that this call for a new approach may be seen by some as a cost cutting exercise. Insufficient thought has been given to how much money will actually be required to deliver the high value countryside, providing sustainable biodiversity and ecosystem goods and services on which our quality of life relies.

12. The reality is that the delivery of public goods and services across Europe may actually cost more than the current Pillar 1 budget.

THE REFORMED CAP

Q2. *What has been your experience so far with the reformed CAP? What has worked well and less well? And where can lessons be learned?*

13. The Woodland Trust experience of the reformed CAP so far has been mixed. We strongly support the recent reforms however we are concerned about some of the detail in the implementation.

14. The inefficiencies of the current system in achieving sustainable land management, and the need for a new approach is exemplified by the case of GAEC (Good Agricultural and Environmental Condition) in England. We have three examples to describe:

14.1 The new reformed CAP aims to be more environmentally aware and through agri-environment and the England Woodland Grant Scheme provides for an expansion of the tree and woodland resource in England. However GAEC 12 prevents the growth of trees and scrub on land not in agricultural production even where it is beneficial to wildlife and woodland to do so. A derogation may be applied for to allow for this but the bureaucracy involved renders this a significant disincentive.

14.2 Ancient trees are not adequately protected under GAEC. While GAEC 16 and 17 mention the importance of ancient trees both only reinforce existing legislation. This existing legislation has significant loopholes which result in the loss of ancient trees across the countryside.

14.2.1 In terms of the felling licences under GAEC16, the felling of a single ancient tree will easily come under the exemptions of a felling licence (the cutoff regarding the amount of wood that can be felled without requiring a licence) and so the loss of these historic trees continues un-recorded.

14.2.2 In terms of Tree Preservation Orders (TPOs) under GAEC 17, we have a number of concerns. Firstly the system is too slow to place TPOs where ancient trees are threatened; secondly the are too few resources to protect the trees needing protection and lastly the "dead, dying and dangerous" loophole in the TPO legislation is significant as a great proportion of ancient trees are dead or dying- however this does not reduce their amenity value and in many cases actually increases their biodiversity value.

15. As such we believe the lessons that could be learnt are in the detail of implementation. Firstly the detail should be checked back against the spirit of the regulation to ensure they match and secondly the effectiveness of mechanisms to protect environmental features needs to be assured.

THE SINGLE PAYMENT SCHEME

Q3. *Do you consider the Single Payment Scheme to be a good basis for the future of EU agricultural policy? What changes might be made at the EU level to the Single Payment Scheme, including to the rules governing entitlements, in the short and/or the longer-term?*

16. The Woodland Trust strongly supports the recent reforms to the CAP, however we believe reform should go further.

17. We believe that the new decoupled Single Payment (even when it eventually becomes tied solely to the area of land for which it is paid), will not be a good basis for securing sustainable land management. This is firstly because the Objective of Pillar 1 is not sustainable land management and secondly because of the detail of its operation, as we describe in our response to Q2 above.

18. As such we believe now is the time to move towards a single Sustainable Land Management policy for Europe, as described in our response to Q1 above.

MARKET MECHANISMS

Q4. *What short and longer-term changes are required to the CAP's market mechanisms? Suggestions made by the Commission have included re-examination of certain quotas, intervention, set-aside, export refunds and private storage payments*

19. Our main concern in relation to short term changes to the CAP's market mechanisms is the abolition of set-aside.

20. Following decoupling there is limited market rationale for set-aside and therefore it is likely to be abolished as a result of the forthcoming CAP "Healthcheck" in 2008.

21. The Woodland Trust has three main views on the future of set-aside:

    21.1 Set-aside is an outdated production reduction mechanism, it therefore has no place in a modernised, decoupled CAP. However where set-aside land is currently delivering high quality wildlife or public benefits, this should be protected for the future, rather than simply lost as set-aside goes in 2008.

    21.2 We support the principle of a % of the farm being managed for wildlife and that this be a condition of payment.

    21.3 We would like to see more imagination in the management of land for wildlife on farms, such as regeneration of scrub and trees adjacent to woodland, without the risk of loss of SPS. This would buffer the existing woodland providing discernible wildlife benefit in terms of resilience to the existing habitat.

22. In order to protect the benefits currently accruing from set-aside for the future we believe that before abolishing set-aside a comprehensive stock take of both rotational and permanent set-aside must be undertaken so we know what environmental benefits it is providing and where these are being provided.

23. Mechanisms to retain the existing environmental benefits include cross-compliance or agri-environment schemes, as in the Welsh Tir Cynnal example, whereby a percentage of the farm is managed for wildlife.

24. In this scenario the maintenance of the biodiversity benefits is a condition of the payment (rather than an option eligible for further payment). In this way the benefits of set-aside can be retained for the future without further squeezing the Pillar 2 budget.

25. In addition we would like to see more imaginative use of set-aside, in the current scenario in England scrub and woodland is not allowed to regenerate on set-aside without the Single Payment being lost. The goes against the new reformed CAP's aims of greater environmental awareness and provision of public benefits.

RURAL DEVELOPMENT

Q5. *What is your view on the introduction of the European Agricultural Fund for Rural Development (EAFRD)? Do you consider that it is meeting its objectives thus far? Is it suitably "strategic" in nature, meeting the needs of rural society as a whole rather than being restricted to aiding the agricultural industry? How well is it being co-ordinated with other EU and national policies on regional and rural development?*

26. The Woodland Trust strongly supports the introduction of the EAFRD, as it provides for the protection and enhancement of our countryside.

Q6. *Is there a case for a higher level of EU financing of rural development? Do you have a view on the extension of compulsory modulation from Pillar 1 (Direct Payments) to Pillar 2 (Rural Development)?*

27. The Woodland Trust strongly believes that rural development measures should receive significantly higher levels of funding because of the need to enhance the countryside in order to deliver a range of public benefits.

28. We were disappointed with the budget that was agreed in December 2005 which cut the amount of funding allocated to the EAFRD.

29. We also believe that the competitive nature of negotiations for the division of funding between Pillar I and Pillar II is counter productive to the aim of making agriculture more sustainable.

30. In addition we do not believe there has been adequate analysis and evidence of the amount of funding needed to maintain agricultural landscapes and deliver targets for biodiversity. As stated in our response to Q1 above it is possible that the level of funding needed to maintain a high value countryside, deliverying a wide range of ecosystem services, may actually be more than the current Pillar 1 budget.

31. The recent disagreement between the European Commission and the European Parliament over the percentage of voluntary modulation the UK would be allowed to introduce also demonstrated the difficulty of trying to fund two sets of policy objectives. Establishing a single fund for Sustainable Land Management would end this debate.

ENVIRONMENTAL PROTECTION AND CLIMATE CHANGE

Q8. *To what extent has the system of cross-compliance contributed to an improved level of environmental protection? How is it linking with other EU policy requirements such as the Water Framework Directive?*

32. The Woodland Trust believes it is too soon to determine if cross compliance has resulted in an improved level of environmental protection.

33. As with other industries, simply complying with Regulations and Directives should not enable farmers/ foresters to claim public monies. However where these Directives are aimed at supporting public goods and services there is a need for public support as the farming industry is unlikely to be able to internalise all of the costs associated with full compliance.

34. The Woodland Trust does not believe that cross-compliance is adequately linking to the Water Framework Directive requirements. Work on these two areas appears to be in parallel rather than joined.

35. In addition to this, the issues we have raised regarding GAEC 12, tree felling and TPOs under Q2 are all relevant here.

Q9. *How can the CAP contribute to mitigation of, and adaptation to, climate change? What do you consider the role of biofuels to be in this regard?*

36. The CAP could contribute to the adaptation of climate change through helping to create wildlife friendly landscape across England. In the short term we believe that this cannot be achieved without a substantial incease in funding for Pillar 2. In the longer term further reform of the CAP into a sustainable land management fund, is required in order to achieve this.

37. The CAP could also contribute to climate mitigation measures through carbon storage, for example by using minimum tillage techniques to prevent carbon loss from soil.

BIOFUELS

38. The Woodland Trust finds that continuing support for production for biofuel crops is incongruous with decoupling CAP funding from production of other crops.

39. We are also concerned that such support could result in intensification of production and could feasibly add to green house gas emissions, for example through increased use of artificial fertilisers.

40. It is essential that biofuels are properly certified both for their carbon savings and to avoid damage to habitats, landscape, and soil and water resources.

BIOENERGY

41. With regard to the wider bioenergy arena we support mechanisms to develop biomass markets, our comments in paragraphs 39 and 40 also apply here.

42. In addition we are concerned about a blanket approach to biomass and the generic assumption that all biodiversity will benefit and that this is a strong rationale for developing biomass markets. This is clearly not the case, as individual species requirements are vastly more complex and variable than any one form of management in woods might be able to deliver.

43. Some types of management in some woods may create conditions that will benefit biodiversity but this is not true in all woods. Much woodland management, such as the clearfelling and replanting of ancient woodlands with conifers in the 1960s, has devastating effects on biodiversity which we now spend much time and money trying to restore.

44. In semi-natural woods where there has been no intervention for some time, there is a risk that re-introducing management for biomass production could have negative effects on biodiversity, just as it is claimed that it might have positive benefits.

45. Biomass production, with the proper checks and balances, is an excellent objective in itself for managing woods and this should be recognised rather than confused with a biodiversity rationale.

FINANCING

Q10. *The Commissioner has expressed her dissatisfaction at the financing agreement reached by the Member States at the December 2005 Council. Do you consider the current budget to be sufficient? Do you consider co-financing to be a possible way forward in financing the Common Agricultural Policy?*

46. The Woodland Trust believes that the 2005 EU budget deal represented a disappointing outcome for the environment and sustainable rural development measures—the current budget is not sufficient.

47. We believe it is imperative that agri-environment schemes across Europe receive the levels of funding required to deliver a high value countryside. We believe that the amount of funding needed is greatly underestimated.

48. The Woodland Trust believes that the cost of protecting and enhancing our environment should be shared by the EU and national governments but allocations to member states must be made using an equitable, needs based approach.

SIMPLIFICATION OF THE CAP AND OTHER ISSUES

Q12. *How could the CAP be further simplified and in what other ways would you like to see the Common Agricultural Policy changed in the short and/or the long term?*

49. We believe the CAP could be further simplified through reform into a single sustainable land management fund. Please see our comments above in relation to this.

June 2007

Printed in the United Kingdom by The Stationery Office Limited
3/2008   389053   19585

ISBN 978-0-10-401235-2